One To Remember

The Relentless Blizzard
of March 1966

Douglas Ramsey & Larry Skroch

Front cover photograph: 1947 Ford near Langdon, North Dakota, after March 1966 blizzard. Photo by James Zettel.

Back cover top photograph: Northern Pacific train north of Linton, North Dakota. Courtesy of State Historical Society of North Dakota.

Back cover bottom photograph: Clearing snow at the Russell Quale farm north of Driscoll, North Dakota. Harley Hettick, Bismarck, photographer. Courtesy of Elwyn B. Robinson, Department of Special Collections, Chester Fritz Library, University of North Dakota.

The text is the same as the first printing, except for a few minor revisions.

Published by Valley Heritage Press, P.O. Box 12872, Grand Forks, ND 58208

Second printing 2005.

ISBN 0-9635253-1-X

Printed in the U.S.A

The Authors

The authors grew up on farms in North Dakota. We met at the University of North Dakota in 1984.

Douglas Ramsey was born at Riverdale, North Dakota. He graduated from Valley High School in Hoople, North Dakota. After graduation, he attended the University of North Dakota. Most of his education was acquired in the winter months.

He received a bachelor and master of arts degrees in history from UND. He also has received a bachelor of science degree in meteorology from UND. His master's thesis was entitled, "A History of the Northern Dakota Railway Company." He farms and works near Crystal, North Dakota.

Larry Skroch was born in Oakes, North Dakota. He graduated from Sargent Central High School in Forman, North Dakota. After graduation, he served three years in the United States Army.

He attended North Dakota State School of Science at Wahpeton, North Dakota and received an associate of science degree in pre-law. After that, he attended the University of North Dakota. He received a bachelor degree in social science and a master degree in history. His master's thesis was entitled, "A History of School Reorganization in Sargent County Since 1947." He was a member of the North Dakota National Guard. Since July 1988, he has worked for Burlington Northern Railroad and Burlington Northern Santa Fe Railway as a brakeman and conductor.

Acknowledgements

The drive to record the heritage of our region has come from Professor D. Jerome Tweton. He gave us guidance on organization and structure. He encouraged us to write a town-by-town story layout.

For inspiring us to undertake this project, we would like to express our appreciation to the professors who taught in the History Department at the University of North Dakota at one time or another. These include Richard Beringer, William Gard, Thomas Howard, Stan Murray, Robert Wilkens, Gordon Iseminger, Glenn Smith, James Vivian, Playford Thorson and D. Jerome Tweton. This appreciation is also extended to Leon Osborne and his crew at UND's Regional Weather Information Center (RWIC). Their enthusiasm for meteorology is contagious. We would also like to thank William Dando and Douglas Munski of the UND Department of Geography.

Thanks are due to the staff of the Chester Fritz Library at the University of North Dakota, especially the services of the inter-library loan division. Their generosity allowed us to start our centennial project. We want to thank Betty Gard and Sandy Beider for their assistance. The Elwyn B. Robinson Special Collection allowed us to use material from its archives.

We are indebted to all the daily and weekly newspapers of the region for allowing us to quote freely and the use their photographs. Special thanks go to the *Bismarck Tribune, Fargo Forum, Grand Forks Herald,* and the *Aberdeen American-News.*

We would like to thank the staffs at the South Dakota State Historical Society in Pierre; North Dakota State Historical Society in Bismarck; the Minnesota Historical Society in St. Paul; the Provincial Archives of Manitoba; and the Western Canada Pictorial Index, both in Winnipeg. The North Dakota Department of Transportation provided some wonderful pictures as well.

Individual thanks go to Diane Lindseth and Toni Vanasek of the Grand Forks Public Library, Mark Piehl of the Clay County Historical Society in Moorhead, and Bruce Cameron for providing the information on the history of Arctic Cat Enterprises.

The authors wish to thank all those who have shared their family stories of the blizzard with us. We regret not being able to use all of them.

We are indebted to the people who have shared their family pictures with us. Those people include Jim Benjaminson, Don Dalzell, Jim and Betty Kunkle, Jim Zettel, M. O. Dahl, Ron and Betty Knotts, Paul "Cookie" Litzinger, Dean Younggren, Jim and Millie Rickard, Juli Becker, Lori M. Elhard and Ruth Johnson.

We like to thank Bev Rosencrams for storm copies of the *Grand Forks Herald* and Carolyn Eckley for the pictorial, *Red River Rampage.*

A special thanks goes to Mike Lunak for his help in solving our computer problems. Mike also provided material on the activities of the Great Northern Railway. Dale Lasch provided material on the operations of the Northern Pacific.

The design people at Knight Printing in Fargo did a wonderful job. In Grand Forks, Jean Clayton helped the authors immensely and made the printing process an enjoyable experience.

Table of Contents

History is not made only by kings and parliaments, presidents, wars, and generals. It is the story of people, of their love, honor, faith, hope and sufferings; of birth and death, of hunger, thirst and cold, of loneliness and sorrow.

Louis L'Amour
Sackett's Land

Preface

Family stories are important keepsakes.

The Ramsey family has a story from the days of the Great Depression. The supply of money back then was tight. Having five dollars in your pocket made you feel rich. One winter, whenever residents in the Ramsey neighborhood went anywhere they would take a five dollar bill with them in case they needed it. The five dollar bill was passed around the neighborhood this way. It was never spent, but having it there in case of emergencies had to provide a psychological boost.

The Skroch family has a story that dates back to the winter of 1884. Frank John Skroch was born October 10, 1860, in Popielow Upper Seliesa, Poland. He came to the United States with his parents in 1882. They first settled in Independence, Wisconsin. The next year, Frank Skroch moved to Watertown, South Dakota. Frank, a carpenter, built many of the early buildings around Lidgerwood, North Dakota. The following story was written down by one of his sons, Ted.

Frank Skroch related the following:

> In the winter of 1884 I was caught in a blizzard on the way back to the farm where I was staying.
>
> I walked from the farm to Watertown, 46 miles, to get some stock in the morning. I left after dinner and when I had walked about 16 miles back it started to snow, I couldn't see much but I happened to be near a strawpile which was used to shelter cattle. I had to dig my way through the snow but I got under it. That was 4 p.m. The following day at 3 p.m., I finally crawled out and walked to the nearest farm.

North Dakota celebrated its centennial in 1989. Before the centennial, we talked about our parent's stories.

In October 1988, we decided to write three books on natural disasters that have affected the Dakotas, Minnesota and Manitoba. This would be our centennial project. Readers could learn about the experiences of other individuals, many miles away from their hometown.

For information the authors have relied heavily on the daily and weekly newspapers. The editors, journalists and news correspondents are important voices in our narrative. Memories, fresh in the minds of the people, were published just days after the event. Just as important, the authors have included stories not told in the newspapers.

Doug was intrigued by his parent's blizzard stories of the March 15, 1941. Our parent's generation has remembered that blizzard the most. That would be our first book. The second natural disaster we would write about was the hardest decision to make. We chose the 1950 Red River Valley flood over the Fargo tornado of 1957 and the 1979 Red River flood. Our choice for our last book was an easy one. We would write about the greatest blizzard of our generation. That storm was in March 1966.

Looking For Candles In The Window: The Tragic Red River Valley Blizzard of March 15, 1941, was the title of our first book. That storm, an intense Alberta Clipper, killed forty people in North Dakota and thirty-one in Minnesota. Eight Canadians also died in the blizzard. It was a fast moving storm that was accompanied by little new snow. The sudden change of temperature and visibility was astonishing. Many more people would have died had the storm lasted more than seven hours. Published in 1992, the blizzard is remembered mostly by the grandchildren of the pioneers of our area.

Our second book, *The Raging Red: The 1950 Red River Valley Flood,* covered the flood that led to the construction of the floodway around Winnipeg. Known as Duff's Ditch, the floodway was completed in 1968. For Winnipeg, the largest city in the Red River Valley, the 1950 flood was the worst flood of the twentieth century. According to Colin Hersle, National Director of the Red Cross for the United States, "the worst disaster of its kind in the history of North America." The 1950 flood set all-time crest records in the North Dakota communities of Akra, Cooperstown, Fordville, Minto, Park River, Grafton and Walhalla. In Minnesota, records were established for Thief River Falls and Roseau.

People in the Red River Valley area endured seven blizzards in the winter of 1996-97. The spring flood of 1997 broke many of the flood records in the drainage basin of the Red River of the North. *The Raging Red,* was published in 1996.

The 1966 blizzard was a different type of storm than the one in 1941. Unlike the 1941 storm, which roared in from the northwest, the 1966 blizzard came from the southwest. Besides moving slower than the 1941 blizzard, it produced a much greater snowfall. Temperatures in the 1966 storm did not drop sharply like the 1941 blizzard. In 1966, cold temperatures, in the wake of the storm, lasted for only three days. After that, the highs were well above normal for a couple of weeks. The result was a rapid thaw.

This blizzard has its own place in weather history. *ESSA II* was launched on February 28, 1966. This weather satellite marked the successful completion of the first worldwide weather forecasting network. The first pictures were received on March 2, 1966. Cameras from space revealed the massive cloud formation of the oncoming storm over the central United States.

The human cost of the 1966 blizzard was high, eighteen lives were lost. Warm temperatures saved many others who waited out the storm in their vehicles. Financially, hundreds of farmers and ranchers suffered livestock losses.

Day in and day out, local weather observers have recorded temperature and precipitation totals. Meteorologists and climatologists have used their data to study the weather. For the most part, their work goes unnoticed. The 1966 blizzard put a face on the weather observers. Their figures are highlighted in our study.

Snowmobiles became of age during the blizzard. The vehicles were no longer regarded just as winter toys.

For all of us, the journey of life has many days. The blizzard froze a moment in time and left distinct memories for many of us.

A severe blizzard, even in modern times, can be a very dangerous experience.

A Look Back at the Times

One popular expression of the times was, "Don't Trust Anyone Over 30." Between 1946 and 1964, seventy-six million people were born in the United States. Members of this new generation would become known as Baby Boomers. In 1960 there were 24 million people between the ages of 15 and 24. Almost half the people in the United States were under the age of 26 in 1966.

Dr. Benjamin M. Spock influenced our parents with his books on childcare. He urged parents to "trust themselves," and "that parents know more than what they think."

Dr. Joyce Brothers and Ann Landers gave social advice. Ann Landers' first newspaper column appeared in September 1955.

New parents relied on Gerber's baby food, a product that had been around since 1929. Procter and Gambles began selling Pampers, a disposable diaper, in 1961.

For many young boomers their first reading experiences probably came from the many Dr. Seuss books, written by Ted Geisel. Dr. Seuss published *The Cat In The Hat* in 1957. Another early favorite was *Green Eggs and Ham*. They advanced to the mysteries of the Hardy Boys, Nancy Drew and Brains Benton. Other adventure series of the times included Trixe Beldon and the Bobbsey Twins. Clair Bee's sport books, featuring Chip Hilton and his pals, became eagerly awaited Christmas gifts.

Growing up, children played baseball, football and hockey outside. Children rode their bikes everywhere. A popular tag game was called "Red Rover, Red Rover, Come on Over." For wintertime amusement, there was "Fox and the Goose" and "King of the Hill."

Hot Wheels, Matchbox Cars, Tonka Toys, Barbie Dolls, GI Joe soldiers, Etch and Sketch sets, Slinkys, Silly Putty, marbles, and were common toys. Monopoly and Checkers were big. Older boys wanted BB guns.

The raising of an antenna on the top of house marked a special occasion. With just three major networks (ABC, CBS and NBC) it would be rotated around to get the best reception for the family's favorite channel. In 1950 the number of American households with a television set was 9 percent. Ten years later, that number had climbed to 89 percent. Most boomers have watched black-and-white TV.

Before going to school children turned on their television set to learn some of life's basics lessons from Captain Kangaroo (Bob Keeshan) and Mr. Green Jeans. That show on CBS ran from October 3, 1955, to December 8, 1984.

Cartoon character favorites included: Bugs Bunny, Elmer Fudd, Daffy Duck, Road Runner, Wylie Coyote, Yosemite Sam, Taz, the Tasmanian Devil, Tweety Bird and Sylvester, Yogi Bear, Huckleberry Hound, Rocky and Bullwinkle, Quick Draw McGraw and Mr. Magoo. Superheros ran the gamut from Superman, Batman, Spiderman and Wonder Woman, to Underdog, Mighty Mouse, Space Ghost and the Fantastic Four. The Adventures of Johnny Quest, The Jetsons and the Archies were Saturday morning choices, as well.

American Bandstand became very important. Teenagers learned the newest fashions, hair styles and how to dance to the latest songs. Bandstand started out as a local program in Philadelphia in 1952. Dick Clark joined the show in 1956. *American Bandstand* went national on ABC stations in 1957.

A time when houses had TV antennas. This photo of 7th Avenue North Grand Forks, North Dakota was taken after the March 2-5, 1966, blizzard. The Paul Litzinger family lived across the street from these two houses. Their son Mike and his friends remembers the forts and tunnels they dug. They had a lot of fun playing in the snow. Virgil Hill, light heavyweight champion of the world, lived in the white house for a time. Courtesy of Mr. and Mrs. Paul Litzinger

Alaska and Hawaii became states in 1959. Alaska became the 49th state on January 3, 1959, and Hawaii, the 50th on August 21, 1959.

The landscape of American cities started to change in the late 1950's and early 1960's. Businesses selling fast food targeted major streets in cities and larger towns. The early chain stores, Sears, J. C. Penny, and Montgomery Ward, began having competition from large discount stores like Kmart and Wal-Mart.

On October 4, 1957, the Soviet Union launched *Sputnik I*, the first man-made object to orbit the earth. The following month, *Sputnik II* carried Laika, a dog, the first animal into space.

The first successful American satellite to be launched into space was Explorer 1, which was sent up on January 31, 1958. The delivery vehicle was an United States Army rocket.

On July 29, 1958, NASA, the National Aeronautics and Space Administration, was formed.

On April 10, 1959, seven men were introduced to the American public as "Astronauts." They were all veteran test pilots between the ages of thirty-two and thirty-seven. Their names were: Alan B. Shepard Jr., M. Scott Carpenter, Virgil I. Grissom, Walter M. Schirra Jr., John H. Glenn, Jr., L. Gordon Cooper Jr. and Donald "Deke" Slayton. These men were part of Project Mercury, the program that tested the ability of both men and space-craft in suborbital and orbital flight.

Except for one individual, this core of men flew the Project Mercury space missions of the United States. That individual was "Deke" Slayton. A heart murmur would ground him, but not forever. "Deke" Slayton finally went into space in 1975.

The Soviets photographed the far side of the moon on October 4, 1959. The pictures from *Luna 3* gave the Soviets a great deal of prestige.

Alvin Ray "Pete" Rozelle was elected commissioner of the National Football League in January 1960.

Louis L'Amour, a native of Jamestown, North Dakota, had his first Sackett novel, *The Daybreakers*, a paperback edition, published by Bantam Books in February 1960. Before he died on June 10, 1988, he wrote over one hundred books, including seventeen Sackett novels.

In 1960, a Lidgerwood, North Dakota, native Z'dene Trinka received acclaim for *Medora: The Secret of the Badlands*. The book was illustrated by Orabel Thortvedt who grew up on the family homestead, five miles northwest of Glyndon, Minnesota.

At the 1960 Winter Olympic Games in Squaw Valley, California, the American hockey team won the gold medal.

On May 9, 1960, the Food and Drug Administration approved the use of a oral contraceptive pill, known as Enovid, developed by Gregory Goodwin Pincus. Before long, it was simply known as the "Pill." By the end of the decade, the number of women taking birth control pills in the United States had reached six million.

In the 1950s, 25 percent of all 18 year-olds were married in the United States. In 1960, there were 17,000 unmarried couple living together. By 1970, the number of unmarried couples living together had reached 143,000.

In 1960, the FDA approved Albert Sabin's oral polio vaccine. Between 1951 and 1955, almost 200,000 Americans, mostly children, were affected with polio. Sabin's vaccine was considered more effective than Jonas Salk's vaccine for polio.

The technique for CPR was demonstrated at John Hopkins Hospital in Baltimore, Maryland, in 1960. The first heart pacemakers were designed.

Theodore Maimen invented the laser. Americans wrote with felt-tip pens, played on Astro Turf, and drank Coca-Cola from a can. Lycra, a spandex fiber, was introduced to the public. United States's first nuclear aircraft carrier, the *Enterprise*, made its maiden voyage.

OPEC, the Organization of Petroleum Exporting Countries, was organized in 1960. The initial member countries included Iran, Iraq, Kuwait, Saudi Arabia, and Venezuela.

The birth of rock 'n' roll harkens back to the mid 1950's. The first number one rock 'n' roll single was by Bill Haley and the Comets in the summer of 1955. The breakthrough song was "(We're Gonna) Rock Around The Clock". Although released in 1954, it took the movie *Blackboard Jungle* (with the song in it) the following year to make the song a hit. Bill Haley and the Comets' first top forty hit, "Shake, Rattle and Roll" came out in August 1954.

The charting of rock 'n' roll songs began around that time. Billboard magazine listed pop singles in three charts; Best Sellers in Stores, Most Played by Jockeys, and Most Played in Juke Boxes.

But the format as we know it today goes back to August 4, 1958. On that date, Billboard magazine started listing a "Hot 100" that combined the best selling and most played pop singles.

Rock 'n' Roll continued to evolve throughout the 1960s. Juke boxes were still around and quite popular. Television played a role in making stars of musicians. The emergence of FM radio stations, more music and less talk, stimulated the industry. Disk jockeys became almost as famous as some of the singers.

A native of Fargo, North Dakota, Robert Thomas Velline, (better known as Bobby Vee) secured a place in the history of Rock and Roll when on February 3, 1959, Buddy Holly, Ritche Valens and J. P. Richardson ("The Big Bopper") died in a plane crash outside of Mason City, Iowa. They were on their way to perform at a show in Moorhead, Minnesota. That night, Vee and his group "The Shadows", made their first public appearance, as replacements for Holly and the others.

Months later, the band signed with Liberty Records. In September 1960, Bobby Vee's, "Devil or Angel," made the Billboard charts, to be followed by "Rubber Ball," a hit three months later.

Elvis Presley was discharged from the United States Army in 1960. Presley had three No. 1 Billboard Hits that year, "Stuck On You"; "It's Now Or Never"; and "Are You Lonesome Tonight."

Other popular songs of 1960 included two big hits for Sam Cooke, "Wonderful World"; and "Chain Gang." It was the year

Roy Orbison wrote and sang, "Only the Lonely."

Some of the TV shows that premiered in 1960 included: *The Flintstones*; *My Three Sons*; and *The Andy Griffith Show*.

Gunsmoke was the number one show on television in 1960. *Gunsmoke*, a longtime radio hit, premiered on television on September 10, 1955, and ran until 1975. *The Flintstones*, the first prime-time cartoon, was a takeoff of the *Honeymooners*.

In September 1960, Cassius Clay, later known as Muhammad Ali, won the light-heavyweight boxing gold medal at the Summer Olympics in Rome. Wilma Rudolph became the first American women to win three gold medals in track and field events.

That fall, the National Football League had competition. The American Football League began its inaugural season.

The Pittsburgh Pirates won the 1960 World Series. For drama, it was one of the best. Bill Mazerowski hit the home run that won the seventh game of the Series, 10 to 9 over the New York Yankees. The fallout from that loss was that after 13 years of managing the Yankees, Casey Stengel lost his job.

Hollywood lost Clark Gable, but Jane Fonda, Peter O'Toole, Alan Bates and Albert Finney made their acting debuts in 1960.

While celebrating one hundred years of American filmaking in 1998, The American Film Institute named one hundred films as "America's Greatest Movies." Three 1960 movies made their list. These were *The Apartment* (Billy Wilder), *Psycho*, (Alfred Hitchcock), and *Spartacus*, (Stanley Kubrick). *Psycho* was Hitchcock's last movie that was shot in black and white. *The Apartment*, won immediate honors with an Oscar for "Best Picture."

On November 8, 1960, a young charismatic man was elected President of the United States. John Fitzgerald Kennedy defeated Richard Millhouse Nixon by just over 100,000 votes in the closest presidential race since 1884.

The old Star Lite drive-in theater in Grand Forks, North Dakota. ca. Fall of 1956 A Lee-Evanson photo.

The Philadelphia Eagles defeated the Green Bay Packers, 17 to 13, in the NFL championship game. In the AFL championship game the Houston Oilers beat the Los Angeles Chargers, 24 to16.

At his chilly inauguration on January 20, 1961, President John Kennedy declared: "Let the word go forth from this time and place ...that the torch has been passed to a new generation of Americans," and "Ask not what your country will do for you, but what you can do for your country."

President Kennedy's catch-phase for his new programs was the "New Frontier." On March 1, 1961, he established the Peace Corps, an organization where volunteers helped people in underdeveloped nations.

On April 12, 1961, the U.S.S.R. became the first country to put a man in orbit. Yuri Gagarin, a Soviet air force major, orbited the earth in 1 hour and 48 minutes. He parachuted down into a pasture in Russia. The cosmonaut's capsule, *Vostok 1*, smoldered nearby from the heat of reentry.

After World War II, U. S. foreign policy leaders came up with a strategy to deal with the rise of communism. In short, it was a policy of "Containment."

In April, 1954, President Eisenhower said, "South Vietnam is like a domino among other dominoes, or nations, in that part of the world: if one of them falls to the Communists, then the rest of the democratic nations of Southeast Asia will inevitably be brought down too."

Vietnam became a diplomatic nightmare. Before the war, France controlled Vietnam, Cambodia, and Loas, known as Indo-China. Japan held Indo-China, during the war. The French reestablished their control, but there was an ongoing battle with Vietnamese nationalists. In 1945, the Democratic Republic of Vietnam was proclaimed by Ho Chi Minh. While this was going on, there was a civil war between the Vietnamese.

The Weather
HIGH THURSDAY 45-55

Grand Forks Herald

FINAL HOME
EDITION

VOL. 81, NUMBER 168 — GRAND FORKS, NORTH DAKOTA, WEDNESDAY, APRIL 12, 1961 ★★★ — PRICE TEN CENTS

RUSS PUT MAN INTO ORBIT

Daring Red Astronaut Feat Turns Page In Human History

Hailed As Step To New Goals

Flight To Moon Nearer, Writer Says

By ALTON BLAKESLEE
Associated Press Science Writer

NEW YORK (AP)—In an awesome, daring and thrilling ride, a Soviet astronaut has just turned a momentous page in human history.

For, says Moscow, he has realized the ancient human dream of vaulting into space and safely back home again.

New Goals Ahead

Still ahead, but closer now, lies the goals of leaping to the moon or Mars; or beyond, in the space oceans of so many tantalizing mysteries.

Human exploration of space may well reap untold and surprising new benefits for all people. Or space could become, perhaps, just an extended arena for the political-military testings of men since history began.

The Soviet Union is first, so recently as the result of a powerful firstpar-plan or as calculated to drive ahead.

In 108 Minutes

DRAWING PROVIDES rough idea, in absence of any specific details from Soviet sources, of Russian spaceman's trip around the world. Drawing does not purport to be in scale. Moscow has not specified where spaceman took off, nor where he landed. (AP Wirephoto)

Forge Ahead In Race For Space

By BEM PRICE
WASHINGTON (AP)—The Soviet Union's success in putting a man into earth orbit has given it a running lead in the race to control space.

Accuser Points At Eichmann

Outburst Brings No Reaction From Prisoner

JERUSALEM (AP) — Israel's attorney general pointed a finger at Adolf Eichmann today Wednesday and vowed that Jewry always will remember him as the man who succeeded in part in carrying out the Nazi plan to exterminate Europe's 11 million Jews.

"There is no pardon and there can be no forgetting," Atty. Gen. Gideon Hausner cried out, his voice ringing with emotion.

Upholds Trial Right

Minnesota Redistrict Bill Passed

ST. PAUL (AP) — The Senate Wed., by a vote of 43-24, passed a bill dividing the state into eight congressional districts in place of the present nine.

Minimum Wage Bill Approved

WASHINGTON (AP)—The Senate Labor Committee Tuesday approved a minimum wage bill to raise the floor to $1.25 an hour from $1 and bring four million additional workers under the law.

4 Injured In Texas Tornado

DALLAS, Tex. (AP)—A tornado flattened a gas station and injured four persons near the north edge of Dallas late Tuesday.

Comic Dictionary

MIDDLE AGE — The period when every woman is just the age she would like to be — and doesn't.

First Man In Space

THIS IS RUSSIAN Maj. Yuri Gagarin, history's first man in space. The Russians rocketed him around the earth in an orbit taking slightly less than 10 minutes, and brought him back safely to a prearranged spot in the Soviet Union. (AP Wirephoto via radio from Moscow).

Describe Life Of 1st Space Man

LONDON (AP) — Moscow television presented a picture of the Soviet Union's first space man Wed., describing him as a man with "a good, honest smile."

U.S. Beaten By At Least 2 Weeks

CAPE CANAVERAL, Fla. (AP) — The Redstone rocket which the United States had hoped would boost the first man into space stands on a launching pad here.

Motorist Gives Up His Jackpot

Market Lost, 139 Oil Wells May Shut Down

'People' Inside

Space Traveler Lands Safely At Target Spot

MOSCOW (AP) — The world's first astronaut has orbited the globe for more than an hour, reported back that he was feeling fine, and then returned safely to receive the plaudits of scientists and political leaders alike. He was in the air an hour and 48 minutes, including an hour and 29 minutes in orbit.

A five-ton spaceship carried Maj. Yuri Alekseyevich Gagarin, 27, father of two daughters. He took off at 8:07 a. m., Moscow time and returned at 10:55 a. m., Soviet officials reported.

Skeptical On Date Of Flight

MOSCOW (AP)—A Soviet astronaut has orbited the globe for more than an hour and returned safely to receive the plaudits of scientists and political leaders alike.

Won't Oppose U. N Debate On China

LONDON (AP) — In a reversal of long-standing policy, President Kennedy's administration has decided not to oppose U.N. debate next fall on Red China's bid for a seat in the United Nations.

Liz Taylor's Family Returns

LOS ANGELES (AP) — Elizabeth Taylor's family was back to gather Wednesday.

Today's Chuckle

Success tips: Start at the bottom and wake up.

Reprint of the front page of the Grand Forks Herald, April 12, 1961. Courtesy of Grand Forks Herald

In 1950, the Soviet Union and China recognized Ho Chi Minh's government, but the United States and Great Britan did not offer recognition.

In May 1954, the Viet Minh defeated the French at Dien Bien Phu. President Dwight Eisenhower supported the French, but Eisenhower revoked the idea of massive intervention to save the French forces at the end.

Vietnam became a divided country, and one of the places where the Cold War played out.

President Kennedy ordered the first direct military support to South Vietnam in May 1961. He sent 36 army helicopters with air and ground support crews, 400 Green Berets soldiers, and 100 military advisers.

On May 5, 1961, the United States launched its first manned space vehicle. Astronaut Alan B. Shepard Jr. rode a *Mercury 3* capsule, named *Freedom 7*, into space. Shepard's suborbital flight lasted 15 minutes and 22 seconds.

On May 25, 1961, in a special message to Congress, President Kennedy said: "We are behind, and it will be some time before we catch up. ...I believe this nation should commit itself to achieving the goal, before the decade is out, of landing a man on the moon and returning him safely to earth."

After Kennedy's challenge, the United States and the Soviet Union became involved in a race to put a man on the moon. For national defense, space became an important battleground. Spy satellites became part of our early warning systems.

Construction of the Berlin Wall began in August 1961.

There was a "white" America and a "black" America.

The first "Freedom Rides" took place in April 1947. Although the attention highlighted the social problems of the United States, there was no change.

In 1961, there was another wave of activism. Freedom Riders were attacked in one hundred Southern cities. In the long run,television coverage of the violence pushed the civil rights movement forward.

Already partners with Richard and Maurice McDonald of San Bernardino, California, Ray Kroc bought the franchise rights for McDonalds outright for 2.7 million dollars in 1961.

Jean Nidetch invited six of her friends to lose weight. Nidetch's plan included low-fat proteins, lots of fruits, and weekly get-togethers for moral support. Nidetch and two friends incorporated Weight Watchers, two years later in 1963.

Mattel came out with an 11 inch Barbie Doll in March 1959. In 1961, Barbie was given a doll-boyfriend named Ken.

Detroit teenagers, Florence Ballard, Mary Wilson, and Diana Ross, signed a contract with Motown Records in 1961. Motown Records was founded by Berry Gordy in 1959. The group was called the Supremes.

Elvis Presley stopped touring in March 1961. Presley spent the next eight years making movies. Altogether, he starred in 31 feature films throughout his career. Elvis's first film, *Love Me Tender*, opened at New York's Paramount Theater on November 15, 1956. Musically, Presley had a No. 1 single with "Surrender" and nine top forty songs in 1961.

Other '61 Billboard No. 1 hits included: "Runaway" (Del Shannon); "Travelin' Man" (Rickey Nelson); "Runaround Sue" (Dion);

"Hit The Road Jack" (Ray Charles); "Please Mr. Postman" (The Marvelettes); and "The Lion Sleeps Tonight" (The Tokens).

Bobby Vee's "Take Good Care of My Baby," became a No. 1 song. He had No. 2 hit, "Run to Him," as well.

Neil Sedaka's sang "Calender Girl," and "Happy Birthday, Sweet Sixteen."

Patsy Cline topped the charts with, "I Fall to Pieces" and "Crazy", the latter written by Willie Nelson.

Lawrence Welk, born in Strasburg, North Dakota, was a musician and band leader. He had a TV musical variety show from 1955 to 1982. His sound became known as "Champagne Music." In 1958 Welk wrote "Calcutta." Three years later, "Calcutta" was a No. 1 Billboard Hit. It featured Frank Scott at the piano.

In May 1961, Bantam published the second Sackett novel by Louis L'Amour. This one was titled *Sackett*.

In honor of the centennial of Dakota Territory (1861-1961), the North Dakota Institute for Regional Studies, Fargo, North Dakota, published William C. Hunter's, *Beacon Across The Prairie: North Dakota's Land-Grant College.*

Theodore H. White finished writing, *The Making of the President: 1960.* (White won the Pulitizer Prize for it in 1962.)

The world loss the great talents of Ernest Hemingway, Dashiell Hammett and James Thurber in 1961.

Hollywood mourned the loss of Gary Cooper, but Burt Reynolds, George Segal, Warren Beatty, Gene Hackman, Joe Pesci and Ann-Margret had their first movie roles.

West Side Story, won the Oscar for Best Picture. The movie was directed by Robert Wise and starred Natalie Wood, George Chakiris and Rita Moreno.

Three 1961 movies, *Breakfast at Tiffany's*; *The Hustler*; and *West Side Story* made AFI's America's Greatest 100 movies list in 1998.

Other well-liked movies that year included, *Judgement at Nuremberg*; *Two Wowen*; *The Guns of Navarone*; *A Raisin in the Sun*; *Comancheros*; and *Voyage to the Bottom of the Sea.*

On April 29, 1961, Americans heard, "... the thrill of victory, the agony of defeat," for the very first time. It was the premier of ABC's *Wide World of Sports.*

For sports, the year 1961, is best remembered for Mickey Mantle's and Roger Maris's chase of Babe Ruth's home run record of 60 home runs in one season. Maris started slow, he did not hit his first home run until the twelfth game of the season. Late season injuries forced Mantle to drop out of the race. But on October 1, 1961, Maris hit his 61st home run off Tracy Stallard, a Boston Red Sox rookie, to break the record. Unfortunately for Maris, the Commissioner of Baseball Ford Frick had an asterisk placed by the record. This was done to show that it took Maris 162 games to break the record. The asterisk would be removed later. Babe Ruth had clobbered 60 home runs in a 154 game schedule in 1927.

Maris, born in Hibbing, Minnesota, lived in Grand Forks, North Dakota, for a while. In Fargo, North Dakota, he played sports for Shanley High School. In 1949, Maris ran four kickoffs back for touchdowns in one game. This national high school football record remains unbroken to this day.

Maris played for the Fargo-Moorhead Twins in the Northern League in 1953. In 1956, as a 22-year old rookie, he signed his first pro contract for $15,000 with the Cleveland Indians. Two years later, after playing for Cleveland and Kansas City, Maris joined the New York Yankees. He was the American League's Most Valuable Player in 1960. Maris also won a gold glove for fielding.

The Twins and Vikings came to Minneapolis in 1961.

The Washington Senators finished in fifth place in 1960, and they drew nearly 750,000 fans. In 1961, the Washington Senators became the Minnesota Twins. They played in Metropolitan Stadium, built in 1956 as a minor league ballpark. The seating capacity was improved to 30,000. In the spring of 1961, Harmon Killebrew signed a contract for $22,500. He hit 46 homes run and drove in 122 runs. Bob Allison had 29 home runs and 105 RBI. Earl Battey won a Gold Glove for catching. Camilo Pascual was the pitching ace. They finished the year with 70 wins and 90 losses. On June 13, 1961, Sam Mele replaced Cookie Lavagetto as the Twins manager. The ball club attracted 1,256,723 fans in the inaugural season.

The Minnesota Vikings became an expansion team in the National Football League in 1961. Minneapolis had been granted a franchise for the American Football League's season in 1960, but waited one year to join the well-established National Football League. (Their franchise rights then went to Oakland, thus creating the Raiders.) Like the Twins, the Vikings played in the "Met." Their first coach was the "Dutchman," Norm Van Brocklin. They had a 21 year-old rookie quarterback, Fran Tarkenton. The Vikings shocked the football world in their first regular game when they defeated the Chicago Bears, 37-13. George Shaw started at quarterback for the Vikings, but Fran Tarkenton entered the game late in the first quarter. Tarkenton threw four touchdown passes and ran for another score in the big upset. The Vikings won a total of five games in their first two seasons.

From 1961 to 1964, Herb Carneal announced Minnesota Viking games on the radio. In 1962, Carneal became the radio analyst of the Minnesota Twins. In 2002, he celebrated his 41st year as the "Voice of Twins."

On February 20, 1962, John Glenn Jr. became the first American to orbit the earth. Aboard a Mercury 6 flight, named Friendship 7, Glenn circled the planet three times. The flight lasted 4 hours, 55 minutes, and 23 seconds.

Walter Cronkite replaced Douglas Edwards as news anchor for CBS's *Evening News* in April 1962.

Marilyn Monroe died of a overdose of sleeping pills on August 5, 1962.

With federal marshals as escorts, James Howard Meredith enrolled in the University of Mississippi on October 1, 1962. Meredith had been denied admission in 1960 because he was black. In June 1962, a federal court ruled that he could not be denied because of his race. Meredith's enrollment led to the desegregation of other universities in the South.

In October 1962, the United States and Soviet Union stood on the brink of nuclear war over missile bases in Cuba. Military units were put on the highest level of alert. Urgent Cabinet meetings discussed war options. Both countries made strong demands. Anxiety escalated with an air and sea quarantine of Cuba. The White House and Kremlin issued ultimatums to each other. The battle was taken to the United Nation. There, Adlai Stevenson, United States Ambassador to the United Nations, presented photographic evidence of the missile complexes in Cuba (which had been shot from U-2 spy planes) for the whole world to see.

The break in the deadlock came when Premier Nikita Khrushchev sent two letters to President Kennedy. Robert Kennedy suggested that the President should ignore Khrushchev's first letter and respond to the second letter. This letter had an conciliatory opening. To settle the crisis, President Kennedy agreed to remove missiles from Turkey, while Premier Khrushchev removed the missiles from Cuba.

Former First Lady Eleanor Roosevelt, born October 11, 1884, died on November 7, 1962.

More new products hit the market in 1962. Polaroid came out with color film. Easy Bake Ovens, Sprite and Lear Jets were sold.

Kmart and Wal-Mart opened their first discount stores.

Yves Saint-Laurent established his fashion house.

H. Ross Perot founded Electronic Data Systems.

One of the favorite folk groups of the 1960's, Peter, Paul and Mary, had their first top 40 hit in 1962. Peter Yarrow, Paul Stookey, and Mary Travers first hit was, "If I had a Hammer (The Hammer Song)". The song was written by Pete Seeger and Lee Hays of The Weavers in 1958.

The Beach Boys, a band from Hawthorne, California, featuring the Wilson brothers, Brian, Carl, and Dennis, their cousin, Mike Love and friend Al Jardine had their first hit, "Surfin Safari."

The 4 Seasons, a group from Newark, New Jersey, featuring Frankie Valli as the lead singer, Bob Gaudio, Nick Massi and Tommy DeVito, had their first No 1. hits, "Sherry" and "Big Girls Don't Cry." During the Christmas season, their version of "Santa Claus Is Coming To Town," made the Billboard charts.

Other Billboard No. 1 hits included: "Johnny Angel" (Shelley Fabares); I' Can't Stop Loving You"(Ray Charles) and "Roses are Red (My Love)" (Bobby Vinton.) Other popular songs of 1962 included: "Twist and Shout" (The Isley Brothers); "Twisting the Night Away" (Sam Cooke); "Teen Age Idol" (Rick Nelson); "The Wanderer" (Dion); and "Return to Sender" (Elvis Presley).

In September 1962, a group known as the Beatles released their first single, "Love Me Do," in England. The song reached No. 17 on the British pop charts. Their second single, "Please Me," went to the top. Their third single, "From Me to You," was also a No 1. hit. John Lennon, Paul McCartney, Ringo Starr and George Harrison would soon be famous.

June Carter wrote, "The Ring of Fire," in 1962. For seven weeks, the song was a No. 1 Country hit for Johnny Cash in the summer of 1963. Cash and Carter started working together in 1961 and were married in March 1968.

TV premieres in 1962 included: the *Tonight Show* (starring Johnny Carson), *Combat*, the *Beverly Hillbillies*, and the *Merv Griffen Show*.

The *Beverly Hillbillies* became an overnight sensation. It was the first comedy to hold top billing since, *I Love Lucy*.

The first, ninety-minute TV western, the *Virigian*, aired on NBC stations.

Robert Redford and Robert Duvall made their acting debuts in 1962. Tom Cruise, Jodie Foster, Demi Moore and Wesley Snipes were born.

Lawrence of Arabia, (David Lean) won the Oscar for Best Picture in 1962. It was named one of America's best 100 movies by American Film Institute in 1998. Two other 1962 movies received the same honor, *The Manchurian Canidate* (John Frankenheimer) and *To Kill A Mockingbird* (Robert Mulligan).

Other popular movies of the year included: *The Longest Day*; *The Miracle Worker*; *Requiem of a Heavyweight*; and *Birdman of Alcatraz*.

The first James Bond movie, *Dr. No*, starring Sean Connery, was seen on the big screen. Connery was paid $30,000 for the picture. The first Bond girl was Ursula Andress.

Two great writers did not live out the year. Gone wereWilliam Faulkner and Hermann Hesse.

Silent Spring, one of most influential book of the 20th century was published in 1962. Its author was Rachel Carson. She revealed the harmful effects of pesticides on the natural world. The U. S. Environmental Protection Agency banned DDT in 1972. Carson was one of the pioneers in the modern ecological movement.

Another Jamestown, North Dakota, writer became noteworthy. That year, Lois Phillips Hudson wrote a novel that has been compared to John Steinbeck's, *The Grapes of Wrath*. Hudson's book, *The Bones Of Plenty*, described the fate a midwestern farmer of the 1930s.

Louis L'Amour novel, *Lando* about Orlando Sackett was published by Bantam Books in December 1962.

Ross & Haines, Inc., Minneapolis, Minnesota, reprinted *Forty Years A Fur Trader: The Personal Narrative of Charles Larpenter 1832-1872*, and Hiran Martin Chittenden's, *History of Early Steamboat Navigation on the Missouri River: Life and Adventures of Joseph Labarge, Pioneer Navigator and Indian Trader*.

On the national scene Helen Gurley Brown's *Sex and the Single Girl* was an instant best seller. Eventually, the book was published in 28 countries.

For sports, the year 1962 is best remembered for some personal achievements. Jim Beattie ran the first sub 4-minute indoor mile in Los Angeles. Wilt Chamberlain, a member of the Philadelphia Warriors, set the NBA scoring record for a single game with 100 points against the New York Knicks. Maury Wills stole 104 bases for the Los Angles Dodgers to break Ty Cobb's record of 96 steals in a single season. In golf, Jack Nicklaus, a 22-year old from Columbus, Ohio, defeated Arnold Palmer to win the U.S. Open.

Life magazine ran it first cover issue that dealt with Vietnam on January 25, 1963. Stationed in Vietnam at that time as a military adviser to the South Vietnamese army, was a fellow named Colin Powell.

Patsy Cline died at the age of 30 in a plane crash on March 5, 1963.

The legal system of the United States was adjusted on March 18, 1963, in a landmark case. In *Gideon versus Wainwright*, the Supreme Court ruled that all indigent defendants are entitled to court-appointed legal counsel in criminal cases.

After playing for the Boston Celtics for fourteen seasons, Bob Cousy, star guard, retired. Cousy went out as a champion. The Celtics defeated the Los Angles Lakers, four games to three, on April 24, 1964. It was their fifth straight title.

On May 5, 1963, the first black cadets graduated the United States Air Force Academy.

The last Mercury flight took place on May 15, 1963. Aboard the space capsule was L. Gordon Cooper Jr. He set a new endurance record 34 hours, 19 minutes, and 49 seconds and orbited the earth 22 times. This flight provided the first television pictures of outer space for the United States. Overall, there were nine Mercury flights.

Freedom Marchers, black and white, came to Washington, D.C. on August 29, 1963. The rally turned out to be the milestone event for Civil Rights legislation. Black leaders visited with President Kennedy in the White House. With the Lincoln Memorial in the background, Bob Dylan, Joan Baez and Peter, Paul and Mary sang songs. Jackie Robinson and Josephine Baker appeared on stage. Reverend Dr. Martin Luther King Jr. spoke:

> *I still have a dream, It is a dream chiefly rooted in the American Dream.*
> *I have a dream that one day this nation will rise up and live out the true*

meaning of its creed; we hold these truths to be self evident, that all men are created equal. I have a dream that one day on the red hills of Georgia sons of former slaves and the sons of former slave-owners will be able to sit down together at the table of brotherhood. ...

On Sunday morning, September 15, 1963, a bomb exploded against the outside wall of the Sixteenth Street Baptist Church in Birmingham, Alabama. The explosion killed four black girls, Addie Mae Collins, Carole Robertson and Cynthia Wesley, all 14, and Denise McNair, 11. It was the work of Ku Klux Klan.

A hotline between Washington and Moscow was set up in 1963 to avoid communication delays that might led to accidental nuclear war.

The United States Post Office, in order to speed up the sorting of mail, went to a five-digit zip-code numbering system.

The first diet soft drink, Tab, came on the market. Consumers could buy trimline and pushbutton telephone models. Cassette tape recorders became available. Green Giant came out with boil in the bag vegetables.

Doctors performed the first human lung transplant in 1963.

A Minnesota native had an impact on the music world that year. Bob Dylan, born Robert Allen Zimmerman in Duluth and raised in Hibbing, voiced the unrest of the young with a song titled "The Times are A-Changing." Although Dylan wrote and recorded "Blowing in the Wind," it would become a Billboard hit not for him, but for Peter, Paul and Mary.

Other 1963 No. 1 hits included: "He' so Fine"(The Chiffons); "I Will Follow Him" (Little Peggy March); "My Boyfriend's Back" (The Angels); "Blue Velvet" (Bobby Vinton); and "Sugar Shack" (Jimmy & the Fireballs).

Motown Records signed a 12-year old blind musician, Steveland Judkins Morris. That year, the record company released his first album, *Little Stevie Wonder*. One of the songs, "Fingertips-Pt 2" climbed to the top of Billboard chart.

The Beach Boys hit songs in '63 included: "Surfin' USA," "Sufer Girl," "Little Deuce Coupe," and "Be True To Your School."

Richard Berry recorded "Louie Louie," in 1957. It was a hit song for the Kingsmen in 1963.

The Crystals had two very popular songs, "Da Doo Ron Ron(When He Walked Me Home)" and "Then He kissed Me."

Lesley Gore had two hits, "It's My Party" and "Judy's Turn To Cry."

Sam Cooke sang "Another Saturday Night."

Martha & the Vandellas's "Heat Wave" climbed high in the Billboard charts.

Elvis Presley had at least one top single from 1956 to 1962. That streak was broken in 1963, but Elvis still had four songs on the Billboard charts.

New TV programs included: *General Hospital*; *My Favorite Martian*; *Petticoat Junction* and the *Fugitive*. With host Marlin Perkins, *Wild Kingdom* premiered on NBC stations.

Alan Alda, Kurt Russell, James Caan and John Huston had their Hollywood debuts. Sidney Poitier became the first black to win an Oscar for Best Actor for his role in *Lilies of the Field*. That year, there was another Alfred Hitchcock classic, *The Birds*. Frankie Avalon and Annette Funicello starred in their first beach movie, *Beach Party*. The second James Bond movie, *From Russia with Love*, played in theaters.

Robert Frost, famous American poet, died in 1963.

It would be a good year for North Dakota in regional books. Bernt Lloyd Wills, Professor and Chairman of the University of North Dakota Geography Department, wrote *North Dakota: The Northern Prairie State*. Edward C. Blackorby's, *Prairie Rebel: The Public Life of William Lemke*. Blackorby was a Professor of History at Wisconsin State College at Eau Clairie. North Dakota Institute for Regional Studies in Fargo, North Dakota, published Orin Alvia Stevens's, *Handbook of North Dakota Plants*. Lantern Books in Alexandria, Minnesota, published Erling Nicolai Rolfsrud's *The Story of North Dakota*.

Another British novelist became famous after writing *The Spy Who Came in from the Cold*. His name was John le Carre.

Betty Friedan's *The Feminine Mystique*, raised the tide for the women's movement in the United States. Three years later, Friedan founded the National Organization For Women.

Television news came of age in 1963. For the first time, that year, more people said they got their news from TV than from newspapers. On September 9, 1963, the *Huntley-Brinkley Report*, on NBC stations, expanded from 15 to 30 minutes. CBS went to the half hour format, right away. ABC waited until 1968.

The Los Angeles Dodgers swept the New York Yankees in four games to win the 1963 World Series. Sandy Koufax struck out fifteen batters in one of the games.

TV sport fans were introduced to "instant replays."

Sniper bullets, fired by Lee Harvey Oswald, killed President Kennedy on November 22, 1963, in Dallas, Texas. Dan Rather, a young journalist working in Dallas broke the news. Newscaster David Brinkley, thinking of America's loss, said "It was too big, too sudden, too overwhelming, and it meant too much."

Lyndon Baines Johnson became President of the United States 98 minutes after President Kennedy died.

The Chicago Bears defeated the New York Giants in the NFL championship game. It would be George Halas's last championship title.

The Pro Football Hall of Fame was founded in Canton, Ohio.

In the mid 1960s, 40 percent of adults smoked in the United States. On January 11, 1964, smoking became less glamorous. Luther L. Terry, the United States Surgeon General, reported that smoking caused lung cancer and heat disease. Terry's statement was based on the findings of ten independent biomedical reseachers. Two years later, Congress required cigarette packages to print the following U.S. Surgeon General warning: "Caution: Cigarette smoking may be hazardous to your health."

The use of poll taxes in federal elections became unconstitutional on January 23, 1964, with the ratification of the 24th Amendment.

On January 25, 1964, the Beatles had the top song "I Want To Hold Your Hand", in the United States. The following month, they came to New York.

On February 9, 1964, the Beatles appeared live on the *The Ed Sullivan Show*. That year, the Beatles would have five more No. 1 hits: "She Loves You"; "Can't Buy Me Love"; "Love Me Do"; "A Hard Day's Night"; and "I Feel Fine."

The success of the Beatles led the way for other English groups, in what would become known as the "British Invasion." These included the Rolling Stones, The Animals, Dave Clark Five, the Hollies, the Yardbirds, Gerry and the Pacemakers and Hermit's Hermit. Those groups paved the way for the Who, Cream, Led Zeppelin, Black Sabbath, Emerson Lake and Palmer and Jethro Tull.

THE FARGO FORUM

DAILY REPUBLICAN AND

Moorhead News

Colder

Fargo-Moorhead and Vicinity — Diminishing cloudiness this afternoon, high 24. Occasional cloudiness tonight and Saturday. Colder tonight, low zero. (Weather details on Page 2.)

Vol. 86, No. 5 · FARGO, N. D., FRIDAY EVENING, NOVEMBER 22, 1963 · Price Ten Cents

Shot Down in Dallas Caravan

KENNEDY ASSASSINATED

(AP Wirephotos)

President John F. Kennedy Slumped Down In Back Seat of Car After Being Shot Today. Mrs. Kennedy Leans Over President As Unidentified Man Stands On Bumper.

President Kennedy, Mrs. Kennedy, and Gov. John B. Connally as they rode in the caravan shortly before the assassination.

Gov. Connally Shot; Johnson Escapes Gunfire

DALLAS (AP) — President John F. Kennedy, thirty-sixth president of the United States, was shot to death today by a hidden assassin armed with a high-powered rifle.

Kennedy, 46, lived about 30 minutes after a sniper cut him down as his limousine left downtown Dallas. Newsmen said the shot that hit him was fired about 12:30 p.m. (CST). A hospital announcement said he died at approximately 1 p.m. of a bullet wound in the head.

Automatically, the mantle of the presidency fell to Vice President Lyndon B. Johnson, a native Texan who had been riding two cars behind the chief executive.

There was no immediate word on when Johnson would take the oath of office.

Asst. presidential press secretary Malcolm Kilduff said Johnson was not hit. The new President previously had been reported wounded.

✣ ✣ ✣

Kennedy died at Parkland Hospital where his bullet-pierced body had been taken in a frantic but futile effort to save his life.

Lying wounded at the same hospital was Gov. John Connally of Texas, who was cut down by the same fusillade that ended the life of the youngest man ever elected to the presidency.

✣ ✣ ✣

Connally and his wife had been riding with the President and Mrs. Kennedy.

Kilduff told newsmen that Gov. Connally, a Democrat, was wounded in the right chest in the same ambush that felled the President.

Connally was rushed into surgery for a two-hour emergency operation.

The First Lady cradled her dying husband's bloodsmeared head in her arms as the presidential limousine raced to the hospital.

"Oh, no," she kept crying. Connally slumped in his seat beside the President.

Police ordered an unprecedented dragnet of the city, hunting for the assassin.

They believed the fatal shots were fired by a white man, about 30, slender of build, weighing about 165 pounds, and standing 5 feet 10 inches tall.

The murder weapon was reportedly a 30-30 rifle.

✣ ✣ ✣

Shortly before Kennedy's death became known, he was administered the last rites of the Roman Catholic Church. He had been the first Roman Catholic president in American history.

Even as two clergymen hovered over the fallen President in the hospital emergency room, doctors and nurses administered blood transfusions.

Kennedy died of a gunshot wound in the brain at approximately 1 p.m. CST according to an announcement by acting White House press secretary Malcolm Kilduff.

The new President, Lyndon Johnson, and his wife left the hospital a half hour later. Newsmen had no opportunity to question them.

✣ ✣ ✣

The horror of the assassination was mirrored in an eye-witness account by Sen. Ralph Yarborough, D-Tex., who had been riding three cars behind Kennedy.

"You could tell something awful and tragic had happened," the senator told newsmen before Kennedy's death became known. His voice breaking and his eyes red-rimmed, Yarborough said:

"I could see a Secret Service man in the President's car leaning on the car with his hands in anger, anguish and despair. I knew then something tragic had happened."

Yarborough had counted three rifle shots as the presidential limousine left downtown Dallas through a triple underpass. The shots were fired from above—possibly from one of the bridges or from a nearby building.

One witness, television reporter Mal Couch, said he saw a gun emerge from an upper story of a warehouse commanding an unobstructed view of the presidential car.

Kennedy was the first president to be assassinated since William McKinley was shot in 1901.

It was the first death of a president in office since Franklin D. Roosevelt died of a cerebral hemorrhage at Warm Springs, Ga., in April 1945.

Roosevelt had been enjoying a vacation when he

KENNEDY SLAIN

(Continued on Page 2, Col. 4)

FORT WORTH, Tex. (AP)—Soon after President Kennedy was assassinated today in Dallas, a white man in his mid 20s was arrested in the Riverside section of Fort Worth in the shooting of a Dallas policeman.

The man, who has black curly hair and who wore a red shirt, denied that he was connected with the assassination of the President.

President John F. Kennedy

New President, Now 55, Had Long Congress Career

Vice President Lyndon B. Johnson, who succeeds John F. Kennedy as President, is 55.

He has had a long career in Congress before winning the vice presidential nomination in 1960.

Johnson was elected to the U.S. House in 1937 and in 1948, at the age of 40, won election to the Senate.

Four years later the Senate Democrats chose him minority leader. That was at the beginning of President Dwight D. Eisenhower's administration when the Republicans were in control of Congress. During the next three Congresses, the Democrats were in the saddle and Johnson was elected majority leader.

At the Democratic national convention in 1960, Johnson had been a serious contender for the presidential nomination. He was strongly supported by Southern delegates but lost out to Kennedy. The later received 806 votes to Johnson's 409. The number required for the nomination was 761.

Kennedy chose his vanquished rival for second place on the ticket.

Johnson was regarded as one of the top dark horse candidates for the Democratic nomination for President in 1956, but he was not an announced candidate. The convention chose Adlai E. Stevenson as standard bearer.

Some of Johnson's Senate colleagues thought him overbearing as majority leader and accused him of running a one-man show; others were lost in admiration for his efficiency.

It was generally agreed that he had formidable assets in his personal charm and commanding bearing, his capability for logical argument, his shrewd timing and sure political sense amounting to a touch of genius at times.

Exhausted by his hard driving duties as majority leader, Johnson suffered a "moderately severe" heart attack seizure in the summer of 1955 and spent several weeks in a hospital.

Johnson made a strong comeback and in a few years appeared fully recovered. He said in 1960 that his health, in the estimation of his physicians, was "too good."

"They say I feel too good and go too much and work too long," he told a news conference.

Johnson was born Aug. 27, 1908, near Stonewall, Tex. When he was 5, his family moved to Johnson City, founded by one of his grandfathers.

When Johnson finished high school, he was tired of studying and made a trek to California. Upon his return, books still had no appeal and he went to work as a laborer on the highways, driving a truck and shoveling gravel.

Lyndon Johnson of Texas Becomes President

He finally went back to school at Southwest Texas State Teachers College at San Marcos, working as a janitor and college secretary to pay his expenses. He received his bachelor of science degree in 1930.

Johnson got into politics when he went to Washington in December of 1931 as secretary to Rep. Richard Kleberg of King Ranch fame.

Johnson won a special election to Congress in 1937 after the death of Rep. James P. Buchanan, defeating 10 opponents.

Johnson's first bid for a Senate seat in 1941 was a failure. He lost to Gov. W. Lee O'Daniel. In 1948 he emerged victorious over Gov. Coke Stevenson for a Senate seat by a margin of 87 votes out of almost a million cast.

His wife is the former Claudia Taylor, who is more familiarly known as Lady Bird, a name given her in infancy by her nurse.

Mrs. Johnson, daughter of a wealthy family, owned a radio and television station in Austin. There are two children, Lynda Bird and Lucy Baines.

Runaway Rail Car Kills 2

COLORADO SPRINGS, Colo. (AP) — A runaway power car hurtled off the famous Pike's Peak cog railway Thursday, carrying two workers to death.

Four companions leaped to safety when the brakes failed and the car started its uncontrolled descent down the 14,110-foot mountain.

Downtown Area Stunned by News

The afternoon program of the Farmers Union convention was canceled. President Ed Smith said there will be a memorial service at 7:15 today. Details on Page 2.

A scene of fun and music was transformed into one of sadness and indignation today when the word of the President's assassination reached delegates of the North Dakota Farmers Union convention in Fargo.

A band was playing a lively noon concert when Ed Smith, Farmers Union president, stepped up to the microphone in Memorial Auditorium and said, "I have tragic news."

He told the gathering that news bulletins from Dallas reported that the President had been shot. "We do not know if it was fatal or not."

A single gasp rang through the throng of people and the chatter and gaiety stopped. The band disappeared behind the stage curtain.

Smith told the delegates that he would keep the delegates informed and then arrangements were made to have radio news broadcasts piped directly into the auditorium.

At that time there was still no word that the assassination attempt was fatal.

Transistor radios popped into view throughout the auditorium. People sat in silence, as if they were in church.

When the word came that two priests had said the President was dead, another deep sigh ran through the hall.

One woman standing in the outer lobby fainted. She was given emergency aid and regained consciousness. She was taken to St. Luke's Hospital.

Men and women wept unashamedly.

"This is terrible," one man declared indignantly. "What is this country coming to?"

President Smith announced that the opening of the afternoon session would be delayed until 2:30.

"The convention must go on," he said gravely.

And on the streets and in stores downtown the reaction was the same: People were stunned.

Many didn't believe the word-of-mouth report.

One woman in a cafe was told the President had been shot. She smiled at what she considered the "joke," and remarked, "He deserved it."

Moments later she heard the report over the radio.

She put her hand to her face.

"Oh, my God," she said.

Mrs. Agnes VanMeer, 910 7th St. N., Fargo, told a Forum reporter on the street just before word came that the President had died:

"We've lost the war! The President has been tough enough to put the pressure on both Castro and Khrushchev. . . They are afraid of him."

She said the vice president must start the job over.

She said she is an independent politically.

Most Fargoans found the shooting almost impossible to believe.

"This doesn't happen in this country," said one man, forgetting that several presidents has either been assassinated or been the target of killers.

Norman Hall, 1625 3rd St. N., entered a local barber shop just after hearing the news. He shook his head. "It's too hard to believe . . . It's hard for me to explain myself," he said.

The flag on the Broadway flagpole was lowered to half mast at the news of the President's death, and a band concert scheduled tonight at Shanley High School was canceled.

Dr. Joseph Knutson, president of Concordia College, closed all offices and dismissed classes. He announced that a memorial service will be held in the College Auditorium at 8 p.m. today, Rev. Carl Lee, college pastor, presiding. The public is invited to the services.

At 2 p.m. Farmers Union President Smith was attempting to cancel the remainder of today's program, if he could legally do so under FU bylaws.

The Farmers Union also was attempting to get in touch with U.S. Sen. Quentin Burdick D-N.D., who was to address the convention tonight, and who was en route this afternoon by plane to Fargo. It was expected that Burdick would return to Washington immediately.

* * *

At the Comstock Hotel in Moorhead, the reaction was the same—stunned, shocked unbelief.

No one said anything for a

DOOWNTOWN

(Continued on Page 2, Col. 3)

GOV. JOHN CONALLY
Wounded by Assassin

Stunned Gov. Guy Lauds JFK

"I am stunned at the announcement of President Kennedy's death. That this sort of thing can happen in the United States in 1963 is almost unbelieveable," Gov. William Guy said at Omaha, where he is attending a conference.

"President Kennedy was a man whose contribution to the peace and progress in the world was only beginning to be felt.

"I join all North Dakotans in sincere mourning for a great man whose dedication to his country will never be questioned.

"We sympathize with his young family who now bear the brunt of the sorrow which all of us feel personally."

Front page of the Fargo Forum, November 22, 1963. Courtesy of the Fargo Forum

Cassius Clay excited the boxing world when he stopped Sonny Liston with a seventh-round technical knockout in Miami in February.

President Johnson sent a request to Congress for 962 million dollars to fight poverty in America on March 16, 1964. Thirty million families had an income of less than $2,000.

On April 5, 1964, General Douglas MacArthur died.

Mini skirts became fashionable in 1964.

Stores stocked Kellog's Pop Tarts, Diet Pepsi and the GI Joe Doll for the first time.

Plastic surgeons started using silicone gel sacs for breast implants.

On July 3, 1964, President Johnson signed the Civil Rights Act of 1964. It forbid racial discrimination in employment, public accommodations, union membership, and federally funded programs.

The Palestine Liberation Organization, PLO, was organized. Egypt's president, Gamal Abdal Nasser, was the moving force behind the creation. Yasir Arafat became PLO chairman in 1968.

At the Summer Olympics at Toyko, Japan, American Don Schollander won four gold medals in swimming. There was a buzz around Jim Ryun, the 17-year mile runner for the United States in the 1,500 meters race. It would not be his day. Peter Snell, from New Zealand, would emerge with the gold medal in the race.

United States's involvement in Vietnam took another turn on August 2, 1964. Americans were informed that North Vietnamese torpedo boats fired at American destroyers in the Gulf of Tonkin. Our navy destroyed two ships and damaged one other boat.

Two days later, another attack took place. In response, Johnson had the North Vietnamenese oil tanks and torpedo boat bases at Vinh bombed.

On August 7, 1964, Congress overwhelmingly passed the Southeast Asia Resolution, better known as the Gulf of Tonkin Resolution. Now, the President of the United States had full Congressional authority "to take all necessary measures to repeal any armed attack against the forces of the United States and to prevent further aggression."

Ford came out with the Mustang in 1964.

Probably, the most anticipated release of 1964 was published on September 27. The Warren Commission Report concluded that Lee Harvey Oswald fired three shots from the easternmost window on the sixth floor of the Texas School Book Depository building on Elm Street in Dallas. Furthermore, the report stated that Oswald had acted alone in the assassination of President John F. Kennedy.

Whitey Ford, Mickey Mantle and Roger Maris, played their last World Series as New York Yankees. The St. Louis Cardinals, with Ken Boyer and Bob Gibson, defeated them four games to three.

Louis L'Amour, had two more books on the market in 1964, *Mojave Crossing* and *Hanging Women Creek*. The price of these Bantam paperbacks was 40 cents.

Hiram M. Drache, born in Meriden, Minnesota, and a Professor of History at Concordia College in Moorhead, Minnesota, had his first book published, *The Day Of The Bonanza: A History of Bonanza Farming in the Red River Valley of the North*.

Two other regional books were published in 1964. One was Roral B. Hassrick's, *The Sioux: Life and Customs of a Warrior Society*. The other was John Upton Terrell, *Black Robe: The Life of Pierre-Jean DeSmet missionary, explorer, pioneer*.

The Animals, with Eric Burden singing lead, recorded a song, "The House of the Rising Sun" that stayed No. 1 on the charts for three weeks in September 1964. Roy Orbison's,

"Oh, Pretty Woman" knocked The Animals off the top spot. Three weeks later, the new top single was Manfred Mann's, "Do Wah Diddy."

The Supremes, had their first three No. 1 hits, "Where Did Our Love Go"; "Baby Love"; and "Come See About Me." Their song,"Baby Love," claimed the top spot for almost all of November.

Leonid Brezhnev replaced Nikita Khrushchev as chairman of the Central Committee of the Communist Party on October 14, 1964.Khrushchev's downfall had its beginning in 1963 when his agricultural programs brought famine to the Soviet Union.

On November 3, 1964, Lyndon Johnson was elected President of the United States. It was an electorial landslide for Johnson.Democrats controlled both houses of Congress with large majorities.

There were many new shows on television in 1964. The programs included: *Let's Make A Deal*; *Jeopardy*; *Bewitched*; *Gilligan's Island*; *The Munsters*; *Flipper*; *Gomer Pyle, U.S.M.C.*; *Twelve O' Clock High*; *Voyage to the Bottom of the Sea*; *Daniel Boone*; and the *Addams Family*.

In the 1964-65 television rating season *Bonanza* which had premiered on September 12, 1959, replaced *Beverly Hillbillies* as the most watched show. It was the first western on TV shown in color. *Bonanza* remained on top until the 1967-68 season.

Rudolph the Red-Nosed Reindeer, premiered on NBC stations on Sunday, December 6, 1964. Written by Robert May, the song was made famous by Gene Autry.

In the fall of 1964, Peter Jennings, the son of the vice president of the Canadian Broadcasting Corporation, was contacted by ABC. Jennings, only 26, already had a good reputation as a reporter-anchor in Canada. That fall, Jennings covered the civil rights movement in the South for ABC. Trying to capitalize on the youth market, Elmer Lower, president of the ABC news division, offered Jennings the anchor spot for the *Evening News*. Jennings accepted the job offer late in the year and stayed until Frank Reynolds took over in early 1968.

Arthur "Harpo" Marx, Alan Ladd and Peter Lorre passed away in 1964. Also, Ian Fleming, the British writer who created the James Bond's character in his books, died. That was the year, *Goldfinger* was released.

James Earl Jones, Donald Sutherland, Roy Scheider, John Houseman, Julie Andrews and Raquel Welch made their film debuts in 1964. Andrews won an Oscar for Best Actress in the film, *Mary Poppins*, directed by Robert Stevenson.

Three 1964 movies made AFI list of 100 best movies.The films included: *Mary Poppins*; *My Fair Lady*; and *Dr. Strangelove or: How I learned to Stop Worring and Love the Bomb* (Stanley Kubrick).

George Cukor was the director of the Best Picture of the year, *My Fair Lady*. The movie featured Audrey Hepburn and Rex Harrison, he won the Oscar for Best Actor.

John Ford's last movie, *Cheyenne Autumn* was released in 1964. It featured scenes from Monument Valley in Utah.

Ronald Reagan made his final appearance as a actor in *The Killers*. Two years later in 1966, Reagan was elected Governor of California.

Clint Eastwood starred overseas in *A Fistful of Dollars*, the first so called, "Spaghetti Western." The movie was not released in the United States until 1967.

One other notable movie of 1964 was based on Eugene Burdick-Harvey Wheeler's best seller. After the Cuban missiles crisis, *Fail Safe*, seemed more real, than fiction. Henry

Fonda played the President of the United States. He had to drop an Atomic Bomb on New Fork City because Moscow had been bombed by mistake.

Dr. Martin Luther King received the Noble Peace Prize on December 10, 1964, in Olso, Norway. He was recognized for initiating the concepts of non-violence to the American civil rights movement. Only 35 years old, Dr. King was the youngest recipient of the award.

Sam Cooke was shot to death by a female motel manager on December 11, 1964, in Los Angeles.

The Beach Boys had their first No. 1 song, "I Get Around." Their other hits included: "Fun, Fun, Fun"; "When I Grow Up (To Be A Man)"; and "Dance, Dance, Dance." Brian Wilson stopped touring with the group that December.

In 1964, there were more 17 year-olds in the United States than any other single age group. They faced the possibility of going to Vietnam. By the end of 1964, the number of solders in Vietnam had reached 16,300. President Johnson escalated the war because he did not want to be the first American President to lose a country to the Communists.

On January 4, 1965, in his State of Union address, Lyndon Johnson said, "The Great Society rest on abundance of liberty for all. It demands an end to poverty and racial injustice." He asked for federal support for urban renewal, health care, education and the basic needs of the poor.

On February 13, 1965, President Johnson ordered a vast bombing campaign against military targets in North Vietnam, Operation Rolling Thunder. The first two battalions of marines landed at Da Nang's air base in March. General William Westmoreland, commander of American forces in Vietnam, continuously requested additional troops.

Malcolm X, born Malcolm Little, was killed on February 21, 1965. He was assassinated by rival sects of a Black Muslin organization.

After Project Mercury, the next phase to get a man on the moon was Project Gemini. More powerful rockets and two-man capsules were required at this stage. The astronauts needed maneuvering and docking skills with other spacecraft.

The first two Gemini missions were unmanned rocket tests.

On March 23, 1965, Virgil I. Grissom and John W. White flew the first-manned Gemini mission. They were in space for 4 hours and 53 minutes.

At Lewistown, Maine, Cassius Clay retained his world heavy weight title with a first round knockout of Sonny Liston in May 1965.

On June 3, 1965, James A. Mcdivitt and Edward H. White II lifted off, aboard *Gemini 4*, into space at 11: 16 a.m. During the third orbit, 150 miles above Australia, White made America's first spacewalk. His stroll on a gold-coated cable lasted 20 minutes.

Mcdivitt and White circled the earth 62 times in four days. They raised the American endurance record to 97 hours, 56 minutes, 11 seconds. Americans were thrilled, but the Soviets had made their spacewalk three months earlier.

In June 1965 at San Diego, Jim Ryun beat Peter Snell in a mile race. Ryun's winning time of 3 minutes 55.2 seconds would be the best time for an American high school student for thirty-six years. (On May 27, 2001, at Eugene, Oregon, Alan Webb broke Ryun's record.)

Medicare legislation was passed on July 30, 1965. President Johnson invited former President, Harry Truman, 81, to the signing ceremony. Truman was the first President to recommend that a federal program be established to provide health insurance for the elderly, as part of Social Security.

On August 6, 1965, President Johnson signed the Voting Rights Act of 1965. The legislation prohibited states from using poll taxes, literacy tests or other techniques to curtail voter registration among minorities.

In the second week of August, riots broke out for five days in Watts, a black section of Los Angeles. Property damage in Los Angeles was estimated at $40 million.

Soon afterwards, riots broke out in Chicago.

The Beatles's *Rubber Soul* album came out in 1965. The No. 1 singles on it included: "Eight Days A Week"; "Ticket to Ride"; "Help" and "Yesterday."

The Supreme had three No. 1's, "Stop! In The Name of Love," "Back In My Arms Again" and "I Hear A Symphony."

The Rolling Stones had their first two No. 1 songs, "(I Can't Get No) Satisfaction" and "Get Off My Cloud."

A new duet, Sonny and Cher, had their first No. 1 hit with "I Got You Babe." They had four other songs in the top forty.

The Beach Boys came out with "Help Me, Ronda," a No. 1 single, and "California Girls."

The Bryds, a Los Angeles folk-rock group consisting of Roger McGuinn, David Crosby, Gene Clark, Cris Hillman and Mike Clarke, had two No. 1 hits, "Mr. Tambourine Man" (Bob Dylan) and "Turn! Turn! Turn!(To Everything There Is A Season).

The Monkees, Davy Jones, Mike Nesmith, Peter Tork, and Mickey Dolenz, became a group in 1965. They later starred in a television series, *The Monkees*, 1966-1968.

Bob Dylan had three singles in the top forty that year. "Like a Rolling Stone," climbed to No. 3 on the charts.

Barry Mcguire sang a protest song, "Eve Of Destruction", which went No. 1 in September 1965.It was written by P.F. Sloane.Other Billboard. No 1 hits of the year included: "Downtown" (Petula Clark); "You've Lost that Lovin' Feelin" (The Righteous Brothers); "This Diamond Ring" (Gary Lewis & The Playboys) "My Girl" (The Temptations); "Mrs. Brown You Got A Lovely Daughter" (Herman's Hermits); "I'm Henry VIII, I Am" (Hermit's Hermits); and "Hang On Sloopy" (The McCoys).

The music industry mourned the passing of Nat "King" Cole,and Spike Jones.

In 1965, the following TV programs had their debuts: *The Big Valley*; *Days of our Lives*; *Green Acres*; *Get Smart*; *I Dream of Jennie*; *Wild, Wild West*; and *Hogan's Heroes*.

Bill Cosby became the first black to have star billing in a new dramatic series, *I Spy*. Efrem Zimbalist, Jr. played Inspector Lew Erskine on Quinn Martin's *The F.B.I.*, which started a nine year run on ABC that year.

Diana Rigg replaced Honor Blackman in the British TV series, *The Avergers*. She played Mrs. Emma Peel, the brilliant amateur sleuth who becomes John Steed's partner. The show was first seen on ABC stations the following year.

Edward R. Murrow of CBS News died in 1965. It was the same year, Americans mourned the passing of Winston Churchill. Murrow reported on the noble stand of British people and the Prime Minister during World War II.

Hollywood lost David O. Selznick, a man best remembered for producing *Gone With the Wind*. Stan Laurel of "Laurel and Hardy,"passed away as well. Woody Allen made his acting debut.

Two 1965 movies made the AFI list of 100 greatest movies in 1998. The first film, *The Sound of Music*, directed by Robert Wise, received the Oscar that year for Best Picture. The other film, *Doctor Zhivago*, was directed by David Lean.

Other movies that were well-liked included: *Cat Ballou*; *The Battle of the Bulge*; *The Spy Who Came In From the Cold*; *Thunderball*; *Von Ryan's Express*; *Shenandoah*; and *The Sons of Katie Elder*.

The Bedford Incident, directed by James B. Harris, had a strong Cold War storyline.

Ralph Nader became famous after his book, *Unsafe at Any Speed* came out. Soon, he was America's leading consumer advocate.

Apple Jacks, Gatorade, and Spaghettios came out in 1965. That year, people started wearing soft contact lenses. Lava lamps provided lots of amusement. Fiber optic telephone cables were developed.

The Astrodome opened in Houston, Texas.

The Gateway Arch, which stands next to the Mississippi River in St. Louis, Missouri, was designed by Finnish-born American architect Eero Saarinen in 1948. Although Saarinen, 51, died suddenly in 1961, the memorial to westward expansion was completed in 1965.

Gemini 5 astronauts, Gordon Cooper and Charles Conrad Jr., roared into space on August 21, 1965. They orbited the earth 120 times in eight days. Cooper and Conrad lost eight pounds and came back with beards. More importantly, they beat the Russian endurance record in space.

In October 1965, the *Gemini 6* mission, with Walter M. Schirra Jr. and Thomas P. Stafford had to be aborted. They were supposed to dock with a Agena target rocket, but the rocket failed to reach orbit.

The first major battle in South Vietnam between United States troops and the North Vietnamese Army occurred on November 14-16, 1965. In the Battle of Ia Drang Valley, 305 Americans lost their lives. Harold Moore, in his book, *We Were Soldiers Once and Young* depicted the battle. Moore wrote:

> *Now the dying had begun in earnest, in wholesale lots, here in this eerie forested valley beneath the 2,140-foot-high crest of the Chu Pong massif, which wandered 10 miles back into Cambodia. The din of battle was unbelievable. Rifle and machine guns and mortars and grenades rattled, banged and boomed.*[1]

On December 4, 1965, Frank Borman and James A Lovell, Jr. reached orbit aboard *Gemini 7*. On December 15, 1965, Gemini 6 crew lifted off in their rocket. While circling the earth, the pilots of the two spacecrafts practiced their maneuvering skills.

They finally flew in close-formation for 185 miles. At one time, the two crafts were only one foot apart. The Gemini 6 flight lasted only 25 hours, 51 minutes, 24 seconds.

Borman and Lovell raised America's endurance record in space to 330 hours, 35 minutes, and 13 seconds. They traveled a distance equal to 12 round trips to the moon and performed 17 experiments. Lovell took a photograph of Cape Kennedy from 140 miles up in the air, and the launch pad was visible.

A Charlie Brown Christmas, was first broadcasted in 1965. The special was written by Charles Schulz, the creator of the beloved *Peanuts* comic characters, Charlie Brown, Snoopy, Woodstock, Linus and Lucy.

The Green Bay Packers won another NFL championship.

Joe Nammath, star quarterback for University of Alabama, signed a lucrative contract(over $400,000) with the New York Jets of the American Football League.

In November, 50,000 protesters marched on Washington, D.C. Some of Johnson's advisors began having second thoughts on their role in Vietnam.

By the end of 1965,the number of American troops in Vietnam had increased to more than 180,000. With no end of the war in sight, the anti-war movement in the United States became more vociferous.

In the first week of January 1966, members of the 173rd Airborne Brigade started search-and-destroy operations in the Mekong Delta region of South Vietnam. Two weeks later, 20,000 troops of the First Cavalry Division, aided by South Korean marines and South Vietnamese infantrymen, began another search-and-destroy campaign.

On January 12, 1966, *Batman* premiered on ABC. The show aired on Wednesdays and Thursdays. Adam West and Bert Ward played Batman and Robin.

On January 31, 1966, the Soviet Union launched *Luna 9*. Three days later, their unmanned spacecraft made a soft landing on the moon. The United States lost another "first" in space to the Soviets.

The first No. 1 Billboard hit of 1966, "The Sounds of Silence," belonged to Paul Simon and Art Garfunkel. The folk-rock duo came from New York City. In 1957, they recorded as Tom and Jerry. They split up in 1964 when Garfunkel went to graduate school. Meanwhile, Simon went to England and performed solo. They reteamed in 1965, and "The Sounds of Silence" became their first hit. "Homeward Bound," was another hit in February and March 1966.

The Mamas & The Papas, formed in Los Angeles, featured John Phillips, Michelle Phillips, Denny Doherty, and Cass Elliot. On February 5, 1966, "California Dreamin'," made the top forty Billboard chart. The song peaked at No. 4.

In February 1966, Robert Kennedy expressed concerns about the war in Vietnam. This was Kennedy's first public breach with President Johnson on this matter.

After six weeks of fighting in the Mekong Delta region of South Vietnam against nine Communist battalions of two search-and-destroy campaigns, military commanders reported the "body count" to be 1,342 enemy soldiers killed, 633 captured, and 1,087 suspected Vietcong taken prisoner.

Chapter I
The South Dakota Experience

Rapid City, Ellsworth Air Force Base, Box Elder, New Underwood, Wasta, Wicksville, Owanka, Enning and Wall

The Missouri River divides South Dakota roughly in half. In general, the land west of the Missouri River is best suited for grazing livestock, and the soil east of the river has allowed farmers to raise crops and animals. Among its residents the words "West River" and "East River" are popular terms to describe the geographical division of the state.

The Black Hills is a nature's wonderland in southwestern South Dakota and north-eastern Wyoming. This elliptical-shaped region is about 60 miles wide and 125 miles in length. Two-thirds of the Black Hills lies in South Dakota. The geological forces that shaped the Rocky Mountains made the Black Hills as well. The deposits of granite rocks, red sandstones, clays and limestones have been washed by wind and rain for centuries.

Coniferous forests of Black Hills Spruce and Western Yellow Pine provide a home for a wide variety of wildlife. Common small animals include the cottontail and wood rabbits, squirrels, raccoons, chipmunks and porcupines. Larger ones include the mountain goat, mountain sheep, buffalo, elk, wild burro and bobcat. Also, there is an abundance of game fish. Wild plum, cowcatcher, and juneberry are familiar shrubs. Traditional herbs include horse mint, thistles and violets. The region contains three particular vines, the woodbine, the bittersweet and the wild grape. The wild grape became the pattern for most Black Hills Gold jewelry.

Red Cloud's Treaty of 1868 stipulated that all land west of the Missouri River to the Big Horn Mountains in Wyoming was reservation land and closed to settlement.

The discovery of gold sparked a rush of white settlers to the region. The Black Hills Treaty of 1876 opened the Black Hills and the land north of it for settlement.

Rapid City dates back to February 26, 1876. On February 23, Samuel Scott, John W. Allen, James Carey and John R. Brennan departed Palmer Gulch, north of Harney Peak. The group, led by Scott, looked for a suitable location for a townsite. Three days later, the party found the site in the foothills along Rapid Creek. Rapid City was first called "The Hay Camp," by the miners and prospectors. That name did not last. Eventually, it was named for its geographical location, neighboring Rapid Creek.

Gold attracted the first settlers, but the railroads provided growth and stability. In 1880, the Chicago and Northwestern Railway reached Pierre, and the Chicago, Milwaukee, & St, Paul Railway arrived at Chamberlain. These railroads became known as the Northwestern and Milwaukee, respectively. The two railroads did not cross the Missouri River. The land west of the Missouri River in South Dakota was mostly reservation land. In 1886, the Fremont, Elkhorn, and Missouri Valley reached Rapid City from Nebraska.

The Dawes Act of 1887 allowed reservations to be broken up. Indian families were allotted 160 acres and additional lands were set aside for schools, churches and agencies. Surplus land, then could be sold. In South Dakota, west of the Missouri River, tracts of land opened for settlement in 1889, 1904, 1907, 1908, 1909 and 1911.

In 1905, the Northwestern and Milwaukee railroads started their push towards Rapid City. The Milwaukee crossed the Missouri River first and reached Murdo in 1906. Both railroads reached Rapid City in 1907.

The State School of Mines was established by a territorial enactment of March 7, 1885. The South Dakota legislature authorized funds for a State Cement Plant in 1919. A meat-packing plant and flour mill was built in Rapid City. With 42,399 residents, Rapid City, seat of Pennington County, was South Dakota's second largest city in 1960.

Over one and a half million visitors made their way to the Mount Rushmore National Memorial in 1965. Doane Robinson, best known chronicler of South Dakota history, first came up with the idea of portraying an epic scene out on the granite fronts of Mount Rushmore. Robinson thought about the faces of Old West explorers, like John Fremont, Jedediah Smith, Kit Carson and Jim Bridger.

Mount Rushmore, located three miles west of Keystone, has an altitude of 6,200 feet. The mountain was named for Charles E. Rushmore. He was a New York attorney, who represented eastern interests of the Etta Mine, located south of Keystone. Very rich in tin, Etta Mine was opened in 1883 by Dr. S. H. Ferguson and L. W. McDonald. Rushmore on an inspection tour asked the guide, What's the name of the nearby mountain?" With no name in mind, the guide in jest said, "Mount Rushmore," and the name stuck.

Robinson contacted Gutzon Borglum, an American sculptor who just had finished a monument on Stone Mountain, Georgia. Borglum came to the Black Hills on September 24, 1924. The following day, Robinson and Borglum visited several sites on Harney Peak. Borglum liked Robinson's idea, but he had a different vision. He imagined the busts of George Washington and Abraham Lincoln. Later on, Borglum suggested adding the faces of Thomas Jefferson and Theodore Roosevelt. He made the heads proportionate to men 465 feet tall.[1]

President Calvin Coolidge attended the ground breaking ceremony on August 10, 1927. Charles E. Rushmore donated five thousand dollars to start the project. South Dakota school children collected pennies, nickels and dimes. Congress authorized funds several times for the monument.

After Borglum's death on March 6, 1941, the work was completed by his son, Lincoln, that October.

What was occurring in space generated a lot of interest in the 1960's. The Soviets proved that the surface of the moon could support a manned spaceship. On January 31, 1966, the Soviets launched *Luna 9*, an unmanned 3,000 pound space probe toward the moon. It touched down there three days later.

The Soviets launched a *Cosmos 110* satellite on February 22, 1966. To study the effects of weightlessness, they strapped two dogs in the spacecraft. Breezie and Blackie, the names of the two dogs, became famous around the world.

Meanwhile, the United States space program suffered a tragedy. On February 28, two American astronauts, Elliot See Jr. and Charles Bassett II, died in a jet crash in St. Louis. They had been slated to pilot *Gemini 9*, whose launch date was tentatively set for May.

Thomas Stafford and Eugene Cernan, the backup astronauts for *Gemini 9*, landed safely in a trailing jet.

The average age of soldiers in Vietnam was nineteen, eight years younger than those in World War II and Korea. On March 1, President Johnson made a bid for peace in Southeast Asia, but at the same time, continued to pledge our support for South Vietnam.

Johnson warned the Communists not to "suppose that our desire for peace springs either from weakness or from hesitation."

Rapid City averages about 33 inches of snowfall a year[2]

In late February 1966, residents of the Black Hills gave little thought to the swirling winds in the upper atmosphere. Meteorologists, however, were tracking a low pressure system that had moved into Montana on February 28.

On Tuesday, March 1, the *Rapid City Daily Journal* published the following weather forecast:

> *Snow is expected in the Pacific Northwest, the Rockies, and the north-*
> *east part of the nation. It will be warmer in the Southwest and colder*
> *in the Rockies and New England. South Dakota's forecast read: Scattered*
> *light rain or snow. Turning colder. High 30-42.*[3]

Sunny skies over Rapid City, gave way to drab clouds. Eventually, a trace of precipitation was recorded. Despite the cloud cover, the city had a high of 35 degrees.

By midnight, a weak low pressure system was located over southwestern Montana. It was moving quickly in a south-southeastward direction. The low was intensifying, according to new pressure readings. Behind this system, an arctic high air mass pushed temperatures down in northern Montana and North Dakota.

Rapid City residents went through their normal routines on Wednesday, March 2. Snow was reported in Montana, Wyoming, and Nevada. The precipitation was expected to spread into the Dakotas.

The five-day forecast for Rapid City stated:

> *Temperatures will average from 10 to 15 degrees below normal highs of*
> *about 39 and normal lows near 16. The colder temperatures should mod-*
> *erate early next week.*
>
> *Snow is expected early Thursday and again on Saturday with three or*
> *more inches expected.*[4]

On this day in 1965, Air Force pilot Captain Hayen J. Lockart was shot down, north of the Vietnamese Demilitarized Zone. He was our first POW of the war in Vietnam.

Robert McNamara, Secretary of Defense, indicated that the number of U.S. troops in Vietnam had reached 215,000, with another 20,000 on the way.[5]

Radio stations throughout the United States played the "Ballad of the Green Berets" in March 1966. The folk song was written by Staff Sergeant Barry Sadler, a combat veteran of Vietnam. In his heartfelt voice, Sadler sang:

> *Put silver wings on my son's chest,*
> *Make him one of America's best,*
> *He'll be a man they'll test one day-*
> *Have him win the green beret.*

"The Ballad of the Green Berets" reached the top of the Billboard Charts on March 5. For the next five weeks, it remained the Number 1 hit in the United States.[6]

By noon, there was snow and rain showers in the Dakotas. Moving towards Colorado, the low deepened. Meteorologist revised their forecasts and issued precautionary storm warnings.

Courtesy of RCA Records

Earl Thomas, a salesman for Ceco Steel, left his home in Rapid City, Wednesday afternoon. He had some contacts to make in North Dakota.

People made plans to watch the premier of high school production of *The Music Man,* on Friday night.

Bud Deutscher and Nick Eckes, U.S. Weather Bureau meteorologists, went to their station at the airport, located about ten miles east of Rapid City, Wednesday afternoon. As a precaution, Deutscher and Eckes brought extra food and warm clothes.

With bad weather approaching the area, civilians who worked at Ellsworth Air Force Base, were allowed to leave early in the afternoon. Farmers and ranchers moved livestock to barns or nearby corrals.

Snow started to fall in Lead and Deadwood. Spearfish reported snow later in the day.

By midnight March 2, the storm system was centered over Pueblo, Colorado. The low continued to gain strength. The path of the storm was uncertain. If it continued on its present course, Oklahoma and Texas would soon be affected. If the low turned straight east, Nebraska, Kansas and Missouri faced the onslaught of bad weather. If it veered north, the Dakotas and Minnesota would feel the impact.

It didn't take long for meteorologists to receive their answer. The storm was steering a northeasterly course. There was an abundance of warm moist air flowing into the central plains from the Gulf of Mexico and pushing north. When the warm moist air collided with the colder air of the trailing high, the result could be heavy precipitation. Barometric readings continued to fall. This meant there was the possibility of very strong winds on the horizon.

The storm arrived that night. The spruce forests of the Black Hills were cloaked under a blanket of heavy snow.

Deutscher and Eckes were not relieved, when their shift ended late Wednesday night. Fred McNally, chief of the Rapid City Weather Bureau, told their replacements to stay home. Visibility and road conditions were bad.

On Thursday morning, March 3, the residents of Rapid City checked the weather information. They learned that blizzard conditions would last most of the day in the west. In central and northeast South Dakota, blizzard conditions were expected to continue through Friday morning.

By Thursday morning, 12 to 24 inches of snow had fallen on the higher elevations of the Black Hills. Lower elevations recorded about 7 to 12 inches. Wednesday night's lows remained in the mid twenties.

Deutscher and Eckes reported that blizzard conditions had developed around midnight. Visibility was between zero and one-sixteenth of a mile. The weathermen figured Rapid City had received 7 inches of snow. "It looks like we're getting three feet," one of them said, "but we're not."[7]

Storm announcements, including school closings, disrupted regular schedules on Thursday. The post office was open, but no mail was received or sent out of Rapid City. No garbage was collected. City hall and courthouse offices were closed. City hospitals provided health care with limited staff. After several hours of business, the First National Bank closed its doors . The American National Bank and Trust maintained its regular hours. The Rushmore State Bank never opened its doors.

Flights into and out of Rapid City's Municipal Airport were canceled on Thursday. Bus schedules were curtailed as well. The westbound Jackrabbit Line bus, which ran from

Minneapolis to Pierre and on to Rapid City, arrived in town at 7 a.m., five hours late. The Continental Trailways bus from Denver reached Rapid City at 8 a.m., only two hours behind schedule.

Ed Hawley, Highway Department maintenance superintendent at Rapid City, indicated that two plows had left Rapid City on Thursday morning. They were called back. Hawley said, "As soon as the wind dies down we will be in business. But until then there's no use in getting the plow out there and getting it stuck." Explaining further, he declared that, at times, the wind was blowing at over 50 mph.[8]

The *Journal* reported that "their switchboard was lit up like the proverbial Christmas tree most of Thursday morning." Their subscribers wanted to know the status of Thursday's edition. The staff began putting the paper together, ninety minutes behind schedule.

Newspapers were delivered to city carriers early in afternoon. As for home delivery, the parents of the carriers made the final decision.

No papers were delivered outside of Rapid City on Thursday.

The Rapid City Police Department grounded its fleet of cars. They handled emergency calls with four-wheel drive vehicles donated by local residents. Chains were put on the vehicles and two-way radios were installed. They transported key medical personnel to area hospitals.

Deutscher and Eckes reported that wind gusts had reached 62 mph in the forenoon. Thursday afternoon, wind gusts of 71 mph were recorded. The center of the storm, stalled over central South Dakota, and the barometric pressure dropped again. With this information, the weathermen did not expect the weather to improve until late Friday or Saturday.

Residents overwhelmed the phone system in Rapid City on Thursday. M. A. Peterson, local manager of Northwestern Bell Telephone Company, indicated that the slow dial tone was caused by an overload of its circuits.

Mrs. Arlene Thomas, wife of Earl Thomas, waited for a phone call from her husband. She was home with their children, Susan and Robert.

City firemen had a busy day Thursday. At 1:29 p.m., they took a man to the hospital to see his wife who had just been in a car accident. Meanwhile, other firemen responded to a house call where a television set had started on fire and was smoking.

A half hour later, the fire alarm rang again. Eleven minutes later, the firemen reached the trailer home of Mr. and Mrs. Dan Shaeffer. Although the firemen did their best, they could not save their home. The couple stayed with the Sven Hansons, owners of the trailer court, until the storm was over. Then, they moved in with other relatives in Rapid City.

How bad was the storm? The firemen were twenty feet away from the burning trailer and they could not see it. A pump froze up on one of their trucks.

After this fire Thursday afternoon, the firemen spent several hours transporting blood from the blood bank to the hospitals. Normally, the blood bank director made the deliveries, but he was stormed in at home.

At 4:50 p.m., the firehouse received a frantic call from a homeowner on East Boulevard. Strong winds had broken a large window on his house, and snow was being blown into the interior of the structure. Fireman placed a tarp over the hole.

Two hours later, firemen took the body of Mrs. Eliza Hellekson, 86, to the Hobart-Catron funeral home. Her husband, Oscar Hellekson, had passed away in 1962. The Hellekson's lived on a ranch near Faith before moving to Rapid City in 1951. The couple had three daughters and two sons, twenty grandchildren, several great-grandchildren and great-great-grandchildren.

About the time local residents were ready to eat supper, the power lines came down on Fairmont Boulevard. While utility crews repaired the damages, firemen protected the site.

The phone in the firehouse rang again and again. A furnace overheated on East Main at 7:58 p.m. A clothes dryer started on fire on Oak Avenue at 8:20 p.m. At 8:33 p.m., Mike Seupert, a sick boy, was taken to the hospital.

Around 9:30 p.m., an off duty firemen, Kenneth Johnson, called the station. Johnson was also an officer in the South Dakota National Guard. He mentioned that the National Guard had an ambulance they could use. They picked up Johnson and the ambulance at the National Guard facilities. It was their last excursion for the day[9]

The police were involved in an impromptu act of kindness on Thursday. A stranded family, with little money, showed up at the police station. The officers took up a collection for them. The grateful family checked into a rooming house.

Norton Lawellin, a representative of Montana-Dakota Utilities, remarked that his company's transmission facilities were okay, but utility repairmen were being hampered by the weather.

Leo Hadcock of the Black Hills Power Company reported that Rapid City had two trouble spots, one in the north end of the town, the other in the south. Hadcock said, "Our biggest problem is getting crews and equipment to those areas to find the trouble. With the winds blowing as they are, two wires can bump together, causing a momentary power outage. But the equipment at their sub-station will soon put the lines back into service."[10]

Power was lost outside of Rapid City.

The North Nike site, located three miles north of the Ellsworth Air Force Base, lost its electricity at noon on Thursday. The place was home for fifteen Air Force families and the Hillcrest School For Boys.

Snowdrifts at the North Nike site, were reported to be 7 feet high on Thursday.

The Civil Engineering Squadron kept the runways and other critical areas open at the Ellsworth Air Force Base. Pilots of the B52's and KC135's remained on alert. They waited out the storm in nearby shelters.

In western South Dakota, Minutemen missile crews were not relieved during the storm. The launch facilities were underground and self sufficient.

Military and civilian personnel who lived off base were advised not to report until highways and access roads were open.

Bud Deutscher and Nick Eckes remained on duty at the airport. They talked about past historic blizzards that had struck South Dakota. The most recent one was in 1949. Fred McNally, their boss, remained on duty for seventy-six hours during that storm. The weather station did not have equipment to measure wind gusts in 1949. Unofficial reports from Ellsworth listed winds at 100 mph. South Dakota had one fatality in that storm.

With no letup of the blizzard in sight, Deutscher and Eckes wondered if they could beat McNally's record. Thursday night, the weathermen called the manager of the Airport Cafe. They wanted permission to break into the storeroom to get some food. They received the okay.

The employees of Bennett-Clarkson Memorial Hospital could not go home, Thursday night. Other individuals were stranded there as well. People slept on extra mattresses that were scattered around the staff lounge and in the X-ray department. Others passed the night away on emergency carts and cushions taken from chairs.

Everyone did not stay in the hospital. Seven individuals made a short dash in the blizzard. They spent the night at the home of Dr. Arthur Lampert.

The strong winds began to take their toll on the second night. A half hour past midnight, Friday, March 4, the electricity went out at Rushmore Junior College, located six miles northeast of Rapid City. Three families and five students struggled to stay warm. They had no heat, lights, or running water.

As of 8:00 a.m. Friday, Deutscher and Eckes had been on duty for 41 consecutive hours. They expected winds of 30 to 60 miles to last most of the day. Thursday night's low was 6 above. Rapid City's high on March 4 was 19 degrees. With the wind chill factor, temperatures remained below zero. Brief snow flurries left .1 inch of precipitation.

The *Journal* published its paper on Friday, but no deliveries were made outside of Rapid City.

Tornadoes spun down in Alabama and Mississippi, late Thursday night. The first reports out of Alabama indicated that one person had died and eleven were injured. In Jackson, Mississippi, and the rural counties to the east, the death toll was at 57 (as of 2 a.m. March 4), and the number of injured victims reached 411.

Local police officers feared more even more deaths in Scott County, Mississippi. Larry Parks, announcer for WQFT-FM at Forest in Scott County, said, "many homes are just gone...and the people in them are missing, too."[11]

Residents learned that two famous television comedians had died within hours of each other on March 3, 1966. Fame had come late for William Frawley and Alice Pearce. Frawley became well-known after playing Fred Mertz on the *I Love Lucy Show,* and Bub, the housekeeper, on *My Three Sons.* Pearce became famous for portraying Mrs. Glayds Kravitz, the nosey next-door neighbor to Darrin and Samantha Stephens on *Bewitched.*

Residents had problems making long distance connections. Down lines in other parts of South Dakota prevented many phone calls from going through.

There was a power outage at the Ellsworth Air Force Base. Backup sources, however, generated power for the critical areas of the base.

Friday morning, on-duty firemen picked up off-duty firemen at their homes for the shift change. They transported five nurses to the Sioux Sanatorium.

The phone rang at the firehouse in Rapid City at 10:25 a.m. Firemen worked their way to an East Denver residence. Smoke was rolling out from under the trailer. The firemen immediately discovered the cause of the fire. The heat tape wrapped around the water pipes started the insulation on fire. They quickly extinguished the fire. The home suffered no other damage. Around 11:30 a.m., the firemen picked up a discharged patient at the hospital and gave him a ride home.

The temperature in the warmest room at the Hillcrest School For Boys had dropped to 42 degrees Friday morning. Looking outside through the whirling snow, its occupants glimpsed snowdrifts at least 8 feet high. Everyone had gathered in one room. They ate cold meals and heated cups of coffee with candles. Maurice Williams, headmaster at Hillcrest, had a sick boy with chills and a bad cold.

The Air Force families faced similar troubles at the North Nike site. There was a shortage of food in some of the households. Several families gathered together in one house. That place did not require electricity for its heat.

The warmest room at Rushmore College was the kitchen. By Friday morning, the temperatures in the bedrooms hovered around 30 degrees. The residents piled on blankets and slept with their clothes on. After they woke up, they headed for the kitchen. The boarders had plenty of food and drinking water, they bottled ten gallons before power was lost. Their dirty dishes were washed with melted snow. To pass the time, they played Monopoly and listened to a transistor radio. They had a kerosene lantern, but only a few hours of fuel.

Ralph Fenner, the night custodian at North Junior High, went to work at eleven o'clock Wednesday night. Thursday morning when his shift was over, Fenner found himself stormed in. He spent the day at the school. There was plenty of food in the school cafeteria. Thursday night, he went back to work. Friday morning, he still could not leave the school.

Earl Thomas did not call home on Friday. His wife and children remained hopeful.

By Friday noon, Rapid City officials were ready with plans to dig out the city. Mayor Henry Baker addressed the media. First, he thanked the people who had volunteered their four-wheel drive vehicles which the police had used for emergency runs. Then, he praised the people who volunteered the use of company equipment for digging out the town. Many others said, "they would help out any way they could." Finally, Mayor Baker commended the townfolks for being good natured about the situation. In a prepared statement Baker said:

> We'll be working 24 hours a day, straight through the weekend and by
> Monday morning when business places open we hope we'll have the snows
> cleared. We are going to concentrate on the main streets and the streets
> into the schools over the weekend, working both Saturday and Sunday,
> getting them plowed out and the snow removed. Today and tonight, one of
> our biggest problems in clearing the streets will be dealing with cars stuck
> in the drifts. Snow is drifting around them and increasing the difficulties.
> Unless people have a very good reason they shouldn't take a chance on get-
> ting their cars out on the streets and becoming stuck.[12]

Friday afternoon the winds let up somewhat. As the visibility improved, city, county and state crews started clearing the streets. Although several plows had been out earlier in the day, the main effort did not start until well into the afternoon. Ralph Fenner made it home Friday afternoon.

The weathermen at the Rapid City airport were relieved at 3:00 p.m. Starting Wednesday afternoon, Bud Deutscher and Nick Eckes had been on duty for 48 straight hours.

The strongest sustained winds Thursday and Friday were 56 and 48 mph, respectively. Visibility was one-eighth mile or less for thirty hours straight in the 1966 blizzard.

The winds finally died down Friday evening. Huge drifts were left in the wake. People made trips to the closest store for groceries and cigarettes.

Residents at North Nike site and the Rushmore Collage spent another night without heat and power. It was a cold night, the recorded low was 7 degrees.

With daylight Saturday morning, the hard work of digging out began in earnest. There was some sun, light winds and an eventual high of 24. Although Rapid City was on the southwest edge of the storm, 8 inches of snow fell in the area. The precipitation contained .83 inches of water.

A snowplow, working one quarter of a mile west of Faith on Highway 212, noticed a partially buried car in the ditch. Upon further investigation, a body was discovered in the vehicle.

The individual was identified as Earl Thomas, the missing Rapid City salesman. Authorities believed Thomas died of asphyxiation sometime on Thursday. The news was broken to his wife.

Earl Thomas, born in 1912 at Pembina, North Dakota, was an all-conference center for the North Dakota State University football team. He married Arlene Johnson at Winnipeg, Manitoba, in 1936. They came to Rapid City in 1956. Survivors included his wife, three children, Mrs. Dean Koch of Imperial Beach, California, Susan and Robert, both at home, and his mother, Mrs. Anne Larson of Ekalaka, Montana. His funeral was held on March 8, 1966.

Saturday morning, Harold Irish, Pennington County Civil Defense director, dispatched a plow to the North Nike site. Drifts, 10 to 12 feet high slowed the advance. In the meantime, food was air dropped to the Air Force families. They shared their bonanza with those at the school. Power was still out.

A family that lived at the Rushmore College dressed warmly and walked into Rapid City. They reported on the conditions there.

Later in the afternoon, the road was cleared to the college.

Power would be off until Saturday night, so people left the campus. Afterwards, Bill Jung, school registrar, said:

> We were lucky in that we did make it through the first day of the blizzard. The kitchens were warmed from the heat of the gas-operated stoves, so we could go in there for a while to get warm. Some snow did gust into the buildings. They weren't built for blizzards conditions. They are constructed of concrete blocks with wooden ceilings, and the wind did blow through cracks between the blocks and ceilings.[13]

Pennington became the first county in South Dakota to enact "Operation Bulldozer." This plan originated in August 1965. Representatives from the South Dakota National Guard, the State Civil Defense and heavy equipment contractors believed they could combine the resources of private companies and public agencies. Personnel and equipment would be shared, and payment for services would be at cost. Participation was strictly voluntary, and it would be run by the Associated General Contractors, Highway and Heavy Chapter.

Saturday morning, Harold Irish announced that four local contractors would help clear snow. As part of "Operation Bulldozer," they opened up most of the county roads and the hangers at the Rapid City Airport. They broke trails to cattle herds in Rapid Valley.

A State Police radio report indicated that primary roads in the Black Hills were open, but travel was not advised as many overpasses on Interstate 90 were still blocked by large drifts. In some places, only one lane was cleared. The announcement emphasized that the men clearing the highways needed time to do their work.

The Rapid City's Street Department had an abundance of calls. Residents were informed that a single path would be cut through all the streets. A thorough cleaning would be done, later. If possible, the city wanted vehicles off the streets.

Snow removal was very time-consuming. Equipment operators worked at a slow pace because parked vehicles were hard to see in the drifts. Downtown on Main and St. Joe Streets, the snow had to be hauled away in trucks.

Although it seemed odd, some individuals parked their cars on their lawns Wednesday night. By thinking ahead, they avoided the extra work of getting their cars off the streets.

With warm temperatures forecasted for Monday, some people decided not to dig out their vehicles. The sun and chinook winds would do their work.

It was a marvelous time for children. They explored the huge drifts and played on them with their friends. Jim Wilson showed his son, Tom, and his son's friends, Jimmy and Greg Keck, and Craig Meier how to build an igloo on their North Brook residence.

National Guard helicopters flew over eastern Pennington County Saturday. Members searched stranded vehicles. To their relief, they found no dead bodies.

The three commercial airlines of Rapid City, Western, North Central and Frontier Airlines resumed their regular scheduled flights on Saturday. That evening, Continental Bus Line reported that its bus from Cheyenne had arrived in Rapid City only thirty minutes late.

Relief came to North Nike site late Saturday afternoon.

While a snowplow worked on snowbanks on the way to the housing site, a rural electric cooperative truck arrived from another direction. At 5:00, power was reestablished. That night, the snowplow opened up the area.

The recovery process continued on Sunday, March 6. National Guard helicopters continued their search for bodies. The Civil Air Patrol had planes up in the air.

Cattlemen in Rapid Valley suffered losses, but it was too early to tell what the actual losses for Pennington County would be. Saturday's reports appeared optimistic because only a few ranchers had been contacted.

Walter Taylor, a Rapid Valley rancher, believed that the number of actual dead cattle would not be as great as during the 1949 blizzard, but "condition losses" probably would be heavier. Explaining his point, he said, "the blizzard which began Wednesday night was preceded by a slick, gummy sleet which soaked the animals to their hides. Ice formed over their eyes and noses, causing suffocation and blindness. Many animals wandered and eventually were forced off their feet."[14]

Another longtime Rapid Valley rancher, William M. Anderson, said, "I have seen nothing like it in 47 years of ranching." Anderson and his son, Wayne R., had a feeding operation in 1966. He indicated that the cattle in their feed lots came through the storm without difficulty. It was a different story for the 400 cattle, he had out on the range. His hired hands had not located all his cattle by Saturday night and some were dead.

On Monday, it was business as usual in Rapid City. Sunday night, the thermometer dropped to 4 above in Rapid City. But, mild chinook winds Monday helped to push it up to a high of 57 for the day. The contrast between huge piles of snow and warm temperatures was quite amazing.

A Rapid City man, Dennis Christenson, had quite a scare. His account was reported in the *Journal* on Monday. Late Wednesday night, Christenson was traveling on Interstate 90 near New Underwood, when the storm hit the region. A short time later, he became stranded when his car stalled. After a lot of thought, Christenson decided to leave his car. The snow stung his face as he made his way in the darkness.

First, Christenson located a feedlot, and shortly afterwards he stumbled upon a truck. Here was shelter at last. The keys were in the vehicle. The truck started, and the warm heat drained some of the cold out of his body. Mr. Christenson had no thoughts of leaving again.

With the arrival of daylight, he discovered that he was only fifty feet away from a trailer home. The family inside the house noticed him about that time. A bundled man dashed out to the truck and invited Christenson to wait out the storm in their home. Saturday morning, Christenson returned home.

Charles Harkins, a Rapid City man, was stuck in his car in downtown Sturgis during the storm. Harkins worked a long time trying to get it free. He gave up and walked several blocks to a cafe. Harkins needed medical attention, as his feet were frostbitten.

Box Elder was founded in 1907 when the Northwestern Railroad reached a general store on Box Elder Creek on its way to Rapid City. The population of the town boomed after Ellsworth Airforce Base was activated in 1950. By 1960, the town had a population of 150, compared with 30 in 1940.

There was little movement in Box Elder during the blizzard. Power outages caused some hard times. On Saturday, the local residents shoveled out their homes and vehicles. A State Highway Department rotary plow, working east out of Rapid City, cleared a lane on Interstate 90 to Box Elder. Over the weekend, other key roads around town and to the base were cleared. The West River Electric Cooperative restored power to its customers. There was some cattle losses in the vicinity.

New Underwood, located about twenty miles east of Rapid City, was named in honor of one guy's business partner. In 1906, Isaac Humphrey donated the right-of way-across his land for the price of one request. He wanted the town to be named Underwood, for his partner Johnny Underwood, but as there was already another Underwood at that time, the "New" was added.

Walter D. Miller came from New Underwood. After South Dakota Governor George Mickelson died in a tragic plane accident in 1993, Miller, Lieutenant Governor at the time, assumed the top office.

New Underwood, home for 462 people in 1960, became a snow trap durint the storm. The town lost power, Wednesday night, March 2. Soon afterwards, residents lost their phone connections. New Underwood was isolated on Thursday and Friday.

George Weitzel, a resident of New Underwood, had business in Mobridge on Wednesday. The storm caught Weitzel on State Highway 63, near Timber Lake, South Dakota. He decided to wait out the storm. On this trip, Weitzel had worn oxfords and a light top coat. He had no food, overshoes or extra blankets in the car. Weitzel ate the fine snow that drifted into his vehicle. He was marooned in his car for seventy-two hours.

After the storm ended on Saturday, the O'Leary brothers went out to feed their cattle. They discovered Weitzel in his car. The Timber Lake ranchers took Weitzel back to their home. They gave him warm clothes and hot food.

Saturday morning, the State Highway plow reached the New Underwood exit around nine o'clock. There were drifts 16 to 18 feet high between Rapid City and New Underwood on Interstate 90. A safe distance behind the plow, was a caravan of twenty-five cars and trucks.

Cattle were buried alive at the livestock pen at Western Feeders, Inc. Residents of New Underwood rallied to the cause. They freed some cattle just in time. Dead animals were discovered in the frantic diggings. By Monday, livestock losses in the feedlot had exceeded fifty head.

New Underwood's Main Street had snowbanks between 6 and 10 feet deep. In other parts of the town, drifts were close to 25 feet high. One of the first tasks assigned to the town's lone bulldozer was to forge a path to the highway.

Ken Norgard, *Journal* photographer, was one of the first outsiders to reach New Underwood after the blizzard. He learned that its residents had encountered no emergencies during the storm. He said, "I walked to the top of a snowdrift, looked into a hole where someone had been digging–and at the bottom was a Cadillac." Norgard visited with some of the town's oldtimers. In their opinion, the present situation was, "the worst they had ever seen."[15]

Doane Robinson wrote, *A History of the Dakota or Sioux Indians,* published in 1904, Robinson had a hand in the naming of Wasta. Its name comes from a Sioux word, "waste or wastah" which means "good."

In 1960, Wasta had 196 residents.

Wasta received 8 inches of snow during the blizzard. Residents on the West River Electric Association suffered through a long power outage, Thursday afternoon to Saturday afternoon. Their telephones went dead several hours after the power failure on the WREA system. There was some livestock losses in the area.

Wicksville, Owanka and Enning had experiences similar to Wasta. The Golden West exchanges at Wicksville and Enning lasted only a couple of hours on emergency power. Then, the batteries froze and cracked. Acid dripped on the floors at the telephone exchanges. The floors were torn up and replaced later on. The WREA power failure was directly related to troubles on the Bureau of Reclamation lines, according to Cone Hunter, local manager for the WREA.

Wall, established in 1907, acquired its name because it is located near the high wall of what is now known as Badlands National Monument. Located in eastern Pennington County, Wall became famous for its drugstore. The source of fame began in 1935. Dorothy Hustead realized that many motorists had been bypassing their hometown of Wall. Her husband's drugstore had been struggling to make ends meet. So, in the style of the popular Burma Shave road signs, they decided to put up their own signs: "Get a soda. Get root beer. Turn next corner. Just as near. To Highway 16 and 14. Free ice water. Wall Drug." Eventually, over a million people would stop in Wall each year.[16]

In 1960, the population of Wall was 629.

In early March 1966, the residents of Wall looked forward to upcoming events. *Operation Crossbow,* starring Sophia Loren, George Peppard, and Trevor Howard was scheduled for the weekend of March 5, at the Riata Theatre.

Young boxers who worked out in the basement of the American Legion Hall had a fight card at Martin on March 5. Joe Crawford, the fight promoter, expected eight of the boys from Wall to fight there. The following week, they would fight at home.

A square dance jamboree was set for March 11.

Bishop R. Garrison announced that Reverend Kenneth L. Harlgrove would be the new Methodist minister for Wall and Wasta beginning March 15. Pastor Harlgrove had been in Presho since 1961. He replaced Rev. John Jacoway who had taken a position in Mitchell in January. Reverend Harlgrove would move to Wall.

Wall's basketball fans traveled to Kadoka on March 2 for the District 30 Basketball Tournament. The roads and highways were slippery. That morning, light rains fell. Temperatures fell. The rain turned to sleet. The countryside was coated with a thin layer of ice. The precipitation turned to snow. Some fans who did not make the trip listened to the game on the radio.

The Wall Eagles played Midland in their opening game. Wall's Coach Ken Poppe said, "The game did not go as they wanted." The final score was Midland 56 Wall 47. For seniors, Rodney Gunn, Tom Rollands and Gary Sebade, it was their last game.[17]

In the middle of the night, the winds picked up and it snowed.

Storm announcements, including school closing, were heard in Wall Thursday morning. Weathermen on KPLO-TV in Rapid City expected the blizzard to last Thursday and most of Friday. Wind gusts up to 70 mph were reported in the region. The forecasts predicted 8 to 10 inches of snow.

Around noon, the lights in many homes snapped on and off. After their lights flickered, people found and placed their flashlights and transistor radios in a handy spot.

Two hours later, power from the WREA failed completely.

The Golden West Telephone Cooperative depended on electricity from the WREA. After the emergency batteries at the local exchange were drained, Wall residents heard nothing when they picked up their phones to use them.

The editor of the *Pennington County Courant* said:

> *The great exodus started late Thursday afternoon. Residents who lived in the government trailer headed for the Joe Knapp Hill Crest camp. Their storm trek was several blocks. Around town other families left their homes at different times on Thursday and Friday. The homes of Doug Calhane and Dave Whitwers provided shelter for six families. Many other families, like Calhane and Whitwers, shared the warmth of their homes.[18]*

The Harold Mortensen family of Wall went to bed, early Thursday night. A gas stove in their kitchen provided the only heat for the house. His wife, Elsie, woke up about 4:30 in the morning. Harold was gone. She found him unconscious by the oven. Mrs. Mortensen struggled out the door and across the street to a neighbor's house. There, the distraught wife talked to Joe Crawford.

Mr. Crawford went for help. Just before sunrise, he went to the Highway Shop. Crawford told the maintenance men that Harold needed help.

A rescue plan was quickly organized. An oxygen tank was needed, so they plowed a path to Bill Walsh's home. Then, they plowed their way back to the Mortensen place. For an hour and a half, they tried to awaken Mr. Mortensen.

Meanwhile, Mrs. Mortensen and her three children were taken next door to Boyd Kitterman's place for first aid. Mrs. Mortensen did not respond well to the treatment for carbon monoxide poisoning. Luckily, the children were not affected by the dangerous fumes.

Mrs. Mortensen was taken to Rapid City in an ambulance. Getting her there, was another ordeal.

The end of the storm came Saturday morning. Here's how the *Pennington County Courant* editor described the aftermath:

> *Saturday morning, the storm was over and the sun came out bright and clear. The power, however was still off, but came on for an hour, and then off until eight o'clock Saturday night.*
>
> *The day was spent with mixed emotions. Most folks were grinning and bearing the losses that they had sustained and the tremendous work that the storm had "put on their door step."*
>
> *Many places had attics well filled with snow. Sheds and garages with only a small crack had the building blown full of snow.[19]*

Besides snow removal, residents had to fix broken water pipes that froze.

Mrs. Mortensen returned to Wall, Saturday night.

Area ranchers lost livestock in the blizzard of January 8, 1949. Overall losses from the March 1966 blizzard were much higher. Individual losses ranged from a few head to forty, or more. Frank Walker, John Swanson, Eddie Geigle, George Knapp, Darwin Knapp, Walter Whitcher, Leo and Dennis Foster and others lost cattle due to the 1966 blizzard.

On a happier note, some ranchers found their cattle intermixed with other herds.

Harold M. Mortensen's funeral was on March 9. He was 42 years old when he died of asphyxiation.

Custer, Hill City, Hermosa, Fairburn, Buffalo Gap, Hot Springs, Edgemont, Igloo, Provo and Oelrichs

Custer, the county seat of Custer County, and the oldest city in the Black Hills began as a boom town. Reports of gold in the Black Hills surfaced as early as 1834. Horatio H. Ross, one of General George A. Custer's mining engineers, discovered gold on French Creek on July 27, 1874.

According to Mrs. Annie D. Tallent, the first white woman in the Black Hills and author of a historical treatise on the Black Hills, an estimated 11,000 people came to the Black Hills between November 15, 1875, and March 1, 1876. In a couple of weeks, Custer's population dropped from an estimated 6,000 people to 30, after gold was discovered in Deadwood Gulch in February 1876.[20]

Wind Cave, breathtaking with alternating currents of air rushing in and out, was discovered by a hunter in 1881. The land was claimed by a private individual in 1900. Private ownership of the cave spurred a national controversy.

The federal government took possession of the cave and surrounding lands on January 9, 1903. It became Wind Cave National Park. In addition to the foregoing park, Congress created the Jewel Cave National Monument in 1908. The park, located twelve miles west of Custer, contains two similar caves, Jewel and Casper.

South Dakota created Custer State Park, a forest and game preserve of 91,400 acres, in 1913.

Unlike many other gold and silver boom towns, Custer enjoyed a rebirth. In 1960, the city had 2,105 residents. Besides a tourist mecca, Custer is home for logging companies, sawmills and planing mills.

Custer had light snow flurries on March 3, .21 inches of precipitation. Custer's high for the day was 24 above. The evening low of 3 degrees. The *Custer County Chronicle* reported winds of 25 mph in town on Thursday.

On Friday, the winds were calm in Custer. The town experienced colder temperatures, the high and low for the day was 9 above and minus 1, respectively.

All city streets and roads were open and school was held.

Hill City escaped the "big blizzard of 1966," accordingly to the *Custer County Chronicle.*

Hermosa, Fairburn and Buffalo Gap, communities located in the eastern half of Custer County, experienced stormy weather. Snows were light and scattered. The hardships were minimal, compared to other areas in South Dakota. Blocked roads were reported in the area. Local ranchers lost some livestock.

For over 250 years, the Cheyennes and Sioux waged war for control of the Black Hills. The Sioux won the last battle and that place became known as Battle Mountain. They used the Black Hills for hunting grounds; the springs and streams for bathing, and the trees for firewood. The tribes, however, settled mostly to the west and south of the Black Hills.

Battle Mountain is located near Hot Springs. The territory was coveted because of the nearby warm springs, the Indians called them "Wi-wi-la-ka-ta" (Springs hot). President Grant opened settlement to the Black Hills with a proclamation on February 28, 1877.

Probably, the first white men to discover the hot springs were part of the Jenney Scientific Expedition of 1875. Walter P. Jenney, a geologist, was sent by the United States government to determine how valuable the mineral resources of the Black Hills were. Other members of the group included Colonel Dodge, Professor Henry Newton and Dr. V. T. McGillicuddy.[21]

Hot Springs was platted by the Hot Springs Townsite Company in December 1882. A stagecoach station and hotel were built in 1883.

Located along the Fall River, Hot Springs was home to 4,943 people in 1960. The South Dakota's Soldiers Home, the National Home for Disabled Veterans and the Battle Mountain Sanitarium were built here. Soldiers with tuberculosis were treated in the facilities.

Hot Springs averages about 36 inches of snow annually.[22]

A high of 51 degrees was recorded on Tuesday, March 1.

There was a change in the weather on Wednesday. Colder temperatures brought a light mixture of rain and snow. That precipitation ended late in the afternoon. Light snow fell very early Thursday. Overall, about three inches of snow fell in Hot Springs. Highs on March 3 and March 4 were in the mid twenties. The brisk winds caused ground drifting, but traffic was not effected.

According to the *Hot Springs Star*:

> The winds blew during the blizzard days but there were no additional snowfalls and business went on as usual. The schools were in operation with no more than the usual number of absentees.[23]

Relatives and friends of the late Senator Francis Case attended the dedication ceremony for a new bridge over the Potomac River in Washington, D. C. on April 20, 1966. Senator Case had served many years on the Senate committee that governed the Capital City. Fellow South Dakota Senator, George McGovern was instrumental in getting the bridge named the Francis Case Memorial Bridge.

Edgemont lies southwest of Hot Springs near the Wyoming border. The area is famous for the Native Americans prehistoric artifacts that have been found nearby. The first white settlers aptly called one area, Flint Hill.

Edgemont had 1,772 people living there in 1960. The Black Hills Ordnance Depot was established there in 1942.

Edgemont received 3 inches of snow early March 3. With the accompanying winds, it was enough to shut down all public schools in Edgemont and nearby Igloo. The Black Hills Army Depot was closed for the day. Road conditions were poor, it took one trucker three hours to make a fifty-mile trip between Newcastle, Wyoming, and Edgemont.

Lead, Deadwood, Spearfish, Sturgis, Bear Butte Valley, Hereford and Belle Fourche

Lead, located in Lawrence County, gained fame as the headquarters of the Homestake Mine. Prospectors scrambled into Deadwood Gulch after Thomas Carey discovered placer gold there in February 1876. While most of the gold seekers looked around Deadwood, some prospectors came to the present-day site of Lead. That spring two brothers, Moses and Fred Manuel, staked out mining claims in a little draw called Bob Tail Gulch. They located their famous claim on April 9, 1876.

Later on, William Randolph Hearst, the newspaper baron, acquired the Homestake Mine. The company owned 110,000 acres of land in South Dakota and adjacent Wyoming. The Hearst family spent a quarter of a million dollars on a beautiful opera hall, now known as the Homestake's Amusement Hall. A library, a hospital and a museum were other gifts to the town.

Smoky Jones, a prospector, plotted the townsite of Lead. Antonio Weber opened a store. In the spring of 1877, Peter Gushurst, the first man to be married in Lead, opened another store. Gushurst became an important businessman in the Black Hills.

In 1960, Lead boasted a population of 6,211.

In 1965, South Dakota led the nation in gold production. The Homestead Mine was the country's biggest gold mine at that time. The company employed about 1,300 people from the surrounding communities.

Late Wednesday, March 2, the storm reached Boulder Canyon. Two inches of snow fell. On Thursday, Lead recorded 22 inches of snow and 4 inches on Friday. Overall, the blizzard brought 28 inches of snow, the precipitation amounted to 1.52 inches.

High winds shut down most activity in Lead on Thursday and Friday. On those days, highs of 13 and 9 and lows of -2 and -1 were recorded.

Homestake Mine employees, working the Wednesday night shift, took shelter in the Armory. Miners on the day shift, those that made it, worked around the clock.

Thursday morning, snowdrifts, 6 feet high, were common around Lead. City plows kept Main Street open most of the time on Thursday and Friday. But, at times, the snow and winds overwhelmed the snow removal crews.

Over the weekend, other primary streets and residential areas were plowed open.

Lead averages 105 inches of snow a year. There was another blizzard on March 22, 1966. That storm brought another 24 inches of snow. Lead recorded 57 inches of total snowfall in March 1966, the most of any town in South Dakota.[25]

Mrs. Raymond Quilling lived on a farm, about six miles east of Lead, near Yellow Creek. After the storm broke, she wanted to see if a pregnant cow, expected to give birth at any time, was okay.

As soon as she found the cow, the animal attacked her. Battered and bruised Mrs. Quilling hobbled back to the house. The cow had just calved, when Mrs. Quilling came upon the scene. Needing medical attention, she called the Highway Patrol. They picked up several doctors and made a blizzard run in a four-wheel drive vehicle. They brought Mrs. Quilling to the St. Joseph's Hospital in Deadwood, where she recovered from her injuries.

Deadwood, the most famous city in the Black Hills, is closely associated with the old west. The discovery of gold in November 1875 by Ed Murphy spurred a rush of other prospectors. Two months later, there were 40 placer-mining claims in Deadwood Gulch.

On April 26, 1876, the city of Deadwood was laid out. Saloons and gambling houses seemed to go up overnight. It was a gamblers paradise, Ironically, that is true even today as well.

On August 2, 1876, Wild Bill Hickok was shot in a saloon by Jack McCall. Calamity Jane, another celebrated figure of the area, passed away on August 2, 1903.

Deadwood, the seat of Lawrence County, had 3,045 people in 1960.

Deadwood residents woke up to a blizzard, Thursday morning. The city received 21 inches of snow during the blizzard. The water content of the snow was high. Overall, the storm dumped 3.97 inches of moisture.

The tremendous amount of snow paralyzed Deadwood. Schools and businesses were closed for two days.

Lawrence County Sheriff Richard McGrath rescued several people in vehicles stalled in Boulder Canyon. They waited out the blizzard in the sheriff's office.

McGrath's officers, in a four-wheel drive vehicle, picked up Mrs. Garis Cleveringa on Thursday. She had labor pains. They took her to St. Joseph's Hospital where she gave birth to a son.

Spearfish, located fourteen miles northwest of Deadwood, was platted in the spring of 1876. Captain C. V. Gardner brought the first quartz mill to the Black Hills in 1877. Quartz mining involved the use of heavy machinery to crush rock or quartz containing gold. This form of mining replaced panning and sluicing for gold. He also opened a flour mill in Spearfish in 1879 with Porter Warner.

Spearfish Creek is famous for its Speckled Trout. The federal government established a fish hatchery in Spearfish.

The Black Hills *Passion Play* draws tourists to the amphitheater every summer.

Spearfish was home for 3,682 residents in 1960.

The greatest temperature variation in a brief span in South Dakota's history occurred on January 22, 1943, at Spearfish. At 7:30 a.m., the temperature was 4 degrees below zero. Two minutes later, it was 45 degrees above zero. This weather phenomenon, now, has a name, the "Spearfish Chinook".[26]

In 1965, the Spearfish Spartans high school wrestling team finished fourth at the state tournament.

On February 26, 1966, the Spartans finished third in the state wrestling tournament at Watertown. John Johnson won the 120 pound weight class. Roger Langer, 98 lb class, and George Anderson, 154 lb class, had second place finishes. Doug Fuller came in third at 112.

On March 3, Spearfish received 19 inches of snow. Blizzard conditions lasted for 36 hours. The storm ended Friday morning. Drifts, 3 to 6 feet high, were common in Spearfish. Except for a few trucks, there was no traffic during the storm. The few downtown businesses, that opened on Thursday, closed early. Public schools were closed on Thursday and Friday. There was no classes at the Black Hills State College in Spearfish on Thursday. Classes were held on Friday, for those who could make it.

One weather observer joked, "I don't know how much snow we got, I couldn't get it to hold still long enough to measure it."

Snowplows were confined to the city until conditions improved.

Roads leading into Spearfish were officially closed until Friday noon.

It was business as usual for stores in Spearfish on Friday. Supplies, like bread and milk, ran low as trucks from distribution centers did not reach Spearfish until Saturday or Sunday.

Police Chief Bud Litschewski reported, "there was no accidents or trouble during the storm." On Saturday morning, the city front-end loader plowed into a big drift near the intersection of Spartan and Woodburn. To the amazement of the driver, there was a car buried underneath. The car, a 1957 Ford, belonged to Hurshell E. Cordell, Jr. The vehicle was a total loss.

A couple, with a six month old baby, were stranded between Belle Fourche and Spearfish on Thursday. Their harrowing ordeal came to an end on Friday when they reached Spearfish.[27]

The first settlement in the neighborhood of Sturgis was known as Camp Sturgis, a military campsite for General Sheridan's troops. After major improvements were completed, the place was renamed Fort Meade. Two miles west of Fort Meade, a settlement took hold. Sturgis received its name in October of 1878, after General Sturgis, the commander of Fort Meade.

Sturgis hosts the annual Black Hills Classic Cycle Rally. This event started in the late 1930's when "Pappy" Hoel, the local cycle dealer, and his friends got together for a few days of racing at the fairgrounds.

Sturgis, the seat of Meade County, had 4,639 inhabitants in 1960.

The early March 1966 blizzard dumped 26 inches of snow on Sturgis on Thursday and Friday. Wind gusts reached 70 mph.

Schools and businesses in Sturgis were closed for those days.

Considerable drifts blocked highways and roads in the area.

Power and telephone lines were down in eastern Meade County. residents. Bear Butte Valley residents lost their power for two days. Ranchers could not water their livestock, most water pumps were electric.

Hereford needed help with its snow blocked roads because its snowplow was broken down.

Saturday morning, Henry Cooper, the owner of the Sturgis Lumber and Grain Company, shoveled snow in front of his business. About 9:00, he had a heart attack. Cooper, 61, died as a result. Cooper left behind a wife, a son and two daughters. Survivors also included a brother and six sisters. Cooper's son, Thomas, had recently completed two years of service in the Peace Corps in Africa.

What happened at the Sturgis Airport was hard to believe. Snow found a way into a closed hangar, Inside, drifts were 10 feet high. The weight of the snow, snapped the wings and tail sections on five planes. The front door of another hangar was left open. Here, the snow whirled through the building. There was no damage to a plane stored just inside the door. The high winds destroyed an uninsured plane on the runway. There was another plane tied down close by. That one was not harmed. Unofficial estimates of the damage was pegged to be about $15,000.

Sergeant William Daney, a local resident and member of the South Dakota National Guard, was hurt in the aftermath. The mishap occurred forty-one miles south of Lemmon, South Dakota. Sergeant Daney was operating a front-end loader when his machine struck a bridge abutment. The tractor flipped over and he was trapped underneath the loader. He suffered a broken pelvis and leg. Sergeant Daney recovered in Five Counties Hospital in Lemmon.

Many newspaper editors had comments about the great blizzard of 1966. They offered advise and insights. Bob Lee, editor of the *Sturgis Tribune* wrote:

Bad Enough

The worst blizzard in Meade County's history?
Worst than the memorable Big Blizzard of 1949?
That's what some people are saying about the storm that hit here last
Wednesday and continued until Saturday. There are differences of opin-

ions, however, in making comparisons. Nobody's around who can recall the historic blizzard of 1888 which covered the entire state and which took a big toll of lives.

But everybody remembers the blizzard of 1949 and the recent storm is most often compared with it. Whether or not last week's storm was worse depends on how each person made out during the two blizzards. Those who suffered hardship or loss of stock in 1949, but who weathered last week's blizzard in better shape naturally claim the earlier storm was the "worst ever." Conversely, those who suffered most last week claim it was the most destructive.

The blizzard of 1949 lasted longer and it was much colder than during last week's storm. But, judging from scattered reports, certain sectors of our region, particularly the northeastern part of the county, were harder hit last week. It will be quite a while before the livestock losses of the two blizzards can be compared. Stock that survived the recent storm may have been debilitated to the extent that they will die later and some of them may lose their calves.

In any event, last week's blizzard was bad enough and we can do without another one like it for quite a while. Shoveling out was the big chore in both rural and urban areas. Main highways and city streets were quickly cleared, but the individual home owners still had a big job in shoveling out to them. Unfortunately, there just wasn't enough publicly-owned equipment to do the work for everybody. In most cases, it was a "do-it-yourself" project and mountains of snow were moved by individual effort.

South Dakotans are generally pretty weather-wise and most of them stayed indoors during the blizzard. It will be noted that the deaths occurred among people who were caught away from home when the storm hit or who wandered out during the storm. There was tragic loss of lives among people who got lost only a short distance from their ranch homes in the blinding snowstorm.

The importance of staying in a car when it is stalled in a blizzard rather than taking off afoot was also demonstrated in last week's storm. There were cases where people survived because they remained in the cars and instances where people died because they did not.

An exception was the death of a Rapid City salesman who died in his stalled car near Faith. But his death was attributed to carbon monoxide poisoning rather than freezing. The wisdom of keeping emergency supplies and equipment in the car trunk during the winter months was also demonstrated again last week. We have often wondered why some enterprising merchant hasn't designed a "blizzard pack" containing food, a heating unit and other emergency supplies that could easily stored in the trunk of a car. We think there would be a market for it in this country.

The enforced seclusion in their homes was enlightening to many men who normally are at work during the daylight hours. They had a chance to see the "soap operas" they wives are subjected to on television during the day and it was almost enough to drive them out into the blizzard. Then there were the kids who were out of school because of the storm. Young-

sters are naturally restless when they have to stay indoors for any length of time and in some cases they were a trial too. But, at least, they were safe – from the blizzard if not from their fathers' wrath. The menfolks certainly must have gained an insight into the daily routine of their house-bound wives. They didn't envy them either.

Their isn't much a man can do around the house during the blizzard. We found something to do, but we wouldn't recommend it. However, it was better than staying inside and listening to the wife preach about our earlier negligence. So we put on the storm windows.[28]

According to Art Vandall, civil defense and rural emergency preparedness specialist for the Cooperative Extension Service at South Dakota State University, Meade County ranchers lost 7,000 head of cattle and about 10,000 head of sheep. Vandall believed, "more animals died of suffocation rather than from starvation or exposure."

After animals were dug out, ranchers had to keep a close eye on their herds for bloat problems and pneumonia. Dr. Weldon Glenn, extension veterinarian at South Dakota State University, said, "Bloat problems following a blizzard has been a rather new experience for stockmen in most areas of South Dakota." Bloat is caused by several factors, first starvation followed by overeating or overwatering; second bloat could result from an imbalance of micro-organisms in the rumen of the animals. Fortunately, ranchers could treat their animals for bloat and pneumonia.

Contamination from dead animals was an important concern in the aftermath. South Dakota had only three rendering plants in 1966. They were located in DeSmet, Watertown and Sioux Falls. In the aftermath, the three sites were overwhelmed with dead carcasses.

Dr. M.D. Mitchell, of the State Livestock Sanitary Board, said, "rendering trucks are being directed to areas where dead animals lay near farmsteads." Information was being provided, and his office would help as much as possible. Vandall advised livestock owners that if dead animals were not picked up, they should pull the animals to high ground to avoid contamination of water supplies and other areas.[29]

U.S. Highways 85 and 212 converge at Belle Fourche, and it is the northern entrance to the Black Hills. Visitors have discovered Belle Fourche's Old West charm.

With 4,087 residents in 1960, not much has changed in Belle Fourche over the years. It was a prominent catttletown in its early days. One can still see the ruts that the Texas Longhorns made along the Belle Fourche River. Since 1918, around the Fourth of July, the town has celebrated its heritage with the Black Hills Roundup.

Belle Fourche is the county seat of Butte County. The local economy still depends on cattle and sheep, the town is an prominent center for shipping wool. Livestock auctions are big draws.

Belle Fourche was on the western edge of blizzard. The general opinion of the area was, "We were lucky." The town recorded just about an inch of precipitation between March 2-4. Most of the snow came on March 3.

Despite receiving little snow, snowdrifts, 4 feet high, were common around town. The biggest one, 7 feet high, stretched across Union Street. On Eleventh Avenue, near the Lutheran Church, another snowbank was over 5 feet high. As elsewhere, stalled cars were buried in snow. Some vehicles had to be moved before work crews could plow the streets.

Livestock losses in the Tri-State area was light.

By 1966, many small towns and cities had snow removal equipment. The editor for the *Belle Fourche Bee*, Marion Lucca, mentioned this important fact. Lucca noted:

Nice Work, Quick Work

At 8 p.m. Thursday, the wind was whipping snow into huge drifts in every corner of town. Traffic, except for an occasional determined driver or a "four-wheel drive" vehicle, was at a standstill. It wasn't a fit night out for man, beast, or machine.

At 7 a.m. Friday, the snow had stopped falling but the wind still was churning the snow at a 30 miles per hour clip and the drifts continued to build.

By noon Friday, by judiciously picking your way, you could go almost anywhere in town and you didn't need a four-wheel drive unit to do it.

By Saturday noon, travel conditions were already returning to normal.

We think that's quite an accomplishment on the part of the city snow removal crews.

This involved clearing a traffic way on more than 60 miles of streets, many of them clogged with parked cars as well as four foot drifts, and it was done with two loaders, two graders, and four trucks.

County snow removal crews, because of wind and drifting, had to wait longer to start, but once they started, they too made record time in cleaning out the traffic ways.

Ten or 15 years ago, a storm such as the one which struck last Wednesday night would have tied up traffic for a full week. Now we count the clearing time in hours.

It wasn't simple and it wasn't easy. Men and machines had to work around the clock. There were tie-ups and breakdowns but the work went on.

We owe these people a vote of thanks, you and I. They did a fine job and deserve recognition.[30]

On Saturday, March 5, Belle Fourche's high school boys basketball team, the Broncs, defeated the Spartans of Spearfish by a score of 63 to 57. Mike Black, the top scorer in the Black Hills Conference, finished with 27 points. Coach Lou Graslie's squad finished the conference season at 12 and 0. It was the second straight year, that the Broncs had gone undefeated in conference play. Their regular season record was 17 - 3.

They were favored to win the Class A Section 8 Tournament at Spearfish. The opening game on March 10 featured Spearfish against Lead. Spearfish won that contest. Belle Fourche beat Sturgis in the second game to set up the championship game.

The Broncs did not disappoint their fans the following day. They defeated the Spartans.

The Broncs went to the South Dakota State Class A Tournament at Sioux Falls on March 17. Tickets prices for students was $3.65 and $8.00 for adults. They met the Webster Bearcats in the opening game of the tournament. Here, their luck ran out. The Bearcats defeated the Broncs by a score of 63 to 42.

Kadoka, Long Valley, Wanblee, Belvidere, Interior, Swett, Martin, Allen, Vetal, Pine Ridge, Batesland, Tuthill and Norris

Kadoka, the county seat of Jackson County, promotes itself as the "Gateway to the Badlands." The Badlands National Park comprises 50,000 acres in a strip forty miles long and twenty miles wide. The town's name stems from the mispronunciation of a Sioux word meaning, "Hole in the Wall." The Badlands Petrified Gardens are located nearby. Kadoko was established in 1906 with the arrival of the Milwaukee.

Large crowds have attended the World Outhouses Races, an event sanctioned by the World Outhouse Racing Association.[31]

Kadoka had 840 residents in 1960.

Kadoka weathered sleet the morning of Wednesday, March 2, 1966. With a high of 40, the sleet turned to rain by noon. Falling temperatures in the afternoon turned the rain to snow. Light winds whipped the snow around. That night blizzard conditions developed after strong winds struck the area.

The storm lasted until Saturday morning. Wind gusts reached 70 mph.

Ivan Colburn, official weather observer of Kadoka, figured 10 inches of snow, 1.72 inches of moisture, fell during that period. Colburn said, "Temperatures, although cold, did not drop much below the zero mark during the storm."

The editor of the *Kadoka Press* wrote:

> The end of the storm was welcomed Saturday by every resident in the area. It will be talked of for years to come, but few will want to experience another one like it in the future.[32]

Early in the storm, Kadoka lost its power. Some residents stayed home and wore heavy clothes. For long periods of time, they remained in bed with lots of blankets on top of them. Most of the residents, however, went to houses with different sources of heat.

Electricity was restored in Kadoka on Saturday morning. The power failed again at 6:30 Monday night and stayed off until 2 o'clock Tuesday morning.

Kadoka became a safe harbor for many travelers. After the storm broke, many truckers and other motorists stayed at Jeff's Truck Stop. The entrance of the station had a huge drift in front and the south side of the cafe was buried.

By Saturday afternoon, highways and roads west of Kadoka had been cleared of snow. Traffic resumed slowly in that direction. It was a different story, going east. Traffic backed up at Kadoka because U.S. Highway 16 near Stamford remained blocked. At one time, there were over sixty trucks lined up on the highway. That's not counting the cars, mixed in the long line of vehicles.

During the storm and afterwards, all the motel rooms were quickly taken. Residents of Kadoka welcomed visitors into their private homes, once it became known that there were no vacant rooms anywhere in town.

Bob and Bill Fugate dug their father's automobile out of a giant snowbank in front of Badlands Petrified Gardens east of town.

Nearly every stockmen in the vicinity encountered livestock losses. Old-timers believed the March 1966 blizzard was one of the worse livestock storms they could remember. Losses varied from ranch to ranch.

Ranchers who had the greatest financial losses included Mike and Dike Borbely who ranched west of Kadoka. Also, Donald Handcock, near Long Valley, Kenny Weaver, near Wanblee and Frank Walker, near Interior, had big losses.[33]

Fritz DeVries ran a feedlot for yearlings east of Belvidere. On Saturday, twenty-five dead animals were counted quickly in the immediate area of the feedlot. Some animals broke out during the storm and died at the doorstep of the DeVries home. A reporter speculated the death toll might reach 50 when the rest of the livestock was checked. "Its probably more like 100," said Mrs. Devries, "but we don't know." Most of the livestock losses occurred on Friday. Mrs. Devries said, "we could hear the yearlings, but we couldn't see them. We couldn't even see the hayrack that stood 30-40 feet from the house. There was nothing we could do."

A row of ten dead yearlings was found on the ground between a huge drift and shed. Numerous others were found in the feedlot, only their feet poked out of the snow.

On Saturday, the Devries and men from Belvidere scooped cattle from drifts with a front-end loader and hauled them to the barn where a heater was set up.

Huge chucks of ice covered the mouths of animals in the feedlot. Mrs. Devries said, "We tried to beat the ice away. It was caked on. I heard about some people using jack handles to get it off."[34]

On March 8, the voters of Kadoka Independent School District approved a bond measure to remodel the school gymnasium. The State Highway Commission awarded construction bids for Interstate 90 projects near Kadoka.

Mr. and Mrs. Alvin Kampfe from Long Valley lost their power at noon on Thursday. Their electricity stayed off until Saturday afternoon. The family had an electric range. Their water was pumped by a electric motor. They had gas heat, controlled electrically.

The Kampfe's handled the crisis by moving their old wood stove back into the house. They had heat and could cook food. For lights, the Kampfe's used kerosene lamps. A transistor radio provided news and weather reports. Water was obtained by melting snow on the wood stove.

Interior is a small community located near Sheep Mountain in Jackson County. The town is famous for its rodeos. Prehistoric dinosaur fossils have been found nearby.

The town had 179 people in 1960.

Interior's troubles did not end, when the storm swept out of the area. After the brief cold snap passed, warm temperatures returned to the area. On March 10, the White River broke out of its banks. Water, from the river, came within one mile of town. The next day, there was an eight-mile long ice jam on the river. Several head of cattle and a flock of chickens drowned in the floodwater on the George Carlbom ranch. Water covered the first floor of their home.

The town's well became inoperative in the blizzard. The well was repaired after the storm ended. Mrs. Lane Johnson, wife of Interior's police chief, turned the water on in her house, and mud oozed and spatted out of the spigots on March 11. Floodwater from the White River had backed up into the well. The local authorities shut the well off. Residents filled their cream cans and gallon jars with water at nearby ranches. School was canceled that Friday.

Interior's water problems lasted about a week.

Martin, founded in 1911, is the county seat of Bennett County. The town was named after Eben Martin of Hot Springs, a South Dakota Congressman from 1908-12.

In 1960, 1,184 people lived there.

On Wednesday, March 2, 1966, the city recorded a high of 35 degrees. During the day, a light mist came down. At times, it was a little heavier. Temperatures fell later in the day.

The ground glistened with a thin layer of ice. Light snow flurries masked the slippery undercoat.

When residents woke up on Thursday, they had time for an extra cup of coffee. With the storm outside, people had no reason to rush anywhere. They listened to weather reports and storm cancellations. There was no school.

On Thursday, a tourist with a wife and small children tried to leave Martin during a brief lull in the storm. State Highway, Patrolman, Steve Polich, guarded the west exit of U.S. Highway 18. He stopped the tourist and advised the family to turn around. The tourist did not want to do this. There was an heated discussion. To end the matter, Patrolman Polich told the man, "If you don't turn around, you're going to jail and stay for court."

Patrolman Polich had tried to tell the tourist, the road was blocked ahead. "Of course, he couldn't have gotten out of town anyway," Patrolman Polich said.[35]

Martin residents believed that between 2 to 4 inches fell on Thursday and Friday. Further east in Vetal, the locals insisted that more than 4 inches had fallen.

Vehicles were stuck in Allen, Swett, Batesland, Martin, Vetal and Tuthill. Most of the roads were blocked by Thursday night. There were marooned vehicles along state and county roads.

The storm came at the worst possible time for Mrs. Dick Marshall, an expectant mother who resided three miles west of Batesland. Mrs. Marshall needed to be near a hospital, so her family notified County Sheriff, Clyde Rayhill. Sheriff Rayhill informed the state highway snowplow operators of the situation. On the west end of Martin, a mammoth drift formed on U.S. Highway 18. The equipment operators hammered away at the hard drift near the OK Motel. They broke through about 7:30 Friday night. In another hour and a half, they had a wider path. Shortly afterwards, Sheriff Rayhill followed a snowplow out of Martin. They reached Batesland about 11:00 p.m. After that, it did not take long to the Marshall's residence. The group arrived back in Martin around midnight. It was not the right time, however, for the baby.

The lights of a snowplow saved the life of a fifteen year old girl. Susan Thomsen, daughter of Mr. and Mrs. Allen Thomsen, who had a chronic asthma attack. Mr. Thomsen noticed some lights east of his place on Highway 18 at 2:00 a.m. Saturday. The family had no phone.

Mr. Thomsen walked one mile in the direction of the lights. When Thomsen was close, he noticed a snowplow stalled in a big drift near Elmer Solid's place. He found Sheriff Clyde Rayhill, behind the plow in his police car. They talked. The sheriff drove as close to the Thomsen's place as he could. They picked up Susan and took her to the hospital in Martin. She was released on March 11.

Saturday morning, the skies were clear in Martin. Temperatures did not rebound much, the high was only 18. With light winds, the digging out process started in earnest.

State Highway 73, running north from Martin to Kadoka, was blocked early Thursday and remained closed until Monday morning.

There was no mail delivered to Martin on Thursday and Friday. Incoming mail from the south was reestablished, Saturday afternoon. No mail arrived from the north until Monday morning. Outgoing mail had the same interruptions.

There was no long distance telephone service at Martin from Thursday night to Sunday night. Most of the local calls went through. In rural areas around Martin, telephone service was sporadic at best.

Information was passed along on police and citizen band radios. After the police radio station lost power, the only radios that worked were in police vehicles.

Power was lost in Martin and other towns in Bennett County. The emergency plant in Martin was started on Thursday. It provided some power for residents. It ran through Saturday. The outages in other Lacreek Electric areas varied town to town and their outlying areas. The length of the outage depended on emergency power capabilities along with wire and pole damages. Most areas had regular power by Saturday afternoon.

On Saturday, Lacreek Electric hired a plane and flew workers over its lines. On Sunday, the power company hired a plane and helicopter. Finding trouble spots, the helicopter landed and the utility linemen made their repairs before moving on.

The strong winds broke twelve poles in the area. In many other cases, power was lost because the lines became tangled and shorted out.

On March 10, the *Bennett County Booster II* reported losses of 10 to 15 per cent of cattle in Bennett County which meant 2,000 to 2500 dead animals. One week later, the extension service of South Dakota State University indicated that Bennett County losses were less than 1,000 head. Animals not found right away, in some cases were presumed dead.

John Hippen and his hired hand were reported missing on Saturday morning. A search party was organized. They were found in the cab of Hippen's tractor. It was half buried in a big drift on Lacreek Refuge. The two men stayed warm by heating a propane branding iron burner.

Early Thursday, Charles "Sonny" Livermont injured his leg in an accident. Livermont lived north of Vetal. He would have gone to the hospital right away, but the blizzard was going full blast. His phone was out.

Saturday evening, Livermont's luck changed after hearing a dial tone. Livermont called Sheriff Rayhill who arranged a plow escort. Sheriff Rayhill picked up Livermont around 10:30 and took him to the hospital. Charles Livermont was discharged from the hospital on March 10.

Meanwhile, State Patrolman Steve Polich made an emergency run to the Blackpipe area. Following a plow, Polich picked up Mrs. Carl Allard. Patrolman Polich took her back to the hospital in Martin. Six hours later, Mrs. Carl Allard gave birth to a baby girl, Cindy Lou.

On Monday, March 7, Martin 's Warriors brought home the 3rd place trophy from Sturgis when they defeated New Underwood, 67 to 65, in the Region 8 basketball tournament. Martin's Ed O'Bryon's hit the winning jump shoot with 38 seconds left.

Martin's "Tornado Disaster Exercise," scheduled for March 6 and 7, was changed to March 20 and 21. Organizers of the event indicated the city had not recovered from recent blizzard. Also, some streets and highways, needed for the exercise, were still blocked with snow.

On March 17, Arlo G. Swanson, State Director of the Farmers Home Administration, confirmed that two-thirds of South Dakota had been declared an emergency area. Ron Walker, FHA supervisor for Bennett and Shannon Counties, said "This means that farmers and ranchers may now apply for emergency loan assistance through the County FHA Office located in Martin." Loan money could be used for essential home and farm operating expenses, replacement of livestock or repair of buildings damaged or destroyed by the blizzard. The interest rate for the loans would be three percent.[36]

Cecil Jones, Soil Conservation Service, announced that Lowell Schlecht, Fred Cozad and Dr. Theodore Roman devised a plan to protect Martin from blizzard winds in the future. Tree windbreaks would be planted west and northwest of Martin in the spring of 1967. Once large, the trees were supposed to stop drifting snow in the fields, leaving Martin with less of a problem.[37]

> *"Look at–Look at Mills! Look at Mills!*
>
> *"Mills is coming on! Mills is coming on! What a tremendous surprise here. Bill Mills of the United States wins the 10,000 meters... a tremendous upset."*

ABC Sportscaster Bud Palmer with the call

Billy Mills won the gold medal in the 10,000 meter race in the 1964 Summer Olympics in Tokyo, Japan. In that race, he improved his personal time by 45 seconds and set an Olympic record of 28:24.1.

On March 19, 1966, Mills was in Pine Ridge for the dedication ceremonies of the Billy Mills Community Center. He was accompanied by his wife and daughter. The event, sponsored by the Oglala Sioux Tribe. Mills was born on the Pine Ridge Reservation and graduated from Kansas University in 1962. He was also a Marine officer for three years and now an insurance representative for Equitable Life. Mills said, "This is one of the greatest honors that has been bestowed upon me. I think my greatest thrill, next to winning the gold medal, has been to return to my hometown here and participate in the dedication."

Tuthill was founded by J.B. Tuthill in 1920. Tuthill ran the post office and operated a store. In 1960, the town had 40 residents.

Mrs. C. E. Ford, *Bennett County Booster II* news correspondent for Tuthill, reported that Tuthill had lost telephone service and experienced power outages. According to Mrs. Ford, these problems along with severe livestock losses, made local news appear to be minor and insignificant.

Norris, located in Mellette County, was founded in 1910 by P.H. Putnam, a pioneer storekeeper. The Post Office Department picked the name of the town from a list of four names that Putnam sent in to them. Norris was the name of one of Putnam's nephew.

In 1960, the town had a population of 40.

On March 10, the *Bennett County Booster II* published the following story by Mrs. Loyd Letellier, its correspondent for Norris. She wrote:

> *"You cannot do a kindness too soon because you never know how soon it will be too late."*
>
> *It seems that news is rather scarce and what has been reported is of a similar nature – thankfulness that we did not fare any worse during the storm and the losses were not worse than they were. It is amazing that anything could survive amidst the fury of a storm like the one just past. There is the humorous side too, like when looking out of the window we saw a bull in the apple tree. He had nonchalantly walked on the snowbank and was standing in the top of that tree. On the next look he had just as calmly wandered back to the barnyard. And then we heard about a cow that walked out of a snowdrift where she had been eating as though nothing unusual had happened. That one had a sad ending for the next day the cow was dead. The two litters of newborn pigs who were brought in by*

the oven at Stoddard's were carefully fed but died. That is a lesson to all of us who use the gas oven for heating while the electricity was off. The party line system of visiting "every hour on the hour" proved to be a popular pastime while we were unable to get out. Not to be forgotten is the helpfulness of neighbors in every way possible. So the Blizzard of '66 has gone on its way to be remembered by those of us who experienced it. Enough of that–now for a few items here and there around Norris. ...

Rushville, Nebraska; Merriman, Nebraska; and Cody, Nebraska

Rushville is located about twenty-four miles south of Pine Ridge, South Dakota. Despite the weather, Mrs. Elmer Throne, a 51 year-old woman, left White Clay, Nebraska, about 5:00 Thursday afternoon for her home in Rushville. Six miles south of White Clay, her car stalled after hitting a drift on Highway 87. Mrs. Throne left her vehicle and started walking back to White Clay. She battled the storm for three miles. Her body was found along the road by Randy Thies, a White Clay coworker, about 11:30 p.m. Lester Jensen, the sheriff of Rushville, investigated the death. Mrs. Elmer Throne was Nebraska's only storm victim in this blizzard.

About eighteen miles straight south of Martin, is the town of Merriman, Nebraska.

In 1960, the place had a population of 285.

There was a power outage in Merriman. At the Sand Motel, five couples waited out the storm. Mr. and Mrs. Larry Ellis, hotel managers, started calling people, right after the power went out. They made other arrangements for their guests. Four of the couples went straight to jail. It was one place that was warm and available. The Ellis's took the senior couple a private home.

Leora Morsett, Merriman news correspondent for the *Bennett County Booster II*, in the March 10, 1966, edition, said:

Wednesday everything iced up by evening, it snowed and blew until Saturday morning. A lot of people without power, and finally no water, phone service to Gordon was out. It kept Evert Leeper's short wave busy. On Saturday Mrs. Weimer called for Help. Ray Weimer had gotten caught in a power take off. A plane from Gordon came and took Ray to Gordon hospital. Last reported he had severely injured his shoulder.

Cody, Nebraska, is located about twenty-four miles east of Merriman. Cliff Watts, a representative of the Bank of Cody, counted 126 dead cattle between Cody and the South Dakota border, in a five-mile stretch. Watts maintained that losses south of Cody were light.[38]

Philip, Faith, Maurine, Dupree, Eagle Butte, Lantry and Ridgeview

Located in Haakon County, Philip rests at the junction of U.S. Highway 14 and State Highway 13. The county, organized in 1914, was named after King Haakon VII of Norway.

In the days of the Old West, sheep and cattle ranchers fought over a water hole that never went dry. Today, the Silent Guide Monument reminds visitors of the range feuds.

Philip is the county seat. Another source of income for the residents, 1,114 in 1960, has been the manufacturing of machine tools.

The Philip Knights of Columbus and the United States Fish and Wildlife Service joined forces to rejuvenate Giant Canada Geese in South Dakota. Sixteen geese, eight mated pairs, were released in a one-acre tract of fenced land at Wagoner Lake in late February 1966. Members of the Knights of Columbus had built nesting platforms near the small dam next to the Philip water plant. An artisan well provided the necessary year-around water supply. Similar undertakings have been done near Belvidere and Wall.

The "Scotties", Philip's high school boys basketball team, won the District 30 Championship Basketball Tournament in late February. They defeated teams from Interior, Kadoka, and Midland.

Mike Hanson was averaging 17 points a game for the Scotties.

The weather was nice in Philip on Tuesday, March 1, the high rose to 37 above.

It was a little colder on Wednesday, the high was only 30. Philip received 0.3 inches of precipitation. The light rain was mostly sleet. The Scotties had a good practice.

The *Pioneer Review* said, "Local residents awoke Thursday morning to find the area blanketed by one of the most severe blizzards ever." It was "another chapter in the already long book of Dakota blizzards."[39]

The storm passed from the area late Friday night.

On Friday, power went out in half of the city, but the electricity was restored, later in the day.

Local calls were completed in Philip. Problems in other areas prevented most long distance from going through. There was some structural damages in the area as well. Between Philip and the airport east of town, there were 45 broken telephone poles.

Rural residents were not as lucky. Many lost power and the use of their telephones.

At three o'clock Thursday afternoon, Tom Garguil, of Torrington, Wyoming, parked his rig at the holding pens for Philip Livestock Auction. He unloaded the cattle in the terrible weather.

Garguil figured he could make it back to Rapid City. Out on the highway, Garguil quickly changed his mind. He turned back and went to Jake's Sinclair service station.

On Friday, Garguil's truck stopped running after snow plugged the air cleaner. Getting cold, he entered the station through a broken window. Then, Garguil called the chief of police, Gay Moses. Moses told Garguil that Jake Hoff owned the station. Garguil phoned Hoff to let him know that he was staying at the station. On Saturday, workers at Jakes Sinclair started Garguil's diesel. He left Philip at 4:00 p.m.

The legendary stork landed at the doorstep of the Neal Hagler's home around 6:00 Friday morning. The Haglers lived on the Bob Lampert's farm, seven miles south of Philip. Mrs. Hagler started having labor pains. They were in a middle of a blizzard. The roads were blocked and their telephone did not work.

Neal Hagler dressed warm. He left their trailer home and headed for the Lampert's home, about a quarter of a mile away. Mr. Hagler made the journey safely. After explaining the situation, Mrs. Bob Lampert (Shirley) returned with Mr. Hagler.

With no medical advice, they delivered a baby girl at 10:00 Friday morning. The happy couple named her Becky Lynn.

On Saturday, the snowplow reached their place. The Woodall ambulance was right behind it. Mrs. Hagler and Becky Lynn were taken to the Hans P. Peterson Memorial Hospital in Philip for checkups. They were dismissed from the hospital on March 9.

Saturday was sunny. The temperature climbed to 32 above in Philip. It was a busy day for everybody. Some families could not get out of their homes, until their neighbors shoveled them out.

Range cattle drifted downwind in the storm. The animals were hard to find after the blizzard. Initial cattle losses for Haakon County were estimated at 10,000 head. Actual losses in the county were considerably less. On March 17, the extension service of the South Dakota State University placed Haakon County livestock losses at over 1,000 head.[40]

On March 7, the Region 8 Basketball Tournament was played in Sturgis. With the Class B tournament scheduled for later in the week, the regional tournament would be a one-day affair. Philip beat New Underwood, 99 to 57, in their afternoon game. Mike Hanson led the way with 21 points. Provo downed Martin in their game. Philip downed the Provo Rattlers, 86 to 65. Toward the end of the game, the excited fans from Philip chanted, "We're Going to State." Mike Hanson scored 19 points and Bill Schilling added 15 points for the winners. The last time the Scotties had made an appearance in the state tournament was in 1948.

The team left for Sioux Falls on March 8. Coach Frank Ochsner had two days to prepare his squad.

Fans who could not make the trip, watched the action on television. On Thursday March 10, Philip lost their first game to Hayti. In 1965, Hayti placed fifth in the tournament. The Scotties won their second game against Cheyenne-Eagle Butte. With less than a minute to go in the consolation game, Frederick had a one point lead over Philip. To get the ball, the Scotties had to foul.

On March 17, Postmaster E.C. Colvin of Philip announced that application forms for supplemental Medicare benefits were available at the post office. President Johnson declared March as "National Medicare Enrollment Month". To get the program started, some two and a half million application forms were sent to nearly 34,000 main post offices in the United States. Through direct mailing and other means, the Social Security Administration had contacted about 16 million elders in the United States. The Social Security Administration figure there were about 19.1 million people who would be 65 or older on July 1st, 1966. Cost for the program was $3.00 a month.

Faith, located in the Northeast corner of Meade County, had a population of 591 in 1960. The town is in cattle country. There's a highway marker that declares on the vast prairie, "deceit finds no place to hide and man is known for his true stature." There's a historical marker that states, "Our grass is unsurpassed anywhere, producing beef, the backbone of our existence.[41]

Faith residents believed the 1966 blizzard surpassed the 1949 blizzard. Carv Thompson, said "while snow on the level may not be so deep as 17 years ago, drifts 15 feet high in town of Faith seem to top the earlier landmark storm."

On March 3, the town lost its capacity to pump water. The pumps at Lake Durkee failed that morning. Emergency supplies were soon used up. Work crews could not reach the plant. Residents melted snow, then boiled it, for several days.

One rancher, in the Faith area, reported having five hundred head of cattle scattered in all directions. Fifty of them gathered at the store at Maurine.

On Saturday, the city water supply was reestablished.

City bulldozers cut fire lanes through town. Workers dallied with snow for days.[42]

Communities are small and far apart in Ziebach County. It is part of the Cheyenne River Reservation. Dupree, the county seat, was named for Frederick Dupree (Dupris). Dupree (1818-1898) was a express runner for the American Fur Company. He married a

Cheyenne woman and settled in the area. Fred and his son, Pete, have been credited for saving the buffalo from extinction. The Duprees started their herd with orphaned calves they picked up on the prairie. The buffalo in the Dupree herd multiplied to 57 by 1901. Scotty Philip purchased the entire herd and moved the animals to his ranch north of Fort Pierre that year.

In 1960, Dupree had a population of 548.

Ranchers in Ziebach County lost 4,000 cattle and 7,000 sheep on account of the blizzard, according to a survey conducted by the extension service of South Dakota State University. The figures were released on March 17, 1966.

Eagle Butte, lies west of Oahe Reservoir on U.S. 212 on the Cheyenne River Reservation in Dewey County.

On January 22, 1966, the Cheyenne-Eagle Butte Braves record stood at 3 wins and 10 losses. Coach Francis Zacher knew his players had lost close games and were getting better.

On February 26, 1966, the team won the District 8 High School Basketball Tournament in Eagle Butte. On their way to the championship, the Braves defeated teams from Dupree, McIntosh and Bison.

On Wednesday, March 2 freezing rain fell in the morning. According to the latest weather forecast, the rain was supposed to turn to snow and strong winds were expected.

Eagle Butte closed their schools at noon. At seven o'clock that evening, blizzard conditions developed.

Thursday morning, Ben Ganje of the *Eagle Butte News* made the following comment to the *Aberdeen American-News*. "You can't see across the street here. It's the worst since 1949."

Ganje figured the winds were about 40 mph and thermometer read 21 above.

Local basketball fans assumed the storm would end before regional play in Aberdeen on Friday. They were wrong. The regional tournament was postponed until Monday, March 7.

On March 10, the *Eagle Butte News* described the blizzard:

Thousands of Dollars Worth of Cattle
Lie Dead On Snow-covered Prairies

Last week's historic blizzard, which started with a sleet storm on Wednesday afternoon, and finally tapered off on Friday evening, was the worst storm in Dakota history, according to long-time residents.

At the end of the three day storm, we had received approximately 30 inches of snow, with winds up to 80 miles per hour.

Most of the time, it was virtually impossible to see even across the street. Many people were snowed in their homes, that is, snow was piled so high in front of doors that it was impossible to get out without going through a window, or calling upon outside help to shovel them out.

Nearly all streets in town were blocked with drifts up to fifteen feet high.

On Main street there was an enormous drift in front of Eagle Butte News and the Coast to Coast Store, Municipal Building, NYC Office, Zacher's Variety and Drug Store. These had to be shoveled out soon as possible on

Saturday to alleviate the pressure on the plate glass windows from the tremendous load of hard packed snow.

The drift in front of the Junior High School building was so big that snowplow crews gave up an attempt to go through the middle of it, and were able, finally, to break a road through at the extreme east side of the street.

On Saturday after the storm ended, people turned out to help shovel out the community. Many residents in both Lantry and Eagle Butte helped to shovel out the hangers which housed planes belonging to Dean Hunt and Marion McDaniel. These planes were used to fly endless hours over the ranches and communities in the area, checking to see if anybody needed assistance. ...[43]

Two mothers gave birth to sons at home during the blizzard. On March 4, Mr. and Mrs. Gerald Frame, of Dupree, had their baby boy. The next day, Mr. and Mrs. Nathan Bagola, Bear Creek, had their son. After the roads were cleared, the mothers and infants were transported to the Eagle Butte Public Health Hospital for checkups.

Mr. and Mrs. Ralph Vrooman and son lived two miles east of Eagle Butte. On Friday, the furnace in their house was not working properly. Just before dark, Mr. and Mrs. Vrooman decided to check their barn for a place to stay if they moved out of the house. The walk was treacherous in the storm.

While they were in the barn, their nine-year old son, Robin, heard urgent warnings on the radio about carbon dioxide poisoning from malfunctioning furnaces.

Now frightened, Robin decided to go to the barn to be with his parents.

Meanwhile, Mr. and Mrs. Vrooman left the barn. They did not see their son fumbling in the snow. Robin had lost his cap and gloves. Blinded by the snow, the couple struggled toward the house.

They were surprised when they almost stepped on their son.

Mr. Vrooman said, "If we had walked just a few feet away, we would never have seen him."[44]

Paul Hinzman, the local Civil Defense representative, obtained heavy equipment and hired operators to clear roads to farms and ranches where fuel and food was needed. People were helped by members of the Community Action Program.

As elsewhere, snow had gotten into attics and water damages occurred.

The Cheyenne-Eagle Butte Braves defeated the Onida Comets, 76 to 54, Monday afternoon in Aberdeen. The other Regional 2 game featured Eureka and Cresbard. Eureka won and remained undefeated. They played the championship game, that night.

Donovan Pretty Weasel gave the Braves the lead, 47 to 46, with a minute and a half left in the game. Eureka shot and missed. The rebound was grabbed by Veri Mcbride. Coach Zancker's team controlled the ball, until they got fouled. They made both free throws. Eureka set up their favorite play, but missed the shot. The Braves grasped the rebound and ran the clock down to seven seconds. Terry Alters was fouled and he sank both free throws for the Braves. Eureka's final shots was off the mark.

On March 10, the Braves rags to riches story continued in Sioux Falls in South Dakota Class B Tournament. Their first round opponent was the team from Parker. The Braves applied their press, but could not stop Parker's Dale Husman. Parker won the game. On Friday, the Philip Scotties defeated the Cheyenne-Eagle Braves. They lost their last contest to Scotland, 73 to 50.

The Public Health Hospital in Eagle Butte issued a warning on March 24. The statement concerned livestock that had died in the recent blizzard. It said, "The freezing of the animals was not sufficient to stop spoilage of the meat." It is advised, "Under No Circumstances should the meat be used for food."[45]

Ridgeview, located east of Eagle Butte in Dewey County, was so named because the site rests on the divide between the Cheyenne and Moreau Rivers. Ridgeview was once part of the largest ranch operations in South Dakota's history. The Diamond A held one-and-a-half million acres of land under lease in its peak. Life for the Diamond A ended in 1939.[46]

In 1960, the number of residents was placed at 40 individuals.

In 1966, Ridgeview recorded the greatest one-day precipitation in South Dakota for the month of March. The community received 3.88 inches of precipitation on Thursday, March 3. The snowfall was estimated at 20 inches. With .21 inches on Wednesday and another .14 inches on Friday, the three-day total for Ridgeview came to 4.23 inches. Overall, 24 inches of snow fell during the blizzard.[47]

Bison, Prairie City, Glad Valley, Chance, Isabel, Firesteel, Timber Lake, Glencross and Trail City

Bison, the seat of Perkins county, was named after the shaggy creatures who at one time roamed the Plains in the millions. An early settler, George Carr, ran across a pile of bison skulls and bones. That discovery was the impetus for the name of the town which was platted in 1907.

In 1960 Bison had 457 residents. South Dakota Highway 8 ran east-west through Bison in 1966.

The Bison Cardinals basketball season ended in Eagle Butte on February 26, 1966. The Cardinals finished second in the district tournament. They defeated Isabel, a team that had lost only six games all year, in the opening round. Then, the Cardinals had a one-point victory over Faith. They lost the championship game to the Cheyenne-Eagle Butte Braves.

On Wednesday, March 2, 1966, the mercury in Bison reached 28 degrees. Fine snow fell in the afternoon. Then, strong winds, 50 to 73 mph, developed along with more snow. Visibility remained near zero until Friday night. By the time the storm ended, 16 inches of the white stuff had fallen on Bison. The *Bison Courier* top headline after the storm read, **"HISTORY'S WORST BLIZZARD HITS HERE."**

There was no public school on Thursday, Friday and Monday.

Mr. and Mrs. Jim Hanson lived on a farm west of Bison. During the storm, fuel for their furnace ran low. But, the Hansons remained warm and comfortable under their electric blankets.

Few hardships were reported in Bison. There was no power and phone outages in Bison. The town's two grocery stores opened their doors, several times during the blizzard. When the supply of milk ran low, the local cafes shared their supplies.

Sheriff Howard Chapman kept abreast of the latest news during the storm with his short-wave radio.

West River Electric transported telephone personnel to and from work via snowmobile during the storm. This was the age of party lines and there was a lot of chatter. Residents, however, could not make long distance calls until March 8.

Mr. and Mrs. Bryce White closed up the Highway Cafe, connected to the Mobile Station in Bison, after the storm brought traffic to a standstill.

Normally, the Whites ate their meals at the Highway Truck Stop, so they had little food at home. The couple soon ran out of food. Mr. White decided to walk to the cafe, a quarter of a mile away, for some supplies. Following the telephone wires, White soon cleared the grain elevators.

Then, the power of the strong winds surprised him. He turned back to the shelter of the buildings. Then, White stopped. Several times, he bucked the strong winds. Each time, White came back to the shelter of the buildings.

But, he had to make it. So, White made one last valiant effort. He reached the cafe. When he arrived home with food supplies, he was plastered with snow.

The couple had a mess after the blizzard. They had broken water pipes in the Highway Cafe. Snow piled up in the kitchen and throughout the cafe. Repairs were made on Saturday and Sunday. On Monday, the cafe reopened for business.

The public telephone booth at the Highway Truck Stop was three-quarters full of snow. The snow had to be cleaned out before the phone could be used.

Mr. and Mrs. Cliff Long kept the City Cafe open during the storm. It was a safe haven for those who wanted meals and hot coffee. Thursday night, Mrs. Long tossed and turned while trying to sleep in one of the cafe booths. They went home, Friday night. In case someone needed food or milk, the Longs left the cafe unlocked. When the couple arrived Saturday morning, several regular customers were already making coffee.

KNDC, radio station at Hettinger, North Dakota, stayed on the air for the duration. The station broadcasted weather warnings and forecasts, and news of what was happening in the storm region. Most of all, KNDC passed on personal messages during the blizzard. For those in the countryside without power, KNDC was heard on transistor radios.

Women fared better than men during the storm. The *Bison Courier* wrote:

> *One feature of the three-day storm was the 'togetherness' it brought upon families who have probably not been together that long for years. Many told of their search for entertainment and activities to while away the long days. Among working women, whose time at home is limited, cookie jars were filled, homemade bread and pies were baked, handiwork brought out and much reading done. Radio and television kept all informed on storm effects and news items. Youngsters and men-folks suffering from 'cabin fever' welcomed the let-up Saturday, however, and flocked outdoors.*[48]

Late Friday night, a path was plowed through Bison's Main Street. Traffic could go only one way. Only a few people were out and about as the weather was still unsettled.

On Saturday morning, a meeting was held at the County Agent's Office at 9:00 o'clock. Members attending the meeting included the Civil Defense Director of Perkins-Harding Counties, E. M. Rowbotham, Major Davis, representing South Dakota's National Guard Headquarters, Major Williamson, Captains Ashmore and Zimmer, Sgt. Otterberg from the Lemmon National Guard unit, the Board of Perkins County Commissioners, and Paul Bishop, Chairman of County Agricultural Defense Board, and other authorities.

Tasks were assigned at the meeting. Lemmon National Guard members would open the Athboy road with their heavy equipment. State Highway Director, John Olson, dispatched a state snowplow from Bison to help the National Guard clear the Athboy Road because State Highways, 8 and 73, had already been plowed.

Ranchers, Wayne and Neal Everidge, had about 1,800 animals to feed and water. They could hire out privately owned equipment operators for snow removal. Or they could wait their turn, to get plowed out by county or National Guard equipment under the direction of the Civil Defense Director. Ranchers would not be billed for the work, if they took this route. Individual counties would be billed for the number of hours worked in their domain.

Business fronts on the north side of Main Street could barely be seen in the huge piles of snow. Business owners, employees, and volunteers made snow steps, tunnels and paths to different stores. Small tractors with scoops cleared snow off sidewalks. City employees and the Heck Construction Company hauled snow away.

One of the biggest drifts in Bison was south of the Neil Van Den Berg home. Another impressive snowbank was near was the Cliff Long residence and Lee Kolb's machine shop.

Saturday afternoon, there was a break in the water mains in Bison. City leaders took some men off their snow removal duties to look for the leak. Workers discovered the fracture below the city's water tower, but hours had elapsed in the meantime.

Repairs could not be made right away. Water was put in the mains at certain times, then shut off. Until repairs were made, residents watched their usage.

After the storm receded, Kenneth Woll walked over to his father's place. Recently, Ole Woll had been a patient in the hospital in Bismarck for three weeks.

Kenneth Woll found his father, but he was dead. The phones were out at the senior Woll's residence, so Kenneth Woll walked over to the Bryon Matthews place.

Matthews drove to Bison and reported the death to Sheriff Howard Chapman. Then, Matthews telephoned the mortuary. After that, arrangements were made for a snowplow to clear the road to the farmstead. The Evanson ambulance picked the body up.

Some family members were not notified until Monday night and Tuesday. Long distance telephone calls could be made at that time.

Authorities concluded that Ole Woll had suffered a heart attack on Thursday night. Mr. Woll, a longtime resident of Scotch Cap community, was buried beside the grave of his wife at Prairie City on March 10.

Jim Haggart, a local pilot, was very busy after the storm. Haggart crisscrossed the area, checking for distress signals. To quickly locate their livestock, ranchers hired Haggart to fly them around.

Dead animals were observed at fence corners over the entire area. The *Courier* reported most ranchers "lost 40 or 50 sheep, and stock were being dug out of draws."[49]

Reid Simons, near Glad Valley, and Vern Carmichaels, down at Surveyors Creek, lost a number of sheep.

Men at the Kenneth Randall ranch noticed an air hole in a snowbank. The drift was 12 feet deep. They widened the cavity and discovered a yearling sheep. Utilizing a Farmhand, the men pulled the animal out of the hole.

Frank Matson indicated the livestock losses around Prairie City were light. Overall, he said, "most people in the area came thru the storm well."[50]

Local school teacher and south Chance rancher, Earl Engebretson reported being snowbound with drifts, 20 feet high.

At the Beryl Veal ranch, Mrs. Veal went out the kitchen window after the storm. During the storm, they followed a rope that was strung between the house and the barn. Late

Friday night, the Veals opened a trail to their cattle. They used a tractor equipped with a scoop.

Several weeks after the blizzard, Elbert Bently, Perkins County agent, listed cattle losses at two percent and sheep losses at four percent. Overall, Bently estimated Perkins County livestock losses at 1,700 head.51

In 1910, the Milwaukee Railroad came to Isabel. The town was named for one of the daughters of the railroad officials. Located in Dewey County, Isabel had 488 inhabitants in 1960.

James Lemer, son of Mrs. Rose Lemer of Isabel, finished his two year hitch in the army in February 1966. Upon his discharge, Lemer flew from South Vietnam to Oakland, California.

When Lemer went to Vietnam in 1964, the trip took 27 days by boat. He drove a diesel truck near Guinhon, about 180 miles south of Saigon. Lemer worked twelve hour a day, seven days a week, with army engineers.

He said, "The country gets extremely hot and was well over 100 degrees when he left and it would get even hotter." He is glad to be out of the army and he "would never do that again."

Lemer said, "the South Korean Tiger Division in South Vietnam appears to be an exceptionally good outfit. They are primarily equipped with the American World War II Carbine. The primary infantry weapon of the South Vietnamese is the American M-1. The American Marines and Army infantry use the M-14 while the paratroopers of the 101st and 173rd use the M-16. The 1st Cavalry also has the M-16."52

The *Isabel Dakotan* published its thirteenth anniversary issue on March 3, 1966. The newspaper enjoyed a circulation of three thousand. For individuals without a subscription, the weekly newspaper was a dime. The following news brief appeared in the *Dakotan* on March 3:

Blizzard Howling Across Dakota Plains, Snow Falling

A wicked blizzard is howling across the plains here. The storm moved in during the afternoon Wednesday. School here closed down at noon as visibility in the country was greatly reduced by then and it was apparent that a full-scale blizzard was on the way.

*A very strong north wind is driving the fine, wet snow with considerable force. Livestock caught in the open may be in trouble.*53

Thursday morning at 6 o'clock, Beth Dougall, manager of the Co-op Store in Isabel, opened for business. Dougall came to work because she lived only a couple of blocks from the store on mainstreet. Dougall said:

Later in the day, I attempted to go home. It was north against the wind. I found out that I could not travel the few blocks straight down the highway to my house. The storm was so severe that I could not see, and found myself lost on Isabel's mainstreet. At one time, I thought I was traveling due north and found myself in Helmuth Schnable's machinery lot. I was angling off to the east. Later on, I was traveling down the highway going north, and I found myself on the porch of the Woodcock house. This was west instead of north. That was enough! I turned around and returned to the store and stayed there until Friday night when the storm let up. I don't know if I would have had enough strength to have moved enough snow to get into my house. Ed Monnens and his sons, Tim and Larry, walked me home. They shoveled the snow from the doorway and removed the screen-door so it would not stop anymore drifting snow.[54]

The *Isabel Dakotan* wrote, "For most people, this was the worst storm within memory. Worse than either 1949 or 1960. It may go down in history as the most devastating storm ever experienced here–even worse than the storm of 1888."[55]

Darrell Card, resident of Timber Lake and banker in Isabel, was stormed in at the bank. Card also operated a two-way radio. Just recently, Card had a high antenna installed on the bank building for his two-way radio. Ed Waddell's and Gene Schnabel's radio towers down were blown down by the strong winds. During the storm, Card acted as a relay station.

Mr. and Mrs. Dick Flemming, monitored their set during the storm. Afterwards, Mr. Flemming who worked for an elevator in Isabel delivered medicine for livestock.

Eugene Schnabel had a small portable two-way radio. On Saturday, Schnabel discovered his band of sheep trapped in snow at the Ernest Pladsen ranch. He summoned additional help over the radio and saved about half of them.

Attics in Isabel were permeated with snow. After the snow melted, homeowners had water problems.

Local contractors and heavy equipment operators were very busy after the blizzard. Usually, there was little work for them, this time of the year.

In Isabel, there were drifts as high as some houses. A week after the storm, Mrs. Leon Tuttle said her car was still entombed in snow. Charles Dahl, another individual, who has been busy digging out his Pontiac said, "It will be the middle of August before I get it out."[56]

In Isabel school was closed for a week, from the afternoon of March 2 to March 9.

On March 9, Alfred Cowan, a local rancher, looked for his cattle out on the range. Leading his tired saddle horse, Cowan was approached by Donald Knodel and two men from Boulder, Colorado. They sold Ski Doo snowmobiles. They informed Cowan of dead cattle in the area. The salesmen mentioned seeing live animals on the tops of hills. Cowan was pleased to hear the good news. Then, Knodel uttered his sales pitch. Cowan bought a snowmobile right on the spot. He sent his horse home. After the Colorado men left, Cowan continued his search on the speedy Ski Doo.

The Gerhardt Heck family, rural Isabel, lost several head of cattle in the storm. Another loss, a puppy, was harder on the family.

Days later, Heck worked inside his granary. He heard a noise. Heck dug out a section in the snow and poked a long stick under the granary. He heard a whelp. A little bit later, the young dog popped out. The puppy had scratched its way to freedom, after seeing a little daylight.

Herbert Lippert, Dewey County agent, believed that the livestock losses in this county had the possibility of being as high as thirty-five percent of the entire stock population in the immediate aftermath of the blizzard.

On March 14, that number was down to twenty percent. Lippert, working out of Timber Lake, said "the loss was over a million dollars. By this date, sixty percent of the livestock owners had been contacted. The number of animals that were confirmed dead included 8,000 cattle (4,800 calves, 1,600 yearlings and 1,600 cows); and 2,000 sheep.[57]

On March 17, a representative from the Small Business Administration stopped in Isabel. In 1966, however, people could not get SBA money to make repairs caused by a disaster.

On March 24, homeowners, L. L. Heinrich, Andrew Knodel, and Oscar Reich, had snowbanks 10 to 15 feet high near their places. Above normal temperatures had sunk the piles and made them hard.

Firesteel is located about fifteen miles northeast of Isabel on State Highway 8. The town was named for nearby Firesteel Creek, which rises in the northern part of Ziebach County and flows north into Corson County to join Grand River. There is lignite coal in the area. "Rock that burns," according to the Native Americans.

In 1960, the town had a population of 50 people. .

North of Firesteel is where Ed Bickel had a ranch in March 1966. After the storm, Bickel used a snowmobile, a Ski Doo, to check his livestock.

On March 16, Mr. Bickel discovered two cows buried in snow. He rescued the animals, but one died, shortly afterwards. Bickel's most valuable tool, the Ski Doo, was now ineffective. The first week after the blizzard, temperatures averaged 8 to 14 degrees above normal. After that, the highs were 12 to 18 degrees above normal for another week.

Besides the financial losses, farmers and ranchers encountered another problem, the disposal of their dead animals. Stockmen had a hard time recovering bloated animals near rivers, streams, creeks and gullies. Soft ground limited the use of heavy equipment.

As the snow disappeared, the sight of dead pheasants became very common. Local residents believed only a few birds survived the blizzard.

Timber Lake, seat of Dewey County, was named for the nearby lake. The Milwaukee Road arrived on May 10, 1910. Its another community on State Highway 8.

In 1960, Timber Lake's population was 624.

On March 5, 1966, once the blizzard had passed, the depth of snow on the ground at Timber Lake was 38 inches. This was the greatest depth of snow on the ground of any reporting station in South Dakota for the month of March 1966. In the March 2-5 blizzard, Timber Lake recorded 4.41 inches of precipitation, of which 3.50 inches came on March 4.[58]

A Timber Lake rancher, Frank Maciejewski Sr., suffered a financial loss estimated at $125,000. Maciejewski lost between 600 and 700 head of cattle and about 400 head of sheep. His cattle bunched up against a shed in the feed lot and smothered.[59]

Mr. and Mrs. Ralph Hacecky, lived near Timber Lake in March 1966. On Wednesday night, the elderly couple went to coal shed. After filling their pails with coal, Mr. Hacecky stepped out into the storm. He disappeared in the blowing snow. He was 74 years old. Mrs. Hacecky stood in the storm for a moment. She had second thoughts about her chances of making it back to the house. She went to the chicken coop, beside the coal shed. The blizzard was relentless. She stayed there until Saturday morning. Mrs. Hacecky had a horrible time, thinking her husband was dead.

Mrs. Hacecky shoveled out of the chicken coop. She looked for their house. It was gone. There was a huge snowdrift in its place. She dug in the pile until she found the house. Mrs. Hacecky heard some noise, so she dug deeper. Did she hear, her husband moving about? Her heart soared with hope. Mrs. Hacecky shoveled deeper and deeper.

What a wonderful reunion it was. Mr. Hacecky was totally exhausted, but he made it back to house, Wednesday night. He thought his wife had died in the storm.

House in northwest Timber Lake almost completely buried in snowbank five days after the storm. Courtesy of Aberdeen American -News.

Maciejewski feedlot five miles from Timber Lake. Courtesy of Aberdeen American-News.

On March 10, the couple were still using a window to get in and out of the house. Their truck had 12 feet of snow on top of it. Mr. Hacecky wondered how he was going to get to town and get some more coal.

Mr. Hacecky and his dog stand on top of a snowbank approximately 20 feet high between wind powered battery charger on left and chimney of his house at the right. Courtesy of Aberdeen American-News.

The Gordon Quinn family lived near Timber Lake in March 1966. Gordon Quinn, the Dewey County ASCS office manager, watched the blizzard pile snow higher and higher. He lived in a two-story house.

Francis, Gordon's son, lived in a mobile home about 11 yards from his father's place. Francis and his wife had five children, the youngest was ten days old. By Friday night, the mobile home was buried. The roof cracked under the weight of the snow. Francis tried to get out of the mobile home, but the door was buried under snow. Earlier, he had placed a table over the top of the door. With a desperate heave, he moved the table enough to get out.

Afraid to leave his trapped family, Francis threw snowballs at his father's house. He attracted his attention. Gordon smelled stove fumes, their chimney was clogged. One by one, Francis handed the children out through the hole in the snow. Each time, Grandpa took them back to his house. The couple left, after the children were out.

Glencross, a little town in Dewey County with 45 residents in 1960, is located just off State Highway 8. In 1919, Conrad Matern established a store on a site where two small narrow valleys intersected. Hence the name, glens cross.

Mr. and Mrs. Leo Aberle of rural Glencross, expected another child in early March. Already blessed with twelve children, the couple had planned to go to the hospital, Wednesday afternoon. The storm came up and they never left the ranch.

On Thursday, the blizzard showed no signs of letting up. Mrs. Leo Aberle was ready to give birth. They had a link to the outside world, their telephone still worked.

Mrs. Francis Card, a registered nurse, instructed the nervous father over the phone. Mr. Aberle delivered their thirteenth child, a boy. In a phone conversation with a reporter, Aberle was asked if the episode had frightened him. He replied, "I don't want to do it again."

The horrible weather continued on Friday. Aberle had lived his whole life near Glencross. Commenting on the blizzard, he said, "this one is as good as any of them."[60]

In 1960, Trail City had a population of 75 residents. The town is located near a popular watering place on an old cattle trail. Cattle companies used to drive their herds past here on their way east to Mobrige for rail shipment. The community is along State Highway 8.

Louie Merkel, a rancher south of Trail City, feared the worst.

After the storm, he looked for his herd. Merkel searched a long time without luck. As the hours passed, his hopes faded. Merkel headed out toward the badlands. He stopped at the edge of the hills and honked the horn. This was a signal for the cows to come and feed. In a bit, the cattle started coming up out of the bottoms. Merkel called the moment, "The most beautiful sight I have ever seen."

Buried in a snowdrift over 20 feet high after the storm is a quonset on the John Reinbold ranch northwest of Trail City. The building, along with some machinery stored inside, suffered some damage when part of it caved in under the weifght of the snow. Mr. Reinbold suffered swollen feet from walking, and blisterd hands from shoveling snow and carrying hay on a pitchfork to feed his livestock. Courtesy of Aberdeen American-News.

Carrying bales of hay after the blizzard to feed the livestock on the Jack Holzer ranch northwest of Trail City. Left to right in the photo are Eugene, James and Thomas Holzer. Courtesy of Aberdeen American-News.

Lemmon, Thunder Hawk, Keldron, Morristown, Watauga, McIntosh, McLaughlin, Mahto, Wakpala and Little Eagle

Lemmon was established when the Milwaukee Railroad arrived in 1907. The town was named after George Lemmon, one of South Dakota's most famous cowboys. Between 1857 and 1946, Mr. Lemmon handled almost a million head of cattle. Lemmon was inducted into the National Cowboy Hall of Fame, founded in 1958. Mr. Lemmon organized a three-day jamboree in 1908 that celebrated the Fourth of July which attracted five thousand people.

By 1960, the town, located in Perkins County, had a population of 2,412.

Lemmon was home for a New York couple, Kathleen Norris and David Dwyer. Norris's maternal grandparents, Frank Totten, a doctor, and his wife, Charlotte, a school teacher, built a house in Lemmon in 1923. After the death of her grandparents in 1974, Norris and her husband, Dwyer, a poet, moved to Lemmon and settled in their grandparents house.

Kathleen Norris wrote a book, *Dakota: A Spiritual Geography*, It was published in 1993. Norris talked about the immediate area and how the couple came to appreciate rural life in West River County.

The Co-Op Oil Station and Freymark Clothing Store were being torn down in late February 1966. The demolition project was expected to be completed by May. Meanwhile, the Hamburger Hut and Pat's Place were getting ready to move into different facilities.

The A & W Root Beer Drive Inn at Lemmon was up for sale in March 1966. The building was built along Highway 12 in 1960.

On February 25, Lemmon's high school boys basketball team, the Cowboys, defeated the Black Devils of Hettinger, 49 to 47. The Cowboys lost to the Dickinson Trinity Titans, the following day.

That weekend, the members of the Lemmon National Guard, the 211th Engineers Company, had a Command Inspection. Colonel T. I. Spalding of Huron, Commanding Officer of the 109th Group at Rapid City, headed the inspection team.

The Lemmon Cub Scouts held their annual Blue and Gold dinner in St. Mary's Church on Sunday. Junior members were recognized at the award banquet. The day was a warm and pleasant, the high reached 47 degrees.

KBJM, a new radio station in Lemmon, had planned to be on the air on March 1. The grand opening was postponed because the operating license from the Federal Communications Commission never arrived as expected. The station manager, James Schimke, said, "The station will begin transmission as soon as the license arrives."

The weather forecasts for the area changed on Wednesday, March 2. The morning forecasts predicted additional snow and strong winds late Wednesday and Thursday. That night, blizzard warnings were issued for Thursday and Friday.

With cloudy skies the thermometer worked its way up to 27 degrees in the morning. Lemmon recorded .30 inches of precipitation for the day. Early in the evening, the blizzard struck Lemmon.

The mail truck left Lemmon at 6:00 p.m. on Wednesday. The truck did not travel very far. The carrier took shelter in McIntosh. Other motorists looked for places to wait to get out of the storm.

Lemmon recorded 14 inches of snow on Thursday.

Postal workers, Bernard Grossmann, George Pixler and Glenn Schnell, battled their way to the post office on Thursday morning. They sorted what little mail that was on hand and conversed with the few hardy customers that picked up their mail.

Postmaster Vincent Hanrahan, Mr. Pixler and Mr. Schnell came to work on Friday. The post office received no mail on Thursday and Friday. Mr. Hanrahan delivered newspapers to the houses that he passed on his way home.

On Thursday and Friday, peak wind gusts at Lemmon fluctuated between 80 and 100 mph. The highs for those days were 19 and 14, and the lows were 6 and 2. The storm let up late Friday night.

Mrs. Vance Stewart, local weather observer, recorded 24 inches of snow in Lemmon during the blizzard. The water content of the precipitation amounted to 2.13 inches. Lemmon averages 33 inches of snow a year.

There was no long distance telephone service available in Lemmon after Wednesday night. Service was restored Sunday evening. High winds toppled the 320 foot microwave tower near Stephan. This prevented Mrs. Stewart from relaying the weather information to the United States Weather Bureau.

Local calls could be made during the blizzard.

Lemmon was a safe haven for many stranded motorists. They went to Phil's Truck Stop on Highway 12, Ray's Motel and the Kuilman's Motel. Also, the hotels, the Yellowstone and Palace, were full. Mrs. Adam Rott and Mrs. Godschalk cooked food for their stranded guests.

On Main Street, some people made their way to Pat's Place.

Donald Becker, night patrolman, came to work Wednesday night. He remained at the police station until Saturday afternoon.

As the weather permitted, the police officers checked on elderly individuals who lived alone. On one run, they discovered that the fire in Mr. T. A. Tharaldson's stove had went out. The West River pioneer suffered from the cold, so they took Mr. Tharaldson to Five Counties Hospital for treatment and care.

Lemmon residents lost their electricity twice. The first outage lasted for forty minutes on Thursday night. On Friday, between 2:00 p.m. and 4:00 p.m., the power went out again. This outage was caused by a transmission failure at the Glenham substation. Montana Dakota Utilities workers redirected the source of power. After the switch, Lemmon's power came from western sources.

At ten o'clock Friday night, the massive task of snow removal began in Lemmon. The command center was set up at police headquarters in Lemmon. It was a coordinated effort, based on priorities.

On Saturday, the Cowboys final regular season basketball game against Spearfish was canceled.

County and state crews were out in full force on Saturday. National Guard equipment operators were called in for extra duty. Contractors worked for Civil Defense teams, private businesses, and local individuals. The matter was made easier because many residents volunteered their time and equipment.

The Willard Ottman family lived at 811 Sixth Avenue West in Lemmon. Their house was buried with snow up to the roof. Mr. Ottman and his two sons shoveled many hours after the blizzard.

Local residents, Mrs. Morris Wise and Rodney, Mrs. John Goeres and Loren traveled to Rapid City prior to the storm. Returning home on Wednesday, Wise's car developed engine trouble north of Sturgis. Help came in the way of a passing motorist. A gentleman gave Mrs. Wise a ride back to Sturgis where arrangements were made to get her car fixed. Mrs. Wise tried to pay the man for his troubles, but he refused the money. Then, the man gave Mrs. Wise his business card. He said, "All I ask is that you look up my good friend, Dud Hogoboom and give him my greetings."

After the car was fixed on Wednesday, they started back to Lemmon. Soon afterwards, the storm came up. Mrs. Wise and her passengers decided to wait out the storm in Newell.

After the highways were cleared on Saturday, Mrs. Wise and her companions started for home. They heard storm news on the car radio. The good samaritan who had helped them on Wednesday was one of South Dakota's storm victims.

Passing through Faith, they noticed the car of Earl Thomas. Mrs. Wise said, "I couldn't help but think if he hadn't stopped to help me, he might still be alive."[61]

By Saturday night, most of the streets in Lemmon had a single path cut through the snow. Drivers needed to use extreme caution because traffic was one way.

Lemmon received incoming mail from the west on Saturday afternoon. Lemmon residents picked up their mail at the post office between March 5 and March 10. On March 7, mail from the east arrived in town. Mail carriers resumed deliveries on rural routes on March 8.

The massive piles of snow delighted children, but a young boy was hurt on Sunday. Peter Froelich, 10, son of Mr. and Mrs. William Froelich of Lemmon, severely injured two vertebrae when he slid on an aluminum saucer off the family garage on to First Avenue West.

Lemmon's rotary plow ran until it threw a rod on March 7. Repair parts for the engine were flown in by the National Guard. After a major overhaul, the plow was put back in action.

On March 7, Lemmon's city council held a brief meeting. Mayor Simon Wahl was not there, so Council President Glenn Stanley ran the meeting. After discussion, the council designated the polling places for the upcoming city election on April 19. They approved the purchase of the Wheeler Manufacturing Company Building, for $6,000, to house city equipment. The old shop would be torn down.

People were concerned about snow on sidewalks. Mr. N. Krause, city attorney, believed the city had a legal obligation to remove the snow off certain sidewalks. With that opinion, the council instructed Fred Johnson, Street Foreman, to remove snow from the designated areas after his crews had finished clearing snow away from the fire hydrants.

On March 8, the Lemmon Cowboys played in the Section 3 Basketball Tournament in Mobridge. They lost to the Aberdeen Golden Eagles.

In other news on March 10, the Perkins County Commissioners awarded its fuel contracts. Winning bids included: Bison Implement, regular gas 14.9 cents per gallon; Standard Oil Company, Diesel No. 1 and burner fuel 14.15 cents per gallon, Diesel No. 2 and burner fuel, 13.15 cents per gallon; Lemmon Gas Company, propane gas 13.4 cents per pound. The highway superintendent was authorized to make the oil and grease purchases.

Phil Blank, agricultural specialist of the First National Bank, contacted the clients who had livestock. Blank discovered that 29 of 51 patrons had no losses at all. Many lost one to six head. Harold Deans, a rancher near Keldron, had substantial losses. Robert Kressly who ranches near Lemmon lost 30 head. Others with significant losses included John Riedy with 16, and Gus Sonn with 10 head.

Walter Storm, farmer northeast of Lemmon, lost twelve small hogs to drowning. The Storms said, "snow blew in the hog shed and melted from the animal heat."[62]

Thunder Hawk, located ten miles east of Lemmon on U.S. Highway 12, is named for the nearby Thunder Hawk Butte. The butte was named after Chief Thunder Hawk, a noted leader of the Sioux who had lived in the area.

Thunder Hawk experienced the same hardships of other communities in Corson County. Area residents had some livestock losses.

One such individual who suffered financial losses was Ernest Robbins, a farmer south of Thunder Hawk. During the storm, the roof of his barn collapsed. The fallen timbers killed some cattle that were inside the building.

Keldron, 25 residents in 1960, is located about eighteen miles east of Lemmon on U.S. Highway 12. Keldron, founded in 1909, derives its name from the word caldron, which means a large kettle or warm place or shelter. The town is nestled in a ring of hills which protect it. It looks like a huge kettle from the top of the hills.

Southeast of Keldron, the home of Art Lindquist was almost covered with snow. The weight put tremendous pressure on the walls. Members of the family heard the walls "creaking." Once their situation became known, their neighbors showed up with shovels. They went to work. Before long, National Guard members arrived at the farm to help out. They saved the Lindquist's home.

Morristown sprang up as a shipping point on the Milwaukee Railroad in 1917. That year, 30,000 head of cattle arrived at the C-7 Ranch from the Morris Packing Company to fatten up on the range. Nels P. Morris was head of the packing company and part owner of the C-7 Ranch. Hence, the name.

Morristown, located twenty-three miles east of Lemmon on U.S. Highway 12 in Corson County, recorded a population of 219 in 1960.

Saturday morning, planes from National Guard and Civil Air patrols crisscrossed the countryside. A spotter noticed the word, "HELP" traced in the snow at a farm yard about two miles south of Morristown. Authorities were notified because the plane did not have skis to land. The roads in the area were clogged with snow. Sunday morning, Darrell Zentner walked across the snow-blasted prairie to see how his neighbor, Clarence Grate, had weathered the blizzard. Once there, he found his friend, Clem, lying on the ground near his pickup. There was nothing the boy could do. Clarence Grate, a 58 year-old cattle rancher was dead.

Corson County Coroner, Cecil Hanson said, "Mr. Grate died of a heart attack sometime Saturday afternoon or evening." Apparently, Grate had been shoveling corn into the back of his pickup when he had the stroke. The truck was still running when Darrell Zentner discovered the body. J.D. Kesling flew the body to Timber Lake.

Since the death of his spouse on September 28, 1963, Grate had lived alone. He was buried beside his wife in the Isabel cemetery. Surviving relatives included six children and eleven grandchildren.

Mrs. Helen Sutton of rural Morristown had no livestock losses, but the family had its share of troubles. Mrs. Sutton and the hired hand, James Conger, carried feed in sacks to the cows in the barn. They worked eighteen hours a day, during the three-day storm.

Jack Sutton, her son, fell getting off the school bus at McIntosh, after the storm. Mrs. Bob Nehl took Jack to the hospital. He was confined for five days with a cracked elbow.

Watauga, a Sioux name meaning "foam or "foaming at the mouth," is another small town in Corson County that is located along U.S. Highway 12. Watauga had a population of 85 in 1960.

South of Watauga, the Vernon Dickenson family was snowed in for four days. On Sunday, Mr. and Mrs. Dickenson drove a tractor to Watauga. The first people they ran into were Mr. and Mrs. Glen Hendrickson. "See," Vern told his wife, "Those things are people I have been telling you about."

The Dickensons had to make a trip to McIntosh. Something strange happened in their barn. They needed a hoist, or anything that could get a cow out of the rafters. Snow blew in their barn during the blizzard and the snowbanks got higher and higher. Some cows in the barn had nowhere to go. They ended up on top of the drifts. One cow got hung up, over the rafters. The Dickensons liberated the cow, but it died afterwards.[63]

McIntosh lies about a mile south of the North Dakota border and forty-two miles east of Lemmon. U.S. Highway 12 and South Dakota Highway 65 meet at McIntosh. As the seat of Corson County, the town took its name from a subcontractor for the Milwaukee Railroad, the McIntosh Brothers. In 1909, they were building grades across Standing Rock Indian Reservation for the Milwaukee Railroad.

McIntosh had 568 residents in 1960.

Blizzard conditions developed before Alvin Jacobs could get to his ranch northeast of McIntosh in early March 1966. He was stranded at Selfridge, North Dakota. His wife,

Mrs. Jacobs, their son Larry, age 20, who worked at a garage in McIntosh, and Mary Ann, were at home. Larry and Mary Ann worked outside in the storm. They shoveled the snow away from the front of the barn doors. Once they had them open, they dug a path to their cattle. Then, the teenagers used the shovels to chase the cattle into the barn. Afterwards, Mrs. Alvin Jacobs said, "I don't know how they did it." They were credited with saving the family herd.[64]

On March 5, Robert Knispel, a North Dakota cattle rancher about fifteen miles north of McIntosh, searched for his cattle. Knispel located some animals, but many were missing. After feeding the ones he found, he continued to look for others the rest of the day.

Knispel received a call from McIntosh on Sunday. During the blizzard, Knispel's cattle drifted downwind, and the animals were on the outskirts of McIntosh when the storm ended. Local residents herded the livestock into the state machinery parking lot. It had an enclosed fence. The Knispels came to McIntosh and took their cattle home.

On March 7, Kenneth Neumiller and David Utter operated a state snowplow, west of McIntosh on U.S. Highway 12. While plowing, a white snow cloud hugged the highway. Something hit the snowplow. After stopping, they noticed a vehicle turned on its side. Two young girls were inside. The driver of the car was Roslie Kendrick, 19, Minneapolis, and her passenger was Donna Peterson, 18. They were lucky to suffer only cuts and bruises.

John Powell, Corson County Agent in McIntosh, compiled the information for the livestock losses of the county. The data was sent to Brookings. The extension service of the South Dakota State University released the results of the study on March 17. Corson County lost 8,500 cattle and 1,500 sheep.[65]

Founded in 1909, McLaughlin had a population of 983 in 1960. Located in Corson County, McLaughlin has two highways passing through it, U.S. 12 and S.D. 63. The city was named after Major James McLaughlin, an Indian agent assigned to the Standing Rock Reservation in Dakota Territory in 1881.

On March 1, 1966, McLaughlin residents enjoyed a high of 41 degrees. There was little snow left on the ground.

On March 2, the high, 33, for the day came early. Snow started to fall around 10 a.m. The precipitation was light and fine. Local radio stations broadcasted storm warnings.

School officials called in their bus drivers at noon. An hour and a half later, school was canceled for the day.

Traffic around McLaughlin was about normal until 4:00 p.m. Blizzard conditions developed quickly after that time. Wind gusts up to 60 mph, hit the area.

By 8:00 p.m. the highways and roads in the area had big snowdrifts. The streets in McLaughlin had waist-deep snowbanks. Traffic came to a standstill.

On Thursday, people could barely see across the street in McLauglin. If anybody moved outside, only short walks were made. The high for the day was 30.

Two local men tested Mother Nature. Tom Knudson was stranded in McLaughlin on Wednesday. Knudson and Stanley Hepper headed out for the sale barn, located northeast of town, Thursday morning.

After passing the depot, they became separated in the storm. Tom, confused about his location, ran into a flag pole. At first, he thought the flag pole was the school yard.

Then, he remembered that the Harn factory had a flag pole. With that in mind, Knudson started walking in the whiteout. He kept walking and walking. He passed his destination and did not know it.

Knudson came across a fence and followed it. Before long, he trudged upon a gravel road. Could he be as far north of town as the Kenel road? If that was the case, he could walk for many miles and not find shelter. Knudson knew he could not stand still. He took off again.

Suddenly, the sun broke through in an opening. During the brief lull, Knudson thought he recognized something in the distance. If this was Gullickson Locker, he knew where he was.

Knudson turned and started back. He stumbled into a parked truck. Knudson figured the vehicle was probably parked near the sale barn. He took off again. Knudson soon reached the barn.

Mr. Hepper survived his ordeal as well.

Just before 7:00 a.m. on Friday, McIntosh had a power failure. For the next three hours, the lights snapped on and off many times. After that, the residents had no power.

Montana-Dakota officials indicated the breakdown came after the heavy transmission line of the Bureau of Reclamation east of the Missouri River went dead. Employees could not redirect power to McLaughlin. The switches to western power sources had frozen up in the blizzard.

Many homes in McLaughlin became cold on Friday. As elsewhere, some residents moved in with their neighbors who had other heat sources. Other residents stayed in bed and used all their blankets and warm clothes to keep warm.

On Friday, the thermometer registered a high of 16. That night, the low was 5 above.

Around midnight, the blizzard started to lose its fierce grip on McLaughlin. The storm brought 20 inches of snow to McLaughlin.

Power came back on for a short period at 1:30 a.m. Saturday. After that, the electricity snapped on and off. By daylight, the current was steady.

As the visibility improved, people were astonished at the height of some of the snowbanks. The digging out process began in earnest.

By Sunday night, state highway crews had opened U.S. Highway 12 in the area.

On the morning of March 2, Mr. and Mrs. Otto Mettler traveled to Lemmon to celebrate their daughter's 20th birthday at the Emanuel Stugelmeyer home. Joanne Mettler worked at the Hamburger Hut in Lemmon. What happened to the family during the blizzard was in many newspapers. Here's what the *McLaughlin Messenger*, Merle E.Lofgren, editor, wrote:

Plight of Three Lost In Storm Main
Concern of People 2 Days and Nights

It was almost like hearing a voice from another world for Mrs. Don Howe Sr., of rural McLaughlin when she tried to call her son in rural Mahto Saturday and heard the voice of Mrs. Otto Mettler on the line. Mrs. Mettler with her husband and six-year-old son Lyle, had been missing since about 4 p.m. Wednesday and not been heard from after that time until Mrs. Howe heard Mrs. Mettler on the line. The Mettlers had walked home earlier that morning but were unable to call out on their phone.

People all over the nation had heard of the missing Mettlers on radio and television. The nearest help, their neighbors and the people at McLaughlin, had born the burden of having to sit helpless through 70 hours of storm without being able to do anything to help. Many people had given up hope the three would be found alive.

Mr. and Mrs. Mettler had gone to a birthday party in Lemmon during the day and stopped at McLaughlin at 3 to pick up Lyle who attends school there. They filled their new car with gas at the Farmer's Union Oil Station and set out for home.

Another son, Earl, and a neighbor boy, Bob Kramer, were in McLaughlin with the Mettler's pickup for some repairs.

There are several roads the Mettlers use from time to time to get to their ranch 13 miles northeast of McLaughlin. They could go through Mahto. They also turn east a mile north of McLaughlin and go south on one of two roads. There was no way of knowing for sure which road they took.

Earl and Bob got to the Mettler ranch and found the car was not there so they went to look. They got stuck at the Elmer Hertel farm. From there they called back to McLaughlin and concern grew. Phone calls were made to farmers who live along the road and Clifford Plank and several other farmers walked along the road as far as they could but could see no car off the road.

The state highway crew with foreman Dave Babbit tried to organize a rescue party but it became obvious they could not get vehicles started and into the storm.

At the Hertel farm they had torn gears out of the Mettler's pickup trying to force it through the snow. Small tractors were started but got stuck. They went the next morning to the Elmer Hertel farm and started a big tractor but it got stuck as they could not see to avoid the huge drifts.

At 11 p.m. Friday night a rescue party started making it up in the blinding blizzard at McLaughlin. A county blade with a plow on front was put into service. The crew and volunteers went out in the binding snow and blizzard digging equipment out of the snow and getting it out into the open. They started out with the patrol, a front end loader with four wheel drive, two trucks with plows and a pickup.

Mr. and Mrs. Otto Mettler and their boy took the road home people for some reason guessed they would least likely to use. They went east on the Kenel road and then south to the old Ehnes place. From there they turned east. The car started to get stuck and tore up a chain and finally slid into the ditch just about two miles from home.

They had eaten at the birthday party and had fifty cents worth of candy with them. They had some blankets in the car which Mrs. Mettler had put there for just such emergencies. They also had a shovel. These items did a lot to save their lives.

During the night, Wednesday the car was covered over with snow. They opened a window and poked holes in the snow with the shovel to get air into the car. The motor had stopped about an hour after they got stuck.

Five times while they were stuck, they shoveled their way out by dragging snow into the back seat, and Mr. Mettler thought of trying to walk home but each time the storm was too violent and they settled down to wait some more.

The candy was rationed to the little boy and they all ate snow. They said they were neither very hungry or very cold. Lyle did not complain through *most of the long, cramped wait, except the last night when he thought they should go home the next morning and get something to eat.*

There was no radio in the new car. Mrs. Mettler said she and Lyle sang a Sunday School song, "Jesus Loves Me."

Early Saturday morning they started to walk home. Mrs. Mettler and Otto each held the corner of a quilt and Lyle walked between them.

Bob and Earl came along after Mr. and Mrs. Mettler and Lyle left and saw their tracks going for home so they went on to the farm.

The next day Lyle had a little fever but the three who were storm bound in a car for about 70 hours show no ill effects of their long entombment in the snow.

Eventually, the rescue party was notified of the good news. Max Cooper, Sunday editor of the *Aberdeen American-News*, told the family that their disappearance in the storm had worried tens of thousands in the midwest. Mr. Mettler replied, "I was some worried myself." He said, "If they had seen Earl they would have traveled to the ranch with him and would have made it easily." Furthermore, during those lonely three nights and two days, "We said quite a few prayers."

Cooper asked the McLaughlin rancher about the thousands of dollars worth of cattle lying dead on his ranch. Mr. Mettler told Cooper, "I can always raise more cattle." Mettler figured he lost around 50 head, a $15,000 loss. It was about half of his herd.[67]

The storm was harsh to the Otto Mettler's neighbors as well. By March 8, the White Bull family had burned their furniture and all the posts they were able to dig out of their fences. They were out of food. That night, two members of the family walked over to the Otto Mettler farm where they received food supplies.

Like the White Bull family, other farmers and ranchers were still isolated. Additional roads would be cleared in a couple of days.

On the morning of March 8, a plane flew to the Donald Schott farm, northeast of McLaughlin, to pick up their sick baby. Also, the plane made another rescue flight to the Lind Olson farm, southwest of McLaughlin. Mr. Olson had a heart attack.

Afterwards, Merle E. Lofgren, said: "Radio does a good job of warning people, it alone is not adequate. Many people do not listen to their radios. Even those who do listen can easily miss the spot storm announcements."

Lofgren suggested that the Civil Defense should have a study on better ways of giving storm warnings. He offered some ideas. Local police could announce weather warnings on their car's loudspeakers, just like they do for summer storms. Stores with public address systems could relay storm warnings. Places where people gather could have storm warnings posted. Finally, a neighbor to neighbor telephone system could be set up–the Civil Defense director in each region could call some people, then they would call five neighbors and repeat the process until everyone was notified.[68]

Lofgren noted his personal observations:

I and Willis Lenerville, the Mammoth Printer of McIntosh, were trapped on main street in McLaughlin in the old blue pickup about 7 p.m. as we tried to go home. The banks kept closing in on us. First, we could run up and down the street a couple of blocks before our course was blocked. Pretty soon our run was less than a block long. We finally broke and made a run for it in the pickup and got firmly stuck two and one-half blocks from home. We were soaked and exhausted when we got home even though we stopped and warmed up and got our breath at the Clarence Sauer house on our way home (and right kind they were to we weary wayfarers.)

Thursday I devoted to making all-day soup while the little wife stirred up bread and rolls and such. At noon she put her bakery in the oven. After dinner she set the alarm on the stove to remind her to do something. When the alarm went off she was not in the kitchen but I was there pitching things into the soup. I hit a few buttons to turn off the alarm and unfortunately turned off the oven in the process. The bread and rolls, half done, did not live up to Momma's expectancy when she went to the stove to pull them out. They were joiners. The top crust joined the bottom crust during the cold snap in the oven.

Friday was frustrating. Son Paul jumped out of bed and switched on TV for cartoons. Television didn't work due to no electricity. The kids about twisted the dials off the set before we abandoned the house for the sanctuary of the home of our friendly neighbor who had heat.

A person found out how habit forming electricity is during the day as he would go into a room, and without thinking flip the light switch. No radio, no television, no cooking, no lights, no hot water–a storm is quite an advertisement for the people who sell electricity.[69]

Townspeople have a close relationship with their neighbors in the country. Merle Lofgren wrote:

The story of the storm is a sad and yet a happy story. It is a sad story of the loss of livestock, both in financial loss and in suffering to animals. It is a happy story in which many lives were in danger and were not lost.

It is a story of people who had their life's work in their cattle and had the cattle wiped out by the storm. People who had borrowed money to start their cattle herds and were just getting out of debt, found their work of many years wiped out. A young farm wife said, "We have been careful and worked hard for 14 years and everything we saved during those years is gone."

Their cattle herd is the bread and butter of farm families in this country. For that matter, it is the bread and butter of the people who live in town. People here figure cows on the range are better than money in the bank. Take care of your cows and they will take care of you is an old Dakota motto. People have a special attachment for their animals.

No wonder men and whole families cried Saturday morning when they shoveled out to their herds and saw the legs of animals sticking out of the drifts. The work of many years was gone in two days and nights on many farms.

Yet, there were many happy endings and we may be so tied up in our tears we cannot see them. The whole country rejoiced when Mr. and Mrs. Otto Mettler and their little son were found. Many people went out in the storm to try to save their stock. We could be plowing through drifts looking for people instead of animals.

There were many heroes of the storm. People went out of their way to help their neighbors. People worried about their neighbors and helped them.[70]

On the night of March 2, 1966, a 121 car Milwaukee Road freight train bogged down in heavy snows between McLaughlin and Malto. L. M. Boughner (Lefty), engineer, tried to free the train, but there was too much snow catching the bottoms of the cars.(Just like a car, a train backs up and goes ahead many times.) After failing to free the train, the brakeman uncoupled the power which consisted of four engines. The engineer opened up the throttle, and they cut a path to McLaughlin. They waited out the storm there.

The conductor and brakemen remained in the caboose. They had heat, water, and what food they brought along for the trip.

The following morning, a work train with a snowplow was ordered in Mobridge. After busting drifts for hours, the snowplow reached the caboose of the stalled train and the men were rescued. The caboose was pulled back to Mobridge.

Steam operated rotary plow. Courtesy of Aberdeen American-News.

Officials of the Milwaukee Railroad gave in to the blizzard on Friday, March 4. Not faced with snow problems for years, the Milwaukee faced a big challenge to get its tracks cleared in the aftermath.

In the mid 1950s, railroads switched from steam to diesel. The Milwaukee Railroad had a rotary plow at Aberdeen that still operated on steam. On Saturday, the rotary plow left Aberdeen, but the train crew soon learned they did not have adequate water supplies to keep the boiler working. They stopped at Bowdle to take on water, but the town had no water reserves to give them. In addition to this, the rotary plow was experiencing other mechanical problems. So, after reaching Mobridge, it was left there.

Steam powered rotary plow in action just east of Mahto March 9. For over a week, sixty-one drifts blocked the Mobridge-Lemmon section of the Milwaukee line. Courtesy of Aberdeen American-News.

Milwaukee officials tried to free the stalled freight train from the west, as well. On Saturday afternoon, an extra worktrain was ordered, the train had two engines with a 60 ton V-plow in front and a caboose. L.M. Boughner was the engineer and the fireman was Ed Mauck.

The railroad hired extra men to shovel snow. They rode in the caboose with the conductor. The diesel engines roared into a thick bank of snow, located just west of the overhead on old Highway 1 about a quarter mile west of Lemmon. The train stalled in the massive drift. Snow caved in around the engines and the men were trapped inside.

Diesel fumes soon saturated the cab. The men knew the fumes could kill them and time was running out. Meanwhile, men from the caboose dug frantically down to the cab of the engine. By the time the men in the caboose broke through to the engine, the trainmen inside were almost unconscious.

In that move, the engines had derailed. Besides that, the tracks were torn up. Carmen and maintenance of way workers were sent to the site. More men, some came as far as away as Chicago, were hired to shovel snow.

On Sunday and Monday, the tracks were repaired and the engines were put back on the rails.

By 11:30 p.m. Monday, the stalled Milwaukee freight train was freed and pulled to the siding at McLaughlin.

To clear the tracks west of Mobridge, the Milwaukee used small charges of dynamite. The chief clerk in Aberdeen said:

One drift is 3,500 feet long and ranges in depth from 5 to 20 feet. The battle with the drifts is compounded considerably by alternating thaw and night freeze, creating ice that plugs snow removal equipment. The equipment is taking a beating and we use it as long as we can and then repair it. Specialists have been flown in to help with the equipment. The dynamite is used to break up the ice and give the plow something to chew on. The road is utilizing two rotary plows, one working from each end of the problem.[71]

On March 12, the Milwaukee Road resumed normal operations on its mainline west of Mobridge.

Wakpala is a Sioux word that means "small river" or "creek."

Superintendent Julius Werle and two Wakpala teachers were rescued March 3 at 11:30 a.m. Lewis Smith, a game warden, reached their stalled car with a snowmobile. A spokesman at the Mobridge Police Department said they'd been too busy there Thursday morning to take down first names. Dale Lewis and Mr. Bockel were with Julius Werle.

Little Eagle had 200 residents in 1960.

Lorne Maxon, a rancher near Little Eagle, told the McLaughlin Messenger that the latest blizzard was, "The worst I have ever seen, and they could not get out of their yard for three days. Its first time, they have not been able to travel along the river with a team."

Frank, Lorne Maxon son, said, "The first time I ever had to shovel out horses." They cleared their yard with a team of horses. Then, they checked their cattle with the team. Maxon said, "Their loses were light."[72]

Mission, Winner, Burke and Bonesteel

Mission, located in Todd County, was founded in 1915 by S. J. Kimmell. There was a number of church missions in the area. That's how, the town acquired its name. The Rosebud Indian Reservation, named for the wild roses that grow in abundance in the area, takes up all of Todd County. The county was named after Captain John Blair Smith Todd, a cousin of Mary Todd, the wife of President Abraham Lincoln. A West Point graduate who served in the Mexican War of 1848. Afterwards, he became a prominent lawyer in Yankton. Todd promoted the creation of Dakota Territory. He was the first elected delegate of Dakota Territory.

Mission had 611 inhabitants in 1960.

Local residents experienced the March blizzard of 1966. The storm lasted two days in the area, March 3 and 4. Winds gusts reached 60 mph.

People lost their electricity. Water pipes froze in some of the homes. Snow worked its way into attics. Residents had water damages, after the snow melted.

East of Mission on U.S. Highway 18, near Joe Assman's place, a family of four from Casper, Wyoming, became stranded in the storm. The good news was that they were pulling a airstream mobile home. The family took shelter in the mobile home. Before long, a driver of a Flanery's truck joined them. Somewhat later, a man from Texas pounded on the mobile home door. He left and brought back his wife and their two-week old baby.

While the highway was being plowed, they were guests at Joe Assman's home.

Late March 4, Mrs. Calvin Jones Sr. experienced labor pains. The nearest hospital from Soldier Creek was sixteen miles away in Rosebud.

At 3:00 p.m., Mr. Jones helped his wife get in their car. Bob Fuller and Bob Delibero, VISTA workers, were already in the back seat. Milton Walking Eagle and Leslie Lance, neighbors, followed behind in Ruth Moccasin's car.

The group left, shortly afterwards. Visibility was near zero. Calvin Jones drove with his head out of the window, to see the edge of the blacktop.

Jones car stalled in a snowdrift, north of Rosebud. The men went to work and shoveled the car out. They cleared a path for the second car.

The group arrived at the hospital, between 5:30 and 6:00 p.m. They were just in time. At 7:15 p.m. March 4, Dorothy had twins, a girl and then a boy. It was the second set of twins for the family.

Saturday morning, Kenneth Tulloss, Parmelee, encountered numerous drifts on the way to hospital in Rosebud. His wife, Betty, was expecting a baby. They arrived at the hospital about 9:30.

Three hours later, Mrs. Kenneth Tulloss gave birth to a baby boy.

Todd County livestock losses exceeded 1,000 head.

Winner, the county seat of Tripp County, had 3705 residents in 1960. The surrounding area is famous for its good pheasant hunting. In 1907, Lamro was the county seat. In 1907, the Northwestern Railroad extended its tracks from Bonesteel to Dallas. The railroad survey in 1909, missed Lamro by about two miles. A new town sprang up along the railroad right-of-way. That town, was named Winner. The line between Dallas and Winner was completed in 1910-11.

On March 1, 1966, the high in Winner was 47 degrees. The thermometer reached 40 on March 2. Winner recorded a trace of precipitation that day.

Mrs. Rollin Key, volunteer observer for the U.S. Weather Bureau at Winner said, "The storm, which turned into a full-fledged blizzard about 4 p.m. Thursday, maintained wind gusts over 60 mile-per-hour mark for a 36 hour period before letting up early Saturday morning." Mrs. Key thought this storm was "the worst one in the last fifteen years."73

Winner received 6 inches of snow. The strong winds created snowbanks, 20 feet high in places. Fields were swept bare.

City officials adopted emergency measures late March 3. Local authorities advised all residents to stay in their homes on Friday. Although visibility was near zero, the city's snowplow operator forged a narrow path to the hospital, fire station, and other key businesses. Residents who ran short of critical items were supposed to call local law enforcement centers. They would, if possible, bring the items to their homes. To aid in such deliveries, police had the use of four-wheel drive vehicles from private citizens.

Tripp County Sheriff, James Storms, was notified that a local milk truck driver was missing Thursday night. Lloyd Lovejoy's last known stop was in Carter, and he never showed up in Mission, the next stop on his run. Eventually, Lovejoy was found safe at the Joe Assman's farm, seven miles east of Mission. There was no phone at his place, so Lovejoy could not contact others.

By Saturday night, Winner's main streets were opened for business. Some rural roads remained blocked for almost a week.

The auto show, sponsored by the Rosebud Auto Dealers Association, at Winner High School auditorium on Sunday was a great success. A crowd of over five thousand turned out for the event. The Browning Family and Ben Norman provided the musical entertainment.

Dr. Gerald Verley, a Winner dentist, received orders to report for active duty on March 7.

Area ranchers suffered some livestock losses.

Pheasants losses ran much higher than other years.

Burke, located about ten miles northwest of Bonesteel on U.S. Highway 18, is the county seat of Gregory County. The town was founded in 1904 and named after Charles Burke of Pierre. Burke was elected to the State legislature in 1895 and 1897, a member of Congress from 1899-1907 and 1909-1915. In 1921, he was named Commissioner of Indian Affairs.

The first three days of March 1966, came in like a lamb in Burke, (population of 811 in 1960). Mrs Wayne Norberg had started teaching kindergarten classes to twenty-nine students who would be attending Burke Public schools. The classes were being held in the Baptist Church with two sessions, 9:00-11:30 a.m. and 2:30-3:00 p.m.

Local residents put money aside for the Easter Seals campaign. Governor Nils A. Boe declared March 1 to April 10 as "Easter Seal Month" in South Dakota. Rapid City's Rene Ripplinger, daughter of Mr. and Mrs. Alex Ripplinger, was the 1966 Easter Seal Child for the South Dakota Society for Crippled Children and Adults. In 1965, 476 crippled children and adults received funds from that year's drive.

Blizzard conditions developed late on Thursday, March 3, in Burke. Friday night, the storm reached its peak. On Saturday, the winds tapered off and the skies cleared.

Burke had sporadic power outages. The longest spell without electricity was one hour.

A used mobile home at G & G Trailer Sales was flipped over by the strong winds. Nearby, a camper was overturned. Also, two brand new trailers were severely damaged when the wind gusts pushed them together.

L. M. Vander Knur's hangar at the airport drifted full of snow. The weight damaged one wing on his plane.[74]

South Dakota experienced a land rush just after the turn of the century. In 1904, several million acres of land opened up for settlement. Prospective homesteaders had to register at the land office in Bonesteel. In July 1904, 35,176 people filed for a chance at 160 acres, but there was only 2,500 land claims. Lottery winners purchased their land at four dollars per acre.

The boom times brought trouble. On July 20, 1904, the good citizens chased the gamblers and thieves out of town. For local residents it became known as the "Battle of Bonesteel."

Located in Gregory County, Bonesteel is close to the Nebraska border on U.S. Highway 18. East of it, is the Fort Randall Dam on the Missouri River.

In 1960, 452 people called Bonesteel home.

In June 1965, voters in the Bonesteel school district approved $95,000 for a new school gymnasium with class rooms and kitchen facilities.

In the first week of March 1966, voters approved an additional $40,000. for the project. Construction costs were higher than expected.

The thermometer climbed to 43 degrees on March 3 in Bonesteel. That night, the blizzard struck Bonesteel. Leo Neilan, local weather observer, recorded .04 inches of precipitation. In the beginning the precipitation was light rain. Thursday's night low was 20 above.

On Friday, the recorded high was 22 degrees. Before the storm ended on Saturday, 3 or 4 inches of snow fell in Bonesteel. Wind gusts were estimated at 60 mph.[75]

Snowdrifts in Bonesteel were between 6 and 8 feet high. Streets, running east and west, had the higher snowbanks.

Some livestock losses occurred in the area.

Pheasant loses were expected to be high.

On Monday, Coach Joe Laber's Bonesteel Tigers defeated the Wagner Red Raiders, 48 to 46, to earn the Region 7 third place trophy in Yankton.

Laborers filled out applications forms for openings at the Fort Randall Dam. They also had to take a civil service exam. Pay was advertised at $2.27 per hour for grade W-3 and $2.12 per hour for grade W-2.

Draper, Vivian, Presho, Kennebec, Lower Brule and Fort Pierre

Draper, located in Jones County, was named for a Milwaukee Railroad conductor, C.A. Draper. Usually, officials received that honor. The town was founded in 1906.

Draper's population in 1960 was 215.

Saturday morning, State Highway snowplow crews opened Highway 16. Plowing between Draper and Vivian, Lee Cox and Bob Evans stopped when they noticed a car, almost buried with snow. Inside, they found a couple from Michigan who were cold and hungry.

Frank Libner, working with Cox and Evans, had been following the plow in a car. Cox and Evans cleared a path to the hospital in Murdo. Libner drove the couple to the hospital where they recovered from their ordeal.

Located in Lyman County, Vivian was named for Mrs. Harry Hunter (Vivian) whose husband was a prominent lawyer, land agent, and representative of the Milwaukee Road when the town was founded in 1906.

Like Draper, Vivian had a population of 215 in 1960.

During the blizzard, Vivian received 7 inches of snow.

Another test of endurance took place west of Vivian. Jerry Parkinson, executive secretary of the Board of Charities and Corrections, waited thirty-six hours in a snowbound car.

Saturday afternoon, the frozen body of Freemont Sands was found beside a fuel barrel on the Ray Guthrie farm, south of Draper. Sands, 66, was a bachelor who cared for the livestock on the ranch. Details of the death were incomplete because there still was no telephone service in the area on the morning of March 8.

Presho, a town of 881 residents in 1960, is located in Lyman County. The town was named after J.S. Presho who operated a ferry across the Missouri River at Yankton in 1862. Presho was a boom town in 1905, the first bank went into operation eight minutes after the first lot was sold. The bank consisted of two barrels with a plank and a six-shooter to protect the cash.

Parents came to school, instead of their children, on February 28, 1966. Parent-teacher conferences in South Dakota are usually held on the last Monday in February. Parents picked up their children's report cards. Superintendent Frank Blaine met with some of the parents.

According to law, fish houses had to be off the ice on South Dakota lakes by March 5. Notices were printed in all local newspapers. Load limits on various highways and roads were being posted for the spring thaw.

Seaman Apprentice Sylvester LaRoche, Jr. was aboard the USS *Bronstein*, an antisubmarine escort ship for the *Yorktown* in March 1966. The Seventh fleet battlegroup was in the South China Sea. The navy apprentice was the son of Mr. and Mrs. Sylvester H. LaRoche of Route 2, Reliance.

Stores would have their windows decorated with posters for Poppy Day, now known as Memorial Day, later in the spring.

The storm affected Presho, before it hit. Wednesday night, residents could not make long distance phone calls.

Thursday night, blizzard conditions developed in the area.

Presho received 3 inches of fine snow and wind gusts of 70 mph. The storm passed out of the region on Saturday.[76]

There was no interruption of local phone service during the blizzard. On Monday, long distance service was back.

Presho experienced intermittent power outages. The longest lapse, ninety minutes, came Friday night. In the rural areas, the electricity was off longer.

Mike Sweeney, Pat Uthe, Pete Swinson, Claire Peterson, Gerald McClannahan and Forrest Houseman reacted quickly to problem in Presho. The electric motor that ran the city's main water pump burned out, during a period of low voltage. Sheriff Lee Roberts contacted the authorities in Winner with the police radio. They contacted the radio station in Winner. A short time later, Presho residents were urged to conserve water. A motor was taken off a secondary well and reinstalled on the primary well. On Saturday, water was restored to the mains.

Carbon monoxide warnings were issued on radio stations. People were instructed to make sure their chimneys, especially on trailer houses, were clear of snow and ice, otherwise poisonous vapors would find there way back into their homes.

Mr. and Mrs. Robert Gallant and Mr. and Mrs. Ted Jamisons had blockages at the Al Blocker trailer court. They cleared their chimneys and avoided the dangerous situation. Another man was really worried. Pat McKeever opened his trailer door and let fresh air into the home. He spent Friday night, on a couch near the front door with a pencil jammed in the doorway.

At the Rex Brown farm, Dennis Enright suffered facial burns in his trailer home when the furnace exploded. He received medical attention.

Stranded people left Presho, Saturday afternoon and Sunday. Most of the motorists ate at the Frontier Drive Inn Cafe. Gerald McClannahan kept the dinner open, even with the power and water shortages.

There was no incoming mail on Friday and Saturday. Rural deliveries depended on the road conditions, some places went almost a week without mail service.

Farmers and ranchers in the area lost livestock.

The March 1966 blizzard made Lee Sibson a firm believer in shelterbelts. He had planted a short belt of trees near his buildings and feed pens. Although Sibson lost six head, he figured the shelterbelt saved his herd of 250 cattle. After the storm, Sibson made plans to extend the shelterbelts around his place.

Kennebec, county seat of Lyman County, was established in 1905. Some people thought the town was named after a Milwaukee Railroad official. Several early settlers have told a different story. They said one of the founders of the town became stuck in heavy gumbo with a loaded wagon and attempted to back onto firmer ground. A bystander shouted "Can no back! Can no back! " and from this incident the town took its name.

In 1960, Kennebec was home for 372 people.

Before the storm, Kennebec received .16 inches of precipitation. Those readings were for Wednesday and Thursday. The temperatures were amiable, the highs for those days were 38 and 35.

Kennebec experienced blizzard conditions on March 4 and March 5. On Saturday, Kennebec recorded another .15 inches of precipitation. The town had the same high, 21 degrees, on Friday, Saturday and Sunday. The *Advocate-Leader* said:

> *In the immediate area less snow came and aside from drifts in sheltered*
> *areas, the roads were mostly clear. However, due to the powder-fine snow*
> *it was impossible to see beyond the front of a car and impossible to walk*
> *against it at any measurable distance.*[77]

Laurel Houcin helped cleared the streets with a Farmhand.

Kennebec experienced a minor power outage on Friday. As elsewhere, the residents could not make long distance phone calls.

Senator James Abdnor, campaigning for re-election for another term in the South Dakota State Senate, was stormed in with many others at Kadoka. The elective districts were redrawn in 1966. In the last election, Senator Abdnor represented the counties of Haakon, Jones, Lyman, and Stanley. But, the new 24th Senatorial District included the counties of Haakon, Jones, Lyman, Mellette, Washabaugh, Bennett, and Jackson. Kennebec is Abdnor's hometown.

A week later, the newspaper said, "Everyone is pretty well shoveled out and with only a few lame backs there was no serious consequences to residents."[78]

Around 1750, the Sioux acquired their first horses. With the horse, the Sioux inhabited a large area of land from western Minnesota to the Rockies. The Sioux trailed the buffalo herds into Nebraska and Kansas on the south and Wyoming and Montana on the west. The heart of their domain was South Dakota.

Their most prosperous years, 1820 to 1850, coincided with the best years of the fur trade on the Upper Missouri. Trade goods improved their lives, but contact with whites brought smallpox and other diseases for which they had no immunities.

After 1850, thousands crossed their hunting grounds on the way to Oregon and California. In 1851, the Teton Sioux, (Minniconjou, San Arc Oglala and Brule tribes) signed a treaty in which they promised to stay north of the Oregon Trail.

In popular culture the Sioux are perceived as the daring buffalo hunters of the prairies. The Teton Sioux tribes were the most well known. In English the name "Teton Sioux" translates to "Dwellers of the Prairie." The word, "Sioux" was a uncomplimentary word used by the Ojibwas to identify their arch rivals.

Originally, the Sioux Nation was composed of seven major divisions: the Oglala, Sichangu, Miniconjou, Hunkpapa, Sihasapa, Itazipcho and Oohenonpa. They lived in related groups called "tiyospayes," in effect an extended family. A number of tiyospayes formed a band, In turn, grouping of bands formed tribes. There were fourteen tribes: Two Kettles, Minniconjou, Black Foot Sioux, San Arc Ogala, Hunkpapa, Brule, Yankton, Yanktonai, Hunkpatina, Assiniboine, Mdewakantowan, Wahpekute, Sisseton and the Wahpeton.[79]

Their livelihood depended on the buffalo herds. In 1830, the number of buffalo ranged between 60 to 75 million, a conservative estimate. The herd was broken up when the

Central Pacific joined the Union Pacific in 1869. The northern herd had about a million and a half animals, and the southern herd had close to five million.

The southern herd disappeared first. In a five year span, 1871 to 1875, buffalo hunters shot around 5 million animals. Among those involved in the slaughter were Wyatt Earp and Bat Masterson.

By 1883, the buffalo herds in South Dakota had disappeared.

That year, the last big buffalo hunt took place in South Dakota. In 1886, the number of buffalo that remained was less than one thousand.

The Lower Brule Reservation occupies parts of Lyman and Stanley Counties. The headquarters is located in Lower Brule The town of Lower Brule is located in Lyman County. In 1960, the place had 150 residents.

Late in the afternoon of Thursday March 3, 1966, the winter storm reached the area. The precipitation and strong winds knocked out the power in half of Lower Brule at 7:30 p.m. Winds of 70 mph were reported in the area.

Friday morning, the power was still out in half of the community. Outages occurred on the other side of town. One failure was four hours long.

A number of families moved into the school as houses lost heat. Houses that had heat became shelters for others. Some individuals sought refuge in Chamberlain's motels.

The power outage on Thursday night caused another problem, the pump that supplied water for the community stopped running. Friday night, Lower Brule ran out of water.

Friday evening, Alex LaRoche had to be hospitalized at Community Bailey because he had labored too hard in the snow.

The blizzard finally ended Saturday March 5. Lower Brule received 4 inches of snow. The strong winds left some impressive snowbanks in its wake. That afternoon, the digging out process involved everyone.

On Saturday, the lights snapped back on at 6:00 p.m., and soon afterwards, the city had water again. Herbert Flute was hospitalized for exhaustion, the snow had gotten the best of him.[80]

The first known explorers of South Dakota were Frenchmen, the Verendrye brothers. Francois and Louis-Joseph Verendrye explored the land west of the Missouri River in 1742-1743. They left a lead plate on a bluff overlooking Missouri River.

Historically, there were three forts built on the west side of Missouri River in what is now Stanley County. The first one was known as Fort Teton. It was built by Joseph LaFramboise around 1817. Fort Teton was replaced by Fort Tecumseh. It was named for the famous Shawnee chief who assisted the British during the War of 1812. Fort Tecumseh was establish about 1822 as a trading post. Old Fort Pierre, a military post, was built just north of the other two forts in 1832. It was named for Pierre Choteau Jr., of the American Fur Company which established the fort.

In 1960, Fort Pierre had a population of 2,649.

The Fort Pierre High School boys basketball team, the Buffaloes, placed third in the District 24 Basketball Tournament at Fort Pierre on February 26, 1966. The Buffaloes downed the Murdo Coyotes twice during the regular season, but lost the semi-final pairing to Murdo, 60 to 57. In the consolation game, Fort Pierre defeated Vivian, 85 to 61.

One noted South Dakotan who had first-hand experience in the March 1966 snowstorm was Roy Houck. He lived on his Triple U Ranch west of the Missouri River, about twenty-five miles northwest of Pierre.

Originally from Gettysburg, Mr. Houck had been ranching for many years. To help his cattle make it through the winter, he would keep them on land he owned next to the Missouri River in Potter and Walworth Counties. They would be protected there out of the wind in the brush and big cottonwoods.

But, trouble was brewing in the 1950's for the Houck family. The Army Corps of Engineers was constructing Oahe Dam at the time. When completely filled, it would flood most of the Missouri River bottom lands between Bismarck, North Dakota, and Pierre, South Dakota.

So, the Houcks sold that land and purchased the new ranch which was west of the Missouri River. The acquisition was done in two phases, the fall of 1959 and the spring of 1960. The Houcks called their new home, the Triple U ranch.

Roy Houck had been interested in buffalo since he was a child. One fourth of July, his father took the family in a Model T Ford down to Pierre for the celebration. That same day, they visited Scotty Philip's herd of buffalo west of the Missouri River. Roy was determined to have some of his own one day.

Scotty Philip had started his herd of buffalo by purchasing the entire herd of animals from the estate of Frederick Dupree (Dupris) of Dupree. He brought the buffalo to a 15,000 acre pasture on his ranch, immediately north of Fort Pierre.

On the first day of the storm in 1966, the Houcks were in the process of vaccinating 600 calves. The day started out with a light rain. The vaccination of the calves was done under the supervision of Dr. Nod, a veterinarian from Gettysburg. He had three helpers with him to assist with the work.

Besides Roy Houck and his wife Nellie, other people on the ranch at the time included Roy's son, Jerry and his wife Lila, their three small children and four hired men.

As they continued to vaccinate the heifer calves for brucellosis that day, the men didn't pay much heed to the weather. In addition to being preoccupied with their work, the wood-plank corrals and the barn provided some protection from the wind.

Conditions slowly deteriorated. The morning's fog and mist had given away to a biting sleet by noon. By the time darkness settled in, the precipitation had changed to a driving snow. The thermometer continued its downward slide all day.

It was a different story when the men were finished. As soon as they left the protection of the corral, the wind knocked them back a step.

The rate of the snow coming down was now so great that Dr. Nod and his helpers couldn't make out their car parked in the middle of the yard. Snow was now piling into drifts around the yard. The drifts next to the machine shed, were already 2 feet high.

For the remainder of the blizzard, Dr. Nold and his assistants were snowbound in Roy Houck's basement.

When he arose the next morning, Roy Houck discovered that the ranch was without power. To restore electricity, Roy and Jerry trudged through zero visibility to a machine shop. Getting there wasn't easy. Let Dale Lewis, author of *Roy Houck Buffalo Man*, describe it:

> Roy bundled up, no cowboy hat today, and out they went. As they waded through the snow alongside the house, the wind was swirling the snow into drifts now already waist deep. They stayed within four feet of the house and once at the fence they followed it down past the corner of Jerry's house. From there on, it was about one hundred feet of open space across the yard to the shop.

Visibility was zero. There was little chance of getting lost in the yard. Buildings, fences and corrals were everywhere. They were bound to run into something familiar from which they could get their bearings. Roy didn't worry about Jerry or himself, but still when you can't see your gloved hand in front of you, it makes a person a little concerned.[81]

An International 300 tractor was stored at the machine shop. After starting the tractor, they attached a portable generator to it. The men then drove the tractor through whiteout conditions, until they came to the light pole that was located between their respective homes.

While the generator had sufficient power to operate the furnace at either Roy or Jerry Houck's places, it couldn't run both at the same time. In order to keep both houses as warm as possible, the two families alternated its use.

In the early hours of the second full day of the snowstorm, all of a sudden, the tractor quit. Roy thought it was out of gas. But it wasn't, solid ice encased the whole motor.

They got another tractor going, a Farmhand equipped International H. They used it to pull the stalled tractor back to the warm confines of the machine shop.

It didn't take Jerry Houck long to get it running again. He then came up with a bright idea. Leave the International 300 equipped with the portable generator running in the shop and run the power through the welder outlet at the shop over to the light pole and on into the two houses. Eureka! it worked.

Feeding all those men took some creative effort on the par of Nellie and Lila Houck. Among the one-pot meals they came up with were chili and stove top stew. As she had a Bernz-o-matic stove equipped with two burners, Lila felt that it was easier to prepare meals for the men at her place. Nellie agreed with her.

Dr. Nold and his crew spent considerable amount of time playing poker with the Houck's hired men in Jerry Houck's basement. To have access to the light upstairs, they set the card table at the bottom of the basement stairs.

Roy Houck spent the majority of the blizzard in his own house-answering letters, handling paperwork or doing some reading. But concern about the fate of the 2,000 head of livestock on their ranch, had him up on his feet about every fifteen or twenty minutes. He walked back and forth, going from one window to another.

As the blizzard stretched from one day into another, Roy Houck pondered, "How long can these critters hold on without feed.?" With that many animals around, a bad snowstorm could bring financial ruin to them.

Jerry Houck and Frank Till stayed down at the shop during the day, when the blizzard was on. Frank Till kept the barrel stove there well supplied with fuel. They fed the cattle as best they could during the storm.

The shifting of the winds to the northeast had the Houcks worried. The ranch was set up to protect their cattle from northwest winds. Now the animals would be forced to locate some new shelter. The deep snow would make it hard for them to maneuver.

After the snowstorm had passed, the Houcks and the others shoveled open the doors to the hangar on their ranch. A huge hard-packed drift lay in front of it. The shovelfuls of the white stuff consisted of large blocks of snow and ice. Inside the hangar was a Piper Super Cub airplane and two Austin-Western road graders equipped with V plows.

After getting inside the hangar, Jerry Houck put skis on the Super Cub. After enough snow had been shoveled, Jerry Houck took off in the airplane. He wanted to see how the livestock had fared in the blizzard.

The plows opened lanes to the haystacks. It didn't take them long to realize, that skirting around the big hard snowbanks was easier, than trying to force the plows through them. Thus, the path to the haystacks was anything but straight.

Jerry Houck returned from his flight to report that the cattle either bunched or had been scattered. Unfortunately, there were some dead ones. Some of the Houcks' cattle, along with their neighbors', got out and wandered as far as Fort Pierre.

On his flight Jerry Houck saw their buffalo (the Houcks had seventy of them in March 1966), and they appeared to be doing alright. He also noticed what appeared to be something unusual, on top of a ridge in the snow were three half circles about a hundred yards apart.

The following day, the Houcks opened the four mile drive to the Mission Ridge Road. This allowed the veterinarian and his crew to finally go home.

Later in the day, after saying goodbye to Dr. Nold, Roy and Jerry Houck made their way on foot to check out those half circles in the buffalo pasture. Dale Lewis relates what they found:

> By examining the track they found that the buffalo had formed in a herd on top of the ridge facing the storm. It was known that buffalo form a V with the biggest bulls on the forward edge of the V and the cows and calves snuggled in the center. As the storm progresses, the front buffalo is constantly being replaced and rotated back down the line. As the snow drifted in behind them and threatened to cover them over, the herd, in unison, simply moved up the ridge another hundred yards and made a new stand.[82]

Roy and Jerry Houck watched in amazement as the buffalo frolicked about in the deep snow. When it came to eating, the shaggy beasts simply pushed aside the deep snow with a single snap of their neck. Exposed below them was buffalo grass.

It took quite a few days, for semitrailers to haul away the dead cattle from the Houcks' ranch and their neighbors. While the Houcks' losses were bad enough, they were staggering for their neighbors.

Most of the cattle the Houcks lost were due to the absence of a bacteria in a cow's stomach. It assists the cow in the digestion of food. The cattle starved during the lengthy blizzard. This starvation led to the death of the bacteria. Because of this, even when some of the cattle were fed after the storm, they bloated and then perished. Roy Houck lost fifty head this way.

The March 1966 blizzard led Roy Houck to thinking about what course his family should take in the future as far as livestock were concerned. A couple weeks after the blizzard, he gathered his family together–his wife Nellie and their four children, Tom Barbara, Jerry and Kaye. He suggested they get rid of the cattle and concentrate exclusively on buffalo. All of them concurred with the idea.

After they got rid of the cattle, the Houcks expanded their buffalo herd. By 1988, they had 3,500 animals. This very large herd caught the attention of Kevin Costner and others who were looking for such a herd to film in their upcoming movie, *Dances With Wolves*. Much of the filming for that movie was done the following year on the Triple U ranch.

Chamberlain, Pukwana, Mitchell, Salem, Sioux Falls and Lennox

In 1880, the Milwaukee extended its line from Marion to Chamberlain, just over 111 miles of track. Chamberlain, the seat of Brule County, attracted its first settlers at that time. A director of the Milwaukee, Selah Chamberlain, enjoyed the honor of having the village named after him. Before that, the place might have been known as Makah Tepee or "mud house" by the Indians since a recluse resided in a dugout or mud house at that locality.

A highway bridge was built across the Missouri River in Chamberlain in 1925.

In the 1960 census Chamberlain had 2,598 residents.

In January 1966, the Chamberlain high school boys basketball team, the Cubs, started a winning streak. The Cubs had twelve straight wins going into the Region IV Tournament at Mitchell, scheduled for March 8-9.

On March 3, the skies were blue in Chamberlain. Although it was windy, the high was 41. As local residents went about their business, they talked about the blizzard west and northwest of Chamberlain.

That afternoon, a basketball team from Rapid City stopped in Chamberlain on their way home. They had participated in the Catholic Invitational Tournament in Mitchell. They learned there was no travel west of Murdo, located about seventy-five miles west of Chamberlain on U.S. Highway 16. Here, they found a place to stay.

The skies turned pale, dumping light rain. It was getting colder outside. Robert Knox, official weather observer for Chamberlain, measured the precipitation at .23 inches. That amount was before 6:00 p.m.

By 7:30 p.m., strong winds and snow had reduced visibility to a "matter of yards." The most powerful gusts came in at 60 mph. That night, the low settled at 25 above.[83]

Police set up a road block at the U.S. Highway 16 bridge. They allowed only emergency travel through. Lodging facilities had a run on business.

There was some traffic on Friday morning. The police maintained their road block on Highway 16. The town cafes attracted most of the people that were out. Friday night, big drifts plugged intersections in Chamberlain. Only a few vehicles were able to move around town.

Blizzard conditions lasted throughout the day. Top wind gusts reached 60 mph. Robert Knox figured Chamberlain received 2 inches of snow, .20 inches of precipitation. On Friday, the high was 30 degrees and the evening low was 10.

The following column appeared in the *Chamberlain Register* on March 10, 1966. It said:

Di's Doodles

At the time you are reading my column this week, the weather outside may be beautiful. The sun might be shining warmly and a slight breeze could be blowing. Perhaps this is not entirely true either, but the weather last weekend was an entirely different story.

On Friday morning, the announcement came over the radio that because of the blizzard, there would be no school. At first, the thought of no school was thrilling to the ears of all CHS'ers. But when the realization that not only would there be no school on Friday, but also no fun all weekend finally hit everyone, this thought was no longer so thrilling.

It is quite a different feeling to many of us to have to stay at home on weekend days and nights without a thing to do. And this feeling is one that is not too welcome.

On Friday afternoon, a bunch of us attempted to brave the storm. Very warmly dressed, we stepped out of our comfortably warm house directly into three feet of snowdrifts. After a while we started for home with the thoughts of a warm house abundant in our minds. We returned only to discover that there was a temporary power failure and that the furnace had gone out. There we were–freezing cold with no way to warm up!

But, perhaps, it is a good thing that this blizzard did come. It's a good reminder to us to appreciate the lovely Spring weather that will be soon here. At least, I hope it would be here because it may be rather hard to keep up my optimistic outlook for long![84]

There was some property damages at the Gilbert Mobile Homes, trailer park east of Chamberlain. Friday afternoon, the strong winds tipped a 12x50 Crest Home on its side. The trailer landed on the steel steps of another trailer.

George Gilbert indicated the trailer was covered by insurance and it would be returned to the factory to be rebuilt. Gilbert said, "It was the only the second time, that gusts have been powerful enough to flip a trailer at the lot."[85]

On Saturday, Chamberlain received another 2 inches of snow. It was the coldest day of the storm, the high was 19 degrees. Conditions improved, as the winds died down. Saturday afternoon, there was a burst of activity.

The following editorial was written by Edwin J. Buckingham, Jr. He wrote:

Nature's Display

"Bring us back some snow, Buck"

Those words came to mind while looking into the wind-suspended snow curtain Friday afternoon. The request came some 20 years ago when we were preparing to leave California for a furlough trip back to Grand Forks, North Dakota.

Nancy and Ned Leisy, the two little youngsters where we roomed while stationed at Camp Roberts, had never seen snow and were intrigued by the idea. It was the only thing they wanted from North Dakota. Unfortunately, even in January, we couldn't fill the order. Of course, they've seen the white stuff themselves since then. He is now flying jets for the Navy and Nancy is a housewife and makes occasional vacation trips into areas of the mountain snows.

In any event, even if one could have taken a handful of snow back to Paso Robles, California, it would have given the youngsters no more real concept this element that the blind men received from the elephant.

Snow is something that everyone should see in its own stormy element at least once. . . preferably from the snug base of a tight cabin warmed by a wood-burning fireplace. It is a show of natural power that puts man-made accomplishments back into perspective.

A typhoon at sea is impressive, even riding the edge in a rolling pitching ship. A tornado earns full respect. A real midwestern blizzard, however, reaches the spectator through all senses. It is especially true of the wind element as one actually sees the wind in the whipping, swirling, driving snow. It adds another dimension to the power song of the shouldering, shouting wind familiar in the other types of storms.

A prairie blizzard can be brutal and costly. It can levy disproportionate penalties for unpreparedness. It can smother a space age back into primitive survival conditions.

It can also break the routine humdrum and give hurried, harried citizens some time of enforced, unplanned moments when they can take stock of themselves and visit unrushed with others. The freezing blasts can actually thaw communications between complete strangers marooned by this caprice of nature.

And the aftermath is a strangely sculptured land of white in almost surrealistic patterns. There are contrasting barren places and towering, high-ridged drifts. In some places, the piled snow is shaped like sand dunes of the ocean areas. In others, it stretches out narrowly as though patterned on the straining neck and lifted mane of a racing palomino.

Then, in contrast to the forceful forms of the drifts, there will be small "backwaters" of calm where the falling snow has been allowed to settle softly on pine branches and build undisturbed to small mounds like cotton Christmas tree decorations.

A blizzard is many things. Each such storm is different, but to one who has seen many, it seems that there is no other display devised by nature quite comparable.[85]

On Sunday, George Winchester and Game Warden Gene Dominlack drove to the airport. They took off in Winchester's plane. Gerald McLeish flew with John Keller in plane owned by Chamberlain Aero, Inc. The men made an aerial survey of Brule County. They had radio contact with the police vehicles.

Sunday afternoon, Ray Steckelberg hitched up a team of horses to a bobsled. He gave the local Cub Scouts and den mothers sleigh rides. Steckelberg attracted a lot of attention. Before long, he picked up other youngsters who enjoyed the experience very much.

As the street department cleared more and more streets, Steckelberg had fewer snow-covered roads to drive the bobsled on. Everybody had a good time, so he decided to take his sled to the hills for moonlight rides. That is, as long as the snow lasts.

Civil Defense Director, Art Foster, reported that Otto Kroupa had lost fifty-five head when they wandered into a creek at the height of the storm. Otherwise, Brule and Buffalo Counties had no serious livestock losses. Foster said, "There might be later scattered reports of losses, but most came through well."[86]

The Section IV Basketball Tournament in Mitchell could not start soon enough for Cub fans. On March 8, Chamberlain faced Miller. The game was intense. Miller converted 25 of 56 shots from the field, and Chamberlain made 22 of 70 attempts. The margin of victory came at the free throw line. Miller sank 11 of 20. Chamberlain dropped 20 of 25. Chamberlain edged Miller by a final score of 64 to 61.

Roger Hammerbeck led the Cubs with 26 points. Bill Hogarth and Norm Almond had 14 and 13 points, respectively. Almond led the team with 9 rebounds. Hammerbeck had 8 boards. The winning streak for the Cubs had reached thirteen.

On March 9, Cub fans drove to Mitchell. Mitchell defeated Huron in overtime on Tuesday night. Playing on their home court, the Kernels were favored to win the championship game.

The crowd noise was unbelievable. Chamberlain outnumbered the people from Mitchell, according to some Cubs fans. At the end, the Cubs won their fourteen straight game, 84 to 54. In the championship game Hammerbeck scored 29 points and pulled down 17 rebounds. Almond had 16 points and 8 rebounds. Ken Soulek finished with 13 points and 7 rebounds and Hogarth scored 12 points and 8 rebounds.

Chamberlain was in the South Dakota Class A Basketball Tournament.

Two days after the blizzard, Chamberlain experienced above normal temperatures.[86] The following highs and lows were recorded by Robert Knox, official weather observer for Chamberlain:

March 8	47	31		March 12	58	27
March 9	55	33		March 13	66	32
March 10	57	28		March 14	64	30
March 11	52	33				

On the morning of March 16, the Cubs left Chamberlain for Sioux Falls. They had a big sendoff. Mark Casey, Chet Swanson. Dr. Robert Winjum, L.Dale Larson and Joe Beyer held up a sign the read, "Our Champs." The sirens blared as team bus left. They were scheduled to play the Canton Hawks in the second game of the tournament on March 17.

Chamberlain had a loud and robust cheering section. Some fans brought cowbells to add to the noise. The entire team wore identical blazing red sport jackets off the court. Of all the teams there, the Cubs stood out the best.

Weeks earlier, Coach Elton Byre submitted his resignation as basketball coach. Byre would continue teaching in the Chamberlain system.

After finishing their warmups, the Cubs and Hawks received the final instructions from their coaches. In the first half, the Cubs played better than the Hawks. At one time, Chamberlain had a 12 point lead, but Canton fought back to make the half time score, 32 to 29. Two minutes left in the third quarter, the Hawks took their first lead. Both teams led in the fourth quarter. With five minutes left, the Hawks went ahead of the Cubs. They held on for the win, 61 to 54.

On March 18, Chamberlain recorded a high of 82 degrees, the highest recorded temperature in South Dakota for the month of March. Many of the residents, however, were in Sioux Falls.

In the consolation game on March 19, Chamberlain lost to the Class A pre-tournament favorite, Rapid City, 65 to 61. The Cubs finished the tournament in sixth place.

Pukwana, founded in 1881, was named by Miss Richards, a relative of a Milwaukee Railroad official who was visiting the area, when the railroad was being built to Chamberlain. At the time, the site was covered with water. Somebody suggested that they give the site an Indian name that means "frog pond." Richard did not like that idea, so she recommended Pukwana from Longfellow's "Hiawatha." Pukwana has a Indian derivation which means "peace pipe" or "smoke of peace pipe."

In 1960, the town had a population of 247.

The blizzard struck Pukwana late on March 3, but the first night of the storm brought no precipitation. The blizzard lasted well into Saturday. Mrs. Emmett Healy, official weather observer, recorded .15 inches of moisture on Friday and .41 inches Saturday. Healy calculated Pukwana received about five an a half inches of snow. The area experienced 60 mph winds.

In the aftermath, Pukwana recorded colder temperatures than Chamberlain on Sunday and Monday nights.[88]

Mitchell, seat of Davison County, was established in 1879. The town was named for Alexander Mitchell, general manager of the Chicago, Milwaukee and St. Paul Railroad at that time.

Mitchell became a regional trade center. It was the center of a pinwheel, a railroad expression with goods coming from all directions. The Milwaukee, on its way to Chamberlain, arrived in 1880, and it built another line between Mitchell and Aberdeen in 1881. The Milwaukee also constructed a line between Mitchell and Scotland Jct. in 1886. There was another spoke in 1887, the Northwestern Railroad extended the tracks from Salem to Mitchell.

Dakota Wesleyan University, an independent Methodist college, was established in 1885.

The first Mitchell Corn Palace festival was held in 1892. It has been an annual event since 1902. John Philip Sousa and his famous band provided the entertainment in 1904. Lawrence Welk's band performed often at the festival. The outside murals and decorations are changed yearly.

In November 1904, Mitchell challenged Pierre for the right to be the capital of South Dakota, but they lost the vote. For a change, people took advantage of the railroads. Prior to the election, the Northwestern supported Pierre and the Milwaukee favored Mitchell. The railroads gave voters free transportation to Pierre and Mitchell. The two cities attracted over one hundred thousand visitors, that year. Drinks were cheap, the railroads had a hand in that.

Mitchell had 12,555 residents in 1960.

Mitchell averages about 22 inches of precipitation a year. The city's annual snowfall averages is 32 inches.[89]

On March 1, 1966, Mitchell had a high of 42 degrees. The next day, the temperature rose to 47. There was some light precipitation, .06 inches. That night, the low was 7 degrees.

On March 3, Mitchell recorded a high of 45 degrees. Bad weather was on the horizon. Strong winds and falling temperatures in the afternoon was a warning sign. That evening, 1.2 inches of snow fell, .06 inches of moisture. One headline that morning in the *Daily Republic* read: **"Crippling Storm Hits In Dakotas, Minnesota."**[90]

Thursday night or early Friday morning, the blizzard moved into the area. Many residents probably looked outside during the night and saw the stormy conditions.

At 7:00 Friday morning, the thermometer in Mitchell read 11 above. Winds were between 35 and 50 mph. Throughout the day, 11 inches of snow fell. Before long, snowbanks were 8 to 10 feet high.[91]

All schools in Mitchell were closed. City, county, state, and federal government agencies were closed as well. State Highway snowplows were held in check. Street department personnel were sent out on emergency runs only.

For the most part, the telephone service in Mitchell was normal. At times, there were too many phone calls. This cause a overload, and people had to wait to get a dial tone.

Mail was not delivered on Friday, but residents could pick their mail up at the post office. One mail truck from Sioux Falls reached Mitchell. After unloading, the truck left immediately for Sioux Falls.

Some *Daily Republic* carriers delivered their papers. Jerome Wolf, a substitute newspaper delivery boy, loaded the papers up in an old sled. He was dressed warm, only his eyes could be seen. Wolf delivered the papers, when only a few people were out.

Friday afternoon, Warren Rice drove cautiously in the 1000 block on West Havens. Rice pulled over to help the driver of a stalled vehicle. After a quick talk with Leroy Bitterman of Mitchell, Rice went behind Bitterman's car to push. The pair started rocking the vehicle and was making progress. Then, another car ran into the rear of Bitterman's car. The driver of that vehicle was Wayne Dodds, another resident of Mitchell. Dodds did not see Bitterman's car in the snowstorm. Rice was hurt in the accident. He had to be taken to the hospital. Luckily, Rice's injuries were not serious. The vehicles had only minor damages.

Manager D.T. Solum, of Northwestern Public Services, dispatched NWPS crews to Letcher. There were reports of power outages in that area. Wet snow, sticking to the wires, created the problems.

Intercounty Electric Association of Mitchell also sent out work crews to the Mt. Vernon and Carthage areas. They indicated the roads were not that bad, but visibility was so poor that it required a great deal of time to check out the troubles.

Donald Fitzler, a resident of Mitchell, was in Vermillion, Friday morning. Deciding to return to Mitchell, Fitzler called his wife and told her he was coming home. If he couldn't make it, he would call.

At 11:30 a.m., Fitzler started confidently out of Vermillion. The storm did not appear that bad in the daylight. He had a warm car. He was halfway home, when he passed Menno on U.S. Highway 18.

Fitzler planned on turning north, once he reached State Highway 37. He knew he had made a mistake in leaving Menno. Fitzler drove very slowly along the edge of the highway in zero visibility.

He almost hit a school warning sign. Fitzler made up his mind to stop at the school, if he could find it. Straining hard to locate the school, Fitzler almost went into the ditch a couple of times. A pause between wind gusts, cleared the skies somewhat for a brief moment, Fitzler just happened to be at the entrance to the school.

He drove in about 2:30 p.m. He waited three hours for the storm to clear, but there was no letup. Driving in the blizzard after dark, was not an option. Fitzler thought about his wife and two children at home. He had made a promise (to call his family), he could not keep.

The school offered his best chance for survival. Fitzler used a pair of scissors to pry open the lock on the door. Inside, he found the school to be warm.

Saturday morning, there was no traffic moving. The weather was bad, but not as harsh. He wanted to leave, but decided to wait some more. Fitzler said, "he played the piano, read history books, and watched the snow swirl around a nearby tree."

Fitzler's wife and children waited with all their fears.

That afternoon, snowplows opened the highway. Fitzler had been at the school for almost twenty-four hours. He followed the traffic behind the snowplows into Mitchell. There, he and his family had a happy reunion.

Fitzler said, "I won't do it again." Although he did not leave a note at the school, Sharon No. 10, Fitzler planned on stopping on his next trip in that direction. He was sure, "it won't be snowing, the next time he goes by."[92]

A trace of snow fell on Saturday. The strong winds did not wane until that afternoon. Total snowfall for Mitchell was 12 inches. Snowbanks were 10 feet high. Cold temperatures followed the storm. Saturday night, the low was zero.

Ted Anderson, Intercounty Electric Association Manager, indicated there was no power outages in the major centers, but about 120 farms were out of power in four counties. He said, "There were 80 farms in Miner County, 9 in Sanborn, 15 in Hanson County and 5 in Davison County." Anderson had five repair crews out. He expected most of the farms would have their power restored by Saturday night.[93]

About fifteen miles west of Mitchell on State Highway 38, there was a four-car crash on Saturday. According to State Highway Patrolman, Ron Noordsy, a car driven by Leroy Alt, Billings, Montana, tried to get around a semi-truck, stuck in the snow. Alt's vehicle became stuck. Within minutes, three other cars collided with each other and Alt's vehicle. Noordsy said, "visibility was poor at the time of the collision."

Alt's car damages was estimated at $400. For Richard Baerg, Capital Hill, North Carolina, and Gerald Holmer, Faulkton, their damages were placed between $600. and $700. Theodore Lerew's car had only minor damages. There were no personal injuries.[94]

Nationally, the Civil Air Patrol was created in 1942. Mitchell's CAP unit was organized around 1954. The local club owned two planes, two powerful radio units, and citizen band radios in 1966. Additional planes that were used on various missions came from some members and their friends. Pilots who flew civil defense projects were reimbursed for oil, fuel, and overnight lodging.

Dick Tracy, executive officer for CAP in Mitchell, reported their unit was placed on "Red Cap" alert at 11:45 a.m. on March 4. The mobilization order came from Major General Duane Corning, State Director of Civil Defense, who acted on orders from Governor Nils Boe. Once local CAP units are alerted, they must maintain radio contact with major units because flight patrols are coordinated at the higher levels.

The Civil Air Patrol in Mitchell operated with a skeleton staff, from noon Friday until three o'clock Saturday afternoon. During this time, other members and volunteers were on standby.

On March 6, the Mitchell CAP had a very busy day. They had six planes up in the air. They had radio contact with other authorities.

Past and present media broadcasts told farmers and others how to mark symbols in the snow. One panel, can be two or three hay bales together, meant a doctor was needed. Two panel meant medical supplies are needed. An "F" meant food or water was needed and an "L" meant fuel was needed.

The Mitchell CAP did not participate in any rescue attempts on Sunday. They gained experience working with other units and authorities.[95]

Salem, seat of McCook County, was settled in 1880. There are several versions how the town acquired its name. O.S. Pender, the first storekeeper and postmaster, named it for his hometown of Salem, Massachusetts. Others thought Salem was named by J.H. Brown, at the urging of E.F. Drake. Salem is a Hebrew word meaning "peace." For a time, Salem was called Melas (Salem spelled backwards) because residents did not want their town to be confused with another town called Salena. After Salena died, the original name was taken up again.

McCook County was named for Edwin S. McCook, Union General in the Civil War and secretary of Dakota Territory 1872-1873. He was a member of the celebrated family of "Fighting McCooks" of Ohio. During the war, six of them became generals.

In 1873, Edwin McCook and Peter P. Wintermute, bitter political rivals, had a gunfight in Yankton. McCook was killed in the gun play. Wintermute was charged for murder. In the trial Wintermute was found guilty, but the case was appealed. He was acquitted in the second trial. The judicial system of the Dakota Territory had passed its first test.

In 1960, the town 1,188 residents.

Montrose ended Salem's high school boys basketball season in district play in late February 1966.

According to the *Salem Special*, "The worst blizzard in years hit the area with a terrible impact Friday morning." The area received 4 inches of snow and had wind gusts up to 65 mph Thursday night and Friday. The storm did not wane until noon on Saturday.

Local events, including school, were canceled and postponed. "Absolutely no traffic moved in or out of Salem from late Thursday night until about Saturday noon."[96]

On Friday and Saturday, Sheriff Harold Lockwood's office was flooded with phone calls concerning road conditions.

Highway Patrolman, Doug Gallipo, indicated stranded motorists stayed at lodging facilities, gas stations, and private homes. Gallipo said, "no serious accidents or incidents were reported."

Drifts in Salem were at least 6 feet high.

Salem and the nearby farms weathered the storm in good shape. Local power suppliers, McCook Electric Cooperative and Northern States Power, reported no serious problems during the blizzard. Lad Karei, NSP manager, said, "We were very, very fortunate indeed." Friday afternoon, Jerry Westoff, McCook line superintendent, dispatched a McCook crew to the substation near Farmer to be in position to fix problems. There was no trouble.

A East River Power Electric Cooperative crew stayed at the substation near Spencer on Friday and Saturday. The cooperative had access to power from different sources. If one source failed, the men could hand operate the switch which redirected energy.

Northwest Bell's local manager, W. E. Melcher, reported their storm damages consisted of only broken lines. One line went down northeast of Salem near the Pete Weber farm. Snow 4 feet high buried that line. At Bridgewater there was trouble on three lines. One wire fell at Canisota and two at Marion. Melcher stated, "all services had been reinstated by 5:00 p.m., Monday."[97]

John Stefvater believed he lost 125 head of cattle when he could not find his livestock. At $250.00 a head, the herd was worth over $31,000.00. Eventually, all were found and only one had died. Stefvater had gotten quite a scare.

Several farmers in the area reported the losses of some young stock.

Sioux Falls, named after the falls of the Big Sioux River, was settled in 1857. A subsidiary of the Northwestern Railroad arrived in 1878, when the line between Valley Spring and Sioux Falls was completed. The following year, Sioux Falls and Salem were tied by tracks. The Milwaukee Road arrived in 1879 from Beloit, Iowa. Another 34 miles of track connected Egan and Sioux Falls in 1881. A Great Northern Railroad subsidiary linked Sioux Falls to Minnesota communities in 1888. The Great Northern united Yankton and Sioux Falls in 1894, and Rutland and Sioux Falls in 1905-1906.

Sioux Falls, the seat of Minnehaha County, developed into South Dakota's largest population center.

In 1883, Sioux Falls College, supported by Baptists, was established in the city. Augustana College, maintained by Lutherans, had its beginning in 1884, but not in Sioux Falls. It was located first at Canton, but moved to Sioux Fall in 1917.

The city became a major outlet for the cattle, hogs, and sheep. In 1909, the John Morrell Packing Company built a vast meat processing plant here.

The State School for the Deaf and State Penitentiary are located in Sioux Falls.

In 1960, Sioux Falls had 70,500 inhabitants.

The storm brushed Sioux Falls on March 4. The impact of the blizzard was minor. Just over 3 inches of snow fell, that day. Northerly winds ranged between 25 and 50 mph. Friday's high was 27 degrees and the low bottomed out at 13 degrees.

Poor visibility reduced traffic and commerce. All schools were closed in the city. Friday morning, several passenger flights to southern and eastern destinations departed the Sioux Falls Airport. Later flights that day were canceled.

Early Friday, one of KSOO's five transmission towers blew over in winds of 35 mph. Located five miles southeast of the city, the tower was 220 feet high. The TV station, Channel 13, reported that the tower was used for nighttime operations only, and daytime programming was not affected.

On March 5, blizzard conditions lasted late into the day. Another inch of snow fell. Ground drifting slowed down traffic in the city. The high and low for the day in Sioux Falls were 19 and 9.

After the storm exited the area, the trailing high ushered in colder temperatures. Most Sioux Falls residents escaped the hard work of digging out on Sunday.

Sioux Falls Civil Air Patrol participated in the aerial search of South Dakota. Cliff Foss, a Sioux Falls farmer-pilot, flew around the McLaughlin area on March 6. This was one of the hardest hit areas of the South Dakota. Here's his report:

> The steer was standing as if frozen stiff as a statue. I landed my ski plane, and knocked away a 16-inch piece of ice that was around the animal's mouth and nostrils. Then I pried away more ice to get its eyes open.
>
> The steer seemed to come to its senses with a start and, in its fright, it almost lunged over me as it ran away.[98]

Lennox, located south of Sioux Falls in Lincoln County, was established in 1879. The town was named for Ben Lennox, private secretary to the general manager of the Milwaukee Railroad.

Lennox was home for 1,353 individuals in 1960. After the early March 1966, blizzard, the *Lennox Independent* wrote:

> Although Lennox and the rest of this part of the state escaped the brunt of the severe blizzard which hit most of Sioux Dakota this past weekend, everyone in this locality was well aware of the nearness of the storm with all the news media devoting much time and space to current developments.
>
> Striking the western part of the state with tremendous furry on Thursday of last week, the storm seemed to be far removed from here and early reports were almost impossible to believe as folks in this vicinity were enjoying temperatures in the 30's. But by Friday the tail end of the storm had reached down into this section and it was deemed advisable to call

off school, considering the dimensions of the storm to the west and north. However, only about two inches of snow fell here, causing only minor drifting....[99]

There was national coverage of the blizzard. People who lived in other regions of the United States contacted relatives in the storm area. Lennox residents reported receiving letters and telephone calls from anxious relatives. For example, Marlyn Musch of Alamogordo, New Mexico, contacted his sister, Mrs. Harley Steener, on March 4. Linda Steever, a college student at Sterling, Kansas, called her parents, Mr. and Mrs. Harley Steever.

Lake Andes, Armour, Corsica, Parkston, Freeman, Yankton and Vermillion

Lake Andes was founded in 1904, it was named for the nearby Lake Andes. The lake, located one mile northeast of the town, was named for Edward Andes, a surveyor for the American Fur Company, or for an early trapper named Handy who settled near the lake. If the second version is right, the lake was known as Handy's Lake, then Andy's Lake, and finally Andes Lake or Lake Andes. Wheeler and Lake Andes battled for the seat of Charles Mix County. Lake Andes won that honor.

In the early days of the automobile, Lake Andes was a popular camping spot. In the Big Band era, the pavilion at Lake Andes hosted lots of dances and celebrations.

According to the 1960 census, the town had a population of 1,097.

Lake Andes residents have a history of weathering bad storms. For them, the blizzards of January 3, 1949, and March 7, 1950, stand out. A long string of snow events, between February 17, 1962, and March 12, 1962, brought the Lake Andes area 42 inches of snow. During that span, the lows ranged between 21 degrees below zero and 28 degrees below zero.[100]

On March 4, 1966, Mother Nature struck again.

The following article appeared in the *Lake Andes Wave*, Ervin E. Palmer, editor and publisher, Ethelyn A Palmer, co-editor:

BLIZZARD HITS LAKE ANDES

Operations "heave-ho" got into full swing in Lake Andes Sunday morning as snow removal crews began to clear the many plugged streets of the city.

The rampaging storm struck this community about 11 p.m. Thursday night, leaving the shelter areas with huge drifts.

Nearly every street in the city was blocked by drifts. Church and High Streets were blocked by huge drifts from First Avenue to the oil road at the west edge of the city, leaving those residents marooned in their homes until the winds died. Many automobiles will be left in garages until the snow thaws. Church Street was also plugged between Third and Fourth Avenues. Several big drifts blocked School Street in front of the school house and on to Seventh Street. Clearing operations started early Sunday morning and by late evening almost all city streets were open to travel, some only one-way traffic.

Drifts on the sidewalks on the north side of Main Street were approximately four feet high by 5 p.m. Friday. Ironically enough, the street was bare, as was the south sidewalks.

Travel was virtually at a standstill all day Friday and part of Saturday. Businessmen ventured downtown Friday to their places of businesses, but cafes, grocery stores and service stations were about the only establishments transacting any business. Needless, to say, school was dismissed Friday.

Total snowfall here amounted to ten inches, as recorded by weatherman Frank Kozak. Temperatures ranged from 11 to 16 during the blizzard but dipped to five below zero Monday morning. The high Monday was 35 degrees and Tuesday snow was melting fast with the 40 degree temperatures.

Lake Andes residents were without mail service from Thursday afternoon to Sunday when a mail truck was able to get through.

Some residents reported shingles had been blown off their roofs and some antennas were downed.

Motorists from near and far were marooned here during the two-day storm. Mrs. Verle Allen reported 12 units at the Sands Motel were occupied with stranded motorists who planned to leave Friday morning but were unable to leave until Saturday. Harriet Holcomb reported eight motorists marooned at the Hotel Andes from Thursday to Sunday. A couple of them tried to leave Saturday but returned and waited until Sunday. Mrs. Lyle Bergin said three traveling men were stranded at the Circle H. Motel from Thursday to Saturday afternoon. Travelers were from Alva, Oklahoma, Austin and Minneapolis, Minnesota, Fremont and Norfolk, Nebraska, Sioux City, Iowa, Bridgewater, Mitchell, Rapid City, Sioux Falls, Huron, and Yankton, South Dakota.

Emery Cooper suffered a heart attack Friday in the height of the raging storm and Dr. Nelson was summoned. It took the doctor one hour to reach the Cooper home in the storm. Mr. Cooper was taken to the Douglas County Memorial Hospital Saturday. Dr. Nelson was also called to the Odegard home Friday afternoon to care for two-year old Tammy. Mrs. Ronnie Leasure was taken to the Wagner hospital Saturday morning when efforts to get her to the Armour hospital failed. She gave birth to a nine pound baby boy that night.

Mrs. Fyle Nelson was taken by ambulance Saturday night to the Wagner hospital after suffering an asthma attack.

In all the incidents the Sheriff's officials and State Highway Patrolman assisted in getting the vehicles through the snow storm.[101]

Mona Evans wrote a column about rural life in the *Lake Andes Wave*. Her column was entitled "A Bit of Corn Chatter." She mentioned the 1966 blizzard. Evans wrote:

Hello Neighbors!

My remarks about the storm can be summed up in two words, "Oh boy!?! Just hope everyone was safe and snug inside as the blizzard howled. I felt so helpless as the menfolk went outside to care for the animals. With the coffee pot going full blast, I baked bread and rolls. Then made noodles to go with the old rooster for supper. With magazines from a good friend and the catalogs, we passed the day. With TV so poor, the children played monopoly and cards. At least our telephone didn't go out and we could visit with the neighbors.

I got out to take movies and our yard is full of snowdrifts as high as the chicken house. The big haymow door fell down from the suction of the wind so we have plenty of snow inside, too. When the boys opened the door Saturday morning, snow was waist deep, so had to scoop out. Our milk truck had to go around, too. At least the separator got a workout. Thank goodness the R.E.A. didn't go off. We lost only a small calf and count ourselves lucky.

Work is getting back to normal again with school for the children. Mr. Sun will have a job melting the snow in everyone's yards. Must get this ready for the mailman. See you next week–God willing.[102]

Armour, seat of Douglas County since 1894, was settled in 1886. It was named for Philip D. Armour, the Chicago meat-packing tycoon and railroad director. In acknowledgement of this honor, Mr. Armour donated a bell for the town's first church.

In 1960, the town had a population of 875.

The Armour Packers defeated the Lake Andes Eagles, 73 to 42, in the District 27 Basketball Tournament in Wagner on February 23, 1966. In their next game, against Geddes, the Rams scored the last three points and won the game. The Packers met the Ravinia Bears in the consolation game and it went into overtime. Again, the Packers had hard luck at the end. They lost the game by two points. The Wagner Red Raiders won the tournament.

For the month of February 1966, the mean temperature in Armour was 18.8 degrees, or 3.8 degrees below normal. The high of 52 on February 28 raised the average. That month, Armour received .53 inches of precipitation, .17 inches below the average.[103]

On March 3, the residents of Armour went to bed thinking they had escaped the much-heralded blizzard. The *Armour Chronicle* said," Many were, indeed surprised Friday morning when they discovered the wind blowing and snow flying. It was almost impossible to see all day Friday because of the blinding storm."[104]

The blizzard lasted two days in the area. Armour received .03 inches of precipitation on March 3, no reading for March 4, and .40 inches on March 5.

Power was out for an hour and a half in Armour.

During and after the storm, about 90 households on Douglas Electric lines had power outages. A Douglas County snowplow was assigned to Douglas Electric, to help expedite their repairs.

An area east of Armour, lost their electricity 1:30 a.m. on Friday. A Douglas Electric crew tried to reach the site of the problem, Friday morning. The snowplow operators and linemen turned around, after going a half-mile in thirty minutes. On Saturday power was restored at 11:00 a.m. A broken phase in this occurrence affected seventeen consumers.

Friday morning, two other sections lost power. One area was west of Armour and the other was south of the Harrision Substation. Overall, it affected forty-one families. Power was restored Saturday afternoon.

Friday night, a broken phase caused problems for twenty-two members north of Armour. They had power again on Saturday night.

Saturday morning, three homes on west State Highway 44 lost their power when a hot line clamp came off. The families had their power restored later in the day.

Saturday night, a transformer in the Hillside area failed, and eight families lost their electricity. Douglas Electric repaired the problem, as soon as possible.

Northwestern Public Service customers lost power for an hour, Friday afternoon. Just west of Armour, the strong winds whipped one of the wires off the poles.

County Agent, Norman Telkamp received several reports of minor livestock losses in the aftermath.[105]

Corsica, located in Douglas County, was founded in 1905. The town was named for the island of Corsica. A number of Corsicans built the railroad track between Armour and Stickney for the Milwaukee Railroad in 1905.

The town had 479 residents in 1960.

Mrs. Don Menning, rural Corsica, was overdue with her pregnancy.

The Mennings left their farm at two o'clock, Friday afternoon. Their car stalled in the snow, seven miles east of Platte on Highway 44. At eight o'clock, Don Menning walked to the Frank Bechen farm home. They came back for Mrs. Menning.

When Mrs. Menning started having labor pains, they called the highway department and state police. Help was soon on the way. Dr. L.P. Mills was along on the emergency run. They reached the Bechen farm at 1:00 a.m. Saturday. There, Mrs. Menning had a boy at 5:00 a.m. Mother and child were taken to the Platte Community Memorial Hospital, after the roads were cleared.

Parkston, located in Hutchinson County, was named by the first townsite owner, R.S. Parke. The Milwaukee built a line from Yankton to Scotland Junction in 1882 and the line was extended to Mitchell in 1886. Parkston benefitted from the expansion, it is located halfway between those points.

In 1960, the town had a population of 1,514.

Parkston did not get a lot of snow in January-February 1966. The main excitement was the high school boys basketball team. The Trojans had a very good team, they were ranked second in the final State Class B poll. Their only losses came in back-to-back games against Scotland and Menno, 58 to 57 and 65 to 63, respectively.

They faced a major hurdle in the District 22 Basketball Tournament in late February. Alexandria, the 1965 Class B State Champion, stood in their way. The Beavers also won the state title in 1963.

The matchup between Parkston and Alexandria was something special. Gerhardt Buenning led the Trojans in their biggest victory of the year, 63 to 60. Buenning said, "Alexandia's Mel Thomas is the best individual and by far the top defensive player I've ever played against and Terry Settje (Scotland) is a close second."[106]

It was warm in Parkston on March 3, the mercury climbed to 47 degrees. Basketball fans drove to Mitchell to watch the first round of Region 6 Basketball Tournament on Thursday. Parkston defeated the Plankinton Pirates in one game. The Woonsocket Redman beat the Murdo Coyotes in the other game. The competing teams for the championship game had been decided.

That night, Parkston recorded .13 inches of precipitation. Wind gusts increased later that night.

It was not business as usual in Parkston on Friday and Saturday. Mother Nature acted up in a bad way. **"Vicious Blizzard Hits Entire Area,"** according to the headline in the *Parkston Advance*. The article said, "The blizzard which hit the Parkston area last Friday and Saturday, brought 4 to 5 inches of snow, which blew into drifts 4 to 5 feet deep. The gale-force winds piled the snow high and lots of livestock suffered."[107]

Parkston received a total of .53 inches of precipitation on Friday and Saturday. The bulk of that total came on Friday.

The game between Parkston and Woonsocket was rescheduled for Monday at Mitchell.

Mr. and Mrs. Vincent Kurtenbach lived twelve miles northwest of Parkston. Mrs. Kurtenbach was expecting a child. Saturday morning at 6:00, the National Guard received a call to break a path to the Kurtenbach farm.

Visibility was still poor. Master Sergeant Hurrl Welch and Sergeant First Class Roger Appel drove a county dump truck, loaded with gravel. Dr. Porter followed the vehicle in his Scout. Near the Sandhoff Brothers farm, the dump truck made a quick, hard stop. Dr. Porter skidded into the back end of the truck. Dr. Porter was not harmed. Although the radiator and fender were damaged, the scout could be driven.

There was a stalled car in the middle of the road, only the top of the car was discernible. They managed, it was not easy, to get around stranded vehicle.

Meanwhile, a snowplow from Ethan was dispatched to clear the roads to the Kurtenbach farm. They lost sight of the road and went into the ditch. The snowplow was delayed for a while.

The National Guard members and Dr. Porter reached the Kurtenbach place. Dr. Porter left his Scout there. They arrived back at the St. Benedict Hospital in Parkston at eleven o'clock. Two hours later, Mrs. Kurtenbach had a baby girl. The Kurtenbachs named their daughter, Judy Ann.

Before the storm was over, the cleanup of Parkston was planned out by Mayor Allan Schilling and others. Work crews began clearing the downtown business district at 3:00 a.m. Sunday morning. Men and equipment from the Weidenbach Construction Company were utilized. The main roads, into and out of Parkston, were cleared by county snowplows.

Bill Isaak said, "he had to come home in time for the blizzard, so he could get his daily exercise." Like many others, Isaak had to shovel out. Bill and his wife just returned California. They were there for two months.

Faith Lutheran Church services were called off on Sunday because Reverend Eberhardt could not reach the church.

Earlier in the week, Reverend John Hamstra attended a meeting in Omaha. Coming home on Saturday, he waited out the storm in Marion. Reverend Hamstra did not make it back to Parkston in time for the Presbyterian Church services on Sunday.

Mr. and Mrs. George Stirlings celebrated their 65th wedding anniversary on Sunday. Some family members could not attend because of travel conditions.

On March 7, the fire alarm sounded at the Parkston Fire Department. A small blaze was reported at Veen Sisters' home. The fire was quickly put out. During the blizzard, snow crept into the attic. After the snow melted, water dripped down into a light socket which started the fire.

A large caravan of cars left Parkston for the Corn Palace on Monday. The people drove to the Corn Palace.

With a tough zone defense and ball control, the Redmen held Parkston's center Gerhardt Buenning, a senior, to 3 points in the first half. Dan Heisinger scored 11 points for the Trojans. Allan Thury and Bruce Maxwell hit outside shots for Parkston. At halftime, Parkston had a 7 point lead.

In the second half, Buenning came on like a freight train. He scored 13 straight points for the Trojans. Maxwell dominated the boards, he had 16 rebounds for the game. Buenning finished the game with 24 points and 9 rebounds. Parkston pulled away for an easy win, 55 to 38.

On March 10, Parkston was almost a ghost town. Most of the residents were in Sioux Falls. Their first opponent was from Frederick. The Vikings led all Class B schools in scoring average, 75 points a game. The Vikings also had a dominant center, Lee Wilson, and good outside shooters.

Both teams started fast. Parkston had a 6 point lead, after one quarter. The Vikings pulled ahead in the second quarter. They held it, into the fourth quarter.

With 6:17 left in the game, the Trojans pulled even. Buenning and Wilson led their teams down the stretch. With 7 seconds left, Buenning sank two free throws and tied the game at 58.

In overtime, Dan Heisinger made a layup, but Wilson sank two free throws. That was all the scoring.

With a minute left in the second overtime, Buenning put Parkston up by two points. Wilson, however, evened the score with 39 seconds left.

In the third overtime, Buenning and Wilson matched baskets. Allan Thury was fouled with 15 seconds left, he made both free throws. The final score was 66-64.

Afterwards, Coach Ken Liveris said, "We thought Alexandria was the toughest team we had seen all season but today (Thursday) we faced the best team we've been up against all year." Buenning ended the game with 34 points. Heisinger and Thury scored 17 and 10 points, respectively. Wilson, a junior, led the Vikings with 28 points.

On Friday, Bryant and Parkston met in the second round. The Bryant Scotties defeated the Scotland Highlanders by one point in their first game. It was an exciting upset for the Scotties.

The Scotties led the Trojans at halftime, 23 to 22. The Trojans came out of the break, with fire in their eyes. Parkston's increased its defensive pressure and took control of the boards. The Scotties scored only 7 points in the third quarter. Bruce Maxwell had a big quarter for the Trojans. The Scotties could not stop Buenning in the fourth quarter. Parkston won 57 to 42. Buenning and Maxwell had 25 and 17 points, respectively.

Parkston faced the Hayti Redbirds in South Dakota's Class B championship game. Hayti played in the 1965 Class B State Tournament. Hayti defeated Philip and Parker to get to the final game. In the final state Class B poll, Hayti was ranked fourth.

The Redbirds started the game with a stout zone defense to shut down Buenning, but Coach Ken Liveris anticipated this tactic. Liveris told his players, "to shoot from the outside, and give Buenning a rest. If they couldn't hit, we'd work it into him."

Coach John Bruce strategy worked for a while, Buenning had only one point in the first quarter. Dan Heisinger, Jim Nelson and Bruce Maxwell, however, hit shot after shot for the Trojans. Bruce said, "They needed to hit from outside to break our zone and they did. Maxwell, Nelson, and Heisinger killed us."

After the Trojans broke the Redbirds zone defense, Buenning scored often. The game remained close, until the middle of the fourth quarter. Then, Hayti ran into foul trouble. Dave Fordyce, Terry and Scott Shelsta fouled out of the game. Buenning finished the game with 23 points and 19 rebounds. Maxwell had 21 points and 8 boards. Terry Shelsta led the Redbirds in scoring with 28 points. Also, Dave Fordyce and Rich Jensen added 15 and 10 points, respectively.

Parkston had won their first Class B South Dakota title, 68-55. In 1949, Parkston lost to Miller in the championship game. The Trojans also had success in State Class A Basketball Tournaments in 1954 and 1955. In those years, they finished second and third, respectively.[108]

Freeman, settled in 1874, bears the name intended for the town of Menno, located ten miles to the southwest. Railroad officials accidentally switched name-boards for the depots. Freeman is named for an early settler of Menno, and Menno's name stems from the large settlement of Mennonites, founded by Menno Simons, at Freeman.

The morning of January 12, 1888, was balmy and rainy. Later on, the warm temperatures turned bitter cold. The heavy rain turned to sleet and then, corn snow. Vicious winds came and lashed the countryside. The unexpected blizzard lasted for fourteen hours. Five school children from Freeman died in the storm, the death toll in the Dakota Territory was at least 112. (Later, residents of Freeman built a monument to honor the five school children. Their names were John Albrecht, Peter Graber, Henry Kaufman, John Kaufman and Elias Kaufman.)[109]

The rural mail carriers of Freeman abandoned their horses in the early 1900's. Instead, they delivered mail in Hutchinson County riding Indian motorcycles.[110]

In 1960, Freeman's population was tabulated at 1,140.

Freeman was shut down on March 4, 1966. The blizzard passed out of the region, Saturday afternoon. Freeman received about 5 inches of snow.

The storm left some impressive drifts, The John P. Kleinsasser's home on north Main in Freeman had drifts as high as the roof. The *Freeman Courier* figured it "was the most photographed scene after the storm."[111]

The Yankton Sioux ceded 14 million acres between the Missouri and Big Sioux River in 1858. The first reservation in South Dakota was created in Charles Mix County for the Yankton Sioux in 1859.

Yankton was settled in 1858, it was named after the Yankton Sioux who inhabited the land.

Congress created Dakota Territory on March 2, 1861. North Dakota, South Dakota, Montana and Wyoming came out of that region. The law, called the Organic Act, allowed the President to name the governor. President Abraham Lincoln appointed Dr. William Jayne, his family physician, the first governor of Dakota Territory. Jayne selected Yankton as the temporary capital.

In March, 1862, the first legislature officially named Yankton as the capital. That year, Yankton became the first city in South Dakota to be incorporated.

The Dakota Territory became much smaller with the organization of Montana Territory in 1864 and Wyoming Territory in 1868. In 1882, a small area along the Niobrara River was transferred to Nebraska.

In 1868, the iron horse reached Sioux City, Iowa. By the time settlers in South Dakota were in need of railroad services, Congress ended its policy of land grants. The Union Pacific had no interest in Dakota Territory. So, the leaders in Yankton took matters in their own hands. The voters of Yankton County passed the bond bill that created the Dakota Southern Railroad. In February, 1873, the Dakota Southern reached Yankton, and South Dakota had its first railroad service. In 1881, the Dakota Southern merged with the Chicago, Milwaukee, and St. Paul Railroad.[112]

In 1883, nine men, members of a capital commission, held a clandestine meeting that lasted five minutes on a train moving through Yankton. At that meeting, Bismarck was chosen to be the capitol of Dakota Territory. The group later became known as the "Capital on Wheels" commission.

This move angered a lot of people. After that, there was a strong push to divide Dakota Territory into two states. On February 22, 1889, North Dakota and South Dakota were created.

The first highway bridge over the Missouri River in South Dakota was constructed in 1924.

The man who gave a generation of Americans a name, those who lived through the Great Depression and fought World War II, came of age in Yankton. On May 27, 1958, Tom Brokaw graduated from Yankton High School. The Brokaw family came to Yankton, when Tom was fifteen. Tom's father, Red, had worked at the Fort Randall Dam project for almost ten years. They lived in Pickstown. Red Brokaw continued working for the U.S. Army Corps of Engineers at Gavins Point Dam. He built riverside parks and camping sites.

Tom's first summer job in Yankton was at a boat and bait shop below the dam. He was paid $35.00 a week.

Brokaw's first broadcast experience came at age sixteen on radio station, KYNT, in Yankton. As a teenage volunteer, he introduced and played rock and roll 45 rpm records. In November 1956, Brokaw reported the results of a local precinct as KYNT covered the 1956 presidential, congressional, and local elections. He said it was a "life-altering experience."

Meredith Auld, Miss South Dakota in 1959, and Tom Brokaw were married in Yankton on August 17, 1962. That year, they left South Dakota.

Brokaw began his journalism career in Omaha and Atlanta. In 1966, he joined NBC News. Brokaw became a White House correspondent. From 1983 to 2004, Brokaw anchored *NBC Nightly News with Tom Brokaw*. He wrote three best sellers: *The Greatest Generation, The Greatest Generation Speaks,* and *An Album of Memories.*

Yankton had 9,279 residents in 1960.

Yankton had a high of 53 degrees on March 1, 1966. The next day was pleasant, but not quite as warm.

On March 3, residents of Yankton talked about the blizzard that swept into West River country and their agreeable weather. The high reached 51 degrees. That night, light rain fell from the cloudy skies. It was windy. Yankton recorded .05 inches of precipitation.

On Friday morning, strong winds, anywhere from 35 to 60 mph, hit the area. Yankton was on the outside fringe of the blizzard. The winds died down Saturday afternoon. Official precipitation, .10 inches, was listed for the storm. Estimated snowfall was about 4 inches. Although there was considerable drifting, the drifts were not very deep. Friday's and Saturday's highs were 36 and 19, respectively.

There was no school in Yankton and area towns. Yankton Colleges, however, did not call off classes. North Central Airlines called off all flights into Yankton. Inter City Bus Lines canceled all its runs. Yankton firemen answered three calls on March 4.

Six miles west of Madison on State Highway 34, a Yankton businessman, Albert E. Herrboldt, was found dead in his car on March 5. The vehicle was completely buried, except for the car's radio antenna. The vehicle was discovered about 2:00 p.m. Saturday by four men from Junius, Glen and William McGillivray, LeRoy Tolly and Frank Young. They were watching a snowplow working in the area when they discovered the car, one fourth of a mile east of Junius. Herrboldt was 64 years old. The cause of death was asphyxiation from carbon monoxide. Survivors included a wife and two children, Also, a brother and three sisters.[113]

Vermillion was established in 1859. The town's name likely came from old Fort Vermillion, an American Fur Company post that was founded in the vicinity in 1835. Another possibility, its name derived from the Vermillion River.

Education in the Dakota Territory had roots in Vermillion.

The territorial legislature authorized the University of Vermillion in 1862, but provided no funds. So, Vermillion citizens raised money for the establishment of University of Dakota. That year, the first classes were held in the courthouse.

The first permanent school house in Dakota Territory was erected here in 1864.

In 1881, Congress granted 72 sections of public land to Dakota Territory "for the use and support of a university when it should be admitted as a State to the Union." In September 1883, classes began on the campus. In 1891, the name of the college was changed to the University of South Dakota. Some famous graduates of the college included, newscaster Tom Brokaw, Miami Dolphins football owner Joe Robbie, and founder of the national newspaper *U.S.A. Today*, Allan Neuharth, born in Eureka, SD.

In 1920, Congress passed legislation that required new American instruments to drop a half step in pitch to conform with European standards. Arne Larson, a musician, started collecting antique flugelhorns, different violins, and other unique musical paraphernalia.

In 1943, Larson taught music in Brookings. Throughout the years, his musical collection grew and grew. Larson's big house in Brookings was full of stuff.

In 1966, the University of South Dakota offered him a faculty position and a home for his cache of memorabilia. Today, the Shrine to Music is a world-class museum.

Vermillion was on the outer edge of the storm that came on March 4, 1966. It lasted two days. According to the *Vermillion Plain Talk*, "The strong winds and blinding snow made traveling difficult and kept most residents huddled about a fire."[114]

The city, according to the 1960 census had 6,102 citizens, received an inch of snow on Friday and two inches on Saturday. Without a lot of snow, it basically was a ground blizzard in Vermillion. The highs for those days were 33 and 23.

The weather had a role in a couple of car accidents.

On Saturday, March 5, John Roning, Athletic Director of the University of South Dakota, introduced the new head football coach for the Coyotes. Joe Salem, 27, had been hired from the University of Minnesota where he had been an assistant backfield coach. Salem, a native of Sioux Falls, replaced Coach Marv Rist. Private business opportunities enticed Coach Rist to leave.

Wessington Springs, Alpena, Woonsocket, Artesian, Fedora, Ramona and Madison

Wessington Springs, first settled in 1876 and called Wessington, is the county seat of Jerauld County. In 1882, the Post Office Department changed the name to Elmer. Local residents did not like that name, so they changed it to Wessington Springs.

In 1960, Wessington Springs was home for 1,488 residents.

Thursday night, March 3, 1966, Dick Costello and his wife, Mary Lou, went to Huron for an evening of bowling. Light snow started to fall as the rural couple of Wessington Springs finished bowling. They walked to their car and left for the farm.

The light snow became much heavier. The winds became stronger. The pleasure of the evening was quickly forgotten. Their eyes focused hard on the road. Numerous drifts had built up across the highway. They were in trouble.

The storm arrived in Wessington Springs. The Costello children waited for their parents to return home. The hours passed, each one longer than the other. They called family friends in Huron to see if their parents were there. Nobody had seen or heard from them. The children figured their parents were on their way home. They called their grandmother, Mrs. Agnes Costello. She stayed calm and reassured them.

The bright headlights showed little in the wind-driven snow. Each mile was a struggle, and the Costellos were closer to home. Their car went into the ditch, about three and a half miles north of the Beadle County line on Highway 281. They were one mile north of the Virgil road. Their home was six and a half miles away.

They were alone with their thoughts. They had a battle with the initial fears of being stranded in a winter blizzard. Dick Costello ran their car at intervals, so they had some heat. They thought about their children, Penny, 17, Susan, 15, and the 12-year-old twins, Charol and Sheryl.

Daylight offered no escape for Dick and Mary Lou Costello. The hours passed. Their vehicle was running out of fuel. Pretty soon, they would not be able to start their car.

The Costello children waited at the farm. Their phone went dead. They were worried, the hours passed slowly.

Mrs. Agnes Costello called Sheriff Dale Easton of Jerauld County. Easton said, "When we first learned that they were missing Friday afternoon, we just couldn't get out. You couldn't see your hand in front of your face so an effort to go out and hunt for them would have been impossible."

Before their car ran out of gas, Dick and Mary Lou made an important decision. They had an extra can of gas. They knew that if they put it in the car, it would not last long. A make-shift stove would be their best option.

They burned a tiny bit of gas in their car's ashtray. The fast but short-lived flame gave off precious heat. The fumes blackened the inside of their vehicle.

They were cold. It stormed all night, but the Costellos were determined to survive. They poured a few teaspoons of gas in their ashtray and lit it. Although the heat was not much, it gave the couple a sense of control.

Sheriff Easton said, "When the weather started to clear Saturday morning, I called Mike Mebius and members of the Wessington Springs fire department. We decided to go out and look for them."

Mebius, an employee of Tri-County Electric Association, drove the company snowmobile. Other volunteers who participated in the search included Fire Chief Don Cameron, Don Keeton, Dale Lieschner and Jerry Anshutz of the Wessington Springs Fire Department and Deputy Sheriff Bob Brockman.

Sheriff Easton said, "We found the Costello car out in the field beside the road. We rushed them right into the hospital here." It was around 9:30 a.m.

The doctor treated them for exposure. He was awed by their story. "This resourcefulness undoubtedly was a factor in saving their lives or at least averting more severe injury," said the doctor.

"After we got their parents back to town," Easton added, "the Wessington Springs Fire Department's rescue unit went to the Costello farm with the help of the State Highway Department and the County Highway Department to bring the children back to Wessington Springs."

Afterwards, Sheriff Easton had praise for members of the Wessington Springs Fire Department who helped in the rescue, Art Maxwell, county highway superintendent, and Dale Powell, head of the State Highway Department crews at Wessington Springs.Easton said, "This could have been a lot more serious."[115]

After visiting their parents in the hospital, the children stayed with their grandmother. Dick Costello was released from the hospital that weekend, but his wife was not released until later the following week.[116]

Alpena, located in Jerauld County, was platted in 1883. It is believed that C. H. Prior, townsite agent for the Milwaukee Railroad, named the town after Alpena, Michigan.

According to the 1960 census, Alpena had 407 inhabitants.

Frank Wuestewald, an employee of the Armour meat packing plant in Huron, left his home on the edge of Alpena at 3:30 a.m. on Friday. He worked the early shift. It was dark and the weather was bad. Warm in his car, Wuestewald figured he could make the twenty minute drive, but left plenty early just in case.

Driving east on Highway 32, Wuestewald drifted off the highway, about two and a half miles from home. He started walking back to Alpena. He hiked about twenty steps, and stopped. The brutal weather was too much. Wuestewald headed back to the shelter of his car.

Once there, Wuestewald was glad he chose to remain with his car. He had a full tank of gas and several blankets in the car. He thought about his wife and small children at home, Thersa, 9; Ellen Ann, 6; Kathy May, 2; and Benny, nine months. Their son, Arthur, 20, was just out of the service and at home.

One hour passed, then another. The strong winds vibrated the car. Snow lashed at his vehicle. The daylight hours ticked away, ever so slowly. After dark, it was more lonely. Wuestewald was somewhat warm in the car, but not comfortable enough to rest. Wuestewald became weary.

Friday morning, Mrs. Frank Wuestewald knew something happened to her husband when he did not call. She said, "During the anxious hours, there was little we could do but pace the floor, hope for the best, and try to reassure the children that their daddy would be found safely."

During the storm, Sheriff Dale Easton received emergency calls. One of then concerned Frank Wuestewald. Sheriff Easton borrowed an REA snowmobile and went looking for him. Sheriff Easton had no luck finding him in the storm.

Saturday morning, Wuestewald braved the weather again. Heading west toward Alpena, he stumbled upon an abandoned farmhouse, a quarter mile from his stalled car. Wuestewald was cold and hungry. Inside the house, he was out of the wind. He gathered papers and rags. He burned the precious material in an old cast stove.

The blizzard, finally, letup Saturday afternoon. At first, the huge snowbanks were curious. Once people started shoveling, the snow was a burden.

The phone rang at the Darrell Ochsner residence. It was from a local resident who had been out on Highway 32. The motorist had seen an abandoned car in the ditch near his farm. There was nobody inside the vehicle. Ochsner, Gilbert Hotchkiss, and Mr. Peterson loaded up in a pickup truck. They headed for Ochsner's old place.

They found Frank Wuestewald, standing close to the stove. A half hour later, there was a family reunion in Alpena.[117]

On Monday, Wuestewald was assigned a new position at the Armour plant. The change was made because someone just retired. Arthur rode to Huron with his father to look for work. Frank was glad Arthur was not along on Friday.

Alpena residents came through the storm like many other small towns. There was no school on Friday. The town was isolated until state and county crews cleared the highways and roads. There was a return of business, getting through the snow was a mixture of nuisance and amusement. Church services were not held on Sunday. Considering the circumstances, the locals were pleased with the handling of the mail.

First known as Milwaukee Junction, Woonsocket was named for Woonsocket, Rhode Island, by Charles H. Prior. The seat of Sanborn County, Woonsocket was settled in 1883.

In 1960, Woonsocket had 1,035 residents.

On February 19, 1966, the Woonsocket Wide Awake Hose Company held its annual firemen's ball at the city auditorium. The Max Hargens orchestra provided the music.

On Monday, February 21, Woonsocket defeated Fedora in the opening game of the District 21 Basketball Tournament in Huron. Dick Authier and Jim Collignon led the Redmen in scoring.

On Tuesday Woonsocket played the Lane Trojans, the winners of the Pony Hill Conference championship. Going into the tournament the Trojans had a record of 17 wins and 3 losses. Coach Ralph Weddle's squad won the game, 67 to 51. Dick Authier, Darwin Reider and Jim Collignon scored the bulk of the Redmen's points.

Going into the championship game, Woonsocket had a team record of 16 wins and 5 losses. Their opponent, Wessington Springs, was ranked No. 1 in the Class B poll.

Coach Weddle played control the ball for the entire game. In doing so, the Spartans had fewer chances to score. They hit 6 of 7 to start the game. At the half, Woonsocket led 19 to 15. In the third quarter, Frank Larson made two baskets to give the Redmen a 25 to 17 lead. Dick Authier increased the lead with a pair of baskets. With a 11 point advantage, the Redmen worked the clock with each possession. Coach Chuck Kirchmeier put the Spartans in a full court press with four minutes remaining with the game. Woonsocket won the championship, 43 to 34.[118]

Wednesday night, March 2, a thunder shower with light rains went through Woonsocket.

On Thursday, Woonsocket residents kept a constant check on the weather because other parts of South Dakota had blizzard conditions. Basketball fans left early for the Corn Palace for the Region 6 Basketball Tournament. Woonsocket would take on the Murdo Coyotes.

The game started at seven o'clock. Woonsocket had a one point lead, with four minutes left. Jim Collignon connected on two long jumpers and Bill Ball's driving lay up put the Redmen up by seven with 2:29 left. Woonsocket won the game 51 to 46. Their next opponent was Parkston.

Thursday night, the blizzard continued eastward.

It left approximately 12 inches of snow in Woonsocket. Overall, the amount of moisture was measured at .80 inches. Wind gusts were reported at 78 mph. Woonsocket had drifts of 10 to 12 feet high.

Three miles east of town at the Siedschlaw parking lot, a new mobile trailer home was completely destroyed when the twister-like winds rolled it over.

Grocery stores ran out of bread on Friday. During the storm, one family ran out of fuel. Households north of Woonsocket lost phone services for a little while. In Sanborn County, nine farms lost their electricity.

National Guardsmen helped in the local snow removal. Some township roads remained blocked, for almost a week.

On Sunday, people from Woonsocket participated in a cattle roundup. They were friends of G.E. Davis, his herd was pastured about seven miles north of town. Wandering blind in the storm, the cattle broke out and strayed in different directions. Icicles as long as 3 inches had formed on their eye lids. Although the animals looked rough, they were expected to recover from the effects of the blizzard.[119]

Before the blizzard struck, Ernest Reimer fertilized 270 acres of alfalfa ground on Jim Easland's land. County Agent, Don Scherschligt, said "I don't think Ernie could of timed a fertilizer application any better, as the snows melting on that alfalfa ground will put the phosphorous into a soil solution ready to go to work. Congrats to you, Ernie, for a well planned and executed move. You should get 5 ton per acre off of there like you did two years ago."[120]

Located in Sanborn County, Artesian was settled in 1883. First called Dianna, the town received its present name because it is located in the center of a great natural artesian basin.

In 1960, it was home for 330 people.

A ewe sheep survived eleven days buried in snow on the Otto Olson farm, north of Artesian. The animal was discovered when Otto Olson and Robert Hetland walked across a snowdrift on March 15. They freed the ewe.

Fedora was settled in 1896. Located in Miner County, Fedora was first known as Miner or Miner Center. There are two explanations for its name. One of the most popular items in the general store owned by Chris. Winters was the so-called "Fedora" hat. ("Fedora," a play by Sardou in 1882–the hat style was worn by one of the characters.) The settlers like the sound of the name, so they circulated a petition for it. The other theory is that the town was named for the wife of a railroad mail clerk.

Fedora had a population of 100 people in 1960.

Late on March 3, blizzard conditions developed in Fedora. Snow fell on Friday, making the storm more dangerous.

Darrel Page, an employee of a service station in Fedora, scowled at the blizzard. He was nervous and worried. Mrs. Darrell Page, 24, was about to give birth for the first time.

Friday night, the time came to take her hospital. About 8:30, Page called Highway Patrolman Steve Kenoyen for help. Kenoyen called Miner County Sheriff, Eugene Kolbach. Both men were at Howard, located east of Fedora on State Highway 34. They needed a snowplow, so they called Bob Chase, State Highway Department employee, at Howard. They worked their way to Fedora. Meanwhile, Donald Lager and Gerald Johnson, friends and coworkers of Darrel Page, learned about the medical emergency, so they came along on the ride.

From Fedora the three-vehicle motorcade traveled west to the Junction of State Highway 37 and turned south. They battled drifts up to 10 feet high. Their progress was very slow. About eleven miles north of Mitchell, the motorcade stalled in the snow. It was about 3:00 a.m. Saturday. They radioed the Mitchell police and requested further assistance.

Wayne Heidinger, Harold Thue, and Gene Kirton, linemen for Intercounty Electric Association, picked up Dr. Preston Brogdon, Pages's family physician on the company snowmobile. The four men arrived at the scene.

Huge drifts made the return trip, impossible. Eleven people were stranded, so they radioed the State Highway Department shop in Mitchell for a rotary plow.

The rotary plow arrived at 7:00 a. m. The motorcade arrived safely in Mitchell at 7:30. That morning, Dr. Brogdon said, "the Fedora woman is expected to have the baby sometime today, and she is fine." At the hospital Darrel Page said, "I'm going to remember this for a long time to come. We're real thankful we got the cooperation."[121]

Located north of Madison in Lake County, Ramona was platted in 1886. It was named by a group of Swiss settlers for a family by the name of Ramon who settled in the vicinity.

In 1960, the community was home for 247 people.

There was trouble at the Alf Manthey chicken ranch, located at the edge of Ramona. Manthey was deeply concerned about snow piling up on the roof of the 88 by 230 foot building that housed 12,000 capons. He stayed in the building to keep an eye on things. A loud cracking noise woke him up. A corner of the roof had collapsed, ripping gas, electrical and water lines. Luckily, there was no explosion. Besides property damages, Manthey lost between 1000 and 1500 birds. He restored the heat, but it was only a short-term fix.

On Sunday, Manthey made arrangements to truck the remaining birds to Marshall, Minnesota. They would be sold there.

Madison, seat of Lake County, was settled in 1873. It was named for Madison, Wisconsin. The town was called New Madison until 1881.

The Milwaukee arrived in Madison, from Pipestone, Minnesota, in 1880. The following year, the line was extended to Woonsocket. The Milwaukee built a stretch of track between Woonsocket and Wessington Springs in 1903.

In February 1966, 1.8 million college students held draft deferments. On February 25, it was announced that the Selective Service college qualification tests would be given on May 14, May 21, and June 3 at 1,200 locations throughout the continental United States, Hawaii, Alaska, Puerto Rico and the Canal zone. College students and high school students graduating this year were eligible, but individuals had to apply by April 23. Under the new deferment procedures, local draft boards could review class standings and test scores of students to determine deferments. Washington expected one million students to take the deferment exams in 1966.[122]

On March 2, 1966, Harold Woldt, Wentworth; Walter Michaelson, Faye Crabbs, John C. Rath and Fred A. Procknow, all of Madison, were members of the local draft board. They served without paid.

Within five days of their 18th birthday, all boys had to register for the draft. Each registrant was given a number and placed in a file. Then, a questionnaire, asking personal information, was sent to the registrant. It was completed and returned. The registrant was then classified. If the individual was classified 1A and over the age of 18 years and 9 months, he was eligible for a pre-induction examination. The order in which the youths were asked to report for physical examinations was determined by date of birth.

For March 1966, South Dakota's draft quota was 88, compared to 79 in February and 110 in January. The Defense Department determined the number of men needed for the protection of the country. Numbers were broken down for the states and then, the local draft boards.[123]

On March 3, the following headline said it all, **"Major Snow Storm Misses Local Area."** The research farm reported .15 inches of rain, Wednesday night. Occasional rain or snow was expected on Thursday. Occasional snow and colder temperatures, Thursday night.

On Friday, cloudy skies and colder temperatures were expected.

On Friday, the following Associated Press News Brief appeared in the *Madison Daily Leader:*

HEAVY FIGHTING IN VIETNAM

Two battalions of US Marines are reported engaged in heavy fighting with the Viet Cong on the South Viet Nam coast near Quang Ngai. They're said to be clashing with an enemy force also of about two battalions. A Marine bomber and two helicopters supporting the ground forces were shot down. The US stepped up the air war against North Viet Nam, American planes ranging far north of Hanoi to pound a rail line leading in from Red China. There also were heavy air strikes in South Viet Nam.

Again, the headlines said it all, **"Blizzard Slugs Madison Area; Weather Does About-Face; 10-Inch Snow; Drifts High."** Madison received 10 inches of snow before the Daily Leader went to press. Winds were between 30 and 60 mph. Drifts around town were already 4 feet high. School closings and other storm announcements were made.

The *Daily Leader* offered a rare look at one weather aspect of the blizzard. Newspapers and climatological data listed only the daily highs and lows. But, the *Daily Leader* provided hourly temperatures, gathered by Northwestern Public Service. Many communities had mild temperature readings prior to the storm and temperatures cooled off gradually. Here's the *Daily Leader* chart:

Hourly Temperatures

Thursday		Friday	
Noon	36	Midnight	30
1 p.m.	38	1 a.m.	28
2 p.m.	38	2 a.m.	26
3 p.m.	38	3 a.m.	20
4 p.m.	38	4 a.m.	18
5 p.m.	36	5 a.m.	14
6 p.m.	36	6 a.m.	12
7 p.m.	32	7 a.m.	12
8 p.m.	30	8 a.m.	12
9 p.m.	30	9 a.m.	12
10 p.m.	30	10 a.m.	12
11 p.m.	30	11 a.m.	12

Source: *Madison Daily Leader,* 4 March 1966

Madison received 2 more inches of snow, before the blizzard ended on Saturday. Overall, Madison recorded 12 inches. Snowfall total for other communities included: Franklin, 9 inches; Wentworth, 6 inches; and Chester, 4 inches.[124]

Sheriff Norman McGillivray said:

We were terribly busy. Saturday was the worst, early in the morning until midnight. His office averaged about one call every two minutes Saturday. Most persons were concerned about highway conditions.[125]

During and after the blizzard, Osterloh Service and Olsbo Service were very busy. Jerry Osterloh said, he and two other men pulled between 50 and 75 cars from the snow during the weekend. Charles Breuer of Olsbo Service estimated his station pulled and pushed about the same number. Breuer could not pull one vehicle out that was stuck. It was a Caterpillar tractor bogged down in the snow, about four miles northeast of Madison.[126]

Pierre, Harrold, Onida, Highmore, Stephan, Miller, Wessington, Huron, De Smet and Brookings

Pierre, seat of Hughes County and State Capital, was founded in 1878. At first, the town was known at Mato. In 1880, a shipment of household goods was sent from Bismarck to "Pierre on the east side of the river, opposite Fort Pierre." That name took hold and lasted.

Fourteen states and parts of others were part of the Louisiana Territory in 1803. Except for the extreme northeast corner, all of South Dakota came in that deal. Initiated by President Thomas Jefferson, the United States government purchased the land drained by the Mississippi River from France (Napoleon) for fifteen million dollars, less than three cents an acre.

Reverend Thomas D. O'Gorman wrote the standard text, *History of the Roman Catholic Church in America* in 1895. On April 19, 1896, he became the consecrated bishop of Sioux Falls. Bishop O'Gorman, born in Boston, received his education in France. Interested in French exploration of the West, Bishop O'Gorman became familiar with French source material on that subject. In January 1903, at a State Historical Society meeting, Bishop O'Gorman told the story of the Verendrye Plate for the first time. He suggested that it might be found within fifty miles of Pierre. In February 1913, two school children found the plate on a hill overlooking Fort Pierre.

On October 1, 1889, Pierre was named the temporary capital in the first state election. Other cities in the hunt included Huron, Watertown, Sioux Falls, Mitchell, and Chamberlain. Voters of South Dakota selected Pierre, the other choice was Huron, the permanent capital in 1890. Pierre withstood another challenge with Mitchell for the capital in 1904. Construction of the capital began in 1907. It was finished in 1910.

In 1960, Pierre had 11,200 residents.

On February 26, 1966, a Saturn 1B rocket, was successfully launched into orbit. It was the first unmanned Apollo spacecraft test. The flight lasted 39 minutes. The capsule touched down in the south Atlantic Ocean. Three 83-foot parachutes softened the fall and it was recovered by the aircraft carrier, *Boxer*. The next unmanned Apollo mission was scheduled for June.

In 1961, the entire American figure skating team, 18 members, died in a Brussels plane crash. At the World Figure Skating Championship in Davcs, Switzerland, the Americans made their comeback in February 1966. The team won five medals at that event. Peggy Fleming, a 17-year-old-high school student from Colorado Springs, Colorado, won the gold medal in the women's competition.

At Pierre's FAA Airport, the high for March 2, 1966, was 32 degrees. That afternoon, it started to snow at 3:00. The precipitation was wet and clingy. Soon afterwards, the northerly winds became much stronger.

The residents in the northeast section of Pierre experienced power outages, that evening. Caked with ice, the power lines on the 7,200 watt service up Hillger's Gulch, north of Capital Lake, banged together and shorted out.

One Evans street resident said, "It looked like the Fourth of July on a grand scale. The lines lit up like neon tubes and the entire valley from one end to the other would be a string of blue flame."[127]

On March 3, the snow turned to drizzle at 2:30 a.m. Thursday morning, the high for the day was recorded, 33 degrees. The freezing mist fell all morning.

The *Daily Capital Journal* headline, **"March Sheds Clock Of Deception With Fast-Moving Storm,"** would soon be ironic. Here's the March 3 weather forecast:

> *Blizzard and heavy snow warnings continued. Northwesterly winds 30-50 m.p.h. today and tonight, gradually diminishing Friday. Blizzard conditions with considerable blowing or drifting snow in many sections today, diminishing slowly tonight and becoming partly cloudy Friday. Local accumulations of an additional four inches of snow or more in some sections, and one to four inches in other sections. Colder today and tonight. Highs today in the mid 20's and lows tonight zero to 12.*[128]

Electrical problems continued to plague Pierre and Fort Pierre. Power crews restored service for some households, but many others lost their electricity. It was a running battle.

Utilities Commissioner, Elwin Hull, said, "the swinging lines would short, and then in a few seconds, a switch would close off the service. After a few more seconds, the switch would cut the service back on. This caused the continually interrupted service."

Hull informed the public that the city power crews worked all night, and cut the power service from Hilgers's Gulch off altogether. He said, "We brought power in from a different direction." Hull stated, "There will be some damage from the shorting out of the 7,200 watt service north of Riggs school. You can't short out that much power without there being some burning. I would guess we have to replace a half dozen or so loops between the poles."

Furthermore, "Some parts of Pierre were not restored until this morning. By noon, a block or two in the extreme part of the city were all that remained without service, but new calls indicate new problem areas."[129]

Power interruptions were reported in Fort Pierre.

Blizzard conditions developed Thursday afternoon. As temperatures fell, the drizzle turned to snow.

A rural Pierre couple, Mr. and Mrs. Vernon Olson, were in Pierre on Thursday. They left Lariat Lanes as the storm was developing. The Olson's lived a couple of miles north of Pierre. They never made it home. Eight children waited at home.

According to Rich J. Burke, local Northwestern Bell manager, the long distance telephone service from Pierre to Blunt, Onida, Agar, Presho, Murdo, Draper, and Vivian have been interrupted because of the ice storm. Burke was uncertain when repairs could be made with the weather conditions, but all available workers in the area have been dispatched. He told a reporter, "Poles are broken north of Pierre. There is about one inch of ice on the wires south of the city."[130]

SNOW SNUFFS OUT ACTIVITY
Rural Pierre Couple Rescued Early Friday

That was the headline for the *Capital Journal* on March 4. Mr. and Mrs. Olson were found around 9:30 a.m. in their car, north of the Oahe Speedway near Pierre. The couple had been stranded for seventeen hours. They stayed warm by burning paper and bits of cardboard in their car.

Deputy Sheriff Frank Weldin and State Patrolman Louis Fratzke departed Pierre at 10:30 Thursday night to search for a party of four missing on U.S. Highway 14. Five miles east of Pierre, they found Wesley and Kenly Olson, Bernard Ree and Robert Miller inside a vehicle. On the return trip, Weldin's patrol car stalled out. They radioed for help. Louis Harding and Civil Defense Director, Jim Mulloy, came in a wrecker. They made it back to Pierre at 2:30 a.m. Friday.

Almost 6 inches of snow fell on Friday, 2 inches were recorded on Thursday. The high was the day 20 degrees.

Schools were closed in Pierre and Fort Pierre. Most businesses had radio announcements of their closures. Radio station KCCR lost its power, but station KGFX transmitted storm messages and notices. Only a few people manned the state capital. City and county offices were closed for the day.

Residents in the northeast section of Pierre had no power Friday morning. An employee at the power plant said:

> We had power all night, but this morning, it went out in the northeastern section of the city served by the 7,200 volt line up the gulch north of the capital building. Our boom truck with the buckets is down and out of commission at present, and our linemen have tried and just can't climb poles in this weather. I doubt if much can be down until the storm subsides.[131]

Deputy Sheriff Frank Weldin said, "Friday morning that the Civil Defense microwave tower wasn't working properly, and it is feared that it has blown down." Also, the police "radio" power was erratic, and Friday morning only local ranges were effective.[132]

Friday afternoon, residents found their homes getting cold so they called the National Guard. John Dewell, National Guard officer, said:

> They moved about 380 people, beginning about 1 p.m. Friday. We got our first call about that time, and sent out our ambulance. Calls started coming in with increased frequency after that, and by 4 p.m. we were in full scale emergency. A call was sent out for the National Guardsmen in the area, and 20 men and 8 officers were able to reach the auditorium. We used two 2 1/2 ton trucks and eight 3/4 ton trucks to shuttle people from their homes to those of friends or to hotels.
>
> They wound up the evacuation about 3 a.m. Saturday, and left several vehicles at the police station for use in case of any further calls. Their last call came Saturday morning from the Bernard Metzinger family about six miles east of Pierre on Highway 14, and they were able to bring them to safety.[133]

The Riverview Trailer Court area, the Government Housing area in northwest Pierre, and the northeast portion of the city had power outages. The last area was without power for twenty-eight hours, and temperatures reached the freezing mark in many homes.

Mrs. James Likness, Pierre correspondent for the *Daily Plainsman* (Huron), was among those evacuated by the National Guard in Pierre. The following is Mrs. James Likness experience:

> "What's it like to ride with a baby in your arms, huddled in an unheated National Guard truck?"
>
> "It's something that I wouldn't want to go through again," said, Mrs. James Likness, mother of five.

When the power failure blacked out, the Likness home, the family decided to evacuate. Mrs. Likness, with Mary, 3 months, Paul 3 1/2 , and Karen, 6, boarded the National Guard truck while Mr. Likness and the two oldest children, Mike, 10, and Steven, 8, went to a neighbor's house.

"There was no heater, no defroster, no nothing in the cab of that truck, but we were being carried through the snow by the most helpful and understanding Guardsmen. We were headed to a friend's house, plowing through the snow, and came on a stalled car blocking the intersection. There was nothing to do but to back up for a block and try another route. You had to lean out the window to see where you were going.

"We changed plans and headed to the Lutheran parsonage where Rev. and Mrs. E. L. Bursagel had offered to put us up. Two Guardsmen helped carry the children–the baby wrapped in her blankets–through the knee-deep drifts to the door. And we spent the night in the warmth and hospitality of the parsonage.[134]

On Thursday morning, Dick McCaughy, Cleo Krier and John Dyce left Pierre for the Armstrong ranch in the Hays area where they worked. Just after turning off Highway 14, their vehicle became stuck. No matter what they did, they could not get it free.

The men were alone on the prairie.

They were lucky in one aspect, they had brought lunches. To wander out in the storm, was not an option. Their vehicle provided shelter from blizzard. Temperatures fell, but it was not bitter cold.

The storm was relentless.

They decided one of their lunch pails could be used for a makeshift stove. Venturing a short distance from their vehicle, the men pulled four fence posts out of the ground. It was not an easy chore. They chopped up the fence post with a pocket knife and a tire iron. They burned Dyce's small step ladder. For blankets the men used the leather seat covers of the vehicle.

Saturday morning, a highway maintenance crew discovered the marooned party. Dick McCaughy, Cleo Krier and John Dyce were taken to Midland. The men contacted their families. Then, they enjoyed hot mineral baths. They were slightly dehydrated. The effects of smoke inhalation was more of a concern. The men arrived back in Pierre, on Sunday afternoon at four o'clock.[135]

Pierre received 9 inches of snow during the blizzard.

Power was restored on March 5. Long-distance telephone service was restored on March 8.

Governor Nils Boe activated the Civil Air Patrol. In the immediate aftermath of the blizzard, having planes and helicopters up in the air was important. Using South Dakota National Guardsmen for snow removal was vital for many communities. The use of contractors' equipment at cost eased the financial burden of the authorities who had to pay the bills.

Governor Boe was in Washington on March 7, for a hearing on having underpasses constructed on Interstate 90 for cattle and machinery. Before the hearing, Governor Boe met with representatives of the Bureau of Indian Affairs. When the meeting was over, Bob Bennett, assistant BIA director, said "all available equipment under BIA jurisdiction would be put into use in Ziebach County." Bennett told Governor Boe that the BIA would authorize $50,000. to assist on the reservation.[136]

Late March 7, Governor Boe declared areas of South Dakota as "major disaster areas." Boe said, "I am using the term to permit the immediate use of all disaster loans and funds that might be available to public bodies as well as to private individuals." Civil Defense funds of the state would be tapped. With little damages to public property, federal aid would be little.[137]

Harrold, settled in 1881, was named for Harrold R. McCullough, a Northwestern Railroad official. Located in Hughes County, the town had 255 residents in 1960.

Mrs. E. Zeller, reporter for Harrold, said:

> This vicinity experienced the worst snow storm in many years, it struck here Thursday evening and lasted through Friday and Friday night, letting up and clearing but still blowing some Saturday piling drifts at least 10 feet high. Electric power was off in the country up to 36 and 42 hours, phone service was restored in most areas by Monday. Wind shifted to the south, southeast Monday and caused some drifting again.[138]

Onida, seat of Sully County, was settled by former residents of the state of New York in 1883. The town's name is a modification of Oneida, New York.

Onida had 843 residents in 1960.

Onida won the District 7 Basketball Tournament on February 23, 1966. The Warriors defeated the Agar Hi-Pointers in the title game, 56 to 47. Rich Niehoff, Joe Kub and Mike Young led Coach Jerry Kassin's squad in scoring. They advanced to the regional tournament in Aberdeen.

The Region 2 Basketball Tournament was wiped out by a three-day blizzard that struck on March 3.

Here's what The *Onida Watchman* said:

> The big blizzard of 1966, which may go down in history as the worst ever, especially in the West River area just across the Missouri River from Sully County, struck here late Thursday afternoon and seemed to grow in intensity until it abated during the early morning hours on Saturday.
>
> Though there are reports of heavy livestock losses just west of the river, losses in Sully are considered to be light in comparison. There were no reports of great hardships or suffering of county residents other than some extremely anxious hours and discomfort due to chilly homes because of electrical power outages as the result of the ferocious storm.[139]

Onida had a standby power plant. It was used for the greater part of two days. Rural residents were not as fortunate.

Onida lost telephone services for almost a week. Northwestern Bell repaired telephone lines that were knocked down. The microwave tower at Stephen Mission was partially blown down and a temporary tower had to be constructed.

No one knew for sure how much snow fell in the area during the storm. The official U.S. Weather recording equipment located near the *Watchman* building was buried in a drift, 7 feet high. Local weather observer, Herbert Tebay, received many inquires about how much snow fell in the aftermath of the blizzard. With a big smile on his face, Tebay replied, "Guess it must have been about seven feet."[140]

On Monday March 7, the Region 2 Basketball Tournament resumed play in Aberdeen. Onida met Cresbard in the consolation game that night. Onida won by two points, 67 to 65. Rich Niehoff, a senior, scored 38 points for the Warriors. The Warriors finished their season with a record of 20 wins and 4 losses.

Unconfirmed reports indicated that Clayton King, East Sully rancher, lost over 100 head of cattle. Also, Billy Pullman lost at least 13 cows and perhaps over 100 head of pigs. There were other reports of minor losses of livestock.

Pheasant loses for Sully County were considered moderate to severe.

Highmore, known from 1880 to 1882 as Siding No. 5., is the seat of Hyde County. The origin of the town's name is uncertain. The townsite rests on the highest ground in South Dakota on the Northwestern Railroad (1903 feet above sea level) east of the Missouri River. Others have said it was named for a surveyor, a member of a famous English family of interior decorators, who worked for the railroad and billed goods to this point under his own name. Another version suggested it was named as a result of a foreign worker's attempt to describe the rising slope of the land by repeating "high more, high more."

In 1960, Highmore's population totaled 1,078 residents.

The Highmore high school boys basketball team, the Pirates, lost their final game of the regular season to the Harrold Cardinals, 53 to 50, on February 15, 1966.

The *Highmore Herald* moved into a new building, built by Frank Hawkins, on main street on February 19. The *Herald* shared the building with the law firm of Heidepriem and Widmaver.

On February 24, the Pirates won the rematch with the Cardinals, 90 to 60. The next day, they became District 16 champions. Dave Parlin's last second shot lifted the Pirates over the Wessington Warriors, 44 to 42.

Highmore received a trace of precipitation in the afternoon of March 2. The high for the day was 33 degrees.

Highmore residents could not make any long distance telephone calls after 4:00 p.m. James Olson, Sully Buttes Telephone Cooperative, said, "large amounts of ice coupled with high winds and heavy snows contributed to lost communication services."[141]

At the regional tournament in Huron, Dave Parlin sank two crucial free throws in the last minute of the game. The Pirates had a one point lead, 56 to 55. Doland called time out with six seconds left. Kenny Ruschenburg tipped the ball toward the basket with three seconds left. Doland won the heartbreaker, 57 to 56.

The Highmore cheering section made it home without any problems Wednesday night.

Hyde County Librarian Nellie Rudd had a pleasant surprise. A library book was returned 20 years overdue. At a penny a day, the fine would have been $73.00. The book had been found in one of the rooms at the Hill Hotel which recently had closed its doors. Rudd renewed the book and canceled the fine.

On March 3, the temperatures did not fluctuate much in Highmore, a high of 33 degrees was recorded. That afternoon, wet snow started to fall. Highmore received 4 inches of snow. That evening, blizzard conditions developed and the low fell to 25.

The Highmore faithful were rewarded at Huron. The Pirates shot 78 percent in their final game, 90 percent in the third quarter. Highmore defeated De Smet, 70 to 62, winning the Region 4 consolation trophy.

Highmore school officials decided to keep the basketball players, cheerleaders, and students in Huron. They stayed at the Marvin Hughitt Hotel. One teacher said, "They let out a big cheer when it was announced they would be staying overnight." Highmore had eight teachers acting as chaperons. Fans of the team stayed at the hotel as well.

Thursday night, some people in Highmore heard their boosters had stayed in Huron, thru the efforts of local C.B. radios operators. On Friday, storm announcements informed others that the Highmore following was safe in Huron.

The main circuit breaker at the Highmore exchange was tripped many times. Olson indicated that the normal load on the board was about 18 amperes. During the storm, over 40 amperes of current were consumed. As a result, the Sully Buttes Telephone Cooperative requested people limit their calls.

Other Sully Buttes exchanges experienced service failures.

In the Highmore area, about one hundred farms, lost their electricity for twenty-four hours.

The storm ended Saturday morning. Numerous drifts, up to 16 feet high, were left behind.

Jon Boller and John McDermott, boys from Highmore, climbed the huge drifts on the grounds of the high school. The *Highmore Herald* said, "In fact, the drift was high enough to put them on the roof of the four-room annex back of the high school building. In attempting to get off, they slipped in between the eighteen foot drift and the wall of the building and into the drift."

Dick Hamlin, putting chains on his car, heard their screams. In a few minutes, he pulled the boys out. The *Herald* said, **"Dick Hamlin Plays The Hero's Role."**[142]

On Saturday, Highmore students walked over to the Elks Club. They played pool and cards and drank lots of pop. Several of the teachers purchased underwear, socks and handkerchiefs. Others were asked why they did not use the laundromat. One of the teachers replied, "We all wore suits and it would be a little difficult to wash them. Besides, what would we wear while our clothes were being washed." Another teacher said, "Next time I go anywhere, I'm going to at least bring a toothbrush."

William J. McDermott, publisher of the *Highmore Herald*, stayed at the Marvin Hughitt Hotel. McDermott remarked that basketball fans of South Dakota have had a history of being stranded away from home because of Mother Nature. He recalled the 1951 blizzard. That year, Highmore hosted the regional tournament. The storm stranded 2,400 people in the community. McDermott said, "About 1,000 people stayed overnight in the auditorium, sleeping on the floor and bleachers, while the rest were taken in by the town's people. There were as many as 50 staying in some of the homes." Storms in 1954 and 1957 also blocked roads for Highmore fans.[143]

Sunday morning, the Highmore crowd left the hotel, fourteen cars returned to Highmore at 11:00.

By Sunday night, Sully Buttes Telephone Cooperative had restored communications to most of their customers. Blocked roads prevented some repairs.

On March 8, eight caterpillars started to open roads to forty-three Hyde County farms and ranches.

In the initial report to state and federal government agencies, Hyde County estimated the storm damages between $250,000. and $300,000. Livestock and poultry losses were as follows: 1,000 cattle, 25 hogs, 300 sheep and 1,000 chickens.[144]

On March 10, 1966, the *Highmore Herald* top headline said, **"Area Digs Out From One Of History's Worst Storms."** If this would have been an ordinary blizzard, the top story would have been **"Governor Boe Announces Candidacy For Second Term."** Nils A. Boe was elected to the South Dakota Legislature in 1951, 1953, 1955 and 1957. He was Speaker Pro tem during the 1953 session. During the 1955 and 1957 sessions, Boe was Speaker of the House. Elected Lieutenant Governor in 1962, he served under Governor Archie Gubbrud. In November 1964, President Johnson, a Democrat, carried South Dakota, but Boe, a Republican, became Governor of South Dakota by a margin of just over 8,000 votes.

Amateur radio operators relayed messages during the storm. The following individuals were recognized in letters to the editors: Mr. Nicholas and Mrs. Jim Hancock of Ree Heights; and Mrs. Kenneth Ferris, Mervin Mewes, Robert Namanny, Lon Hurd, George Wheelhouse and Simon Kusser, all of Highmore; Hap Hazzard of Wessington; Eldon Willeiwiet of Chamberlain; and Vern Collins and Bruce Hammill of Miller.[145]

Stephan, located in Hyde County, was named for St. Stephan, patron saint of Hungary. A Catholic mission was built there.

The town had a population of 61 in 1960.

Stephan was in the news during the blizzard. Northwestern Bell Telephone Company reported the nearby 320 foot microwave tower had blown down in the blizzard. Management suspected something was wrong when 250 long distance circuits going through Pierre went out simultaneously in the storm.

On March 5, a highway crew, opening a blocked road, noticed the fallen tower and contacted the phone company. Richard Devereaux, South Dakota manager, sent a replacement portable tower via a truck. The tower could be set up in twenty-four hours. In the meantime, Devereaux said "calls were being rerouted over other long distance circuits."[146]

Miller, the seat of Hand County, goes back to 1880. It was named for Henry Miller, first settler here and founder of the town.

In 1960, Miller had 2,081 residents.

The following story about the Howard Jensen family was written by Millard F. Seaman, superintendent of the Sunshine Bible Academy at Miller. Seaman wrote:

A SHELTER IN THE STORM

Blizzards are not new to South Dakota. It would be an exceptional winter on the Great Plains that didn't produce at least one snow-swirling storm churning across the vast   expanse of wind-swept prairies. For as long as most of us can remember, old timers have been carefully casual as they compared each wintry blast unfavorably to the storm to the storm of '88. That is, until March 4, 1966. From that date, a more severe standard of ferocity has been established.

The suffering and hardship of any blizzard is difficult to describe. The total picture of what happened in '66 will probably never be known. However, I am sure there are few tales that can rival the experiences of the Howard Jensen family in south Hand County for composure, ingenuity and courage.

All Day Thursday, March 3rd, the radio kept forecasting an impending storm. That morning visibility in Rapid City was zero with winds at 65 m.p.h. At noon, Pierre closed their schools. Still, at Miller, it was a nice day; there was little indication that a storm was coming. On the Howard E. Jensen farm, 21 miles southeast of Miller, everything was as usual. The boys got home from school and the chores were finished. Fifty-two year old Howard, his wife, Glayds, and their six children were enjoying a pleasant evening at home. Their neighbors, the Parmelys, Clark, Ruby, and five children–stopped over for a visit. About 11 p.m., when the Parmelys left for their home approximately three-quarters of a mile northeast of Jensens, it was evident the weatherman knew what he was talking about. The wind had switched to the northwest; it was snowing and blowing. Jensens gave the Parmelys time to get home, and before going to bed called on the telephone to be certain they had been able to make it.

About 5 o'clock Friday morning, Curtis, 17, the oldest of the five boys and one girl that make up the Jensen family, woke up with the distinct smell of smoke irritating the nostrils. The Miller High School senior proceeded downstairs and checked the basement door. He found increasing amounts of smoke coming from that area of the basement that housed the fuel-oil furnace. Then he raced to his parents' bedroom shouting, "The house is on fire!"

Howard Jensen recalls that his first thoughts were of his family. He and his wife hastily drew on part of their clothing as Curtis went to rouse the other children. Throughout the ensuing hours, the quick thinking and calm decisions of the head of the house were without doubt, the main factors that kept the tragic situation from being even worse. Fifteen-year-old Kenny, the most vocal of the family, recalls that he put on a shirt, pants, socks, and two overshoes–not mates. He was assigned the task of starting the cars which were parked in the garage approximately 50 feet southeast of the house. The plan was to leave with the family. By the time the smaller children got downstairs, the house was fast filling with smoke. Especially, bad was the kitchen area on the south side of the house above the furnace dense with eye-smarting vapors. It was impossible for the family to follow Kenny through the south door, so Jensen instructed everyone to lock arms and exit through the north door.

At the thought of going out of the house, 12-year-old Jane, a seventh-grader, broke into tears. "Oh, my Tammy doll!" she wailed. In patience, her mother instructed, "Okay take one quick look." The smoke was too much; the doll could not be found. Howard used the seconds to grab an armful of clothes which he thrust into the hands of several of the fellows. As they stepped through the north door, the wind, which was now gusting to near 85 m.p.h. caught the clothes, tearing them loose. Everybody had all they could do to hang on to each other as they headed for the cars.

In the garage, Howard recalls that he counted noses; all were present and accounted for. Both cars ('57 & '62 Plymouths) started, and Howard made one last trip to the south entry to get more clothes–a pair of coveralls, a parka and some rubber boots which he brought to the car. Curtis and 13-year-old Alan were in the '57. They backed it out and headed for the nearby road; but before long, as they waited, the blowing snow caused the car to begin to miss and soon it stopped altogether. Kenny backed the '62 out of the garage, but while trying to turn around, got stuck. The others pushed it out. The gauge revealed a shortage of gas, and they headed for the gas pump bout 150 feet south from the house in the direction of the barn. Here, the swirling snow proved too much for the newer Plymouth, and it, too drowned out.

The cool-headed father again appraised the situation. It was apparent now that they would be unable to leave the place. It would be too cold to keep the family in the cars. The best chance would be to try to get to the barn. They must keep calm. First, Curt and Alan must be brought from the '57. Kenny, wearing only a light jacket and no shoes—just overshoes—fought his way back and informed his brothers that they were going to try to get to the barn. As the three boys went past the house, they noticed that the west window of the kitchen had broken and flames were sucking out past the fuel-oil and bottle-gas tanks.

Huddled in the '62 Plymouth, the family of eight held another conference. Would it be possible to get to the barn? Alan and Kenny volunteered to see if they could find their way in the blinding snow. Kenny recalls that he couldn't even see the granary as they walked past it. The barn was not visible until they ran into it. Alan stayed at the barn while Kenny returned for the others. He carried five-year-old Daryl; Curt picked up Gregory (age six) and Howard took 12-year-old Jane, who, fortunately, is not as large as some seventh graders. It was all the three could do to make it back to the barn with their burdens. After a brief rest, Kenny returned once more to the car to bring his mother to the barn. Time-keeper Alan—the only one with a watch—recalls that it was 8:25 (nearly two and a half hours of desperation and struggle) when they deposited the three smaller children in a wheel-barrow full of ground feed and covered their bare feet in an effort to keep them warm. Everyone was wet clear through. Although it was none too warm in the barn, it was a big improvement over being out in the snowdrifts.

They opened the barn door and let the 20 milk cows in. Curt went up in the haymow and threw down about 10 bales of hay which were scattered in the feed aisle between the two rows of milking stanchions. Then, everybody crawled into the hay, trying to keep warm.

It was the eight-grader, Alan, who got hungry about noon and decided he would have some warm milk. Soon, the other boys and Howard joined him; they milked most of the cows, separated, and fed the calves as well as the children. A single cup served the family as a community bowl.

Staring reflectively across the room Sunday evening, as a group sat around the Parmely's dining room table. Kenny, who usually does not lack words, mused, "You can't tell it-how it happened; it was awful!" Mrs. Jensen, who had just returned with those who had taken Curtis to the hospital, adds, "It was the quietest thirty hours in the history of our family. I never knew Kenny and Alan could be so still." All testify that the whole experience didn't seem real. They found some gunny sacks and wrapped the little bare feet, but Gladys says, "They just wouldn't stay on". Howard reflects, "If it hadn't been for the cows in the barn, it would have been much worse; their heat kept us from freezing."

Curt, who was the best dressed with overalls, parka and boots, went upstairs and threw down more hay to feed the cows, and to make a better bed for the night. The storm's intensity had increased all day. There was no electricity, therefore, no heat and no light. As darkness crept upon the desolate group, Howard assigned the "sleeping" arrangements. Curt, the oldest, would sleep on the outside and be responsible for his sister, Jane, who was next to him. Six-year old Greg would lie between Jane and his mother, with five-year-old Daryl between Gladys and the father. "It was too cold to sleep," Mrs. Jensen volunteered. "You couldn't get warm enough to rest." She tells how she would warm the bare feet of first one boy and then the other between her legs until they would doze off.

Sometimes in the middle of the night, Daryl roused and asked, "Daddy, did anybody turn off our electric blanket?" Assured by his father that everything was all right, he crawled a little deeper into the hay. The older boys report that they didn't get much rest. Kenny said, "It was too noisy to sleep." Howard adds, "You would be surprised at the noise there is in a barn at night. First, a cow would moo, then a calf would bawl or a sheep would cough. It was quite a night!"

About 7 a.m. Curt went up to look out the haymow window and announced the storm was getting "a little better". About the same time, Greg got sick, and shortly after, Daryl, too, was vomiting. Howard recalls, "I knew then we had to do something." Some of the clothes he had brought to the car had been left when the family fled to the barn. Curt went for them. Meanwhile, Mr. and Mrs. Jensen decided that two men should go. They would try to get to the road and then decide whether to head northeast to Clark Parmely's–their "nearest" neighbors–or go east and south to Elden Winter's. There were at least three drifts, 12 to 15 feet high, between the barn and the road; but, they made it. The wind continued to blow the snow off the graded road; they could see where they were going. The cutting wind and snow swirling in their faces made the 15 degrees temperature seem much colder. They would take a few steps into the wind and then be forced to turn their backs to wipe the snow from their faces and move ahead again. Both men froze their noses and patches on their faces, but they fought on. About 8 o'clock Howard stumbled through the kitchen door at Clark Parmely's; Curt was right behind him. They were wet and tired, but they had reached help.

Clark took up the story as we sat around his table. "It was storming, so we were late getting up. We were just getting dressed when Howard walked in and announced, "We've had some tough luck... our house burned down!"

Ruby reacted first, "Where is the family?"

"In the barn", was Howard's reply.

Is everybody all right?"

Assured that they were, but that they needed help, Clark finished dressing. As he walked past the kitchen, he checked the cookie jar–the only thing he could think of to give them to eat. It was empty, so he proceeded outside to see if he could get his tractor out. He carried five gallons of gas to the barn where the tractor was stored; he wanted to be sure he had enough. A trailer, which was used to haul ground feed, sat in the barn with three or four bushels of grain in it. This was shoveled into a trough and the three men were ready for the trip. Ruby had packed a large box with blankets, clothing for the children, and some bread and butter; other bulky clothes were tied together with a rope. Within an hour from the time the men left the barn, Clark's tractor was parked, heading up-wind, in the Jensens' drive, idling fast so as not to be drowned out by the snow. Curt carried the box, and Clark and Howard the bulky clothes as they climbed back over the huge drifts to the barn.

Mrs. Jensen recalls, "When I saw the fellows again, I was overjoyed, but the sight of those little stockings and shoes was more than I could take; I broke down and cried."

It took nearly a half hour to get everybody ready for the trip to Parmely's. Then, carrying the little ones, the entire family proceeded to the tractor and trailer. Everybody sat on the floor of the trailer. Clark reflects, "I used 4th gear going back–I wasn't too sure of the trailer hitch, and I know how rough a trailer ride can be." He had used road gear going down; it hadn't taken long.

Howard smiled and added, "He wouldn't have had to be so careful; nobody complained about the ride."

Clark, with chocked emotion, recalls, "When I saw the corral gate and the outline of the trees, I knew we had made it." The storm was still raging and in the open visibility very poor.

Ruby was ready for the frosty crew when it arrived. She reasoned that after so long with no solid food, they would want something warm, but not to heavy. The water was hot and in less than five minutes, eager little hands were spooning warm oatmeal, and empty tummies were welcoming warm toast. Glayds recalls, I remember what Howard said, "I like oatmeal, but I never tasted any as good as Ruby had that morning!" His sentiment was echoed by the entire Jensen family.

About 11 o'clock Clark, Howard, and the three older Jensen boys (wearing additional clothes) were on their way back to the Jensen farm to take care of the livestock. Ruby and the Parmely boys were busy with their own chores. Kenny modestly reports, "Clark and I milked those 18 cows; I think Clark got a couple more than I did." (Sunday morning Clark could hardly open his hands; he was used to electric milkers.) Howard, Curt, and Alan, were digging sheep out of the snow. Twenty-two ewes with lambs were under a hayrack that had been turned upside down. "By the time we got them out, we were soaked to the skin, and I do mean the skin," Howard relates.

About three o'clock the men returned to Parmely's for dinner. While Clark fed some of his stock, the Jensens rested. At 5 p.m. the three older boys went back to the farm with Clark to do chores. Howard had taken about all he could. As the boys began cleaning the barn, Clark went to the Winter's to try calling R.E. A. on the telephone. They needed electricity to pump water for the cattle. The phones were still out, so Clark went home and fed some more of his cattle until he went for the boys about 6:30.

In order to get hay for the cows, it was necessary to climb on top of the snowbank at the south end of the barn and shovel out the haymow door. Several bales of alfalfa were dragged to the stock cattle, huddled in bunches around the yard. Also, they had to shovel down into the south barn door to get cattle into the east side of the barn. With the help of Clark's cigarette lighter, the cows were able to find their way back to the stanchions. About 8:30 the men returned to Parmely's for supper. They were just finishing eating when Clark remembered a bunch of sheep with their eyes frozen shut; they could drift over the fence during the night.

If they could get them into a shed, they would thaw out by morning. At 9:30 Clark and the boys, who had been able to get most of their clothes dry, headed for Jensen's for the fourth time. It didn't take too long this time. The snow was shoveled out and the sheep driven in out of the blowing snow. About 10:30 they were back at Parmely's and Alan went to open the gates so Clark could get one more load of hay for his cattle.

Saturday night baths were quite an ordeal for the two families crowded into the Parmely farm home. The little ones went first, and by midnight everyone was bedded down. Even those on the floor didn't mind. It was much better than the feed alley in the barn. It was warm and everyone was ready to rest.

Sunday morning, Howard was feeling better and able to go with the boys to do chores. However, Curtis was not feeling well, and the thermometer revealed a temperature of 102 degrees. Kenny recalls, "It was hot in bed Saturday night, but Curt couldn't seem to get warm." Clark cleaned snow from his driveway so that they could get the pickup out, feed a few more of his cows and then headed across the pasture, approximately one and a half miles, to use the telephone at the Cronin sisters. He got in touch with R.E. A., his mother, and the sheriff, to report the situation that existed. Hand County sheriff, Bruce Hammill, was prompt to get action started. The Hand County snow equipment headed south to help dig out. The National Guard was alerted to collect and deliver food stuffs and clothing. By two o'clock, farmers and friends of the area were plowing their way through. Neighbors, including a group from Sunshine Bible Academy, followed the sheriff and road crew to the farm where, for the remainder of the afternoon, shoveling snow was the order of the day. Mr. Rostern, county highway superintendent, personally operated the big snow scoop that dug through the three large banks, ranging from 10 to 15 feet high, between the road and barn which served as shelter for the stricken family.

The words of Sheriff Hammill to Mrs. Jensen, as he checked at the Parmely home to see what could be done for Curt, still ring in the author's ears. "We can be thankful everyone is alive. Everything else can be replaced." A simple organization was set up; Mrs. Mary McCarthey is in charge of clothing collection, and Mrs. Jim Perrington responsible for food. Mr. and Mrs. Clark Parmely are caring for the family who were still in *their home. Ruby assured everyone that Jensens could stay as long as they wanted, but everyone knew it couldn't be forever.*

To lose one's home and personal belongings is a great loss at any time. To have it happen in the midst of the worst blizzard in South Dakota's history is almost too much to image. The help of friends means much at a time like this. Gifts of food and clothing are greatly appreciated. Considerable money will be needed to buy even the essentials to begin housekeeping again. The First National Bank has agreed to receive gifts designated for the Howard Jensen Emergency Fund.

Tears of appreciation welled up as the Jensens were given new Bibles by local Gideons, indicating the nature of the faith that carried them through the Blizzard of 1966. That same faith will provide a shelter as they re-gather their courage, reorganize their efforts, and continue on to face the storms of life.

About 3 p.m. Sunday, a neighbor, Richard Moser, headed west from Jensen's barn. He paused to examine several dead lambs protruding from the snow along the fence. Then, as he continued over a snowbank, his leg dropped into a soft spot in a drift. Pulling his leg out, he saw a lamb covered with snow. In a few minutes, a shovel had freed the sheep and he went scampering to join the others. You could tell he belonged to the Jensens. He wasn't complaining about what he had been through. He was happy to be alive and free![147]

Wessington, began as a water station for trains, aptly named Aqua, in 1880, is located in Beadle County. In 1882, the town was renamed, for the nearby Wessington Hills.

In 1960, 378 people called Wessington home.

On February 26, 1966, the Wessington Rural Fire Association learned a new fire truck with a 1,000 gallon tank would cost approximately $3,200. The cost of installing the water tank and transferring current equipment to the new truck would cost another $1,000. Exact specifications were drawn up by a committee. It was decided to request an additional $200. from the seven townships that were participating in the purchase.

Mr. and Mrs. Walter Palmer received word that their grandson, Raymond Conzemius, had been wounded in Viet Nam. PFC Conzemius, a U.S. Marine, was now aboard a hospital ship. Other local residents in the military included Dean V. Hedge, Doug Horn and Clifford Matthews.

There was some light rain late March 2, .05 inches were recorded.

The storm blew into Wessington around 9 p.m., March 3. Wessington received approximately .40 inch of precipitation.

Wind speeds reached about 60 mph, Friday morning. Blizzard conditions existed all day Friday and Friday night. On Friday and Saturday, another .89 inches of precipitation were recorded.

There was little activity in Wessington on Friday.

There was no mail deliveries on Friday and Saturday.

Some livestock was lost in the vicinity.

Talk about being away at the right time. Mr. and Mrs. Ward Radcliffe and John returned to Wessington on Sunday. They had been on a six week trip to southern California, Oregon and Washington. Ward's sister's, Amy of Hot Springs, South Dakota, and Rose of

Amarillo, Texas, accompanied the trio. They visited relatives and friends who used to live in the area. Some of the former residents included: Lyle Luschens, George Heilmans, Orval Swartz, Lee and Milt Hutchinson, Perry O'Neal, Art Boldt and Joe Bushongs.

The Howard Jensen family tragedy touched the hearts of local residents that included Gene Evans. Mrs. Jensen was Gene's sister. People donated cash, clothing, and furniture for the homeless family. Gene stored all the stuff, until the Jensens had another place to live in.

Huron was first settled in 1880. Marvin Hughitt, President of the Northwestern Railroad named the place after the Huron Indians of the Great Lakes.

Huron, the seat of Beadle County, was named for William Henry Harrison Beadle. A native of Wisconsin, Beadle was a Brigidier General in the Civil War, but is more famous for his role in the development of public education in the Dakotas. As territorial Superintendent of Public Instruction, from 1879 to 1885, he devised a financial plan with guarantees for the support of the common schools. It was incorporated into the Enabling Act of February 22, 1889, the Omnibus Bill that authorized statehood for North and South Dakota, Montana, and Washington. The origin of the school land system had its beginnings in 1785 when Congress passed a statute devoting section 16 in each township "for the maintenance of public schools within the said township." Aware of "school-land" corruptions in the past, Beadle doubled the amount of public lands, set selling conditions, and guaranteed the proceeds from impairment or loss by writing strict provisions.[148]

Huron had a population of 14,180 in 1960.

The Huron high school boys wrestling team had a great year, in dual meets they were 11-1. The grapplers won their regional tournament and finished fourth in state on February 26, 1966. Coach Ray Wellman squad was led by co-captains Nels Peterson and Tim Stahly. Stahly placed third in state while Peterson and George Havens took fourth place honors. Besides Peterson and Stahly, other regional crowns were won by Dale May, Steve Vosler, John Hanson, and Rod Thompson.

On February 27, Richard Petty, 28, won the Daytona 500 for the second time. The NASCAR event attracted a crowd of 87,840. Although rain cut the race short by five miles, a new speed record of 160 mph was set. The old record of 154 mph was set in 1964. From Randleman, North Carolina, Petty drove a 1966 Plymouth. Carl Yarborough, Timmonsville, South Carolina, finished second in a Ford. The third place driver was David Parson, Spartanburg, South Carolina, in a Dodge. In 1965, Petty stayed away from major NASCAR events because hemiheads, used in Plymouths and Dodges, were banned on the circuit.

The Minnesota Twins began spring training on February 27. The Twins and Dodgers played in the 1965 World Series. The first two games were at Metropolitan Stadium. The Twins beat Don Drysdale in the opener, 8 to 2. Then, they defeated Sandy Koufax, 5 to 1. The Dodgers won the next three games in Los Angeles. The Twins returned to Metropolitan Stadium and won game six, 5 to 1. The Met was packed with 50,596 screaming fans for game seven. Sandy Koufax took the mound for the Dodgers and the Twins started with Jim Kaat.

After the fourth inning, the Twins were down by two runs. In the fifth, the Twins had runners on first and second with one out.

Zoilo Versalles lined the ball sharply down the third-base line. It looked like a sure double, but Jim Gilliam, the Dodger's third baseman, dove for the ball and snared it. He scrambled to his feet and forced the runner out at third. The next batter for the Twins grounded out. Harmon Killibrew hit a single with one out in the last of the ninth, but Kaufax struck out Earl Batty and Bobby Allison to end the game. Koufax, one of the greatest left-handed pitchers in baseball history, had pitched a three-hit shutout with ten strikeouts on just two days rest. In 1966, the Twins had two promising rookies, Cesar Tovar and Rod Carew, trying to make the team in spring training.

Admiral Chester Nimitz, commander of naval forces in the Pacific Theater in World War II, died on February 28, 1966.

Local boxing fans hoped see the upcoming heavyweight title fight between Cassius Clay and Ernie Terrell fight at Huron. Promoters in Huron placed a bid for the fight with Main Bout Inc., owner of the closed circuit television rights after they turned down Chicago's offer.

On March 1, the Huron Tigers high school boys basketball team lost to the Watertown Arrows, 67 to 63.

On March 2, Robert A. Wallace, assistant Secretary of Treasury, announced the new President John F. Kennedy half dollars pieces would contain 40 percent silver. The original half dollars, were 90 percent silver. Most of the original coins that came out in 1964 had disappeared from circulation. Wallace believed they had become mementoes of the late President.

The *Daily Plainsman* mentioned the possibility of bad weather on March 2. The article said:

Heavy Snow May Spread Over Region

March came in like a lamb, but don't let that fool you. He was actually a lion in disguise. Soon after the sweet little thing arrived, the weathermen issued an urgent bulletin–stockmen beware a storm center is moving into the state from the southwest bringing with it the possibility of heavy snowfall.

Scattered reports of snow have already come in from various parts of South Dakota today and its expected to spread over the entire state during the day.

In central South Dakota the forecasts calls for considerable cloudiness with occasional rain or snow through Thursday. And if that's not enough there will also be a strong northeasterly winds today and tonight, gusting up to 40 mph.[149]

On March 2, Huron recorded a high of 39 degrees. It started to drizzle about 3:30 p.m. The mist turned to a light rain, an hour later. For most of the day, winds were around 30 mph. That night, it rain hard between 10:00 and 10:30. The precipitation tapered off around midnight. The official low at the airport was 35 degrees.

The blizzard in Dakotas dominated the front page of the *Plainsman* on March 3. The leading headline said, **"Lion-Type Blizzard Hits Much of State."** Secondary headlines declared **"3 Missing, Train Stopped by Storm; Winds, Ice, Cause CSD Blackouts."** It was called a **"History Book Blizzard."**

The weather forecast for Huron and Vicinity read: "Cloudy with strong northwesterly winds and intermittent snow tonight. Clearing Friday. Colder tonight and Friday, low temperatures upper teens; high Friday mid 20s.

On March 3, local residents had to pay a penny more for milk. The price of a quart of milk was now 25 cents and a half gallon of milk was raised to 46 cents. Stores in Huron increased their prices, after stores in Sioux Falls hiked their prices. It was first price increase in seven years.

Grocery ads for the O.P. Skaggs Food Store, located on the corner of 3rd Street S.E., appeared in the *Plainsman*. The following specials were advertised:

Ice cream	one half gallon	69 cents
Oranges	one dozen	69 cents
Tomatoes	pound	19 cents
Bananas	pound	10 cents
Potatoes	ten pounds	29 cents
Carrots	two pounds	21 cents
Ground Beef	pound	49 cents
Chuck Roast	pound	49 cents
Bacon	pound	79 cents
Coffee	three pound can	1.98

On March 3, Huron's high of 41 degrees came in the morning. The winds were strong and the skies were cloudy.

Light snow began coming down in Huron at 8:47 p.m. Shortly afterwards, the snow became heavy. For Huron, that was the beginning of the blizzard.

The Region 4 Basketball Tournament ended about an hour later. Tournament and school officials had been constantly checking the weather. De Smet, Bryant, and Doland and their fans left Huron.

Travel in and out of Huron came to a stop, late Thursday night. Flights were canceled and buses were grounded. There was no rail service. Motorists quickly filled the hotels and motels.

Friday morning, William Wells and Eugene Fowler, walked to work. Wells, the Huron weather bureau chief, and Fowler, assistant weather observer, left for the airport, three miles out of Huron, at 6:00. They arrived at 7:30.

Wells told a *Plainsman* reporter, "they saw dozens of cars stalled or waiting to get through the snarled traffic, particularly along Dakota Avenue." Peering out of an airport window, he said, "It looks like the dickens out here." Wells gave the reporter the latest forecast and added, "Let's just say things are slightly ungood outside."

The weathermen were not the only ones to make it to work at the airport on March 4. Glenn Huset and Robert Tillery, FAA employees, drove out to the airport. Don Friese, the airport manager, was there bright and early. "He should be," Wells said, "he lives out here."[151]

The storm delayed the publication of the *Plainsman* on Friday. With the holdup, the paper carried the latest news of the blizzard. Across eight columns the top headline read, **"State Shuts Down In Severe Blizzard."** Other key headlines, **"State Shuddering Under Big Storm,"** and **"Weather Bureau Terms Blizzard One of Worst."** The entire front page was devoted to the blizzard.

William Wells declared, "this to be one of the worst storms on record as the wind reached 56 miles per hour this morning." Wells indicated that blizzards in 1962 and 1965 had heavier snowfalls, but the winds were not as strong as in this one. He indicated this storm was the first statewide blizzard in the 1965-66 winter.

Early on March 4, the Weather Bureau revised its storm warnings. Instead of "a blizzard warning," it was upgraded to "a severe blizzard warning." Another 4 to 6 inches of snow was expected before the storm letup on Saturday.152

On Friday, Huron experienced winds between 35 and 55 mph. The highest recorded gust was 67 mph. By noon, Huron had received 6 inches of snow. The high for the day was 22 degrees, and Friday night's low was 10.

Friday morning, Mrs. Robert Glowac checked the temperature of her two-year old son, Bobby. The reading on the thermometer was 104 degrees. She promptly called her husband, a pharmacist at Osco Drug. They discussed Bobby's high fever.

Robert Glowac contacted the police at 9:18. The police told the pharmacist to get the medicine ready, and they would have someone pick it up. They had a emergency vehicle and driver standing by for such calls.

Howard Bill, owner-manager of Eastside Cities Service, had volunteered to drive his four-wheel drive jeep on emergency runs. Bill picked up the antibiotics at the drugstore and headed out in the blinding snowstorm.

Just like Howard Bill, J.L. Groves was on another emergency run for the police. Both drivers had white four-wheel drive pickups.

Howard Bill turned a corner and started down the street. All of a sudden, Bill jerked his steering wheel as a vehicle barreled down on him. The other vehicle turned away, just as fast to avoid a crash.

It was just "in the nick of time."

They recognized one another, after their blood pressure had returned to normal. Bill and Groves were amateur radio fans and both vehicles had CB radios. Bill picked up his mike. He radioed a quick, "I'm sorry," to Groves. Likewise, Groves relayed his apologies. Bill and Groves resumed their mercy runs. Afterwards, "The white trucks were almost invisible," said Bill. "The whole town was white and neither of us saw–or expected–the other."153

Ray Keelin, another volunteer, helped out in the blizzard in the same way. Archie French and Gary Phillips helped Bill on his runs. Throughout the storm, they delivered prescriptions, picked up doctors and nurses, and even pushed a police car back to the station.

A couple from Canada had registered at one motel. There, the manager humorously said, "He didn't know if they came on their own or had been blown in."

The Traveler Motel had a Kansas man who was trying to get to Valley City, North Dakota, for the Winter Show. The manager jokingly said, "But I guess he got his show here."154

Windows in the Ben Franklin and J. C. Penney stores were blown out Friday morning. Damages for the Ben Franklin store was estimated at "hundreds of dollars." For Penney's, the loss was placed at about $1,000.

The Farmers and Merchants Bank time-temperature sign was destroyed, when its moorings gave way to the high winds. Their losses were around $9,000.00.

On Friday morning, Larry Rogers went to pick up his son Randy, 15, who worked at the Double II Cafe. He drove cautiously because visibility was bad even in town. Rogers thought he hit something on Third Street. He went a little further and stopped at a gas station to take a look. Rogers peaked under his car. He saw the head of a women and another part of her body in a white coat. Rogers had a fright. What was he going to do? A hard look under the vehicle revealed the woman to be a mannequin. It had blown out of J. C. Penny's store window. Rogers pulled the rest of the dummy out from under the car. Then, he picked up his son.

The Huron weathermen felt the sting of the blizzard every time they went outside to read the thermometers. Wells and Fowler knew long before their shift ended, they would not be going home Friday night.

The power failed at the airport Friday at 4:45. They contacted an airplane captain and received permission to grab all the blankets and pillows out of a passenger plane.

They started up an emergency generator. With it running, the weather bureau instruments continued to work. The generator provided another important service, it kept their coffee pot brewing.

Wells and Fowler had brought dried soup mix when they came to work, Friday morning. The men ate the soup, along with left-over rolls.

Saturday morning at 4:00, the power came back on at the airport. Fowler said, "it got a wee bit chilly out here."

Robert E. Wilkens, manager of Northwestern Public Service Company, indicated part of southwest Huron lost power for a short time on Friday afternoon. Also, there was a power outage in north Huron, Friday evening. A city snowplow opened paths to the troubled spots. The power company emergency team consisted of twelve linemen and four or five members from the office. They restored power to most residents of north Huron within three hours. Power was restored to some homes around midnight and to others on Saturday morning.

Wilkens reported that Iroquois, Cavour, and Yale lost electricity at the height of the storm on Friday. Power was restored to those places within four hours of the outages.

William Van Tassel, manager of Northwestern Bell Telephone Company, informed the public that most of their troubles were caused by swinging lines. Other storm damages included a broken axle on two line trucks and a burnt out generator on the aerial bucket truck.

The waning hours of the storm in Huron came Saturday afternoon. The storm had deposited 13.7 inches of snow and a low reading of 10 degrees.

Other notable blizzards in Huron's past included storms on March 7, 1950, and March 2-3, 1951. The first one brought 9.7 inches of snow, winds up to 62 mph, and low reading of 3 above. The second one came with 8.4 inches of snow, wind gusts up to 40 mph, and a temperature reading of 2 degrees below zero.

The digging out phase started Saturday afternoon. Norman Ambrosius, city street commissioner, had crews working twelve hour shifts. Arrangements were made with private contractors for snow removal. Also, machines and equipment operators from Huron National Guard, 153rd Engineer Battalion, were thrown into the campaign. The following men were activated on Saturday: Larry T. Teuber, Gordon T. Lanam, Verlyn J. Wipf, Leroy Atkins, George Soule and Gilbert Magge. They drove two front-end loaders, a bulldozer and a three-quarter ton truck.

Ambrosius reported that all streets in Huron were opened by Sunday night. On Monday, trucks started hauling tons of snow to a four-block dump site west of Ravine Lake.

County highway crews had opened all county roads by Sunday night, according to M. R. Cheeseman, county highway superintendent. The biggest drifts, up to 14 feet high, were in the Lake Byron area.

Sunday night, Ambrosius released the private contractors who worked in Huron.

On Monday, Lt. Col. James R. Hydahl, commander of the 153rd Engineer Battalion, announced that the six soldiers left Huron to work in the Selby area.

Pheasant losses were considered light in Beadle County.

On March 10, the board of education approved construction contracts for the new Huron Senior High School. Work was scheduled to begin on April 1. The main contractors were Jacobson Construction Company, Lawson Plumbing and Heating, Lothrop Electric, all of Huron, and Schmit Plumbing and Sheet Metal, Pierre. The total amount of contracts awarded was $1,831,268.

On March 13, local boxing fans learned that Classius Clay-Ernie Terrell heavyweight fight would not be in Huron. As things turned out, Clay fought George Chuvalo on March 29 at Toronto. Clay won the fight and met Terrell later in 1967.

In other sport news that day, Tony Oliva, two time batting champion of the American League in his first two years in the big leagues, ended his holdout with the Minnesota Twins. Oliva received $18,000.00 in 1965. Although terms were not disclosed, Oliva signed for about $30,000.00 in 1966. This left Jim (Mudcat) Grant as the only holdout left. Grant wanted $41,000, he had made $21,000.00 in 1965.

De Smet, seat of Kingsbury County, was named for Father Pierre Jean DeSmet (1801-1873), "Apostle of the Indians." He was an Jesuit missionary from Belgium, explorer and pioneer. From 1848 to his death, he devoted much of his missionary efforts to the Sioux of South Dakota. The Sioux named their friend, "Black Robe."

The Northwestern Railroad went through De Smet in 1880, the year it was platted. Three years later, the town was incorporated.

A couple, married in De Smet, became famous. Here's the public notice of their wedding:

MARRIED

at the residence of the officiating clergyman, Rev. E. Brown, August 25, 1885, Almanzo J. Wilder and Miss Laura E. Ingalls, both of DeSmet. Both the contracting parties are well and favorably known in DeSmet, both having located here before there was a town and they will start in their new career with the best wishes of all. May their pathway be ever bright with no clouds to dim the sunshine of their happiness is the wish of the NEWS.[155]

In 1932, Laura Ingalls Wilder published her first book, *Little House in the Big Woods*. She wrote other "Little House" books. Almanzo passed away in 1949, and Laura's death came in 1957.

On September 11, 1974, *Little House on the Prairie* debuted on NBC stations, staring Michael Landon, Karen Grassle, Melissa Gilbert and Melissa Sue Anderson.

Another famous person from De Smet was Harvey Dunn.

In 1960, the population of the town was placed at 1,324.

In late February 1966, the De Smet Bulldogs captured the District 15 championship with victories over, Iroquois 74 to 49, Tulare 65 to 57, and Hitchcock 71 to 63. Leading scorers for the Bulldogs included Doyle Spader, Steven Kracht and Arlen Wallum. Their head coach was Don McCaskell.

On March 2, in the Region 4 Championship Tournament in Huron, De Smet faced the District 14 champion, the Bryant Scotties. The Scotties shot the lights out in the fourth and won the game, 66 to 47.

The next day, De Smet lost the consolation game to Highmore.

The basketball team and their fans made it home just in time. On Thursday, the weather in De Smet was mixed. Although the winds were blustery, the town had a high of 40 degrees.

The De Smet News said, "The storm experienced in this area was the weakened tail of what is considered the worst storm of recorded history in northern South Dakota and in North Dakota. "The end of the blizzard came late Saturday afternoon.156

On Friday, the high was 33 degrees and 1.06 inches of precipitation fell. On Saturday the mercury rose to 22 degrees and another .20 inches of precipitation was recorded. Overall, De Smet received a total of 7 inches of snow. Maximum wind gusts ranged between 60 and 70 mph.

Kingsbury County experienced some power outages. Electricity was restored to Iroquois after a Northwest Public Service Company employee redirected the power supply. A number of farms in the county lost their electricity as well. Roland Anderson, manager for Kingsbury Electric Co-operative, sent men out twice to restore power to some farms.

County and state snowplows escorted power company trucks, carrying an emergency power plant, for the Johnson Home at the country farm. By the time they got there, the power was back on.

On Saturday, there was medical emergency at the Leslie Ellingson farm, south and east of the Piriet school on U.S. Highway 14 east of De Smet. They took Boyd, a six-month old baby, with influenza to the hospital.

No mail went on Friday and Saturday, but some came in on Sunday. William Coughlin opened the post office on Sunday morning. De Smet's two rural mail carriers had a hectic day on Monday.

The Wullum's lost five head of cattle.

In 1966, South Dakota had three rendering plants, they were located at De Smet, Watertown and Sioux Falls. Vern Belzer, manager of the De Smet Rendering Company, indicated the number of cattle coming in jumped sharply on March 9. Belzer said:

> We have 200 head of cows and an unknown number of calves and sheep piled up. I imagine in a couple of days we will have 500-600 head waiting for processing.
>
> At first the livestock losses didn't seem too heavy, but now it seems to be worse than what was expected–about what the newspapers have indicated.[157]

The following story about the 1966 blizzard was written by Mrs. James Combs, a local resident. Mrs. James Combs wrote:

What's It Like?

> It's like hearing on the radio for over a day that a terrible blizzard is raging in the western part of the state and will hit where you live, but when it doesn't come as soon as the forecast says, deciding it is going to miss us.
>
> It's going to bed one night with it real nice outside, and a half hour later hearing the blizzard hit with the horrible wind. It's wondering if all the kids and adults who had gone to Huron for the Regional basketball game will make it home safe, and being thankful it was the night before that the band had to play there, and that your son is safe at home tonight.
>
> It's remembering that last night it rained "cats and dogs", with thunder

and lightning-even some hail-and how glad you were to see those buses drive up to the school house at eleven o'clock after waiting a half hour for them to come with the safe return of your boy.

It's marveling that now just 24 hours later you're in a blizzard that later is called "the worst in history". It's wondering how you could have been so stupid as to not get food in town this afternoon when you were there, instead of thinking "I'll do my weekly shopping on my usual day."

It's wishing the neighborhood men could have located that shotgun pellet, that is probably causing your phone to be dead for two days now. It's wishing your husband was home with you and the three children, instead of gone to Arizona to be with his parents for their golden wedding anniversary.

It's getting up the next morning and shutting off the upstairs and tacking a blanket over the north door to help keep out the 60-to-70 mile-per-hour wind that goes right through your house, which sits in the open with no protection.

It's checking again to be sure there is enough fuel oil and coal to last a week if necessary, but knowing the one box of cobs to start the kitchen range is going to be used very carefully-wishing the cobs and the cattle were at this place instead of a mile and a half away and recognizing it may get colder later on, so instead of using precious cobs to start the fire now, to get by as long as we can with just the oil stove in the living room.

It's bundling up warm and staying in the one room to keep warm. It's realizing by noon you have to start the kitchen stove. It's having the suction caused by opening the south door blow the living room stove door open and having soot fly all over. It's being smart enough after that when it is necessary to carry in more oil for the stove, to hold the stove door shut while the kitchen door is open, but still having smoke roar out of the kitchen stove from the suction.

It's rationing out what little milk you have to your boy, who is taking pills for a sore throat, these to be taken with a glass of milk. It's ice frozen to your son's eyelashes after being outside for just a few minutes for oil, making him realize what you said about not trying to get down to the other place to take care of the cattle is pretty wise after all. It's explaining to three kids that if the cattle die it doesn't matter; we won't risk our lives for cattle. It's comforting a little girl who is sobbing she doesn't want her kitty to die.

It's hearing the radio messages: "If anyone knows the whereabouts of these people please call this number; they were last seen so many hours ago". It's praying over and over for protection from our Heavenly Father.

It's going to the phone dozens of times and knowing it won't work but picking it up anyway and hearing the dead silence.

It's looking through the peep holes in the windows and seeing the drifts blow higher and higher.

It's the realization that if one of the children gets sick there is nothing you can do. It's peeping out at a car just a week old and knowing it can't help you in this blizzard. It's the knowledge that modern man for all its advances is utterly dependent on God.

It's deciding whether to take a bed apart and move it into the living room with the cot and davenport–thereby being able to shut off the northwest bedroom to help keep warm. It's looking over the basement for bits of wood to burn when the cobs run out.

It's the children's skeptical look when you tell them people have burned furniture to keep warm. It's a little girl saying "I wish my daddy was here", and a mother who probably wished it more than the little girl, but assuring her we would be all right.

It's nerves as taut as a rubber band stretched tight. It's children getting yelled at for no reason. It's the electricity going off at four-thirty and immediately wondering how you could have been so stupid as to sit there all that time and not have run water into your pans just in case it did go off–that all the water you have is what little is left in the electric pressure pump. It's kids being awfully thirsty all of a sudden and knowing that now you must ration the water. It's being sure the electricity will be off the duration of the storm.

It's lining up the old oil lamp and candles and getting supper eaten before it gets dark. It's realizing how much the radio meant to you. It's knowing the refrigerator and freezer doors must not be opened any oftener than necessary.

It's being thankful our heat isn't dependent on electricity, either by the heat itself or for a blower on a oil or gas furnace. It's a son who says when our drinking water is gone we can melt snow.

It's being so happy when at six-thirty just as it is getting dark the electricity suddenly comes back on. It's the comforting voice on the radio and the music that helps to calm the nerves. It's the pajama-clad little girl "dancing" to the music and the boys who laugh at her antics. It's the precious lights to see by.

It's a boy roaring with laughter at the radio announcer's words of "if you go outside and look up you won't see anything; if you look around you won't see anything, but if you look down you might see your feet." It's a mother who thinks its too true to be funny.

It's the laying awake for hours in the middle of the night and listening to the fury of the storm and the mournful wail the windmill head makes as it turns in the wind. It's being thankful the children are young enough to sleep through it.

It's your boy telling you the next day that as soon as the wind goes down he is going to walk to the other place to take care of the cattle, and the hard time you have convincing him that we are all staying right here until someone comes to us. It's assuring them that as soon as possible someone will come to check on us. It's knowing that relatives and friends are worried about us and wondering if I'd be dumb enough to try to get to the cattle. It's wondering if your husband knows what is going on here and if he is wondering the same thing, out there in the land of sunshine.

It's the children that want to go out to play as soon as he wind goes down to about 30 miles per hour. It's their way of saying "I'm tired of being cooped up in the house."

It's the sound of something late in the afternoon and looking to see the truck coming in the yard and the happy shouts of us all "Someone's here; someone here!" It's the sight of your brother-in-law and his friend whom you just met several days before, who had to go by tractor to town from his place–and the milk and bread they brought from their own supply cause there wasn't any left in the stores. It's the never being so glad to see anyone in your life. It's the good news that the road is open from here to town.

It's the experienced help of two men and the 12-and-14-year-old boys to dig the snow away from the front of the barn door so the cattle could get out to eat and drink. It's the men sweeping out as much of the snow as possible from the car engine and telling us to let it run for at least a half hour to melt off most of the rest of it, so we could go back to the other place after awhile to shut off the water for the cattle. It was the discovery on checking the fuel gauge on the car after they had gone. We would have to go to town for gas for the car. It was the getting out and seeing all the snowdrifts every place else.

It was calling my husband from town, and instead of asking him to cut his vacation short by a day, telling him to.

It was the only being able to say "It's a mess" when he asked what it is like. It was a surprise that he knew nothing of the storm until his sister called that morning to tell him she would fly there the next morning if the wind went down, to be with the folks for their celebration.

It was wondering if our part of the nation was so unimportant that the blizzard didn't make national news or if they were so busy visiting they hadn't even turned on the news. It was hoping later he would understand my curtness on the phone and realize it had been an ordeal, those days of blizzard.

It was waking up the third morning to no wind, and knowing it was all over. It was the reports on the radio of the storm causing deaths. It was nerves that went limp as a wet flag. It was the silly tears that flowed when it was all over and we were all right.

This and so much more was the blizzard of '66. The blizzard that this mother and three children will never forget.[158]

Brookings was platted in 1879. Before the townsite was laid out, it was known as Ada. W. H. Sinner, an early settler, suggested the new town be called Brookings, to honor Judge Wilmont W. Brookings. A native of Maine, Judge Brookings (1833-1907), was a lawyer, a member of the territorial legislature of 1863 and associate justice of the Territorial Supreme Court from 1869 to 1873. He promoted the Southern Dakota Railroad, the first railroad in South Dakota. Brookings directed the building of the Minnesota Wagon Road, a United States military wagon road across South Dakota from the Minnesota border to Fort Pierre to Crook Creek Agency in Montana. He was a member of the Constitutional Conventions of 1883 and 1885. Brookings published the *Sioux Falls Leader* from 1883 to 1885. Also, he built a canning factory and linen mills.

In 1879, the Northwestern extended its line from the Minnesota state line to Volga, located six miles west of Brookings. The Northwestern connected Watertown and Brookings in 1880. That year, the east-west extension between Volga to Pierre was built.

In 1881, Dakota Territorial legislature designated Brookings as the site for an agricultural college. The legislature appropriated $25,000 to establish the college in 1883. In September, 1884, the State College of Agriculture and Mechanic Arts (to be known later as South Dakota State University) held their first classes. South Dakota's agricultural experiment station and agricultural extension service are here.

Hobo Day, a SDSU football homecoming theme, was held for the first time in 1912. Since then, it has became an annual tradition for homecoming weekend.

In 1929, SDSU's campus landmark structure, the Campanile, was built. It was a gift of Charles Coughlin, a graduate of the school in 1909.

South Dakota Art Museum is located in Brookings. One of the artists featured is Harvey Dunn (1884-1952) who grew up near Redstone Creek south of Manchester in Kingsbury County. Like Norman Rockwell, Dunn was a famed illustrator for the *Saturday Evening Post* and other major magazines.

"The prettiest 70 acres in South Dakota," are located in Brookings. That's what people have said about the McCrory Gardens. They were named for Sam McCrory, former head of the horticulture department at SDSU.

Brookings, the seat of Brookings County, had a population total of 10,558 in the 1960 census.

On February 12, 1966, Army Sp5 Duane A. Smith was assigned to the 568th Medical Company in Vietnam. Smith graduated from Elkton High School in 1961. He attended SDSU, before joining the army in October 1962.

SDSU announced that the school had set a new enrollment record (4,393 students) in the spring of 1966.

On March 1, 1966, Brookings recorded a high of 47 degrees. The next day, the thermometer rose to 40.

On March 3, the weather in Brookings remained nice. The high for the day was 41. According to the weather forecasts, the storm would move into the eastern South Dakota, late Thursday night or early Friday morning.

Temperatures in Brookings dropped slowly on Thursday. The winds picked up, but what little snow that was left had a hard shell. Late in the day, snow fell. There was a last minute rush to get food, cigarettes and alcohol.

The worst blizzard to hit Brookings in many years developed in the dark of the night. W.A. McWilliams, local weather observer, estimated 10 to 12 inches of snow fell in the vicinity, and winds gusts reached 55 mph on Friday. The precipitation for March 4 amounted to 1.50 inches.

Snow fell again on Saturday. The winds finally died down, late in the day. As the skies cleared, colder temperatures settled in. McWilliams estimated 2.75 inches of precipitation fell between Thursday night and Saturday night. Overall, Brookings received about 20 inches of snow.

There was no school in Brookings County on Friday. Classes were called off for SDSU students. Local radio station, KBRK, repeated public announcements.

Businesses in Brookings closed their doors at noon on Friday.

North Central Airlines canceled its flights in and out of Brookings on Friday and Saturday morning.

On Friday and Saturday morning, there was no bus service.

No rural mail deliveries were made on Friday and Saturday. Likewise, mail from out of town did not arrived in Brookings on those days.

The storm delayed the publication of the *Brookings Register*.

At the request of Brookings Police Chief, Douglas Filholm, city street crews kept the four main traffic arteries in town open during the blizzard. They plowed paths on Main and Medary Avenues (north and south) and Sixth and Third (east and west).

Brookings County Sheriff Edwin Cunningham reported his office was "quiet" during the storm.

The North Central Conference Wresting Tournament was scheduled for March 4-5 at the SDSU gymnasium. Because of the weather, teams from the University of North Dakota, North Dakota State, and Morningside did not show. That left four teams, South Dakota State, University of South Dakota, Augustana, and State College of Iowa, to battle for the title. The tournament was rescheduled for Saturday afternoon and Saturday night.

State College of Iowa captured the first NCC wresting title in 1964. South Dakota State claimed the championship in 1965. On March 5, SDSU added another championship banner for Coach Warren Williamson.

In an public announcement on March 5, 1966, Delbert Bjordahl, the owner and manager of a proposed building project in Brookings said, "Construction of a new 68-unit apartment complex in northwest Brookings is scheduled to get underway as soon as weather permits, with some of the units ready for occupancy in the fall." He said the complex would be called Westgate Apartments. Bjordahl added, "It will help fill the housing needs of SDSU and the city of Brookings."[159]

Gettysburg, Gettysburg Air Station, Lebanon, Gorman, Tolstoy, Hoven Onaka and Faulkton

Gettysburg, the seat of Potter County, was platted in 1884. It was settled by Civil War veterans of the Union army. The town was named for the famous Battle of Gettysburg, fought on July, 1-3, 1863. The Northwestern Railroad arrived here in 1887.

Gettysburg had 1,950 residents in 1960.

The Iversen Brothers had a large cattle operation near Gettysburg. Clarence and Elmer Iversen had a young calf that refused to drink its milk. Trying what had worked in the past, Clarence put his hand in the milk and then stuck his hand in the calf's mouth to get it interested in drinking. The calf bit Clarence's hand. Elmer tried the same thing, but the calf was not interested in drinking. Elmer's hand was scratched at the time. A couple of days later, the Iversen's sold the troublesome calf.

Somebody near Highmore bought the calf. The calf died, soon afterwards. The veterinarian sent in a sample of the head to be tested. As it turned out, the calf had rabies. Clarence and Elmer Iversen needed medical attention in February 1966.

For six weeks in 1966, Gettysburg High School had a foreign exchange teacher from Lucerne, Switzerland. Miss Elisabeth Stockly taught German. While in Gettysburg, she stayed with Mr. and Mrs. Coe Frankhauser.

On March 2, Miss Stockly was in Eagle Butte. She talked about Switzerland and showed slides of her country. By the time Miss Stockly had reached Gettysburg, the weather had turned nasty.

Next couple of days, Miss Stockly made a documentary tape of the blizzard for her Swiss students. She had many slides of the snowbanks in Gettysburg.

The following story was written by Gerald Larson, mechanical superintendent for the *Potter County News*. His commentary was entitled "Larsony." Jerry Larson wrote:

Hello–

How about that?

The snow, I mean.

I do hope that all of you in the snow area were able to be in, out of the blizzard. And for you people out of the territory, former residents who left here, you may have seen as much snow here in Gettysburg when you lived here, but you never saw it come as it did. I have talked to seven old timers and found none who could remember anything like it. As far as I am concerned, once in a lifetime was enough.

Boy how we "crowed" when the schools, and nearly everything else from Mobridge north to Bismarck and farther yet, were all closed up because of a snow storm on Thursday. We had some snow Wednesday evening and Thursday dawned nice and clear. The radio reported zero visibility at Mobridge and Aberdeen, but we could even have school. I laughed at the radio announcer who told all the kids in their town to send "sympathy cards" to the Gettysburg kids because they had to attend.

So Thursday morning I shoveled off the walk which had a few good size drifts in it, and was silently congratulating ourselves for having missed the "big blow." But there was something in the air–rumors–a terrific storm at Philip–winds at 60 miles–Mobridge with 20 inches already on the level. It was heading for Gettysburg. It was a big one–etc. So most people headed for home.

And it came–with a vengeance. Thursday night I could just see across the street–and by Friday morning I couldn't even see my car which was only about 15 feet from my front door. The snow did not come down–it went across–at about a line perfectly horizontal to the ground, pushed by a veritable hurricane of wind. And the drifts were already getting huge.

I decided to check on my neighbors, Lil Adams, in the trailor next door and Bill on the corner. Wow–Lil had a drift about two-thirds of the way up her door–shoveled enough to be able to knock–she was happy to see me–I assured her I would get her out if she got snowed in–but I was only joking– I thought.

And then to work–for a while–and then the power went off. Which was wasn't too unexpected because it usually does once or twice during a storm, for at least a few minutes. This was at 10:30–by 1:30 it was starting to get cold in the house. And the radio said that MDU denied any large outage of power–just a few local outages. However, by 4:00 they were admitting that practically everywhere from Gettysburg north into North Dakota was out, and they could do nothing until the storm subsided–sometime Saturday morning. So we had a half of a day and a full night to look forward to without electricity. Not a pleasant thought with a 60-70 mile an hour wind and no visibility outside. And no heat inside.

But we could cook. And have hot coffee–hung a blanket in the doorway to the back of the trailer to keep the heat up front–and used the oven to furnish heat–(which I afterwards found was quite common practice) managed to keep it about 55 so was thankful that we could do this–and then the fire went out. I couldn't believe my tank would be empty–but had to go outside to see. My tank was buried under six feet of snow and believe me, I had a hectic time, but finally got it dug out and it was empty. Thankfully, I had a small tank for emergency use, but it had been used several times so I had no idea how much gas was in it. But I had to change over to it. So we would burn the oven for half an hour until it got to about 58 and then shut it off until it got too cold for comfort. Finally went to bed about 11 to conserve gas. And still no let-up–maybe a little, because I could see my car, but not much farther. Got up at 1:30 to light the oven for a while–it was 40 so decided to turn on a faucet to keep the pipes from freezing. Up again at 5 and this time it was 36 and about this time I started to get a little worried. But on looking out the front window I could see the News office so I took heart.

By this time we had been in the storm for almost 36 hours, 18 of it without no electricity. Up again at 7 and decided to check on Lil and Bill again. And found an oddity–Bill's back door had no snow near it at all–and Lil's door, only 25 feet or so away, was completely out of sight. A drift about 9 feet high and 10 wide and all across the yard had her completely buried. So I dug her out. She was happy to see me, and the feeling was mutual.

By now the storm had subsided– and a few heads were starting to pop up around town. And then my spare bottle of gas went dry. And the streets were all drifted in–what a mess of snow. I have never seen the likes of it. But finally, with the assistance of Alie Hericks, managed to get to the station for a new bottle–and by the time I had it connected the power came on. Great day in the morning.

And I must take back any aspersions I have cast at our city because they moved snow and opened streets like I never believed they could. By Monday morning main street looked almost normal. My hat is off to the whole crew for a job being well done.[160]

According to William R. Owens, editor and publisher, in the history of *Potter County News* there has been only one issue that devoted the entire front page to one subject and dominated several other pages. The historic issue was published on March 10, 1966. The top headline said, **"All Emerge from Killer Storm Cold but Undaunted."** Owens reported that 100 extra copies were printed and it was not enough.

The *Potter County News* said:

Gettysburg and Potter county weathered a massive three day blizzard apparently without losing a human life, but with a 24 hour power shortage.

Winds up to 100 miles an hour accompanied 1.94 inches of moisture in 17 1/2 inches of snow.

The storm began Wednesday evening of last week, let up Thursday, and hit with increased fury that evening. It raged all night, with the power supply beginning to flicker Friday morning, going out shortly before noon for a 24-hour period.

The wind and snow gradually Friday night, and by Saturday noon people were able to be out and moving around.

Walt Hagenlock estimated the snowfall at 17 1/2 inches, gauged from the 1.94 inches of melted moisture. He estimated drifts up to 12 feet high.

Temperatures did not reach below zero until after the storm had sub-sided. The thermometer was 19 above on Thursday, 2 above on Friday, and zero on Saturday. Sunday and Monday it reached to six degrees below zero in the storm's aftermath.

Without electricity to trigger thermostats, and with the killer storm raging outside Friday and during the night many residents were caught without heat.[161]

The Radar Station there clocked wind gusts over 100 mph. At one time, the winds were up to 130 mph. The national wire services picked up the story, and Gettysburg was pinpointed on the national map.

The Gettysburg Fire Department was manned during the blizzard. After the power went out, during the blizzard, Leonard Koch, city policeman, dug out Mrs. Burt Schutterle and moved her to the Alfred Nagel residence.

Bud Roesler called Sheriff Eldon Umiker, Friday afternoon at 3:30. His wife was expecting and needed to be taken to the hospital. The phones went dead shortly afterwards, so Sheriff Umiker walked to the home of County Highway Superintendent, Ed Packard.

The two men walked to the county shed to get a snowplow. They plowed a path to the hospital and then to the Roeslers house.

Sheriff Umiker stood outside on the fender of the plow and acted as a lookout. They got Mrs. Roesler to the hospital about 9:50, that night. (Sunday afternoon, she had a baby girl. The couple named her Pammv Staria.)

Saturday morning, the sheriff received word that Mrs. Ronnie Tanner was very sick. Packard and Sheriff Umiker departed in the county's loader-snowplow. About three miles west of Gettysburg, the plow blew a tire.

Clifford Warwick and Jim Kane started out in a truck plow. Packard and Sheriff Umiker followed in a pickup. Ollie Hericks and Don Soper were behind them. Soper had his "weasel," a tracked snow vehicle, loaded on Hericks' truck.

Meanwhile, Bob Beach, a state snowplow operator had been working close to the Tanner place. He called Pierre and received permission to make a detour to Tanner farm.

The Gettysburg rescue party reached the Tanners. They learned the snowplow had just taken Mrs. Tanner to the hospital.

During the storm Don Soper's "weasel" was kept busy. Northwestern Bell used it for a trip to Seneca. Cam Wal Electric used the snow tracked vehicle for a run to Agar.

The hotels and motels in Gettysburg sheltered 140 people, 57 at Hotel Windsor, 38 at Evelyn's Motel, 35 at the Trail Motel and 11 at the Sage Motel. Some guests at the Sage Motel could not get out of their rooms and had to be helped out through windows.

Those at the Windsor ate well, thanks to the generosity of the Flanery meat truck driver. Evelyn's guests did not suffer in the power outage because of an old range in the kitchen and an old Warm Morning coal stove in the basement. The motel also had a fireplace and plenty of wood.

Evelyn heard a strange sound, outside of the motel. Thinking, someone trying to get to the office from the cabins, Evelyn stepped out with a bright flashlight. Soon, a small dog showed up at her doorsteps.

One of Potter County's biggest snowbanks was at the Chalmer Hottman farm, located fourteen miles east of Gettysburg. The drift was estimated at 900 feet long, 14 to 20 feet high. A car and two tractors were completely buried in it.

Gettysburg residents had plenty of water during the power outage. Mayor Carl Schiefelbein said the city had two tanks that held 600,000 gallons of water in storage.

The family of Alfred G. (Bud) Collins had headaches and stomach pains, Friday morning. They felt better, later in the day. They had other worries, their power was out.

On Saturday, the family had a relapse. But, the family had electricity, again. Now, they thought about carbon monoxide poisoning. They walked over to the Frank Fransen house and called the doctor. He told they to stay out of their home. Their chimney had clogged up. Carbon monoxide fumes had built up in the basement, when the furnace was running. Eventually, the poison gas affected the rest of the house. Sherman Crane cleaned their chimney.

Most homes in the country lost their electricity.

Gettysburg had phone service in town, but at times the local circuits were overloaded. Some rural and long distance lines went down in the storm.

Residents of the Oahe Manor fared well during the storm. After the power failed, their auxiliary generator provided emergency power. From Thursday afternoon until Saturday afternoon, the staff at the Manor was Mrs. Elizabeth Meyers, LPN, Mrs. Emma Stangi, aid, Mrs. Evelyn Stotz, aid, Lloyd Dreyer, maintenance, and William Kennedy, administrator. Dreyer and Kennedy walked to work in the blizzard, Friday morning. Emma Stangi prepared all the meals until Saturday afternoon. Dreyer worked around the clock to Saturday afternoon. Evelyn Stotz stayed up Friday night, making sure the residents were comfortable. Someone smelled smoke in the Manor Friday morning. Ted Stroup walked there and investigated the alarm. Nothing serious was found. On Sunday, there was no services because the minister could not make it to the Manor.

Mrs. E. H. Collins stayed warm after the power went out by crawling into a sleeping bag. A. L. Rogers moved into his camper on Friday.

Bill Owens told how his family stayed warm in his column entitled, **"Back Wash."** Owens wrote:

> When our house began to get cold Friday afternoon, due to the failure of our electricity activated oil furnace, we had an idea. It ia an old coal furnace that had been converted to oil heat many, many years ago. Why wouldn't it burn wood? We went into the space under our house that we laughingly call a basement, and discovered a lot of scrap lumber we had forgotten about. It was an earlier home remodeling and we had stashed it for future do-it yourself jobs.
>
> We threw a few pieces into the furnace in the current do-it-yourself project, lit it, and found that it did a fine job of heating. So every three hours or so we'd throw in some more. And the temperature in our house never got below 58 degrees. We sat around bundled up most of the time and read. Lou found some candles and we read by candlelight Friday evening. [162]

Many homes in Gettysburg ended up with snow in their attics.

Neil Nauman had two planes damaged in the storm.

The awning on Cliff's Jewelry buckled under heavy snow.

Merle Collins reported using a post auger to find his pickup after the blizzard.

Postmaster Marvin Smith reported the last mail truck arrived at 10:00 a.m. Thursday. The next one, came Sunday evening.

Classes at the elementary school were canceled on Monday. Water pipes broke in the building, due to the power outage.

According to Francis Buckley, Potter County Agent, livestock losses were estimated at about 100-150 head of cattle, 250 sheep and 40 hogs. These were revised totals. Otto Anderson lost 15 head of cattle. Wray Hall, Jim Brown, and Raymond Larson each lost a few cattle. Bill Buechler lost a yearling that accumulated too much ice. Eldon Smith lost about 100 fat lambs.

Game Warden, Duane Pomplun, said:

> It would appear that as far as the pheasant population is concerned we're in trouble. I have made a pretty thorough search of some of our better pheasant areas and the loss is running 50 to 70 percent due to our famous blizzard. The birds just couldn't coup with the blinding and suffocating snow. The dead birds that I found are far away from cover way out in the open. Most shelter belts and cover areas just weren't wide enough or big enough to protect the birds. A few of the game cover areas that the department put in years ago, saved quite a few pheasants, but not enough I'm afraid. Its a crying shame too, because we had a good supply of brood stock to go into the hatching season with.[163]

The Gettysburg Air Station had a separate power plant. People who lived in the residences still had no power because the connecting wires shorted out when the strong winds played havoc with them.

Bettye Gillings wrote the following:

> The families here and the Base Personnel, who worked the duration with little relief, are thankful to come through the storm with no serious hardships or injuries. All houses were without power and heat at some time. Several families escaped the fumes and smoke of faulty furnaces to stay with neighbors. Food, blankets, and medicine were pooled to make the best of it.
>
> Saturday with the drifting snow just an excuse of the winds of Friday, a tired husband home from the radars, told his wife that they were now enduring "a typical South Dakota blizzard." When she asked "what the heck did they call that thing yesterday?" He said, "Oh–they haven't found a name for that yet."
>
> The first vehicle from town seen Sunday in Base Housing was a milk truck, a most welcomed sight. Many families enjoyed a Sunday drive to Gettysburg to shop and locate friends. We do hear that one pastor's morning congregation consisted of one cow, however the cow was very reluctant to leave.
>
> Monday the Base Civil Engineers cleared the Base housing attics of snow aided by a volunteer bucket and shovel brigade.[164]

Lebanon, located in Potter County, was platted in 1887. The town was originally called Webb for a New York capitalist who requested that the name be changed to Lebanon for a range of mountains in Syria. Another version suggested it was named after Lebanon, New York.

In 1960, Lebanon's population was figured at 198.

Mrs. A. C. Baum, *Potter County News* correspondent for Lebanon in March 1966, mentioned the blizzard in her column. Mrs. Baum wrote:

> *Wednesday evening, March 3 ushered in snow and wind. By Thursday afternoon Mr. Sun appeared and the weather looked to be clearing. By about three o'clock the blizzard struck. Thursday evening telephone service came to a stand still, during the early morning hours most of the residential district was without electricity, until Saturday evening. With Friday's high wind and zero visibility the business places took a snowbound holiday from work. Many homes heated by electricity oil furnaces became rather cool, some charted 20 degrees. Some folks stated they spent much of the time in bed, while others moved in some other type of heat, still others moved into basements where they had a discarded oil or wood burning stove.*
>
> *The snowfall clogged streets and roads, buildings and corrals were blanketed. Many farmers reported spending hours shoveling out to get to their tractors and farm hands. in the immediate vicinity, loss of cattle and sheep was light, although the animals looked rough from lack of water and feed. The pheasants no doubt were among the greatest casualties. Monday's drifting snow closed many roads which were previously opened. Rural route patrons received their first mail since Thursday on the Tuesday delivery. The Lebanon streets have been plowed out so most citizens can drive from their homes, although many large banks still block the regular paths of traffic.*[165]

There was no school in Lebanon on Thursday and Friday because of the storm. On Monday classes were not held because of boiler difficulties at the school.

Gorman was named for its founder, R.T. Gorman. The town, located south of Gettysburg in Potter County, was settled in 1910.

Mrs. Alma Jones covered Gorman for the *Potter County News* in 1966. Mrs. Jones wrote:

> *March came in like a lion in sheep's clothing. Tuesday morning was mild, but by night the weather had changed. Wednesday there was snow and an east wind of thirty six miles an hour, and a livestock warning. Thursday was fairly calm until about 4:30, when snow and wind began. Friday was a raging blizzard (about sixty miles an hour wind) with zero visibility. Saturday morning the fury of the storm had diminished leaving huge snowdrifts and colder temperatures, but there was still a ground blizzard. Sunday was the calm after the storm, and everybody was busy at the tremendous task of digging out buildings and equipment. A strong southeast wind on Monday caused drifting of the snow but warmer temperatures.*[166]

Tolstoy, located in Potter County was founded in 1907.

It was named by Doane Robinson for the Russian writer, Count Tolstoy. The town had 142 inhabitants in 1960.

Tolstoy lost power and phone services. Residents waited out the storm in their homes.

Mr. and Mrs. R. C. Berg, residents of Onaka, who operated the grocery store in Tolstoy were stranded at the store Thursday, Friday, and Saturday. They returned to Onaka

Sunday morning. After parking their car on the edge of town, the couple walked to their house. The streets were not plowed out, yet.

Hoven, founded in 1883 and incorporated 1907, was named for the owner of the town-site, Peter or Matt Hoven. The town, located in Potter County, was home to 568 people in 1960. Long distance telephone service was lost March 3. Hoven had power outages as well as Onaka

Faulkton, seat of Faulk County, was platted in 1886 by the Western Town Lot Company. That year, the Northwestern extended their line from Redfield to Faulkton. The city and county were named for Andrew J. Faulk, the son-in-law of Walter A. Burleigh. Faulk was governor of Dakota Territory from 1866 to 1869.

He played a pivotal role in the opening of the Black Hills for development.

In 1960, Faulkton's population was placed at 1,051.

Faulkton and Onaka recorded weather information for South Dakota's Climatological Record in 1966. Data for Faulkton was recorded 1 mile northwest of the town.

The first precipitation of the storm, .04 inches of moisture, for Faulkton came late on March 2.

Mrs. Lyle Giesen said, "It was blizzardy at Faulkton Wednesday night, but snowing had stopped and the wind had died down Thursday morning."[167]

Thursday afternoon, blizzard conditions developed. Faulkton received .94 inches of precipitation. The high for the day was 33 degrees. The evening low was 25.

Faulkton recorded .60 inches of precipitation on Friday. The storm reached its peak. After a high of 27 degrees, the temperatures fell to 3 degrees below zero that night.

Onaka, located in Faulk County, derives its name from a Sioux word which means "places" or "inserts." According to the 1960 census, 65 people lived in Onaka.

The weather observer for Onaka recorded only precipitation totals. On March 4, 1966, the community received 1.88 inches of precipitation. The town lost long distance telephone service Thursday morning, March 3.

On March 14, 1966, Douglas Wallace, Faulk County Agent, said, "animals are continuing to die in Faulk." Wallace placed loss estimates between $175,000 and $200,000 for livestock. He figured an estimated 600 cattle, 1,200 sheep, 30 hogs and 1,000 chickens had been killed.[168]

Pheasant losses in Faulk County were considered severe.

Redfield, Doland, Clark, Garden City, Watertown, Castlewood, Clear Lake, Bemis and Goodwin

Redfield, named for J.B. Redfield, a well-liked official of the Northwestern, was platted by the Western Town Lot Company in 1880. There was a post office there in 1879, but it was known as Stennet Junction.

Redfield, Spink County seat, had a population of 2,952 in 1960.

Wrestling fans of Redfield attended the South Dakota State High School Wrestling Tournament in Watertown in late February 1966. They had witnessed the amazing wrestling career of Greg Schmidt, son of Mr. and Mrs. Milton Schmidt, rural Rockham. In 1963, as a freshman, 95 pound weight class, Schmidt lost his first wrestling match. Schmidt next loss was in the state finals. In 1964, Schmidt was undefeated in the same weight class. The following year, he never lost at 103 pounds.

Going into the 1966 state tournament, Schmidt was undefeated in the 112 pound class. Other teammates going to state with Schmidt included Gerry Neu, Chris Esser, Randy Joyce and Fran Esser.

Schmidt won another state title. He set the South Dakota high school wrestling record for 68 straight wins.(The national record for consecutive wins at that time was 74.) Schmidt joined Norman Neu who won titles for Redfield in 1958, 1959, and 1960. Norman Neu was there, as Milbank's wrestling coach. Chris Wagner coached the Redfield Pheasants.

The blizzard struck Redfield shortly after 6:30 p.m. Thursday. The storm lasted until Saturday morning. Thursday's high was 36 degrees and on Saturday it was 15 degrees. Local weather observer, Francis Taylor, estimated that 5 or 6 inches of snow fell. Overall, .70 inches of precipitation was recorded. High winds were judged to be about 60 mph.[169]

On Thursday, employees of Northwestern Public Service Company left Redfield for the Loyalton area. They sought shelter in Faulkton and stayed there until Saturday.

On Friday, Redfield, homes in east and north sections of town, experienced a power outage at 12:30 a.m. The high winds broke tree limbs in Redfield and the branches fell on the power lines. NWPS linemen fixed the problem in one hour. Redfield had other brief and sporadic outages in the storm.

Spink County Sheriff, Winston Barness, received a call from Jack Kennedy, game warden station at Redfield, at 3:30 a.m. Friday. His wife was ready to give birth. Sheriff Barness and Deputy Sheriff Dean Waddington left in Waddington's car. A snowplow led the way. Their emergency run was successful. They also guided Dr. Patterson to the hospital. Mrs. Jack Kennedy had a boy.

They also rescued Duane Hunter, a Huron man, stranded at the Einer Johnson farm, located five miles north of Redfield. Hunter was taken to the Redfield Community Memorial Hospital. He had suffered an appendicitis attack.

Redfield street crews went to work early Saturday morning. Traffic resumed at noon on Saturday in Redfield.

Sunday morning, snowplows worked four hours digging through a drift, just north of the Clayton Welke's farm, located four miles north of Redfield along U.S. 281.

There was no major livestock losses in the Redfield area.

On March 8, the Redfield Pheasants met Mobridge in the second game of the Section 3 tournament at Mobridge. The high school boys basketball team came away with an impressive win, 74 to 36. They faced Aberdeen in the championship game the following day.

Doland, located in Spink County was founded in 1882. The town was named after F. H. Doland, a Northwestern Railroad director who, at one time, owned the land on which the town was founded.

In 1960, Doland had a population of 481.

One resident who grew up in the small town became a national figure.

The youngster, the last of four children, was born in a room over the drugstore in Wallace. The boy started the second grade in Doland. His father was a druggist. For extra money, he did some veterinary work. The boy grew up behind the soda fountain and helped his father vaccinated hogs, cattle and poultry.

In high school, he played football, basketball, ran the half mile, acted in school plays, played baritone horn in the band, and became the star of the school's debate team. In 1929, he graduated as class valedictorian.

Father and son shared a common interest and that was politics. Doland is Republican country, but the father won respect as a Democrat. He became the mayor of Doland. In 1928, the father went to the Democratic National Convention in Houston, Texas, to nominate Al Smith. The father came away more impressed with the man who gave the nomination speech, Franklin Roosevelt.

In the fall of 1929, the boy went to the University of Minnesota to study political science. Times were tough for the family, two years earlier the family had to sale their home in Doland. They rented another one. His brother, Ralph, a college student at Dakota Wesleyan in Mitchel for two years, came home and worked in the family business, so his younger brother could go to school. The boy's wit earned him a part time job at Swoboda's Drugstore in Minneapolis.

After his freshman year, as agreed, the young man returned to Doland, Ralph went to the University of Minnesota where he assumed his brother's job at Swoboda's. After Christmas, 1930, the young man returned to the University of Minnesota and worked with his brother at Swoboda's. Their time there would be short.

South Dakota experienced hard times in 1927, the ensuing years brought little crops and numerous bank closures. In 1931, his father sold the drugstore in Doland and made another go of it in Huron. After final exams in March 1931, the brothers left college and returned to Huron.

In the winter of 1932, the youngest son enrolled at Capital College of Pharmacy in Denver, Colorado. He passed a six-month, day and night intensive course of study. He came home to the family business. Later that year, he met his wife to be at one of the dances at the Huron College. His life was the drugstore, but a break with the family business was coming.

In 1936, newly married to Muriel Buck, the young man enrolled at the University of Minnesota. Later on, he graduated magna cum laude from that school. Next, he earned a master's degree from the Louisiana State University. While there, his debating partner was a future U.S. Senator from Louisiana, Russell Long.

In June 1940, this fellow returned to Minneapolis. That fall, he joined the University of Minnesota Debating team, another member on that team was Orville Freeman, a future governor of Minnesota and later Secretary of Agriculture.

When World War II started, he was classified as 3-A, the classification given to men with wives and children. He was now 30 years old. This individual was appointed assistant director of Minnesota War Manpower Commission in 1943. Now classified as 1A-Limited, he tried to get in the Navy and Army in 1944, but was rejected again. He failed the physical for color blindness, suffered a double hernia in the past, and had some scars on his lungs.

Politics kept the young man from getting his doctoral degree. He ran for mayor of Minneapolis in 1943, but came up short. Two years later, he was elected mayor of Minneapolis.

At the 1948 Democratic national convention in Philadelphia, he spoke about civil rights. Later that year, Minnesotans sent him to Washington, D.C. as a United States Senator.

In 1960, he lost the Democratic primaries to John F. Kennedy. Four years later, he became Vice President of the United States under Lyndon B. Johnson. His name was Hubert Horatio Humphrey Jr. (May 27, 1911- January 13, 1978).

In 1965-66 season, Doland began its wrestling program. Scott Vogel and Dan Wilson qualified for the state tournament in February 1966.

In late February 1966, Doland won the District 13 Basketball Tournament and advanced to the Region 4 Basketball Tournament. The Wheelers won the regional title in 1965. .

On March 3, Doland, with a school enrollment of 160, faced the Highmore Pirates, a school of 226. Doland earned a one point victory.

On Thursday night, they faced the Bryant Scotties. This time, they were the big school, Bryant had an enrollment of 68. The crowd at Huron was estimated at 4,000 people.

Doland and Bryant battled for supremacy. The contest was close, very exciting to watch. The Bryant Scotties came away with a 57 to 51 victory.

School officials checked the weather one last time. It was snowing in Huron, but Doland was less than an hour away, about fifty miles.

The caravan of buses and cars left Huron. It was a large group, about 250 people. They pulled out of Huron at 10:30 p.m.

Traveling north on Highway 37, the Doland party ran into weather that was getting worse by the minute. The buses and cars moved slower and slower.

Members of the Doland caravan stopped at the intersection of state Highways 37 and 28. That location featured a combination gas station and cafe. The place was known as Pheasant City.

They mulled over their options.

People on three buses and some cars, about 85 individuals, decided to stay put and wait out the storm at the service station.

The stranded fans picked out places to sleep on the main floor and in the basement. The youngest member of the group was the son of Mr. and Mrs. John Albrecht, he was four and a half months old.

Two bus loads of people and some other fans in cars left Pheasant City.

It did not take long for the storm to wilt the confidence of the travelers. One of the buses and a number of cars stopped, just two miles north of Pheasant City at the farm house of Mr. and Mrs. John S. Hofer. It was after midnight. The Hofers had a big surprise, but they welcomed about eighty-eight people into their home.

The last bus and a few cars continued their struggle. As before, Mother Nature won. Their ordeal came to an end ten miles south of Doland. The vehicles pulled into the driveway of Mr. and Mrs. Burt Mason. The farm couple had about eighty visitors. The Mason's hospitality soon became a family affair. About twenty-two individuals were taken to nearby home of their son, Duane Mason.

Earl Hanson, stranded at the service station at Pheasant City, told the *Daily Plainsman* on Friday morning:

> *Everybody was accounted for and that the group were a bit pooped from lack of sleep and a bit disappointed at the tournament loss. The persons just milled around and made no attempt to sleep during the night. Often they went outside for a bit of fresh air and to watch the snow blowing across the countryside. Food was no problem as there was plenty of coffee, rolls, and cookies at the station.*[170]

In Doland several individuals attempted to get to work on Friday, but they returned to their homes. Some stores were opened for business, but there was no traffic.

Spink Electric Co-operative reported one phase out on a line from the La Delle sub-station. Power was lost when the tie wires broke in the wind and the phase wire came in contact with other wires. The outage happened early Friday morning and it affected about 15 farms southeast of Doland. Repairs could not be made in the blizzard. Power was restored around 11:20 Saturday morning.

Also, Spink Electric reported individual outages on farms.

Saturday morning, a state snowplow started clearing U.S. Highway 281, north from Redfield to Aberdeen about 9:00 a.m. After that was done, the crew returned to work on U.S. 212 between Redfield and Doland. Spinks County Sheriff Winston Barness contacted the state operators and had them clear a lane on state Highway 37 to Pheasant City, first.

On Saturday, Mrs. Harold Kline of Doland, stranded at the Mason home, talked to the *Daily Plainsman* about their experiences. She said:

> We never had it so good. We had color television, and even an electric piano, and we even had wall-to wall sleeping. Those who took refuge at the Hofer home probably will send a resolution of gratitude to the Hofer poultry flock. They had enough eggs on hand to keep the group fed indefinitely. Here, also, sleeping was the major problem, with every nook and cranny of the Hofer home put to use by the weary basketball fans. The trip into Doland Saturday morning was extremely difficult, and at times poor visibility threatened to halt the trip.[171]

The streets in Doland had drifts 8 feet high.

Clark was named for Clark County, which was named for Newton Clark, a Territorial legislator. It is the county seat. The Northwestern Railroad came to Clark from Watertown in 1881. The next year, the line was extended to Redfield. The community was first called Clark Center.

In 1960, Clark had 1,484 residents.

On February 26, 1966, the Clark Chamber of Commerce sponsored its annual Free Pancake Day in Clark. The event drew over 900 people.

Blizzard conditions developed late on March 3, 1966. Before the storm hit, Clark had a high of 37 degrees. The storm ended Saturday afternoon. Overall, the storm brought .82 inches of moisture.

The efforts of engineers Terry Kos of Henry and Howard Hilldahl of Garden City kept KDLO-TV station on the air. Kos worked over 33 straight hours without relief. He started at six o'clock Friday morning. Bart Kull, local announcer, made two regular newscasts from his home in Clark, plus eight special broadcasts. Afterwards, Kull said that around 200 calls were received at the station or at his home. They dealt with stranded individuals, cancellations and information for National Guard members. Kull condensed the information and called the station where it was taped for broadcast.

During the blizzard Chief of Police, John Sterner, worked out of City Hall. With the help of a state snowplow, Sterner transported relief workers for the Clark Nursing Home. He delivered medicines to other residents of the city.

Mrs. Willen, administrator of the Clark Nursing Home, worked twenty-five straight hours. She praised the efforts of Sally Wagner, Janet Palewski, Janet Miller and Linda Balley who stayed on duty for seventeen straight hours. They cared for forty-four patients. Strong winds forced snow down the ventilating stack of the emergency generator and water dripped down on it. Mrs. Willen draped blankets over the generator to catch the water.

The city hired out its snow removal. The operators started clearing the business district on Sunday morning. By Monday, most of the city streets were opened.

The *Clark County Courier* said, **"All Safe, But Storm Provided Anxious Moments in County."** A number of county residents were stranded in Huron, where they attended the Regional basketball tournament. Ardean Graff of Clark started for home after the game. Graff turned around after traveling a couple of miles.

Frank Seater, Stan Logan, and Tong, Clark's AFS exchange student, watched the basketball games in Huron. Tong said:

> *I was frightened for never have I known such wind. We had a room in the top story of the hotel, and I thought the building would tip over due to the strong wind.*

He was amazed with the amount of snow that piled up outside the hotel door. Their car was buried in the parking lot.[172]

Sheriff Hulscher received many phone calls Thursday night from people who had missing relatives.

The blizzard overwhelmed John Olson, Jim Gerhardt Jr., Randy Stevens and Mike Makens. They spent the night in a car nine or ten miles south of Clark on old highway 25. Toward morning, they caught a glimpse of a farm light, about a quarter of away. With visibility near zero, they waited for daylight. The boys arrived at the Gloe's house about 7:30. They called their homes.

Just prior to this, Dale Stevens and Jim Gerhardt started for Doland in a four-wheel drive pickup. They reached Doland and called their homes. They learned the boys were safe. They returned to Clark. Then, they picked up the boys at the Gloe farm.

West of Garden City, near the John Foster farm, there was a snowdrift about a mile long. It was too big for the state and county snowplows. Officials ordered in a caterpillar.

Watertown was founded in 1875 and platted in 1878. John E. Kemp, one of the first settlers, named it after his hometown in New York.

The Northwestern Railroad extended its line from Gary to Watertown in 1873. A Great Northern subsidiary linked Watertown and Huron in 1888. The Minneapolis and St. Louis line reached Watertown in 1884. From there, it went to Aberdeen and Leola in 1907.

The seat of Codington County, Watertown, had 14,077 residents in 1960. One of inhabitants was Terry Redlin, born on a farm near Watertown in 1937. When Redlin was fifteen years old, he lost a leg in a motorcycle accident. He graduated from Watertown High School in 1955. One year later, Redlin married his high school sweetheart, Helene Langenfeld. Later, the couple moved to Forest Lake, Minnesota. Redlin enrolled at the School of Associated Arts in St. Paul. He designed playing cards for Brown and Bigelow. The couple returned to Watertown in 1960. They stayed for six years, Redlin worked as an architectural illustrator. Redlin loved the outdoors, especially the area around Lake Kampeska. In his free time, he enjoyed painting scenes of wildlife.

In February 1966, the Watertown high school boys wrestling team was ranked No. 1. Coach Gene Schlekeway's team won the Eastern South Dakota Conference Wrestling Tournament. Watertown was 12-1 in dual meets in the regular season, and the Arrows won the tough Fargo Quadrangular. They qualified nine wrestlers for the state tournament. Watertown finished second at the state tournament in 1965.

South Dakota had forty-six high school wrestling programs in 1966. The state tournament was held in Watertown on February 25-26, and thirty-six schools had athletes there. The first state tournament was held in 1958.

In the last six years, the state wrestling tournament had been won by a West River team. Rapid City was the two-time defending champion. Before that, Spearfish captured the title four years in a row.

When the tournament ended Saturday night, five points separated the top four teams. Watertown had 46; Rapid City 45; Spearfish 43; and Brookings 41 points. It was Watertown's first state wrestling title. Bruce Asmussen, John Larson, Brian Asmussen, Gene Benthin, Loren Leonard and Keith Engels brought the championship home for the Arrows.

On March 2, Watertown had a quarter inch of rain. That day, the high reached 33 degrees. Winds ranged between 20 and 30 mph.

On March 3, the *Watertown Public Opinion* said:

Fierce Storm Dips Deep Into Region

March came in like a lamb Tuesday but let out a roar Wednesday in northeast South Dakota which sounded more like a lion.

The result was rain and snow which disrupted travel and communication throughout a widespread area.

Much of the South Dakota shuddered under a heavy load of new snow and blizzard conditions, when the storm rammed straight east through the state. ...[173]

On Thursday, the mercury rose to 38 above in Watertown. "The storm struck Watertown on the heels of a mixture of rain, drizzle, fog and sleet late Thursday afternoon and early in the evening."[174]

Watertown was host to Class B Region 3 Basketball Tournament.

The Conova high school boys basketball team stayed in a Watertown motel, Thursday night.

On March 4, the *Public Opinion* said:

Activity Slowed By Vicious Storm

Schools were closed, highway travel went by the boards, streets were snow-choked, and fresh snow swirled out of the north on wind logged at from 35 to 50 miles an hour at the Watertown airport.[175]

A physician for St. Ann Hospital in Watertown resided at Lake Kampeska. He was trapped by the storm. In contact with the hospital, the doctor had a patient who needed emergency surgery on Friday. Visibility was almost zero. The doctor took off on his snowmobile. Meanwhile, two volunteers on snowmobiles owned by Crouse Universal Rentals left Watertown. They met the physician about halfway and gave him a ride to the hospital. The operation was successful.

Saturday morning, at 8:15, Watertown reported winds between to 25 to 35 mph. Visibility was near zero in the fore-noon hours. Watertown received a total of 6 inches of snow. The wind gusts peaked between 55 to 60 mph. The winds subsided late on Saturday. The high was 16 above. The evening low was 4 degrees.

Drifts were 10 feet high in places.

There was a snowbank, 20 feet high, at the entrance to Stony Point.

Residents of Lake Kampeska were snowbound for almost forty-eight hours. The Codington County rotary snowplow cut through the tightly-packed drifts, Saturday night.

Mrs. Mathew Langenfeld and Mrs. O.A. Jeffers won the grand prizes of the "Red Owl Sweepstakes." Mrs. Langenfeld won a 1966 model car, and Mrs. Jeffers received a stereo system.

Castlewood, located in Hamlin County, probably was named by the daughter of J.S. Keator of Davenport, Iowa, who located the townsite. She liked "Castlewood" because it was the American home of Henry Esmond, the hero in a Thackeray's novel of the same name. When the Northwestern connected Watertown and Brookings in 1880, the town had a railroad.

In 1960, Castlewood had a population of 500.

Late Friday night, many phone calls were made to get Mrs. Allen Kannas, Castlewood, to the Memorial Hospital in Watertown. She was ready to give birth.

Operators of two state snowplows pulled out of Hayti. They cleared a path to U.S. Highway 81, and then traveled north.

Two counterpart crews left Watertown. They plowed south on U.S. Highway 81.

State Highway 22 runs through Castlewood and connects to U.S. Highway 81. This junction is located about four miles west of Castletown. The snowplows cleared this route as well.

The Castlewood police accompanied the car carrying Mrs. Allen Kannas. The four plows met about halfway and provided an escort to the hospital.

They arrived at the Hospital at 2:00 Saturday morning. Four minutes later, Mrs. Allen Kannas gave birth to a baby boy.

Clear Lake, seat of Deuel County, was named after Clear Lake which is located one mile east of the town. The community was settled in 1884.

The population of Clear Lake in 1960 was 1,137.

Laron Stoltenburg, Bob Gjere and Darrell Halse represented the Clear Lake Cardinals in the 1966 state wrestling tournament. Stoltenburg defeated Dennis Larive of Lead and lost an overtime decision to Scott Bruce of Sioux Falls Washington. Gjere pinned Rod Thompson of Huron, the region 3 champion, but lost a 6-1 decision to Steve Sona of Sioux Falls Lincoln. Haise lost a 7-0 decision to Tom Reidy of Lemmon.

In Clear Lake, the storm began on Thursday afternoon, March 3. The high that day was 28 above. The blizzard lasted about forty-eight hours. Jake Wentezell, local weather observer, measured 5 inches of snow from the storm. This came to .29 inches of precipitation. On Friday and Saturday, the highs and lows were 15 and 10 and -3 and -2, respectively.

Schools were closed in the county on Friday. There was very little business.

Bemis, named for P. W. Bemis, a pioneer settler, had a population of 50 in 1960. The community, located in Duel County, is northeast of Clear Lake.

On Thursday, Patrolman Elmer Drapeau, who was located at Clear Lake, went to Watertown to help direct traffic at the regional basketball tournament. Afterwards, Drapeau ended up in a ditch filled with snow, near Kransburg. Drapeau was rescued by another highway patrolman from Watertown. He made it back to Clear Lake on Sunday.

About midnight Thursday, Loren Krause and Allen Benson left Clear Lake. Returning to Bemis, their car motor stalled. They stayed in the car, because the storm was so bad. They were near the Odin Hetlet place, located about three-quarters of a mile from the highway. Herb Krause telephoned Sheriff Armond Vik, Friday morning at 6:30. Shortly afterwards, Sheriff Vik, Albert Voss and Clarence Oswald, county highway workers, and Bill Kruse began their search. They found the boys in the car. They were "cold, but otherwise all right." They were taken to Bemis. Sheriff Vik said, "it would have been impossible to reach them without the help of the snowplow.[176]

One accident occurred in Deuel County on Friday. Six miles north of Clear Lake on Highway 77, a truck driven by Wayne Vivant of Wahkon, Minnesota, stalled in the snow as it was traveling north. A car driven by Edward Bauer, Aberdeen, ran into the rear of the truck. Visibility was zero at the time of the accident. Nobody was hurt. Sheriff Vik followed Benny Neuman's highway plow to the crash site. The truck was pulled out by snowplow crew. Estimated damages, according to Vik, were around $700.00.

Goodwin, located in Deuel County, had 113 residents in 1960.

Hattie Washburn of Goodwin wrote the following poem. Washburn wrote:

Blizzards

Folks speak of the blizzard so long ago
In the year eighteen-eight-eight,
When so long and fierce did the winds blow
That many met a frozen fate.
The fierce, wild blizzard swept across the plain
When the Dakotas were still one,
And many knew worry's distress and pain
Before that dreadful storm was done.
Though we now have roads that are smooth and wide
And heated cars that swiftly go,
Fate will many a traveler betide
When they are closed by drifting snow.
Some speak of such storms as though quaint and old,
As a thing that will come no more;
But weather that once blew so fierce and cold
May yet repeat the same thing o'er.
We have swift planes that streak across the sky,
Great ships that sail upon the sea,
But when nature does her instruments ply
Man is helpless as he used to be.
The great disaster of our present year
Shows that it is so very true;
Travelers have the same stress and fear,
As awful as they ever knew.[177]

Mobridge, Selby, Akaska, Java, Glenham and Lowry

Mobridge obtained its name from a telegrapher's contraction of the abbreviation for the Missouri and bridge. Mobridge was founded in 1906. The Milwaukee extended its line from Glenham to Mobridge in 1907. That year, the railroad started construction of a railroad bridge across the Missouri River at Mobridge.

For years, South Dakotans had been trying to have Sitting Bull's remains brought home from his burial site at Fort Yates, North Dakota, to the area he grew up in, the Grand River vicinity near Mobridge.

The failure of regular methods brought about an unusual one in April 1953. A night-time raid at that time achieved the desired results, or did it? With the backing of Sitting Bull's relatives South Dakotans dug up his bones at Fort Yates and then dashed back across the state line.

The reinterment was done on the west side of the Missouri River not far from Mobridge. Sitting Bull's remains lie in a steel vault which was covered with twenty tons of concrete. The last feature was done to ensure that the Hunkpapa medicine man's bones would not be moved again. Controversy ensued when some North Dakotans claimed that the wrong bones were taken from Fort Yates.

The bust of Sitting Bull on the grave marker was designed by sculptor Korczak Ziolkowski, the person who started the Crazy Horse Monument in the Black Hills.[178]

Nearby is a monument to another famous Indian, Sakakawea, or "Bird Woman." She was the Shoshoni woman who accompanied Lewis and Clark on their famous expedition. Most historians agree that Sakakawea perished near here at Fort Manuel Lisa in 1812.

In 1960, Mobridge had a population of 4,391.

On March 10 the front-page headline of the *Mobridge Tribune* said, **"DETERMINED WORST IN HISTORY; Livestock Losses in Area in Thousands."**

The *Tribune* said:

> But for plain, old-fashioned misery, the March 2-3-4 storm had all the earmarks of the classic blizzard as described to every newcomer to the Dakotas. Temperatures were what could be considered mild Wednesday in comparison to the chill days of the winter to date. Then the snow began to fall and the wind came up, to set the stage for the wildest two days anyone could recollect.[179]

The blizzard made the national news. Photographers from the *Huntley-Brinkley Report* came to Mobridge several times to film storm scenes. The Art Smith place was featured, but local residents were disappointed on March 7. That day, the Bismarck TV station broadcasting the story lost its network connection, just before the program was to be aired.

On March 2, Winston Hall, local weather observer, recorded a high of 30 degrees for Mobridge. During the day, .74 inches of precipitation, or 7.3 inches of snow, fell. That night, the evening low was 23 degrees.

On Thursday, the high was 25 degrees. That night, the low was 10 above. Hall figured .85 inches of precipitation, 8.9 inches of snow, came down. Wind gust ranged between 50 and 60 mph.

The *Aberdeen American-News* contacted someone at the railroad office in Mobridge, Friday morning. The Mobridge man told the newsman that Mobridge had 55-66 mile winds, 20 inches of snow and mountainous drifts on Main Street.

"How is it in Aberdeen," he wondered.

The newsman mentioned 40 mile winds, several inches of new snow, and visibility so bad you could barely see across the street. "Well," he sighed as the conversation ended, "I'm glad to hear you have half-way decent weather in Aberdeen."[180]

On Friday, the high for Mobridge was 16 degrees, its coldest day-time high of the storm. Hall concluded that 15 inches of snow, 1.88 inches of moisture, fell that day.

Before the storm letup on Saturday, another inch of snow, .13 inches of precipitation, was added to the grand total. Overall, Hall calculated that 3.60 inches of precipitation had fallen during the week of the storm. According to official climatological data, Mobridge recorded 32.2 inches of snow, but 34 and 35 inches of snowfall were mentioned in newspapers reports.

Local police used motorized sleds on emergency runs. At the height of the storm, the vehicles were parked inside.

The *Tribune* said, "One man was advised to spend the night at the hotel as his family felt he couldn't make the 10-block walk to his home in the blizzard. Another lost his sense of direction right in town and had to locate a street sign to find out where he was."[181]

The tremendous amount of snow put some people in danger. The chimneys on their houses were completely iced over, forcing residents to leave.

The strong winds drove snow through ventilation vents. Most attics filled up with snow. Homeowners carried the snow out in buckets, many stopped shoveling their driveways and sidewalks and took care of this problem first.

Mobridge's water plant lost its power source after a connecting line went down. The city had enough water in storage to meet its needs while the line was reconnected. Mobridge was more fortunate than other communities in Walworth County because its power supply was uninterrupted during the storm.

The digging out process was hampered by strong winds on Monday. Streets, roads and highways that were plowed had to be plowed over again. For a while, streets were one-way tunnels. School officials canceled school for several more days.

Digging out a buried car. Two Mobridge women, Mrs. Donald Idler and Mrs. Ben Welder, employ shovels and a tub to remove snow from around the Idler car. With snowbanks everywhere, finding a place to deposit the snow was a problem. Courtesy of the Aberdeen American-News.

Eastern approach to Mobridge on U.S. 12 on March 8. Both top and bottom photos courtesy of Aberdeen American-News.

Children enroute to school carrying flags on long poles so they could be seen at intersections. Virtually all of Mobridge's streets had snowdrifts, 10 to 15 feet high, on them. Quite a few motorists tied flags to their radio aerials for the same purpose.

On the first day of the blizzard, Mrs. James Crump saw a pheasant huddled behind a fence post trying to escape the howling winds and biting snows. Jim went outside and caught the bird. After a while, the pheasant settled down in the Crumps home. Family members fed the bird bread, oatmeal and water. After the storm ended, the Crumps house guest was ready to leave. They took the bird outside. The pheasant squawked, before he flew away. The Crumps figured that was his way of saying, "Thank you."

Founded in 1900, Glenham was so named because it was located in a glen, a narrow, secluded valley. The town had 171 residents in 1960.

Gloria Walth, Connie Cameron and Jane Schlomer went home with Gerhardt Schlomer after school on Wednesday. They attended a birthday party for Marilyn Schlomer. They stayed at the Gerhardt Schlomers home until the storm was over. Early in the storm, the Schlomers lost their power. Most of the time, they had no heat and lights. Gloria Walth and Connie Cameron returned to their homes on Saturday. Jane Schlomer went home on Sunday. Afterwards, the girls said, "They would not forget this party in a hurry."[182]

The Kenny Thomases reported most of their livestock had survived the blizzard, but 40 sheep was still missing. Also, the family heard from their son, Robbie, who had arrived in Vietnam.

Selby, the seat of Walworth County, was named after a Milwaukee Railroad official. The town was established in 1899.

By 1960, the population of Selby had grown to 979.

Selby hosted the District 6 Basketball Tournament. Eureka and Selby met in the title game on February 26, 1966. Going into the tournament, the Eureka Trojans sported a 20-0 record. To get to the championship game, the Trojans defeated the Herreid Yellowjackets and the Bowdle Bobcats. The Selby Lions reached the finals by knocking off Pollock and the Wakpala Sioux. Eureka won the game, 74 to 69.

Two children, one from Selby and one from Java, needed medical attention, Thursday afternoon, March 3. Patti Lynn Tisdall, year-old daughter of Mr.and Mrs. Don Tisdall of Selby, had a fever of 106 degrees. Susan Goetz, 10-year old daughter of Mr. and Mrs. Ray Goetz of Java, had severe pains on her left side.

Bob Idler and Albert Schmidtgall of Selby led the way in a state snowplow. Joyce Tisdall and Patti Lynn rode in Ed Schanzenbach's car that was driven by Larry Schanzenbach and Jim Knecht. The occupants in the second car included Susan, Mr. and Mrs. Ray Goetz, their son Jim, and uncle Julius Wolf. The trip between Selby and Mobridge took two hour in the white-out conditions.

Susan underwent an appendectomy. She was well after the surgery. With medical attention, Patti Lynn's temperatures returned to normal.

Don Tisdall's job had taken him away from home at the time. He worked for D&D Construction along with Larry Sulzle and Dennis Madden, all of Selby. They were snowed in at Timber Lake. After the blizzard, Deiser Construction was part of the snow-clearing operations in Dewey County.

Local U.S. Weather Observer, A. M. Hoven estimated the total snowfall for Selby at 24 inches, 1.72 inches of precipitation. Unlike Mobridge, Selby received no snowfall on March 2. Selby recorded .82 inches of precipitation on March 3 and March 4.

The last day of the blizzard, March 5, Selby amassed the most precipitation, .90 inches of precipitation. Before the storm hit, the high in Selby was 34 degrees. Sunday night, the coldest reading was 8 below zero.

The *Selby Record* was a family newspaper in 1966. Ida Clement was the editor and her husband, Fritz Clement was the publisher. Each wrote their own column. Bruce Clement, their son, was the newspaper's photographer. Ida's column was called **"Office Cat,"** and Fritz's column was **"In The Dog House."**

Ida Clement wrote:

> *The big storm which began blowing from the northeast on Wednesday and did not subside until Saturday evening was the worst in the memory of Old Timers in this area. None could remember one that lasted so long.*
>
> *We were able to get to downtown Thursday but there was little activity in town and all Lenten services and meetings set for that evening had been canceled. When we went home late Thursday afternoon, a big drift in front of the garage prevented Fritz from putting the car inside and Bruce found the same situation when he got home. None of us ventured out that evening. Around 8 p.m., we had a terrific flash of blue-white light near the house which seemed to go all thru the place like a flash of lightning, and off went our electric power.*
>
> *We checked and found some of our neighbors were also affected although the Schlomers across the street from us and those in their block were okay. In reporting to the MDU man, Emil (Shorty) Wolf in Selby, we learned that a sector in the east end of town was also affected as were some of the blocks to the north of us. However, Shorty and his helper were around soon to check on the situation and found the storm had torn off a street light wire and caused a short circuit which threw out this area of town. He had to make a trip to the substation east of town where a fuse had blown and about an hour and a half or so later we again had power. During that time the temperature in our house had dropped from 75 to nearly 65.*
>
> *The storm raged all night with visibility practically zero and the next morning the wind shifted to the northwest and showed no signs of abating. Windows were beginning to frost over or be plastered with snow and we could not see out most of them. About 10:30 a.m., Friday the power again went off and this time it stayed off and we were without heat, light, radio (our transistors had been left at the office!) and TV and phone service was in and out. Later, without power for some hours the phone system went dead and we did not even have the means of communication. We felt completely isolated.*
>
> *During the day while we had telephone communication, we got in touch with Denny Zabel and had him contact Ron Stroh, whose trailer is located not far from our office and had him check on things there. None of us left the house that day. Late in the afternoon, Hank Schlomers across the street from us, called and invited us to come over there for the night as they had a bottle gas kitchen range in their basement recreation room and were keeping warm with that. However, it wasn't too uncomfortable in our house, around 50 degrees and we decided to stick it out for the night. We dug out all the quilts and blankets we could find and went to bed about 7 p.m. We had plenty of candles and managed to warm a few cups of water on a candle warmer and plenty of food in the house so there was no worry on that score.*

With the power off, and no pumps working the city's water supply was exhausted during the night and shortly after midnight we had no water. I was afraid it might have frozen up but when we checked on the temp in the house and basement it was around 40 degrees and up, so decided it must be the water supply.

During the day, while we still had phone service we kept checking in with the neighbors and though some were without heat, everyone was managing to keep warm mostly by staying in bed.

Saturday morning, the wind had abated so that you could see for a block or two in town and Bruce donned heavy clothing and started for the office to check on things there and get his transistor radio. Shortly after he returned, Hank Schlomer came over to invite us over for pancakes, sausage and coffee,–our first warm meal since Thursday evening. We found the Robert Krogstad family and our next door neighbor, Margaret Reuer had spent the night with them and were also there for breakfast.

While we were at the Schlomers, the Herb Himrichs and Mrs. Jeff Meester checked in. The Meester family had spent the night with the Himrich's who operated their gas furnace manually and so kept the house warm. Hank Schlomers went to several of the other homes in the neighborhood whose doors were drifted shut and shoveled a path to their doors to check on them.

It wasn't just in our neighborhood. Margaret Powell, who works in our office, said Jim Digman was around with a shovel Saturday morning checking on her and her mother and others in that part of town. And that was the case all over town. There were many Good Samaritans. There were many other instances, too, of neighbors moving in with neighbors. It wasn't just friends or relatives–none could take a chance of walking farther than next door or across the street.

Saw several sparrows before and after the storm, and was surprised that somehow, they managed to survive. Jeff Meester rescued one in his yard and took it in his house were it proceeded to make itself at home while the Meesters were staying at the Himrichs. It even ate part of one of Marge Meester's pies and also rendered the rest of it unfit for consumption.

Our power was restored for a time about noon Saturday after a 26-hour outage but there was still trouble and it kicked on and off most of the afternoon. Late that afternoon it came on to stay and everyone soon had their homes cozy and warm and were thankful and happy to have warm meals again.

Stores in town opened Saturday and Sunday so people could replenish their supplies. A few farmers were able to get to town Saturday. Bread and milk supplies were exhausted almost at once.

Saturday night was a wonderful night–calm after a 4-day roaring storm, and so quiet and restful and warm. I sometimes wonder if the Good Lord doesn't send these storms so that we will appreciate more fully, the creature comforts which He has blessed us.

The sun shone on Saturday but the wind was still kicking up lot of snow as it was still gusting up to 25 and 30 miles an hour and more at times.

Sunday was clear and calm and the temperature rose to a point where the snow thawed away from windows and some of it began to slide off the roof. There were no services at any of the churches so folks spent the day digging trenches through the drifts in their yards, the kiddies were out having a big time sliding on the mountainous drifts, and many folks were busy taking pictures of the drifts.

Everyone was happy to hear the news Saturday that the Otto Mettler family at McLaughlin were safe, as well as Supt. Werle of Wakpala and the two men with him, one of which was Dale Lewis, former Bowdle publisher. Also the three Fort Yates coaches. Most of the people who wisely remained in their cars survived.

Many people, remembering other storms, used the old trick of tying ropes to one another or to a door of the house before leaving it to check on things at their farm buildings and thus were able to find their way back safely.[183]

Some residents who had no other means of heating food, fired up their charcoal grills in their garages and cooked on them.

The Edward Gregers family had an oil burner in their basement. They hauled it upstairs and used it to keep their house warm. The Gregers had a number of their neighbors in for part of the storm.

The Ernest Hayford family and Mr. and Mrs. Flemmer spent Friday night there. Saturday morning, the Gregers served hot breakfast to the Hayford family, the Femmers, the Delbert Schley family and his mother, Mrs. Wilfred Stoick and children, Mr. and Mrs. William Bauder and Mrs. Lawrence Stahlecker, Joan and Kevin.

Mrs. Emily Himrich kept her house warm during the blackout by burning wood in a range in her basement. Friends and neighbors who enjoyed the comforts of her home included Mr. and Mrs. Verne Bohlander, Mr. and Mrs. Henry Aman, and the Howard Goehring and LuVerne Berreth families.

Fritz Clement admitted he was somewhat of an old timer. Like other old timers, he did not think weekend blizzard was the worst one, but it was the longest one. Furthermore, he believed many factors have to be considered in comparing blizzard of different ages. Every generation will make a "good argument" for the ones they remember.

Fritz Clement wrote:

But in my book, the one we had last week was a dinger with horns and I don't care for a repeat performance. We getting along just fine until the power went off and it began to get cold enough to send us to bed before our usual bedtime. We were fortunate, like many others in the area, to have good neighbors who were concerned about the welfare and did everything they could to make us more comfortable. There were a lot of nice little favors that were done during the storm, many of which will never come to light, but it is comforting to know that when there is a disaster such as the one that hit us last week, there are those who are ready and able to lend a helping hand to others and in that respect, the Clement family is duly grateful.

Now, with the storm over, the big problem of the day is what to do with all the snow that is piled up in drifts here in Selby and other cities as well as the countryside. Work was commenced Tuesday morning of clearing Main street and if weather holds out the work should go quite rapidly. At a city council meeting Monday night, it was decided to take care of Main street first (except in cases of emergencies) and then began work on some of the side streets. Most of the city streets were opened with bulldozers so that fire trucks would get around in case of a fire and also to make available access to homes for fuel delivery trucks. Nothing has been done on Highway 103 by state crews but that is expected to come later. Some of the drifts on the highway are almost 20 feet high and special or heavy equipment will be necessary to open them. Your Dog House is sure that if everyone is cooperative and will exercise a little patience, the job will be done eventually and without needless suffering. In the meantime it is recommended that cars or trucks use the existing facilities only when necessary to avoid congested streets which might lead to serious accidents.[184]

At the Berens Hotel, guests slept on davenports in the lobby and in the social room in the basement where five extra beds were set up. The Stroh Hotel found some space for nine extra visitors. The Auburn was overcrowded as well. Their guests kept warm by hand-feeding the stoker in the furnace. With a LP gas range in the kitchen, they had hot meals. A number of other people came in for meals.

Nine men who stayed at the Bennett's Hill Top motel had a rough time after the power went out. There was no heat in any of the units or in the Bennett home. Huge snowdrifts blocked the doors to five rooms, so they were unoccupied. The men heated soup over candles for their meals.

On Sunday, the cleanup operation had its first full day of work. Some streets in Selby were not cleared until March 10 and 11. Equipment capable of handling the biggest snowbanks arrived at that time.

A number of people in Selby found snow in their attics on Sunday. Humorously, the *Record* said, "it took steps to remove it."

The homes of Del Schapekahm and Wayne Cheskey were located south of the courthouse in Selby in 1966. After the blizzard, their front yards had huge drifts with pieces of roofing and tree branches scattered on top. The roofing came off the courthouse.

The post office dealt with the backlog of mail on Monday and Tuesday.

School was called off in Selby on Thursday, March 3. Courses resumed on March 8, except for kindergarten classes. There was no school bus service on March 8.

August Thorstenson, of Selby, received bad news from his son, Calvin, a rancher northeast of Wakpala on Monday. They had lost at least 75 head of cattle and most of their 200 head of ewes. August Thorstenson called Pierre, and a helicopter was dispatched from Ellsworth Air Force Base Tuesday morning. The crew picked up Mr. Thorstenson in Selby. Then, the crew went to Mobridge for medical supplies and a veterinarian. After that, the pilot flew to Calvin's ranch. The helicopter was handy, while it was there.

Loy Miklos, a farmer southeast of Selby in the Spring Valley community, came to Selby on March 8. Miklos observed a number of dead cattle south of their place but he did not know whose they were. A number of Miklos's cows escaped death in a straw shed which was nearly filled with drifted snow. The animals climbed the drifts to the roof and ate a hole in it. During the storm, Miklos and several of his children were able to get to the barn by hanging on to each other. They followed landmarks in the yard including building and fences. Miklos said, "That a few feet away from a building, you could not see a thing and lost all sense of direction unless you had something to hang on." Furthermore, Miklos stated "he had never seen so much snow in his life. South of his father's place, between two hills, the snow had filled in the space until it was level between them and he estimated there must be 50 or 60 feet of snow filled in there."[185]

State Highway 103 was opened the evening of March 9. It took the biggest state highway V-plow to do the job.

Initial cattle losses for Walworth County were estimated between 3,000 and 3,500 head. Damages were expected to exceed one million dollars. A week after the storm, John Skogberg, Walworth County Agent, revised figures. The latest estimates were placed at "about 1,000 head of cattle, 100 head of sheep, 50 head of hogs and 1,000 chickens, representing a loss of about $200,000."[186]

Walworth County pheasant losses were reported as severe. Dead deer and antelope were seen in the county, but the numbers were not great.

Java, located in Walworth County, has been called the "Coffee Town." Named by the officials of the Milwaukee Railroad, it is not known if Java coffee had anything to do with its naming.

In 1960, the population of Java was 406.

The Wakpala Sioux ended the Java Panthers high school boys basketball season in the opening round of the District 6 Basketball Tournament in Selby on February 24, 1966.

On Sunday afternoon, March 6, Bruce Clement, *Selby Record* photographer, and Ronnie Stroh drove to Java to take some pictures. They reported seeing mountainous drifts all over the town. The two men saw residents carrying coal by the bucket and fuel oil by the can to their houses. People's coal chutes and fuel tanks were buried in snow.

Located in Walworth County, Akaska is a corruption of a Sioux word that in one dialect means "a women who lives with several men," but in another one it means "to eat up."

According to the 1960 census, Akaska was home to 90 people.

On March 2, 1966, the evening services at the Zion Lutheran Church in Akaska were canceled because of bad weather. There was no school in Akaska on Thursday and Friday.

Wayne Eiteneier, local news correspondent for Akaska in the *Selby Record* wrote:

> The storm hit Akaska about 4:00 p.m. Wednesday afternoon and grew worse during Thursday and Friday. During Thursday and Friday visibility was zero. At times you couldn't see your porch steps. It was a storm that no other blizzard, even the one in 1949 could be compared with. Even the older people who have seen many said this about the storm.
>
> As of this writing, we have a fairly good contact with the rural area, and the loss of cattle is light. We have no emergencies as far as illnesses with people are concerned,–for this we can be thankful.
>
> The total amount of snow that we have is about 23 inches. Sunday morning found residents digging out. Ervin Rueb should be thanked also for helping get roads open by using his tractor and scoop and clearing many streets and yards. We do have many high drifts, but I'm sure that the ones that completely the Carl Kuehl garage, and completely fill the driveway and partly cover the garage at the R.C. Heier place are the biggest.
>
> The storm is over and even if we do have much snow, we can be thankful that we have no great cattle losses such as the west river area has.[187]

Friday morning at 10:30, the power went out in Akaska. It was off until 6:30 Saturday evening. Eiteneier described their situation:

> During this time all but a few homes in town were without power and heat, and everyone who had an emergency heat source, such as kerosene or bottle gas stove, moved to their basements, ate by candlelight, and listened to transistor radios. The following moved in with neighbors while they had no substitute for heat: The Marvin Bergs and the Emil Ballenskys went over to the Max Weiss home; Mrs. LaRue Goetz, Elizabeth and David went to the John Hubers; Fred Ritter to C.B. Kalmbachs, Mrs. Ritter to Gottfried Kalmbachs; Pastor and Mrs. Herrmann over to Erhard Kilbers; Mr. and Mrs. Rudy Heier went to Mrs. Christ Heiers.

> Several things happened during the storm: At the Marvin Berg home, the chimney filled with ice and caused fumes in the house. They went to the Max Weiss home on Friday evening, the day the chimney filled up. And another not so bad, but uncomfortable ordeal was that during the height of the storm, John Hubers ran out of fuel.

> A special thanks is extended to Erhard Kilber, Rolland Rieger and Calvin Schilling, who during the storm, went from house to house to see how the people were faring and helped those who needed to be moved to different places. No words can express the appreciation that the residents of Akaska feels towards these men.[188]

There was no school in Akaska on March 7 and 8.

Lowry, located in Walworth County, was named for an official of the Minneapolis & St. Louis Railroad in 1907 when the early settlers and railroad officials met. At first, they considered the name Andersonville, for Lars Anderson, a homesteader, but decided it was too long.

The town was home for 44 people in 1960.

Cam Wal REA at Selby reported that the Lowry area had lost power several times during the blizzard. Power went out on Wednesday at 8:00 p.m. and was off until 4:00 p.m. Thursday. The other outage was between 10:45 a.m. Friday and 12:45 p.m Saturday.

Ipswich, Bowdle, Hosmer, Roscoe, Beebe, Loyalton, Mound City, Pollock, Leola, Eureka and Wetonka

Ipswich, the seat of Edmunds County, was most-likely named for Ipswich, England, the birthplace of Charles H. Prior, a Milwaukee townsite agent. Another source indicated that Prior named it for a Massachusetts city. The town was settled in 1883, the year the Milwaukee extended its line to Ipswich from Aberdeen. Three years later, the Milwaukee laid another 30 miles of track to Bowdle.

Ipswich was home for 1,131 people in 1960.

In late February 1966, Ipswich met and defeated Polo in the first round game of the District 5 Tournament. In the semi-final the Ipswich Tigers lost to Cresbard, 43 to 34. In the consolation game on February 28, Coach Marvin Seyer squad fell to the Leola Pirates, 53 to 46. Curt Sylte and Tim Schumacher led the Tigers in scoring.

Dianne Kay Murkuson, daughter of Mr. and Mrs. Robert Murkuson, died from the injuries she suffered from a car-train accident. She married Kenton Eisenbeisz of Bowdle on June 25, 1965, and the young couple moved to Aberdeen, afterwards. Gary Murkuson,

Ipswich forward, missed the Leola game because he attended the funeral of his sister who was only nineteen at the time of her death.

On February 28, over 330 people attended the second annual Ipswich Community Hospital dinner. Dr. Walter Kitzler and his wife were introduced to the public. The couple planned to move to Ipswich from Webster in April. They purchased the Harley Taylor residence. Doctor Kitzler made arrangements to set his office up in the Geffre building.

On March 2, the storm began with a mixture of rain and snow. The high for that day was 34 degrees. The initial precipitation, that which fell before 6:00 p.m., amounted to .14 inches. It left the streets and walks covered with a sheet of ice. After that, an estimated 5 or 6 inches of wet snow fell late Wednesday night. Strong winds brought blizzard conditions.

There was a power outage in Ipswich between 7:00 and 10:00 p.m.

Thursday morning, Ipswich Public and Holy Cross schools were closed. Traffic diminished as the storm intensified. According to weather records, Ipswich recorded .79 inches of precipitation.

Temperature readings and precipitation were not recorded for Friday. Weather records showed Ipswich getting 1.25 inches on Saturday. The storm ended Saturday afternoon.

Ipswich lost power again on Friday morning. It went off at 10:45 a.m. and was off until 12:45 p.m Saturday. According to Victor Baker, Montana Dakota Utilities Company manager in Ipswich, the main cause of the failure was a fault at the substation east of Glenham. Baker said, "Several attempts were made to reach the substation and correct the fault, but due to zero visibility and driving snow, with winds up to 60 miles per hour, the men were driven back to cover."[189]

Al Gimbel, district manager for MDU at Ellendale, North Dakota, said, "Rain, which preceded the snow in areas south of here, caused most of the physical damages when it froze on lines. Icing conditions and wind caused three caused three broken poles, 10 to 12 snapped crossarms and several wire breaks in a stretch from the Barnard corner to Leola. Between Leola and Ipswich there were 32 spots where the wind literally blew wires off insulators."[190]

At 6:30 Thursday night, Mr. and Mrs. Dave Dockter and daughter, from Cresbard, became marooned in their vehicle two miles south of the Edmunds county line on Highway 45. Mr. Dockter walked to the William Haller farm, two and a half miles away off Highway 20, to get help. By the time he reached the Haller place, there was no hope of returning to get his wife and daughter.

Calls were made to Faulk County Sheriff Kenneth Wherry and Highway Patrolman Chuck Benson. They drove out in the storm, but got stuck about 8:30 p.m. Using the radio in their vehicle, the men contacted Edmunds County Sheriff, Clarence DeWald, for assistance.

Sheriff DeWald contacted Miles Miller, Game Warden Dick Marko and John Hein. The four men left Ipswich in the F.E.M. snowmobile. About a mile out, the motor of the vehicle started having problems, so they turned around. They headed out in a car, but the weather forced them to turn back, again.

At 9:00 Friday morning, Sheriff DeWald and Walt Haux followed a state snowplow in a pick-up truck equipped with a short-wave radio. Art Uttenhove and Edmund Jung drove the plow toward the Dockter's car. They turned around, after going four miles. This round trip in the storm took three hours.

Sheriff DeWald had something else to worry about on Friday. Faulk County Sheriff Kenneth Wherry and Highway Patrolman Chuck Benson were reported missing. The two lawmen had been out in the storm, trying to locate two school buses carrying children home in the Cresbard area that had disappeared.

Wherry and Benson had found the school buses. The children were safe, but they spent Friday night in an abandoned farm house.

On Saturday, the Ipswich quartet made another attempt to reach the Dockter's stalled car. Again, Uttenhove and Jung led the way in the state snowplow. DeWald and Haux followed in a pickup truck.

The state highway department from Faulkton was out, looking for Wherry, Benson and the Dockters. They found both parties around noon. To keep warm, Mrs. Dockter ran the car at intervals until it ran out of gas. Then, they moved around as much as possible to avoid freezing.

The Ipswich men were contacted and they turned around.

Merrill B. Bebermeyer's, editor of the *Ipswich Tribune*, wrote:

Home Spun Slants
Heard and Seen Through My Bifocals

The blizzard last weekend had its humorous as well as more or less dangerous incidents. The weather certainly brought out a spirit of neighborliness that can be found best in small towns like ours. It will probably be impossible for the Tribune to report all of the visiting that was done over the blizzard days but there were many times when good neighborliness was shown.

Walking over the drifts Sunday morning we found a number of interesting stories. The Alvin Evans family reports one. The drift north of the house, twice the height of the roof, completely blocked the doors. The family was getting cold during the electric outage when Mrs. Sylvia Germain contacted them and offered the facilities of her home next door which she found able to heat quite comfortably.

LEAVE THRU WINDOW

Unable to leave their house the Evans family found an exit by way of window. Daughter Peggy climbed out, shoveled the door clear and the family were able to get out, including Joan who was on crutches. After the storm abated they returned to their own home.

The high drifts posed some dangers to youngsters enjoying the sport of sliding. The height of the drifts permitted power and telephone lines to be in reach. The youngsters were warned not to touch any lines and avoid danger.

The hugh drift north of the softball field was so high that the city gave up trying to open it to traffic. Close by the home of Joe Nigg to the west got cold during the storm, Joe reporting that his house temperatures got down to what it was outside, in the twenties.

Mrs. Katherine Gisi who lives a block north of Father Bormann Memorial Hall with her sons, found out that the temperature in the home of the Sisters was getting low. Hence she brewed up a gallon and more of coffee which she sent over to help the women keep warm. Other cases of gift coffee we heard which made for the "Good Neighbor Policy."

LIVED IN SCHOOL BUS

In the north edge of Ipswich the Dan Braun family and their neighbors, the Joe Gauers with their small baby had the problem of keeping warm. They solved it in a novel way. Dan, who drives one of the school buses, thought that would be the best way to keep warm, so the two families got together and kept warm in the bus. It was a little crowded and cramped for the youngsters but they were comfortable. Dan had the foresight to have the bus well filled with fuel.

We heard of one Ipswich man who went to bed with a knit cap on his head to keep his head warm. In our house we didn't have any heat either but my bald head kept quite comfortable. Many bone is a poor conductor of cold.[191]

People were amazed with a large drift, estimated at 14 feet high, just north of the Ipswich Softball Field.

On Sunday, all stores in Ipswich were closed, except Thares Grocery which opened up in the afternoon.

To raise money for charities, bowlers from Ipswich squared off against bowlers from Ipswich, England. The two towns started playing in 1964. Ipswich, South Dakota, won the honors that year and in 1965.

On March 6, 1966, the international competition was held for the third time. In the two previous matches, trans-Atlantic phone connections allowed the bowlers to keep track of the scores after each round of games. In 1966, storm damages prevented the hookup.

Sunday night, Lee Hopkins, secretary of the Men's Bowling Association in Ipswich, South Dakota, sent a cablegram to Ipswich, England, with their scores. Local men who participated included Stu Holdhusen, Tony Thares, Leonard Engler, Lee Hopkins, Bryce Herrick, Darold Owens, Norbert Jangula, John Hein, Earl Swanson and Morris Dehnert.

Ipswich, South Dakota, won the bowling match in 1966. On March 15, they received a credit transfer of $25.00. James Sargent, promotions and public relations controller for Ambassador Bowling Limited in Ipswich, England, concluded in his letter of congratulations to Lee Hopkins by saying, "Once again, many congratulations to you and your bowlers and let's hope that next year we can manage to establish telephone communications and perhaps even victory."[192]

The cleanup of Ipswich was an around-the-clock operation.

By Sunday, most roads in Ipswich were open for one-way travel. Something else, happened. In the process, a tractor dropped in a well pit and broke a shut-off value. Water erupted. The city's fire truck pumped the excess water into a storm sewer for twenty-two hours. To repair the break, Ipswich hired the Independent Drilling Company of Aberdeen.

Mayor S. G. Fischer thanked the Virgil Oban Construction Company and Glen Jones and his crew for the use of their private equipment. Also, trucks from David Hales Construction hauled snow away from downtown areas. The Dehnert Brothers, Ipswich Lumber Company, Taylor Implement, Doug Eilers and others provided much needed help.

Ipswich was one of the few towns in the area to have school on Monday.

An aerial survey of livestock losses was conducted by the chairman of County Commissioners, and Dennis Bunde, Edmunds County Agent. Harley Taylor flew the plane.

Initial reports of livestock losses in Edmunds County were fairly accurate. Cattle losses were expected between 1,000 and 1,500 head and 500 to 1,000 sheep.

One week later, the totals had changed, 1,000 head of cattle and 500 head of sheep. Bunde stated, "Value of losses including personal property in Edmunds County has been placed at $500,000. but may go slightly higher."[193]

Pheasant losses in Edmunds County was reported as moderate to severe. There were other reports of dead wildlife.

Bowdle, located in Edmunds County, was platted in 1886. The town was named either for C. C. Bowdle, a pioneer banker of the town, or Hon. G. M. Bowdle of Mitchell. The community had 673 residents in 1960.

Bowdle recorded just over a quarter inch of precipitation on Wednesday and Thursday. On March 4, the town recorded 2.80 inches. On Saturday and Sunday, another three-quarters of an inch fell.

Bowdle lost its power at 10:45 a.m. Friday. It was off for twenty-six hours. A Montana-Dakota Utilities crew from Mobridge fixed the problem at Glenham. The emergency batteries at telephone exchanges soon failed.

Located in Edmunds County, Hosmer was founded in 1887. The town was named for the wife of a Captain Arnold, her maiden name was Hosmer.

In 1960, 433 people lived there.

The finals of the District 5 Basketball Tournament featured the Hosmer Tigers and the Crestbard Comets at the Aberdeen Civic Arena on February 26, 1966. Hosmer came from behind to defeat Roscoe in the first round. Against the Leola Pirates, Tom Job made a short jumper in the final seconds of overtime. The Eisenbeisz brothers, Tom and Dave, and Tom Job led the Tigers in scoring. The title game was tied at halftime, but Hosmer had a tough third quarter, the Tigers scored only two points. The Comets went on to win the game, 49 to 32.

A week later, Hosmer experienced a blizzard which left some of the biggest drifts in Edmunds County. Afterwards, some locals figured the drift on main street in Hosmer was 22 feet high. Like Bowdle, Hosmer endured a power failure for over a day. The electricity went out around 10:45 a.m. March 4, and was not restored until 12:45 p.m. March 5. Without power, the phone system broke down.

One of the storm victims in South Dakota was Albert Herrboldt of Yankton. He had lived in the local area for many years. Albert Herrboldt was a former Edmunds County Auditor and Treasurer. Family survivors in Hosmer included a brother and sister, Art Herrboldt and Mrs. Gotilieb Walth.

Named for Roscoe Conkling, U.S. Senator from New York (1867 to 1881), Roscoe was founded in 1877. The Milwaukee Railroad extended westward from Aberdeen to Ipswich in 1883. Roscoe enjoyed rail service, once the line was built to Bowdle in 1886. The rail line from Roscoe to Eureka and Orient was completed in 1887.

In 1960, there were 532 people living in Roscoe.

Roscoe's weather observer, William Lammle, talked about the 1966 blizzard and other storms. It was published in the *Ipswich Tribune*. Here's William Lammle's commentary:

> Wednesday's weather was a prelude to the bad weather, with some fog, light rain in the form of drizzle and some snow with it. The temperature was 30 above, which formed a glaze on roads and streets. Wind velocity became 45 miles per hour and the barometer dropped rather fast, getting down to 29 by afternoon. By 5:00 Wednesday visibility got down one-fourth mile and snowfall was moderate to heavy, and cancellations of activities were reported on radio and TV stations.

The conditions prevailed all night Wednesday and by Thursday morning 10 inches of wet snow was on the ground. Roscoe streets and roads were bladed during the day. Visibility became very bad Thursday afternoon and then became worse. The wind shifted to the northwest with a velocity of between 55 and 60 miles per hour, with more snow and visibility reduced to zero.

At 11:00 a.m. Friday, light and power was cut off. Most of the telephones went out. Water pressure began to get low, due to the lack of power. It was 26 hours before power was restored.

Saturday morning, March 5 the skies were clear, but only after 18 inches of snow had fallen, from which 2.88 inches of moisture was measured. Nearly everyone tried to get out and see what it was all about, something like ground hog day, Lammle remarked.

The observer said, It doesn't happen here, but it did. There are older pioneers than I am who may recall blizzards to compare with this one. As for me, its the second one. February, 1922, I recall was equal to this 1966 blizzard at which time several children froze to death near Eureka, but the duration was shorter. The modern living conveniences didn't prevail, people were more cautious, and believed it can happen.

"Incomplete reports on the storm are numerous, and it may take several more weeks before they are complete. However, at this time four people lost their lives in this 1966 blizzard. Some survived, which was a miracle.

"In our own community reports of livestock losses runs into thousands of dollars. These are some of the losses reported. Sam Johnle of Onaka lost 12 head of cattle. Perry Downer 14 head, Otto Hieb of northeast of Hosmer 50 head. Another report said a farmer south of Hosmer lost 50 head. Earl Hettich of Roscoe reports losing one cow. People in the west river area got hit the hardest, with some ranchers said to have lost all of their herds. Some lost 100 and more.

"Some stories of the storm border on the humorous, others not very pleasant. A number of families grouped together in one home where no electricity was required. Several families had to crawl out through windows because of blocked doors. Some families stayed in bed all day (Friday) due to lack of heat in the house. Some saved the trouble of dressing in the morning by keeping their clothes on.

"Sunday, March 6 streets were open to one-way traffic and people started to move about. Some drifts are ten to twelve feet high. Traffic again is beginning to move, and should be about normal in a few days.

"We should all praise the radio and TV stations and the civil defense for their part in broadcasting to the public. Congratulations! There however is a note of warning to the public to heed and notice these warnings on weather reports when they are given. This storm was in the making for several days before it arrived here. Don't think it can't happen here. It did! [194]

For the most part, Highway 12 between Roscoe and Ipswich was clear after the blizzard, except for a troublesome spot, two and one-half miles east of Roscoe, near the Dick-

Looking towards Roscoe's city park on March 6. Viewing the snowbanks are Sharon Pischke and Mona Genzlinger, two Roscoe school teachers. Courtesy of Aberdeen American-News.

hault farm. On Saturday, Sheriff DeWald reported that eight semi-trucks and several cars were stalled in the area. The vehicles were pulled out, Saturday afternoon.

Beebe, located in Edmunds County, was named for a pioneer banker from Ipswich, Marcus Beebe. In South Dakota, only four towns were named for bankers.

Before the storm ended, people were advised to put signs on the snow for planes to see. They were told a blanket was the distress signal for medical assistance. Hay bales, or anything else, in the shape of a "F" meant they needed food. If they needed fuel, the signal for that was an "L."

Christ Sauer, 63, a rural Beebe resident, had chest pains. On March 4, Dennis Sauer, his son, wanted to take his father to the hospital, but the blizzard prevented that.

Flying northeast of Roscoe, Harley Taylor and Duane Torrence spotted two blankets laid out on the snow on Sunday. They were over the Dennis and Christ Sauer farm, two and a half miles north and one mile west of Beebe. Taylor and Torrence were part of the Aberdeen CAP squadron. Taylor, a pilot, flew his own plane.

Clarence DeWald, Edmunds County Sheriff, received the call. Sheriff Dewald drove out to the Art Zambo's place. Zambo had a four-wheel drive truck. The two men climbed in the truck and departed for the Sauer farm. Near the Edwin Bauer farm, they encountered a drifts too big for Zambo's truck. They were close to Sauer place, so DeWald and Zambo started walking. Bauer joined the other men, and they transported Christ Sauer to the Ipswich Community Hospital.

Loyalton, located in Edmunds County, was named for a group of Union soldiers from New Hampshire who settled in the vicinity in 1877. The small community had 34 residents in 1960.

Mrs. Clyde Allbee, news correspondent for Loyalton for the *Ipswich Tribune* in 1966 wrote:

> On Wednesday the wind started to blow and started to blizzard, cleared off and on Thursday afternoon we really got a blizzard that didn't let up until Saturday evening. Many a farmer was without electricity, so no water. But do believe that the cattle got the worse of it–without water.[195]

There was no school in Loyalton on Monday, March 7. Mrs. Helmuth Kirschenmann, teacher, indicated the school had furnace trouble and windows, blown in by the storm, needed to be repaired.

Mound City, the seat of Campbell County, acquired its name from near-by Indian mounds.

In 1960, Mound City had a population of 144.

David Ritter, 10 year-old son of Mr. and Mrs. Marvin Ritter who lived south of Mound City near Sand Lake, suffered an appendicitis attack on March 4, 1966. With the blizzard raging outside, the family had one thing going for them. Mrs. Ritter, a registered nurse, knew what was best for her son.

Saturday afternoon, rancher-pilot, Bill Eliason of Gettysburg was asked to fly to the Marvin Ritter farm. Eliason and his neighbors, Webb Jones and Bob Smith, worked tenaciously to get the frozen doors on the hangar open. To get the plane out, they had to shovel lots of snow in front of the building.

Meanwhile, a snowplow worked its way towards the Ritter farm. Behind the snowplow, there was a state patrolman. When they were almost there, he called Gettsyburg. Eliason was informed the snowplow was three blocks away from the farm.

The boy was taken to the Mobridge hospital where he underwent an appendectomy.

In 1966, Miss Stella Allen, Mound City correspondent for the *Selby Record* reported the following:

> The past two Sundays have been very busy ones for many people in Mound City and the Mound City area. On Sunday March 6, help was needed at the Ralph Ritter, Ben Heiser and Milton Deibert farms to dig out livestock. Ralph Ritter lost approximately 100 head of cattle when a pole barn roof collapsed; Heisler lost 15 steers, 1 bull and 2 hogs, and Deibert, 5 steers. Lots more livestock was lost in the area, but reports were not available.
>
> This Sunday, the 13th, thawing snow and opened culverts brought an abundance of water into the new courthouse grounds where drainage had not been provided, and water drained into the basement damaging old records filled there, and to the lawn on the grounds. Men, women and machinery worked diligently to remove snow and water to make adequate drainage possible. The county bulldozer was pressed into service and brought some relief when it cut down the high drifts north of the courthouse.[196]

The first unconfirmed reports out of Campbell County indicated cattle losses between 8,000 and 10,000 head. Mike Madden, Campbell County Agent, revised the totals, one week later. Madden estimated about three percent of the animals in the county were causalities of the storm, about 1,200 head.

Pheasant losses in Campbell County were considered severe.

Pollock, founded in 1901, was first called Harba. The town was renamed for a pioneer settler, James Pollock. The Soo Line arrived in 1902. Pollock was home for 417 in 1960.

On March 2, 1966, Pollock recorded 6 inches of snow, .40 inches of precipitation. The high for the day was 31 degrees. Blizzard conditions developed late in the afternoon.

The storm continued on March 3, the high reached 25 above. Pollock received another .42 inches of precipitation. The low, that evening, dropped to 10 degrees. Wind gusts reached new heights.

On March 4, the winds remained at peak levels for most of the day. After reaching a high of 17 degrees, the temperatures declined to zero, that night. No precipitation was recorded for the day.

On Saturday, another 7 inches of snow fell in Pollock. Overall, Pollock recorded 1.46 inches of precipitation. The town recorded a grand total of 16 inches of snow during the blizzard that ended Saturday afternoon.

Leola, McPherson County seat, was named for Leola Haynes, a daughter of one of the pioneer families. The town was settled in 1885. The Minneapolis & St. Louis Railroad, known as the "Louie," arrived in 1906 from Watertown. Early in 1907, the extension was opened for business.

Eureka was first named St Petersburg by the German-Russians homesteaders of the vicinity. The town was platted on October 3, 1887. Charles Preffer suggested the name Eureka to the Milwaukee Railroad. Eureka, a Greek word, means, "I have found it."

According to Bob Karolevitz and Bernie Hunhoff, "For a time, Eureka was reputed to be one of the largest wheat shipping centers in the world with twenty or more elevators in operation."[197]

Wetonka, another town named by Doane Robinson, was founded in 1906. Its an Indian word that means, "big sun" or "to grow big." The Minneapolis & St. Louis, was its railroad connection.

In 1960, the number of residents in the towns in McPerson County included Leola, 833; Eureka, 1,555; and Wetonka, 46.

On March 2, Leola recorded the most precipitation, .48 inches. That day, Wetonka received .18 inches and .04 inches fell in Eureka.

On Thursday, Eureka recorded 1.70 inches. Leola received at 1.02 inches. Eureka, the only site that listed snowfall, estimated their snowfall total at 15.4 inches. Leola's and Eureka's highs were similar, 30 and 26. That night, there was a big difference in their lows. In Leola thermometer read 23 above, but it was 3 degrees below zero in Eureka.

Leola had a high of 23 and a evening low of 8 degrees on Friday. In Eureka the high and low was 13 and -6. Precipitation was about the same, .35 inches for Leola and .20 inches for Eureka. Snowfall for Eureka was measured at 8.2 inches. Wetonka received no precipitation on Thursday and Friday.

On Saturday, Wetonka recorded, .88 inches. Leola's precipitation amounted to .15 inches. Overall, Eureka received 27 inches of snow, before the storm passed out of the area on Saturday.

Leola and Wetonka lost their power for an hour and a half Thursday night. Power was restored when an employee of Montana Dakota Utilities redirected power at Bowdle.

McPherson County experienced another power outage on Friday. This one lasted much longer. In Leola, Eureka and Wetonka the electricity went out around 10:45 a.m. and it was off to about noon on Saturday. The main cause for this blackout was a fault at the substation in Glenham.

Leola lost its long distance telephone service Thursday morning.

On March 14, Wayne Nesby said "Direct storm-kill figures stood at 900 head in McPherson." Nesby believed that total could go as high 1,200 head with weakened animals still dying in the county. One McPherson rancher told Nesby, "he will be lucky if his loss is less than $25,000.[198]

Pheasant loses in McPerson County from the storm were considered severe.

There was a report of some dead antelope in the Leola hills.

Aberdeen, Columbia, Groton, Westport, Barnard and Frederick

Aberdeen, seat of Brown County, was established in 1881. It was named for Aberdeen, Scotland, the birthplace of Alexander Mitchel, president of the Milwaukee Railroad at that time.

In 1960, Aberdeen's population stood at 23,073.

On March 1, 1966, Americans learned that the Soviet Union landed the first man-made object on planet Venus. The satellite, *Venus 3*, was launched on November 16, 1965.

Meanwhile, the United States planetary exploration program suffered from a financial squeeze. In 1962, *Mariner 2* came within 21,648 miles of Venus. At that time, scientists learned Venus had a surface temperature of 800 degrees, and the cloud cover surrounding the planet prevented the surface heat was rising and escaping. In 1965, *Mariner 4* made the first close approach to Mars and relayed pictures of the planet. Most of NASA budget, however, was being funneled to the manned spaced programs. Congress cut the budget for NASA, as the cost of the Vietnam War was soaring.

In other news, the Malcolm X murder trial continued in New York. One of the assassins, Talmadge Hayer made a dramatic courtroom confession. He testified that he fired a 45-caliber automatic at Malcolm "about four times", after he had been felled by a shotgun blast.

In March 1966, Jay Hanna Dean, better known as "Dizzy," was notified he would not be rehired as a baseball announcer for the upcoming summer games on national television. Dean was a great baseball pitcher for St. Louis Cardinals in the 1930's.

On March 2, Aberdeen had a high of 36 degrees. Old man winter returned, late in the afternoon. The U.S. Weather Bureau local forecast read:

> Aberdeen: Snow this afternoon, tonight and Thursday with strong easterly winds resulting in blowing and drifting. New snow accumulation of four inches or more likely with hazardous driving conditions tonight and Thursday morning. Snow diminishing to flurries by Thursday afternoon. Colder. High today 32, low tonight 20 to 25, high Thursday near 25. Chill factor 0 degrees at noon.[199]

Mayor Cliff Hurlbert of Aberdeen informed local residents that a letter from North Central Airlines had arrived at his office. The letter indicated jet service was now scheduled for the fall of 1967. The airline indicated that Douglas Aircraft Company was delivering its DC-9 jets ahead of schedule and "we sincerely urge your city to make every effort to implement a construction program which would provide an adequate runaway for jet service." Aberdeen had been scheduled for jet service in the spring of 1968. Considering the news, Mayor Hurlbert said, We have to be in position by 1967. We will have to find a way. If necessary, a bond issue would be asked of the voters."[200]

It started snowing in Aberdeen about 3:00 Wednesday afternoon. Before the day was over, 6 inches of snow fell. It contained .59 inches of moisture. The winds fluctuated between 26 and 44 mph. At one point, visibility was down to one-quarter of a mile in the Hub City.

Temperatures remained warm in Aberdeen, it was 26 degrees at midnight.

City snow removal crews started clearing the streets at 2:00 a.m. March 3. In an half hour, the snow turned to rain. Throughout the morning, it rained and drizzled. The winds remained blustery.

The Highway Department issued a travel advisory. It said: "all roads in the Aberdeen district were wet Thursday morning and travel is most instances was difficult to impossible."[201]

The bus depot in Aberdeen reported that the strong winds blew one of their buses to the wrong side of the road in the icy conditions.

There was no disruption of North Central Airlines passenger flights into Aberdeen on Wednesday afternoon and Thursday morning. Scheduled flights out of Aberdeen to Rapid City and Pierre were canceled Thursday morning because those cities reported blizzard conditions.

On March 3 the local forecast said:

> *Aberdeen: Cloudy this afternoon with no important temperature change; high today 37. Cloudy with strong northerly winds developing late this afternoon and tonight with snow flurries and considerable blowing and drifting. Temperature falling with a low by Friday morning of zero to 10 above. Gradual clearing Friday with diminishing winds and much colder, high near 10 above. Hazardous driving conditions will continue in the areas west and north of Aberdeen.*[202]

On Thursday, the *Aberdeen American-News* covered the blizzard that had struck the Dakotas and assigned additional resources to its coverage.

Mike Vogel, sidelined since December 30, 1965, was ready to return to action for the Aberdeen High School basketball team. Coach Frank Bohall wanted Vogel to play in the last regular season game at Huron, Friday night. Aberdeen and Huron were tied for fourth place in the Eastern Conference with seven wins and four losses. The Tigers won the first matchup, 52 to 50, at the Civic Arena.

Aberdeen's high on Thursday was 36 degrees, the official reading came from a site at the airport. As the temperatures fell, the rain and drizzle turned into snow pellets. Around 4:00 p.m., the snow pellets turned to snow. About that time, the winds became much stronger. According to the local media, that was the beginning of the blizzard in Aberdeen.

By Friday morning, the United States Weather Bureau upgraded the "blizzard warnings" to "severe blizzard warnings."

Northerly winds of 40 to 60 miles per hour with snow and colder temperatures were expected for Friday and Friday night.

That afternoon, the temperatures, with the wind chill factor, were expected to be 35 to 40 below zero and 45 to 50 below zero Friday night.

The *American-News* published its daily on Friday, despite the blizzard conditions. There was not much activity in Aberdeen on Friday. That fact was brought home with the lead story. The headline read:

How A Blizzard Closes Up A City
Hub Is Ghost Town In Swirling White Stuff

Bob Overturf, *American-News* staff writer, wrote about his experience with the storm, prior to his arrival at work. Overturf penned the following article:

Snow . . . Snow . . . Snow . . . Wind and Cold
Ways To Say Winter Pile Into Drifts

THERE'S A heck of a lot of ways to say winter in Aberdeen, but they all pile into one big drift.

Snow. Snow. Snow. Snow.

Plus a little wind and cold.

Take Friday morning, for instance. With visibility just a little under zero and a wind that would take the shingles off the roof if they weren't frozen down.

First statement of condition comes from pop who can't get the front door open to let the dogs out early in the morning.

"Nuts!" To put it mildly.

NEXT, THE kids come downstairs to get breakfast.

"No school at Ipswich, None at Bowdle. No school at Mobridge. No classes at Bath. No school at etc., etc., etc.," says the announcer on the local radio station.

Back to pop. Just in from trying to start the car.

"Nuts!" To put it even more mildly.

"No school at Ellendale. None at Webster," continues the announcer.

"Please, mister. Common fellow." The kids are in a circle around the radio. The littlest guy folds his hands in silent prayer.

"No school at crackle-snapple-pop," goes the static, caused by some far off wire being attacked by near-zero wind blowing billows of snow.

THE KIDS are stone-quiet as the announcer finally comes back on the air. " een, where there will be no private or public schools," says the studio voice.

"D'ya suppose?" asks the oldest kid. Was it really Aberdeen? Maybe he'll repeat it?"

Pop, again. He's still trying to get the front door shut.

"Nuts!" Again putting it very, very mildly.

He gives up and goes in the kitchen for his 14th cup of coffee. He adjusts his long underwear he hasn't worn since a river fishing trip a year-ago February. Puts on a second sweater and gulps down one last hot shot of coffee.

"Yippee!" screams the kids. "No school. No school. No school!" The announcer has come through.

BLEARY-EYED mom, hearing the last merry note from the radio station heads for the coffee pot herself, girding herself for a long cold winter day with a house full of vacationing kids.

Uptown, a lone businessman who has struggled through drifts and gusts, eyes the snow covered piles of abandoned cars and the absence of people. He sighs and re-locks his door.

Meanwhile, pop, struggling to see past the hood of his car as he proceeds slowly down 6th Ave., has a comment or two.

"Nuts!" Still putting it mildly, of course.

RADIO SAYS, "No city hall, no courthouse business, no county commissioners, no stores open."

Pop finally climbs through a half-block of snow, from his stalled car, pushes open the door of the door of the newspaper office where he will probably be for the next three days and through frosted chin whiskers, "Hi, gang. Where's the coffee?"

Pop no longer puts it mildly.

He explodes.[203]

Friday morning at 7:00, the thermometer read 10 above at the Municipal Airport. Wind gusts were reported as high as 58 mph.

On Friday morning, Brown County Sheriff, Bernie Kopecky, drove out into the storm to pick up Mrs. Anton Piatz, an expected mother who lived three miles west of Aberdeen. The short run was a long struggle. Sheriff Kopecky battled the weather for five hours, getting Mrs. Piatz to the hospital.

At 3:00 p.m., Aberdeen recorded its daytime high, 17 degrees above zero. Snow amounts were greater than expected. The city recorded 10 inches of snow, amounting to 1.23 inches of moisture.

View of First National Bank driveup teller's windows in Aberdeen. Courtesy of Aberdeen American-News.

Brown County Sheriff Bernie Kopecky on a snowmobile that he used to search for people believed missing in the blizzard, when motor vehicular travel proved impossible. Courtesy of Aberdeen American-News.

According to the *American-News*, "Police, fire, and volunteer blizzard fighters bucked growing drifts and rock-bottom visibility Friday on emergency runs." The police used a National Guard four-wheel drive truck to deliver prescriptions. The vehicle got stuck in the snow on one run, but the patrolman walked the final five blocks and transferred the medicine. Somewhat later, a state highway snowplow pulled the National Guard vehicle out for the police.

The Civil Air Patrol manned its radio during the storm. Using a four-wheel drive vehicle, the Aberdeen unit also disbursed prescriptions, hauled doctors and nurses to and from the hospital, and ran other tasks.

A snowplow was assigned to the fire department for the duration of the storm. The operators stayed at the fire station. The firemen responded to two calls during the blizzard. One was a car fire by the Radison Hotel. The other run was to a trailor home where a space heater overheated.

The Aberdeen-Huron basketball game was canceled Friday night. The game was not rescheduled because sectional play started on Tuesday.

Early Saturday morning, the winds had settled down to 25 to 37 mph. The snow stopped falling in Aberdeen at 8:30. The local media considered that the end of the blizzard. For the day Aberdeen recorded .28 inches of precipitation, 2.9 inches of snow.

The Harry Warfield farm north of Aberdeen.

Traffic on 8th Avenue NE in Aberdeen on March 6. Both photos courtesy of Aberdeen American-News.

Digging out on 8th Avenue NE in Aberdeen. Courtesy of Aberdeen American-News.

Aberdeen residents digging out vehicles. Both photos courtesy of Aberdeen American-News.

Facing south on North Lloyd Street in Aberdeen. Courtesy of Aberdeen American-News.

For the residents of Aberdeen, the blizzard was just over forty hours. Overall, Aberdeen received 18 inches of snow, between March 2 and March 5.

Operation Bulldozer, the state-wide employment of heavy equipment contractors for snow removal operations, was utilized in the Aberdeen area.

One house near 8th Ave North and Arch Street had its doors blocked with huge drifts. The family was trapped inside. When people walked by their home, they banged on their front windows. After a while, someone came over with a shovel and freed them.

Pheasant hunting brings millions of dollars into South Dakota. According to R.A. Hodgins, director of the Department of Game, Fish and Parks, the state's ringneck population in the fall of 1965 had dropped to 3.5 million, or 28 percent below the 1964 figure.

On March 6, biologists checked southwest Brown County and southeast Edmunds, northeast Faulk, and a corner of Spink County for pheasant losses. They found lots of dead birds, but many others had survived the storm.

Also, on Sunday afternoon one man drove to Cresbarb and he counted birds on the trip. Monday morning, that individual reported his findings to the *Aberdeen American-News*. He saw about 300 dead birds and about 900 live ones.

On March 7, the Game, Fish, and Parks Department personnel began aerial observations for pheasants losses. As travel conditions improved, the department conducted grounds checks. Game Warden B.J. Rose of Aberdeen reported storm-kill percentages of 25 to 33 percent in the Aberdeen area on March 8.

That sample area extended on a line between Columbia and Cresbard. Rose said, "The kill looked to be about 10 percent in the Columbia area and rose as it went southward to about 50 percent near the end of the checking line. The kill varied greatly, all along the line. Those pheasants which were in a large areas of good winter cover came out of the

SOUVENIR EDITION

The 1966
BLIZZARD

Aberdeen American-News

Aberdeen, South Dakota   March 15, 1966

Page 1   Fifteen Cents

CATTLE, OUTSIDE IN the blizzard, wore snow masks when the storm ended Saturday morning. Ice and snow covered their eyes. Icicles hung from their lips and in some cases their mouths were frozen shut. An important ranching tool after the blizzard was an axe (or hammer) which was used to break the ice off the cattle's faces. This photo was taken near Glenham Saturday morning by Eldon Merkel.

Neighborly Shooting . . . Oregon Trucker Learns Fast

Newsman Told Of Laughter, Terror, Courage

By MAX COOPER
American-News Sunday Editor

IT WAS almost exactly the way I thought it would be when I met Frank Maciejewski on the storm-battered Maciejewski Ranch near Timber Lake — a few rods from where hundreds of his dead calves were piled up against a fence.

A Summation Of The Big Storm

Blizzard Of '66 Was A Killer Out Of The West

By Del Griffin
American-News Staff Writer

IT CAME out of the west, this brawling, bawling wild one. It sucked up air, gulped water from the Gulf of Mexico and blew. It staggered noisily around in the Dakotas for awhile before it drifted quietly away.

Souvenir Edition of Aberdeen American News, March 15, 1966. Courtesy of Aberdeen American-News.

storm pretty well. Smaller flocks in smaller areas, however, were in some instances almost completely wiped out."[204]

~ On March 8, the Aberdeen High School basketball team, the Golden Eagles, traveled to Mobridge to face the Lemmon Cowboys in the opening game of the Section 3 Class A Tournament. The Eagles advanced to the championship game, 63 to 47. Mike Vogel scored 8 points in his first appearance since December 30. Terry Durnil led the team in scoring with 11 points.

Redfield and Aberdeen met in the championship game. Early in the fourth quarter, Redfield led Aberdeen by 8 points. Late in the game, Dan Wollman scored three successive baskets, it gave the Eagles a one point lead. The Pheasants tied the game with a free throw. Redfield held the ball for the final shot. It was off the mark.

The game went into overtime. Dan Cavanaugh won the tip for the Eagles and they controlled the ball until the final seconds. Tom Olson drove in for the winning shot. He made the basket, but the referee gave Olson a charging foul, after releasing the shot. Redfield's Alvars Silins sank both free throws.

The game went into double overtime. Nobody scored as the clock dwindled down to 10 seconds. Redfield played for the last shot. They missed the shot, but Tom Powers grabbed the rebound for the Pheasants. Powers went up with another shot, but Mike Vogel blocked it. The play resulted in a jump ball. Vogel tipped the ball to Terry Durnil who fired a long desperation shot. It missed, but Vogel sprinted down the court. Just before time expired, Vogel caught the rebound off the backboard and put it. The Golden Eagles advanced to the Class A Basketball Tournament in Sioux Falls.

Pheasant losses in Brown County on March 12 were considered light.

Columbia was settled in 1879, but the town was called Richmond at that time. It was named for Richmond, Illinois. Another town in Dakota Territory already claimed that name, so the Post Office submitted a list of substitute names. C.P. Peck and William Townsend picked the new name.

The population of Columbia in 1960 was 272.

In a special election on February 28, 1966, the voters in the Columbia Independent School District approved the plan that would close the school in Columbia on July 1, 1966, and send the students to the Groton High School or someplace else. Superintendent Harold T. Nelson indicated that emotions were mixed in the community, 87 voted in favor of the proposal and 67 against the issue. Currently, the high school had an enrollment of 61 students.

The following account was provided to *Dakota Midland News Service*. A journalist interviewed a person from Columbia. The article said:

> When the electricity went off and many of the homes were left without heat and cooking facilities, the men banded together to bring members of heatless households to homes where space heaters or manually operated furnaces were still in use.
>
> The men went out in the storm several times to get persons who couldn't walk through the storm alone and brought them to friends houses.
>
> Extra food was prepared and all available bedding was rounded up. One home housed 17 persons during the storm.
>
> Three men headed for the Fritz Meints home at the north city limits and the Pete Heitzigs home a little further east when they learned the heat had gone off at these houses.

> *The trio met the group walking toward town after their tractor and trailer in which they were riding in had stalled. Those on foot joined the trio in the truck and turned back to town. When the truck became stalled all occupants started out on foot once again.*
>
> *When the trio failed to return to town after a reasonable length of time, five more men went in search of the party and located them about a block north of town. All were brought safely into homes in town.*
>
> *During the storm, the stove in the post office went "boom" and scattered soot and smoke. The women in town went to work to clean up the mess and the post office was ready to handle mail again by Monday morning when the trucks once again were moving on the roads.*[205]

Westport and Barnard, had 100 residents in 1960. Westport was named after a Milwaukee Railroad official. Founded in 1906, Barnard was either named for Frank H. Barnard, the landowner of the townsite or for Horance Barnard, an early settler.

Hecla (444 resident in 1960), another town in Brown County, was founded by the Western Town Lot Company in 1886. It was named for a volcano in Iceland with the same name.

On March 3, 1966, there was no school Westport, Barnard and Helca.

During the blizzard, Westport and Barnard endured a power outage.

Although Frederick was platted in 1881, it was not settled until the following year. The town was named for a son of a Milwaukee Railroad official. Its population was figured at 381 in 1960.

In February 1966, Frederick won the District 4 Basketball Tournament by beating Columbia and Hecla.

Although there was no school on Frederick on March 3, 1966, the high school boys basketball team was in Webster to play Roslyn in the opening game of the Region 1 Basketball Tournament. Roslyn defeated Garden City, Waubay and Bristol in the District 2 Basketball Tournament. Despite the weather, there was good turnout of Viking fans at Webster. So far, the team was 21-1, its single loss came in overtime to the Britton Braves on January 11.

Coach Roger Prunty went to his bench in the second half, the starters had built a big lead. Britton won the second game. The team started back to Frederick, but they stopped in Aberdeen.

Many of their fans took shelter in Aberdeen as well. Among those who stopped there were Gayle Maunna, Sheryl Breitkreutz, Lynne Eissinger, Frederick cheerleaders, along with Mr. and Mrs. Ralph Cranage and Scott Post of Frederick.

The four girls were interviewed Friday morning at the Alonazo Ward Hotel Coffee shop. The girls said:

> *"Last night we got to about half a mile north of Aberdeen and had to turn around and come back. We picked up three kids who had been at the bowling alley and gave them a ride back to town. They were all frost covered, even though they had just walked a little way. There were 10 of us in the car."*

They were riding in Cranage's car, a police car. Mr. Cranage used the red lights all the back to Aberdeen. Miss Breitkreutz said:

> *"My dad has told me about winter storms like this but I never believed him."*

Another one said:

> *"Its quite an experience, a lot of fun, but I wouldn't want to do it again."*[206]

Frederick lost its long distance phone service Thursday night. The town experienced a minor power outage on Friday. Winds, up to 60 mph, left drifts 12 to 15 feet high in Frederick.

South of Frederick, the strong winds swept a semi-truck into the ditch, Thursday night. Three men were marooned until Saturday afternoon. To keep their feet from freezing, the men took their boots and shoes off. Then, they placed them on each others chests.

According to the men, they prayed many times during their 33 hour ordeal. They had a package of gum for food.

Phone service to Frederick was restored Monday evening.

That night, the rematch took place in Webster. Coach Roger Prunty and the starting five wanted to get back to Sioux Falls for the state tournament. In 1964, the Vikings played in the tournament and finished in seventh place. At that time, Coach Prunty was an assistant to Bob Sorenson. In the 1965-66 season, he became the head coach. Sorenson took a teaching job in Pipestone, Minnesota. Prunty was a 1960 graduate of Westport High School and he attended Northern State College. Russ Podal, a sophomore, and Lee Wilson, a freshman, were starters on the 1964 team and Stan Mikkonen, Roy Glover and Darrell Golnitz saw action off the bench.

Frederick led Britton Braves, 53 to 50, with 5:30 left in the game. Wilson converted three straight shots and the Vikings led 59 to 50. After that, the Braves had to foul to get the ball back.

Another basket by Wilson and six straight free throws by Glover and Golnitz sent the Vikings back to the state tournament. The final score was 69 to 63. Wilson had 28 points and Glover had 15. Golnitz, added 11, and he held Britton's ace, Wayne Schlekeway, to 9 points in the first half.

School in Frederick was resumed on March 8.

According to the *Frederick Brown County News*, Daryl Bender and some men caught a deer near the station on the hill. They removed the snow and ice from its face. Many pheasants were killed in the area.

Britton, Veblen, Newark, Kidder and Eden

Britton, founded in 1881, is the county seat of Marshall County. The town was named after Isaac Britton, the general manager of the Dakota and Great Southern Railroad.

In 1960, Britton had a population of 1,442.

In February 1966, Britton won District 3 Basketball Tournament Class B Championship Tournament. The Braves defeated Groton, 66 to 53, and Langford, 67 to 58. In the championship game, Pierpont outshot Britton in the field, but the Braves made 25 of 31 free throws. The hometown team came out with a victory, 62 to 51. Wayne Schlekeway, Dick Medley, John Prchal, Dennis Smart and Wayne Cusick started for Britton. Their coach was Bill Amacher.

On March 2, Britton recorded a high of 34 degrees. It was the fifth straight day, that temperatures rose above the freezing mark.

Light snow fell that night, Harvey Dugdale, the local weather observer recorded it as a trace of precipitation.

That week residents could shop in two new stores. Ternes Clothing opened up for business in the Skogmo Store. Mr. and Mrs. Tony Ternes were the proprietors. The Ben Franklin Variety store had their grand opening as well.

In the Region 1 Tournament at Webster on March 3, they met the Corona Midgets, newly crowned District 1 champions with victories over Peever, Veblen, and New Effington.

For most of the day, the weather was decent. The town had a high of 34 degrees. Blizzard warnings were issued for northeast South Dakota Thursday and Thursday night. Despite the weather, their fans traveled to Webster, that evening.

Blizzard conditions developed that night.

The Britton Braves did not disappoint their fans, as they defeated Corona, 71 to 49. Frederick downed Rosyln in the other game. After the games were over, most of the people stayed in Webster.

Two cars full of people left Webster for Britton. In one vehicle was Mr. and Mrs. Archie Kilkner and their sons, Boyd and Dennis, Tom Polkinghorn and Dale Wilgers. Jim and Bruce Anderson, Mahlan Satrang, and Don Gooding were in the another one. Traveling north on State Highway 25, they slowed down to almost a crawl. Five miles south of Britton, they turned east and headed for the Duane Thayer farm. Both parties were glad to reach the farm yard in the near-zero visibility. The house was not occupied at this time, so they stayed in their cars, Thursday night.

Friday morning, the door to the farmhouse was forced open. Inside, they had a pleasant surprise, heat. The Thayer family had kept the furnace running on low, so the pipes wouldn't freeze over the winter. Later, the boys left for Britton in one of the cars. Shortly before noon, the boys reached Britton. They notified the authorities of the situation out at the Thayer farm.

Friday afternoon, Sheriff Ed Friebel and Patrolman Jerry Boyer worked their way to the Thayer farm. They transported the stranded fans back to Britton.

The annual South Dakota Wool Growers Association meeting, scheduled for March 6 in Britton was canceled. Russell Dull, Amherst, was reported missing. Dull left Sisseton Thursday at 9:30 p.m.

The storm ended Saturday morning. Harvey Dugdale estimated Britton received 7 inches of snow in the storm, 1.05 inches of precipitation.[207]

Otter Tail Power Company experience a power outage at 3:00 a.m. Friday. After that, Britton's local plant took over the load. Parts of Britton were without power for 45 minutes and just a couple of minutes in other areas.

Bob Perry, local manager of the telephone company, reported that 252 telephone customers lost the use of their phones. Just west of Britton, twelve poles were knocked down by the high winds.

Russell Dull left Sisseton about 9:30 p.m. Thursday. Dull headed west on State Highway 10. He drove slowly, very slowly, along the shoulder of the road. At times, he stopped and waited for the visibility to clear a little.

After a while, Dull was stuck in the snow. And he was lost.

On Friday, the storm did not let up. Dull started his car at intervals. The hours dragged on and on.

Saturday morning, Dull had some gas left in his car. He used it to get warm. Later on, the storm letup.

That afternoon, Dull left his car and walked to the Janisch Tavern. Dull had left State Highway 10 and turned onto the Buffalo Lake road. He never saw the road signs in the blizzard.

Cleanup up in Britton began at 3:00 p.m. Saturday. The biggest drift, 6 to 8 feet high, was on the south side of the Thorp Auto Company.

The business district was cleared by 10:00 a.m Sunday.

State Highway 10 was blocked on the west edge of Britton and by the Clifford Reyelts farm. East of Britton, big drifts formed on the highway by the city dump entrance road.

County highway crews went out for a couple of hours on Saturday. They were out all day Sunday. Most county roads were opened on Monday, but not for long. Blustery winds filled the cuts back up. There was another round of plowing on Tuesday. By Wednesday noon, all county roads were open except the Buffalo Lake road, according to Robert Stadler, temporary highway superintendent. Stadler figured it would be open late Wednesday night.

Snowplow crews thought the Kidder road was the "toughest" to open in the aftermath.

By Monday night, phone service was restored to all customers, except for a few families where extensive work was required.

Livestock losses were light in Marshall County. Dalton Docter lost 18 head of cattle, about $5400.00 worth. Otto Turk suffered a loss of 12 head of cattle. Delvin Weiker reported the death of 9 butcher hogs. Both Loren Grupe and Dick Moeckly lost a couple of head of cattle on their farms. Moeckly's cattle-feeding shed blew down in the storm, but only one animal was there when the structure collapsed.

Game Warden, Harvey Binger, acknowledged the death of some antelope. Fortunately, he said, "other animals in several herds in the area survived the winter storm." Binger estimated pheasant losses at 20 to 25 percent.

On March 10, the Marshall County Commissioners held their regular meeting. They placed county storm losses at $250,000.[208]

Veblen, located in Marshall County, was founded in 1900.

The town was named J.E. Veblen, one of the first homesteaders near the town site. George Anderson and Dan Hill of Veblen persuaded a Minneapolis banker, Julius Rosholt, to invest in the Fairmount & Veblen Railway in 1912. Construction of the line was completed in 1913. In 1915, the Soo Line purchased the Fairmount & Veblen Railroad.

Veblen had 437 residents in 1960.

The Veblen high school boys won the Whetsone Valley Conference title for the 1965-66 season. The Cardinals compiled a 11-4 regular season record. The team was coached by Bud Lewis.

During the morning of March 3, 1966, Veblen lost its long distance telephone service.

Newark was settled April 1883. P. O. Howell, an early resident named it for Newark, New Jersey.

Kidder, located in Marshall County, was founded in 1885. The Great Northern Railroad went through the town, that year. The town probably was named for Jefferson P. Kidder, a Congressman for Dakota Territory between 1875 and 1879.

John Kotschavor donated 10 acres of his land in Eden Township in 1895 for a townsite, a church, and a cemetery in Marshall County. The place became known as Eden Park. The Fairmout & Veblen Railroad extended their line from Veblen to Grenville in Day County in 1914. Businesses from Eden Park moved to the railroad and the place became known as Eden.

In 1960, the Marshall County towns had the following populations Newark, 39; Kidder, 61; and Eden, 136.

The power went out in Newark and Kidder at about 4:30 a.m. on Friday and it was not restored until noon on Saturday. Eden's power outage lasted from 1:00 a.m. to 7:00 p.m. on Saturday.

Webster, Bristol, Waubay, Rosyln and Pierpont

Webster, seat of Day County, was platted in 1881. The town was named for J.B. Webster, the first settler. The Milwaukee Road extended its line from Big Stone to Webster in 1880. Webster received a rail connection to Aberdeen the following year.

Bristol, named by C.H. Prior, townsite agent for the Milwaukee, for Bristol, England. Located in Day County, the town's first settlers came in 1881. R.P Brokaw helped lay out the town of Bristol, which had been called simply Section 70 by the railroad surveyors.

Waubay was established in 1880, it was first known as Station 50 on the Milwaukee. Later that year, the town was renamed Blue Lake. In 1885, the town had its last name change, Waubay. At one time, Waubay had eleven grain elevators.

Rosyln, located in Day County, was platted in 1914. The town is named after two nearby lakes, Rosholt and Lynn Lakes.

Located in Day County, Pierpont first settlers arrived in 1883. The town was named for a Milwaukee Railroad official.

On February 6, 1940, Tom Brokaw was born in Webster. His first memories are from Bristol and the Brokaw House Hotel. His great-grandfathers, Richard Paterson Brokaw and Tom Conley had settled in Day County. In the early 1880's, R.P. Brokaw began construction on Brokaw House Hotel in Bristol.

Another Webster native who went on to become famous was Myron Floren. A world class accordionist, he joined the Lawrence Welk Orchestra in 1950. Eventually, he became Welk's second in command. From 1955 to 1982, Mr. Floren's virtuosity on the accordion could be seen weekly on national television, first on the ABC television network and then later in syndication. In later years, he made regular appearances at the Norsk Hoskfest in Minot, North Dakota.

According to the South Dakota Game, Fish and Parks information guide, Enemy Swin Lake, located north of Waubay, gave up three record fish prior to 1966. Leroy Nelson caught a 33 lbs., 8 oz northern pike in 1939. Nelson holds the second oldest fishing record in the state.(The oldest record on the books is the catch of the biggest brown trout in Rapid Creek in the Black hills in 1928.) John Yunker holds the record for the largest white (silver) bass, 3 lbs 14 oz., in 1964. In 1965, John Vincent pulled in the largest rock bass in the state. In the fall of 1965, Jerry Roitsch shot a big whitetail deer, four and a half miles northwest of Lily. The Boone and Crockett Club figured it might rank as high as fifth for non-typical whitetail deer in North America with a score of 244.8 points.

In 1966, Day County led South Dakota in fur sales and licensed trappers.

The Waubay National Wildlife Refuge is located in Day County. The name "Waubay," is an English corruption of a Sioux word meaning "where wild fowl build their nest." The refuge is an important breeding ground for the thousands of ducks and geese that fly over the area.

In 1960, Webster had a population of 2,409; Bristol 562; Rosyln 256; Waubay 851; and Pierpont, 258.

On February 28, 1966, Webster suffered its first conference loss of the season to the Sisseton Redmen, 68 to 58. Earlier in the year, Webster beat Sisseton, 63 to 56.

Their upcoming game with Milbank on March 4 was very important. A victory over Milbank would ensure the Cats the Northeast Conference title outright. If they lost, Sisseton and Webster would share the conference crown.

On March 2, highways and roads in northern half of South Dakota were not in the best shape because of rain and drizzle. There were reports of glare ice.

Snow and high winds on March 3 compounded the problem.

There was no school in Webster on Thursday.

The blizzard struck Thursday night. Webster recorded .27 inches of precipitation that day.

The storm was relentless on Friday. More snow fell, .68 inches of precipitation. Webster's high of 31, came early in the day. That night, the low was 10 degrees.

The weather was still bad, Saturday morning. Webster recorded another .44 inches of precipitation. Overall, Webster received 12 inches of snow. Saturday's high was 15 degrees.

Businessmen on the west side of Main who had lots of work ahead of them included Horton Wagner of Lindrud Stores and Lyle Hansen of Webster Cafe. A car parked south of the Klein Hotel on Sixth Avenue was completely buried, except for the tip of the car's aerial. Several other cars were buried in the same drift.

James Johnson, an employee of Langager Implement, was overwhelmed by the storm between Webster and Watertown. He pulled his truck over and spent the night in it.

Day County suffered major telephone damages. Outages were reported in Roslyn, Webster, Waubay, and Bristol. Telephone crews from outside the area assisted local workers. The reporter for the *Webster Reporter and Farmer* wrote:

> Northwestern Bell Telephone manager Paul Robson said that major damage to the telephone lines was reported in the Roslyn area. Roslyn was without services from Saturday until Monday and rural areas northwest, southwest, south and east of the community lost service.
>
> The long distance lines and connecting lines between Rosyln and Webster were repaired first and Minnesota crews came in Tuesday to replace aerial cable damaged by the storm. The high winds caused the aerial cable to whip in a circular motion and break in several places.
>
> Robson said he hopes repairmen can repair the broken cable by today (March 9) and expects to have the cable which feeds all the lake lines and rural patrons south and east of Roslyn in operation by Friday (March 11). An underground cable will replace the aerial cable, but will not be buried until the spring thaw.[209]

Lake Region Electric reported power outages on their rural lines between Thursday and Saturday.

During the blizzard, two water mains broke at Bristol. Part of the city had no water until the repairs were made.

Some cattle strolled into Bristol, Saturday morning.

The cattle shed at the Maynard Sigdestad farm, near Bristol, collapsed in the blizzard. Friends and neighbors came over with shovels and tractors to free 19 animals trapped inside the building on Saturday. They worked carefully. By noon Sunday, the crisis was over. Sigdestad lost only four head in the disaster.

Another individual who lost several head of cattle was John Skaare.

The *Reporter and Farmer* published the happenings of Piermont. Here's the Piermont News:

> School and most of the stores in town were closed Friday because of the severe blizzard. Many homes west of town were without electricity and some families having bottle gas heat in their basements had to move down there during the storm.
>
> Much snow fell here and banks blocked roads and yards, but with many men with tractors and snow scoops, most of it has been removed and roads are opened.[210]

The following blizzard inklings were written by Larry Ingalls of the *Webster Reporter and Farmer*. Ingalls wrote:

> How about that snow flurry we had last week.? It is being pegged as the worst blizzard since 1888, but of course that doesn't count in this area because we didn't get enough snow. It really did seem pretty tough Friday, but we were surprised to find how little snow there was out in the country.
>
> The towns and farm homes with tree groves really caught the snow while the plowed fields looked like they just had a little frost on them.
>
> Boy, the city really cleaned up Main Street and nearby side streets in a hurry. By Sunday morning the streets were so clean you couldn't even tell there had been a blizzard.
>
> The street openings had their bad moments however. I'll bet I shoveled the south end of by driveway out at least four times Saturday. I'd open it up and an hour later a plow would come along to move snow further off the streets. It seemed like most of it was dumped in my driveway or sidewalk entrance.
>
> Our family happened to be in the process of moving when the storm hit and it proved to be rather comical. We got our furniture and most of our other belongings moved Thursday afternoon, but our clothes, pots and pans and other odds and ends were in the other home. My wife Jan would call the shop every once and awhile and the conversation would go thusly: "I need the small frying pan next to the large one in the upper left drawer on the left side of the counter. You might also bring a couple of diapers for Pam and the distilled water for the iron is in the second bedroom."
>
> Two hours later: "I forgot about the ironing board, and if you want a change of clothes for tomorrow you had better get some out of the closet. While you're at it grab the broom, my green coat, Pam's pajamas, the box of Cherrios and the clothes hamper."
>
> I even took my suit along Saturday afternoon, but to no avail. They didn't have church Sunday.
>
> Grace Nerger from Nerger's V-Store didn't let the storm bother her. She walked the six blocks to work Friday morning and I saw her on the way

home again that night. I had to take a second look to make sure it was her though, because she had a paper sack over her head as protection against the wind. The eyes, nose and mouth were cut out of the sack so she could see and breath.[211]

With the sectional tournament later in the week, Webster and Milbank had no interest in making up their game.

Webster's first round opponent at Watertown on March 10 was against their arch rival Sisseton. In 1965, Sisseton defeated Webster in the championship game and went on to the state tournament.

In 1966, Webster defeated Sisseton, 60 to 55. Clyde Hagen led Webster with 24 points, he was 11 for 11 at the free throw line.

Webster faced Milbank who had routed Watertown by a score of 57 to 43. Milbank led Webster for most of the game. When the final buzzer sounded the score was 37 to 37.

After gaining possession of the ball in overtime, Webster went into a stall. With four seconds left, Larry Syhre sank a 20-foot set shot. It sent the Bearcats to the state tournament. Hagen, a forward, poured in 21 points for the Bearcats. Dick Maynes finished with 14 for Milbank.

Coach Bob Swanhorst's squad had nine seniors, the team took a 17-3 record into the state tournament. Swanhorst was an impact player for Cresbard in the Class B State Tournaments in 1956 and 1957. He led Cresbard to the title in 1957. Swanhorst scored the most points in a championship game. That record was still his in 1966. After high school, Swanhorst became a starter for Augustana College.

The last time Webster played in the Class A State Tournament was in 1954. That year, the team finished seventh and was coached by Hobe Richards. Webster made its name in South Dakota basketball in the Class B tournaments in the 1940s. Webster with Coach Houk won the Class B State tournament three years in a row, 1946-48.

On March 16, about 200 fans gave the Cats a big sendoff to Sioux Falls when the team left at 7:00 a.m.

Webster canceled school for students in grades 7-12 on March 17 and March 18, so they could attend the state tournament. Arrangements were made for adults and students to ride buses to Sioux Falls, $1.50 for adults and $1.25 for students for the trip.

Sioux Falls Washington and Rapid City were the favorites of the pre-tourney talk because of their school size and records. Webster, Belle Fourche, Canton and Chamberlain all were about the same size.

On March 17, Webster and Belle Fourche, 19-3, played the first game of the tournament. Webster had too much for Belle Fourche. The Bearcats won 63 to 42. Clyde Hagen and Mike Thompson led the team with 16 and 14 points. Dean Johnson, a junior, scored 10 points off the bench. Larry Syhre brought the ball upcourt and directed their offense. He also netted 9 points. In the second game, Canton surprised Chamberlain. In the evening session, Aberdeen upset Rapid City and Sioux Falls came from behind to defeat Pierre.

On March 18, the Bearcats led the Canton Hawks by three points at half time. Late in the third period, Webster took charge of the game, despite the hot shooting of Canton's guard, John Eidsness. Webster advanced to the championship game with a 56 to 47 victory. Hagen scored 30 points and pulled down 22 rebounds. Aberdeen pulled off another upset win over Sioux Falls Washington.

Saturday night, Webster and Aberdeen played in front of 9,000 fans. The Bearcats and Golden Eagles liked to control the ball. Aberdeen came out in a man-to-man full court press. They scored the first two baskets of the game. The Eagles led after one quarter, 12 to 11. The Cats scored the first basket in the second quarter to take the lead. Webster never trailed again, they had a six point lead at halftime. In the final minutes of the game, Coach Bob Swanhorst cleared his bench. All twelve players played in the championship game. Webster won by a score of 51 to 32. Hagen scored 23 points and Ron Jacobson and Mike Keller finished with 11 and 9 points. Syhre handled the full court press of the Golden Eagles. Hagen was named most valuable player of the tournament.

It was the first Class A title for Webster. Coach Swanhorst said, "It was a pleasure working with these guys, and I'm sure hate to see those seniors go. But we have some good sophomores, and I hope we can be back here next year." The players on the championship team included Dean Johnson, Craig Saylor, Randy Lindquist, Bill Kehrwald, Larry Syhre, Norm Baumgarn, Mike Thompson, Ted Gerriets, Maris Birzneiks, Ron Jacobson, Mike Keller and Clyde Hagen. Colin Conley, student manager, and Larry Luitjens, Assistant Coach, were other members of the team.

Sunday afternoon the Cats, now being called "Hagen's Heroes," were welcomed back to Webster. The *Reporter and Farmer* said, "By the time the bus carrying the players and their coaches reached Webster there were an estimated 500 honking cars trailing behind in a eight mile line."[212]

Claire City, Hammer, New Effington, Victor, Rosholt, Sisseton, Peever, Wilmot, Summit and Corona

In the northern part of Roberts County, the building of Fairmount & Veblen Railroad helped establish five towns in 1913. Claire City was named by A. E. Feeney, one of the four donors of the townsite. Hammer was named for Gunder and Ivor Hammer, the town was built on their land. New Effington was named for the nearby abandoned town of Effington which was named for the first girl, Effie, born there. Victor was named for Victor Township, organized by Victor Renville in 1892. Renville was the son of Gabriel Renville, chief of the Sisseton Sioux, and grandson of the first Victor Renville who lived with the Indians in this area before white settlement. Rosholt was named for Julius Rosholt.

In 1960, population totals for Claire City, 86; Hammer, 45; New Effington, 280; Victor, 40; and Rosholt, 423.

Long distance telephone service was disrupted for New Effington and Claire City, the morning of March 3, 1966. That morning, fog reduced visibility.

Sisseton, Roberts County seat, was platted in 1892. The town had 3, 218 residents in 1960.

There was a trace of precipitation in Sisseton on March 2, 1966. The thermometer rose to 33 degrees, and the mercury fell only five degrees for the evening low.

On Thursday, Sisseton received .61 inches of precipitation, a mixture of freezing rain and snow. School was called off. Temperature wise, the high was 35 above and the low was 28. Blizzard conditions developed when strong winds hit the area late in the afternoon.

On Friday, there was very little activity.

On Saturday, the storm receded and expired. Before it did, Sisseton recorded another .97 inches of precipitation.

On March 14, Joe E. Schuch, Roberts County Agent, stated, "There were no storm-related livestock deaths in Roberts County."

Pheasant losses were moderate to severe.[213]

Peever, named after T.H. Peever, an early-day resident of Sisseton who bought the land and named the town for himself, is located in Roberts County. The Milwaukee Railroad arrived in 1893.

The 1965-66 basketball season for the Peever high school boys ended in the District 1 Tournament in late February 1966.

Blizzard conditions developed, Thursday evening, March 3. That night, the residents of Peever enjoyed the warm comforts of their homes. Peever had a population of 205 in 1966.

Early Friday morning, the town faced its worst nightmare. There was a fire. The local volunteers responded as quickly as possible. The Town Hall, the social center of the school and town, was burning. Calls went out to the fire departments in Sisseton, and Browns Valley, Minnesota.

In Sisseton, the alarm rang at 6:30 a.m. The Sisseton fire department quickly made arrangements for an escort. A state highway snowplow led fire truck in near-zero visibility.

The fire volunteers in Peever did everything they could, but flames crackled in the strong winds. The fire expanded to other buildings.

The firemen from Sisseton arrived in Peever at 9:00 a.m. Their Browns Valley counterparts arrived just ahead of them. By then, the fire was out of control.

The combined forces of the three fire departments stopped the fire from advancing to additional buildings. After the fire ran its course, most of the buildings on Peever's business block had been destroyed. Lost were the Town Hall, the municipal liquor store, the Peever Post Office, including records; a vacant building which was formerly Wren's Tavern; and Bucklin's Tavern.

The loss was partially covered by insurance.

Wilmot was named for Judge Wilmot W. Brookings by C.H. Prior, Milwaukee townsite agent. The railroad built a branch line from Milbank to Wilmot in 1882. That branch line was extended to Sisseton in 1893.

In 1960, the town was home for 545 people.

The Veblen Cardinals earned a tough win by overcoming the Wilmont Wolves, 53 to 49, in the first round of District 1 Tournament at Webster on February 24, 1966. The next day, the Wolves defeated the Peever Panthers by a score of 55 to 42. On Saturday, the Wolves battled the Summit Eagles for fifth place. The game was decided in the final seconds of a double overtime game. Dale Faeth shot the ball as the buzzer sounded. It went in the basket. The Eagles had a thrilling two point victory over the Wolves.

The blizzard of 1966 made a deposit at Wilmont. Drifts were 12 feet high around town. Some were on the north side of David Babb and Rex Rensberger homes. Another home that was surrounded by giant drifts was the H.J. Christianson home. The Herman Jurgens home on the south side was buried to the roof, the doors and windows were completely covered. The west wing of the new Wilmot Community Home had snowbanks level with the roof.

On March 3, 4 inches of snow fell in Wilmot. Warm weather melted some of it. Heavy fog then rolled into the area. There was school in Wilmot on Thursday. On Friday and Saturday, 14 inches of snow fell. The winds died down late Saturday. Throughout the storm, the temperatures remained moderate.[214]

Mr. and Mrs. Gene Frerichs were stranded at Brooks Corner. They left their infant son with his grandparents, Mr. and Mrs. Ernest Frerichs. The couple planned on returning the same day. On Friday, Donald Frerichs rode horseback to Gene Frerichs farm and returned with a supply of milk.

The digging out process began on Sunday and it lasted well into the following week.

Residents were able to pick up their mail Sunday morning.

Milk trucks from the Farmers Co-op Creamery began around the clock service on Sunday. Some dairy farmers suffered financial losses when they ran out of storage. On March 9, milk trucks resumed their normal pickups.

There was no school in Wilmot on Friday and Monday.

Summit, located in Roberts County, was established by the Milwaukee in 1892. First known as Summit Siding, the railroad builders thought it was the highest town in the Coteau range between the Mississippi and Missouri Rivers with an altitude of 2,000 feet.

Summit had a population of 283 in 1960.

On March 2, 1966, Summit had a high of 31 degrees. There was a trace of precipitation.

On March 3, Summit experienced strong winds. School officials called off school on Thursday. Summit recorded .19 inches of precipitation and a high of 33 degrees. Blizzard conditions developed that night.

Around midnight Thursday, a gun boomed in one of the houses in Summit. The bullet from the .22 rifle hit Sylvan White in the stomach. The gunshot wound was an accident.

Details of the incident were explained to the authorities. Roberts County Sheriff, James Sanden, in Sisseton notified medical personnel to get ready for a stomach wound. After lining up a snowplow and the services of a local ambulance, Sheriff Sanden and the others headed out in the storm. The drivers of the emergency vehicles drove with their heads out of the windows. They had to return.

On Friday, they tried again, but the storm forced the party back to Sisseton.

There was no school. Summit received .40 inches of precipitation that day.

Roberts County personnel made another attempt on Saturday. The snowplow hit many drifts on the way to Summit, but the operator could see what he was plowing. Sheriff Sanden and the ambulance made it to White's home. They took the young man back to the hospital in Sisseton. White's wound was serious, but he recovered with medical treatment.

Before the blizzard ended on Saturday, another .20 inches of precipitation fell. Summit had snowbanks 12 feet high.

On Sunday, churches services in Summit were canceled.

The town of Corona was first known as Prior. The Milwaukee townsite agent, named it after himself because he owned the land on which the town was platted. The railroad went through in 1882. A year later, the name was changed to the present one, probably after Corona, New York, which is now one of the borough of Queens, New York City.

In 1960, Corona was home to 150 people. Their high school enrollment was fifty students in 1966.

In late February 1966, Corona residents cheered their high school basketball team, known as the Midgets, on to victory in the District 1 Basketball Tournament. Al Deboer, Mark Wilde, and Dennis Rohlfs led Corona in scoring. In the last ten years, Corona had won the district title six times.

Corona advanced to the Region 1 Basketball Tournament in Webster, scheduled for on March 3-4. Coach Don Akre prepared his squad to face the Britton Braves. Britton had an enrollment of 185 students. It was a David vs Goliath matchup.

Rough weather on March 3 created more jitters. School was canceled in Webster, but the teams from Corona, Britton, Rosyln and Frederick made the journey.

The Braves had too much firepower for the Midgets. Britton defeated Corona, 71 to 49.

The Corona party of 79 people left Webster after the game.

They made it as far as Brooks Corner, a cafe and service station located at the junction of U.S. Highways 12 and 81. Another thirty people were stranded there.

In a way, it was like a homecoming. Mr. and Mrs. Henry Poel who owned and operated the Brook Corner cafe and service station were former residents of Corona. Martha Poel said, people began converging there about 11 p.m. Thursday night after the Region 1 basketball tournament at Webster and continued to arrive through the night. A "final count" showed 109 people jammed into the station as of midmorning Friday. She said, "We're doing the best we can. Practically no one had been able to get any sleep."[215]

Friday morning, two dishpans of pancake batter were made. This left a shortage of milk. One of the people stranded was Forrest Tassler, a driver for Old Home Bread. He opened the truck and sold bread, rolls, cakes and buns. Glenn Trupe, who lived close to the station, brought meat to the station in the middle of the storm.

On Friday, over 760 hamburgers were consumed along with sandwiches, candy, toast, coffee and pop.

Daylight on Saturday brought a slight letup of the storm. Some of Corona students developed stomach flu.

Saturday afternoon, the weather started to clear. There was no traffic by Brooks Corner until late in the day. Snowplow crews from the South Dakota Highway Department and Day County Highway Department cleared snow at Brooks Corner. They opened accesses to the highways.

The Corona party left Brooks Corner for Milbank at 7:30 p.m. They hoped to find sleeping accommodations there. The roads to Corona were blocked.

The last of the stranded motorists left Brook Corner Sunday morning at 10:30.

The local news correspondent for Corona said, "Good neighbors took over farm chores at many places but there were a few farms that could not be reached because of blocked roads."[216]

There was no school in Corona on March 7. That night, the Corona's basketball team and their fans were back in Webster. With one minute left in the game, Corona and Roslyn were tied at 61. Mark Wilde scored a basket and sank two free throws to give the Midgets an exciting win over Roslyn, 67 to 64.

Milbank, Stockholm, Big Stone City and La Bolt

Established by the Milwaukee Road in 1880, Milbank was named for one of its directors, Jeremiah Milbank of New York. The town is known for its granite quarries. Milbank is the seat of Grant County. Milbank's most famous landmark, a wind-operated gristmill, was built by Henry Holland in 1886.

In 1960, Milbank supported 3,500 people.

On February 26, 1966, Milbank residents checked out the train derailment near the Farmers Union Elevator that happened at 12:30 p.m. There were nineteen cars off the rails.

On March 1, the Millbank Bulldogs freshman basketball squad finished their season, when they played Flandreau for the Conference Championship at Webster. The Bulldogs won by a score of 65 to 43. They were coached by Clarence Modlin. He said, "Much credit should be given to Duane Rembold who coached these boys through the seventh and eighth grades seasons and to Roy Jensen who worked with the boys on the B squad...." Richard Dohrer, Marlin Forman, and Gary Feind led the team in scoring. Their only loss of the year was to Clear City by two points.[217]

The varsity team had one regular season game, against Webster on March 4. The Northeast Conference crown was on the line. If Milbank won the game, Webster would share the title with Sisseton, the defending champion. Webster could win the title outright with a victory.

The mercury rose to 37 degrees in Milbank on Thursday. Blizzard conditions were reported in Webster, Sisseton and South Shore. The blizzard soon claimed the final towns of South Dakota late Thursday night. In the first wave of precipitation, Milbank received 2 inches of snow. Most residents of Milbank had retired for the evening, so they were safe in their homes. Travelers, however, were forced off the roads and highways.

On Friday, retail business in downtown Milbank was sparse. Lodging facilities and eating places were busy with stranded motorists. There was no public school. Athletic Director Roy Jensen reported that the Webster-Milbank basketball game was canceled and would not be rescheduled.

Milbank received 4 more inches of snow. The temperatures stayed warm for a little while, Friday's high was 35 above. That night, the low dipped to 11 degrees.

Another inch of snow fell on Saturday. The high rebounded to 19 above. Blizzard conditions lasted well into the day. Overall, Milbank received 7 inches of snow.

Dakota Granite crews had Friday and Saturday off.

Valley Queen milk haulers were pulled off their routes late Thursday. Some milk was picked up late Saturday.

Truck drivers for the Big Stone Cheese Factory stopped collections on Friday. Noon Saturday, they resumed operations.

The annual Milbank High School Sweetheart Ball was rescheduled for March 12.

The Mill Motel had twenty beds, but it was not enough. Mr. and Mrs. Goodwin Youngren, managers of the establishment, allowed guests to use their children's bedroom. The Youngren's children slept on the couch. Several groups of traveling salesmen doubled up in rooms. Mrs. Youngren cooked for several older guests. The other patrons went out for their meals. The Youngrens did not get much sleep. Their switchboard was constantly ringing with calls from worried families, trying to find their missing relatives. Their guests checked in Thursday night and left on Sunday. The Youngrens said they had a group from Arkansas who could not believe what they were experiencing.

Van's Motel's sixteen rooms were full, but many of the guests were regulars from the Midwest. Mrs. Marvin VanDervoort said they had guests from New York and Indiana. Also, staying there was a woman from North Carolina who was in town to take photographs at the Penny store. On Saturday, a snowplow opened their yard so guests could get downtown for meals.

At the Keystone Hotel, Mrs. John Feather reported their sleeping accommodations for twenty were full until Saturday. Their guests passed the time playing cards and visiting in the lobby. Mrs. Feather indicated all visitors were able to get to local restaurants for their meals.

Rooms at the Hotel St. Hubert were usually rented by the month, but the hotel had additional rooms, around twenty-four in all, on a day-to-day basis. Mrs. Vic Amdahl said the only rooms left were on the third floor, and the guests were from Rochester, Aberdeen, Fargo, Chicago and Sioux Falls. Several customers arrived on Friday.

The following week, the *Milbank Herald Advance* top headline said, **"Weekend Blizzard Called Worst Of Century,"** and **"Milbank Last Corner Of State To Feel Fury of Snowstorm."**[218]

One tidbit in the *Herald Advance* said:

> *One of the most astounding feats of endurance we have listened to as tales about the blizzard of the weekend are swapped is that of three Milbank high students who walked to Ortonville Friday evening.*
>
> *They were Jack Giessinger, Bernie Miller and Ron Drobeck. They dressed up real warm and set out along the new highway route and said "it wasn't bad at all." Worried parents found out Saturday morning that they stayed overnight with Jack's aunt, in Ortonville. They were instructed to make the trip home by car.*[219]

Jim Mundwiler, Leonard Stengel and Dr. V. Janavs battled the blizzard on Friday. The doctor was needed at the Robert Pierce, Jr., farm home near Wilmot to deliver a baby. At 2:00 p.m. Robert and his father, Fred, drove to the Pierce school house. They came to the conclusion, a trip to the hospital was out of the question. They went back home to Robert's place.

The Mundwiler ambulance followed a state snowplow into the storm. The Milbank residents left at 2:30 p.m. Four hours later, they were stuck by the Orville Meyers home, still two miles away from the Pierce farm.

At the Meyers residence, Dr. Janavs learned that Mrs. Robert Pierce had given birth to a baby boy, Michael Robert at 5:15 p.m. Robert and his mother, Mrs. Fred Pierce, received last minute phone instructions from another Milbank doctor, Dr. E. A. Johnson. Also, before the birth, the two read instructions from a medical book.

The Milbank men freed their vehicle and started for home. They arrived back in Milbank 10:00 p.m. Mundwiler said, "many times during the trip they were following the plow by sound alone because visibility was so poor. The plow stopped once to put chains on all four tires but still could not make no headway.[220]

Jim Bakeberg of Milbank and three other men left Howard, Thursday night at 6:30. They stopped near Turnerville at 11:30 p.m. They waited ten hours in their car for the storm to clear. Late Friday morning, they arrived at a gas station north of Turnerville. The men joined thirty-five others who were already stranded there. They were among the many, listed as missing in the storm. They could not contact their relatives. Bakeberg mentioned they had nothing to eat from Thursday noon until Saturday night at 8:30 when they reached Milbank.

People have jobs and responsibilities, no matter what their age. Another tidbit in the *Herald Advance* offered a point of view from the eyes of paper boys. It said:

One event arising out of the blizzard which can hardly be appreciated by many folks in town is the delight with which the paper boys greeted the blizzard.

Most of our Charles' friends have paper routes and not one was one bit disturbed about the financial loss which might accrue from the non-arrival of their papers for delivery. If anything, they were glad to pay the price. If there is anything more glorious than snow vacation from school to a paper boy, it is snow vacation from delivering papers.

However, we know the many household city residents would have given their eyeteeth for their regular daily paper to break the monotony of staying home.

Just goes to prove that old saying, "One man's sorrow is another's joy."[221]

After the storm, there was a big demand for bread and milk. Grocers ran out of milk. Normally, Shad's Bakery made pastries on Saturday, but Wayne Schad made bread instead. He even delivered some to the hospital via snowplow, Saturday afternoon. Ordinarily, no baking is done on Sundays, but Orville Webb and Jerome Rieck baked extra goods on March 6 as a public service.

Saturday afternoon, Darrell Thompson, driving a 1965 Plymouth station wagon, left Ortonville for Milbank. He ran into a snowbank on the highway near Van's Motel and became stuck.

Before he could get out of his car, another car slammed into his vehicle, pushing it atop of the drift. Mr. Robert Long, of North Minneapolis, the driver a 1965 Dodge station wagon, had his wife and three children along. Thompson suffered neck whiplash and the estimated damages to his vehicle was placed at $500.00. Mrs Long bruised her forehead and one daughter suffered a minor lip cut. Damages to Long's vehicle was placed around $300.00.

Ralph Scott, head of the city street department, and his six-man crew began the "gargantuan task of snow removal Saturday morning in spite of blowing snow and intermittently blizzardous conditions." Six to eight foot drifts were common around town after the storm.

Six extra men were hired and three additional trucks were utilized in the cleanup on Saturday. Snow was hauled away to the cemetery area.

On Sunday, Streges and George Korstjens supplied five trucks. The men worked from sun-up to an hour after midnight.

They worked ten hours on Monday.

On Tuesday, they worked from 8:00 a.m. till 11:00 p.m.

Grant County road crews had opened the roads by Monday morning. Superintendent H. E. Marquette reported all buses completed their routes.

Milbank lost its rail service on March 3. The last westbound freight that went through Milbank was stopped at Aberdeen. The passenger train left Thursday night, but the next one didn't arrive until Sunday night. Westbound freight trains started going through Milbank on March 8. Herb Walth, depot agent, reported the tracks west of Mobridge were still blocked with snow on March 9. Westbound freight trains were being yarded at Aberdeen. Walth said that was the reason why no eastbound freight trains had not arrived in a week.

Milbank's Civil Air Patrol was activated Friday. Members manned their two CAP radio stations, Dacotah 10 and Dacotah 12, Friday and Saturday. They relayed urgent messages and tried to find people who were reported missing by making numerous inquiries.

One of the most comprehensive air coverage of South Dakota took place on Sunday. The Milbank Squadron's four planes covered an area 36 miles wide running from southwest of Aberdeen to east of Watertown and an adjacent area, also 36 miles wide from Milbank to west of Webster. The local aircraft searched approximately 6000 square miles. Their pilots logged 11 hours and 25 minutes in the air.

Milbank lost the championship game of the sectional to Webster. (Next season, was their year. They won the Class A State Tournament in March 1967.)

Stockholm, named after Stockholm, Sweden, was founded in 1896. The area was settled by Swedish immigrants. In 1960, the community had 155 residents.

The *Herald Advance* printed news of nearby towns. Here's what Stockholm correspondent wrote:

> *The storm which struck here Thursday night curtailed all activities over the weekend. There was no school on Friday. Mail trucks and other delivery trucks were not able to get through on Saturday but by Sunday the wind had calmed and main roads were opened and many of the trucks came through. Seemed odd to get our daily papers on Sunday. There were no services in either the Elim Covenant Church or the Evangelical Free Church on Sunday.[222]*

Named after Big Stone Lake, Big Stone City was the first place the Milwaukee reached in northern South Dakota. In 1880, that rail line crossed the Minnesota-South Dakota border on its way to Webster. Big Stone City and Milbank were bitter political rivals for the seat of Grant County between 1881 and 1883.

Big Stone city had 718 residents in 1960.

Here's what the Big Stone City's correspondent wrote:

> *A blizzard raging over the country the latter part of last week kept most people home, and those who were unable to get home were glad when the roads were open and they could get back. No real hardships or deaths were in our immediate territory and we can be thankful for that. There was a wide spread closing of school, church services and other activities that had been planned. All this adding up to very little local news for the news correspondents.[223]*

Located in Grant County, La Bolt was named for Alfred LaBolt, an early landowner. In the 1960 census, LaBolt had a population of 125.

Here's what the LaBolt correspondent wrote:

> *A severe snow storm struck the state and community about midnight on Thursday and continued through Friday and all day Saturday thus closing all schools on Friday and most business places. No church services were held either at the Covenant or the Grace Lutheran churches on Sunday. Everyone was busy on Sunday shoveling snow; snowplows opened highways and streets. Farmers were busy with their scoops and tractors, continuing on Monday to get their yards and roads open again.[224]*

Chapter 2

The North Dakota Experience

Bowman, Scranton and Hettinger

Located in the southwest corner of North Dakota, Bowman (1,730 residents in 1960) is the seat of the county of the same name.

The Milwaukee Railroad extended its line to Bowman in 1907. The settlement received its present name on January 1, 1908. It either took its name from William Bowman, a territorial legislator or E. W. Bowman, a Milwaukee official.

It began snowing in Bowman at noon Wednesday March 2, 1966. It was the start of a blizzard that would last in the Bowman area until Saturday morning. Commencing that afternoon, winds accompanying the storm would roar for the next three days, finally letting up Saturday morning. Wind gust speeds reached 35 mph at Bowman.

Surprisingly, while the depth of snowdrifts on Bowman streets reached 12 feet, out in the country shifting winds blew highways clear. There were a few drifts in sheltered areas.

The *Bowman County Pioneer* described the effect of the blizzard on the Tri-state area:
> Schools closed. Businesses shut down. Planes, trains, and buses gave up the struggle in much of the area. Police in some communities mobilized snowmobiles as emergency vehicles. Traffic signals blinked in the thick whiteness, directing traffic that wasn't there.[1]

Bowman came through the blizzard with a narrow escape.

On the first day of the storm, a fire broke out in an empty building on Main Street that used to be the home of Buzz's Furniture. Heeding a fire alarm, the fire siren in Bowman rang out at 7 p.m. Responding quickly to the situation, firemen were soon on the scene. They battled the fire in zero visibility and 30 mph winds. Fortunately, the firemen extinguished the blaze before any extensive damage could be done to the structure.

At the courthouse in Bowman, Mike Hirsch, the local weather observer, recorded precipitation from the storm as amounting to .77 of an inch, or between 8 to 10 inches of snow.

A high of 38 was reached in Bowman on March 2, the first day of the blizzard. As the storm continued, temperatures fell slowly but remained above zero. After it had passed, a low of 9 below was observed in Bowman on Sunday morning, March 6.

The weather caught one Bowman resident, Cleon Willette, in Bismarck. To let his family know of his safety, Willette had a message delivered to them over TV.

On March 5, the Bowman Bulldogs and the Scranton Miners finished their seasons in the consolation game of the district tournament at Bowman. Scranton won 47 to 34. Ken Schmit led the Bulldogs with 11 points.

Scranton (358 residents in 1960) lies thirteen miles east-southeast of Bowman.

Scranton began as a Milwaukee townsite in 1907. It took its name from Scranton, Pennsylvania. This was done because both places were the hubs of coal mining districts. The Pennsylvania city was named after three ironworks developers, George Whitfield Scranton, his brother Selden T. Scranton and their cousin Joseph H. Scranton.

Flakes of snow began coming down in Scranton at midday March 2. To make sure children from rural areas made it home safely, the school buses departed early. It wasn't long before weather conditions deteriorated to the state of a blizzard.

For the next two days, blizzard conditions enveloped Scranton. The Science Fair at Scranton, set for March 4, was rescheduled for March 10.

On March 5, Scranton had huge snowdrifts in town. The depth of the snow in places was such that a person could only see the tops of cars as they passed by. In sheltered areas, the snowbanks were vast. Open fields and highways were swept bare.

As the seat of Adams County, Hettinger, lies only four miles from the South Dakota border. The Milwaukee extended its line up through northwestern South Dakota and on into southwestern North Dakota in 1907. Hettinger was a beneficiary of this. That same year, Adams County was carved out of Hettinger County. The latter was named for Mathias Hettinger of Freeport, Illinois. His son-in law, Erastus A. Williams, a member of the territorial legislature, suggested the name.

Hettinger was totally engulfed by the March 1966 storm. It arrived there Wednesday evening. Business and traffic in Hettinger was nil for the next two days. By Friday morning, the doors of business establishments had packed snow 5 feet high in front of them.

The streets had snowdrifts 6 to 8 feet high. Around Hettinger, parked cars were completely buried in the snow.

According to Forthun Florist, the local weather observer, the blizzard had deposited a total of .37 inch of precipitation on Hettinger. The town had a high of 29 on March 2. The thermometer dropped a bit during the storm, but it never fell below the doughnut hole until after the blizzard. Sunday morning, a low of 5 below was reached.

Hettinger's Terry Severson led North Dakota Class A basketball ranks in scoring for the 1965-66 season. He averaged 26.2 points per game.

On March 7, Hettinger and Mandan met in the Southwest Regional tournament in Mandan. At halftime, Mandan led 27 to 25. Hettinger could not keep the pace up in the second half. Mandan won the game 70 to 58. Terry Severson notched 23 points for Hettinger.

Marmarth, Amidon, New England, Regent and Mott

Marmarth, a Slope County village (population of 319 in 1960) on the Little Missouri River, is twenty-seven miles northwest of Bowman.

It all began for Marmarth, when the Milwaukee established a townsite here in the fall of 1907. It's name honored the granddaughter of Albert J. Earling, president of the Milwaukee Railroad. The granddaughter's name was MARgaret MARTHa Fitch.

The March 1966 storm dropped 10 inches of snow (.31 inches of precipitation) on Marmarth. Temperatures began a gradual slide in Marmarth after a high of 40 was reached on March 2.

Amidon (1960 population of 85) lies on U. S. Highway 85, roughly halfway between Belfield and Bowman.

In 1910, it was believed that a branch line of the Milwaukee Railroad from McLaughlin, South Dakota, to New England was going to be extended to Amidon. So, that year, a townsite was established there. The residents named the place "Amidon," after U.S. District Judge of North Dakota, Charles F. Amidon of Fargo.

The March 1966 storm deposited .47 of precipitation on Amidon.

New England (1,095 residents in 1960) is located twenty-five miles south of Dickinson.

New England, the first settlement in Hettinger County, was established in April 1887 by settlers from northeastern United States. Its name reflected from where they came, New England.

The Milwaukee Railroad reached New England in 1910.

New England was on the receiving end of 15 to 20 inches of snow (2 inches of precipitation) from the March 1966 blizzard. Winds reached speeds of 60 mph. The thermometer remained above zero, while the storm raged. A high of 28 was recorded on March 2, and a low of 6 below was achieved on March 6.

The stork arrived during the blizzard for one New England farm family. In expectation of the arrival of their child, Mr. and Mrs. Claire Strom left their farm at 4:10 a.m. Thursday and headed out into the storm. Their destination was St. Joseph's Hospital in Dickinson.

The inclement weather forced them to halt at the Carroll Township school. The Stroms held out hope that once daylight arrived, weather conditions would improve.

Unfortunately, that failed to happen. They set out again, but were forced to turn back. Going past the school, the Stroms came to the Charles Olson farm house, where they took shelter.

At 6:30 that evening, Todd LeRoy Strom, weighing 6 pounds, made his appearance into this world. Assisting with his birth were Claire Strom and Mrs. Olson. During the birth, Mr. Olson had a doctor in Dickinson and Mrs. Lloyd Strom, Hettinger County Health Nurse on the phone.

More help came at noon, Friday, when a Hettinger County snowplow, driven by Clyde Gullickson, made it to the Olson farm. Although, Mrs. Strom suffered some complications after the birth, she was doing better a week later. As for the baby? He came through the ordeal with flying colors.

The New England St. Mary's basketball team advanced to the Class B State Basketball Tournament in Minot. On March 19, they lost the consolation title to Cooperstown, 95 to 74. Dick Ryan led St. Mary's effort with 19 points. The Saints finished the season with a 22-3 record.

In 1960, 388 people called Regent home.

The "Enchanted Highway" runs from Regent, north to Gladstone. Along it are large metallic statues representing such things as Teddy Roosevelt, geese and pheasants.

The Milwaukee Railroad set up a station here in October 1910.

Railroad townsite officials provided the settlement with a regal-sounding name-hence "Regent."

Regent is the birthplace of Byron Dorgan. Today, Dorgan represents North Dakota in the U.S. Senate.

Blocked roads in the Regent area, after the storm, necessitated the use of an airplane to transport Mrs. Hulda Pahlmeyer from the Harold Pahlmeyer farm north of Regent to a place where she could receive medical attention.

The March 1966 blizzard proved to be a trying experience for Farmers Union Oil Company employees in Regent. They had received word that a Regent area farmer needed propane delivered to his farm. First, they had to dig the truck that delivered propane from its snowy imprisonment. That effort required a number of hours. Next, to fill the truck, the Farmers Union employees had to go to the storage tanks which were located across town.

After all this work, no wonder it was late in the evening before they made it to the farmer's place. To top it all off, after going through all that effort, they discovered that the farmer had been in error. He had looked at the wrong gauges on the propane tank.

In district tournament action, Regent was beaten by Scranton, 53 to 50, on February 28. In that game, Craig Newby tossed in 25 points for Regent in their last game of the season.

In 1960, Mott had a population of 1,463 residents.

The selection, promotion and platting of Mott was done in 1904 by realtors from Chicago, the William H. Brown Land Company.

Mott was either named after Lilian Mott, Mr. Brown's secretary or C. W. Mott, a civil engineer and emigration agent for the NP. Mott was served by both the Milwaukee and the NP. The latter terminated its line at Mott. They both reached Mott in 1910.

On February 28, 1966, Dickinson Trinity defeated Mott, 64 to 57. The playoff loss ended their season. Bill Griffen scored 14 points and Blair Bauer finished with 9 points for Mott.

The March 1966 blizzard started in Mott on March 2. The thermometer climbed to 29 above, that day. Precipitationwise, 2 inches of snow fell that day.

Before conditions grew worse in the Mott vicinity, classes were dismissed at 3 p.m. Wednesday.

The onslaught of the storm left Mott with its share of marooned travelers. A refuge for many of them was the Holiday House, a hotel in Mott.

Among the unexpected guests was an NP train crew stranded in Mott. The freight train pulled into Mott on March 2. The blizzard blocked the tracks further east and they could not return to Mandan.

Hotel employees stuck for the entirety of the storm included desk clerks Judy Bucholz, Joe Keller, and Frank Lantz. The hotel cooks and waitresses who were also stranded there were Dela Collins, Genevieve Hanson, Cheryl Lantz and Delores Wanner.

To pass the time while they were stuck at the hotel, people there read books and magazines, played cards and watched television.

Except for the depletion of just a few items, the hotel's food supply carried them through the blizzard without any problems.

Answering the call to duty for the duration of the blizzard was Montana-Dakota Utilities (MDU) area Manager Vern Rogers. Other MDU personnel also on duty for the duration of the storm were Paul Jahner and Fred Kern.

They received only one emergency call during the storm. That came from Warren Schleprogt whose farm was northwest of Mott. He had lost power at his place at 1:30 a.m. Thursday. It would be 7 a.m. Saturday, before the electricity was back on there.

Northwestern Bell Telephone Operator, Virginia Bohn, remained at her post from Wednesday evening until Saturday morning. Another person who remained on duty for a long time was Nancy Fiedler, another telephone operator. Thursday morning, it took a snowplow to get her to work. They were very busy. Their food needs, during the blizzard, were taken care of by Mrs. Bohn's husband. He brought them something to eat on Thursday and Friday.

On Thursday, *Mott Pioneer Press* employees fought their way through the adverse weather to the *Pioneer Press* office. Walter Mundstock walked with a snow shovel in front of his face to soften the blow of 55 mph winds. It took him forty-five minutes to reach the front door. He found a four-foot drift in front of it. Mundstock used the shovel for what it was made for.

During the height of the storm on Thursday, when visibility was down to zero, Mundstrock ventured out into the elements to snap a picture of fellow employees, Dennis Maas and Luke Senn, in the intersection next to the Holiday House. When the film was developed, the men looked like silhouettes in the swirling snow.

On Friday, Bob Carvell received five or six phone calls for drugs. One place that needed them was the Rej Watson residence in Mott. Using the county snowplow to deliver the medicine, George Klein and Frank Srb arrived at the Watson place around 6:30 p.m that night.

The high winds accompanying the blizzard brought down a light tower at Mott's baseball park.

According to Gus Fiedler, Mott's weather observer, the March 1966 snowstorm dumped 8 inches of snow on Mott. This came to 1.20 inches of precipitation. Temperatures in Mott remained above zero during the blizzard.

Snow removal efforts in Mott swung into high gear on Saturday, March 5. Mott city employees, the National Guard operators and local farmers with tractors equipped with snow scoops all helped out. The National Guard equipment and operators were activated for the cause.

They removed the snow from Mott's Main Street, Saturday and Sunday. On Sunday, eight National Guard trucks were being used. Between the heavy equipment and trucks it didn't take long to haul the snow away. The Hettinger County snowplow plowed out Mott's side streets.

Cleanup crews dumped much of the snow in large piles at street intersections. Because of this, Reinhold Schaible, Mott's Chief of police, requested that motorists be careful when traveling down the city's streets.

In the aftermath of the storm there was a heavy run on food staples such as bread, eggs and milk at local grocery stores. Because of this, one local grocery store opened for awhile on Sunday.

The NP train crew departed Mott on Sunday by means of private transportation. The NP would not have the line open to Mott until March 21.

An emergency developed for a Walker Township family near Mott. According to Hettinger County Sheriff, Earl Kramer, two children from the Leo Schramm family had come down with severe virus infections. They were airlifted out by the Mott Flying Service on Sunday.

According to Jack Samuelson of the North Dakota Game and Fish Department, a preliminary check on Sunday revealed wildlife losses from the blizzard to be small. It appeared that deer had tolerated the storm a lot better than pheasants.

It was back to the books for Mott students on Monday. Oscar Peterson, Superintendent of Mott Schools, said that only a few students weren't at school. Their absence was due to blocked roads.

There were substantial livestock losses in the Mott area because of the blizzard. Dead cattle piled up against fences and roadsides.

To check on livestock losses in the Mott area, Hettinger County Sheriff Earl G. Kramer, along with News Director Lloyd Kuehn and photographer Jon Springer of KDIX-TV in Dickinson journeyed on a plowed out county road on March 7. The area they covered extended from about two miles north of Mott to about four miles south of town.

While they saw about a 100 dead cattle and some sheep, Mr. Kuehn was of the belief that the losses wouldn't be really bad.

In talking about livestock that had perished, Kuehn had this to say:

> *In most cases death was due to suffocation and exhaustion. The animals just petered out. . . . Most of what we saw were individual cattle in a lonely struggle against the storm.[2]*

Impassable roads east of Mott on Monday prevented Kuehn from checking on livestock losses near Burt, a village about eight miles east of Mott.

While the storm was on, six head of cattle meandered into Mott. They were located standing beside the PV Producer Service.

Ralph Shults made these observation about the March 1966 blizzard in the *Mott Pioneer Press*:

> *Boy, what a storm! The oldtimers will have to go back a long way to come up with one like we had in this area last week. We thought the one last year was bad (and it was) but this one must have topped it by quite a lot.*
>
> *We didn't have the intense cold but it made up for it by lasting about twice as long. We had lots of snow and lots of wind; fortunately it wasn't quite so cold.*
>
> *I know we have an alley-full of snow at the present time and that goes for much of the rest of Mott. Mrs. Donald Carlson reports that they have a new hoe and a garbage can that the owner may have by stopping at their home. We can understand the garbage can blowing away but it must have taken quite a wind to move a garden hoe.[3]*

Dead cattle along fence line near Mott March 8. 1966. AP wire photo.

Chris Grondahl on snowmobile 16 miles south of Mott along Cedar River. Courtesy of Bismarck Tribune

Golva, Beach, Medora, Belfield, Dickinson and Richardton

Golva lies thirteen miles south of Beach.

In 1960, 162 people lived in Golva.

This NP station was established in 1914. Its name came from townsite owner, A. L. Martin. He took it from the name of the county where it was located, GOLden VAlley.

For awhile, the March 1966 blizzard had people living in the Golva area concerned. But, after learning about how much worse it was farther east (where both the snowfall totals and wind speeds increased), local residents came to the realization of just how lucky they had been.

However, it was a different story for those who departed from the Golva vicinity and ventured east. Included in that group were Jim Brophy, Holger Johnson, John Irons and Ronald Raisler.

They departed from Golva in the wee hours of Wednesday with two truckloads of seed potatoes. Their destination was eastern North Dakota.

Snow began falling, after they passed Bismarck. The winds became stronger.

They made it to Jamestown, but lousy weather conditions prevented them from going further. They remained there for the night. Weather conditions were no better Thursday morning. They decided to leave the trucks at Jamestown and return home by train.

At 9:20 Thursday night, their train stalled one mile west of New Salem. At 5:00 Friday morning, another train took them into New Salem. The four Golva men bunked down over a pool room until late Saturday evening. At that time, a bus took them to Beach. From there, the men returned to Golva.

They had come through their never-to-be-forgotten experience in good shape. As soon as roads were opened, the men intended to return to Jamestown and finish the delivery of those seed potatoes.

No one in the Golva vicinity perished in the storm.

The snowstorm closed Golva's school on March 3. It reopened on Friday, but a lot of the students were absent because of blocked roads.

On March 7, the Golva Tigers lost their District 30 tournament matchup with Gladstone, 71 to 58. Bob Nistler led Golva in scoring with 18 points, followed by Duane Maus with 13 points.

Beach had a population of 1,460 in 1960.

The Northern Pacific (NP) established a station in Beach in 1881. It was named after Captain Warren C. Beach, one of the officers of the military escort for the 1873 NP Survey Expedition.

Residents at Beach enjoyed a high of 40 degrees on March 1, 1966. Some made travel plans for the upcoming Winter Show in Valley City. High school students had ten days left to get their projects ready for the "First Annual Science Fair." That night, it dipped to a low of 14.

On March 2, Beach recorded a high of 25 degrees. The skies were pale. Early in the afternoon, one inch of snow fell. Storm conditions developed late that night.

On Thursday, the high in Beach reached 18 degrees. The town received 4 more inches of snow. Blizzard conditions shut down most traffic. There was no school.

On Friday, the storm blew itself out. Overall, Beach received .40 inches of precipitation. There was school on March 4.

The *Billings County Pioneer* described the worst blizzard in years as such:

It arrived in Golden Valley County last Wednesday, unexpected for the most part, coming in a direction most unusual for a storm of these proportions, the northeast wind accompanying the heavy snowfall making a ghostly and silent whiteness.[4]

The blizzard proved to be a trying experience for the daughter of a Beach couple. Visiting at the home of Mr. and Mrs. Kenneth Kannenberg in Beach at the time of the storm was their daughter, Mrs. K. L. Dedecker of Minneapolis, along with her two small children.

Storm conditions Thursday night, forced the NP passenger train, the *North Coast Limited*, to make an unscheduled stop at Beach. Mr. and Mrs. Kannenberg bade their daughter and grandchildren goodbye at the Beach depot.

But, it was too soon to say their goodbyes. The *North Coast Limited* only got as far as Glen Ullin before it was forced to stop. Mrs. Dedecker and children now had to wait aboard the stalled train until conditions improved.

Relief came, Saturday night. Mr. and Mrs. Kannenberg drove to Glen Ullin and picked up their daughter and the little ones. They gave them a ride to the Bismarck airport.

Dr. Dedecker and a friend were waiting for them at the airport with a light plane. Not many hours later, Mrs. Dedecker and children were back home in Minneapolis.

Concerning everyone's ordeal aboard the train, the passengers and train crew received considerable praise from Mrs. Dedecker. According to her, everyone pitched in and worked together to make the best of a bad situation.

Because of the train's crew efficiency, the passengers lacked neither food or heat.

Eventually, the train's batteries became depleted. The train crew handled that emergency by purchasing four candles in Glen Ullin.

The draining of the train's batteries left the train in darkness. Fortunately, Mrs. Dedecker's kids had brought a couple of little flashlights with them. These were a Godsend to many.

The blizzard left a couple of former Beach residents, Gene Johnson and Cliff Stecker, now of Billings, Montana, stranded for eighty hours at Sterling. They were Garret truck drivers enroute to St. Paul. As their truck came equipped with permanent sleeping facilities for an additional driver, the men weren't in any serious trouble. They simply slept in their rig.

Also, stuck at Sterling was another Beach resident, Mrs. Sally Abernathy. She had been enroute to Valley City for the Winter Show and Rodeo. The rodeo there was put on by her husband, Bob Abernathy. As the approximately 120 traveler snowbound at Sterling had to be fed, Mrs. Abernathy pitched in to help as a waitress.

Marooned by the storm for three days in a Fargo hotel were two Beach couples, Mr. and Mrs. Keith Finkle and Mr. and Mrs. Charles Hardy. They had been attending a Farmers Union Central Exchange stockholders meeting in St. Paul. They made it home Sunday night. Along the way near Valley City, they noticed two trains enveloped in huge drifts.

Also, in attendance at the same convention was a resident of rural Beach, Carl Ueckert. When he realized how bad conditions were becoming, Ueckert made his departure from St. Paul, Wednesday evening. His train stayed in Dickinson for two days.

Another Beach resident attending the Farmers Union meeting in St. Paul was Ray Lingk. His departure from the Twin Cities was one day later than the others. This was because he was visiting relatives in Minneapolis. Mr. Lingk considered his decision to delay his leave for home a fortunate one.

The train he finally boarded, was stopped at Fargo at 3 a.m. Friday. Along with other passengers, Mr. Lingk was put on a faster train.

But, that one was also stopped. In the meantime, on the majority of the passenger cars, the heating system wasn't working properly. Luckily, there was one car where that wasn't the case, and it stayed warm. To warm up, all passengers had to do was walk into that car. Afterwards, they made their way back to their own seats. The railroad provided the passengers with one solid hot meal a day.

A couple of Beach women were aboard the train that was stuck at Cleveland, North Dakota. Sheryl Smith, a student at NDSU in Fargo, boarded the train Thursday night in Fargo. Marsha Kukowski, the other lady, had a job in New York City and was enroute to Beach for a short vacation. Her mother, Mrs. Vera Kukowski, lived at Beach.

After catching a ride from Cleveland to Dickinson, Miss Smith was picked up there Sunday afternoon by her parents, Mr. and Mrs. Frank Smith.

As for Miss Kukowski, she didn't leave the train. Eventually, a pull back of coaches (railroad passenger cars) to Jamestown was done. Then, bus transportation was provided for passengers to Mandan.

The rail line between Mandan and Beach was now open, and Miss Kukowski took the train the rest of the way. She made it home Sunday night.

Most old-timers of the Beach believed this storm was one of the worst ever that stalked across North Dakota.

Beach and New England St. Mary's met in the regional championship game on March 12 at Dickinson. New England defeated the Bucs, 32 to 16.

> "I must say that here, in this country of hills and plateaus, the romance
> of my life began . . . I had studied a lot about men and things before I saw
> you fellows, but it was only when I came out here that I began to know
> anything or to measure men right."[5]

That quote came from Theodore Roosevelt during a Republican presidential rally in 1900 at Medora. Roosevelt came to the Badlands on September 8, 1883, he was twenty-four years old. He wanted to hunt buffalo and to invigorate his health. Roosevelt gained fame in the Spanish-American War of 1898 as a "Rough Rider."

He became President of the United States after the assassination of William McKinley in 1901.

Today, Medora (133 residents in 1960) is one of North Dakota's top tourist attractions.

Medora lies in Billings County, which was named in honor of Frederick H. Billings president of the Northern Pacific Railroad 1879-1881. The town's name goes back to the spring of 1883. That year, Antoine de Vallombrosa, Marquis de Mores started a business venture there. He selected a townsite and named it Medora after his wife, Marquise Medora von Hoffman, the daughter of a Wall Street banker.

The NP built its line through the region in 1881.

Marquis de Mores came up with an idea. Cattle would be raised in the area, then butchered, packaged and shipped eastward in refrigerated cars. His dream ended in failure. Refrigeration, at that time, was not good enough to ensure a good product on the table.

In 1958, an amphitheater was constructed at Medora for the celebration of Teddy Roosevelt's 100th birthday, and a play, *Old Four Eyes*, was held there over the next few years.

The current Medora Musical began when Harold Schaefer bought the amphitheater in 1965. *Starsky and Hutch* star David Soul was in the original cast.

Temperatures in Medora reached a high of 40 on March 2.

The March 1966 blizzard dumped .74 inches of precipitation on Medora. It received .48 inches on Thursday and .26 on Friday. On those days, the highs were 24 and 21 respectively. The coldest temperatures, -3 and -4, came on Saturday night and Sunday night.

A Medora correspondent described the cleanup at Medora after the March 1966 snowstorm:

> Many people helped with the snow removal job on our streets over the weekend, and although we didn't have the terrific problem that some of our neighboring communities have, the workers did a very good job of clearing the snow so us villagers could circulate again.[6]

Almost twenty miles west of Dickinson is the city of Belfield. It boasted a population of 1,064 in 1960.

In 1882, the NP established a station at Belfield. The townsite was platted in April 1883. Among the versions as to how Belfield was received its name was that it was named after Belle Field, the daughter of an NP engineer or after a prairie flower, the bluebell.

Belfield was on the receiving end of .86 inches of precipitation from the March 1966 blizzard.

A Belfield correspondent gave the following description of the March 1966 snowstorm:

> Snow storms may come and snow storms may go but we North Dakotans are going to remember a few of them; and the least of them will not be the big storm of December 1964 and its terrific toll of livestock nor the one we are just recovering from. For zero visibility this one must be a record taker. The human toll would have been much worse if it hadn't been for the comparatively mild temperatures during the storm. It is too soon yet to tell whether livestock losses have been severe.
>
> Mountains of snow are piled up in our grove and I'm presuming that it is similar in other places. Roads do not have the snow on them around here like they did last year though; so clearing them will not be such a problem.[7]

Snow amounts from the blizzard increased east of Belfield.

In District 30 tournament action on March 7, Belfield's season ended with a loss to Sentinel Butte, 54 to 36.

Situated in the heart of oil and ranching country, Dickinson was home for 9,971 people in 1960. Oil wells operate up to the very edge of the city. Interstate 94 (not yet finished in March 1966) passes along the north side of Dickinson. Before Interstate 94 was completed, U.S Highway 10 was the major transportation east-west transportation route across the southern half of North Dakota.

The NP went through the area in 1880. In 1881, their stopping point here was renamed for Wells Stoughton Dickinson (1828-1892), a former state senator from Malone, New York. In the summer of 1882, the townsite was platted.

The March 1966 blizzard made its appearance in Dickinson at noon, March 2. The thermometer registered a high of 28. On Wednesday, winds gusts reached 43 mph. For the day, they averaged 29 mph from the northeast at Dickinson FAA Airport. Snowfall totals came to 2.8 inches or .29 inches of moisture.

The Dickinson area weather forecast for March 3 called for one or two inch accumulation of snow and a letup in winds. The skies were supposed to clear soon.

Unfortunately, things didn't quite turn out that way.

At the airport on Thursday, 9.4 inches of snow, .94 inches of precipitation, fell. Wind speeds in Dickinson that day were from the north and varied from 30 to 46 mph. Dickinson recorded a high of 17 and a low of 6 above on Thursday. The storm did not let up in Dickinson on Thursday.

Schools throughout the area were closed on Thursday. This included elementary, secondary and Dickinson State College.

There was a power outage for a short time in the Suncrest area of Dickinson Wednesday night. According to Elmer Elkins, an MDU electrical engineer, a fuse in a transformer failed there. The blizzard slowed repairs at the transformer. On Thursday, there was no outage of power

To Dickinson's police force, the blizzard was no laughing matter. They warned motorists to refrain from driving on city streets. If they ignored the warning, motorists faced the risk of receiving a citation. The only exceptions allowed were emergencies.

It wasn't easy going for the police either. Thursday morning at 9:00, one of their patrol cars needed help. It was stuck in a large snowbank.

Dickinson's off-duty firemen were notified to return to work.

Except for rail service, no travel at all was advised both in and out of Dickinson. Greyhound suspended its bus operations. At Peck Hill, a place east of Medora, an eastbound Greyhound bus went into the ditch. Rescue came in the form of the North Dakota State Highway Department. Once free, the bus continued on to Dickinson. There, its driver and passengers remained until the storm passed.

Dickinson's truck stops filled up with rigs. To pass the time, some drivers drank coffee and played cards. Others took refuge in motels and a local hotel.

Thursday night, the North Dakota Highway Department issued a no travel advisory for the southern half of North Dakota. Snow accumulations were significant at many locations. Cars driving through the drifts began to stall, as their ignition systems became wet.

Travel conditions on many North Dakota highways remained a question mark after Thursday night. That was because highway snowplow crews were pulled off the roads for their own safety. It was a race with the stork for a couple from Gorham, a hamlet about forty miles northwest of Dickinson. Mr. and Mrs. Mike Baranko departed their farmstead around 3:00 a.m. Thursday and headed for Dickinson. Their automobile stalled in a drift at Emil Evoniluk's place.

Mr. Evoniluk then took the expectant couple to Dickinson in his car. A block and a half from St. Joseph's Hospital, their vehicle got stuck in a snowbank. With assistance, Mrs. Baranko, age 42, traveled the remaining distance on foot. After checking into the hospital at 7:45 a.m., she gave birth to a son, her sixth child, fourteen minutes later. Afterwards, both mother and son were reported to be doing well.

The *Dickinson Press* was having a difficult time Thursday determining whether subscribers had received their papers. A lot of them told the newspaper that because of the weather conditions outside that they had never gone out to see if a paper had been delivered. While carriers had phoned to see if papers had been left at the five pickup spots around town, whether they had picked them up or not was another question. Weather permitting, newspapers not delivered Thursday would be sent out Friday.

On Thursday, two NDSU students from Dickinson, Alan Sandowsky and Tom Goodman, were reported missing. Fortunately, they were located that night. On Wednesday afternoon, the two young men left Fargo by automobile. Upon making it to Valley City, they parked their car and returned to Fargo by train.

The heavy snowfall clogged a house vent at one Dickinson home. Gas fumes from a furnace then spread through the house. Responding to the emergency, firemen cleaned snow from the vent. People were also warned of the problems overheated furnaces could cause for chimneys.

The March 1966 blizzard was deja vouz for Maurice Tessier, a Dickinson television station engineer. A storm during the 1964-65 winter trapped him for three days in a TV transmitting tower, fifteen miles southwest of Dickinson. On Wednesday, March 3, Mr. Tessier was in the same transmitting tower, when that storm broke. He was stranded, once again.

Dickinson experienced blizzard conditions most of Friday. The wind in Dickinson blew from the west northwest at speeds ranging from 29 to 41 mph. A high of 18 was achieved. The city received 6 more inches of snow, .60 inches of precipitation.

It certainly was a busy time for the National Guard unit stationed in Dickinson. Between Thursday evening and 3 a.m. Friday, one of their crews made two dashes to St. Joseph's Hospital with a couple of expectant mothers. In another case, they came to the aid of the parents of a boy with a bad nose bleed.

Other tasks Guardsmen performed included helping people make it to important jobs around Dickinson, delivering food to the hospital and providing assistance to medical personnel attempting to reach there.

A North Dakota Highway Department official on Friday reported that U.S. Highway 10 and Interstate 94 seemed to be open from the Montana line to about Richardton. Another highway open to traffic was N.D. Highway 22, from New England to Killdeer.

After their plans to fly to Kansas City in a charter plane came to naught, Dickinson State College men's basketball team was scheduled to depart on an NP through passenger train on Friday night for Kansas City, Missouri. But, even that departure was postponed. The NAIA District 12 champs were scheduled to play Illinois Wesleyan College at 10:30 p.m. Tuesday, March 8, at the Kansas City Municipal Auditorium.

When it came to making rounds at the hospital on Friday, most of the doctors there walked to the hospital. Dr. Norman B. Ordahl had a different idea. He resided on Empire Road, northwest of Dickinson. Friday morning, Dr. Ordahl traversed the distance to St. Joseph's Hospital on horseback. For a hitching rail, he employed a handrail at the hospital's entrance.

Residents of Dickinson enjoyed postal service on Friday. Carriers forced their way through deep snow to deliver the mail. Out of town, it was something else. There was no rural service. An impediment to mail coming to Dickinson was stalled trains.

In spite of the conditions, cleanup in Dickinson began on Friday. The snow was windrowed on Villard Street, Dickinson's main thoroughfare, to allow for single lane traffic in both directions. Trucks then hauled the snow away.

While some people used shovels to clean off sidewalks, there were places downtown where the snow was drifted 5 feet deep on the sidewalks. To clear the snow away in these instances, front-end loaders were employed. By Friday night, most of the downtown sidewalks had been cleared of snow.

The weather began to improve in Dickinson, Friday night. Out in the country, blowing snow kept visibility down.

Snowfall totals for Dickinson from the blizzard came to 18.2 inches. It amounted to 1.83 inches of precipitation. The low on March 4, was 5 degrees.

A fire broke out in downtown Dickinson, just before midday, Saturday. Doherty Printers, Dickinson Supply and the Western Trading Post were destroyed in the fire. A couple of businesses to the east of them, Vantine Paint and Glass Co. and the Western Grill suffered considerable smoke damage. Firemen had the blaze under control within three hours. A sad aspect of the tragedy was that many small-town North Dakota newspapers had their papers printed at Doherty Printers.

On March 8, Dickinson Postmaster C. Ray Culver reported the return of normal mail service at Dickinson to be at least a week away. Dickinson had been receiving a little bit of mail that had been trucked in from Bismarck. That mail had been airlifted to Bismarck from Minneapolis. The problem was block railroad tracks between Bismarck and Fargo. Until the rail lines were cleared, postal officials planned on using trucks.

Dickinson State ran into a hot shooting Illinois Wesleyan team on March 8 and lost, 86 to 76. They finished the season with a 21-4 record.

In March 1966, Harold Flom resided in Dickinson. He worked in construction for a contractor there. As with many other people Harold was forced to remain at home during the blizzard. Once it had passed, the contractor dispatched a snowmobile to Harold's residence. Harold was supposed to help clear the runways at the Dickinson Airport. He recalls that as he rode on the snowmobile down the street only the aerials of cars were visible above the snow. The vehicles themselves were completely covered by the white stuff.

After reaching the shop, Harold headed out with the road grader for the Dickinson Airport, five miles south of town. The road grader Harold piloted was equipped only with a blade. The road leading to the airport, N.D. Highway 22, was blocked in places.

He had a hard time making it to the airport.

Harold started clearing a runway at the far end. The markers delineating the edges of the runway were buried in the snow. But Harold had done some flying there, and he had a pretty good idea of where the runway was in spite of the deep snow. He set out with the road grader, for the other end of the runway. Upon reaching it, Harold discovered that he was still on the runway, but on the other side of it.[8]

About twenty-five miles east of Dickinson is the city of Richardton (792 residents in 1960).

Richardton began in 1881 as an NP station known as Spring Valley. Platted in the fall of 1882, the settlement was named after C. B. Richard, a passenger agent for the Hamburg-American Steamship Company of New York.

Richardton did not escape the wrath of the March 1966 storm.

Weather records at the Assumption Abbey indicate that Richardton received 12.7 inches of snow, or 1.23 inches of precipitation. Of that total, 10 inches, fell on March 3. Temperatures stayed at zero or above for the duration of the storm there.

Selfridge, Fort Yates, New Leipzig, Elgin and Carson

Selfridge, located in Sioux County, lies fifty-five miles south of Mandan.

Its population in 1960 was 371.

In 1911, the Milwaukee Railroad set up a station here.

At a minimum, the Feist Mink Ranch by Selfridge lost 1000 mink in the blizzard. When all was said and done, their financial loss was thought to be as much as $65,000.

On March 10, the Carson Chieftains beat Selfridge, 72 to 59. Carson finished fifth in the District 31 tournament.

Located on the west side of the Missouri River, Fort Yates had a population of 1,100 people in 1960. It is the seat of Sioux County and headquarters of the Standing Rock Indian Reservation.

On January 11, 1875, the Standing Rock Indian Agency was established. Fort Yates was named for George W. Yates who fell at the Battle of the Little Big Horn. On February 14, 1913, land on Standing Rock Indian Reservation opened up for public settlement.

Jean Mason, the wife of Governor William L. Guy, was born here.

The March 1966 snowstorm dumped 19 inches of snow, 3.06 inches of precipitation on Fort Yates.

One of the most dramatic survival stories of the March 1966 blizzard involved three Fort Yates high school basketball coaches.

On Wednesday evening, March 2, 1966, head coach Harlan Wash, and his two assistant coaches, James Barret and Allen Mitzenberger took in the first day's action of the Southwest Region Basketball Tournament at Mandan High School.

They headed for home around 11:30 p.m. What made them decide to proceed on? Let Coach Wash answer that:

We got over the hill south of town (Mandan) and decided the storm wasn't too bad. So we continued on, and the highway was clear until we had gone far past the airport.

But by the time we'd driven 25 miles, the storm really set in. We passed Junction Inn and by the time we'd gone another seven or eight miles the storm got really bad.

We passed the Solen road junction and decided to wait for the storm to subside and the sun to come up.

We idled the motor until about 9:30 a.m. Thursday then the motor stopped, although we had a good supply of gas, and we couldn't get it started again because we had left the car lights on and had no battery.

They were able to get the motor running again by pushing the car a short distance. In order to have the rear of the vehicle facing the storm, they turned their automobile around. The men were thirty-two miles south of Mandan.

For most of Thursday, the men kept the motor running. But visibility was so poor, they could barely make out the hood ornament.

That evening, the blizzard let up enough to allow them to see a fence line and a few telephone lines.

In the meantime, the vehicle's clutch froze.

With the car's supply of gas reduced to a quarter of a tank, Coach Wash headed out into the elements and brought back three fence posts.

Mr. Wash continued:

We ripped out the car's upholstery to partition off the front seat, then started a fire on the front floor-board at our feet. To get the ash fence posts going, we had to burn the rubber floor mats and some insulation and stuffing from the back seat. At 2 a.m. Friday the car ran out of gas.

For the next twenty-five hours the three men switched positions, sat on each other's feet, and to keep warm they rubbed themselves briskly. And they prayed.

James Barret reminisced about the situation:

> We kept thinking with every sunrise or sunset it would break and we'd be able to find the farm. But it kept on blowing. Pray? You bet I did. Everybody was saying their own prayers . . . it got pretty quiet in that car.

To keep up morale, Coach Wash kept relating the following information to his assistants, "These three-dayers come, but they blow themselves out." Another phrase he repeated was " We're gonna make it."

Mr. Barret went on:

> We had three sweet rolls we divided between us and every once in a while we'd grab a handful of snow. We weren't very hungry, just scared. We knew someone must be looking for us, but we had no radio in the car. Maybe it was best. We couldn't hear how bad it was at all. We knew our only chance was to stay with the car. Yes, I'm thanking the good Lord for my life.

Rescue finally came at around 2:30 a.m. Saturday in the form of a Highway Department rotary snowplow which was accompanied by other emergency vehicles.

The three coaches were then taken to the Mandan Hospital. After treatment for eye irritation and smoke inhalation, it was expected that all three would be released from the hospital, the next day.[9]

After the blizzard North Dakota State Extension Service initiated a statewide survey of livestock losses from the March blizzard. County extension agents provided the numbers. The results were released late in March. Overall, North Dakota livestock losses included 18,905 head of cattle, 7,854 head of sheep and 640 hogs. The report broke down the most severe cattle losses by county. Sheep and hogs losses by county were not mentioned in the press release. Sioux County lost 2,000 head of cattle.

Located in western Grant County, New Leipzig (390 residents in 1960) is seventeen miles east of Mott.

The Milwaukee arrived at this location in May 1910. The NP came in October of that year. New Leipzig was named after an earlier settlement, eleven miles to the northeast. That one took its name from a city in Russia which was named after Leipzig, Germany.

As with other cities and towns in Grant County the March 1966 blizzard hammered New Leipzig. Let the *New Leipzig Sentinel* tell the story:

> Everyone agrees it was bad, but they can't seem to agree as to which was the worst 1888, 1921, 1950 or 1966.
>
> As far as most were concerned last weekend's storm was an all time record breaker. There may have been more snow in a given year, but for a one storm snowfall and blizzard it seems to be the worst. Reports are about 17 inches of snow fell, and the wind blew from Wednesday afternoon until Saturday morning. . . All supply lines and vehicles to the area were stalled.[10]

In its wake, the blizzard left snowbanks as high as 10 to 15 feet in the New Leipzig vicinity.

In Grant County after the storm it took quite a while to open streets in town and roads out in the country. This despite around the clock efforts of snow removal crews. Their work was hampered by a limited supply of equipment.

No matter who won the tournament in 1966, District 31 was assured a new champion. The winner of the tournament for the past 12 years, the Fort Yates Warriors, had moved up to the Class A ranks for the 1965-66 season.

On March 10, New Leipzig faced Elgin in the championship game at Carson. The Tigers lost the contest, 61 to 49.

Not far north of the Cannonball River, near the intersection of N.D. Highways 21 and 49 is the city of Elgin. In 1960, the town had a population of 944.

Elgin began in 1910 as an NP townsite. The Milwaukee Railroad reached here with its tracks the same year. Isadore Gintzler named the settlement after the brand of watch he was wearing, "Elgin."

The March 1966 storm blew into Elgin, around noon, Wednesday. By evening, 6 inches of snow had fallen. Strong winds piled the white stuff up. The majority of Elgin's streets became blocked.

No school classes were held in Elgin either Thursday or Friday.

Blizzard conditions existed all day Thursday and most of Friday.

When the wind eased Friday evening, one Elgin resident with cabin fever swung into action. Alvin Redman was impatient for the storm to be over. He started clearing snow off his sidewalk. Mr. Redman probably was the first person in Elgin to have a snow-free sidewalk Saturday morning.

Snow levels were so deep in Elgin on Saturday morning that quite a few people were forced to use windows as exits. The snow removal process in Elgin was well under way.

Sunday evening, an NP train arrived in Elgin for water and refueling. There were snowbanks west of the depot. The next morning, the train began pushing through these drifts. Unfortunately, the NP train encountered a breakdown that necessitated its return to Mandan.

On Monday, Elgin school buses were filled with only half the number of school children that usually rode on them. Impassable roads helped to keep the numbers down. Heavy drifting of snow on Monday led to the decision to send farm children home at noon.

Monday afternoon, two V-plows helped a Milwaukee train make it through Elgin.

Cattle losses from the blizzard were considerable in the Elgin vicinity. Saddled with the heaviest losses was the Gary Meyer Ranch, located south of Elgin. That outfit was reported to have 14 cows missing. It was thought that a directional change by the wind during the blizzard had brought about this situation. Forced to seek new shelter, the cattle drifted with the wind. In doing so, their eyes froze shut. Tumbling over a river bank, they suffocated in the deep snow.

On March 12, Elgin and Hebron played for third place in the regional tournament at Dickinson. The Dutchmen, under head coach Lester Hintz, won that game.

It would be March 21, before an NP train reached Elgin.

Carson, seat of Grant County, lies fourteen miles east of Elgin.

In 1960, Carson had a population of 501.

The NP built its rail line to the present location of Carson in 1910. Its name is a combination of three early settlers of the area, Frank CARter and David and Simon Pederson.

On March 2, 1966, Carson enjoyed mild weather part of the day. The thermometer climbed to 33 above. That afternoon, the storm arrived. As roads became heavy with snow, vehicular traffic dwindled in and around Carson and finally stopped.

On Thursday, Carson received .55 inches of precipitation. A high of 28 above was reached that day. Blizzard conditions were experienced until Saturday morning.

More snow fell on Friday, .60 inches of precipitation was recorded. The high was 16 degrees, the evening low was 6.

A crisis developed in Carson and two neighboring towns southwest of it, Heil and Leith, on Friday. Around 11 a.m., these communities suffered a power outage. About a mile east of N.D. Highway 49, a short had developed, when high winds had pushed two floating phase wires together.

For many people, this loss of power also meant they were without heat, lights and cooking facilities. While a lot of families took refuge in neighboring homes, others moved into the City Hall and the Orthodox Presbyterian Church in Carson. Adding more blankets was one solution for those who elected to remain in their homes and tough it out.

For cooking, several people chose to put their camping stoves to use. One report had Lloyd Kempf utilizing his charcoal burner in his garage on Friday to barbecue hamburgers.

The power outage forced the editor of the *Carson Press*, Willard Ketterling and his family, to leave their home and take shelter in the Ken Stewart home, a block down the hill from the Ketterling residence. As they burned coal, the Stewarts were not without heat. Although it was but a short distance, it took quite a while for the Ketterlings to reach the Stewart home. They brought with them clothing and their children. Also, spending the night at the Stewart residence was the Les Gullickson family.

It would be around 11 a.m., Saturday before power was restored to these communities. According to C. S. Richards, the MDU supervisor at Elgin, having the power restored as soon as they did was possible only through the cooperation of the residents of Elgin. The only way they could locate the source of the outage was by walking along the power line. The lousy visibility of the storm prevented searchers from spotting the problem, the first time they looked.

Receiving thanks from Mr. Richards and the three affected towns were the MDU crew and others who gave their time and assistance. These included Marvin Dittus, Fritz Hochhalter, Hugh Jacobson, Bill Lince, Jim Martell, Wilmer Pich, Sam Rivinius, Dennis Roth, Marvin Schatz, Otto Wolff, and Harry Zacher. Mr. Richards also thanked the Martell Inc. Co. for providing a big comforter equipped diesel tractor and Bob Well who not only furnished his services but also a four-wheel drive unit.

The storm departed the Carson area, Saturday morning. Before it did, another .25 inches of precipitation fell. According to local weather observer, Jake Stewart, the blizzard had dumped about 17 inches of snow on Carson.

Once the cleanup began, snow removal crews worked around the clock. But, their efforts were being hampered by deep snowdrifts, 10 to 15 feet in height in many instances, and having only so many pieces of snow removal equipment.

As of March 9, train service to Carson still had not been restored. And restoring it would prove to be very difficult.

On March 12, the Milwaukee opened its line through Shields, Raleigh, Brisbane, Leith, Elgin, New Leipzig and further west.

It was a different story for the NP. A cut two miles east of Carson had a snowbank 19 feet high, and it was three quarters of a mile long. The NP arrived with a V-Plow on March 10. The unevenness of the snow caused the plow to jump the tracks and pull to the left. The result was a broken rail. The plow was removed and the tracks repaired.

North Dakota National Guard SGM Ray Schernowski clearing snow in Grant County, March 1966.
Snow removal in Grant County, March 1966. Both photos courtesy of E.B.R. SC, UND

Two days later, the NP returned with a rotary plow. It was very slow going in the wet and hardened snow. A break down west of Elgin forced them to head back to Mandan. Their return was delayed because the track at Solon, next to the Cannonball River, was submerged by floodwaters. It would be March 21, before the NP ran a train the full length of this branch line to Mott.

Grant County suffered heavy cattle losses, mainly from the Carson vicinity on to points east of it. Very few cattle were lost in western Grant County. The southeastern corner of Grant County had the heaviest losses, especially south of Raleigh and around Shields.

The loss of sheep to the blizzard was severe for a couple of ranchers. The number of sheep lost by one fellow near Carson exceeded 200. For another rancher at New Leipzig sheep losses came to 100 head.

A switch in wind direction during the blizzard contributed greatly to the loss of cattle. As long as it blew out of the northeast, the cattle stayed together and didn't move. They did this despite having their eyes and chins encrusted with ice. But a wind switch to the northwest led to their wandering. Unable to see the animals had to deal with fences before they succumbed in large snowdrifts.

Overall, Grant County cattle losses numbered 2,000 head.

Wilbert Ketterling was worried the blizzard had decimated the already declining pheasant population in the Carson vicinity. His fears weren't entirely unfounded as a North Dakota Game and fish Department biologist, Chris Grondahl, estimated pheasant losses between 40 and 50 percent in the excellent southeast range.

Another post blizzard survey was done in southwestern North Dakota. After checking over the Gladstone, Hettinger, Mott, and Reeder neighborhoods, Jerry Kobriger, a Game and fish biologist from Dickinson, was able to locate some dead birds. Along with the pheasant losses suffered in the 1965 blizzard that struck southwestern North Dakota, it did not look good for North Dakota's pheasant population.

Because of grouse and Hungarian partridge's ability make it through tough winter weather alive, Mr. Grondahl didn't think the March storm would bring about an abnormal mortality of them.

Charles Y. Weiser, Grant County Extension Agent called on Grant County cattleman to keep a close eye on their animals for signs of stress. Farmers and ranchers were told to report livestock losses He would report Grant County livestock losses to the extension service at NDSU.

Mr. Asbridge ranched nineteen miles south of Leith. He was out riding his horse, looking for cattle that had disappeared in the storm. After spending the greater part of the day on horseback, he apparently succumbed to a heart attack. He was seventy-eight years old.

Flasher, Hebron, Glen Ullin, New Salem, Almont, and Mandan

East of Carson in southwestern Morton County is Flasher (515 residents in 1960).

This NP townsite was established in 1902 by William H. Brown. He named the settlement after his niece, Mabel Flasher (1880-1934).

Flasher received 1.09 inches of precipitation from the March 1966 blizzard.

The following story is Marcella Schock's personal experience with the March 1966 blizzard:

The Blizzard of '66

I was in a Bismarck hospital with a fractured leg and ankle when the Blizzard of March 1966 hit. I had four small children at home, the youngest being four months old.

During the raging three-day blizzard my husband couldn't get outside to tend to the dairy herd. The milk tank was full, as the milk truck couldn't pick up the milk.

The snow had drifted the barn door shut, so he had to go into the hay mow to get to the dairy herd. The pole barn, where some of the herd was kept, had drifted full of snow.

The range cattle drifted as far away as one or two miles from the yard. Some cattle were found under snowbanks in the spring, when the snow had melted. Banks drifted to 30-plus feet high, making it difficult to get around. The roads were blocked.

My parents had come from South Dakota a day before the blizzard hit, to help our family while I was in the hospital. The day after the storm I was discharged from the hospital. The National Guard had to open roads and a trail in the fields to make travel possible for all the people in our community.

Luckily, we all survived, and were left with a memory never to be forgotten.[11]

On March 10, the Flasher Bulldogs met the Solen Dragons in the District 31 tournament at Carson. The Dragons came away with the third place trophy, 78 to 60.

Situated in northwestern Morton County is Hebron (1,340 residents in 1960). Hebron lies between Glen Ullin and Richardton. As "The Brick City", it is home to the famous Hebron Brick Company which was founded here in 1904.

Established in 1885, Hebron was named after Hebron, Palestine by either Rev. John L. King or Rev. J. G. Koch.

The blizzard arrived in Hebron, Wednesday afternoon. Conditions worsened as the day wore on. By evening, drifting snow made road travel virtually impossible.

By the next morning, huge drifts blocked Hebron's Main Street. The blizzard was at its height on Thursday. The city received 1.05 inches of precipitation. Wilbert Sailer, the Hebron Creamery delivery man, headed out on foot, to deliver milk to those customers who had children.

On Friday, the snowbanks were even higher. To reach grocery stores for essential items like bread and milk, men trudged through drifts that reached up to their necks.

While Hebron was still being hammered by the storm, one person fought his way through large snowbanks to reach a grocery store. After making his purchases, he returned home. Once there, the person realized he had forgotten the groceries on the store's counter.

As getting around Hebron on foot was so difficult during the blizzard, employing a horse made a good substitute. And that is just what Reinhold Kraenzel and Al Schultz did. They rode their steeds down Main Street, when the storm was on.

What were people to do, when they were stuck at home? One Hebron resident, Jane Berg, had these answers:

for some it brought lots of time to take "catnaps", the chance to watch

No school classes were held in Hebron on Thursday or Friday.

Hebron received .75 inches of precipitation on Friday. This brought the storm total to 1.80 inches. Temperatures remained above zero. Wind gusts reached 50 mph in during the blizzard.

The storm began to ease up a little in Hebron on Friday afternoon. Taking advantage of the break, Jane Berg went outside. She shoveled out her driveway and the sidewalks next to her house. The jump start of the cleanup was cabin fever.

On Saturday, the digging out process in Hebron was well under way. It was a daunting undertaking, considering that some of the drifts on Main Street reached heights as much as 6 feet.

By Saturday evening, through the assistance of county and state equipment and a snow-plow furnished by the Richter Construction Company, they had the majority of Hebron's streets open to single lane traffic.

Temperatures at Hebron Sunday morning dipped to 12 below.

Glen Ullin, located on old U.S. 10, about four miles south of Interstate 94 and about forty miles west of Mandan, had a population of 1,210 residents in 1960.

In 1879, the NP established a station at Glen Ullin. On May 12, 1883, prospective settlers showed up at the new townsite. Major Alvin E. Bovay, an NP land agent, came up with the name for the townsite. He chose "glen" for the prefix and "ullin" for the suffix.

The blizzard arrived in Glen Ullin Wednesday night. It didn't leave the area until Friday night. The roughly 18 inches of snow that was dumped on Glen Ullin was whipped around by winds gusting up to 50 mph.

Glen Ullin's population swelled considerable, with stranded motorists. They had other guests also that needed help during the storm.

The NP train, *No. 26, North Coast Limited*, had 131 passengers and crewmen on board it. That passenger train became stuck in 20-foot drifts at Eagle's Nest, a one-time NP loading station five miles northwest of Glen Ullin. They remained there until Saturday morning. Local stores provided food for them. Glen Ullin residents assisted in delivering food to the train.

High winds on Friday dashed hopes of freeing the train from its snowy grave. To keep passengers warm, fuel was delivered to the train.

Miss Patsy Kline, the NP stewardess on the train, sang the praises of the residents of Glen Ullin:

> *I think we bought out all the grocery stores in Glen Ullin. The people in that little town should be commended because I don't know what we would have done without them.*

Another crisis arose for the train crew when the batteries on the train became depleted. They didn't have any electricity. What were they to do? Miss Kline had an answer. *"We bought all the candles the townspeople had–four."*

Despite the seriousness of the situation, the passengers aboard the train were taking it in stride. A statement by one of them typified the response to the crisis by many of them. *"You don't know how interesting it has been, the people on this train are simply fantastic."*

Being marooned near Glen Ullin meant that a few of the passengers aboard the train would miss speaking engagements, wedding and funerals. Their situation was summed by one lady, *"Well, you just have to take things as they come–there's no use worrying and we were warm and comfortable."*

Three sailors from Greece were aboard the train. Their problem was that their ship was scheduled to depart for Greece on March 7. When one of them, a fellow by the name of Pagonis Stravios, was asked about what they were going to do? This was his reply, *"I don't know, but I doubt that the ship will wait for us."*

A different predicament awaited a young guy from Williston. He had been slated for induction into the armed forces on March 4. He had this to say about his situation:

> *Not only am I late, but my buddy has all my money, and he's someplace down the line waiting for me–I hope I'm not AWOL.*

For the majority of the passengers aboard the train, the worst part, of their enforced stay, was a deficient supply of water. The residents of Glen Ullin did furnish the passengers with drinking water, but as for bathing, there wasn't enough to go around. As a bearded man remarked, *"You get to feeling sort of grimy and it's tough on little kids."*

The train was fortunate to have a physician on board. Dr. and Mrs. Paul Rossiter of Sheridan, Montana had boarded the Mainstreeter in Butte, Montana. While the train was stuck at Glen Ullin, the doctor provided medical assistance to four people–two young children who became sick and two passengers who had epileptic seizures.

Dr. Rossiter downplayed his role in the four cases. *"It was nothing serious, just minor incidents that could have been handled without a doctor."*

But, according to an older woman, *"the doctor's presence aboard was a calming influence for everyone."*

One person who was worried and didn't care for their situation was Mrs. Peggy Garrison. She was headed from Seattle to Georgia with her five-year-old son, Billy, to visit relatives. She voiced her opinion:

> *I've seen enough snow to last me a lifetime, and I'll never forget this as long as I live. Everybody kept teasing me about how we weren't going to be out of this mess until Easter–and I thought, 'Oh, Lord!'*

After 54 hours, they were rescued from their snowy tomb Saturday morning.[13]

Another harrowing tale involving a train and the blizzard was related by NP engineer Leo P. Tuhy of Mandan. On Thursday, March 3 Tuhy was aboard an eastbound NP freight train for Mandan. It was a ordinary run, except for the blinding snowstorm.

Soon, it was anything, but normal. The further east they went, the deeper and more numerous the snowdrifts became.

Before the freight train got close to Glen Ullin, the crew received orders to head in at Glen Ullin. The dispatcher informed the crew that the westbound *Mainstreeter, No. 1,* was stuck on the main, ahead in deep snowdrifts at New Salem. Meanwhile, the NP's eastbound passenger train, *North Coast Limited, No. 26,* had stalled in the snow behind them.

The train crew remained in radio contact with K. A. Anderson, NP Superintendent in Glendive, Montana.

Before stopping at Glen Ullin, Tuhy's freight train hit an humongous snowdrift. The resulting collision broke the window on the fireman's side of the engine's cab. Facing forward, the firemen's side of the cab is on the left or opposite side of the engineer's.

Konster Schumacher family of Glen Ullin digs out on March 8, 1966. Photo by Bob Feickert Courtesy of Bismarck Tribune

Men shoveling out NP's Mainstreeter passenger train at Eagle's Nest AP wire photo. Courtesy of Aberdeen American-News

Tuhy exclaimed, *"Snow poured through the broken window with a force you can't imagine."*

Snow began filling the cab. Head brakeman Wiedman was in snow up to his waist. Also, in the cab was the Glen Ullin section foreman.

As the train moved forward, snow poured through the broken window. Soon, three fourths of the space in the cab was taken up by snow.

The situation grew worse. Engineer Tuhy recalls Brakeman Wiedman yelling, *"I can't even move!"*

Unfortunately, the emergency brake valve could not be pulled by the section foreman to stop the train. Snow kept pouring into the cab, forcing him away from the valve.

If the engineer could not operate the brake valve on the control stand, there was a good chance the freight train would plow into NP's, *No. 1*, ahead of them.

By digging frantically, Tuhy found the brake valve. He dumped the air, and the train came to quick stop. A relieved Tuhy remarked, *"It's a good thing, or we would have plowed into No. 1 which was stalled only a short distance ahead."*

Next, the train crew began the process of digging themselves out of their snowy confines. Tuhy continued:

> *"We lost all our flashlights under the snow, so we worked in the dark until we uncovered two lanterns. We can just thank our lucky stars we were told to head in at Glen Ullin, but you know, that's the way the ball bounces."*

In all his years of employment, Tuhy said that he had never experienced a storm like the one in the March 1966.

How did Mr. Tuhy feel after what he had been through? *"Oh, you get used to it, railroading–it's something that does happen sometimes, I guess."* Continuing on he remarked:

> *It didn't bother me, until later this evening–when I started getting my frozen clothes off. Then, it dawned on me what could have happened.*

But Engineer Tuhy didn't have a lot of time to worry about the incident. It was back to work for him. As he noted, *"I'll be going at 6:01 in the morning."*[14]

A Mandan resident wouldn't soon forget the assistance of the residents of Glen Ullin and Mandan. Mr. and Mrs. Ray Husen and their three children moved to Mandan from Detroit Lakes, just three weeks before the 1966 snowstorm. In addition to being an electronics supply salesman, Husen was a ham radio operator.

Returning home from a Montana trip, Mr. Husen encountered fifty stranded motorists east of Glen Ullin. He couldn't go any further.

From where he was stalled, on Friday, Mr. Husen made contact with a ham radio operator in Plainview, Ohio. He asked that person to call Mrs. Husen in Mandan.

While her husband remained in contact with the Ohio operator, Mrs. Husen received a phone call from that person at 6 p.m., Friday.

Efforts were made to free the stalled vehicles, east of Glen Ullin. The equipment was inadequate and those efforts failed.

So, a large highway plow was brought into play. It had the road open to Glen Ullin by 10 p.m. Friday. The stranded motorists returned to Glen Ullin where they spent the night.

Mr. Husen made it back to Mandan the next day.

He was appreciative of the concern shown both in Glen Ullin and Mandan. He remarked, *"I was impressed with the helpfulness of the people in Glen Ullin and also by the kind people in Mandan who called my wife with offers of help."*[15]

In March 1966, Gary Hellman was a senior at Glen Ullin High School. He lived with his family on a nearby farm where they raised dairy cattle. The Hellmans didn't let the storm prevent them from milking their cows. Gary remembers every time he went outside during the blizzard, the snowdrifts were oriented in a different direction. This indicated the shifting directions of the wind.

Their cattle didn't produce a lot of milk during the blizzard. This was partially due to a lack of water. The Hellmans had a pump jack located in the middle of their yard that provided water to the cattle. As the storm raged, they encountered difficulties in getting it to work. The thirsty cows began to bawl.[16]

Although the Glen Ullin vicinity did experience some livestock losses from the blizzard, they were not as high as points further south and east.

The snow removal process in Glen Ullin after the storm was a slow one. Even a week later, quite a few streets were only open to one-way traffic.

On March 8, Glen Ullin met New Salem in the District 29 tournament at Hebron. Glen Ullin lost, 50 to 44.

New Salem (986 residents in 1960) is located about twenty miles west of Mandan.

To celebrate the region's dairy industry, in 1974 a fiberglass statue of a Holstein cow was erected on Crow's Nest Butte just to the northwest of New Salem. It would be just south of this butte, where General Custer and the Seventh Cavalry camped on May 19, 1876, on their way to the Little Bighorn.

On April 6, 1883, New Salem's first settlers arrived at that location via an NP train. The settlement was named after the Biblical city of Salem.

The blizzard made its appearance in New Salem, early Wednesday afternoon. At that time, temperatures began to fall, and the wind increased its velocity. Later that night, there was quite a bit of drifting. On March 2, New Salem received several inches of new snow. That night, the Morton County Implement building had its large front window blown in by high winds.

No school classes were held in New Salem on Thursday or Friday.

The majority of business establishments in New Salem remained closed for the duration of the storm. The ones that remained open, had skeleton crews.

Even as a blizzard raged about them, some people ran short on food supplies. To assist them, the Central Food Market remained open. The same was true, at the Co-op store. Its manager, Bill Weiss, remained there, from Thursday morning until Saturday, ready to help.

Almont, with 190 residents in 1960, and New Salem endured a thirteen and a half hour power outage, Thursday evening until Friday morning. There were a couple of causes of the outage. One was broken insulators near Crown Butte. The other one was at the Glen Ullin Substation. There, compacted snow had caused oil breakers in a cabinet to stick.

Thursday night, Roy Hartman, Henry Kaelerer, and Paul Neidhardt tried to reach a switch, two miles north of New Salem. The switch brought power to Almont and New Salem from Mandan. But, the atrocious weather forced them to turn around.

Another attempt was made, Friday morning. Employing a Farmers Union oil truck, Willie Heid, Eervin Messer, Dale Neidhardt, and Willard Rusch drove north down N.D.

Highway 31 from New Salem. From there, it was a half mile walk to the switch. Friday, at 9:28 a.m., power came back on for Almont and New Salem.

On Wednesday evening, Mr. and Mrs. Clarence Toepke were enroute to their home in New Salem from a business trip to Glen Ullin. They were traveling down old U.S. Highway 10, when their automobile left the road on the shoulder near the Almont turnoff, nine miles west of New Salem. Their defroster and windshield wipers quit working. This made it impossible for Mr. Toepke to see the road. He was trying to get the defroster on the 1952 Ford to work, when they went into the ditch. This happened around 6 p.m. Wednesday.

What were they to do now? Mrs. Toepke provided the answer, *"We kept the motor running, the window open a crack, and got quite a lot of sleep."*

But, at 2:30 a.m. Thursday the car's engine quit; the vehicle had run out of gas.

However, the Toepke's weren't in any serious trouble. It wasn't that cold outside. And, as more and more snow enveloped the automobile, it acted as a cocoon, shielding the Toepke's from the high winds.

Mrs. Toepke described what they did next:

> We made a bed by taking the back of the back seat and putting it on the floor of the front seat. I had on very heavy boots and the one blanket kept us both warm.
>
> In reflecting on their predicament Mrs. Toepke remarked, *"No, we weren't cold, but we were sort of cramped.*

A lack of stockings left Mrs. Toepke with cold feet. But otherwise, she came through the ordeal in fine shape.

Having the knowledge their five year old son Dennis was staying at the Jack Kirchmeier home in New Salem provided solace to Mrs. Toepke. But not knowing where their nine year old daughter, Donna, did concern her. Donna had been in school in New Salem Wednesday afternoon. Unknown to Mrs. Toepke, Donna was also at the Jack Kirschmeier residence.

Rescue for the Toepkes came at 8:30 p.m., Friday. Gary Kreidt and his father George found the Toepkes. As soon as conditions had improved, the Kreidts set out to look for the Toepkes. It turned out their car was only about four blocks from the Kreidt's farm home.

The Kreidts brought the Toepkes to their home. After staying there overnight, the Kreidts took them into New Salem, the next morning.[17]

The March 1966 blizzard turned out to be a painful one for a rural New Salem farm wife. Around 8;30 a.m., Thursday, Mrs. Richard Gappert was in a corral on the Gappert farm assisting her husband. They were attempting to move their animals into a barn.

Mrs. Gappert fell and broke her arm.

The Gapperts were in a bind. Their farm was eighteen miles north of New Salem. They could not run to town in the storm. Help could not reach the farm in a hurry.

So, the Gapperts resorted to treating the broken arm themselves, with help from doctors over the phone. With information from doctors as to the correct procedure for setting splints and knowledge Mrs. Gappert had picked up as a hospital employee herself, they got the job done. Under her direction, Mr. Gappert splinted the arm and applied cold packs. The wood splint came from a board.

Now, all she could do was wait for the blizzard to end to be rescued. It would be a long wait. Fortunately, Mrs. Gappert had the assistance of not only her husband but also her three children. They were Brenda, 15, Duane, 10, and Dwight, 8. In describing the children's efforts, Mrs. Gappert remarked, *"My children were so much help and made the long wait quite comfortable for me."* The children took care of household chores and lent a hand to their father.

Mrs. Gappert's ordeal at the farm came to an end fifty-four hours later. At that time, she was taken to a Mandan hospital. That trip, was not easy. A local road was blocked by drifts, up to 12 feet high. To get around them, Mr. Gappert and neighbors cleared a three mile trail across high ground of fields and the prairie. Their convoy consisted of two front-end loaders and two automobiles.

Additional assistance was furnished by Milton Lennick, Morton County Deputy Sheriff, and a N.D. State Highway Department snowplow.

From the back seat of Deputy Sheriff Lennick's car, Mrs. Gappert said:

> *I really suffered the first night, but that ride across the hills was really pretty rough and my arm started to hurt again.*[18]

The March 1966 storm really hammered New Salem. Snowfall amounts there came to over 25 inches. In some instances, snowbanks were as high as 18 feet. It was reported the moisture content of the snow was ten percent greater than normal.

Saturday morning, the cleanup process got underway.

One of the most dramatic stories of the March 1966 blizzard occurred about a mile west of New Salem. At 9:15 p.m., Thursday night, a NP passenger train, *No. 1*, the *Mainstreeter*, became stuck in eight-foot drifts there. Outside, blizzard conditions raged. Inside

Main Street of New Salem on March 8, 1966. Photo by Bob Feickert Courtesy of Bismarck Tribune

200

were 97 passengers, 92 adults and 5 children. The westbound train had departed from Bismarck around 7:30 that evening.

At 4 a.m., the next morning, the evacuation of passengers back to New Salem began. The power consist, four diesel engines hooked together, came out of Mandan. The locomotives transported fifteen passengers at a time back to New Salem. Passengers made their departure through the rear door of the train. They entered the diesel engine through its nose opening.

According to the train's conductor, A . X. Koch of Mandan, at one time, the train depot in New Salem was filled with 115 passengers and train personnel. Two of the trainmen, Engineer Gene White of Mandan and Fireman Doug Handtmann, stayed in the cab of engine 6506A. Mr. White remained with the train until it was freed from its snowy grave.

From the depot, passengers were transported to the city auditorium. Koch stated that while there, passengers were given food bought by the NP. The passengers used the kitchen at the auditorium to prepare the food. Passengers also had meals at the Bee Hive Cafe. The NP covered the cost of these meals too.

A lady from Dickinson and a family from Seattle were given shelter by Wilmar Held, operator of the PV Producer Service.

Another Good Samaritan was George Olheiser, owner of the Friendly Bar. He provided refuge for seventeen of the passengers in his home.

Late Saturday afternoon the passengers finally departed New Salem by bus.

As for the *Mainstreeter*? Fifty hired hands with shovels began the process of freeing the train from its predicament. Their job was a daunting one. The depth of snow along the train's engine reached as high as the engineer's window. To reduce the terrific pressure of the snowbanks against the train, workers dug deep trenches on both sides of the train. To reach the rails, they dug down as much as 20 feet. This also made it easier for pulling the train back to Mandan.

On Sunday, the train was back in Mandan.

As the crow flies, Mandan lies just across the Missouri River from Bismarck. In addition to being the seat of Morton County, Mandan is home to an important railroad center. Kist Livestock Auction is located in Mandan.

In 1960, 10,525 people called Mandan home. The first settlers arrived in the area in 1872.

There was also a new military outpost a few miles to the south, Fort Lincoln. Moving into the post in 1873 was the 7th Cavalry, under the leadership of Lieutenant Colonel George Armstrong Custer.

The community was first known as Morton, then Lincoln, then Mandan and then Cushman. On September, 26, 1879, the name was restored to Mandan.

Frederick F. Gerard, is believed to have suggested the name "Mandan" after the Indian tribe of that name. Gerard had been a interpreter, trader, and the first white person to reside at present-day Mandan.

During the winter of 1879-1880, an NP train made the first traverse from Bismarck to Mandan on track set on ice across the Missouri River.

On March 2, the weather forecast indicated the skies would be cloudy. Snow, up to 4 inches, was expected for south-eastern and south-central portions of North Dakota. That day, the high was 33 degrees. Colder temperatures and winds of 15-20 mph were predicted.[19]

As the intensity of the storm changed, the weather forecasts were updated over the next three days. The March 1966 blizzard deposited 1.03 inches at Fort Lincoln State Park, four miles south of downtown Mandan. The lowest reported temperature at Fort Lincoln during the storm was 9 above on Friday March 4. Before rebounding, the thermometer slid to 11 below on Sunday morning, March 6.

One of the first Mandan residents to experience the effects of the blizzard was Mrs. Lucille Hendrickson, *Morning Pioneer* Society Editor. She had been at the Bismarck Airport for two hours on Wednesday conducting an interview. While enroute back to Mandan, even though roads were still passable, she became afraid that her car would end up in the ditch.

Mrs. Hendrickson took her automobile back to the airport and caught a ride home with the newspaper's photographer.

Mr. and Mrs. Carl Hendrickson resided on their farm at the bottom of a cliff-like hill next to the Heart River, seventeen miles southwest of Mandan. The heavy snowfall from the storm made their phone line sag to the ground. The end result was that the Hendrickson could hear incoming phone calls but not answer them. The phone continued to ring–day and night. Once the phone rang 100 times in a row. Mrs. Hendrickson related her frustration. *"I spent a terrible 2 1/2 days. I shouted but callers couldn't hear us and became worried."*[20]

On Saturday morning, Pete Voigt, their closest neighbor, snowshoed over to the Hendrickson place and found them to be doing OK.

Clifford Nelson, another one of their neighbors, used his tractor to inspect the Hendrickson's phone line. He got the line up and going by using a piece of barbed wire to patch it.

One Mandan resident, Mrs. Monroe Chase, didn't get very shook up when her husband, a pilot, failed to return home from a flight Wednesday. That left Mrs. Chase, a teacher instructor at St. Joseph' School in Mandan, home alone with her three young children. Having a "don't-worry attitude" about him, and a complete faith in his knowledge of weather helped get her through the storm.

Many times in the past, Mr. Chase had to fly charter flights late in the day. Mrs. Chase thought that was what had happened Wednesday night. With the arrival of the blizzard, she assumed that he had elected to stay with the planes at the Bismarck Airport.

The next morning, Mrs. Chase found out that her husband was missing. Upon learning that, Mrs. Chase phoned Jim Ewers. He was Midstate's chief instructor in Bismarck. Mr. Ewers told her that Mr. Chase, Jay Ehrmantraut and Stan Hetzler had flown from Grand Forks to Harvey on his last charter flight Wednesday.

Mr. Ehrmantraut's wife then phoned Harvey. She was informed that a friend had given the trio a ride to Goodrich. There, Mr. Chase had an automobile. They left Harvey at 6 p.m. As the other two men had business to conduct in Bismarck, the trio set off for the capitol city, eighty miles away. Nothing more was heard from them.

During this time of uncertainty, Mrs. Chase received a lot of phone calls from friends and relative to extend words of support and encouragement. These included ones from a couple of her sisters. They phoned from Tioga, North Dakota, and Seattle, Washington, respectively. Unable to reach Mrs. Chase, her parents, Mr. and Mrs. John Lozensky of Paradise, California, phoned her husband's parents, Mr. and Mrs. Herbert Chase, in Hebron. Others providing support were a Dickinson minister who also happened to be a pilot and was stuck in Bismarck and several Bismarck ministers. Their wait ended Saturday morning when Mrs. Ehrmantraut received a phone call from her husband. The men were safe.

Monroe Chase described what happened once they left Goodrich:

> *An hour later we hit a patch of ice and a gust of wind blew us into the ditch. We were perfectly helpless. There was nothing we could do.*

They had departed Goodrich with a full tank of gas. Continuing on with his story, Chase remarked:

> *Every 15 minutes we ran the car to warm it up. After three minutes we shut it off.*

According to Chase, during their ordeal, the car burned 11.6 gallons of gas. He mentioned how much gas they had left in the tank at that time:

> *We had seven gallons left. We could have lasted another day.*

The trio remained there from 8 p.m. Wednesday until 7 a.m. Saturday. They were in the car for over sixty hours.

The blizzard was letting up at that time, and the men could make out a farm house, a quarter mile away. They made their way to the John Kruger farm..

Approximately an hour later, a snowplow opened the road.

The trio came through their confinement without any ill effects and without food.

Concerning the lack of food, Chase remarked, *"you can get along without that if you have to."* [21]

Even after that ordeal, Monroe Chase didn't return home right away. First, he went to Midstate Aviation at the Bismarck Airport. There, he shoveled out planes and remained with the emergency charters. Mr. Chase didn't make it back to his family until around 8:30 p.m. Saturday. Even then, he didn't hang around long. According to Mrs. Chase, he was back in the air by 7 a.m. the next morning on other emergency flights.

Concerning the men's disappearance in the storm, Mrs. Chase had this to say:

> *Naturally I was very concerned and kept hoping and praying they'd stay with the car. On the other hand I was confident in Monroe's knowledge of the weather, so I wasn't actually worried.* [22]

The American Oil Company Refinery at Mandan chugged through the blizzard full steam ahead, never letting up its production.

In terms of petroleum products, that came to a daily round-the-clock output of 45,000 barrels per day. This was due to extraordinary efforts on part of the sixty-five man work force.

Wednesday night, the midnight shift came aboard for their eight hour shift. Some of them stayed over the next shift at 8 o'clock Thursday morning. Around twenty-five to thirty workers stayed on duty from 8 a.m. Thursday until 4 p.m. Saturday. Other workers arrived at different times to increase the number to sixty-five.

Snow removal operations were handled by the refinery's front-end loaders and blade equipment. They prevented the refinery's grounds from becoming impassable and the road to Mandan open.

When needed, pick up of food and relief workers in Mandan was handled by a panel truck and a four-wheel drive convoy truck.

Additional help with snow removal and opening roads into Mandan were outfits from General Construction. They were associated with the Northern Improvement operation.

That outfit provided assistance to the American Oil Company when it shut down for maintenance.

A company official gave this explanation as to how they were able to keep production up during the blizzard:

> Normally there isn't too much outside work, but workers do have to get
> out in the field to gauge the tanks and guard against overfilling.
> We're generally prepared for emergencies, but not to this extent![23]

On Wednesday evening, upon completion of the basketball game in Mandan, Watford City fans embarked for home. However, the atrocious weather conditions forced them to turn around and return to Mandan that evening.

Some of the fans took refuge in two Mandan residences. One group consisting of one adult and six teenagers stayed at the Harvey Just home. At the time, Mr. Just was caring for his wife who was recovering from recent back surgery. In order to do that, he had taken time off from his job. So now, Mr. Just had to take care of everyone in his house.

The other group which was made up of two mothers and eleven teenagers stayed at the Darrell Krause residence as guests of the Krause family. For Mrs. Krause, a registered nurse, it meant little sleep. Besides working overtime at the Mandan Hospital during the blizzard, she was helping out at home caring for her guests. Between Wednesday night and midday Saturday, it was reported that she had managed to get only five hours of sleep.

Mrs. Krause had been a nurse at the hospital in Watford City before she moved to Mandan. Also working as a nurse there at the same time was one of the mothers who came with the Watford City fans. So, when this group returned to Mandan, they knew they had a place to go.

Staying at the Lewis and Clark Hotel in Mandan on account of the storm were Watford city basketball fans, unable to make it home. In spite of this, the hotel was not completely filled.

Another Mandan inn, the TP Motel had stranded guests there.

It too, still had available rooms.

One hotel that was filled to capacity was the Holiday Inn. Half of the guests staying there were marooned travelers.

On Thursday, the boys high school basketball team from Watford City headed out into the elements in their bus. Their destination was a local gymnasium for a short workout. They returned in the bus.

The storm kept things interesting for the Mandan police and streets departments on Thursday. If needed, they coordinated their movements. They provided transportation for key personnel at their places of employment.

This was particularly true of the hospitals. There, the nursing staffs put in long hours until relieved by replacements. After working the Wednesday night shift, a few of the nurses got some "shuteye" at the hospital the next day. That helped get them ready for Thursday night's shift. Other nurses never left their posts but caught snatches of sleep when they could. Although hospitals in Bismarck and Mandan were filled to capacity, no emergencies developed in any of them on Thursday.

An emergency call came into the Mandan Police Department around noon Thursday. They were asked to transport a choking child to the hospital.

Shortly afterwards, the child's mother, Mrs. Ronald Schuler of 508-1/2 Collins Avenue phoned the family doctor. She complained about feeling faint and reported that the family cat had "passed out."

In response, the doctor told her to open windows and doors. Then, without delay he phoned the police.

With the city snowplow leading the way, Mandan police made two trips in delivering the family to the Mandan Hospital. Their effort required about an hour's time.

After oxygen had been administered to Mrs. Schuler and her four children, they made a good recovery.

Mr. Schuler was not at home when the incident occurred, but at his place of work, Sanitary Plumbing.

It turned out that the Schuler family's asphyxiation had been caused by snow clogging a gas vent.

The *Morning Pioneer* wasn't about to let an historic blizzard keep it from getting out a paper. Before conditions had deteriorated very much, a printing of the next morning's *Pioneer* was done Wednesday.

However, delivering the paper Thursday morning was another story. As the *Pioneer* put it:

> North Dakota's raging blizzard didn't stop the Morning Pioneer from rolling, but it did put an almost "unchopable" ice block in front of delivery operations. As a result, not many newspaper were delivered.[24]

It took a determined effort of around six people from the editorial and printing departments to get Friday's edition of the *Pioneer* out. They all bundled up and made it to work on foot. A few came from quite a ways.

The eight page edition of Friday's *Pioneer* focused its attention on the relentless storm. Mandan residents had various reflections about the blizzard on Thursday.

Acting as his own cook, waiter, and dishwasher for part of the day was Carl Lenz of Vi's Cafe in Mandan. Even if a few of the hamburgers were overcooked, the customers weren't complaining. Just to have a place to eat was enough for them.

For Mrs. Joe Weber of 104 4th Ave. N.E. the storm brought back memories of her wedding day, November 11, 1919. On that day, horse drawn sleighs delivered them to the church for the wedding.

It was an entirely new experience for Modesto del Busto who taught Spanish at Mandan High School and his family, refugees from Cuba. The year before, Mr. del Busto had attended college at Great Falls, Montana. While there, he and his family had encountered wintry weather, but nothing like the March 1966 blizzard.

As he remarked:

> It has been a new interesting experience to see cars covered with snow and the stores all closed. It reminded me of pictures of storms which I used to see pictured in Cuban newspapers but I never dreamed I would one day be just like the pictures.

Henry Hagerott, a farmer of northwest Mandan had this description of the blizzard:

> This is one of the worst blizzards I can remember. In the nearly 40 years I have lived on this place, it's the first time I haven't been able to see the barn or garage from the house.

Mrs. Charles Mischel resided at 1405 Monte Drive in Mandan in March 1966. She hailed from Colorado, so blizzards weren't anything new to her. But never one as bad as the present one. With a baby in their home, milk was a requisite for the Mischels. And they received their milk, when the Foremost delivery man trudged through the elements against a terrific wind to deliver it. He had parked his truck on Sunset Drive and then walked the rest of the way.

Sig Syvrud, a rural Mandan mail carrier, reported Thursday afternoon that he was making plans to deliver mail on Friday. He said:

> If I can make the first six miles out, I will then have a pick of trails and knowing the roads I can perhaps get quite a distance if the wind stops blowing.

Syvrud recalled a bad winter around 1930 when a local farmer subbed for a few months as a rural mail carrier. He got through enormous snowbanks with his farm truck. He was able to do this because he had loaded the back of his farm truck with a few tons of coal. The additional ballast got him through the drifts.

Living at 308 5th St. N. W. in Mandan in March 1966 was Mrs. Fred Reisenauer. In her 23 years of living in Mandan, the March 1966 blizzard was the worst one she could remember being through.

As they came from South Dakota, snowstorms were not a new experience for Mr. and Mrs. E. J. Doering, newcomers to Mandan. But as Mrs. Doering remarked:

> Our children have never experienced such snow and are chomping at the bit to get out and play in those big drifts.

The R. M. Dorsetts of 308 12th Ave. N. E. hailed from Pennsylvania and Texas. Although snow was nothing new to Mrs. Dorsett, this *"is the worst we've ever known."*

A couple from rural southwest Mandan, Carl and Nancy Hendrickson, agreed that the March 1966 blizzard had the most intense winds *"we can remember in our long lifetimes here since the 1880's."*[25]

Good Samaritan deeds were performed during the storm by some Mandan residents. In one case, a 13 year-old boy really went above and beyond the call of duty. From the Mandan golf course, Mr. and Mrs. Steve Dassinger's home was across the Heart River east of Highway 6.

The storm had left the five families on Route 4 snowbound. Two of Keith Keidel's children needed medicine and all of the families residing there were short of groceries.

To remedy the situation on Friday while the blizzard was in full gear 13-year-old Monte Dassinger and Emil Fandrick, who was staying at the Dassinger residence, set off on foot headed for Mandan to obtain the needed supplies.

The situation was exacerbated by the fact that in a couple of the homes the telephones didn't work. One residence was having furnace trouble. Sickness was a problem in two of the homes.

Throughout the course of the storm, Monte Dassinger made frequents slogs through drifts to check on his neighbors.

His father, Steve Dassinger, worked for the railroad. In between calls from the railroad, his stay at home wouldn't be that long.

On Sunday, in an attempt to clear their road to the highway, Monte Dassinger, his mother and Emil Fandrick shoveled about 100 feet of it. They were on the job from 11 a.m. to 5:30 p.m.

At the same time, a neighbor of their, Mrs. James Rask, was doing the same thing. She was clearing the road from her place with a shovel in order to hook up with the Dassinger's road. As her husband was sick, he couldn't lend her a hand. The job was finished Monday afternoon, when the National Guard completed the task of clearing a route to the marooned families.

Another Good Samaritan act being performed when the storm was at its worst, was done by Leon Pytliit, a Mandan Senior High School teacher, and Bob Schulsie, a Mandan Cloverdale employee. They trudged through the deep snow to the smattering of stores that hadn't closed their doors.

After buying twenty-seven half gallons of milk and putting them on sleds, the men set out into the storm. They headed for the 700-block area of Collins Avenue and the Tower Place. At homes in that area, the men would inquire if there were any small children there who required milk. Among their stopping places were homes the men knew had babies or small children present.

In their heavy clothing and icicles the two men were unrecognizable to some of the residents of the homes.

John Oxton, Mandan High School wrestling coach, came up with a novel way of putting chains on the tires of his car. First, he removed the rear wheels from his automobile and took them inside his house. Once inside, he put the chains on the tires. Then he mounted the tires back on his car. A short time later, Mr Oxton was observed traveling in his car down East Main Street in Mandan.

A serious situation was averted by Mandan police. On West Main Street they noticed a lad of about fourteen years of age leaning against a building. Dressed lightly he was without cap, gloves or overshoes. The building was serving as protection from the wind for the boy. To obtain some pins, the boy had trudged over nine blocks. The officers gave him a ride home.

A lady called a Mandan plumbing shop at 8 a.m. Thursday. Her toilet had a leak in it. As she couldn't go anywhere, the lady intended to be home all day. So, that was the day she wanted the repairmen to come to her home and fix it. Unfortunately, the personnel at the plumbing shop couldn't make it out either.

Another lady phoned the Mandan Pfaff Sewing Service requesting that they make a trip to her home to repair her sewing machine. Conditions were such that she had the entire day to sew for her family. The response of the proprietor of the shop was that he had two vehicles on hand, a car and a truck, but that deep snow prevented the usage of either. In spite of terrible conditions outside, the proprietor actually tried (and failed) to answer the call.

Upon awakening Thursday morning, Joe Schaaf, 502 11th St. N.W. Mandan, noticed a snowbank in his driveway whose height exceeded 7 feet. In his neighbor's garage was a snow removal machine that he had recently bought. Upon going over to his neighbor's (F. R. Siegfried) place to retrieve the machine, Schaaf discovered a bus situated in the driveway. One could barely see the top of it.

Cattle losses in Morton County from the storm amounted to 1,900 head.

After the storm, both George Toman, Mandan City Engineer and Delores Pierce, Mandan's Street Commissioner, thanked the city's street department personnel for their hard work in clearing snow.

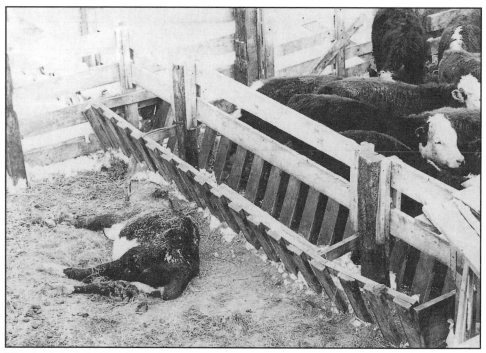

Kist Stockyards in Mandan on March 8, 1966. Courtesy of Bismarck Tribune

By Monday night, March 7, around a third of all Morton County roads had been opened according to the chairman of the Morton County Commission, Roy O. Young of Mandan. If things went right, the remainder would be opened by the following weekend.

He reported that since Saturday morning about thirty-five men had been working to clear roads. They were using fifteen pieces of county snow removal equipment. A lot of the work had been round-the-clock.

Additional help came from the National Guard.

The Holen Construction Company of McClusky was being employed by residents of the St. Anthony vicinity to open roads. St. Anthony is a village that lies fourteen miles south of Mandan.

The Mandan Braves would emerge as winners of the postponed Southwest Tournament. With first year coach Jim Walker at the helm as coach, the Braves defeated the Fort Yates Warriors 65 to 52 in the championship game on March 8. The win ensured a trip to the state tournament being held in Grand Forks.

On March 12, at UND's Fieldhouse, the Mandan Braves roared past Bismarck 84 to 63 to win the North Dakota State Class A high school basketball title (a feat they would repeat in 1967).

Leading the way for the Braves was Bob Green who poured in a record 40 points. In doing so, he broke Phil Jackson's record of 35 points for a championship game. Jackson had set that record in 1963 when Williston beat Grand Forks Central for the title. Green's 17 field goals for the game tied a record set by Rugby's Paul Presthus in a 1962 semifinal game against Fargo Central. The 84 points scored by Mandan broke the 80 point record set by Grafton in 1964.

Center, Beulah, Hazen and Stanton

Center (476 residents in 1960) lies south of historic Fort Clark in Oliver County.

Because of is geographical location in the center of Oliver County, on November 4, 1902, Center was chosen to be the county seat. The following year, H. H. Harmon platted Center.

The blizzard descended upon Center on March 2. When it was done snowing, 12 inches of the white stuff, .31 inches of precipitation had been dumped on Center. From a high of 30 above on Wednesday, the thermometer began its descent at Center. Although temperatures remained above 0 at Center, during the storm, they fell afterwards. Monday morning, the low of 5 below.

On March 7, the Center Wildcats lost their last game of the season in the District 29 tournament at Hebron. New Salem won the game, 55 to 42.

Beulah lies a short distance north of the Knife River.

In 1960, 1,318 people called Beulah home.

In 1914, the NP located a station here. An agent for the Tuttle Land Co., Lee Pettibone, gave the settlement the name Beulah, in honor of his niece, Beulah Stinchcombe Bishop.

The effects of the March 1966 blizzard varied considerably across Mercer County. The further east a person went, the worst conditions became. This was also true for nine townships in the southwestern part of the county. Zap, a town about seven miles west of Beulah had even less snowfall than Beulah.

As for Beulah, it received about 3 inches of snow from the storm. Precipitationwise that came to .17 inches. Before the temperatures started to fall on Wednesday, the high was 32 degrees. Highs of 22 and 19 were posted Thursday and Friday, respectively with lows in the single digits. Once the storm had passed, a low of -10 was reached Sunday morning.

But as Lawrence Joos noted, determining just how much snow fell in Mercer County would have to be an estimate. This was because of the high winds that piled the snow into drifts that varied from 6 feet high to over 10 feet in some locales.

Mr. Roos had this to say about the radio and television coverage of the blizzard:

> Last, but not least, we should be very grateful to the Radio and TV stations for spending so many hours carrying the weather and storm reports. I believe letters of thanks and appreciation to them, would be more than welcome. For without their constant reports the entire state would of been in the dark about the weather and many people would of worried about the safety of their families and friends.[26]

The storm brought about the activation of the National Guard unit at Beulah on March 5 and 6.

Beulah high school boys basketball team finished the 1965-66 season with a second place finish in the District 28 tournament. Halliday edged them out for the championship with a 54 to 49 win. Leading the Miners' attack were M. Blohm and R. Mutzenberger with 14 points each, followed by S. Sailer's 13 points.

The Knife River passes through Hazen (1,222 residents in 1960), which is located on N.D. 200 (N.D. Highway 7 in 1966) over ten miles west of Stanton.

The founders of Hazen were Richard Farrington and Alexander F. "Sandy" Roberts. Mr. Roberts arrived here in October 1882. A portion of the land on which he settled would eventually be incorporated into the townsite of Hazen.

With the establishment of a post office at Hazen on February 12, 1885, Zacariah L. Jones became the settlement's new postmaster. He named the post office after A. D. Hazen, who at that time was Third Assistant Postmaster General. Some people claim the settlement took its name from General William Babcock Hazen (1830-1897), a onetime commander of Fort Buford. In 1912, the populous of Hazen moved to the NP townsite in the same section.

The energy crisis of the early 1970's spurred the energy business and helped to dramatically increase Hazen's population. The 1980 census showed Hazen enjoying a population of 2,376 people.

Snow began falling around 4 p.m. March 2, in Hazen. It was accompanied by high winds that brought much activity in the Hazen area to a halt from late Wednesday until Saturday morning.

The blizzard dumped only about 4 inches of snow on Hazen, but along with strong winds, was enough to reduce visibility there to near zero. Sometimes, the ability to see across streets in Hazen on Thursday was close to nil. Once a person left the protection of the Knife River Valley, visibility was further reduced.

Despite this, the lack of heavy snowfall in the Hazen vicinity did not stop vehicular traffic completely Thursday and Friday. Out in the country, high winds left most highways and township roads clear of snow. Those individuals who had to go work and drive a ways did just that. But, for the most part, if left with a choice, people stayed home.

Temperatures at Hazen during the storm varied between the teen's and single digits above zero.

Mercer County did not receive any incoming mail during the blizzard. Once the mail truck that served Mercer County went back to Bismarck Wednesday evening, North Branch offices would not see it again until about 5 p.m. Saturday. Weather conditions on Thursday prevented local carriers from even trying to make it around their mail routes. On Friday, they were able to get around most of their routes.

It was a shorter work day for quite a few business establishments in Hazen on Thursday. On that day, they shut their doors an hour or so sooner than they ordinarily did.

No classes were held at any school in Mercer County on Thursday and Friday.

The blizzard kept trains from running on the NP line through Hazen from March 2 to March 8. At that time, an NP snowplow pulled into Hazen. Enroute, NP trainmen encountered many hard, but not high, snowdrifts near Hensler. Hensler is located over thirty miles east of Hazen near the Missouri River.

Depth of a number of snowbanks in farm shelterbelts the Hazen area varied from 5 to 8 feet.

In Hazen itself, the blizzard had filled a two block area west of the intersection of Fourth Avenue East and East Fifth Street pretty solid with snow. In the same area, a drift that was a minimum of 5 feet in height was deposited in front of Reinhold Schwinkendorf's home.

At Hazen, the high northeast winds of the blizzard piled the snow up on the north side of the east-west Main Street while leaving the south side of the street with much less snow. Hardly any shoveling was needed to remove the snow from the sidewalks there. On the north side of the street, there were pretty good size drifts in front of the Jack & Jill Store and the Hazen Rexall Drug Store.

Mercer County stockmen emerged from the blizzard with few, if any, losses of live-stock. As of Wednesday morning, March 9 there hadn't been any reports of any livestock losses come into the office of Mercer County Agent, H. R. McKenzie.

It didn't take long to clear the snow from the three main business blocks on Hazen's Main Street. Equipment involved in the cleanup operation included a piece of equipment from the S & R Excavating Company, three machines from the Oster Construction Company of Hazen, and other equipment. The snow was delivered to the railroad right-of-way in a Tournapull-type scraper.

On March 8, the Hazen Bison rolled past the Killdeer Cowboys, 86 to 61. The Bison finished in third place in the District 28 tournament. Pacing the Bison attack were J. Pulles with 24 points, followed by L. Stroup's 20 points.

Stanton (409 residents in 1960) lies on the west side of the Missouri River, not far from the mouth of the Knife River. It is the seat of Mercer County.

The Stanton vicinity has a rich history. When Lewis and Clark arrived here in October 1804, they came upon a Mandan Indian village known as Mah-har-ha.

In 1882, two brothers, James and Thomas McGrath, showed up in the Stanton vicinity. They constructed a log cabin. A post office was set up in that establishment on December 4, 1882.

The McGraths applied their mother's maiden name to the post office. Another version has Stanton taking its name from Abraham Lincoln's Secretary of War, Edwin Stanton (1814-1869).

The NP extended its line to Stanton in 1910.

Stanton was the birthplace of Harold Schafer (1912-2002), a prominent businessman from Bismarck, Medora promoter, and father of Edward Schafer, North Dakota governor from 1992 until 2000.

The Knife River Indian Village, a National Historic Site, is also located near here.

One of the March 1966 blizzard's most dramatic rescues involved four men from Stanton. Three of the men were part of the rescue party, and the fourth person was of the group that was rescued.

Allen Mutzenburger taught history and was an assistant basketball coach at Fort Yates. A Stanton High School and Minot State College graduate, Mutzenburger and two other Fort Yates coaches set out from Mandan to return to Fort Yates Wednesday evening.

Their failure to reach Fort Yates, seventy miles south of Mandan, set off alarms. Especially concerned were Allen and his wife Judy's parents, Mr. and Mrs. William Mutzenburger and Mr. and Mrs. Willmar Schweigert, all of whom were residents of Stanton. A rescue operation was set in motion. Furnishing assistance were three Stanton men, Jim and Vernon Smith, and Lee Stephens.

They set out from Stanton with a pickup and a snow sled at 8:15 a.m. Friday. Lousy visibility forced them to take shelter in a schoolhouse east of Center. Their stay there lasted from just before noon until evening.

Upon arrival in Mandan, the three Stanton men hooked up with the main rescue party and set out to find the missing coaches. With a rotary plow in the lead, the fifteen man rescue crew came upon the stranded men thirty-two miles south of Mandan around 2:30 a.m. Saturday.

Allen Mutzenburger and his wife's parents said the three rescuers from Stanton provided the impetus for starting the rescue party in Mandan in motion.

The March 1966 blizzard hardly affected the Basin Electric Power Cooperative Leland Olds power plant located on the west side of the Missouri River. Of the plant's 45 employees, only two men from Center failed to make it to work. The majority of the workers hailed from Hazen and Stanton. They made it to work without incident. To compensate for the absence of one of the workers from Center, a plant operator had to pull double shifts.

Linton, Strasburg, Hague, Westfield, Hazelton and Kintyre

Emmons County was named for James A. Emmons (1843-1919), a Missouri River boat captain who came to Bismarck in 1872. Emmons served as the post trader at Camp Hancock, present-day Bismarck. The military camp provided protection for the NP work gangs.

Linton was settled in 1898. It was named for George W. Lynn, an Emmons County attorney. However, Mr. Lynn would only agree to a contraction of his name, so "Linton" was chosen.

Linton's growth coincided with the arrival of two railroads. The Milwaukee Railroad arrived in 1902 and the NP came in 1903. The city is a terminus for both railroads.

The *Emmons County Record* published its first newspaper on June 10, 1884. After the 1966 blizzard, Bill Fischer, editor of the *Record*, wrote:

WORST BLIZZARD IN HISTORY

It took just three nights and two days last week for an entirely new–and almost unbelievable–chapter to be added to the weather history of most of North Dakota.[27]

About noon on March 2, light snow started to fall in the Linton area. There was a "rather stiff northeast wind" that Wednesday. Blizzard warnings, for the first time, were heard on the radio that evening. Local weather observer, L. P. Malone, figured the city received .12 inches of precipitation. The high for the day had been 31 degrees. The low that night was 22.

Wednesday evening, the wind blew two conductors into contact with each other and power was lost. Montana-Dakota Utility manager, George Mischel handled the radio while Don Ryckman and George Bosch traveled to the substation just north of Linton in their pickup. They redirected the source of power for Linton. Power now came from the east, instead of the north. Electricity was off for about an hour. They returned to Linton and went to bed.

That night, the winds increased in velocity. To make matters worse, the snowfall became intense.

Ryckman and Bosch did not get much sleep. They received word that a portion of the city was still without power. The two men traced the source of trouble to a spot behind the Dietz Barbershop, on Broadway. They had the problem fixed by 3:30 a.m. Thursday.

Visibility was zero Thursday morning. The high for the day was 24. Winds gusts of 65 mph hit the city of Linton. Malone calculated the precipitation total at .80 inches, about 8 inches of snow. According to the *Emmons County Record*:

"The whole area had been paralyzed and people were living in a world of swirling white."[28]

A NP Railroad crew went to work Thursday morning in Linton. That day, the local had a small train, three boxcars and a caboose behind the diesel engine. They had work to do between Linton and McKenzie. After leaving town, the train was not sighted at the next stop. Authorities were notified.

During the storm, KEM's rural customers were without power for periods ranging from 15 minutes to 3 hours. Some of the outages occurred when power was shut off and interrupted on MDU lines. Thursday morning, a KEM crew battled their way to the John Kelsch farm, 15 miles east of Linton to fix a problem. After that, the utility did not send crews out in the bad weather.

On Thursday, Bill Fischer and others stopped at the Lauinger Cafe for lunch. Scoop Calquhoun, the cook, was on duty. Ralph Schmaltz and Sam Feist were busy as impromptu waitresses.

Ryckman and Bosch spent much of Thursday fixing outages around town.

The wind changed directions Thursday night, at first straight north and then to the northwest. The winds from that direction were just as strong, if not stronger. The official the low for Thursday was 12 degrees.

On Friday, according to the *Record*, "Only a very few Linton people–the same was true in other towns–ventured from their homes, and these went to inspect their businesses and to check their furnaces."[29]

The high on Friday was 17 above. Another .87 inches of precipitation fell.

Friday afternoon, the source of power from the east went out. Another switch at the substation had to be made. An escort was arranged for the MDU men. The county blade and Russ Lawler's bulldozer were pressed into service but the weather was too bad.

John O'Rourke came through with his little snowmobile. With Ryckman as his passenger, they started out on Highway 83. Before long, they were in the ditch and lost. Eventually, they recovered their bearings and reached the substation. Don switched the source of power back to the north. This gave most of Linton electricity again. There still were outages in the northeast part of town. For this, Russ Lawler took Ryckman around town on his bulldozer. After Don made the necessary repairs, all of Linton had power.

Somehow, the stork found its way to the Joe G. Gross farm, fourteen miles east and three miles north of Linton. The telephone was their only option. A call was made to Dr. W. J. Orchard Jr., Linton, for instructions on delivering a baby. Mr. and Mrs. Alois Leier, neighbors of the Grosses, were there to help. Mr. Gross was coached on the procedures.

Mrs. Gross gave birth to the couple's second daughter. They also had four sons. Mother and child were doing fine afterwards.

The winds lost some of their velocity Friday night. The low fell to 8.

Saturday morning, the blizzard dissipated, and colder temperatures came with the clearing of the skies. L.P. Malone estimated the storm had dumped about 24 inches of snow, 1.79 inches of precipitation on Linton. On Saturday, it warmed up to 18 degrees, that night the low fell to 5 above.

The *Record* said:

> Saturday morning many people were unable to get out of their doors because of the drifted snow. Some left by way of windows; others waited for neighbors to shovel them out. The same conditions prevailed on farms, many of which are covered with drifts of almost unbelievable height, width and depth.[30]

Jacob Munsch, 60, was found dead at the Linton Public School around 9 a.m. Saturday by Sam Bollinger, janitor. Munsch left home about 8:00. He walked about five blocks to the school. Munsch was one the school's janitors. Authorities believed Munsch death was caused by exertions in struggling through heavy snow to get to work.

Jacob Munsch, born in Linton on October 23, 1905, a son of Mr. and Mrs. Peter Munsch, had lived in Linton the past twenty-three years. Before that, Munsch farmed twelve miles west of Strasburg. On February 20, 1934, he married Elizabeth Riedlinger in Linton. The couple had one son, Curtis C., a student at Valley city State College, and a daughter, Judith K., a student at Dickinson State College.

One mystery was solved. The NP train crew walked back into Linton. Their train had stalled about three miles north of the city in a big drift on Thursday. Linton Station Agent Gordon Beck reported:

> The train was radio-equipped but being stalled in the deep cut made it impossible to get out a message. The crew lived on rather meager rations during the two days. The train will remain in the cut until all tracks from the north are cleared by a rotary plow.

Linton's streets and avenues were "absolutely impassable." Drifts up to 10 feet were common around town. Many people could walk right to the roofs of their houses from the top of the drifts.

Linton hired Russ Lawler for snow removal. Vic Schiermeister manned a cat equipped with an angle dozer. All tractors with bucket or blade attachments were also put into service. The city's small snow blower proved too small for the job.

Mayor Bob Gaukler had a lot on his mind, during and after the storm. Mayor Gaukler was so busy he forgot about his fuel situation at home and his furnace conked out late at night.

According to the *Record*, snow shovels "moved quickly" out of hardware stores.

Rural families were isolated longer than the residents of Linton. Emmons County operators did their best to clear county roads, but bucker plows were not suitable for much of the work. Rotary plows and bulldozers were needed.

On Sunday, the cleanup continued in Linton. The high for the day was 17 degrees. That night, the thermometer dropped to 16 degrees below zero.

Emmons County Civil Defense Director, Alvin M. Tschosik contacted various military officials and leaders of the state Civil Air Patrol. Heavy equipment from National Guard units opened many roads in the county.

Robert Miller, Reinie Werner and Emil Humann, members on the Hazelton Township board, made arrangements with Northern Improvement Company for the use of three dozers before the storm was over. The machines were put to use right away.

A large Air Force helicopter took stranded people home early on Sunday. It also carried two photographers for *LIFE* magazine. Later in the day, other missions were completed with a smaller helicopter. The National Guard sent a light plane equipped with skis for emergencies.

MDU and KEM utility linemen were busy after the blizzard. A National Guard helicopter dropped KEM men off where outages occurred on Sunday. Their customers were scattered over a large area. That crew consisted of the following men, Bill Kliche, Leo Hughes, Leonard Vetsch, John Dykema, Mattie Vetter, Eddie Wagner, Syl Zahn, Anton Bosch and Terry Martin. Essential repairs were completed by Sunday evening.

The National Guard unit at Linton drilled Saturday and Sunday. They had other duties and some members were placed on alert. Lacking heavy equipment, the Guardsmen brought people to the hospital in their trucks. They aided others who needed help.

Abe Compaan operated KEM's radio day and night during the blizzard. Bruce Bosworth and Bob Martin remained in the office throughout the storm. General Manager George Cornog, returning from the Rural Electric Cooperatives convention, was snowbound in Herreid, South Dakota.

On Monday March 7, Governor William L. Guy, Lieutenant Governor Charles Tighe of Bismarck, Adjutant General L. A. Melhouse, Director Donald Mushik of Civil Defense and three newsmen took a helicopter tour west of Bismarck, southwest to Solen, Selfridge, Fort Yates and then across the river and north through Strasburg, Linton, Tenvik, Hazelton and back to Bismarck. They saw only a few dead cattle and some groups of strays during their flight. Some animals were in belly-deep snow. One of the things they noticed on the observation tour was that the public school houses in Strasburg and Hazelton had drifts up to the second story windows. Governor Guy said:

> It's going to be difficult for many people and livestock until we can get the big hard snowbanks open. One of our real problems is going to be getting rural school bus routes plowed out, especially in cuts and coulees before the snow melts and makes lakes out of these low-lying areas.[31]

Governor Guy made a comment about livestock losses that upset Bill Fischer. Governor Guy remarked, "Frankly, it wasn't as bad as I expected to find it." Responding, Fischer said, "A lot of these animals died right in the barn or right next to the barn. Many of the lost cattle are buried in draws and coulees and couldn't be spotted from the air."[32]

On Tuesday, Governor Guy said, "I regret deeply the impression I left with reporters yesterday. Minimizing the suffering observed in a helicopter tour. This was not my intent. I regard the losses of livestock as extremely severe and the need for help in opening roads and feed supplies as very critical."

Federal funds would not be made available to North Dakota for snow removal. A representative from the Federal Office of Emergency Planning in Denver arrived in North Dakota on Sunday, March 6. Emergency planning funds were made available to local governments to replace local public utilities damaged or destroyed in emergencies. After talking to the representative, Governor Guy said, "We just haven't had the type of disaster that would qualify us for EOP funds."[33]

Governor Guy indicated there was $361,000 in a state contingency fund for such emergencies. The state had to meet all costs of the cleanup from this uncommitted balance. Money had to be left in that fund for other emergencies. Flood forecasters, alarmed by snowfall totals, expected severe flooding in the drainage basin of the Red River of the North. Consequently, a strict monetary cap was set for hiring private contractors for snow removal. Governor Guy helped the residents of the state by mobilizing National Guard units for snow removal.

Fischer estimated Emmons County livestock losses at $200,000.

Lester DeKrey, county agent at Linton, estimated animal losses at about 1,000 head. DeKrey said, "We can account for 850 head and there are a lot of small losses which have not been reported in. I think 1,000 is about right." He indicted that Gene Vander Vorst, who farms in North Dakota north of Pollock, South Dakota, lost about 130 head. DeKrey said, "Others in the area reported losing animals after the storm through a combination of exhaustion and pneumonia caused by breathing snow and dust during the storm."[34]

Monday morning, the National Guard sent a bulldozer to Emmons County. Another one was being transported to McIntosh County.

U.S. Highway 83 two miles north of Linton at NP crossing on March 9, 1966. Courtesy of North Dakota Department of Transportation (NDDOT)

N.D. Highway 13 east of Linton on March 9, 1966. Courtesy of NDDOT

N.D. Highway 13 east of Linton on March 9, 1966. Both photos courtesy of NDDOT

The blizzard interrupted the District 20 tournament at Napoleon. St. Benedict of Strasburg defeated Braddock, 59 to 51, and Wishek downed St. Anthony of Linton, 71 to 57. In other action before the storm, Zeeland outran Strasburg Public, 73 to 45.

Play was resumed on March 7. The Hazelton Tigers, the pre-tournament favorite with a 17-3 record, blew away St. Benedict Knights of Strasburg 121 to 56. Harvey Jahner scored 54 points for the Tigers. Jahner's teammates, Abby Opp, 21, Monte Humann, 17, Terry Gimbel, 16, and Rod Kalberer, 15, scored lots of points. Richard Baumgartner put up 27 points for the Knights.

Tuesday night, the Ashley Aces won a hard fought contest against Napoleon, 65 to 63. Lehr pulled away from Wishek for a 79 to 49 victory and Linton defeated Zeeland in overtime, 79 to 74.

The semifinal games were played on Wednesday. Ashley upset the Hazelton Tigers, 70 to 63. Linton cruised pass Lehr, 72 to 47.

Thursday afternoon, Lehr defeated Hazelton, 81 to 72, in the consolation game. Ashley regained possession of the ball with three seconds left. The Aces called time out. The Linton Lions were up two points. Don Kammerer caught the pass from the sideline and threw up a shot. The championship game ended in a tie.

There was no scoring in the first overtime.

In the second overtime, the Aces took their first lead in the game, 60 to 58. A free throw put the Aces up by three. Linton's John Backhaus cut the margin to one. Ashley scored another free throw, but Backhaus knotted the score.

Linton scored first in the third overtime, but Ashley came back with a basket. Backhaus put the Lions ahead, but Ashley sank two free throws to tie the game again. With 25 seconds left, Linton regained possession of the ball. They worked the clock down to the final seconds. The ball went to Backhaus. He scored with one tick left on the clock. Ashley's last effort failed. Linton won the district title, 68 to 66. John Backhaus led the Lions with 44 points. Backaus made all of Linton's points in the second half and in the three overtimes, except for two points. For Ashley, Ken Retzer hit 21, Bill Thurn, 20, and David Jenner, 10. Linton looked forward to defending their 1965 Region 5 title.

Linton beat Medina in their first regional game. The Lions were one win away from to the Class B State tournament. They were there in 1964 and 1965. Coach Dale Baer started coaching the Lions in 1964. Linton and Wing played in championship game of the regional. Linton won the double-overtime contest, 54 to 53.

On March 17, Linton faced Fessenden, the No. 1 team in the final Class B poll. The Orioles had a 24-2 record. The Lions had a 16-10 record, their overtime victories in district and regional gave them lots of confidence. The Orioles won their eighteenth straight game, 84 to 63, but John Backhaus was the star of the game. He scored 36 points.

Linton met Cooperstown on Friday. A last second shot derailed the Lynxs on Thursday. Linton lost the game, 101 to 81. John Backhaus made 20 of 32 shots and 6 out 7 free throws. Backhaus's 47 points broke the single game scoring record held by Washburn's Don Prouty. In 1956, Prouty tallied 41 points against Hunter and scored 78 points in two games. With 82 points, Backhaus broke that record as well. He established another record, 20 field goals in one game.

Louis Sandwick, farmer northeast of Linton, had five turkeys. Before the blizzard hit, he left the door of an old granary open for the birds. The storm filled the granary with snow. Afterwards, he found three of the birds. On March 13, Sandwick was shoveling snow out of the old granary. During a pause, he noticed a small hole. Sandwick carefully enlarged the hole and discovered two turkeys. They were alive.

Three weeks after the blizzard, Bill Fischer wrote:

WE RAN SHORT

We thought there would be some people who would want to keep a copy of the March 16 Record, in which we carried a large number of blizzard pictures. The demand, however, has exceeded the supply.

There are still a few people who would like a copy of that paper, so we'll pay 15¢ for every one in good condition brought back. AND, we'll sell those same ones for 15¢. There won't be a profit, but some just may be able to get ahold of a souvenir.[35]

At the end of March 1966, the North Dakota State University Extension Service placed Emmons County cattle losses were placed at 1,150 head.[36]

About ten miles south of Linton along U. S. Highway 83 is Strasburg. Settlement in this part of Emmons County began in 1888. Sebastian Bauman, Joseph Baumgartner, Joseph Burgan, Jacob Feist and Joseph Kraft were Strasburg's pioneer trailblazers. The people who emigrated here were Germans from Strasburg, South Russia. In 1902, the Milwaukee Railroad arrived at this townsite, known as Stafford. Within a year, the town's name was changed to Strasburg.

Strasburg is best remembered as the home of Lawrence Welk, (1903-1992). His parents, Ludwig and Christina (Schwahn) Welk immigrated to the United States in 1893 from Odessa, Russia. Lawrence grew up on a farm, a couple miles northwest of Strasburg. When Lawrence was 17, he made a deal with his father for a accordion. He would work on the farm for another four years and turn over all the money he earned at various celebrations to his father during that period. Lawrence Welk left home on his 21st birthday to pursue his musical career. On July 2, 1955, Welk made his debut on national television.

The city had 612 residents in 1960.

Kasper Jacob, son of Mr. and Mrs. Valentine Jacob Jr., arrived in Danang on January 22, 1966. Jacob worked 12 hour shifts unloading supplies on a Pier Team in Vietnam. Jacob graduated from St. Benedict High School in 1963 and joined the United States Navy in June 1965.

In late February 1966, Catholic pastors and assistant pastors in the county approved a plan to eliminate St. Anthony High School at Linton and St. Benedict High School at Strasburg and establish "Emmons Central High School." Classes would commence in the fall of 1966 in the facilities of St. Benedict High School. The high school project did not involve the grade schools. The religious faculty of both schools would retain their positions at the new school.

Mrs. Marcus Richter, Strasburg's news correspondent, wrote:

Another time to write up the news and we still do not have our Record from last week. No doubt it will be coming through tomorrow (Monday, March 7). Of course, you all are well aware of the reason–at least our North Dakota people–the terrible 3-day blizzard which started about Wednesday noon, March 2, and raged until into the night on Friday!

We have snowbanks which are unbelievable. Many had their doors blocked Saturday morning so that their neighbors had to help shovel to get the door open. We were fortunate in that we had electricity, although it went off intermittently at the beginning of the storm. Several were low on fuel supply and, of course, no fuel trucks could move so people were carrying 5-gallon cans Saturday morning. We also had telephone service.

There are many dramatic stories and acts of heroism during this 3-day critical period. Nothing really tragic, that is know at this time, happened in our town. Ten miles to the east of us was the little Welk girl's tragedy. At our Nursing Home, on Wednesday afternoon, the shift got home, but the 11 o'clock shift could not get to work, so they were short on help and, like other public places, each one had to help "beyond the call of duty." Several ladies braved almost insurmountable conditions to get there to do their duty. The most serious condition arose when the chimney became clogged and the Home was becoming gassed. There again repairmen faced almost impossible conditions to get the trouble corrected. Thanks should go to Frank Fiest and Ernie Borr for this. ...

The Strasburg Public School will be closed until repairs can be obtained from Bismarck for the heating system in part of the school. No doubt it will be several days before the country roads can be opened so that the school buses can get the children into school. There was no school at St. Benedict on Monday and Tuesday.

Telephone calls to their parents from Margaret Richter and Darlene Klein at the UND in Grand Forks, informed us that the storm was as bad or worse there and the snow was covering the first-floor windows of the dormitory where they stay. Cooks were not on duty at the cafeterias so students had to help themselves to what they could find. It is the first time in the history of the school that there was no school because of a storm.[37]

Dorothy Corner, manager, received a note of appreciation for the employees of Nursing Home in Strasburg. Here's some of their comments:

Mrs. Carl Roehrich: Time to go to work early Friday morning for Katie Klein and myself. If it would not have been Carl's help we would never have made it. We got as far as Ben Bickler's barn and stopped in for a few minutes to get our breath, then arm in arm we finally made it. We were never so glad to see the Old Peoples' Home in all the time I've worked three years.

Virgina Schatz: Getting there and the three days we spent there was a challenge and I beli eve we all met it to the best of our ability.

Mrs. Max Paul: Got stuck on the way home Thursday night, but still made it.

Margie Goetz: Although somewhat tiring after three full days and nights at the Home, I'm thankful we could be here to give our patients the care and attention they needed.

Kathryn Borr: When I left home Thursday morning, I had no idea how bad this blizzard really was. It was one big snowdrift after the other. I soon real that I had to take it easy if I were to get there. I was one of the many who went through this to help our elderly people.

Ann Burgad: Just couldn't make it.

Katie Rohrick and Rosalie Mattern: It was our turn to cook, so Friday morning we braved the storm. It was rough, but we got there. Spent the night there to be sure that we could be on the job the next morning.

Amy Vander Sluis: Supposed to be on duty Wednesday night, beginning at 11. My brother tried to take me by car, got about two blocks but had to go back. Was amazed Saturday when I got back to work how happy everyone was in spite of the blizzard.

Mrs. Ray Wagner: I got out of the house to go to work but before I knew it, I sat in the snow. After a short rest, I made it to the Home.

Mary Miller: I never thought I'd make it. Fell several times. I thought this is the end of my life.

Irene Buecklet: Opened the door, went back again and tried it, walked a block, thought I had to go back. I will never forget this.

Margaret Geigle: I made it to work on Thursday. Started to go to work on Friday but after walking a half block decided I couldn't make it, so turned back home. Was just too bad. I live on the far end of town from the Home.[38]

The following comments are from several of the patients:

Hjelmer Hanson: The storm was bad but the nurses and aides gave us real good care. I can't help but admire them the way they fought through the storm to take care of us.

Lloyd Iverson: The storm was very bad, the days were very long, but through the cooperation of the nurses and aides and members of the board, everything went okay.

Mrs. Fannie Nelson: The storm was shocking but the workers were wonderful, you'd hardly know it.

Pat Malone: Have been in Emmons County 64 years and this is the worst I have ever seen. But the care here was no different. The workers were good-natured even during the storm.

Molly Coordes and Kathiern Weisbeck: I like to say a prayer of thanks for the help and sacrifice the workers gave us old people; to come every day to work and take care of us. I will never forget what good meals they had for us, with so many things missing. Many thanks to the personnel.[39]

The workers said, "We all thank God we had the guidance and wisdom of Ernie Borr through this trying experience."[40]

Mike Dosch, Strasburg, played an accordion solo on the *Lawrence Welk Show*, Saturday evening, March 5.

Hague, located halfway between Strasburg and Zeeland, was founded in 1902 when the Milwaukee went through the area.

To honor the Dutch settlers, the railroad officials named the community after Hague, Netherlands.

The community had 197 residents in 1960.

Hague recorded 2.5 inches of precipitation between March 2, 1966, and March 5, 1966.

On March 9, 1966, the following article appeared in the *Record*:

6-Year Old Hague Girl
Dies in Blizzard Thursday

The six-year-old daughter of a rural Hague couple became a victim of the fierce blizzard last week.

Carleen, daughter of Mr. and Mrs. Eugene Welk, became separated from her two older brothers on the family farm, about 12 miles east of Strasburg, Thursday afternoon, and was found dead Saturday morning in a sitting position about a quarter of a mile from the farm.

Carleen had accompanied her brothers, Allan, 13, and Duane, 11, out to do chores at about 4 p.m. The three had gone to the chicken coop about 60 feet from the house and then went another 20 feet to the barn where the boys discovered that their sister was missing. Her father, who had gone out earlier to put cattle in another barn did not know of her disappearance until he met the boys. After checking the house, a search was started. A neighbor, Jerome Senger, joined in the search, but it had to be called off by 7 p.m. Others were willing to help, but were unable to reach the Welk farm because of the storm.

Mr. Welk tried again Friday afternoon, but was unable to go far because of the storm. He tried once more Saturday morning and then found his daughter's body and carried it back to a granary. A helicopter from the Minot Air Force Base brought the body to the Kraft Funeral Home at Linton Sunday.

As of Tuesday evening, (March 8) funeral arrangements had not been made because roads in the St. Aloysius area, where the family lives and where the funeral will be held, had not yet been opened.

Carleen, who was six years old on January 25 of this year, leaves her parents; her maternal grandparents, Mr. and Mrs. Mike Schatz, Zeeland; Mrs. Barbara Welk, Strasburg; a sister, Linda, 8, and a brother, Tim, 3, as well as the two brothers mentioned above.[41]

The funeral for Carleen Welk was held on March 12 at the St. Aloysius Church with Reverend Austin Herrmann officiating.

Mrs. C.J. Buechler, Hague's news correspondent, wrote:

Caption to the following news could read:

"TAILS OFF the '66 BLIZZARD"

Adam Ebrle had three ponies in his barn with his cattle during the blizzard–the storm had prevented him from getting out to feed his stock for a couple of days–and when he did get out he found that his three ponies were without tails. Adam is wondering if his cattle actually got that hungry that they mistook the horses' tails for grass.

At the Julius Miller farm. Julius had to dig down to find the shed where he kept his hogs. His coal shed was also covered. He had burned just about everything that he could find, before he found his coal shed. The hogs were still alive, but he thought if it would have been another half hour that they would have been smothered.

Victor Schall was given an unscheduled vacation. He did not get into his garage until Saturday. The snowplow had to open up the alley to get

Main Street of Hague on March 9, 1966. Courtesy of North Dakota State Historical Society

Hague school bus buried in large drift in Hague on March 9, 1966. Courtesy of E.B.R. SC, UND

one of the school busses out, that had been in the garage for repair. Sunday (March 13) the snow was removed from the front of the garage, so he can now be open for business.

Charles Masset had both his Chevy and station wagon completely covered by about four feet of snow. The school bus was also under a huge drift that completely covered it.

At the Joe Klein home, the chimney plugged with snow, so that the oil stove went out. They were without heat. We were fortunate, the power was off only about 4 1/2 hours in all–half hour one day and four the next. ...[42]

Westfield, another Dutch community in Emmons County, was founded in 1884. The early pioneers came from Westfield, Iowa. It is locally known as the "Wooden Shoe Community."

It had a population of 60 in 1960.

Mrs. A. Van Beek, Westfield's news correspondent, wrote:

We here in Westfield are getting back to normal having been without mail or any way of getting out, from March 2 till March 11, when they came and opened up the road, so the mail came on Thursday evening. We still have an enormous lot of snow and water, following the big blizzard. Driveways are still blocked by 4 to 5 foot drifts. Traffic we had through here till Friday a.m. was on foot, and we still have to climb over snowbanks to get to the road, where they can pick us up by car. A lot of cattle in the area were lost during the storm, and now there is a sickness among the ones that survived the storm. Next will be flooding, which already occurred out west, but not too much here in Westfield up till now, but it will be coming in the next few days if weather remains so nice.

School was resumed this Monday morning after 7-day vacation as roads were impassable for the busses to make the routes. ...[43]

Hazelton, named by John Ithamer Roop for his daughter, Hazel, was established in 1902. The town, on a NP line, was home for 451 people in 1960. Hazelton bills itself as the "Flax Capital of the Nation."

Tommy Beastrom spent ten months in Vietnam in the United States Army. In March 1966, he was home after being discharged recently.

Mrs. Jerome Landsberger, Hazelton's news correspondent for in the *Emmons County Record*, wrote:

Several men in the community operated a grocery delivery service Saturday morning with vehicles that could get through the snow. Thanks a lot, men![44]

The Grunefelder Brothers barn collapsed in blizzard from the weight of the snow. They lost between 50 and 75 head of cattle in the snow and fallen timber. Ten days after the blizzard, they found three cows still alive. The animals had enough strength to get up and walk without assistance.

Kintyre was founded in 1905 on the Soo Line. The town was named for the Kintyre peninsula in Scotland. The name comes from the clan name McIntyre and means the head of land. Thomas S. Kleppe, a U.S. Representative and Secretary of Interior under President Ford, was born in Kintyre. In 1965, the population was estimated at 80.

William Grunefelder farm southeast of Hazelton on March 9 1966. Courtesy of Elwyn B. Robinson Special Collections, University of North Dakota (E.B.R. SC, UND)

Collapsed barn on William Grunefelder farm southeast of Hazelton, March 1966. Courtesy of E.B.R. SC, UND

Weiser farm northeast of Hazelton on March 9, 1966 Courtesy of E.B.R. SC, UND

Trailer house owned by Weiser's hired man buried snowbanks on March 9, 1966. Courtesy of E.B.R. SC, UND

Weiser farm northeast of Hazelton, March 1966. Courtesy of E.B.R. SC, UND

Northern Improvement dozer operator Ray Tobiason receiving instructions about three miles east of Hazelton, March 1966. Courtesy of E.B.R. SC, UND

Alice Fallgatter, Kintyre's news correspondent, wrote:

> The worst four-day blizzard is the news this week. Schools were closed, no mail service and many around here were stranded in other towns....
>
> It kept Postmaster Sperle busy taking care of the fires in different places while these folks were stranded. Roads are still blocked in front of most of the homes and some went through the windows to get out to shovel the snow away and neighbors would shovel others out. We were thankful the power stayed on and had telephone service. Many cattle are dead. Some that reported losses were the Grunefelders and J.J. Mochs.
>
> I have lived in Kintyre over fifty years and never saw a blizzard like this with so much snow all at once. Snowbanks as high as the house and there were windows covered with snow. Some have had snow in their attics. I have heard my folks (the C.J. Hoofs who were pioneers at Napoleon) tell of the blizzard of 1888, which was terrible. If this snow goes away as fast as it came then we will need a boat. ...
>
> A National Guard plane came to the Fred Nelson farm Sunday to take Mrs. Wally Nelson to Bismarck to be with her father, Joel Erickson of Steele. Wally Nelson went later when they opened the roads from their home.[45]

Ashley, Venturia, Zeeland, Lehr and Wishek

Ashley, the seat of McIntosh County, was founded in 1887.

The town (1,419 residents in 1960) was probably named for Ashley E. Morrow of the Northwestern Construction and Improvement Company. Others believed Ashley was named for Ashley Morrell, a relative of the townsite owners. The origin of the word "ashley" is an English one that means "dweller in the ash-tree meadow." Ashley displaced Hoskins, located three miles to the east, as the seat of McIntosh County in 1888. Hoskins was the first townsite in McIntosh County. Hoskins and Lake Hoskins were given the maiden name of the wife of Colonel C. A. Lounsberry, historian and founder of the *Bismarck Tribune*. John H. Wishek, came to Bismarck in 1884. Born in 1855 to German immigrant parents in Warren, Pennsylvania, Wishek went to law school at the University of Michigan. After that, he practiced law for five years in Prospect, Ohio. Despite his lack of funds, Wishek joined a group of land speculators, headed by George W. Lilly. That party was interested in McIntosh County, as well as Logan and Emmons counties in North Dakota and McPherson County in South Dakota. Their first venture was Hoskins. Wiskek helped the government surveyors divide the townships into sections.

Usually, railroads turned over the development of townsites to a "land company." Wishek found his niche as a townsite promoter. He spoke the language of the German Russians who settled McIntosh County and the surrounding counties. Displaying a generous civic side, Wishek gave away town lots for churches, parks, and town halls. Wishek was also a businessman, politician and rancher. He owned banks, grain elevators and implement firms. He invested in lumber and coal. Wishek helped secure right-of-way across McIntosh County for the Soo Line. He settled in Ashley.

The Soo Line established a station in Ashley in 1901, but a roadbed was raised there in 1887. On May 31, 1883, the Ordway, Bismarck and Northwestern Railway was incorporated in Dakota Territory. The Board of Directors approved another plan that extended the line to Aberdeen in April 1887. The railroad became known as the Aberdeen, Bismarck and Northwestern Company, but no tracks were laid.

Four railroads, the Minneapolis & St. Croix Railway Company, the Minneapolis, Sault Ste. Marie & Atlantic Railway Company, Minneapolis & Pacific Railway Company and Aberdeen, Bismarck & Northwestern Railway Company, merged in 1888. The brokers of the deal were Canadian Pacific financiers. The new railroad was called the Minneapolis, St. Paul & Sault Ste. Marie Railway Company. It became known as the Soo.

In the 1870's and 1880's the milling industry in Minneapolis implemented technological improvements. Prior to 1880, millers preferred soft winter wheat. After the upgrade in machinery, the millers wanted hard spring wheat. The idea growing place for this crop was in the Dakotas and northern Minnesota.

In the 1880's, there was a clash between the Minneapolis milling industry and Chicago's railroad interests. Minneapolis's future was at stake. An independent route to the eastern seaboard markets helped the development of Minneapolis. The Soo provided that access on January 6, 1888.

The Soo converged into McIntosh County from the east and south. In 1898, the east-west line was built between Kulm and Wishek. It angled toward Bismarck, but stopped at Braddock.

The south-north line was constructed from Pollock, South Dakota, to Wishek in 1901. The Soo extended the line from Braddock to Bismarck in 1902.

The Soo Line Railroad Company was officially created in 1961 with the merger of the Minneapolis, St. Paul & Sault Ste. Marie Railroad Company, the Wisconsin Central and Duluth, South Shore & Atlantic. (In 1990, the CP purchased the railroad.)

On March 2, 1966, Ashley recorded a high of 32 above. The winds from the southeast, switched to the northeast and became stronger. That Wednesday snow fell. According to Ben Steinhaus, local weather observer, 2 inches came down.

School was let out early that afternoon.

One of the school buses did not return to Ashley that evening. City workers kept the street to the hospital open most of the time. Nurses who were there worked double and triple shifts and operated the kitchen. Dr. Roland Fleck walked to the hospital at times.

The *Ashley Tribune* with Walter Froh, editor, wrote:

> It thawed the fore part of last week–up through Tuesday it seemed like spring. Then the weatherman lowered the boom.
>
> Worst blizzard of record–worse than the famous (or infamous) one of 1888, says the weather bureau.
>
> It started Wednesday, growing stronger in intensity through the night, continued all day Thursday, reached its peak that night and raged all of Friday. Friday night it began to lose a little of its force, but was still fierce by any standard. Saturday it began to taper off noticeably and by nightfall was about played out. Sunday dawned beautifully–a bright sun peering down on the landscape covered by the awesome drifts of snow sculptured by the storm. In intensity and duration it was the worst on record.
>
> The blizzard here can be described as savage, the treacherous swirling snow driven by a strong northeasterly wind that later shifted to the northwest, bringing colder temperatures that dipped below zero. At its worst visibility was down to absolutely nothing. It was like a white wall. Walking was not only fatiguing, but one didn't know where he was until he almost literally bumped into something familiar. Out in the open it was terrify-

*ing and hopeless. Objects and buildings could be missed by only a few feet
without being noticed.*

*Drifts were high. Snow collected on eyebrows and face, and eyes froze
shut. No one could survive out in the open for any length of time. Death
by suffocation would have resulted. ...[46]*

Ashley received 19 inches of snow between March 2 and March 5.

The precipitation had twenty percent moisture, snow normally contains about ten
percent moisture. Most of the drifts around town were 6 to 8 feet high, but others were
12 feet high or higher.

Although 70 mph wind gusts were recorded, the winds during the blizzard fluctuated
mainly between 40 and 50 mph.

Ben Steinhaus recorded the following weather data for Ashley. Here's the March 10,
1966, report:

THE WEATHER AT ASHLEY
Ben Steinhaus, Observer

March		H	L	Pre
2	2 in., snow se wind	32	23	
3	9 in., sno, nw blizzard	25	16	.76
4	4 in., sno, str nw wind	18	5	.36
5	4 in., sno, str nw wind	13	4	.37
6	clear, calm	13	-9	
7	str nw wind, blowing sn	22	-11	
8	clear, calm	36	20	

Normal moisture for March   .75
Moisture March 1 to date   1.49
Normal moisture to April 1   1.76
Moisture Jan. 1 to date   1.78

Christ Schlabsz, a farmer who lived northeast of Ashley, experienced trouble with the
oil furnace in his basement. It exploded. Black soot spewed out. The force of the blast sent
the stove pipes flying in the air. They came apart and lost their shape. That furnace heated
his house.

Schlabsz telephoned Albert Klipfel of Klipfel Heating and Sheet Metal at Ashley for
help. Schlabsz needed to remove the burner, clean and set the ignition points and reinstall
it, and recontruct the stove pipes. Klipfel provided the "easy" lessons in seven or eight
phone calls. Schlabsz repaired the furnace.

After the storm, Klipfel went to the farm. He checked the furnace and replaced the
stove pipes. He said:

*"The high wind may have created such a strong chimney draft that the
oil fumes were pulled out of the chimney before they could ignite, building
up an excess amount of oil in the furnace. When it finally did ignite, the
excess fuel caused the explosion."[47]*

Christ Schlabsz had to repaint his basement.

Valentine Neuhardt walked uptown Saturday after the weather had cleared. Neuhardt
lived on the west edge of town. On his way home, Neuhardt started to breathe hard.
Soon, every step was a struggle. He staggered and fell face down in the snow near the
Farmers Union Oil Company service station. Neuhardt was totally exhausted. He lacked

the strength to get up. Snowdrifts obscured the body from those working at the service station.

Milbert (Radar) Bauer was out in his MDU service truck. He noticed a body. It was face down in the swirling snow. Bauer picked Neuhardt up and took him to the Farmers Union Station.

Bauer cleared the snow from the man's nose and face. Neuhardt labored breathing became easier. Neuhardt would have suffocated to death, if Bauer had not found him when he did.

There was more good news on Saturday. The whereabouts of Aaron Haas, the missing school bus driver, became known. Wednesday night, Haas had taken shelter at the farm home of Donald Pfeifer. He had dropped off all of the passengers, except Eugene Pfeifer who later was delivered by car. Haas left the Pfeifer place Saturday night. There was no phone at the farm.

The blizzard created additional work for Cliff Goebel and Elroy Scherbenske. They had over 300 cattle to care for at the Ashley Livestock Sales Company. The animals had been sold on March 2.

Goebel raised cattle on his ranch north of town. He lost one animal because of the storm. Afterwards, Goebel said, *"He has been busier than an ant at a picnic and twice as tired."*[48]

The operators of lodging facilities heard storm stories from their guests. The Hotel Reuther gave shelter to Mr. and Mrs. Keifer of rural Zeeland on March 3. The couple had purchased some cattle in Minnesota. Between Ellendale and Ashley they drove 10 mph with both windows open all the way for better visibility. They were soaked to the bone from the wet snow. After reaching Ashley, the couple unloaded the cattle. Mrs. Keifer told Mrs. Reuther, *"that they would go no further and if no rooms were available would be willing to just sit in the lobby–anything to be out of the blizzard."*

After the hotel was full, a stranded traveler asked for accommodations. The Reuthers gave up their own bed for two nights and slept on the floor. The third night, the guest said, *"Enough of your kindness–tonight you sleep in your bed and I'll sleep on the floor."*[49]

Mr. and Mrs. Fred Maier, operators of the A & F Motel, mentioned the experiences of Reverend and Mrs. Richard Teuscher and their five children, ranging from 8 months to 15 years. The family left Great Bend, North Dakota, located southwest of Wahpeton, enroute to Nebraska to serve a parish there. Fighting snow and visibility, the Teuscher's car stalled ten miles east of Ashley. They were lucky. Adam Schneider came along with his cattle truck. He brought Mrs. Teuscher, the baby and one of the boys to Ashley with him. Soon afterwards, Stanley Dobler of Dobler 66 Service headed toward the stalled vehicle. Dobler towed the car with the rest of the family to town. Mrs. Maier provided meals for the family during the blizzard. While visiting, the Maiers learned that their daughter, Mrs. Roland Nies, had taught one of the Teuscher's boys at Great Bend.

On Saturday, a salesman checked out of the A & F Motel. Before he left, he reserved the right to get his room back if he couldn't get out of town. Mrs. Maier received a phone call minutes later. Mrs. Maier asked the salesman, *"How far did you get?"* He confessed, *"Only down town."*[50]

Ashley street crews had help in the snow removal operations. The city hired Ehley and Frisch Gravel Company to haul snow away.

On Monday, a radio announcement said that Ashley schools were closed until further notices. That information was inaccurate. Classes were held for those who made it in. There was no bus service.

The hospital in Ashley needed an anesthetist nurse for scheduled surgery. Sections of area highways were still blocked with snow. Civil Defense director, E. Oberlander, handled the problem. An Air Force helicopter flew in Mrs. Dennis Liska of Edgeley. After the roads were plowed open on Tuesday, Mrs. Liska received a ride home in a car.

On Tuesday, school buses were sent out on their routes, but some farms were still isolated. Some snowdrifts were too big for the county snowplows, so a rotary plow was needed.

Mail service was curtailed from March 2, to March 8.

Tim Nies, son of Mr. and Mrs. Walter Nies, lived on a farm near Ashley. He was nine years old when the blizzard struck in March 1966. To get out of their house, he left through his sister's upstairs bedroom window. He walked onto a drift and the snowbank stretched all way to the barn. At that time, the family had a new pole barn for their cattle. He remembered the storm had piled snow high around the pole barn, but there was a six inch gap. That gap, probably, saved their cattle from suffocation. They kept their milk cows in the barn. They had hay in the loft, so feeding them was no problem. He can recall digging a tunnel to their kitchen window to let light in the house. Although they lived only a quarter of a mile off the highway, they were stranded for almost five days. They had to wait for the rotary plow from Bismarck to open the road to their farm. After the storm, his father bought a generator that could be powered with the PTO on their tractors. A couple of days after storm, the sun was very bright and warm.[51]

Walter Froh visited a local farm on March 13. He wrote:

> You have to see it to believe it. We visited the Kenneth Lynn farm Sunday afternoon to see the accumulated snow in his yard. Drifts several hundred feet long cover his entire yard. Even the snow in the valleys between his drifts must be six to eight feet deep. During the storm he walked to his barn over the drifts using the telephone wire as a guideline. Sunday, his paths to the various farm buildings were trenches leading from one to another–at the bottom of them was water from the melting snow, mixed with gravel covered softening earth. It was a mess. One wonders how long it will take before it all melts.
>
> After the storm Mr. Lynn called for equipment from Ashley to dig a path to his almost completely buried garage and to uncover his own scoop-equipped tractor.
>
> Mr. Lynn has a standby electric generator in his two-car garage. When the power failed during the storm, he couldn't get into it to start the generator. Fortunately, the outage was only of four hours duration. A number of other farmers with a standby power plant also experienced a similar situation. They didn't believe that the plant might be inaccessible.[52]

County Agent A. F. Bosch estimated that cattle losses to county stockmen will be around "a quarter million dollars in cash at market prices." Initial reports indicated about 1,100 head were dead. There was property damages to cattle shelters as well. The *Tribune* reported Otto Thurn, Alvin Entzi, Daniel Klein, Rudy Nitschke and Edwin Rohrbach had buildings that collapsed during the storm.[53]

Those with confirmed losses included county commissioner Edwin A. Boschee, 48 head, Zeeland, Daniel Klein, Zeeland, 45; Les Sinkbeil, Zeeland, 42; James Brinkman, Wishek,40; Joe F. Weigel, Zeeland, 40; Amos Brinkman, Wishek, 30; and Herman Thurn, Zeeland, 26.

Others with losses between 10 and 20 head included Eddie Heinirch, Edwin Kost, Jacob Kost, Gottlieb Martin, all of rural Ashley; Art Tesky, Milo Sayler and Melvin Fetzer, Venturia; Marvin Huber and Henry Woehl, Wishek, and Walter Ruff, Lehr.

Reuben Helfenstein of Ashley lost 12 butcher hogs during the storm.

Rudy Nitschke, a farmer near Ashley, raised Angus cows. The family's pole barn collapsed from the weight of a 20 foot drift. Nitschke believed the animals were dead under the fallen timbers and snow. After the storm, Nitschke and several of his neighbors poked around the ruins for signs of life. There was none. Thirteen days passed. Someone thought the snowbank wiggled. With no real hopes, the Nitschkes started shoveling snow. They found a stock cow still alive under the collapsed wreckage. The animal appeared to be relatively healthy. They continued their excavation. They found two more cows, one of them was alive. Nitschke believed the animals had a good chance of recuperating.[54]

McIntosh County cattle losses were placed at 1,500 head at the end of the month.[55]

Venturia, located in McIntosh County, was platted by the Minnesota Loan and Trust Company. The Soo went through the here in 1901. John H. Wishek named the town after seeing a freight train wreck near the townsite. Wishek noticed the name on one of the box cars that was on its side. In 1960, the town had 148 residents.

Venturia lost its power. Joachim Ritter, village merchant, stated the outage was between four and five hours. Ritter said, *"Everyone there was quite comfortable."* Main Street was not blocked, but the street leading to it had 20 foot drifts.

Christian Bauer, Friedrich Ellwein, and Heinrich Hafner, Zeeland's first settlers, arrived in 1884. Zeeland, located in McIntosh County, was platted by the Milwaukee Land Company in 1902. The Milwaukee Railroad arrived that year from Eureka, South Dakota. The town was named by local Dutch settlers for the Zeeland province in the Netherlands Zeeland. The name means "sea land."

Zeeland had 427 residents in 1960.

There was a very sick two-year-old boy at the Kurt Reed farm near Zeeland. His parents thought he might have had pneumonia. Captain Robert L. Powell, United States Air Force, landed a helicopter at the farm. The boy was taken to Bismarck and transported to the hospital by a waiting ambulance.

Sebastian Krumm, a farmer near Zeeland, and his family watched the blizzard winds pile snow around their house. After a while, they were trapped inside. After the storm ended, the family escaped through an attic window.

Ernest Oberlander, county Civil Defense director, reported *"that the blizzard covered Krumms's one and one-half story farm house with snow to the point where but a part of the chimney was exposed."* Krumm contacted Oberlander for help to remove the snow. Krumm was afraid the pressure and weight of the snow might collapse the walls or the roof of their home.

The North Dakota National Guard came to their rescue. Members of the Grafton unit were sent to the Linton area. Late on March 8, a bulldozer arrived at Krumm's farm. Men and equipment cleared the snow away from the house.

Wishek was named for John H. Wishek (1855-1932). The town was home for 1,290 people in 1960. Wishek set a new population record in 1980 with 1,345.

Spring seemed just around the corner in March 1966. The *Wishek Star* advertised the following specials for Sailor's Meat Market: Amour Star Picnic Hams, 6 to 8 lbs, for 43 cents; Grade A Fresh Fryers, 3 lbs and over, for 35 cents; and Longhorn Cheese, 59 cents.

Old Man Winter knocked on the door March 2. When people came out of their houses on March 5, that's all they talked. *"Shut in from all the world without."* Raymond Barchenger, editor and publisher of the *Wishek Star*, said that was the phrase that summed up the emotional feelings of the area residents during the blizzard.

With everybody in the "same boat," people were "kind and charitable." The *Star* heard many reports of people calling their neighbors, checking to see if their doors were blocked with snow. If so, they shoveled the snow away. The elderly and those who lived alone greatly appreciated the help.

Wishek provided shelter for stranded people. After the boarding places were full, they stayed in private homes. During the blizzard, the cafes were "kept very busy feeding them."[56]

Mrs. John Ackerman had a unique problem. It was a noisy one. The strong winds deposited lots of snow around her home. After the snow settled, the back doorbell rang continuously. From inside the house, Mrs. Ackerman excavated the unwanted snow. She loaded it into tubs. The bell stopped its chime, when the ringer was cleared of snow.

Near Wishek at the Christ Bauer farm, snow blocked their doors. So, they crawled through the coal bin, over the coal, and through a basement window to get out for chores.

At the Walter Bettenhausen farm, the Bettenhausens tied themselves together with clothesline when they went to the barn. Snow covered their large granary.

N.D. Highway 13 east of Wishek on March 9, 1966. Courtesy of NDDOT

N.D. Highway 13 east of Wishek on March 9, 1966. Courtesy of NDDOT

It has been said, *"Man's best friend is his dog."* Mr. and Mrs. Marvin Huber became lost between their barn and house. They did not know which way to turn in the sea of agitated snow. Their dog had followed them out into the winter chaos. Their pet safely guided the couple back to the house.

Adam Herr, rural Wishek, lost at least 9 head of cattle in the storm. He had a pet turkey. Mrs. Adam Herr's son heard a strange noise doing chores. The sound came from a large snowdrift on the west side of the barn. The lad carefully dug into the pile. He went deeper and deeper. Mr. Turkey walked out, alive and unhurt. Mrs. Herr said, *"This is one experience the bird will not soon forget."*[57]

August Kramlich, rural Wishek, had 4 cows trapped in his barn. The snowdrifts presented a dilemma, that could not be solved quickly. Kramlich removed part of the roof of the barn to save the cattle. How bad was the blizzard? *"Conditions were so severe, the cows were fed their own milk for moisture until water could be brought to them,"* according to Kramlich.[58]

Burnstad, Napoleon, Fredonia and Gackle
Logan County was named for General John A. Logan (1826-1886). After the Civil War, Logan served the state of Illinois as a Congressman and United States Senator. He advocated benefits for veterans and soldiers.

Burnstad, a small community in Logan County, had 55 residents in 1960. The town came to life in 1906 when Christ P. Burnstad donated land for a Soo townsite. Burnstad was known as the "Logan County Cattle Baron of North Dakota."

Burnstad lost power on March 2, 1966. The blackout lasted for seventy-two hours. On March 5, Earl Heck, an Montana-Dakota Utility employee at Napoleon, hired Dale Schulz

SSgt Adams, 366 2nd Ord. Co. NDARNG and crew shoveling out dozer southwest of Burnstad March 1966. Courtesy of E.B.R. SC, UND

and his snowmobile. They went to the substation at Burnstad and he replaced the blown fuse.

The first townsite for Napoleon lasted about a year. George H. Cook, a resident of Steele and a member of the Napoleon Townsite Company, platted it northwest of its present location in 1885. Cook named the place after the president of the townsite company, Napoleon Goodsill (1841-1887). Originally from Minneapolis, Goodsill was another realtor that lived in Steele.

The Napoleon Townsite Company needed access to a railroad. Another site, present-day Napoleon, was picked in 1886. It was along the planned route of the Soo. Prior to the arrival of settlers, Napoleon was chosen to be the seat of Logan County. The first business in Napoleon was a combination newspaper office and store. The paper, the *Napoleon Homestead*, has been in the Bryant family for three generations.

Napoleon had 1,078 residents in 1960. Like Wishek, the city population peaked in 1980 with 1,103. Longtime N.D. Secretary of State, Ben Meier, born on August 1, 1918, hails from Napoleon. Meier was first elected Secretary of State in 1954 and held that office until 1992. It is a longevity record for an elected state official in North Dakota.

On Wednesday, the temperatures hovered around 32 degrees. The forecast predicted snow, strong winds and colder temperatures. That afternoon, adverse weather conditions developed. According to Gladys Peterson, local weather observer, 2 inches of snow, .18 inches of precipitation, fell.

Napoleon let out school at 2:00 p.m. Their school bus drivers ran into tough driving conditions. Ben Marquart had a service contract with the school. Marquart owned three buses. He drove one of the buses and employed two other drivers. Southeast of Napoleon, Ben Marquart got stuck in the snow at the Ignatz Feist farm. Marquart gained access to a car and delivered the children. Then, he came to town in a farmer's pickup.

Baltzer Weigel, a bus driver for Marquart, stalled six miles north of Napoleon on Highway 3 when the motor got wet. Weigel and the children waited for help.

Marquart's third bus, driven by Rudolph Mertz, developed mechanical problems, a few miles out of town. Mertz returned to Napoleon before the engine quit running. The children were taken off the bus.

After drying out the distributor, Ben Marquart and Rudolph Mertz headed north on Highway 3. They pulled the second bus back to Napoleon. Arrangements were made for the children of the two buses to stay in Napoleon.

Tony Kuntz drove another school bus. It stalled near the George Gross farm, fourteen miles south of Napoleon. Meanwhile, Leo Kuntz finished his route. Leo heard that Tony ran into trouble, so he headed out in the storm. Tony and several children stayed with the Gross family until Saturday. Leo waited out the blizzard at the George Bitz farm.

Mail did go out on Wednesday.

Napoleon experienced short and sporadic power outages on Wednesday night. Stranded motorists stayed at the Miller Hotel and Wentz Motel.

On Thursday, Peterson calculated that another 8.4 inches of snow, .84 inches of precipitation, fell in Napoleon. The high for the day was 23 above, the low that night was 11.

Peterson recorded the most precipitation, 1.19 inches, about 10.2 inches of snow, on Friday. Temperatures fell again, the high was 18 above and the low was down to 8.

All businesses were closed in Napoleon on Thursday and Friday, except the Red Owl Store and the Miller Cafe. By Thursday, the front of the Miller Cafe was completely covered with snow. Their customers came and left through the back door.

Sheriff Norbert Mueller organized work parties to aid the elderly and those who lived alone after the storm. Many farmers needed help removing snow. That was another list.

Men who worked for the Napoleon bulk oil dealers carried 5 gallon cans of fuel to homeowners and businesses who ran low or completely out of fuel.

Dennis Kroll, son of Mr. and Mrs. Marvin Kroll, was home alone during the blizzard. He was twelve-years old. His parents fretted every hour of the storm.

Before the storm ended on Saturday, another 2 inches of snow fell, .21 inches of precipitation. Overall, Gladys Peterson measured Napoleon's snowfall at 24 inches., 3.42 inches of moisture. Clearing skies brought colder temperatures. The high for Saturday was 14 above.[59]

Early Saturday morning, Tom Aberle rode Tony Kuntz's snowmobile to the George Gross place. He picked up Tony and they went back to Napoleon.

Later, Tony Kuntz went out to the John A. Bitz farm, seven miles south of Napoleon. He picked up Mrs. Bitz who was feeling ill. He gave her a snowmobile ride to the home of her parents, Mr. and Mrs. Alois Gross. Dr. Goodman made a housecall.

Somewhat later, Kuntz rode his snowmobile to the Joe Wrangler farm, fourteen miles southwest of Napoleon. He gave Mrs. Julius Vetter who was sick a ride to Mr. and Mrs. Joe P. Hilsendeger's place in Napoleon. Her uncle lived there.

Late Saturday night, Tony Kuntz made another emergency run on his snowmobile. This time he went to the home of Mr. and Mrs. Tony Leier, twelve miles southwest of Napoleon. Tony Kuntz transported a sick child to the home of her grandparents, Mr. and Mrs. Carl Leier, in Napoleon.

George Jackson, a farmer who lived twelve miles north of Napoleon, became serious ill at his home on Saturday. The roads to his farm were blocked with huge drifts, so a civil defense helicopter picked Jackson up at his farm. The pilot flew Jackson to Bismarck where he taken to the hospital.

Marvin Kroll, his father, and a neighbor walked several miles to the Kroll farm on Saturday. They were ecstatic after finding Dennis safe at home.

Father Veit loved to ski. On Saturday, he was seen skiing around town. Like many others, he took pictures of the huge snowdrifts.

Snow was not the only thing that drifted in the strong winds. The end of the storm brought people out of their houses. They had special visitors. About 175 head of cattle wandered into Napoleon and the fields north of town. Most of the animals came from the Wes Nickolson ranch, south of Dawson. They were dazed and pelted with snow and ice.

The circumstances provided the townspeople with a rare opportunity. They took part in a cattle roundup on Saturday. The cattle were herded down Highway 3 to a corral at Alvin Scherrs. The animals were fed pellets from the Napoleon elevators.

On Sunday, the Nickolsons brought a stack of hay to Napoleon.

Drifts in Napoleon were 10 to 15 feet high in places.

Bob Foster, pilot for the Civil Air Patrol of Williston, flew a plane to Napoleon on Sunday. Foster picked up Sheriff Mueller. Their air search provided good and bad news for livestock owners.

Lieutenant Jerome Schwartzenberger coordinated the National Guard assistance for help in snow removal.

Marvin Wolf and his caterpillar had plenty of work north of Napoleon. Sunday night, Napoleon had a low of 15 degrees below zero.

Outside mail reached Napoleon on March 7. The previous week's edition of the *Homestead* was placed in the mail that day.

There was another air rescue on Monday. A civil defense plane picked up Mrs. Ignatz Horner. She became ill at their farm home south of Napoleon.

On March 8, a civil defense bulldozer arrived in Napoleon. Sheriff Mueller sent the dozer to local farms that had cattle trapped inside barns.

Rail service was restored on Tuesday. Napoleon lost an exciting game of basketball to Ashley.

Barns at the farms of Frank S. Schumacher, Howard Hunkler and Valentine Wangler collapsed under the strain of the heavy snow on the roofs. Also, the roof of Nelson Brothers barn caved in, smothering about 50 head of cattle.

Those who lost livestock in the area included Joe Leier, Valentine Fettig, Ray Nord, Victor Wald, Rubin Lang, Mike Welder, Roy Glatt, Joe Wolf, Wald Brothers, Baltzer A. Weigel and Marvin Wentz.

On March 10, 1966, Art Schultz, director of North Dakota Extension Service, said *"the Logan County agent personally contacted 86 farmers and 62 reported losses of from one to 35 head."* Furthermore, Schultz said, *"heavy losses were noted along the Missouri River following a survey made by county agents."*[60]

According to the North Dakota Extension Service, Logan County had the highest cattle losses in the state, 3,000 head.[61]

Fredonia began with the construction of an elevator and store in 1904. The Soo townsite was first known as Denevitz, after a settlement in Bessarabia, South Russia. Quite a few of the pioneers who came to the vicinity originated from that area. The opening of a post office on February 1, 1905, beckoned a name change to Fredonia. Douglas Wick in *North Dakota Place Names* indicated the origin of the word, coined from the Latin for place of freedom, is traced to Samuel Latham Mitchell, and was once seriously considered as the name for the United States of America.

A depot was established in the community in 1905.

The town's population in 1960 was 141.

Mrs. Harold Blumhardt developed complications in March from recent surgery in Fargo. Family members contacted Dr. Hill from Kulm and Dr. Roland Fleck of Ashley for advice.

Efforts to reach Blumhardt farm during the blizzard failed.

In the final hours of the storm, a helicopter from Bismarck tried to reach the farm. The attempt was unsuccessful.

Saturday afternoon, neighbors of the Blumhardt family gathered to help out. They pushed and shoveled the family car through numerous drifts over five miles. In the meantime, a county road maintainer, a state snowplow, a truck and the people in them opened county roads until they met the Blumhardts's party fifteen miles from Ashley.

The Blumhardts arrived in Ashley around 5:30. Mrs. Harold Blumhardt recovered her health in the days that followed.

Mrs. LeMore Hehr, a expectant mother, waited for the Air Force helicopter that was dispatched from Jamestown late Saturday morning. Snowmobilers from Fredonia came out with material to light a smoke smudge for the aircraft. High surface winds and poor visibility prevented the pickup.

Snowplows worked their way toward the farm. Mrs. Olaf Holman, Fredonia's news correspondent in the *Kulm Messenger*, wrote:

> Mrs. LeMore Hehr was taken to the Wishek hospital on Saturday during the severe snow storm by her husband and father, Rudolph Ruff and 2 neighbors Wilbert Gutschmidt and Oliver Schlecht. She was taken by truck after other attempts by ambulance and plane failed because of blocked roads and visibility. The Hehr's daughter, Brenda is staying with the Wilbert Gutschmidts.[62]

Saturday afternoon, men from Fredonia formed a work party. Christ Kleingartner, John Coppin, Roland Essig and Roland Rossman. went door to door. They made sure everyone was able to get out of their houses after the storm.

The storm left massive drifts at the Herbert Hehr farm, near Fredonia. The house and barn were locked in snow. To feed his cattle, Herbert crawled through an upstairs window of the barn.

The cattle were trapped for one week. On March 9, National Guard soldiers cleared the snow away from the doors.

Gackle began about six miles south of its present-day location when George Elhard and George Gackle set up a country store and post office in 1903. Originally known as Hackney, the name was changed to "Gackle" on June 3, 1903.

Elhard and Gackle moved their enterprises north to a railroad townsite in the fall of 1904. The NP was about to start the construction phase of the Streeter Branch Line. The NP reached in Gackle in 1905. George Gackle had an impressive career. He farmed about 7,000 acres, owned elevators and sold farm machinery. Gackle had furniture and hardware businesses.

Gackle's population in 1960 was figured at 523.

The snow and winds came as forecasted on March 2. The high in Gackle that day was 31 above. That night, the temperture dropped to 23. Al Hummel, local weather observer, concluded that 3 inches of snow or .33 inches of precipitation fell that day.

John E Peters, editor and publisher of the *Gackle Tri-County News*, said:

> *Travelers were still starting out on necessary travels up until Wednesday afternoon with reasonable assurance of arriving safely at their destinations. But, nightfall brought a different story. By Wednesday night, travelers and all commercial transportation started to bog down. Local freight trains were trapped by drifts between towns, buses stopped for the night, abandoning schedules; mail service pickup failed in a mail blackout that was to last the duration of the 4-day blizzard.*[63]

Norman W. Martin slipped in front of the post office about 5:00 p.m. Wednesday. Martin might have broken one arm in the fall. He could not go to Jamestown to have x-rays taken. He received first aid at home.

Edmund Janke and Willie Geiszler conducted business in Wishek on Wednesday. Coming home that night, the distributor cap on the pickup became wet and their vehicle stalled. Fortunately, someone came along and offered the two men a ride. They stayed at the Albert Muller home, located south of Fredonia.

Clyde Remboldt with the Gackle Locker truck sought refuge in Carrington.

The *Tri-County News* said:

> *By Thursday everyone knew we were in for a blizzard of several days, and though visibility was fair, and many folks in towns walked to stores to replenish bread and milk supplies, streets and highways were clogged at many points with drifts so deep that only hours of digging in the cold biting wind would allow passage. By Thursday folks knew that the digging out was going to be long, long process. Autos were buried, drifts were blocking doors to homes and businesses, and out in the country, farmers were getting concerned about cattle. Some farmers were trapped in town, and couldn't get to their livestock.*
>
> *The wind and snow was steady out of the northeast for the initial part of the 4-day blow, and by Thursday night had built up formidable drifts. A wind shift to the north during the night changed the whole drift structure around, removing some drifts almost as high as houses, and building new ones in different locations, some as deep as 25 feet.*[64]

Temperatures fell from a high of 23 to 16 on Thursday. Gackle received 14 inches of snow, 1.41 inches of precipitation.

On Friday, temperatures dropped ten degrees from 16 to 6. Hummel recorded 6 inches of snow, .68 inches of precipitation.

According to the *Tri-County News*:

> *Friday was the worst day of the blizzard, confining everyone to their homes except for essential maintenance, necessary supplies, and feeding*

and caring for cattle. Weather forecast called for the winds to stop about midnight Friday, and everyone looked for forward to a weekend of digging and replacing dwindling food supplies.

In many cases fuel had to be transported during the blizzard by toboggan in drums or 5-gallon cans to homes or businesses that were running short of fuel.[65]

On Saturday, temperatures fluctuated between 14 and 5 degrees. There was more snow, 5 inches, .46 inches of precipitation. Overall, Al Hummel calculated the storm dumped 28.5 inches of snow on Gackle.

The *Tri-County News* stated:

Saturday dawned with the wind blowing as strong as ever, and while Saturday's portion of the storm was less severe, it was impossible to clear roads, streets or get started on mop-up chores.[66]

Dawn on Sunday was cold and clear. Saturday's night low was 7 below zero. There was no wind. After being coped up for several days, people ascertained the work of Mother Nature. It was a day for taking pictures. Everybody, including the elderly, said, *"that they never witnessed a storm of such severity in all their years of residence here."*

Gackle's fire trucks were dug out. Homeowners and businesses began their snow removal tasks. Most church services were canceled. Sympathetic law officers overlooked the Sunday shopping laws, when businesses opened their doors. According to the *News*:

Farmers and townsmen came to the Fairway grocery store to get groceries with sleds and some carried them on their back packed in gunny sacks.[67]

Local residents who were stranded in other places returned to their homes on Sunday. One such group was the Fischers. On March 2, Mr. and Mrs. Elroy Fischer and Mrs. Fred Fischer drove Fred F. Fischer to the Veteran's Hospital in Fargo. Returning that night, they ended up at the Midway Service Station, located at the junction of Highway 281 and 46. Their three sons waited out the storm at the Malvin Zenker home. On Friday, teachers from Gackle, Mr. Ronald Knauss and Mr. Gale Larson, walked out to their farm and fed the livestock. On Saturday, the farm chores were done by Howard Dockter and Curtis Fischer.

Sunday evening, after the highways were opened, Norman Martin was transported to Jamestown for x-rays. Martin's arm was not broken. He was sent home after the medical examination.

Gackle area residents faced hard times. According to the *Tri-County News:*

There are many people who lost cattle, sheep, pigs, and other things that may be not known until the snow is gone. There were some farmers who were out of electricity as long as 72 hours. It was as low as 35 degrees in their houses. Some people used stoves and ways of cooking and heating that hasn't been used for many years. No heat and no water was the experience of many.[68]

Gerhardt Geisler of Gackle had about $14,000. in damages. Snow collapsed the roof on his machine shed. A combine, tractor and other implements stored inside the building were destroyed.[69]

There was a lot of ground drifting on Monday. That afternoon, Gackle's main street was opened by a snowplow. Tractors with front-end scoops cleared snow off side streets. After a low of 7 below zero Monday night, the area experienced above normal temperatures for two weeks.

Ellendale, Monango, Forbes, Oakes and Ludden

As the seat of Dickey County, Ellendale had 1,800 residents in 1960. From 1899 to 1970 there was a state teacher's college at Ellendale.

Settlers began coming to Ellendale in October 1881 with the expectation of the Milwaukee Railroad building to that site. In 1882, that railroad made it to Ellendale. The town was named for the wife of Milwaukee's superintendent and general manager, S. S. Merill. Her maiden name was Mary Ellen Dale.

The GN built a line to Ellendale in 1887 and on to Forbes in 1905.

The District 3 tournament started on February 26, 1966. In the first round Edgeley beat Verona, 57 to 40, and Fullerton knocked off Forbes, 86 to 39.

Quarter-final games were played on March 1. LaMoure beat Guelph and Ellendale topped Edgeley. Monango defeated Kulm and Oakes routed Fullerton in other games.

Blizzard conditions developed on March 2.

The storm lasted until March 5. Ellendale received 2.31 inches of precipitation, 20 inches of snow. On Thursday night, the winds increased their velocity to 55 and 60 mph. For the next thirty-six hours, the winds remained at that speed. Saturday morning, the winds started to abate. During the storm, temperatures hovered in the 12 to 15 degree range.

One snowbank, 25 feet high, amazed local residents. It stretched across 7th Street North between the homes of Dr. E. F. Bolliger and Ervin Vogel.

The following editorial was written by M. D. Goddard:

The Storm...

made us mad at first. March had come in like a lamb. Tuesday was a beautiful day and it began to look like we were home free.

January and February were not exactly our picture of an ideal winter, with weeks of below zero weather and ordering more fuel at intervals of what seemed like every third day.

But that was behind us now, we thought, as we tore off the calendar on March 1. The sun was warm and bright, and the snow of the preceding weeks had dwindled to a fraction of an inch in most places by the time the sun set Tuesday.

There was a few flakes of snow in the air when we went to work Wednesday morning. This is to be expected early in March. But we began to have somber thoughts when the air was filled with snow an hour or two later.

We forgot about the weather most of Wednesday, which is press day in the weekly newspaper business. There is too much work to allow more than an occasional glance out the window.

By supper time we had a few hundred of the final press run finished and knew that a couple hours work would wrap it up. So we broke for supper, and it was then we realized this was turning into more than a routine spring snowfall.

By the time we lugged the big mail sacks to the post office shortly before 9 p.m., we knew our long hours of the preceding three days had been largely in vain. It was blowing and drifting quite hard by that time and we figured there was small chance of any mail leaving town that night.

Everything you do for three days (and nights) on a small weekly is directed ultimately at the Wednesday night mail deadline. If you miss it–or if it misses you, as happened last week–you always have the feeling you lost the game.

We grumbled a bit to ourself as we left the post office to take one of our employees home, but the grumbling turned into something more violent when we got stuck four times enroute to get home. We never did get the car home. We gave up a few houses away, got it next to the curb and hoofed it the rest of the way.

Thursday morning looked bad, but we bundled up and walked to work, trying to visualize how it would be to change places with our two kids, who were still in their pajamas on the living room floor watching television, since school had been called off.

As a matter of fact, there hadn't been school the previous afternoon, either. When we were in school, there were no rural buses to worry about and we practically never had a storm vacation.

Thursday was almost normal for veteran Dakotans. There was no school or mail (except for the Leader) and a number of the stores closed early for lack of traffic, but there was a surprising quantity of people moving downtown.

The printing business, on any given day, does not depend on people walking in your front door. You can be very busy with work for people who walked in yesterday, or two days ago, or who telephoned to say they need more of what they got the last time.

So we were busy. We didn't walk home for lunch and we missed the poker game some of our business colleagues get up–but mostly it was business as usual and the storm, we thought, was strictly bush league.

We walked home that night without too much difficulty. But it wasn't long before we were aware the wind was shifting and getting stronger. We looked out the window numerous times and soon realized we had been wrong. This was no garden variety storm. It was an old-fashioned killer blizzard.

Friday was a day to be remembered. In our adult life we don't recall another time when we didn't go outside sometime during the day–barring a bout with virus pneumonia about 10 years ago. But we didn't go out Friday.

We've heard people talk about storms when "you couldn't see across the street" and always viewed it as another figure of speech. But now we're a believer, because Friday we couldn't see across the street.

At times we had difficulty seeing the corner of the house next door, and the white fence which borders our front sidewalk, only about 20 feet away from our front window, was indistinct.

We paced the floor and snapped at the kids(who had by this time been caged far too long). We thought of the work we should be doing. But finally, in the afternoon, we gave up and decided to enjoy our enforced vacation.

We found some books and magazines we'd been wanting to find time to read–and we read them.

We thought the wind would go down Thursday night, Friday morning, Friday afternoon, Friday night. But it didn't. It just seemed to get worse. The wind was still howling and the air was filled with snow when we went to bed.

We heard the wind, first thing, upon waking Saturday morning, but the sky was clearer and we could see around the neighborhood through the window.

And what sights we saw. Our car, parked down the street a way, was visible only by the radio antenna. The entire street was one big drift, from our front door to the house across the street. Wind had driven snow and packed it between the inside doors and the storm doors.

We finally bundled up after lunch and went outside into a strange white world. We waded through drifts for a couple of blocks and finally, as we approached the business district, the going became easier. A few paths had been plowed through the almost unbelievable rolling hills of snow.

We got to the store too late for bread, but managed to buy a couple of quarts of skim milk. The atmosphere downtown was strange. People were greeting people with broad smiles, silently congratulating themselves that they had survived, laughing about how they came out to get the necessities("the heck with the kids'milk, I needed cigarettes!"), and exchanging tales how high the drifts were at their place.

The more ambitious people were already shoveling themselves out when we trudged home with provisions. High school kids, who had been wandering around town for three days, were talking about going to the late horror movie that night.

Nobody likes severe storms. Occasionally, a kid will say storms are fun, but they're stretching the truth.

Storms, disasters, emergencies, war, all are grim. People are stranded in storms and die in storms and lose livestock in storms and–at the very least–are inconvenienced by storms.

But all these things have a light side and an enabling side, as if Someone had gotten disgusted with our petty problems and myopic little personal circles, and decided to get our attention–to snap us back to first principles and make us realize the fundamental facts of living, to make us decide what is important and what isn't.

There is sometimes a fine line that separates life from death in war and severe storms–and there is a grim and light side to both. Storms can be dangerous, but humans find enjoyment in danger, which probably explains why some people have fun climbing mountains or driving 150 miles per hour in an automobile.

Storms often bring out the elementary human kindness in people who go around ignoring each other the rest of the time. People in hospitals and nursing homes stay and work around the clock to minister to others when their replacements can't come.

People in hotels, restaurants and gas stations take care of stranded travelers. Neighbors share food and fuel. Radio-TV people send personal messages. Law enforcement people and volunteers risk their lives to help others.

Like any other trying time–you wouldn't want to go through it again, but you're glad you had the experience.

Things are not back to normal by a long shot(we'll be walking to work for quite some time), but before long we'll forget about the storm and return to our old ways–just like we forget the lessons we should have learned from wars.

There are some things we shouldn't forget. And one of them is the Great Blizzard of '66. This one should be remembered.[70]

Mr.and Mrs. Fred Hillius, owners of the Hillius Launderette, were busy at their place of business Friday morning. They heard a loud thump at eight o'clock. Glass flew everywhere. A ringneck pheasant crashed through the plate glass window that faced west. The impact killed the bird. Mrs. Hillius suffered minor cuts and scratches from the flying glass. Hillius boarded up the broken window with scrap lumber.

The blizzard forced about sixty travelers to stay at the Nodak Hotel in Ellendale. Many of their guest remained there for four days. Mr. and Mrs. Leonard Hagen owned the hotel and cafe. Mrs. Hagen reported they had people from as far as away as Texas and Canada. There were numerous truckers. Some couples had returned from winter vacations in the south. She said, "we couldn't have asked for a nicer, more congenial group of people."

One of the stranded guests was a accordion player. He was returning home from playing at an old-fashioned wedding anniversary celebration in Minnesota. On Friday and Saturday nights, the Nodak Hotel had impromptu dances with live music. One of the guests at the hotel "ball" said it was the first time he had danced since 1923."[71]

The Oxenrider Motel filled up during the storm. This place offered no eating facilities, but management helped individuals get some food. Towards the end of the storm, three men fought their way uptown for a restaurant meal. They carried additional food supplies back with them. After the storm, some guests left via the back windows as the wind piled snow up against the front doors.

All communities in Dickey County lost telephone service at some point during the blizzard. The toll lines were damaged near Ludden. Several crossarms were broken and seven or eight spans were completely open. Snowmobiles transported repairmen to the troubled areas near Ludden. Northwestern Bell crews restored all phone services by Tuesday night March 8.

Another group went to the William Gulke farm west of Ellendale where their was a similar incident. Other cattle or machinery sheds protected by trees in the county were damaged from the accumulation of snow.

Miss Carol M. Strand of Ellendale and Kerry J. Nixon of Frederick planned to get married on March 5. Instead of going to the Lutheran Church near Frederick, the bride was stormed in at the home of her parents, Mr. and Mrs. Harold Strand. The Strands lost their electricity and phone service. The blizzard wiped out the championship game on March 4 in Webster. On March 7, Frederick defeated Britton which sent the Vikings to the South Dakota Class B tournament in Sioux Falls on March 10-12. The couple delayed their wedding, so Viking fans could attend the state tournament. The couple was finally married on March 13.

On March 7, Ellendale outscored LaMoure, 71 to 49 and Monango rolled over Oakes, 64 to 38.

On Tuesday, the Cardinals won the district championship, 61 to 45.

National Guard units in Ellendale and Oakes helped in the digging out process. Many farms in the hill area west of Ellendale were literally buried in snow. One spokesman said, *"Some people are really hurting and others are merely inconvenienced. We hope that people who are getting by fairly well will be patient and let us handle the critical cases first."*[72]

Garbage pickup was suspended temporarily because snow blocked the alleys in the business district and residential areas.

M.D. Goddard, figured there would be a big demand for the (Ellendale) *Leader* on March 10. Goddard printed twice their normal run. He thought people would buy an extra copy or two, but he was wrong. The *Leader* sold out by two o'clock that Thursday. Residents purchased 6, 8, and 10 copies at a time. To make up for the shortage, the *Leader* published the same blizzard photos, plus three new ones, the following week.

Ellendale advanced to the Region 1 basketball tournament in Wahpeton on March 11-12. The Cardinals upset Central Cass, 68 to 61. John Walsh took scoring honors for Ellendale with 24 points.

Milnor and Ellendale played the championship game Saturday night. Don Voorhees, one of Ellendale's best scorers, fouled out in the final seconds of the third quarter. With less than three minutes left in the game, the score was 51 to 51. The Cardinals worked the clock down for the last shot.

- Two weeks after the storm, County Agent Robert Hughes appraised Dickey County cattle losses between 400 to 500 head. Estimated monetary losses for 400 head was placed at $80,000. to 100,000. A number of sheep and pigs died in the storm as well.

Stockmen with substantial losses included: Jay Anderberg, Forbes, 90 head; Chris and Victor Bollinger, Merricourt, 64 head; Ed and Newton Davis, Monango, 40 to 50 head; Marshall Hokana, Ellendale, 35 head; and George Haussler, Monango, 45 head.

Game officials estimated that up to fifty percent of the pheasants in the prime southeast range area were lost.

Forbes was established when the GN arrived in 1905. It was named for S.F. Forbes. He operated a general store and later became an GN official.

In 1960, Forbes had 138 residents. Al Gimbel, district manager at Ellendale for MDU, reported the Forbes area lost their power at 4:00 a.m. Friday. It was out until 1:45 p.m. Saturday.

On Sunday, a team of volunteers brought fuel and supplies to the Jay Anderberg farm near Forbes. To get there, it took quite an effort. A ski-plane pilot scouted the best route to the farm. Information was then relayed to the crew of a snowplow. The volunteers traveled behind the snowplow. Mr. Anderberg was snowbound at Mobridge, South Dakota.

There was trouble at the Chris and Victor Bollinger farm, located four miles north of Monango. The roof of the 24x40 foot pole barn collapsed down on 92 head of cattle. Volunteers from Ellendale helped free the animals on Saturday and Monday. The Bollingers and others saved 26 of them.

In 1960, Oakes had 1,650 residents.

Oakes began as an NP townsite. On September 17, 1886, officials named it after Thomas Fletcher Oakes, who, at the time was the NP's General Manager. A business associate of Henry Villard (the primary mover and shaker at the NP), Oakes would go on to head the NP as its president from 1888-1893.

Two other railroads came to Oakes, the Northwestern in 1886, and the Soo in 1887.

On March 1, 1966, members of the Dickey-Sargent and James River Valley Irrigation Districts met with members of the Garrison Conservancy District at the Armory in Oakes. They signed the first contracts that opened the door for irrigation of 40,000 acres of land in the Dickey-Sargent District and 13,000 acres in the James River Valley District. The Garrison Conservancy had already signed contracts with the federal government, so this was the next step.

People looked forward to the upcoming shows at the Grand Theatre in Oakes. *The Saboteur*, starring Marlon Brando and Yul Bryner was booked for March 3, 4, and 5. Elvis Presley in *Harum Scarum* was scheduled for March 6, 7, 8, and 9.

The blizzard struck late on March 2. There was a lull in the storm on Thursday. After the break, conditions were miserable till late Saturday afternoon. Freezing rain was reported east of Oakes early in the storm. The high for Oakes on March 3 was 31 degrees.

Mrs. Carrie Murray, official weather observer, recorded 2.00 inches of precipitation on Thursday. Murray reported a high of 27 and .37 inches of moisture on Friday. On Saturday, the high was only 12 and another .18 inches of precipitation fell. Overall, Murray calculated that Oakes had received 17 inches of snow.

The *Oakes Times* said:

> It was not uncommon to hear someone say they had to crawl out of windows of their houses as they emerged to get at the big shoveling jobs... We were also quite fortunate in that we had no emergency ambulance calls or fires during the storm. Things could have been worse when one looks back on what seemed to be almost unreal.[73]

Lloyd E. Oldenburg, pheasant biologist for the State Game and Fish Department at Oakes, reported the outlook for pheasants was not good on March 5. Oldenburg was out on a snow sled on Friday. He said, *"The snow is so wet, your eyes freeze shut. I hate to think about what it did to the pheasants."*[74]

At the Leo Spitzer farm, located two miles north of Oakes, there was a snowbank 20 feet in depth.

At the A. H. Ellenson farm, about eight miles north of Oakes on Highway 1, there was a big windbreak that stretched from the farmstead east a half mile to Highway 1. The snow piled up on the south side of that windbreak for the entire length. Associates of the *LaMoure Chronicle* climbed it. *"We could look down on the tops of those tall trees."*[75]

Lawrence Dethlefsen lost at least 14 head of cattle.

The following letter, written by Juli Becker, is about the blizzard of '66. She wrote:

> I was working for Cass County Electric Cooperative as Home Service Advisor (March 1955). I had been asked to go outside the service area to give a demonstration on lightning at the Maddock Farm Show at Maddock, N.D.
>
> I left the Valley City office with the temperature warm enough to only need a sweater. I spent the night in Maddock, gave my demonstration the next day and started back to the Valley City office. Stopping for gas in Carrington, the service station attendant asked where I was going as I appeared to be heading south. I told him Valley City. He said, "You're going to run into some bad weather." I debated on staying in Carrington, taking highway #200 (N.D. #7 in 1966) on to #1 to Valley City or going to Jamestown and possibly #I-94 would be more apt to be open.

As I got closer to Jamestown, the road was very heavy with snow. My 1964 Ford Custom was being a snowplow. The visibility was almost zero.

I got to Jamestown and decided the best motel would be one with a restaurant. I went to the top of the hill where there was supposed to be a new one with a cafe. When I got to the top of the hill I could not see anything, and the motel was not visible. I turned around and went back down to the motel at the bottom on the right side of the road.

It was named "Kenney's" (the motel) at that time. I remembered in 1957 the Rainbow Advisor (the girl's organization of the Masons and Eastern Star) and I had stopped at the cafe next door as the lady at the cafe and the Advisor were friends. Lucky for me it was the same lady running the motel, and she had one room left. I went to bed a bit hungry.

The next AM, Mrs. Frandsen woke me with a call that rolls and coffee delivered to the room shortly. I asked WHY? She told me the storm was worse. I then went to where I could see out and discovered I couldn't see across the street. We didn't see Melland's(a store) for three days. I heard later the motel that had a cafe attached had no help and they ran out of food so I was better off. We ate well.

I called the CCEC office to tell them the evening before where I was. I called again in the morning. Willard Grager answered. I then knew that every one in the office of male gender was out and about. Willard would monitor the phones when things were not too bad, but he was the telephone man when it was storming. He told me I was to stay where I was until he gave me permission to come home.

The stores in Jamestown announced they would be open for a certain time. Three salesmen, the sons of Mrs. Frandsen and I went to the grocery store, with the men pushing the car across the bridge and coming back the same way.

When we got back, she(Mrs. Frandsen) and I started cooking. I am not sure how many were at the motel, but we ate well, played a lot of cards, only to wake up the next day to still not seeing across the street. I remember a trucker from Alabama thinking this was the worst area he had ever been in. He had a load of bananas to be taken to Canada. His two buddies were out on the highway north of Jamestown, and he was very frantic about their safety. He had kept his truck running to protect his load of bananas.

The storm abated Saturday P. M. Going out we found all the cars were very compacted with snow under the hood. The men were very helpful in cleaning and running them to thaw them out. Since I didn't have permission to travel, I could maybe have only gotten to Fargo anyway.

I stayed until Sunday. A man from Fargo who worked for US Steel said he would follow me. So we drove in a caravan to Fargo. I had to go thru West Fargo, Fargo, onto Highway(US) 81 to #46 and into Kindred.

It was something I never forgot and am very thankful I went the way I did as I would never have made it to Valley City on the other road and would have been in my car for four days. My folks didn't have a phone so they had no idea where I was. They had no electricity for several days.

I never travelled again in the winter without extra clothes, blankets, and food in the car.[76]

Ludden was a boom town in its early years. The original townsite, founded in 1883, was located one mile west of present-day Ludden. To have a railroad connection, the Northwestern, the town moved in 1886. The townsite owner, Frank Randall, named the town for Mr. and Mrs. John D. Ludden, St. Paul, the couple he stayed with when he attended business college. In 1890, there were 400 people living in Ludden. In 1960, Ludden's official count was 59.

Those who lived south of Ludden were without REA power from Wednesday to Sunday.

Kulm, Edgeley, LaMoure, Verona and Marion

It all started for Kulm in 1891 when the Soo bought 106 acres for a townsite from part of J. Wesley Organ's homestead in Norden Township. Christian Flegel (1859-1937) gave it the name of "Kulm" after his hometown of Kulm, Bessarabia.

Until the Soo Line extended its branch line on to Wishek in 1898, Kulm served as the terminus of the line.

Kulm is the birthplace of Angeline Brown, better known as actress Angie Dickinson. In 1959, she starred in *Rio Bravo* with John Wayne and Dean Martin. In the TV series *Police Woman*, 1974-78, she played Sgt. Pepper Anderson.

In the 1960 census, the population of Kulm was 664.

On March 3, the *Kulm Messenger* carried a picture of Technical Sergeant Daniel H. Van Glader, son of Mr. and Mrs. Donald W. Van Galder of West Candor, New York, receiving the United States Air Force Medal. Sergeant Van Glader was recognized for distinguished airmanship while refueling Vietnam combat aircraft in flight. He was a refueling technician aboard a KC-135 Strato Tanker. His wife Arlene, is the daughter of Mr. and Mrs. Sam Henke of Kulm.

John E. Peters, editor and publisher of the *Kulm Messenger*, wrote:

The great storm of 1966, and it will surely be known as that, had humble beginnings. Some snow and locally blowing winds had been forecast by the weather bureau on Tuesday, March 1, for Wednesday, and the new snow with moderate winds came on schedule Wednesday, with blowing and drifting occurring all day long.[77]

One of the front windows on the Kulm State bank gave way, Thursday morning. Snow filled President Sharpe Pruetz' office. Bank employees put plywood over the hole and they cleaned the bank during the blizzard.

The blizzard wiped out I. H. Pancake Day at Gackle Brothers I.H. dealership on Friday. People would have free pancakes and coffee another day. They would have another chance to meet Gackle Brothers Grain Company's new manager, Rueben Goehring.

On Friday, Mr. and Mrs. Karl Grenz, rural Kulm, left their house to do chores. The couple almost never reached the barn. After that experience, they did not want to take any more chances. Mr. and Mrs. Karl Grenz stayed in the barn until Saturday morning.

One radio voice covering the blizzard came from the local area. Paul Walters, announcer and engineer of KVOX radio, Moorhead, Minnesota, was stranded with Ron Scott at the station's studio in south Moorhead. Walters, better known to the Kulm community as Adolph Puhlmann, the son of Mr. and Mrs. Walter Puhlmann of Kulm, started working at the radio station in 1963. Walters and Scott, since they were stranded, broadcasted around the clock for the duration of the storm. Walters gave a telephone report for the CBS network and radio stations at Detroit Lakes and Kansas City.

The *Messenger* published an article entitled, *"Women Corner."* Edna Okerlund wrote:

> *March 2, 1966 – How can any of us forget. A day that didn't start too unusually different from any other at this time of the year, but certainly changed in a matter of hours. I was real happy to get home about 6 o'clock on Wednesday, but little did I realize that I was going to stay put until Saturday. It was almost unbelievable and while I have seen lots of snow and severe storms here in North Dakota I know that this has been worse than any I have witnessed. There wasn't a street or intersection that wasn't closed and although a little bit of headway was made by clearing a path on mainstreet on Sunday there is much left to be done.*
>
> *After spending three days inside it was quite a treat to get out and get some fresh air and interesting to see the huge drifts of snow. A lot of the local residents were standing around visiting and lots of pictures were being taken of different areas in town where the snow had really piled up.*
>
> *Wednesday evening we had our first and only power outage which sent my husband out to the substation and he still wonders how he ever made it out there and back, because by now the storm was going strong. I was pacing the floor as usual while he was out and certainly was thankful to see him return. By 1:00 we finally retired, but by that time the whole family was up and wondering, why all the commotion was taking place. It was pretty hard to relax knowing that the same thing could happen again and knowing too that there wasn't much one could do if it happened again.*
>
> *Thursday came and the storm raging as badly as it had the night before. There wasn't much one could do but sleep and eat. No one cared to wander very far from home that day. This was the day I managed to get caught up on all the washing and ironing. I didn't have any trouble finding enough work to keep me busy, but I didn't realize that the next day was going to be the very same.*
>
> *While one can't do too much cleaning on days such as these, I did get busy and get that out of the way, hoping I could spend the afternoon on some other favorite project like sewing. After getting through a nice big stack of mending I've been wanting to do, I really became enthused and cut out several articles of apparel only to have my sewing machine break down. This really dampened my day and goodness knows when I am ever going to find that kind of time again, but it sure was fun while it lasted. I finally proceeded to another unfinished project that's been waiting for a nasty day, which happens to be getting my recipes into a book and filing them where I can find them. Although I accomplished much during all this time I was still hoping for the sun to shine because by now I think we were pretty tired of this kind of weather. By Saturday afternoon the storm was showing signs of subsiding and I was beginning to notice that the atmosphere in the house was also taking on a new look. After so many days inside people have a tendency to become a bit cross and cranky.*

Sunday morning dawned to a bright sunshinny day. The day was a bit unusual because of the fact that one couldn't hear any church bells and this is different from any other Sunday morning. We did have some coffee guests too and this helped to brighten our spirits a little bit.

There are those who weren't as fortunate as some of us because of illness or other emergencies, but as a whole most of us can't complain. Farmers, were also unfortunate being hit hardest through loss of cattle.

School has not been in session since Wednesday but will be resuming this week sometime. We don't know just how this will affect their Easter vacation, but I am sure we will know about it soon.

It will be nice to get back to normal living. It may take several weeks, but we'll make it.[78]

Kulm had a high of 36 degrees on March 2, the day the storm hit the area. On March 5, Kulm reported a high of 26 degrees, the day the storm ended. The coldest readings stayed around the teen mark. After the storm, temperatures declined to -5 on Sunday night and -10 below Monday night.

Kulm's storm total came to about 25 inches of snow, 3.24 inches of precipitation.

Snowdrifts, between 7 and 8 feet high, crammed the business fronts in Kulm. Cars were buried all over town. Helmuth Hille's and Jim Weatherly's cars were covered in a drift in front of the Kulm Cafe. They had to dig down two feet to find the tops of their vehicles. Hille, a local farmer, was stranded in town during the blizzard. He lost cattle, around 9 head, in the storm.

Hille and Weatherly were lucky. At the Herbert Davidson farm the family auto was buried in a drift 25 feet high. Victor Orgen Leroy Davidson, Milton Davidson, Erland Blomquist and Clarence Kinslow dug the car out. The weight of the snow caved in the roof and broke the windshield.

One huge drift curved between the Standard Service Station and the *Messenger* building. It was as high as the second-story window of the *Messenger* building. The gas station had two big service doors. Luckily, the snow blocked only one of doors of the garage, really bad. The door with less snow in front of it, was where Robert Buerkley, proprietor of the Standard Station, kept his pickup with portable light plant that he used to start vehicles. After some tinkering, Buerkley fired up city snowplow.

State highway crews faced setbacks in the area. There was a big drift near Monango on Highway 281 that required a long detour. Highway 13, between Kulm and Edgeley, was blocked in two places. The drift at the Schlechts shelterbelt was a quarter of a mile long and 20 feet deep. Another drift near the Edwin Lundgren's farm was almost as big.

It took state highway department crews two days to open the spectacular drift at Lundgrens. They were able to clear the drift at the north edge of Kulm on Highway 56. State operators tried to open the Monango and Schlecht drifts, but failed in their attempts. Those spots needed a rotary plow.

The Ernest Kramlich family near Kulm, received the brunt of the blizzard. Their farmhouse was built in a gulch with hills on the north side. Snow buried the house. To get out from an upstairs window, the Kramlichs shoveled snow into the house. Once outside, they cleared snow away from the window. Then, they shoveled the snow out of the house. They found their dog sleeping against the top six inches of the chimney, the only sign of their house.

Numerous trees around the Kramlich's house prevented the National Guard from clearing the snow with their machinery. Friends and neighbors came to their aid.

Drifts in the shelterbelts and farm yards were high as 30 feet. Conrad Kinzler's chicken coop disappeared in a big drift. Kinzler reported 30 foot drifts at his place.

Schools closed in Kulm at 3 p.m. Wednesday, March 2, and classes resumed on Tuesday, March 8.

Emil Anderson, long-time Kulm businessman, was trapped for three hours in a house fire on March 9. Anderson, 82 years old, was rushed to the hospital in Ellendale. He contracted pneumonia from the ordeal, but his physician, Dr. W. Allen Hill, said death was caused by smoke inhalation. The street to Anderson's house had been plowed out and the firemen were not delayed getting there.

On March 24, John E. Peters discussed the circumstances behind an car accident that took place on Highway 13 in the Schlecht drift. *"It should have never happened."* Peters wrote:

> *The highway department plow opened a single track about 150 feet into the drift, then drove away and were never seen again. Later in the week, Wayne Lundgren and companion driving home from Jamestown, drove into the cut in the fog; perhaps a little too fast, and hit the dead end, going at a fair clip. Knocked his companion unconscious, wrecked his car, etc.*
>
> *Personally, I feel that the state crew that was there and drove off without warning the driving public with so much as a barricade, or sign that the road was blocked was negligent. Since being in North Dakota going on four years, I have noticed this situation several times, and feel that the Highway Patrol's efforts to prod the public into making the highway a safe place to drive will be unsuccessful even if they succeed; mainly because the highway department has a responsibility to help keep the highways in a safe condition, a responsibility that is blithely ignored.*
>
> *I propose a state law that would make it illegal for a state highway crew to leave the scene of blocked road, or unsafe highway situation without leaving behind an approved road danger sign appropriate for the situation or leaving a flag man.*
>
> *You auto travelers are aware that in most states it doesn't take much to warrant the use of a flagman; and for the safety of the driving public, North Dakota should to the same. And with a bracket welded on the side of each state highway truck, the approved signs could always be available to every crew. ...*[79]

The following week in his column, Peters praised the highway department for opening the highways as fast as they did after the blizzard, but reiterated his points on their failure of not leaving warning signs. Peters said, *"Word leaking back to our office on the chastisement of the highway department is about 99% favorable to our position."*[80]

The *Messenger* sponsored a photo contest on March 17. There were two categories, most unusual blizzard scene or most beautiful blizzard scene. The winners would receive $5.00. Individuals who entered the contest included: Lester H. Berntson, Lucille Hettich, Rudolf Ruff, Mrs. Fred Himmerich, Reuben Weil Harry Isaak, Harold Kjos, Jerry Elhard, Eleanora Buerkle, Mrs. Lenhardt Mundt, Gottfried Weiler, Fred Vogel, Henry Miller, Annie LaBrensz, Bertha Ensslen and Michael Herman. The *Messenger* ran many of the photos in their next two weekly publications.

Judges for the photo contest included Mrs. Otto Rutschke, Mrs. Dick Stadler, and Reinhold Harr. On April 7, the *Messenger* announced the winners. Marcene Isaak Puhlmann won the prize for the most unusual blizzard scene with the Isaak's garage photo. Mrs. Annie LaBrensz received the prize for most beautiful blizzard scene with the photo of the Nickisch Funeral Home. Honorable mention prize of two dollars went to Jerry Elhard for several pictures that "showed imagination in photography and appreciation of the drift beauty."

The first settlement near the present-day Edgeley was called Saint George. In 1886, a new location was secured by Richard Sykes, a townsite developer and extensive area landowner (4,500 acres). He not only platted the NP townsite, but also gave the town its name. Sykes was born in Edgeley Park, Stockport, Cheshire, England.

Rail lines from three different companies, the NP, the Milwaukee, and the Midland Continental, met a mile northeast of Edgeley at a place known as Edgeley Junction. The Milwaukee and the Midland Continental terminated at Edgeley.

The Midland Continental Railroad grew out of a plan around 1915 to connect Winnipeg, Manitoba with Galveston, Texas by rail. Existing rail lines went in a generally east to west direction. This venture was a bold attempt to connect the bread basket of Canada and the United States with ports on the Gulf of Mexico. But it never came to fruition. Only the sixty-nine miles between Wimbledon and Edgeley were built. The headquarters of the railroad was at Jamestown.

Edgeley's population peaked in 1960 with 992.

Information published on March 3, 1966, signalled the end of the Midland Continental Railway Company. The article in the *Enderlin Independent* said:

> *Transactions by which the Soo Line Railway company and Northern Pacific Railroad company will acquire joint control of the Midland Continental Railway company through acquisition of all its securities were announced this week by executives of the three lines.*[81]

Coverage of the 1966 blizzard for Edgeley was similar to the reporting of storm in Kulm and Gackle. John E. Peters, editor and publisher of the *Tri County News* and the *Kulm Messenger*, was also the editor and publisher of the *Edgeley Mail*.

According to climatology records, kept at Edgeley Experiment Farm, the area received .30 inches of precipitation on March 2. The following day, another .70 inches of precipitation fell. Most of the snow, 1.54 inches of moisture, came on Friday March 4. Overall, the storm dropped 2.54 inches of precipitation.

The high on March 2, was 36 degrees. Thursday's, Friday's, and Saturday's highs were 28, 25, and 26, respectively. Likewise, the lows were 23, 21, and 9.

The northbound Jackrabbit Lines bus stopped in Edgeley in the evening of March 2. The four passengers and driver stayed at the Star Hotel until late Saturday. To get outside, the managers of the Star Hotel climbed through a second floor window. They dug out the doorways, and their guests left the normal way.

The James Valley Electric snow cat was busy during the storm. Company men inspected their facilities and preformed other vital tasks in the area.

On March 4, a spokesman for Northwestern Bell Telephone Company indicated that the Oakes telephone center was out of service. That center supported other tributaries in southeastern North Dakota including Edgeley, LaMoure and Verona.[82]

Cliff's Tavern lost a window during the blizzard. It was boarded up with plywood. After the storm, the James Ham's Tavern displayed a sign that said, "Closed for Roof Repairs." Pieces of the roof were seen in the snowbanks near the establishment.

The Lyle Berntson farm, just outside Edgeley, had no electricity for 24 hours. A broken wire caused the outage on Friday morning. For heat, Lyle manufactured a temporary stove in the basement.

Some men in Edgeley showed their cleverness. They needed to get their stranded car out of a snowdrift that ran several hundred feet long and 10 feet deep. The men acquired some planks from the lumber yard. They made a gradual slope in the bank. They laid the planks on the snowdrift and drove on them. They shuffled the planks from the rear to the front. Doing this many times, they drove the car out of the snowbank to an open road.

Simon Aberle's pole barn collapsed on 200 head of cattle. It was impossible to get the snow off the roof, or the roof off the cattle. Friends of the family rallied to the cause. They removed the animals that could walk out first. After that, they pulled out 25 or 30 head of injured, uninjured, and dead cattle. Then, they crawled through a hole in the roof into the darkness and listened for any signs of life. All was quiet. Initial reports indicated Simon Aberle lost 38 cows and 18 calves, but Aberle's final total was 66.

The *Edgeley Mail* had a photo contest, just like the one in the *Kulm Messenger*. The following people submitted blizzard pictures: Lila Zimmerman, Anna Roehr, Mrs. Ted Taszrek, Dan Teske, Peal Alford, Mrs. August Krueger, James Mathson, Oral Elhard, Linda Schockman, Delmar Beglau, Edwin Schmidt, Mrs. Philip Prochniak, Mrs. Max Hartwig, Bill Nordley, Paul Senger, Mrs. Glenn Witt, Carol Bitz, Mrs. R. G. Albert, Milton Lacina, Mrs. Harry Brauer and Francis Jacobs.

The judges of the *Edgeley Mail* storm photo contest included Miss Esther Haugen, Mrs. Carolyn Anderson and Mr. Dennis L. Anderson. Bill Nordley's picture of the Riley's car was deemed the most beautiful. Pearl Alford's photo of the wrecker pulling out a buried car at Lanings garage was named most unusual.

The *Edgeley Mail* said:

> Other photos of worthy of honorable mention were Edwin Schmidt, Dick-ey, for his picture of the 200 foot ditch to his machine shed; Oral Elhard, Jud, for the photo of the family digging out their pickup and fuel barrels; Linda Schockman for the picture of the pony standing by the garden gate surrounded by drifts; Mrs. Glenn Witt, Berlin, her picture showing the girls standing in the tunnel entrance to their home; and to August Krueger, Adrian, his picture showing a huge snowbank, that looked like an iceberg floating in the farm yard.[83]

LaMoure, nestled in the James River Valley, came to life in October 1882. The Wells-Dickey Land Company, a consortium of bankers, businessmen, and railroad officials platted this NP townsite. The county and two cities were named for Judson LaMoure, a territorial and state legislator.

In August 1883, the NP's Fargo and Southern Branch was extended to LaMoure. There, it hooked up with the NP's Valley Line which ran from Jamestown to Oakes.

In 1960, LaMoure was home for 1,714 people.

On March 2, 1966, the *LaMoure Chronicle* printed an article entitled, **"News from our boys in Viet Nam."** The following letter was written by SP6 Lester Wolfe, nephew of Walter and Foster Lau of LaMoure. Lester Wolfe said:

I am with a helicopter unit that was sent to this God forsaken part of the world from Fort Benning. We fly the largest helicopter in the army. We started to fly about December 5.

I am a flight engineer on one of the copters. We have 19 choppers in the company and support the whole delta area of South Vietnam to support the troops in the combat area by hauling in troops, guns, ammo, food etc. and bringing out the dead and wounded. We have a cargo area 6 1/2 ft wide, 7 1/2 ft high and 38 1/2 feet long, and can carry 12,000 lbs for about 2 hours.

Only 2 of our crew has been hit with enemy ground fire and both of them were back to work in about three weeks, but our aircraft are something else.

For the 9 days after New Year's eve, we really got worked over; every day we had at least 2 hits and many times as many as 15 or 20 holes but always got back home okay. They can keep their darn bullets. I got my share the last time I was here, back in '62.

We live in quonset huts, have nice showers with hot water once a week, which most troops don't have. The food is A rations and hot all the time. We have a beach just off the end of the runway, where the China Sea is, and if we would not have to go out to the battle zones and fly over the other parts of the country you would never believe there was a war going on over here.

We support two of the American units that are fighting down in this part of the country, the 173rd Airborne and the 1st Inf Div from Fort Riley. For the past two weeks we have been on a big push northwest of Bien Hao. Our crew has been out there now the past four days taking in fresh supplies.

We don't know really who the enemy is. All we can do is if he isn't an American and points a gun at us or shoots at us he is a Viet Cong & we go get him. The VCs go thru the towns and kill the people, take their food and homes & try to take over the country. One minute the VC is a poor old man having rice and the next minute he has a gun shooting at you.

I have 216 days left here. The weather is hot as hell. If it weren't for the breeze, it would really be hot. It won't be long before we'll be getting about three months of rain.[84]

"*An incredible blizzard struck LaMoure County Wednesday at 10 a.m. and raged until Saturday night without a letup, increasing in ferocity steadily until Saturday morning, and then tapering off a little.*" That's how the *LaMoure Chronicle*, Glenn Dill, publisher, described the weather between March 2, 1966 and March 5, 1966.

Local weather observer, Albert Ness, indicated that the LaMoure received 22 inches of snow which amounted to 2.34 inches of precipitation from the blizzard. Winds held steady at 60 mph for many hours.

Just prior to the historic blizzard at LaMoure, Ness received a letter of appreciation from the United States Department of Commerce, Weather Bureau Environmental Science Services Administration at Bismarck. He also received a fifteen year length-of-service award by the Weather Bureau for faithful service in recording temperature and precipitation the past fifteen years. Albert Ness began recording observations in October, 1950.[85]

LaMoure recorded a high of 39 on March 2.

Schools were closed at noon. According to the *Chronicle*, *"it was not a moment too soon."*

On Thursday and Friday, the thermometer reached 27 and 25, respectively. About half the businesses opened their doors on Thursday. There was very little commerce on Friday.

The blizzard spoiled the open house date for Hirds of LaMoure, International Harvester, Ford, etc, dealership. Besides free coffee and donuts, they planned to give away $500.00 in cash and door prizes on Thursday.

Around midnight on Friday, Mrs. Ted Lee needed to be rushed to the hospital. County highway department personnel were called out to handle the job. They had several other emergency runs during the storm.

Saturday afternoon, Doug Peterson hitched up a pair of horses to a sled with a bale of hay. Members of his family went for a ride.

Highway Superintendent, Albert Hurley, reported that most roads near shelterbelts were blocked with snow. For example, Hurley said, *"at Joe Laney's there's a drift about 15 feet deep for the whole half mile of the shelterbelt from No. 1 to his house."*

Snowdrifts were 16 feet high in some places.

The biggest drift in LaMoure was at Mrs. Triepke's place. It was as high as the roof of the house. Someone came over and dug the snow away from her doorways.

Ed Raugusts and Irving Christensons and others crawled out of their houses through windows. Like Mrs. Triepke, other families had their doorways cleared by friends and neighbors when they were blocked inside of their houses.

About half of the LaMoure's merchants in LaMoure did some business on Saturday. A toboggan was used to haul milk from the creamery to the Red Owl Store. Elmer's Bakery had a very busy weekend. A run on bread hastened a second baking.

On Thursday and Friday, Dallas Willey could not send out his trucks to pick up milk for the creamery. Willey's truck drivers struggled with poor road conditions Saturday night and Sunday, but they emptied milk storage tanks of local dairy farmers. Claire Sandness separated all his milk. He kept the cream and fed the skim milk to the calves. Jim Potts, another dairy farmer, had enough bulk tanks to store his milk until Dallas arrived Saturday night. Kenneth Peterson dumped two days supply of milk. He lost a fat steer to the storm. Peterson's cattle yards were so full of snow that the cattle could walk right over the fences. Because of that he kept his cattle in the barn for several days. Peterson's son and hired man shoveled snow out of the cattle yards by hand all day Sunday. Although some farmers had to dump milk, the losses, overall, "were not as great as expected."

Sunday night, Jerry Mangin was hurt in a farm accident clearing snow when he was operating a farmhand. A pin on the cable pulley broke and it snapped. The edge of the pulley cut through Jerry's cap, the earflaps were tucked inside, and opened a deep gash, an inch and quarter long, on his head. The laceration was stitched shut at the hospital. Jerry, a college student, went back to Fargo, late Monday afternoon.

After the storm, Dan Smithwick, local Northwestern Bell Telephone manager, found a way to check the long distance lines in the area. Smithwick rented a horse from Neil Rickford.

Originally known as Elmo, Marion was founded in 1900. It was the terminus for a NP branch line from Casselton. That line had several stations with female names. This one honored the daughter of Charles S. Mellen, President of the Northern Pacific Railroad. Also, there was another Marion. Mr. and Mrs. Louis O. Berg, parents of the first baby born in town, named their daughter, Marion. In 1960, Marion's population peaked with 309 residents.

Verona was settled in 1883, the town was first known as Matson. The postmaster, James J. Stevens, changed the name to Verona at the suggestion of a settler from Verona, Michigan, on June 25, 1886. Between 1907 and 1911, the town had three newspapers. In 1960, Verona had a population of 162.

Mrs. Willis Hanson, Hanson-Verona's news correspondent, wrote:

> It was man and machinery versus mountains of snow, as the area continued "operation dig out" the past week. Heavy equipment of the Civil Defense department was brought into the battle where county snow removal machinery proved inadequate. The Joe Laney, Darold Benson and Duane Pollert farms were finally opened as late as Friday (March 11), when 20 foot drifts some a mile long gave way to a superior power.
>
> In spite of the hardships occasioned by the storm by the storm, the community was very fortunate. There were no tragedies no emergencies that required hazardous attempts to reach hospitals. Livestock losses in Hanson Township were very light and mainly confined to scattered incidents. There was inconvenience but no suffering. Several farm families ran out of bottle gas but housewives used their electric appliances to breach the gap.
>
> Electric lights flickered during the height of the wind but stabilized and there was no power outage. Getting feed to the hungry livestock was the biggest problem. Farmers found there was no substitute for a well constructed barn with a hay loft full of hay for just emergencies. Many farmsteads were surrounded by hay stacks (hauled in the fall) but farmers were unable to reach the hay. Pole barns which had gained in popularity proved the poorest risk.
>
> Verona was hit hard. Mountains of drifts virtually covered the town and everything was at a stand still. There was no equipment which proved adequate to move the drifts and county machinery came to the rescue. An example of the snow's depth was the story of Dick Taylor's pickup which was located in a drift with four feet of snow over the top of the cab. School buses were stopped at main street and pupils trudged to school from there. Cattle losses were reported at the Art Dietrich and R. D. Magill farms. LaMoure County cattle losses were very heavy.[86]

The following story appeared in the *Ransom County Gazette*:

> As people gathered after the blizzard storm stories headed the conversation. A harrowing story with a happy ending concerned three families north of Verona, the Heisers, the Laney's and Christensens and two young men from Fargo. The Heisers went to Fargo the day of the storm and were accompanied by Mark Laney, son of Mr. and Mrs. Joe Laney who had an appointment with an orthodontist and Mrs. Louis Christensen, mother of six. As the storm developed Heiser called the Laney farm and said they

were starting from Fargo and would Laney please go to his place and get the cattle in. Laney and son went to the Heiser farm but were unable to return home. In the meantime the Heiser car ran into difficulty and went into the ditch. Aided by two young men from Fargo they managed to reach home and the safety of the Heiser farm. With the storm howling outside Mrs. Laney was home alone with the rest of the children. Louise Christensen was baby sitting with his family and the young men from Fargo. Mrs. Christensen and Laney and sons were all at the Heisers. After all the anxiety was over and everyone was united with their families, someone remarked it was a good thing Mrs. Heiser was used to a crowd–they have nine children, because she ended up cooking for 17 during the duration.[87]

Peter Houtkooper, Hanson farmer, had a busy week after the blizzard. He noticed a hole in one of the big snowdrifts. Houtkooper thought that was odd, so he took a closer look at the hole. To his surprise, he discovered a young ewe at the bottom. He dug her out and carried her to the barn. The ewe regained its health after being buried in the snowbank for eight days.[88]

Marion hosted the District 4 tournament in 1966, the games were scheduled for the first weekend in March.

On March 2, school in Marion was let out at noon for Parent-Teachers Conferences. The storm was about two hours old.

There was no school on Thursday and Friday. The basketball games were canceled. Marion's news correspondent wrote:

WORST STORM FOR MANY YEARS

Irascible March again lived up to its reputation in North Dakota. Having come in like a lamb on Tuesday with a day of spring like weather, its mood changed abruptly Wednesday morning when heavy snow began falling around 10 a.m. and the worst blizzard in decades roared into the area. The storm continued for four days, piling up huge drifts in towns and farm yards. There are reports of livestock losses at farms in the community with the Knudsen brothers having the greatest loss in this community. An emergency road was plowed open Saturday out of Marion when Clifford Rosland was stricken after walking over snowbanks from the highway to town. Mr. Rosland was taken to the LaMoure Hospital. The new road turns into town south of the old Baertsch farm and enters town north of the school house. It is being used at present, as the street past the Lutheran Church is blocked by an enormous snowbank in front of the church. The street coming into town past Clarence Bubachs is also blocked, but the emergency roads have been plowed out through vacant lots. Old timers say this is the most snow they've seen in Marion and we've seen plenty in some years.[89]

Art Zimmerman of Marion lost 20 stock cows and 5 of last spring's sucking calves. The cattle and snow piled up against the buildings. The *LaMoure Chronicle* described the predicament at their farm as such:

The Zimmermans knew they had to get them out of the lot and into the barn. The only way they could do that was to lead them across a road, down a ditch & back into the yard to the barn. However many of the

258

cattle got mired in the snow on the way and couldn't help themselves, nor was there any way the Zimmermans could get them all out, and so they died. Zimmermans dug out some calves that had been buried for a day and were only visible by being a snow-covered lump in the snow, and they took the calves up to the yard with the loader and cleaned a place, and laid them in the Sunday sun on some hay, and some of these calves, which seemed to be too close to dead to revive did in fact revive & got up as tho by a miracle and are walking around now, but whether they are strong enough to survive is something else.[90]

Charlie Bowen, rural Marion, lived in a basement home. When the storm was over, there was 10 or 12 feet of snow on top of his house. Bowen dug straight up to get out. It was said, "he popped up and down the vertical tunnel like a gopher." Friends and neighbors helped him shovel out. The snow was trucked away. The family lost power for 17 hours in the storm. During that time, temperatures in the house vary only a couple of degrees.

In 1905, the Fargo-Streeter NP branch line served another town in northwest LaMoure County known as Fox. On October 4, 1906, the community changed its name to Jud, to honor Judson LaMoure.

In 1960, the town had a population of 156.

Mrs. Anna Roehr, Jud's news correspondent, wrote:

Well guess most of the news has been received by radio over the great central plains. This village, and I presume a good many others over these great plain states, have had no incoming or outgoing mail since Wednesday or since the now historical storm started. The NP Fargo Streeter eastbound train that serves these towns has been stuck in a deep cut about two or three miles east of Alfred since Thursday. The five man crew stayed in the caboose until Saturday afternoon. They had part of a year old pound can of sardines, two candy bars, coffee which they boiled up with snow water and an orange which they divided until the 5 ran out of fuel and walked to Jud Saturday afternoon where after enjoying a hot meal at Jud Cafe they were put up for the night at the Thorson and Adolph Nitschke homes and Sunday Adolph drove them to their homes in Fargo, Moorhead and Dilworth. ...

Jud is thankful that there are no human tragedys to report but there was some stock lost. One of the heaviest if not the heaviest in the community was on the Henry Forsman farm west of town. A 50 by 25 or 30 foot shelter shed where 70 to 75 head of stock cows took shelter and shed being on the south side of the shelterbelt the storm piled the wet snow on the roof until weight caused the roof to collapse, trapping the animals. On Sunday when around 100 people working in shifts pulled the live ones with ropes by hand as on account of the trees and drifts they were unable to use machinery the count was 40 dead or so bad they had to be destroyed. They were part of a larger herd of heavy stock cows that Mr. Forsman has. ...[91]

Brampton, Straubville, Cogswell, Stirum, Crete, Forman, Havana, Rutland, Gwinner and Milnor

In Sargent County the railroad building race (1886 and 1887) was between the GN and the Soo. However, the first railroad to arrive in what became Sargent County was the NP which reached DeLamere in 1882 and Milnor in 1883. The NP stopped construction in 1883, but Gwinner, Stirum and Crete were established in 1900 when construction continued. The Soo's Oakes branch line reached Forman in 1886 and was lengthened to Boynton, located two miles southeast of Monango in Dickey County, in 1887. In 1890, the Soo depot at Towanda, situated several miles east of Cogswell, was relocated to Cogswell. The GN established the communities of Geneseo, Cayuga, Rutland and Havana in 1886. The Milwaukee Railroad began servicing the communities of Brampton, Cogswell, and Harlem in 1889.

Charles H. Cooper platted a Milwaukee townsite in in 1882. It did not catch on with the early settlers. Charles A. Finch, a settler from Brampton, Ontario, Canada, homesteaded on land just west of the railroad townsite. Finch operated a farm post office, between February 27, 1884, and August 31, 1897. The railroad townsite grew after 1900 and the post office was reestablished on September 1, 1904.

Brampton closed its school in 1955. After that, area children attended classes in Cogswell. The Milwaukee shut down its depot at Brampton in 1958. In 1960, the town had a population of 50. In 1966, Sandy Cooper operated the town store.

Brampton had power and telephone outages during the March 2-5, 1966 blizzard. Mrs. Arlo Helgenson, Brampton's news correspondent wrote:

> Mr. and Mrs. William Bosse and Jerry spent Thursday until Saturday at the Dennis Bishoff home during the blizzard. Also, Mr. and Mrs. Wayne Lunneborg and family spent Friday and Friday evening there.[92]

Straubville, named for Joseph W. Straub, the area's first settler in 1883, was founded in 1886. It was a GN townsite on the Forbes-Rutland branch line. In 1960, the place was home for 10. In 1964, Straubville was selected as a target for low level bombing practice. It was a simulated practice, with electronic devices recording the hits and misses.

Here's the Straubville news after the blizzard:

> Once again this finds us digging out of snowdrifts and after a duration of no electricity or telephone communications things will get back to normal in the near future. Many farmers are still snow bound. Many are still trying to locate cattle, sheep, etc. Many were buried in snowbanks and many strayed many miles from home.
>
> This winter has found this community without electricity and phone service more than any year in the past. This is the first time in 14 years that the postmaster, Mrs. Karven Nepstad, remembers that all mail has been delayed six days. Sure hope it comes thru today.[93]

People have had different opinions on how Cogswell acquired its name. Sources have said it was named for a Soo Line official, or Major Thomas Cogswell, a Revolutionary War hero. Some individuals believed it was for L.K. Cogswell who raised purebred cattle in the vicinity. In 1960, Cogswell had a population of 305.

The Cogswell Gun Club was organized in 1947 by veterans of World War II who lived in the area. That year, the club put on a supper for its members and their wives. They wanted something different, so they prepared wild game, pheasant with homemade pumpkin pies. Cern McCoy, Ralph and Wayne Seelhammer prepared the meal which was served in Columby Hall, the old Catholic hall.

The dinner was a big success and it became an annual event. It was soon the chief fund raiser for the club. They cooked bear and moose but the club eventually settled on everybody's favorite meal. That menu featured soup, salad, buffalo, mashed potatoes with gravy, buns, relish tray and ice cream.

The event outgrew the Catholic hall. After that, the supper was held in the American Legion building and then, the Cogswell Community Hall. The Cogswell Gun Club Buffalo Supper draws a standing-room only crowd of over one thousand people.

In 1966, Jim and Betty Kunkle lived in Cogswell. Jim, a charter member of the Cogswell Gun Club, drove a fuel oil truck. Jim and J.D. Bopp had planned to go to Oakes, Wednesday evening. The men were on a bowling team and it was league night. Jim drove out a little ways to check the road conditions. There was no way they could go. Jim remembered it rained on the second day of the blizzard. On Saturday after the storm letup, Betty took pictures in Cogswell and Forman.[94]

There were people stranded at the Harry Smith farm, north and east of Cogswell. They were celebrating Harry's birthday.

John and Barb Hayen lived on a farm, south and east of Cogswell. John went out to the barn to do chores in the blizzard. When he came back, Barb said, *"His whole body was plastered white with snow, except for his eyes."*[95]

Jane Seelhammer shoveling snow on Main Street of Cogswell on March 5, 1966. Courtesy of Jim and Betty Kunkle

Main Street of Cogswell on March 5, 1966. Courtesy of Jim and Betty Kunkle

Situated exactly in the middle of Sargent County, Forman acquired a nickname, the "Hub City." In April 1883, Colonel Cornelius Hageman Forman (1833-1923) arrived here from Michigan. Four months later, Forman donated land for a townsite that was soon platted. In 1886, it was chosen to be the seat of Sargent County. Before that, Milnor had the seat for three years. Forman was home for 530 people in 1960.

On February 28, 1966, the Sargent Central Cadets traveled to Wyndmere to meet the Fairmount Pheasants. The winner advanced to the District 1 tournament. At halftime, the Cadets posted a ten point lead. After three quarters, the advantage was three.

On Wednesday March 2, the weather turned nasty. The high for the day was 32. Wet snow and strong winds slashed the countryside. Blizzard conditions developed. Forman recorded .32 inches of precipitation.

Temperatures did not deviate much on Thursday, 31 and 23, the high and low, respectively. There was a lull in the storm.

Forman on March 5, 1966. Courtesy of Jim and Betty Kunkle

The brunt of the storm came on Friday. Blizzard conditions prevented the local weather observer from recording precipitation totals. The thermometer reached 25, that night the mercury fell to 12 degrees.

On Saturday, Forman's high was 17. The local weather observer measured 1.84 inches of precipitation and the snow contained about twenty percent moisture. Overall, Forman recorded 2.18 inches of precipitation during the blizzard.

Anthony Volkmuth, editor of the *Sargent County News*, wrote:

> *The storm resulted in the electric and telephone companies being very busy once travel could be resumed. It was reported that there was a mile of telephone poles down in the Rutland area and another 9 or 10 poles down between Forman and Cogswell. By Monday morning crews were more than busy restoring broken poles.*
>
> *There were many homes without electricity during part of the storm. Some served by RSR found themselves out of electricity for about 36 hours,*

with service being restored Saturday afternoon. Several of the communities were also without electricity, returning to service Saturday. Long distance lines were out of order, as well as lines to Havana.

Only a few reports of cattle being lost during the storm. There are also a few scattered reports of other animals being lost during the storm.

Since the storm has passed there are many who are venturing opinions on the seriousness of the storm as compared to other storms received by the area. There seems to be agreement on at least one thing. Anything that comes close to the severity of this storm must be at least twenty years ago. The storm of 1943 is somewhat comparable, but there are many who feel that one must go back to the 1920's. This editor has not gone through a storm in North Dakota that has been as intense as the one experienced this past weekend.[96]

Volkmuth in his editorial, **"Could Be by Tony"** wrote:

This week, of course, the big news is the blizzard that the area experienced last week. Wherever you go this week people are talking about how much snow there is in the farm yards and communities throughout the area.

This writer has been more than amazed at how rapidly everyone dug out from this experience. Once the wind subsided it took little or no time and those from farms were coming to town. Of course, necessity promoted this move, for many were running low on provisions.

Many a time this writer let off a bit of steam concerning how long snow remained on the streets in Forman. This past week end the city fathers proved that it could be done. First off they started clearing Thursday and making it possible for traffic to move about town. Then the big blow came Thursday night and Friday.

This was the first time (Friday) that this writer remembers when no one was concerned about making it to work, for there couldn't possibly be any customers. There were, however, a few hearty souls who ventured to work. It is not known whether they did it out of loyalty or to prove that it could be done.

Any way, back to street cleaning. Saturday the workers were out once again making it possible to move about. This is something that can be pointed to with pride. When the necessity arises everyone is willing to put their shoulders to the grind stone and get the job completed.

Come Sunday people were busy making trips hither and thither to see how much snow had fallen. The latest report we have heard is that 22 inches of actual snow had fallen, with drifts up to 16 or 18 feet being seen in many places.

The pictures of the storm showed the depth of the snow. Yes, people in North Dakota do know how to react when faced with adverse weather.

The storm resulted in fathers spending more time with their youngsters than they have for a long time. Usually, old dad is just too darn busy to have time to sit down and enjoy his off-springs.

This past week end, however, the story was different. After laying around for just so long dad had to find something to do and he figured he could kill two birds with one stone; keeping the youngsters amused and still have something to occupy his extra free time. We'll bet there were more card and kids games played by adults this last week than have been played for many years.

This writer went through his time with the youngsters. Things got to the point that old dad was outside helping the younger set make a snow house. The funny part of it all was the fact that the old man actually enjoyed himself, after resorting himself that there wasn't much else he could do about the entire situation.

Maybe more of this type of storm would get more parents closer to their children and from this a better bond of understanding.

Basketball tournaments became victims of the weather. Very few tournaments scheduled for the week end found the schedules being completed.

Mom was sure glad school got underway again Monday. Seems the week end proved quite trying. Having the youngsters home was bad enough; but dear husband was also around to help torment the dear little wife.

In Short– The shortage of news from neighboring communities will make this issue on the short side. Please bear with us.[97]

Agnes Nelson wrote the news for the *Sargent County Manor*:

No hardships were felt at the Manor during the big storm as both telephone and electric power were in good condition. Some of our staff were unable to get here on Friday morning so only Lorraine Stucker, the night worker, was here on duty but all the residents that could work pitched in and helped during breakfast and during the forenoon, so all went well. Before dinner Glenn Seavert brought some of the staff here in his station wagon and also Mrs. Olstad, the nurse from the clinic, who came to assist with caring for a sick lady here. Glenn also gave taxi service Saturday morning to some of the staff. A big thanks to Glenn and Mrs. Olstad for their assistance.

We had some enormous snowdrifts when the storm let up–too bad we didn't have a toboggan or two so us oldsters could have a party. Can't you just see us sailing down the drifts?[98]

Havana was originally called Weber after Henry Weber, Sr., who settled in Sargent County in 1883. The name was changed to avoid confusion with another GN Railroad station named Weber.

Havana had the best school building in the county before schools were consolidated. In 1960, the town had a population of 267.

The grand opening of the Jack and Jill Store, operated by R. N. Weber, was held on February 18 and 19, 1966. Many people enjoyed the free sandwiches, cookies and coffee. The store gave away lot of prizes as well.

The Havana Arrows had two prolific scorers in basketball in the Wild Rice Conference in the 1965-66 season. Rex Collins led the conference in scoring in the 1964-65 season. In the 1965-66 season he came in second. Collins's scored 300 points in 14 games, 21.4 points per game. Irving Weber averaged 19.6 points per game in conference play, 275 points in 14 games. Weber finished third in the scoring race.

After the blizzard delay, the Arrows pulled off a big upset in the District 1 tournament on March 7. Havana, 4-10 in Wild Rice Conference play, defeated Hankinson, 56 to 46. The Pirates, 11-3, placed second in the Wild Rice Conference. Rex Collins led the Arrows with 29 points and Irving Weber scored 15 points.

On Tuesday, Havana lost their next game to Wyndmere, the host of the District 1 tournament. In the loss, 80 to 57, Irving Weber was high with 28. Paul Bergh and Rex Collins added 15 and 10, respectively. St. Francis of Hankinson defeated the Arrows for the third place trophy the following day.

In March 1993, the North Dakota *REC Magazine* printed blizzard stories from its readers. Doris Gulsvig of rural Havana, wrote about March 1966 blizzard:

> *The blizzard of March 2, 1966, I will always remember. My husband had left to attend a conference in Fargo that morning. About 11 o'clock I received a call that they had arrived safely. Then the phone went out.*
>
> *Early in the afternoon our power went out, and we were left without heat, lights and water. We spent the next three days, huddled around a one-burner oil heater in a basement room, with a small kerosene lamp for light. They were six of us in this room–three teen-aged sons, a 10-year-old daughter and an 8-month-old baby. At night we went upstairs to sleep, where the contrast in temperature was so great it cracked the lamp chimney.*
>
> *Each morning and evening the boys found their way to the barn, where they attempted to milk and care for the dairy herd. With both boys and cows used to a milking machine, this was no easy task. Each time they returned safely I uttered a prayer of Thanksgiving.*
>
> *Sunday morning, March 6. the storm was over, the power was restored and we were able to begin digging out. We thank God for watching over us during this time.*[99]

For about five years, Rutland was known as Steward. That's because Albert H. Stewart donated the land for the townsite. Stewart renamed the town, Rutland, after his hometown in Vermont.

Rutland is noted for having very good baseball teams over the years. When Rutland celebrated its centennial in 1982, the residents cooked one of the world's largest hamburger. It weighted over 1800 pounds.

In late February 1966, the community lost Joseph Kulzer. He left 244 descendants, 14 children, 66 grandchildren, 159 great-grandchildren and 5 great-great-grandchildren.

Lou Sanderson, Rutland's news correspondent wrote:

> *Nineteen Sixty Six is setting a new record in everything, and had just succeeded in putting on the worst blizzard ever seen, one which lasted four days and left 20 foot snowdrifts in the streets of every town. Occasionally you hear some one say, I've seen worse ones," but if they had they would not be here to tell story.*
>
> *One thing was clearly demonstrated, it does not pay to put your eggs all in one basket. The average modern home is depended solely on electricity for heat and light and during this storm it was found necessary for 27 persons to gather at one house, and 19 at another home where they were forced to spend the night, while their home was without light or heat. For-*

tunately everyone stayed at home and there were no casualties; although it was necessary to get along without lights, power, telephones or mail during the four or five days the storm lasted.

On their way to Valley City, the truck in which the Hoflen Brothers were hauling several head of livestock for their own, and some for Gordon Williams of Fairmount, left the icy highway and tipped over; killing one large bull owned by Mr. Williams.

Sunday Mahrer Brothers came from Hankinson with their snow removal equipment and proceeded to cleanup. By working until midnight, they succeeded in opening the streets on Monday things were back to normal. No loss of livestock has been reported; but dead sparrows were found in all trees and it is presumed that no less than 50 percent of the pheasants perished. With the amount of snow we have it is feared that when the snow melts (if it ever does) there will be no way to prevent basements from being flooded. And now, while President Johnson is warring on Viet Nam and poverty, it is high time to declare war on the weather. ...

Train service was resumed here Monday when the first train arrived equipped with a snowplow and extra crew.[100]

In March 1966, Greg Groettum lived with his family, the Boyd Groettum's, on a farm near Rutland. He was in first grade. Greg remembers a huge snowdrift in their yard whose height extended almost up to their yard light. A person could scamper up the drift and touch that light.

The family car was in a garage whose door was open during the storm. Wind driven snow was packed hard around the automobile. Greg recalls that after the car had been dislodged from its snowy grave, a person could see marks of the front end of the vehicle imprinted in the snow.

To reach their livestock inside a barn at their place the Groettums were forced to dig a tunnel through a large drift at the entrance of the building.

Greg recalls that a person could see the school bus coming down the road to their place, but not at the entry to their driveway. The view there was blocked by an enormous snowbank.

With a yard full of snow, the only place for the Groettums to get rid of it was in the ditch.

He heard stories of trains being buried in snow.[101]

Peter Skroch stayed with Mr. and Mrs. Arnold Banish at their place near Rutland during the blizzard. They had a dairy herd. Skroch was there, collecting milk samples, when the storm hit.

Gwinner and Stirum were named for German financiers who were interested in the NP. Crete was originally named Elizabeth by railroad officials, but later named Crete, the nickname of John M. Steele's daughter, Lucretia. This was in accordance with their bargain for the right-of-way across his land.

Gwinner's population increased rapidly between 1950 and 1970, from 195 to 623 residents. By 1980, the town had grown to 725. The rise can be attributed the Melroe Manufacturing Company which opened there in 1946.

Edward Melroe, a Sargent County farmer, recognized that grain ripened too unevenly in the local area for straight combining. This meant that grain had to be cut in windrows and cured before it was harvested. He developed a pickup attachment for combines that lifted the windrows of grain into the combine. The pickup attachment later became standard equipment on Oliver, Gleaner Harvester (International Harvester), and John Deere combines. A family partnership consisting of Edward Melroe, his sons Lester, Clifford, Roger, and Irving, and Eugene Dahl, his son-in-law, started Melroe Manufacturing Company.

In 1957, the company bought the rights and plans for a tri-wheeled loader from the Keller Brothers of Rothsay, Minnesota. The purchase became the foundation of the growing company. Melroe's first Bobcat, M200, came out in 1959.

In 1965, gross sales were over nine million dollars.

In early March 1966, the construction of its new office building with a total floor area of 14,370 feet was just about completed. Melroe employed more than 300 people. Bobcats were being sent to all parts of the world. One was sent to Ethiopia in late February. Some Bobcats were being readied for shipment to Australia. The Melroe machine shop recently added a $13,500. Circular Surface Grinder. The machine polished the faces of clutches and other parts that needed micro finishes.

Ted Dravland, night shift foreman, reported that twenty workers were stranded at the plant during the storm. They kept the ovens lathes and welders going. The men slept in the conference room at the new office building. Al Holmstron, a foreman, made it to the store for food supplies. Several ladies from Gwinner prepared hot dishes and sandwiches for them. And they drank a lot of coffee, someone figured they consumed thirty-six gallons of coffee.

After the storm ended, Jack Johnson, production manager, assigned men and equipment for snow removal. There was huge banks in front of the new office building and in the storage yards. Workers had the front sidewalks cleared on Monday. For three days, they worked around the clock. According to Melroe:

> Twelve Bobcats, two caterpillars and twenty men were used to clean the storage yards alone, which was one big drift after the storm. The total man-hours that were used to dig out after the storm amounted to 768.[102]

The District 1 tournament resumed action on March 7-9. On Monday and Tuesday, North Sargent was beaten by Wyndmere, 91 to 68, and Hankinson, 93 to 78. Gary Jones, a guard for North Sargent, won the conference scoring title. Jones averaged 23.2 points per game, 325 points in 14 games.

The effects of March 2-5 blizzard played havoc with people's telephones for days. On March 15, local Northwestern Bell Telephone Company manager, W. R. Pagel, remarked:

> that troubles right after the storm and a week after seemed never-ending, but things are finally getting cleaned up. The main problems now are pesky ones brought about by moisture having been driven into terminals, wire entrances, drop wires and protective coverings. Where more than one circuit is carried through a cable, moisture between them shorts the wires and causes wrong numbers, garbled messages, static and outages.[103]

Pagel reported that 51 poles went down in a three-mile stretch of line, three miles west of Gwinner to the Stirum corner during the blizzard. In that area the bad weather began with rain instead of snow. The wires became ice laden. Pagel indicated, "the following high winds did a thorough job of wrecking, actually rolling the lines into fields."[104]

Milnor was platted in August 1883. The establishment of this NP townsite came about as a result of a land dispute between the NP and the owners a townsite named Linton, located three miles east of Milnor. Unwilling to meet their price, the NP established a townsite further west. That year, the NP arrived in September. The railroad honored two of its employees, William Milnor Roberts, chief civil engineer, and William E. Milnor, the local telegrapher. Milnor's population in 1960, was listed at 658.

Harrison McCleery, editor and publisher of the *Sargent County Teller* in Milnor, wrote:

The weather - Eckk! - These words appeared on the weather board on TV during the height of the history making storm which raged throughout the midwest for several days last week. A more fitting description was hard to find.

Wednesday found the area engulfed in a furious snow storm causing school administrators to close school early and brought traffic to a near stop. However, Thursday found the weather returning to normal and before midnight the snow removal crews had removed all the snow from Main Street. This was completed just in time for the beginning of what has been labeled the worst storm of the century. Commencing with rain early in the afternoon it soon turned to snow and within a few hours a raging blizzard was in full swing.

Weathermen reporting the progress of the storm could do little to ease the concern of those having dear ones missing in the area as the indications for relief were very slight until late Friday night.

The storm finally broke Saturday afternoon and by 3:00 p.m. people were able to drive through main street.

Clearing of snow began almost immediately and within an hour all available snow removal equipment was in service both in the business district and residential area. However, all banks were not easily moved as can be seen by the pictures in this issue. The north end of main street was blocked by a huge drift as was the bridge just past the school house.

The town as a whole fared well through the storm, on Friday night about 11:00 p.m. the current went off in part of the residential area as well as part of main street. On Saturday morning Otter Tail Power Company made arrangements for the RSR Electric Cooperative line crew to make the necessary repairs and by noon the power was once more restored, thanks to the RSR men. Certainly all appreciated the efforts of these men and especially the people who were without power. But having the opportunity to see these men pile out of the snowmobile (an enclosed vehicle with tracked wheels) and climb the highline poles at the height of the storm and then stop only momentarily to warm up before returning to the task once more, our hats are off boys, thank you much.

Rural areas were not as fortunate with current being off more than 30 hours in some cases. Rain and sleet during the storm had caused lines to snap and circuits to go out.

In spite of the hardships no loss of life was reported in the area. [105]

On March 12, 1966, the championship game of Region 1, featured the Ellendale Cardinals and the Milnor Bison. With less than three minutes left, the contest was knotted at 51. With the ball in their hands, Ellendale played for the last shot. The Bison forced a jump ball in the last minute. Milnor controlled the tip. With thirteen seconds left, Dave Edison received a nifty pass. He scored a field goal. Ellendale still had a chance to even the score. With a couple of seconds left, Dennis Nelson stole the ball from the Cardinals. Milnor advanced state Class B tournament for the first time. (Ellendale won the North Dakota Class B basketball title in 1967.)

Going into the tournament, Milnor was a big unknown. In the final Class B poll, the team was not ranked in the top ten but received votes for honorable mention. Their record stood at 20-4. The Bison had four players who could score points. In Wild Rice Conference play, David Edison, Clint Lonbaken, Dennis Nelson and Dennis Carlson averaged 15, 12, 11 and 10 points per game, respectively. Coach Brent Potts's team finished first in the Wild Rice Conference.

On Thursday afternoon March 17, Milnor faced Cooperstown, another unranked team with a similar record at 20-5. The final minute of the game was fantastic. Cooperstown took a one point lead when Larry Rislov scored with 35 seconds left. It was the eighth time, the lead had changed hands. Less than 10 seconds remained. Clint Lonbaken drove in for a left-handed lay up. The ball bounced into the basket with six seconds left. Milnor won 62 to 61.

On Friday, Milnor played Fessenden, the Orioles were ranked Number 1 in the final Class B poll. Fessenden's record was 25-2. The team had won eighteen straight games. The Orioles had a twelve point lead, late in the third quarter. With 5:55 left in the game, Mark Reddig, the husky 6-1 center for the Orioles, fouled out with 23 points. Milnor was down at the time, 64 to 59. The Bison went ahead, 71 to 70, on a David Edison's shot with 1:03 left. Fessenden's Wayne Mohr sank two free throws with 41 seconds left on clock. Milnor worked the clocked down to sixteen seconds. Edison's shot was off the mark, but the Bison controlled the mad scramble for the rebound. Dennis Nelson put up another shot. It did not go in. Milnor ended up with the ball. Kent Vail, Milnor's sixth man, drove to the basket with four seconds left. He scored on the layup. Milnor held on for the victory, 73 to 72. The Bison became the "cinderella" story of the tournament with their two "story-book" finishes.

Could the magic, happen one more time. On Saturday, Milnor faced Kenmare. The Honkers, 26-1, were in the final round for the fourth straight year. They won Class B state titles in 1963 and 1965.(Ft Yates beat Kenmare in 1964.) Kenmare's only loss in the 1965-66 season was against the Fessenden Orioles in overtime.

The first quarter was close, but the Honkers started to pull away in the second quarter. There was no rally in the second half. Kenmare won the championship, their third in the last four year, 69 to 41.

According to the *Sargent County Teller*:

> Upon their return home the Bison and their supporters were met at Gwinner with an escort of fire trucks and cars. It is estimated over 200 cars were in the procession. Neighboring towns had prepared signs of congratulation and welcome also to greet the returning heroes.

Members of the 1965-1966 Milnor Bison team included the following players: Dennis Carlson, John Lien, Clint Lonbaken, Kent Vail, Greg Mund, Terry Brown, Bob Nelson, David Edison, Dennis Nelson, Steve Murdock, Kit Mund and Charles Spiedel; Student Managers, Arvid Rydholm, Lavern Colby and David Halvorson; Coach Brent Potts.

David Edison made the KLPM all-tournament team.[106]

Lisbon, Elliott, Enderlin

Nestled in the Sheyenne River Valley, Lisbon enjoyed a population of 2,093 in 1960.

Joseph L. Colton (1840-1896) came to the area in 1878 to buy land. In 1880, Mr. Colton established a townsite on both sides of the Sheyenne River. He also constructed a flour mill. Mr. Colton and his business partners, his brother-in-law, George Murray, and John Challey, named the town after their previous residences, Lisbon, New York, and Lisbon, Illinois. The city became seat of Ransom County in 1881.

The southwestern branch line (Fargo to Streeter) of the NP reached the Sheyenne River at Lisbon on December 24, 1882. It bridged the river in 1883. Besides Lisbon, the NP served the communities of Sheldon, Elliott and Englevale in Ramson County.

North Dakota's Soldiers Home is located on a 90-acre tract of land adjacent to the City of Lisbon. It has been in operation since 1893.

North Dakota is one the leading producers of Durum wheat. Snorri Thorfinnson wrote two books, *Sargent County History* and *Ransom County History* for the American Revolution Bicentennial in 1976. Educated in the field of agriculture and a Sargent County Extension Agent for 14 years, Thorfinnson told the story of the first planting of Durum wheat in North Dakota. Thorfinnson wrote:

> *A young farmer named Charles Hitchcock brought his family to Ransom County and settled 3 miles west of the present site of Anselm, or 12 miles northeast of Lisbon. Neither town was there in 1879.*
>
> *In 1882 a Canadian by the name of Christian came here with the intention of homesteading, and working for Hitchcock that summer. In the fall he heard his wife was ill so returned to Ontario, planning to return. He left three small 'shot bags' of wheat that he had brought with him from Ontario.*
>
> *Christian did not return and the wheat was forgotten until Mrs. Hitchcock discovered that mice had found it, where it was stored on the sod wall just under the roof, and eaten part of it. The oldest daughter, Clarice (Mrs. Loken) was told to pick it over and pick out the good seeds. She found only a half a cup. Those seeds were so nice and plump that Mr. Hitchcock decided to plant them in the garden. They were harvested with a pair of scissors. This was North Dakota's first Durum crop.*
>
> *Mr. Hitchcock kept increasing the seed until in 1890 he sold 15 bushels to Frank H. Strong, and planted 40 acres himself in 1891. He harvested 1600 bushels.[107]*

On March 1, 1966, Lisbon residents enjoyed a high of 41 above. It was the third day in a row that temperatures exceeded 40 degrees. That streak was extended on March 2, but the nice weather came to an end.

The following weather report, with comments, appeared in the *Ransom County Gazette* on March 10:

Weather Report Tells Part of Blizzard Story

How do you measure snow depth when its whirling around in the air in crazy-quilt patterns? It isn't easy, even when you have the instruments to do it. Henry J. Smith, our weather recorder, says he measured five inches of new snow last week Wednesday, three inches on Thursday, four inches on Friday and a trace on Saturday. He estimates that at least three inches weren't caught in his instruments. So, by conservative estimate, the snow-fall here amounted to over 15 inches during the three day storm. Instru-mentally or incidentally, this is the weather report for the past week:

Date	High	Low	Precipitation
March 2	40	25	.21
March 3	28	24	.31
March 4	26	13	.31
March 5	17	9	.03
March 6	18	-5	0
March 7	28	-16	0
March 8	41	24	0

Cecil D. Jahraus, editor and publisher of the *Gazette*, offered the following insights and observations:

There were casualties, yet few when you consider the scope of the storm. Here in town it wasn't so ferocious that a hardy soul couldn't grope his way downtown to buy a couple cartons of milk and a loaf of bread, or to compare notes on the storm with others over a cup of cafe coffee.

Checking in for a cup of java at the cafe on Friday morning, I found oth-ers who had gone downtown and couldn't explain why. Some excuses were to ward off the cabin fever, or just to prove they could get from one place to the next if they really wanted to. One fellow had a legitimate reason. His fuel tank was getting alarmingly low and he figured to take a couple can-fuls back with him.

Schools of course were shut down, but with all the scholars snuggled in their homes, another complication resulted. The younger generation practically took over the telephone lines bright and early Thursday and re-ally important calls were held up for aggravating periods, waiting for dial tone.

Lights flickered menacingly, but were out for only seconds at a time dur-ing the storm's fury. Here in Lisbon the Otter Tail Power Company had plenty of juice and johnny-on-the-spot-servicemen to look after things and keep the lines hot. Come to think of it now, the first cup of coffee in the cafe Friday morning was lukewarm because the power was off for a half hour. Repairmen out in back got it dinged up for a hot one before we left.

Some rural people in the county were less fortunate, and had to retire to basement cook stoves to keep reasonably warm.

Looking out a main street window, I watched the progress of two senior citizens who were literally feeling their way to a pub. Even without gale winds to hinder their movement their gait would have been less than sure, but they were fighting the wind and visibility of less than 100 feet at times, and their navigation was obviously made harder by the sting of snow and biting winds on their faces.

The hardier of the two took the lead and graciously allowed the other to hang onto his coattails. Walking east, they came to main street where the full force of the north wind shot down the canyon of Main Street and hit them square. They walked south about 25 feet and evidently decided that was the wrong side of the street on which to be found. To cross the street, they did an about-face. A gust of wind hit them. Knees buckled momentarily and hands lifted skyward. Almost airborne, they regrouped without falling, then shuffled across the street in solid fellowship like a wayward engine and caboose. I thought I heard them clucking happily as they plodded past our window with the gale at their backs. Or was it only the wind? I assume they reached their destination and got energized for the return trip.[108]

On Thursday morning, Martin Thompson suffered a stroke at his home. The ambulance crew shoveled snow to get there. Mr. Thompson was admitted to the Lisbon Memorial Hospital for an extended stay.

Saturday afternoon, Van Lozier was the first one shoveled out in the north end of town. Lozier, with the help of Lorelei and Grover Orr, went grocery shopping for their snowed-in neighbors. Milk and bread were the most requested items.

The city plow started clearing streets.

Howard Bushee, proprietor of the Triple Service, north of Lisbon, played hide and seek with a probing stick. The storm left a drift 100 feet long and 10 to 12 feet high near his establishment. His car was somewhere in that drift. After digging the vehicle out, he discovered the roof had caved and the windshield was cracked from the weight of the snow. Maintaining his sense of humor, Bushee said, "it ran good."

Dick Armstrong's ambulance was summoned to the airport Sunday morning. Earlier, a plane, equipped with skis, landed at Lucca. Orville Huseby and baby, DeLaine, boarded the plane. She needed medical care. The father and daughter were flown to Lisbon. The ambulance delivered the passengers to the hospital.

James Giedd, Lisbon Memorial Hospital Administrator, said, *"eight people carried the load of 15 for two days. The hospital's dining room was turned into a dormitory."* Mainstay RN's were Mrs. Levi Carlson of Nome and Mrs. Kenneth Bachman of Englevale. Inga Nagel and Annie Olk, cooks, and aides Faye Smith and Gusta Evenson were others who pitched in with extra hours. Kay Foss stayed with RN Mrs. Bill Kubus who shuttled back and forth between her home and the hospital. Also, Mrs. W.R. Pagel, President of the Hospital Guild, worked as a nurses aide. When the storm hit, Mrs. John McCann was visiting her mother in the hospital. Mrs. McCann volunteered to help out. She put in many hours doing housekeeping and laundry chores.[109]

According to Mr. Henderson, *"the Soldiers Home received plenty snow, but no serious difficulties. The cleaning women didn't make it out to the home but the cooks stayed right on the job, so everything was very good."*[110]

The news was the same at the Parkside Home. Mrs. Grant Peterson worked over forty straight hours. Mrs. Lorraine Devitt stayed over thirty hours before going home for rest. Mr. and Mrs. Fritz Houge spent Friday at the Home. Lee Bratland helped out Friday and Friday night. Mrs. Bill Schuessler helped with supper Friday.

Monday afternoon, March 7, the Dakota Bus Lines resumed bus service to Fargo. Service was suspended the morning of March 2.

Coach Harry Cline's Lisbon High School Broncos 1965-66 basketball season ended Monday at Valley City in the Southeastern Regional tournament. Wahpeton, ranked in the top ten all season, defeated Lisbon, 77 to 55.

At noon March 8, heavy equipment, belonging to the National Guard, arrived in Lisbon from Devils Lake. The front-end loader, could handle 2 1/2 cubic yards per scoopful. The first drift the operator cleared was in front of the armory. The machine was sent for snow removal operations on area farms.

The Sheriff's office acted as a liaison between the Guard unit and farms in the area. Farmers having trouble feeding their livestock because of snow conditions were given preference. On March 7 and 8, the following individuals requested help at their places: Orin Streich, John Faller, Gary Rieger, Doris Lyons, Gordon Potter, Alex Rotenberger, James Wiltse, Fred Sullivan, Ed Freitag, LeMoyne Olson, Vernon Sweet, Frank Himebaugh, Eric Forsberg, Ed Nicolai, Carl Bjugstad and Orville Pfingsten. The Farmers Elevator in Elliott Township asked for some assistance.

Pheasant losses in Ransom County were between fifty and seventy percent. It was believed that the partridge population was wiped out. Farmers who maintained feeding stations for the birds during the winter months reported seeing only a few bedraggled birds, two weeks after the blizzard.[111]

After the storm, county, township and city agencies met and discussed the challenges of the natural disasters. According to the *Gazette* the results of the meeting indicated the following:

> The biggest problem during the recent blizzard, it was agreed, was the lack of good and adequate communications. It was believed that if the two- way radio system planned for Ransom and Sargent Counties had been in operation county plows and other vehicles could have been dispatched and used more effectively. Preparations for acquiring such a radio system in connection with Civil Defense have apparently bogged down because of lack of departmental government funds.[112]

Mrs. Walter Juhnke, Bale's news correspondent, wrote:

> A storm which many of the older folks say "was the worst they have encountered" hit the area Wednesday and diminished on Saturday. Farmsteads are really feeling the blunt of the storm with snowdrifts of 12 to 14 feet high which blocked barn doors, making it impossible to let farm animals out for two days. Robert Olson took livestock to Fargo on Wednesday and was forced to remain until Sunday. Who did the chores? The Olson's oldest daughter Lynn, as Mike came down with the mumps. Everybody says it won't last long, spring is just around the corner.[113]

Elliott was platted by the townsite owner, Thomas M. Elliott in 1882. He arrived in 1879 from Canada. Elliott, a lover of good horses, designed the site with a race track. The town's population in 1960 was placed at 62.

Mrs. Melvin Urbach, Elliott's news correspondent, wrote:

> Harold Dick was busy Sunday and Monday with his tractor and scoop digging most everyone out from under the snowdrifts that piled up quite high during the four day storm.
>
> Lester McCloud became ill and was taken by Armstrongs Ambulance to the Lisbon Hospital Saturday morning. He was carried by stretcher over the huge snowbanks that blocked most side streets here. The snowplow came ahead first and opened the main street.[114]

Ray Yeager reported a snowdrift that was 20 feet high, just west of the depot at Elliott.

In 1867, General Alfred Terry oversaw the construction of Fort Ransom, a 200-man military post, located three-quarters of a mile west of the town of Fort Ransom. It was abandoned on July 31, 1872. Soldiers could be stationed elsewhere and transported to different areas by rail.

The town of Fort Ransom can be traced back to 1880, but the first white settlers, Norwegians, came to the area in 1878.

In 1960, Fort Ransom had 125 residents.

Mrs. Curtis Olson, Fort Ransom's news correspondent, wrote:

> Due to the blizzard of last week, the news items seem to be scarce. We were fortunate in this community to weather a three day storm without any emergency calls for sickness, fuel oil etc., although the fuel oil trucks have been busy making deliveries after the storm. Harry Peterson suffered a great loss when the roof of the pole barn collapsed due to the snow that accumulated on the roof pinning over 20 stock cows and 50 sheep.
>
> With the aid of a large group of men they rescued the sheep but nearly all the cattle were a loss. Everybody is busy trying to get themselves dug out, but the farmers seem to have the biggest task getting the farm yards shoveled out so they can do their chores and locating tractors and cars that are completely covered.[115]

The *Gazette* covered the crisis at Harry W. Peterson farm, located in extreme western Ransom County. The drift that collapsed the roof of the pole barn was estimated at 25 feet high. Peterson said, "*The fury of the storm kept him from checking his stock during the evening.*" The *Gazette* said:

> When he ventured out Saturday morning there was no sign of the barn except for vapor issuing south end of the 60-foot long structure were the sheep were partitioned off from the cattle. The south end wasn't collapsed quite as badly as the other end and, with some shoveling all of the sheep were freed. Neighbors and volunteers from Fort Ransom got to Peterson's farm and shoveled their way down to the cattle. The bull and five cows were taken from the building alive, but only three cows are expected to survive. The others were crushed. Peterson's property loss is estimated in excess of $5000.00.[116]

Resident who lived along the Valley Road, between Lisbon and Fort Ransom, had their share of difficulties. Mrs. Irene Hoenhause, Valley Road's news correspondent, wrote the following:

> "Diminishing winds by tomorrow," was the weather report on Wednesday when at 3:00 school buses were delivering youngsters due to blowing snow. Twenty-four hours later the report was still "diminishing winds." Of, course, if they reported this long enough it was bound to come true but the severity of the wind and snow on Friday was an unexpected surprise.
>
> Many of the younger generation in the past had listened to tale of buildings being covered over, cattle lost, people dying and thought the old timers were stretching it a bit to make a good story but this long drawn out storm proved it could happen and imprinted an unforgettable lesson on their minds and gave a refresher course. The never blocked Valley Road had up to six foot drifts in spots and was opened up Saturday evening when

the snowplow went as far as the suicide hill. Many of the roads were open but the yards and driveways had as much as twenty feet of snow piled up. Many farms had livestock losses and telephones were out in a lot of places–a Valley line was disconnected in the Lisbon office and few farmers did some checking to find that one,

The Archie and Charles Jorgenson living beneath a hill would be known as the lost farm if another storm hit as their machinery was completely covered. Their driveways look like part of the hills and a few telephone poles stick out about a foot. Their car was pulled onto Valley Road thru a cowyard and thus have transportation facilities. Four year old Stevie called to the Hoenhause and asked if they had room for snow and he was told the river wasn't full yet so it could be hauled there. He also called recently and said he had a news item, his little dog Toolabrook was accidentally run over and died. He felt the Norm Hoabys from whom he received him, would read about it and remember him with another.

Wes Tanner has been a busy man since the storm helping out neighbors and friends with snow problems. Melroe bobcats have been used and he had a chance to ride around a couple of times on this and to let them know the needy people. A sister of Mrs. Tanner, Mrs. Doris Myhra was in town and stayed at the Wesley Tanner home four days. She was escorted by a brother, Paul Hansen and Mr. Tanner Saturday evening to No. 1 where she left for her home at Verona. They also stopped at the Leon Hansen home and chatted. After helping in town he loaded a jug of milk, loaf of bread in his car and drove up the Valley to see how his daughter and family, Clarence Bens were getting along as their road was blocked and no phone. He arrived at the suicide hill and found Rex Brace with his cat and dozer clearing Valley Road and followed it to the farm. Rex cleared the road to Fort Ramson which was greatly appreciated by all as there was up to 15 foot drifts on it.

Johnie Hoaby spent Wednesday night at the Bobbie Guymer home and being a bit stormy on Thursday, Mrs. Guymer attached a walkie-talkie to them so Bobbie could walk Johnie home safely.

The telephone was hot on Sunday as the Cass Clay milk truck did not appear to pick up the brimful milk tanks but due to the road to Fargo not being open until Sunday morning and impossible roads by the farms, a truck that was giving static, Gerald could not get to all the milk. Some of the milk was dumped while others dug out wash tubs and anything that had a leakproof bottom. Chet Larson drove with him on Sunday and he appeared in the Valley, long bearded and tired after only an hour sleep, on Monday morning and took his relief driver, Myles Hoenhause with him. They were in hopes by Tuesday morning all the milk would be delivered to Fargo and Gerald Sletmoe could get to bed.

Mrs. Larry Larson climbed a snowbank and stepped down on the garage roof and shoveled four feet of snow off the building to keep the roof from caving in. She stated it was touching the hi-line wires in their yard and that it was not safe for Brian to play out due to the danger of snow cliffs which resembled the needles of the Black Hills.

> *Wilbur Hanson started for work Friday morning and ended up in the ditch a couple of miles from home but took a chance on leaving his car and walking home. He made it but did have one thing in his favor–the wind was behind him and put him in high gear so he arrived home in record time.*
>
> *Drifts are over some of the buildings and covered windows of the house. Bill Lambrecht said in all his Valley years he has never had so much snow in his yard.*[117]

The townsite that became Sheldon was a good investment for the postmaster of Jenksville, located six miles to the north in Cass County. On June 22, 1881, Barnabus D. Wilcox purchased a townsite for $3200. Within a few days, Wilcox sold the townsite to E. E. Sheldon for $3800.

Sheldon had a population of 221 in 1960.

Mr. and Mrs. Arland Olson lived on a farm six miles east of Sheldon. On Saturday, Mrs. Olson became sick and needed to be rushed to the hospital. The Olsons knew the roads would be blocked at various places. Their neighbors came over to help. Armed with shovels, the party started out in two cars. Mrs. Don McDougall took care of Mrs. Olson in one of the cars. The group could not reach Highway 46, so they took other roads that led to Enderlin. From there, they doubled back to Sheldon. When they encountered drifts too big to shovel, they motored over open fields. Their struggle to get to the hospital lasted seven hours.

On March 9, Mrs Olson's condition was described as "improved."

On August 17, 1891, the Minnesota Loan and Trust Company bought 120 acres from two homesteaders, Ranvel Gullickson and Eleanor Olson. Some of that land was used for a townsite that became Enderlin. How the town came by its name is a subject of debate. Most likely version, Germans who were building the grade for the rail line referred to the terminus as the "end der line." Townsite officials used that expression to name their settlement.

Enderlin was the halfway point between Minneapolis and Whitetail, Montana, on the Soo. In North Dakota, the Soo southeast-to-northwest mainline runs from Hankinson to Portal. Enderlin was a division point for operations west of the Shoreham (major yard in Minneapolis). The second largest Soo roundhouse, 24 stalls, was built here. Train dispatchers and the Division Superintendent worked out of Enderlin in 1966.

It was the birthplace of North Dakota Congressman, Hjalmer Nygaard. Born in 1906, Nygaard was first elected to the office in 1960. After being reelected in 1962, he died in office in July 1963. A special election was held to fill Nygaard unexpired term in October 1963. The man who won that election became well known in North Dakota politics. The winner was Mark Andrews.

In 1960, the town had 1,596 residents

Enderlin was ranked seventh in the 1965-66 final statewide Class B poll. The Eagles were favored to win the District 4 basketball tournament in Marion. The Eagles had a 16-2 record.

Men in Enderlin were growing beards and mustaches for the town's 75th anniversary jubilee. Women were getting their long dresses ready for the summer event.

The storm began with snow falling in Enderlin about noon Wednesday March 2. School was dismissed early. That night, the Metro mail truck that carried mail to Fargo did not arrive at Enderlin.

There was a letup of the storm, Thursday afternoon. Most folks had themselves dug out fairly well by late Thursday evening. Local weather observer, Red Neros put the precipitation total at 1.45 inches.

> "Apparently the break was just a windup for the "Sunday punch," beginning early Friday morning. A howling wind accompanied by an exceptional snowfall whipped huge drifts and filled the air so that visibility was almost zero most of the time." That's how the *Enderlin Independent,* described the weather for March 4.[118]

During the blizzard Elmer Davis, suffering from a heart condition, needed oxygen. Soo roundhouse foreman, Bill Pearthree procured a tank from the Soo Line's supply. Dr. S.C Bacheller administered the oxygen to Davis.

The Enderlin area, according to Otter Tail Power, lost power between 9:00 and 10:00 Friday night. Walt Hanson and Dale Slotten fixed the problem. After picking up their tools, they walked to the Ervin Schmitz farm and repaired the damaged lines.

In the waning hours of the storm on Saturday, Chester Eskelson needed medical care. Eskelson lived four miles west of Enderlin. He was taken to the Lisbon Memorial Hospital by car.

In the columns reserved for the amount of moisture received for the days of March 4 and 5, Neros placed question marks. He said, *"That it had been impossible with all the snow flying about to tell which was new snow, and which was not."* The snowfall had about twice the moisture normally found in snow.[119]

Kent Cable, editor of the *Enderlin Independent,* wrote:

> The storm definitely was in keeping with Enderlin's attempt to find articles of pioneer times. It was one we could have gotten along without, but as we said we found new respect for the old timers who underwent similar storms with a lot less going for them.
> We couldn't help thinking Friday that we were glad not to be living in a sod hut. We didn't have to go outside for fuel, water or any one of a dozen other reasons why our forefathers had to face the storms of their times. Incidentally they didn't have parkas and insulated clothing which we make good use of today.[120]

Roger Schimming, Dayton Fritz and Jervel Moen had Enderlin's streets opened by 10:00 Saturday morning. Although many of the openings were just single lanes, fire trucks could get around town. They worked late into the night and all day Sunday clearing more snow off the streets.

The city hired several truckers to haul snow out of the downtown district. The street department employees had help from nearby farmers who drove their tractors with scoops to town.

Milk was rationed in Enderlin on Saturday. The stores were all out of milk by the end of the day. Only a few people were disappointed. The shortage was over that night when Dagman's Cream Station replenished its supplies from the Lisbon Creamery.

Western Division Superintendent J. A. Welton, Enderlin, reported the Soo restored normal schedules between Glenwood, Minnesota, and Portal, North Dakota, 12 hours after the storm ended on Saturday. Local people were paid to dig out buried trains and switches in Enderlin.

Sunday morning, the Metro mail truck picked up mail in Enderlin and took it to Fargo. Mail for Enderlin came on the return trip.

Gordon Brown, manager of the Moore-Liberty Telephone Company, reported calls overwhelmed their circuits during the blizzard. "Icing conditions, beginning south of Enderlin and becoming progressively worse southward, did cause some difficulty," according to Brown. He said, "all lines were operating properly on Sunday." Normally, there is no voltage in a telephone line, but one of the telephone lines was found to be carrying over 300 volts. Brown figured that particular line must have crossed a power line during the high winds.[121]

School resumed on March 8. Superintendent A. P. Ziegenhagen reported that the buses picked up most of the students. Some farms were still isolated.

The huge drift at the Broadway entrance to Enderlin was opened on Tuesday. The district tournament in Marion resumed play. Enderlin had a bye in the first round.

The Eagles defeated Sheldon on Wednesday, 95 to 51. Arvid Berglund scored 27 points for Enderlin.

The Soo delivered a plow to the Midland Continental Railroad on March 9. Engineer Clarence Bearman and Roadmaster Francis Balmer, Enderlin residents, worked with Midland Continental personnel that cleared the line between Jamestown and Wimbledon. Two GN freight trains, 97-6 and 3-88-28, were rerouted on the Soo Line between Hankinson and Minot. Soo employees were pilots for the trains. The reroutes lasted four days. The GN had to clear drifts, 25 feet high, near Nolan and 35 foot drifts near Pillsbury.

Enderlin won the championship by outscoring Litchville, 68 to 56. Steve Wallner led the Eagles in scoring with 22 points. Vernell Lindemann added 14, Arvid Berglund 13, and Bruce Scheie 10. Chuck Geske, another starter, had 9. Berglund suffered a ankle injury. After that, his play was limited.

The team had no rest. On Friday, they met Milnor in regional play. The game was close, but the Bison pulled away at the end for a 63 to 40 win.

On Saturday with 16 seconds left, Enderlin and Central Cass were tied at 64. Central Cass had control of the ball. They called a time out. Just before the buzzer sounded, Don Bartholomay put up a 25 foot shot. It went in and Central Cass won the game. Coach Ed Schense's team finished the year with an 18-4 record, won the Southeast Conference championship, brought the goat home from Lisbon, and captured the District 4 championship.

Lidgerwood, Mantador, Hankinson, Fairmount, Wyndmere, Dwight and Wahpeton

The city of Lidgerwood is located in western Richland County. In 1885, George I. Lidgerwood purchased some land from Charles H. Sparks. On this land in 1886, the platting of a townsite was done by him and his partners, R. N. Ink and Gen. William D. Washburn. Lidgerwood's name was chosen for the new settlement. He would later enjoy employment as the Soo Line's right-of-way agent.

The GN and the Soo built almost parallel rail lines west, less than a mile apart, through Richland County in 1886. There was hard feelings between the Polish and Irish construction crews along the way. Bosses of the construction crews fanned the hatred. The trouble led to a pitched battle with pick handles as weapons near Geneseo or Cayuga in the adjacent county. It was undoubtedly the biggest battle ever fought in Sargent County.[122]

Lidgerwood had 1,081 residents in 1960.

Marine Pfc Howard Kath, son of Mr. and Mrs. Norman Kath of Lidgerwood, was in Vietnam in February 1966.

St. Francis defeated Lidgerwood in the opening round of the District 1 basketball tournament on March 1. Bad weather interrupted play on Wednesday.

A busload of band members traveled to Wyndmere for the tournament on Thursday. Fans of the Cardinals made the trip as well. When other teams could not make it to Wyndmere, the games were postponed for the second time. Various buses and cars headed for home immediately. Everybody made it.

According to the *Lidgerwood Monitor*, published by C. W. and Louise Frost:

> *Winds, reaching as high as 65 miles per hour, drove falling snow into road-blocking drifts throughout the area.*
>
> *Temperatures dipped only to 15 above. Also helping reduce hardship was the fact that most areas power remained on. Otter Tail Power representatives reported outages totalling 37 minutes out of the Hankinson substation. In the Wyndmere area, outage was somewhat more prolonged. Some REA lines reportedly were out, also.*
>
> *By Saturday afternoon the end of the storm was in sight. Lidgerwood city crews were still digging out Wednesday noon (March 9). Rising temperatures already had greatly reduced piles of snow.*[123]

Northwestern Bell reported 170 households in the Lidgerwood area lost phone services during the blizzard.[124]

Art Gollnick and Loren Zietlow baked bread and other sweets at the city bakery during the blizzard. Lidgerwood had a good supply of bread for the rush after the storm. Milk was in short supply.

Dick Mattson lived seven miles from Lidgerwood. Mattson left his truck in a protected spot. Snow built up on top of the pickup. The snow was so tightly packed that Mattson was able to make two trips to town and back, before the snow started to crack.

Some churches in Lidgerwood canceled services on Sunday. Many of their parishioners were still digging out. A big drift formed behind the Immanuel Lutheran Church.

Harold Helmer was forced to something he did not want to do. Snowdrifts on the Henry Helmer farm were 8 to 14 feet high. Snow blocked the doors of their house. To get out, Harold broke a window in the porch.

Snow piled up in the lee of the buildings on the Roger Thielman farm. One drift edged the top of their pole barn. Another imposing drift formed between the house and barn.

On March 8, Lidgerwood bested Fairmount, 63 to 49. Trinka led the Cardinals in scoring with 18 points.

Two weeks after the storm, J. C. Haas and George Jereska announced the sale of Haas Grocery to Jereska. The transfer of ownership took place on March 21, 1966. Haas operated the store since 1922, the current building was built in 1947.

The origin of Mantador's name is unique. This Soo town was founded in 1886, but the railroad arrived in 1891. In 1960, the town had a population of 98. Douglas Wick wrote: Folklore says that before settlement began a solitary home was here, and its owner would always appear at the door to watch passing trains, prompting the comment "There's the man at the door." No better explanation of the name has surfaced.[125]

In 1966, the new Mantador School was almost completely covered by a huge drift between the old school and the new one. It was estimated at 20 feet high. The town had many other big drifts. Janitor William Theil climbed some of them to get into St. Peter and St Paul Church on March 5. There were no church services on Sunday.

The Ed Reiland farm home near Mantador was just about buried. His yard also had many drifts, 5 to 6 feet high.

In 1880, Richard Henry Hankinson homesteaded land which later the city of Hankinson was founded. Hankinson obtained the rank of Colonel in the Civil War. In 1871, Hankinson was put in charge of constructing a telegraph line from Moorhead to Valley City, and on to Bismarck the next year. He later served as Superintendent of the Northwestern Telegraph Company (later, part of Western Union).

In 1960, Hankinson had a population of 1,285.

On March 2, 1966, Hankinson recorded a high of 38 degrees.

Blizzard conditions developed west of Hankinson, that afternoon. That evening, snow fell in the area. Temperatures bottomed out at 20 above.

Thursday morning, there was no school at Immanuel Lutheran, Hankinson Public School and St. Francis. Television and radio commentators called the latest blizzard, *"the worst one of the century for the Dakotas."* Where was the storm? Hankinson had nice weather. The city had a high of 32.

According to the *Hankinson News*, Grant Helgeson, editor:

> It wasn't until 6 p.m. Thursday night the high winds and snow hit, and continued unabated until about noon Saturday. Traffic and business came to all but a standstill Friday morning as the snow continued and the drifts began to pile up in the sheltered areas. Some businesses here opened Friday morning, but most of them closed early in the afternoon as owners went home to wait out the storm's fierceness.[126]

Peak wind gusts were around 70 mph. Overall, Hankinson received 8 inches of snow, .76 inches of precipitation. Thursday's night low was 25. On Friday, the high reached 35 and then dropped to 14 above. On Saturday, the mercury rebounded to 20 above.

Thursday night, two school buses from Hankinson traveled to Wyndmere for the District 1 tournament. The basketball games had been canceled. They returned immediately, the bus drivers reported the visibility as "very poor."

Ernest Johnson took his three sons and two of their friends went to Wyndmere for same reason. After they learned the games were postponed, they stopped at his parent's home in Wyndmere for a short visit. They stayed too long. They returned home on Sunday.

Friday morning, W.W. (Bud) Engen, local Otter Tail manager, was on duty at 4:00. He needed to make a switch at the Otter Tail 115 KV substation, located four miles north of Hankinson near the Elmer Bladow farm. Leaving at that time, Engen explained his ordeal:

> It was almost necessary to feel every inch of the way. It was only by shining the spotlight from the service truck on the white center line, I was able to keep on the road and at times I lost sight of it. I inched along a few feet at a time and got out innumerable times to check the road. I finally saw a bridge sign on County Highway 1 and realized I went too far. To turn around was a problem. I decided to do it right on the bridge and eliminate the chances of backing off the road. I radioed for help. Leroy Jorgensen and

Grant Baker, members of an Otter Tail work crew stationed in Hankinson, started out in a bigger truck. We reached the substation about the same time, at 6:30 a.m.[127]

On Friday, Jack Braun of Duerr Gas delivered a bottle of gas to a north-side resident. He left his house on the south side of town in his truck. Soon afterwards, his truck was stuck in a drift. He shoveled out and drove until he was stuck in another drift. He shoveled out, only to get stuck in the next drift. Braun's cross-town trip took two hours.

Early Saturday, between 1:00 and 4:00 a.m., the men of the Otter Tail Power Company had another battle with Mother Nature trying to reach the substation north of Hankinson. Mother Nature won, so they waited for help. Snowplows started working at 7:30 and they opened the highway.

A trip to the substation east of Hankinson was made on foot.

Hankinson lost power, three or four times, during the blizzard. The good news, the outages lasted about 30 minutes each time.

Northwestern Bell reported very little trouble in Hankinson, although some rural lines were out during the storm.

Soo Line Depot Agent, Elmer Gabel indicated that no trains arrived on Friday and Saturday. Gabel still worked at the depot on those days. Hankinson had two short wave radio operators, Father Francis Smalley and Gabel. Throughout the storm, Father Smalley sent and received messages on his set. Gabel passed information along when he was not working at the depot.

Grocery stores in Hankinson started to run out of bread, milk and eggs Saturday morning. Trucks that supplied those items did not arrive until Monday. The stores were open for a while on Sunday.

After digging out Saturday and Sunday, movie goers watched, *The Sons Of Katie Elder* at the Avon Theatre.

Street crews and Mahrer Construction Company handled the snow removal around town. Although Main Street was cleared by Saturday evening, it took almost a week for the complete cleanup of Hankinson.

Area farmers sold their milk to the Hankinson Creamery. According to Manager Roland Roeder, there was no pickups on Friday. On Saturday, he stated the can truck left Hankinson at 1:00 p.m. Five hours later, that truck had made it to three farms where they picked up 21 cans of milk. The bulk truck left town late Saturday. This truck took milk from the bulk tanks at eighteen farms. At some farms, the driver had to back the truck into the driveways. With all the snow in the yards there was no room for the truck to turn around. Sunday and Monday were catch up days. Roeder reported the last truck finished the route at 2:00 a.m. Tuesday.

Mr. and Mrs. Grant Helgeson invited their son, Blayne and his family over for Sunday dinner. They encouraged him to bring his camera, plenty of film and his overshoes. Dad had a plan up his sleeve. They would take pictures of snowstorm for the newspaper. That's what Blayne did.

Sunday afternoon, the film was processed. Pictures were printed that night. On Monday morning, the selected photos were taken to Fargo for processing into printing plates. Normally, Grant used the mail, but any slip in connections would have made these pictures practically worthless a week later.

The Walter Klawitter farm, located west of Hankinson just off Highway 11, had drifts, probably 15 feet high. Their home was nearly hemmed in by snow. The family car was just about buried. The Klawitters had a building that housed ducks and geese. Only the top of that building could be seen after the storm. The Klawitters fed the birds through a vent. They had to be careful, power lines about 12 to 14 feet off the ground, were partially covered with snow.

On March 8 Grant Helgenson wrote:

> Ironic as it may seem, after writing snow stories all afternoon, the temperature had risen to a point where water was right up to our front door from the melting snow. And tomorrow, the mercury is supposed to go even higher. We would hate to see what the results would have been if the snow had not been removed from our streets.[128]

The Hankinson Pirates defeated the Lidgerwood Cardinals, 75 to 54, in the consolation game of the district tournament on March 9. For the Pirates, Rettig was high with 21 points, followed by Solid and Teigs with 16 and 15.

Straight south of Wahpeton, fifteen miles, is Fairmount.

The city had 503 residents in 1960.

In 1878, E. Warren Spaulding led more than forty families from Hartford, Michigan, to the Fairmount area. It was called the "Michigan Settlement."

Fairmount was officially established in 1883. It was given the name "Fairmount" after Fairmount Park in Philadelphia by townsite owner, Joseph C. Henvis. He lived in the "City of Brotherly Love" at one time.

Rail service to Fairmount began with the arrival of the Fargo Southern (later the Milwaukee) in the fall of 1884. GN and the Soo Line reached Fairmount in 1886. Before a Soo Line merger in 1915, Fairmount was also served by a fourth railroad, the local Fairmount and Veblen (South Dakota) RR. This situation gave Fairmount bragging rights as being the only place in North Dakota with rail service from four different railroads.

Fairmount was the scene of a deadly tornado in 1965.

Kindergarten classes for the Fairmount Public School system began on Monday, February 28, 1966. That night, Fairmount residents traveled to Wyndmere to watch the Pheasants play the Sargent Central Cadets. The game was decided in the final seconds. Fairmount won by one point, 58 to 57. Jim Bertelsen scored 21 points for Fairmount.

On Tuesday, Fairmount battled Milnor, the Wild Rice Conference champs. Milnor's big fourth quarter gave them a 71 to 53 victory. On Wednesday, blizzard conditions developed. There was a break in the storm on Thursday, the big blow came that night and lasted until early Saturday morning.

According to the *Fairmount News*:

> Transportation in Fairmount was dead from Friday until Sunday. There were no reported emergencies in our immediate area.
>
> Store owners or managers remained on the job to enable customers to buy necessities until a run on butter, bread, milk etc. depleted their stocks.
>
> The big display window and metal awning at the Fairmount Drug collapsed under heavy, moisture-laden snow. Clarence George, pharmacist, said, "It was almost like a tornado.[129]

James Carney, Northwestern Bell manager at Wahpeton, estimated fifty poles went down in one stretch along Highway 81 near Fairmount. He reported 190 customers in the Fairmount area had phone outages.[130]

In 1883, an NP townsite was established in Wyndmere Township.

The settlement took the name of "Wyndmere." The impetus for this name was Windermere Lake, Westmorelandshire, England. That name comes from "wynd", a narrow lane. The other part, derives from "mere", a pool or lake. The name reflected the geograhy of the townsite-before it was ditched and drained.

In 1888, the Soo started construction on the Hankinson-Portal mainline. It intersected the NP line, a mile east of Wyndmere. A settlement started there 1889. The place was known as East Wyndmere. A year later, the majority of the buildings from Wyndmere were hauled to the new townsite. Before long, the community was known just as Wyndmere.

Wyndmere has billed itself as the "Corn Capital of North Dakota." The town's population peaked in the 1960 with 644 residents. N.D. Highways 13 and 18 meet at Wyndmere.

An estimated 3000 people attended the 3rd annual Crop Show at Wyndmere on February 25 and 26, 1966. The Wyndmere Community Club sponsored the event. On Friday night, the 4-H follies, with George Carver as Master of Ceremonies, were presented at the high school auditorium. The awards banquet was held, Saturday evening.

Wyndmere hosted the District 1 tournament. Wyndmere had finished the Wild Rice Conference play with a 10-4 record. Inclement weather interrupted the tournament on Wednesday.

On March 2, Wyndmere High School Band, 34 students, and Mrs. Bruce Anderson, director, appeared at the Woodwind Clinic on the campus of the Valley City State College. Eight chaperons accompanied the band members on the trip.

That afternoon, the weather turned ugly in Valley City. The group left the clinic early. They headed out in a caravan of seven cars. Visibility was poor.

After fighting the weather for a little bit, the caravan stopped and headed back to Valley City. The group stayed at the Rudolph Hotel. As many as seven shared a room. Band members from other schools were stranded there as well.

The blizzard lasted till Saturday. The musicians played cards, games and organized Hootenannies. The Wyndmere teenagers sang songs and Marjorie Dotzenrod played her autoharp. Students from other towns joined the sessions. They washed their clothes at the hotel and used bedding as bathrobes.

The caravan left the hotel, late Sunday morning, and arrived back in Wyndmere at 3:00 p.m.

Meanwhile, the times at home were tougher. According to Les Robinson, Wahpeton district manger, Wyndmere lost its power at 4:00 a.m. Friday. Service was restored 9:00 p.m. Robinson indicated the outage was caused by line trouble, ice and strong winds knocked down some lines. James Carney, Northwestern Bell at Wahpeton, reported 70 homes in the Wyndmere area lost the use of their phones. One section of the town did not have water.[131]

During the blizzard, Otter Tail Power Company and Northwestern Bell had employees working in Wyndmere. Their tinkering prevented complete breakdown of systems.

Thursday morning March 3, there was a fire at the Nels and James Charlson's C-Diamond Ranch. The headquarters of the ranch was located 10 miles northwest of Wyndmere. Overall, the Charlsons ran over 500 head of cattle and about 300 hogs. At the time of the storm, 340 head of cattle and the hogs were located on the main unit. The blizzard caused a series of delays. With their telephone not working, someone drove to town and called the fire department. Snow blocked the driveway of the firehouse, so that was plowed first. By the time the fire department arrived at the scene, the fire at the garage-workshop was out of control. The fire department saved the surrounding buildings.

James Charlson estimated the fire damages at about $15,000. That included the cost of garage-workshop building, the shop tools, and the truck and Bobcat that burnt up inside the structure. Before the flames took over, Charlson's car and a tractor were taken out of the shop.

The cause of the fire was undetermined, but Mr. Charlson thought the fluctuating current had something to do with it. He believed the furnace motor pumped oil into the fire pot, when the voltage was low. When the current surged, it exploded.

One hour after the blaze, Gordon Trana of Wyndmere, representative of the Melroe Manufacturing Company, had a Bobcat delivered to the C-Diamond Ranch.

To get out of the house after the storm, Nels took a window out. He shoveled the drifted snow away from the opening. Only the top section of the house was visible. Nels walked two miles to his son's place to get help. He said, "This was the worst storm he'd seen in 60 years and doesn't care to see another like it."[132]

Game Warden John Violet and Highway Patrolmen Dosch and Evenson helped stranded motorist get out of the storm.

Ed Anderson, John Violet, Doug Thompson, George Carver, Ralph Heitkamp, and Joe Karas manned the ambulance. They had four hospital runs during the blizzard. The ambulance had a two-way radio system. It was used as a base station for coordinating state and county plows.

One telephone employee stayed at the unheated relay station. He was outfitted with a sleeping bag and cot.

According to the *Wyndmere Missile*, Harrison McCleery, publisher, and Jo Ann Peterson, editor:

> Anderson's Service and Ralph's Service furnished batteries and Anderson's Service kept recharging the batteries, so as to keep the relays working for telephone service. It is estimated that Anderson's Service made 50 miles hauling supplies and equipment to the Power and Telephone Companies. Two of the councilmen spent the whole day with them on Friday, doing what they could to help, and also hauled Doug Thompson to the Well House in order to keep the water running. This crew got to bed at 1 p.m. and was called again at 4 a.m. to man the Ambulance for a trip to the Durayne Nelson farm. They also called the State plow and stood by from 4 to 7 before a decision was made not to take her to the hospital.[133]

Mrs. Peter Haugen wrote:

> The Gordon Tranas and Ronald Algaards were Friday guests in the John Violet home during the storm. The water main in that section of the town had a break which made it inconvenient for the residents of that vicinity.

> *With the electricity off many furnaces could not operate and many peo-*
> *ple were guests of neighbors who had heating and cooking facilities.*
>   *Emma Olson and the Robert Foyes were guests in the Clifton G. Foye*
> *home during the storm, the latter has a furnace that operates manually*
> *when the current is off, and also has a coal stove for emergencies.*[134]

Saturday at 5:35 a.m., Mrs. Durayne Nelson gave birth to a 6 pound and 2 ounce baby girl at her home near Wyndmere. Durayne and Karolyn named the child, Darla Jayne. John Bailey and Mrs. Vincent Jones of Wyndmere, a RN, helped in the delivery.

After the roads were cleared Sunday morning, mother and child were admitted to St. Francis Hospital at Breckenridge.

The blizzard knocked the phone out at the David Goerger farm.

He came to Wyndmere, Saturday morning at 9:00. Goerger brought Mrs. Ray Bommersbach, great aunt of his wife. He informed the authorities that his wife was expecting a child. She needed to be taken to St. Francis Hospital in Breckenridge. Later, Mrs. Don Puetz, a nurse, and Mr. and Mrs. Edd Goerger of Barney arrived at the David Goerger farm. State and county snowplows led the city ambulance to Breckenridge. They arrived just in time. Fifty minutes later at 5:00 p.m., Mrs. David Goerger gave birth to a baby boy, Edmund David.

On March 7, there was a lot of activity at the C- Diamond Ranch. The ranch had drifts, 12 to 15 feet high. Three tractors were completely buried in the snow. One hired man operated the Bobcat, clearing snow away from the granary to get feed for the cattle and hogs.

Six members of the Whapeton National Guard, Company C, 231st Engineer Battalion, arrived at the ranch at 3:00 p.m. In charge was 1st Lt. Alan G. Braaton of rural Wyndmere. During the storm, the local unit received approval for calling out 40 men for snow removal operations. On Sunday, the guardsmen transported the loader from Fargo. National guardsmen from the Wahpeton unit that cleared snow at the ranch included Kermit Anderson and David Yaggie, both of rural Breckenridge, Harlan Muehler, Wahpeton, and Virgil Woytassek, Geneseo. They worked around the clock for twenty hours. The guardsmen also helped in the feeding of the livestock. Only the general location of the tractors were known. One was found accidently. The operator of the front-end loader reached into the drift for another big scoop of snow and he hit a tractor tire.

On March 8, they left the C-Diamond Ranch. According to Mr. Charlson, the National Guard members were scheduled to help Ernest Kjar, north of McLeod, Irvin Huseth, Harold Huseth, Gordon Carlson and Kenneth Larson.[135]

Art Johnson, Richland County Commissioner, contacted the authorities in Bismarck for additional heavy equipment for the Wyndmere area on March 9. Bismarck made arrangement with a Fargo contractor. On Thursday, Alan Braaten directed the machine to snow-plagued ranches.

The District 1 tournament resumed play on Monday. Wyndmere had no trouble beating the North Sargent Continentals, 96 to 68. The following day, they stopped the Havana Arrows, 80 to 57.

The championship game against Milnor, Wednesday night, was low scoring and a defensive battle. With about four minutes left in the game, the Warriors had a 8 point lead. Milnor rallied for a 40 to 37 win. Free throws accounted for the difference, the Bison made 12 out of 16, while the Warriors hit only 5 of 18.

The high school basketball team was later rewarded for their good season and hard work. Coach Don Pfaffle and the entire squad watched the Milnor Bison take second place in the Class B Tournament in Minot.

A New York Congressman, Jeremiah Wilbur Dwight (1819-1885), owned 27,000 acres of land in Richland County in 1880. He was from Dryden, New York. With that much land, the GN came to him. That year, tracks were built through Dwight, Galchutt, Colfax and Walcott. On February 2, 1881, John Miller, also from Dryden, became Dwight's first postmaster. In 1889, Miller became the first Governor of North Dakota.

In 1960, Dwight had 101 people living there.

Mrs. Ted Quamme, Dwight's news correspondent, wrote:

> Like all other communities, Dwight residents weathered the long storm, but fortunately with out any dramatic hardship. We were thankful for un-interrupted service in all utilities. The men of the town went in two cars to Wahpeton Saturday morning for medication for Edwin Larson and had to wait for the rotary plow to open the highway by Frank Domms. These same men shoveled out cars for persons who had need to get out soon, and made themselves useful wherever there was a need. Dwight folks say Thank You to these fellows who made living in a small community a feeling of one family. School was dismissed Wednesday afternoon for the remainder of the week. All church activities were canceled. The snowplow early Sunday was a welcome sight, but it took considerable digging to connect driveways and sidewalks with the street. ...
>
> In rural areas where the electrical power was off during the storm, some farmers made use of their tractor radios and batteries by bring them in the house, and where there were oil burners, prepared the family meals on them. Many were without telephone communications, too. This will make us appreciate every day utilities all the more.
>
> Glenn Cooksley who is employed on maintenance at the Science School was on duty constantly from Thursday morning until Sunday night. Part of his work was getting the cooks to work and home again, to keep entrances from being snow blocked, and Sunday the men were on four hour shifts to clear sidewalks and streets on the campus.[136]

According to Northwestern Bell Telephone, James Carney, local manager at Wahpeton, phone service was lost for 60 customers in the Dwight area.[137]

Over forty miles southeast of Fargo is the city of Wahpeton, the seat of Richland County. Wahpeton was the first white settlement in North Dakota after Pembina. In 1960, Wahpeton was the home to 5,876 people.

The Red River of the North is unique in that it is one of the few rivers on earth that flows north. The source of Red River of the North is at the intersection of the Bois de Sioux and Ottertail River in Wahpeton and Breckenridge, Minnesota.

The first person to settle at Wahpeton was Morgan T. Rich who arrived here in 1864. In addition to farming, he ran a ferry operation for people trying to cross the Bois de Sioux near its meeting with the Ottertail River. The completion of a bridge in 1876 ended that business.

More people arrived in 1869, the settlement was named Richville after Mr. Rich. Richville became "Chahinkapa," on October 13, 1873. The English translation of this Indian word means "end of the woods." But that name never caught on, so postmaster Hugh R. Blanding adopted the name of the local Sioux tribe, the Wahpeton Indians, on July 24, 1874. The word "Wahpeton" comes from the Sioux word "wa-qpe-tong-wong." This translates into English as "dweller among the deciduous trees or village of many leaves."

Three rail lines would meet at Wahpeton. The St. Paul, Minneapolis, and Manitoba R.R. (later the GN) came from the east in 1880. Next in 1882, was the Fergus and Black Hills R.R., an NP branch line. Finally, the Fargo Southern arrived in 1884.

Wahpeton is where UND football player and future NFL player, Steve Myhra was born in 1934. A Little All-American at UND, Myhra would later go on to play with the Baltimore Colts. In December 1958, he kicked a field goal in the NFL championship game to send the game between the Colts and the New York Giants to overtime. The Colts would go on to win that game.

Wahpeton has its share of attractions. Many people have memories of riding the wooden horse carousel in Wahpeton. In 1926, there were 150 wooden horse carrousels built. Its the only one of the originals, still operating in the United States. The Richland County Historical Museum contains an extensive collection of Rosemeade pottery, which originally was produced in Wahpeton. The world's largest statue of a channel catfish rests in the 26-acre Kidder Recreation Area north of town.[138]

On March 2, the mercury rose to 35 above. According to the *Farmer Globe*:

> *The March lamb donned the wintery garb of a lion Wednesday, as winds whipped freshly fallen snow to snowstorm proportions. The Wahpeton weather recording station reported between four and five inches of new snow.*[139]

On Wednesday, the Wahpeton High School basketball team was in Valley City to play Lisbon in the opening round of the Southeast Regional Tournament. Wahpeton finished district play with a 13-1 record. Going into the regional tournament, Coach Dan Tehle's squad had a 17-3 won-loss record and was ranked third in the final Class A poll. Mike Berg finished second in the Class A scoring race with an average of 22.2 points. Blizzard conditions developed in Valley City and the games were called off.

Many streets in Wahpeton and Breckenridge were clogged with snow on Thursday morning. City operators started clearing the roads early. To complicate matters, it rained that morning. Reports, received by the *Farmer Globe*, indicated that most county roads were heavy with snow, with some impassable. Schools in the area were closed.

Wahpeton reported a high of 36 degrees on Thursday. That night, the low was 26. The precipitation for the day amounted to .12 inches. There was plenty of blowing and drifting snow, despite the lull in the storm. Thursday evening, the lull was over. Mother Nature struck angrily.

The Wahpeton National Guard unit, Company C, 231st Engineer Battalion, received notification that their unit had been selected as the most outstanding National Guard unit in North Dakota for 1965. Two platoons at Wahpeton and one at Lisbon make up Company C. Captain Donald P.N. Rosley of Wahpeton was in charge.

Wahpeton City Engineer, Ed Johnson revealed that their large plow broke down on Thursday. While repairs were being made, county and National Guard equipment handled snow removal duties.

On Friday, temperatures fell to 17 degrees after a high of 33. Wahpeton recorded .35 inches of precipitation on Friday. Winds were estimated at 50 mph

Phone

Name

Name Karen, T

Request Expires: 03/03

ided at 6:20 p.m. The storm was at its pinnacle.
y Shop at 629 9th Street North. A snowplow was on
low. They could not save the shop, but they stopped
is located at the rear of the Martin Pankow residence.
anes building collapsed from the weight of heavy snow.
the bowling lanes were not damaged because they were
it Diederich.
favorite television shows during the blizzard. Here's Thurs-
evision schedule:

WDAY Channel 6

March 3	Friday, March 4
iel Boone	6:30 *Camp Runamuck*
redo	7:00 *Hank*
i. McLusky	7:30 *Sammy Davis*
Dean Martin	8:30 *Mr. Roberts*
	9:00 *Man from Uncle*

KXJB Channel 4

6:30 *The Munsters*	6:30 *Wild, Wild West*
7:00 *Gilligans Island*	7:30 *Hogan's Heroes*
7:30 *My Three Sons*	8:00 *Gomer Pyle*
8:00 Thurs. Movie	8:30 *Smothers Brothers*
	9:00 Greatest Game

KTHI Channel 11

6:30 *Batman*	6:00 *Rifleman*
7:00 *Gidget*	6:30 *Flintstones*
7:30 *Henry Phyfe*	7:00 *Tammy*
8:00 *Bewitched*	7:30 *Addams Family*
8:30 *Peyton Place*	8:00 Fri. Movie
9:00 *The Baron*	

The blizzard ended on Saturday. Another .05 inches was added to the precipitation total. Overall, Wahpeton amassed 10 inches of snow during the storm.

At the time of the March 1966 storm, Gloria Ebertowski was attending North Dakota State School of Science in Wapheton. Gloria lived in a women's dormitory. The blizzard left such large drifts at the college, that for two days the only means of exit from the women's dormitory was from a second story window. From there, a person jumped down a short distance onto a snowdrift. After two days, food supplies in the dormitory ran low. Relief came, when the college sent a sled loaded with food around to the dormitory.[140]

In March 1966, Bill Mitchell of Crystal, North Dakota, was studying electronics at NDSSS in Wahpeton. His memories of the storm concern more for what happened afterwards. Mitchell had parked his car, a Ford Falcon, at the southernmost part of the parking lot. Once the storm had passed, his car was about the only one that was not buried under piles of snow. Other students began asking him for rides. Being an enterprising student, Mitchell ran a taxi service for two days. He made quite a few trips to the grocery and liquor stores. Mitchell was paid a dollar for each trip. Mitchell said, "*That was a lot of money back then.*"[141]

Saturday night, NDSSS Wildcats basketball team won the Region 13 Junior College Basketball Tournament in Willmar, Minnesota. Region 13 involved teams from Minnesota, Montana, Michigan, and North and South Dakota. In the championship game, the Wildcats upset tourney favorite, Bismarck, 87 to 69. Del Hagen and John Nordgaard scored 27 and 20 points, respectively, for Wahpeton. NDSSS advanced to the National Junior College Tournament in Hutchinson, Kansas, on March 15-19. There were 675 Junior Colleges in the United States in 1966. Only 16 teams advanced to the national tournament.

Around midnight Saturday, the high school basketball team returned to Wahpeton. They spent four days in Valley City and never played a game.

Repairs were completed on the large city plow on Sunday. It was put into action right away. National Guard equipment from Fargo arrived on Sunday.

Richland County Agent, Verne Kasson believed county livestock losses were minor on Sunday.

James Carney reported seventy Northwestern Bell customers in the Wahpeton area suffered outages. On Sunday, Carney indicated thirty men were working to restore their telephone connections, but they were slowed by snow-blocked roads. Carney noted that local service was at full capacity during the days and most of the nights during the blizzard. He said, "*3,100 long distance calls went out of Wahpeton-Breckenridge Sunday, about double the normal amount. That pace was maintained for about three days.*"[142]

The weather did not delay the Southeast Regional any longer on Monday. Wahpeton defeated Lisbon, 77 to 55.

The NDSSS band departed for Hutchinson, Kansas, on Monday.

Under the direction of Joe Intlehouse, the band had forty members. For was the first time, the Science band appeared at a national basketball tournament.

On Tuesday, Wahpeton met the Shanley Decons. Wahpeton pulled away in the second for a 61 to 48 victory. No championship game would be played, the semi-final winners advanced to the state tournament in Grand Forks on Thursday

Wahpeton Mayor, Virgil Sturdevant decided not to seek a third term as mayor in the upcoming April 5 city election. Petitions for the office were being circulated around town. Before Sturdevant was elected mayor in 1958, he served four years as an alderman. The newspaper announcement on came Thursday, March 10.

Wahpeton faced the Minot Magicians, the 1965 state champions. At halftime, Wahpeton trailed the Magicians, 37 to 31. During the break, Coach Tehle urged his players to get command of the boards. Both teams had leads in the fourth quarter. With two minutes left, Wahpeton had a 4 point advantage. They went into stall, forcing Minot to foul. Wahpeton made 10 free throws and won the game, 76 to 62. Mike Berg scored 33 points.

On Friday, Wahpeton faced the Bismarck Demons who were ranked number one in the final Class A poll. At the end of the first quarter, Wahpeton was up by one. The Demons had a 5 point lead at halftime. Wahpeton had another strong third quarter, they pulled ahead by seven. Bismarck bounced back in the fourth quarter. Wahpeton, with a slight lead, worked the clock down. Bismarck pressed frenetically. Wahpeton turned the ball over several times. The game was tied with 48 seconds left. Pressure mounted with each tick of the clock. Wahpeton called time, but the team didn't have any left. A technical foul was called. It gave Bismarck a free throw and the ball afterwards. Wahpeton did not have enough time to rally. Bismarck won the game, 70 to 65.

On Saturday, Wahpeton bounced back from their heartbreaking loss. They defeated Fargo North, 60 to 54, for the consolation trophy. Mike Berg finished with 25 points, he scored 72 points in the tournament. Other key members of the 21-4 team included Lance Wolf, Paul Ferrie, Mark Werre, Dale Bakko and Steve Furst.

NDSSS basketball coach, Ed Werre coached Science teams in the national tournament in 1953 and 1964. On March 15, NDSSS faced Leicester, Massachusetts. The game was decided in the final minutes. The Wildcats lost the tough battle, 81 to 73.

At 6 a.m. on March 16, the Red River of the North crested at 13.94 feet, at Wahpeton. In 1965, the crest reached 14.34 feet in mid April.

NDSSS finished the national tournament with a 94 to 69 loss to Chicago Wilson.

New Town, Parshall, Stanley and Berthold

New Town lies a few miles east of the Missouri River and about twenty-five miles southwest of Stanley. It owes its existence to the Garrison Dam. It was built to replace three towns, Elbowoods, Sanish and Van Hook, that were going to be inundated by Lake Sakakawea.

The Sanish-Van Hook Relocation Townsite Corporation was a group of twenty men, ten each from Sanish and Van Hook who were the financiers who bought 160 acres for the New Town townsite. The platting and building of curbs, streets, and sidewalks was done by the Federal government.

In September 1950, ground breaking ceremonies for New Town were held. New Town became the terminus of the Soo's branch line from Max in 1953. By 1960, the community had 1,586 residents.

The March 1966 storm only gave New Town a grazing blow. This Mountrail city had been enjoying mild weather before the storm. A high and low of 31 and 21 were recorded in New Town on March 2.

On Thursday, it began to snow in New Town. The winds picked up, reducing visibility. New Town students who rode to school on buses were sent home shortly after 12 p.m. Wind gusts at New Town that day exceeded 50 mph. New Town received .10 inches of precipitation. The thermometer reached a high of 24.

However, as midnight approached, the stormy weather in New Town was pretty much finished. There was school on Friday.

The March 1966 blizzard did bring an interruption of freight, mail and television programming to New Town. But that was about it. To compensate, New Town area residents relied on the radio for storm reports.

A municipal officers' conference to be held over the weekend at Grand Forks was the destination of New Town Mayor Mr. McMaster and his wife. They never got there. Lousy weather conditions at Leeds forced them to turn around.

The New Town Eagles finished their season with a win at Parshall on March 5. They upended White Shield 82 to 77 to capture the third place in the District 26 tournament. Leading a balanced New Town attack was Mike Hovey with 26 points and Willis Bancroft with 23 points.

Parshall began as a Soo Line townsite in 1914. The surveying of the townsite was done by a Hidatsa Indian who also drove a local mail stage. His name was George Parshall.

Parshall is widely known for having the lowest temperature ever recorded in North Dakota, -60 degrees F. on February 15, 1936. Less than half a year later on July 12, 1936,

Parshall endured a broiling +112 degrees F. This temperature spread, recorded at one location, is thought to be a world record.

Parshall had 1,216 residents in 1960.

Parshall was just grazed by the March 1966 blizzard. It received an inch of snow on Thursday, March 3, and just a trace the next day, for a total of .06 inches of precipitation. The weather observer in Parshall at that time was C. E. Shubert.

Parshall had more problems with high winds. Visibility was reduced-not by blowing snow, but wind-blown dirt off summer fallow. There was a lot of damage at United Church of Christ in Parshall.

High winds blew in its basement window. Dirt settled over the whole basement kitchen. Now exposed to the outside weather, water pipes in the basement froze up.

Another storm casualty was Lloyd Trulson's windmill at his farm, four miles east of Parshall. Around 4 o'clock Wednesday afternoon, the high wind knocked it over. In the process it landed on a shed.

Temperatures remained moderate in Parshall during and after the storm. A high of 25 was recorded on Thursday and 29 on Saturday. It dipped to 9 below Sunday morning, before rebounding.

Parshall did have one of its residents, Larry Hedberg, who was stranded by the blizzard. A student at Moorhead, Hedberg was enroute back to Parshall via a Fargo to Minot train. It became stuck in a snowdrift, seven miles long. The height of the drift exceeded 40 feet, higher than the domes on the observation cars.

Under the guidance of Coach Bill Fruhwirth the Braves won the District 26 tournament with a victory over New Town. Their win over the Washburn Cardinals, 43 to 41, in the regional tournament at Garrison sent the team the state Class B tournament at Minot.

Things didn't go so well for Parshall at Minot. On March 17, they lost to a hot shooting Langdon team, 52 to 50. Parshall's season came to an end with a disheartening double-overtime loss to New England St. Mary's, 68 to 63.

A schoolteacher from Parshall, Mrs. Ina B. Hall, a mother of eight children was chosen North Dakota's, *"1966 Mother of the Year."*

Stanley is located about half way between Minot and Williston on U.S. Highway 2.

In 1895, the first settlers arrived in the Stanley area. In 1902, George W. Wilson (1858-1935) platted a townsite on land he controlled through scrip.

There is some disagreement as to the origins of Stanley's name. The most accepted version has Wilson naming the townsite after a pioneering homesteader of the area, Col. King Stanley. The other version says the townsite was named after a onetime commandant of Fort Berthold, David Sloane Stanley.

Stanley was selected to be the seat of Mountrail County in 1910. The town had 1,795 residents in 1960.

For the most part, the Stanley area escaped the wrath of the March 1966 snowstorm. There was a trace of precipitation in Stanley on Wednesday and 0.20 the next day. Just over 2 inches of snow fell on those days. Extremely windy, blustery conditions were experienced in Stanley on Thursday and Friday. After reaching a high of 31 in Stanley on March 2, the thermometer began to slide downwards, reaching a low of -11 Sunday morning, before rebounding.

There was the loss of the broadcast signal of both television networks in the Stanley vicinity. Once the storm engulfed most of North Dakota, Stanley did not receive any incoming mail until Monday, March 7.

Berthold is twenty-three miles northwest of Minot.

It had a population of 431 in 1960.

Berthold was established in April 1900. It was a station on GN's mainline. The GN ran a branch line from here to Crosby. The name for Berthold came from Fort Berthold. That settlement was named after a fellow from St. Louis, Missouri, Bartholomew Berthold. He set up a trading post at that location in 1845.

Berthold was on the northern edge of the blizzard. For a while Thursday morning, blizzard conditions prevailed. However, by midday, the weather at Berthold had improved a lot. There still was drifting of snow, but visibility wasn't too bad. Berthold received one inch of snow, .06 inches of precipitation, that day.

Bismarck, Sterling, Sterling Corners, Driscoll, Wilton, Regan and Wing

Bismarck, North Dakota's state capital, hugs the east bank of the Missouri River.

In 1960, 27,670 people called Bismarck home.

The city of Bismarck began as a terminus for the NP. During the winter of 1871-1872, NP survey crews were working on the grade of the rail line east of the Missouri River. The first settlement at the terminus site was a supply depot and survey camp. That location was known as "The Crossing."

The staking of a townsite nearby came next in May 1872. Edwin F, Johnson, chief engineer of the NP, received the honor of having the townsite named after him. It was called Edwinton.

But the NP was experiencing financial problems. German bond holders of the NP helped to keep the rail line afloat. In appreciation for their efforts, NP officials changed the name of the townsite from Edwinton to Bismarck in honor of the "Iron Chancellor" of Germany, Otto von Bismarck (1815-1898). That name change occurred on July 17, 1873.

In succession, Bismarck became the seat of Burleigh County (1873), capital of Dakota Territory (1883) and the capital of North Dakota (1889).

Among the colorful characters who at one time or another lived in and around Bismarck were Grant Marsh, captain of the steamboat the *Far West*, Colonel Clement Lounsberry, editor of the *Bismarck Tribune*, and of course, George Armstrong Custer.

The March 1966 storm arrived in the Bismarck vicinity at 1:00 p.m. Wednesday. At that time, the thermometer read 29 above and the wind gusts reached 33 mph.

The situation became serious enough by Thursday morning that two of the Weather Bureau's personnel in Bismarck were unable to get to their post at the Bismarck Airport. Herbert Monson and Clarence Pruitt returned home, leaving their cars stuck in snowbanks.

L.R. (LeRoy) Nordahl, another Weather Bureau employee, was able to reach the airport at midnight Wednesday, March 2. Working by himself until 1 p.m. Thursday, Nordahl accomplished the job normally done by two people. He did this, in spite of heavy pressure from the public and news media clamoring for information. Nordahl, with the help of the janitors, launched and took a raob. He managed to do this, despite wind gusts close to 60 mph, zero visibility and driving snow.

One member of the news media Nordahl was in contact was the *Fargo Forum*. He told that newspaper that at that time (9 a.m. Thursday) visibility at the Bismarck Airport was zero and the winds were coming from the NNE at 38 to 60 mph. Gusts during the night had reached between 60 and 65 mph. But, at the same time, temperatures remained between 15 and 20 above. By 9 a.m. Bismarck had received 8 inches of new snow.

Nordahl reported the depth of snowbanks ranging from shoulder high at the airport to as much as 8 feet in other locales around Bismarck.

He mentioned the inability of anyone getting to the airport for work Thursday morning. Those who were there would have to remain there until snowplows cleared a path to the airport.

Nordahl said there were numerous automobiles stalled around Bismarck. The piling up of stalled vehicles in downtown Bismarck was preventing any traffic on those streets.

After many efforts, Herman G. Stommel, another Weather Bureau employee, was able to get the Sheriff to take Nordahl home. At the same time, the Sheriff brought Alan C. Hanson and Martin M. Baumann to the Airport as Mr. Nordahl's relief.

Hanson and Baumann worked continuously for thirty-three hours and never missed an observation. This included all raobs. One release was destroyed when the balloon landed in some wires.

The weary men were relieved by Nordahl and Pruitt at 5:00 p.m. Friday. Despite Stommel's efforts, he was unable to arrange transportation for Nordahl and Pruitt to the airport. So, they walked the entire distance from their homes to the airport, a remarkable feat.

At 10 p.m. Friday, Hanson and Baumann were able to return home, when a North Central Airlines employee drove them into Bismarck. They had to walk part way, when the car became stuck in a snowdrift.

Nordahl and Pruitt then stayed on the job nineteen hours, until Dan Meyers and Mr. Monson relieved them. By then, snowplows had opened a few roads.

During the storm, the forecasters and observers at the Bismarck Airport faced, both a lack of food and sleep. They received permission to pick the lock on the door of the restaurant at the airport, and thus solved their food problem.

But, the men couldn't get any rest. As a result, for several days, all were in poor physical condition. Stommel paid the restaurant bill which wholesale came to $2.10.

The *Bismarck Tribune* was founded in 1873. March 3, 1966, was the first time in memory for employees of Tribune that distribution of that newspaper was canceled. Papers were not delivered on Friday as well. While the *Tribune* itself was published, distribution of it for home delivery was stopped. Areas served by carriers included Bismarck and Mandan. By putting out a newspaper on March 3, 1966, the *Tribune* was continuing an amazing 93 year old record of never having failed to publish.

The blizzard on Thursday left Mrs. Gladys K. Toland, hostess at the Grand Pacific Hotel, with a much reduced staff. She lacked a dishwasher, but did have a cook and two waitresses on hand. This reduced food service to the counter and some tables in the back. Peering out at the empty, snow-swept Fourth Street, she said, "this is rough."

No relief had shown up at the Grand Pacific Hotel yet, as of mid-morning Thursday for Leonard Watson, the hotel auditor and night clerk. He had been on duty since midnight.

The Patterson Hotel became a home away from home for marooned basketball fans from Fort Yates, McClusky and Watford City.

Among the stranded visitors at the Prince Hotel was the Dickinson basketball team.

The storm brought about an increase of three to four times the normal load of telephone calls for the local Northwestern Bell Telephone Company office in Bismarck early Thursday morning. This overload resulted in a slow dial tone.

To handle this onslaught were twenty-six telephone operators. Quite a few of them had fought their way through humongous drifts to make it to work. On hand were night operators who stayed past their usual quitting time to assist with the deluge of phone calls. On a normal day, thirty-five girls worked at the telephone office.

For the most part, Northwestern Bell's telephone lines in the Bismarck area were coming through the blizzard in pretty good shape. They were encountering sporadic toll trouble, but nothing major.

The electrical utilities weren't running into any major problems on Thursday, either. According to Montana-Dakota Utilities Company in Bismarck (MDU), the west end of McKenzie had suffered a power interruption. The blizzard had caused short intermittent outages due to "bouncing and kicking" of power lines between Bismarck and Linton, and Bismarck and Beulah.

On the same day, Capital Electric wasn't reporting any problems anywhere.

Personnel at radio station KBOM, which was located between Bismarck and Mandan, were unable to make it through the deep snow to the station early Thursday. As a result the radio station was unable to make its 5 a.m. sign-on. This led to oversleeping by some Bismarck residents whose clock-radios were dialed to KBOM.

The blizzard kept local businesses and banks closed for the day in Bismarck. This proved to be an unpleasant surprise for those few hardy souls who didn't live far away and came to these places to transact business, only to have to turn around and go back home.

In Bismarck, no government offices were open on Thursday. This included city, county, state and federal offices.

Walter Krueger fed cattle on a ranch southwest of McKenzie, a small town eighteen miles east of Bismarck. On Thursday Mr. Krueger reported, *"we haven't even tried to feed today, we might if the wind goes down."*[143]

At their ranch south of Bismarck, Mrs. Gene McCormick reported that calves in a corral were being fed by their hired man. As for stock cows in a nearby coulee, they would have to fend for themselves.

The McCormicks had two children, Monte, 17, and Vicki, 16, who were students at St. Mary's High School in Bismarck. Wednesday evening, they attended the Class A basketball tournament in Mandan. Bad weather conditions forced the McCormick children to remain in Bismarck after the tournament.

Bismarck's fire trucks had chains on their tires for traction in the snow or on ice.

The headquarters for emergency calls in Bismarck were at the Bismarck police department. Working in conjunction with the police department were snowplows from the city street department, an auxiliary policeman's four-wheeled vehicle and a rescue truck from the fire department.

On Thursday morning, a convoy consisting of a snow blade equipped police jeep, the rescue truck and police patrol cars brought a heart attack victim and two pregnant women to local hospitals.

Their progress was blocked at one point, when they were all stuck in a humongous drift. But not for long. Snow graders helped to free them and get them moving again.

Meanwhile, Bismarck motorists were being asked to leave their automobiles at home by E. J. Booth, Bismarck city engineer.

The inclement weather didn't deter one Bismarck attorney, E. Forsyth Engebretson, from trudging through snowdrifts on foot to make it to work Thursday morning. About his effort Engebretson had this to say:

> I wouldn't have tried it if it had been colder. I'm not
> looking forward to going back against the north wind.[144]

One Bismarck television station made a few television viewers irate with its suggestion Thursday evening. It advised viewers to "Stay in where it's snug and warm and watch television." The blizzard had interrupted the station's network programming. So, instead of getting regular programs from the network, the local television station treated viewers to reruns.

There were people in Bismarck Thursday morning, who were not going to let a storm force them to stay at home. They even put a good face on it, exchanging cheerful greetings and pleasantries.

One bundled up individual encountered another person in the middle of a residential street in a track that was filling in quickly. About the track, the first person remarked, "It's not plugged, just a little crowded."[145]

To get Bismarck's water plant into operation, Harry Hanson, its superintendent, made his way on foot from his residence at 822 W. Ave. A to the water plant on River Road. Upon learning of this, E. J. Booth, Bismarck's City Engineer told Hanson not to leave the plant, that a plow would clear a path to him later.

To help snowplows in Bismarck that were involved with emergency runs maintain communications with others, radio trucks were pressed into service to work in tandem with the plows.

The blizzard forced the closing of schools in Bismarck on Thursday. Robert P. Miller, Bismarck superintendent of schools, had been with the local school system for twenty years. According to him, in all that time, weather had never been a factor in closing Bismarck schools. When it came to inclement weather, the school policy had always been to let parents decide whether their children should go to school or not. But the raging blizzard forced the schools to close their doors on Thursday. As Mr. Miller put it, "Even the teachers wouldn't be able to get there."[146]

From 4 p.m. Wednesday on, incoming calls concerning stranded cars flooded the state radio switchboard, according to Ralph Wood, North Dakota Highway Patrol Superintendent.

It wasn't easy going for state highway patrolmen either. One of them, Leonard R. Wentz, set out at 1 a.m. Thursday on U.S. Highway 10 from Sterling heading for Bismarck. Along the way, Mr. Wentz encountered such bad drifting on Highway 10, it took him three hours to complete the twenty-four mile journey.

For the first time that anyone could recall, Bismarck did not have mail carrier service on Thursday. There had been lousy weather other times, but the postman had always delivered the mail. This time it was different. As Bismarck Postmaster, H. D. Dunahy, put it, conditions outside were "impossible."

Because N.D. Governor William L. Guy was vacationing in Arizona during the storm, Lt. Governor Charles Tighe was in charge.

Dan Rassett in Bismarck Tribune parking lot during the blizzard. Courtesy of the Bismarck Tribune

Not many *Tribune* employees were on hand at 8 a.m. at the newspaper plant in downtown Bismarck. Most of those that did show up were people who resided close enough to the plant to able to walk to work. The best turn out of personnel, and a pretty good one at that, were the printers in the composing room.

It was downhill from there. Only six people showed up in the editorial department (usually staffed with eleven people) on Thursday, five on Friday. The business office had a couple of personnel on hand. As for the art, circulation, delivery and press departments? With no one around, they were dark and empty.

The distaff side had only four people on hand. They were Mrs. Louise Thompson, accounting, Mrs. Dora Sdcherger, advertising department, and in the proof room, a couple of emergency substitutes, the Misses Carolyn and Kathy Williams. These teenage proof readers had been pressed into service by their father, Composing Room Foreman, Frank Williams.

Only twenty-five percent of the *Tribune* employees made it to work Thursday. Despite this, they didn't miss any deadlines and were able to dispatch mail editions on schedule.

Even when the storm was at its worst on Thursday, the *Tribune* was delivered to hotels, motels and newsstands on Thursday in both Bismarck and Mandan. This amazing feat was accomplished through the assistance of the Bismarck Cycle Shop and the Broadway Skelly Service.

Employing a couple of Polaris snowmobiles, Tom Schofield, Circulation Manager of the *Tribune*, and the Bismarck Cycle Shop's manager, John Wolf, drove around the Bismarck area to deliver copies of the *Tribune* to people filled hotels and motels. Battling his way through four foot drifts most of the way, Charles Snyder drove a four-wheel drive Skelly service wagon to both the post office and the Northern Pacific Depot, in order to deliver mail edition copies of the *Tribune*.

Snyder was able to make it to Mandan also with final editions of the *Tribune*. On that trip, he was brought to a halt only once. The Northern Pacific Underpass on Memorial Highway was becoming plugged by snowdrifts. Becoming stuck in them, Mr. Snyder dug his way out and proceeded on his way.

On Friday, five people showed up for work in the *Tribune's* business office. Two individuals held down the fort in the advertising department.

Only half of the normal staff of thirty-two made it to work Friday to man the composing, mailing and press rooms and the stereotyping department.

To keep abreast of the breaking storm news, two Associated Press reporters remained at their post in their office Thursday night.

The continuation of the blizzard on Friday raised the concerns of Bismarck area ranchers about their cattle.

The atrocious weather hampered efforts by MDU line crews attempting to restore power east of Bismarck and at New Salem. Thursday night, they failed to reach New Salem in a power wagon.

To drive the fifteen miles from Bismarck east to McKenzie to restore electrical power there, took an MDU crews almost seven hours. Setting out at 9 a.m. Thursday, the MDU crew bucked through drifts until they reached McKenzie at 3:45 p.m.

Crews from MDU were being dispatched in pairs to handle the power outages. Unfortunately, what usually happened was that one of the trucks would stall out, thus forcing the crew to turn back. In the journey to McKenzie on Thursday, only one of the trucks reached its destination.

The terrible weather conditions on Thursday really interfered with *Tribune* Photographer Leo LaLonde's attempts to get some storm pictures. He was trudging through the elements along Fourth Street looking for such photos. But, the swirling snow made the job of keeping his camera lens free of snow just about impossible. As Mr. LaLonde reported, *"It was almost like being inside my wife's washing machine."*[147]

By 12:15 p.m. Thursday, the Weather Bureau station at the Bismarck Airport had received 11 inches of new snow.

The *Bismarck Tribune* was calling the blizzard the worst winter storm to hit North Dakota in almost fifty years. Wind gusts Thursday morning were reaching speeds up to 65 mph.

According to the Weather Bureau office in Bismarck, Thursday morning, the storm center was in a stationary position in central South Dakota. Then, it was expected to begin a slow northeastward movement. Eastern North Dakota was to be the recipient of additional amounts of fresh snow Thursday night. As for a let-up in the storm, the Bismarck weather office didn't see one until Friday morning at the earliest.

Around 9:30 a.m., the FAA tower at the Bismarck Airport received a radio call from a pilot. The pilot informed the tower that at 10,000 feet in the Bismarck he was flying in and out of the tops of the storm clouds.

To maintain essential services in Bismarck while the storm raged, emergency measures were instituted. People and places that needed essential items such as drugs, medical supplies and milk were getting them. There were those families whose small children depended on the nourishment of milk. On Thursday, policemen delivered quarts of milk to them.

A local dairy operation, Yegen's Dairy, didn't shut down during the blizzard. It kept its doors open. Local hospitals received milk supplies from there both on Thursday and Friday. On Friday, with their supply of all staples becoming depleted, local restaurants procured supplies of milk at Yegen's Dairy.

Reaction of Bismarck residents to the blizzard on Thursday varied.

The Jeimer Shjeflos were taking the whole thing in stride. As they reported, *"The house is warm; the freezer is full."*

The Charles Stephensons hadn't been living in Bismarck very long when the March 1966 blizzard arrived. But they were familiar with such storms. After residing in Turtle Lake for quite awhile, they had spent twenty-eight years in Minnesota. Mr. Stephenson remarked, *"We've experienced three-day blizzards like this one. I don't think this one will last that long."*

Coming from Massachusetts, snow wasn't anything new for Mrs. Irene Reynolds. But the combination of snow and high wind were a new experience for her. Residing only a couple of blocks from the grocery store made her happy. She laughingly remarked, *"I felt like an old horse plowing through the street to the store this morning."*

The music director at Standing Rock High School in Fort Yates was Mrs. Reynold's son, Jonathan. Along with eight of his band students he had been to a band clinic in Valley City. On their return Thursday, they had gotten as far as Bismarck before the elements forced them to halt. Although Mr. Reynolds had never experienced a North Dakota snowstorm before, he wasn't going to let it get him down. He remarked, *"I like it here in North Dakota."*[148] It wasn't snowing as much in Bismarck on Friday as it had been on Thursday. However, the winds hadn't subsided and blizzard conditions still existed.

A picture by *Tribune* Photographer Leo LaLonde in the March 4, 1966, edition of that newspaper shows Bismarck's Main Avenue, normally one of the busiest in that city, to be buried in snow and free of traffic.

St. Alexius Hospital in Bismarck received unexpected assistance from a pharmacist in a uniform during the snowstorm. That person was Robert Epstein, a navy lieutenant. His assignment was with the U. S. Public Health Service. In addition to that, Epstein served on the government hospital staff at Fort Yates.

Epstein and Ray Link, a St. Alexius pharmacist, had been at a conference in Iowa. A train brought them to Bismarck early Thursday morning.

Since lousy weather conditions prevented his return to Fort Yates, Epstein helped out at St. Alexius Hospital. His assistance was appreciated, as the blizzard had left the hospital without the services of one of their regular pharmacists.

Some Bismarck Junior College (BJC) students unable to make it home on account of the storm. Although they were stranded there on campus, the students took the blizzard in stride. This was due partly to the school's location on hills along the Missouri River. The high winds of the storm scoured any snow that fell at BJC completely away. So, there weren't any big drifts for the students to dig out of. In fact, the winds were strong enough to blow away gravel and pebbles that ordinarily accumulated on the parking lots' hard surface.

If it ever cleared off, utility crews were ready to go. As O. S. Soma, manager of Capital Electric Cooperative Incorporated put it Friday, *"We're all ready to go as soon as we get visibility."*[149]

Capital Electric had been having its problems with the weather too. Its line between McKenzie and Sterling had been off since around 3 p.m. Thursday. About fifteen customers were without power. According to Soma, individual places at Baldwin, Goodrich and on South Washington Street in Bismarck were encountering outages.

When it was finally over, Bismarck had received 22.4 inches of snow or 1.82 inches of precipitation. The storm had set a couple of records at Bismarck. The 15.5 inches of precipitation received from 1 p.m. Wednesday until 1 p.m. Thursday broke the 24 hour precipitation total that had been set in March 1950. The blizzard's total snowfall of 22.4 inches broke the 19.1 inches set from March 20-22, 1894.

From 1 p.m. Wednesday until around 2 a.m. Thursday, visibility in Bismarck remained at 1/16th of a mile or greater. From then until 1 p.m. Thursday, Bismarck had zero visibility. For the next thirty hour time span (1 p.m. Thursday until 7 p.m. Friday) visibility at the Weather Bureau station at the Bismarck Airport was never greater than 1/8th of a mile. For the majority of the time, it varied from zero to 1/16th of a mile visibility.

Highest wind speed recorded in Bismarck was a 65 mph gust on Thursday. Friday's highest reported gust was 59 mph.

The storm forced all Bismarck schools to close both Thursday and Friday. Students at Bismarck's public schools were looking forward to a spring vacation scheduled for Thursday and Friday March 10 and 11, 1966.

Unfortunately, the loss of class days the previous week forced School Superintendent Robert P. Miller to cancel the spring vacation on Monday March 7. According to state law, for schools to be able to obtain their allotment of state aid, their school year had to run for a full 180 days.

Thoughts were turning to the cleanup that would follow the storm. This is what City Engineer E. J. Booth had to say about it:

> As soon as the storm subsides we're going right to work on it but its going to be slow work. There's a lot of drifting. While some spots have blown clear most of the rest are plugged tight.[150]

It took an all-night effort by snow removal crews, but by Saturday morning Bismarck's airport was operational. Runways had been opened and a path cleared to the new terminal building. That building was completely surrounded by large snowbanks. To get equipment operators to the airport its manager, Raymond Heinemeyer, transported them aboard his own snowmobile. He didn't think there would be any delays in flights scheduled to arrive at Bismarck on Saturday.

As for clearing Bismarck's streets after such an intense storm, it was going to be a mammoth undertaking. Snow removal crews began the task at 2 a.m. Saturday.

It was estimated that the storm cost Bismarck retailers more than a half million dollars per day in lost business Thursday and Friday March 3 and 4, 1966. This included service stations. Even with service calls, service stations didn't make that much money. They had their fixed costs too. Also affected by the storm were dental and doctor appointments that had to be rescheduled.

The following account was written by Glenn Sorlie, publisher of the *Tribune* in March 1966. On Saturday morning, following the blizzard he flew over part of the storm affected area. The following is his description of some of the things he saw on his flight:

> Viewed from 300 feet in the air the rolling area west of Mandan didn't look much different than on any ordinary winter day as I flew with Jack

Operations Map showing location of North Dakota National Guard snow removal equipment around North Dakota, March 1966 North Dakota National Guard Headquarters, Bismarck.

North Dakota Adjutant General L. A. Melhouse on the phone, March 1966. Both photos courtesy of E.B.R. SC, UND

Hughes Junior High School in Bismarck, March 1966

Digging out automobile in Bismarck, March 1966. Both photos courtesy of the Bismarck Tribune

Snowblower in action in Bismarck on March 5, 1966. Courtesy of the Bismarck Tribune.

Watts of Capital Aviation in anattempt to get snowbound shots of the Northern Pacific's storm-bound Mainstreeter Saturday morning.

At least at first glance it didn't. Snow was only stubble deep in many larger fields and last fall's plowed furrows could easily be made out in others.

But a second look showed there's snow out there and plenty of it. Difficult as it is to judge from the air, there was no doubt about the extreme depths of drifts on leeward sides of hills and the huge banks drifting completely across cuts and draws on country roads and highways.

We watched a Northern Pacific work train heading out of Mandan as it churned into drifts covering the tracks about five miles west of the city. The plow-mounted engine and three cars of the train completely disappeared in a towering cloud of snow as it tore into the drift. Another five miles down the track, drifts which appeared to be from four to six feet deep coverd the right-of-way in block long sections. We didn't wait to see whether the plow made it through or not.

A mile east of Judson, an NP engine and heating car sprawled at an angle along one side of the track, completely immobilized. Several small figures wandered apparently looking the situation over but making no progress. The units were derailed Thursday when they went to the aid of the Mainstreeter west of New Salem.

Judson itself looked completely socked in, though plows and shovelers were busily clearing the streets and shoveling out walk ways.

Looking east down Avenue B in Bismarck on March 5, 1966. Courtesy of the Bismarck Tribune

Snow removal on U.S. Highway 83 in Bismarck on March 7, 1966. Both photos courtesy of NDDOT

Snow removal on Boulevard in front of Capitol Building in Bismarck on March 7, 1966

Snow removal on Broadway by Fleck's in Bismarck on March 7, 1966. Both photos courtesy of the Bismarck Tribune

A mile or so west of New Salem we got our first look at the bogged down train.

The engineer had reported Friday that snow was drifting up to the door of his cab. The drift had grown by Saturday to a point where only the front half of the engine poked its nose out of the towering snowbanks. Snow was at roof level along almost the entire length of the north side of the train and it was almost impossible to determine where one car started and the other left off. Efforts were being made to dig out, but it didn't appear as if much progress was being made.

Flying north towards Stanton from New Salem the snow cover seemed to diminish somewhat, though cuts and draws were leveled with drifts. Livestock were evident at farms throughout the area, huddled around shelters and feeding areas.

Highways and country roads appeared remarkably clear in most areas, though at intervals towering drifts blocked the roadways, making travel nearly impossible. An occasional stalled car indicated an attempt had been made to get to town or another farm but with no success.[151]

After the blizzard, Attorney Fred Saefke used his Jeep to get around Bismarck. The vehicle's horn had been inoperable for months while Mr. Saefke waited for parts to come.

Unfortunately, while he was motoring through Bismarck's business district, the Jeep's horn suddenly began to blare nonstop.

In the meantime, Mr. Saefke's attempts to silence the horn were failing. As a last resort he unhooked the wires. Quiet now prevailed.

As to why the Jeep's horn had started to blow, Mr. Saefke was of the opinion that it was due to a short circuit. He thought snow packed around the Jeep's engine caused a faulty connection to become wet sufficiently to induce a short circuit. This in turn activated the horn.

By Monday morning March 7, 1966, utility service was pretty much back to normal in the Bismarck vicinity. Using a line from today's computer age, public utilities in Bismarck's neck of the woods were back "online."

In March 1966, Ed Yelick was the manager of the local Northwestern Bell Telephone Company office in Bismarck. On Monday March 7 he said, *"We are in excellent shape and didn't really have too much trouble."*[152]

While overloaded circuits were the telephone company's biggest problem during and after the storm, by Monday normal operating conditions had returned.

On that day, a large volume of calls kept long distance circuits humming. But Mr. Yelick didn't think they would overload the circuits. That would call for a voluntary ceasing of nonessential calls.

It was estimated that Capital Electric Cooperative had thirty-five outages during the blizzard. The greatest number of outages for Capital Electric, a total of twenty-two, occurred in the McKenzie-Sterling vicinity.

MDU also endured power outages in the storm.

Suffering power outages for several hours in the blizzard were Carson, Heil, Leith, and New Salem.

By Monday, March 7 power had been restored to the vast majority of Capital Electric's and MDU's customers.

The primary task of the Burleigh County Red Cross during the blizzard consisted mainly of assisting servicemen in their efforts to notify their bases of their inability to return there on time.

The aftermath of the March 1966 blizzard was a busy time for pilots.

A joint mercy and rescue operation effort was put forth by wardens from the North Dakota Game and Fish Department and U. S. Air Force helicopter pilots once the storm had passed by.

Around twenty-three sick or marooned people were assisted in this joint operation. The six pilots, five game wardens and Air force crew chiefs logged over twenty-five hours in the air in carrying out their missions.

Donald Mushik, North Dakota state civil defense director made the following remarks about their efforts:

> These Air Force pilots, crew chiefs and game wardens have done a great service to the people of North Dakota. They are no doubt responsible for saving at least a score of lives.[153]

There were other aircraft flying mercy and rescue missions after the storm. On March 5 and 6, a Civil Air Patrol (CAP) unit from Williston were in the air south and east of Bismarck. Major Vern Baltzer, district CAP commander, provided the following statistic for that unit. The airtime for the twenty-six sorties they flew on those two days came to thirty-five hours and eighteen minutes.

People's concerns about loved ones during and after the blizzard was reflected in the volume of civil defense and law enforcement radio traffic. All such traffic in North Dakota is managed by the state radio communication system, headquartered at Bismarck Municipal Airport.

Usually, a month's worth of radio messages for the system comes to about 16,000 messages. On March 2, before North Dakota was enveloped by the *"Blizzard of the Century"*, four operators at the airport handled 500 messages.

But the snowstorm changed that. By the time Monday morning rolled around, the operators had processed 16,777 messages. In that short span, the operators had taken care of as many messages as they normally handled in one month.

In late March, cattle losses for Burleigh County came in at 2,000 head. There were no figures for other livestock losses.[154]

In 1960, Sterling had 50 residents.

The NP constructed a station here in 1873. They gave it the name of Sixteenth Siding. When the first settlers came around 1880, the place was called Ballville. The settlement was renamed Sterling in 1882 after Sterling, Illinois.

In March 1966, Sterling Corners was a business complex located at the junction of U. S. Highways 10 and 83. It consisted of a bar, cafe, motel and service station. The village of Sterling is only a short distance south of Sterling Corners. Although Interstate 94 was under construction in 1966, there was not a completed section of it in the Sterling area.

Sterling Corners became the refuge for many travelers during the storm. It was during the day on Wednesday, when most of them showed up there. Around forty travelers filled up the eighteen unit motel. Resting on the floor in sleeping bags became an option for some; others were taken in at the few nearby homes.

How were the marooned travelers getting along and passing the time? This is what Steve Singelton, 25, of Portland, Oregon, had to say about it:

> We're just great, everybody's making the best of it. We play cards, talk with one another about the world situation and watch television.

Among those holing up at Sterling Corners was Ray Streeter, a newsman for station WMAD in Madison, Wisconsin. In a phone interview with the *Bismarck Tribune*, Streeter

J. C. Pfeiffer farm near Menoken on March 22, 1966. Courtesy of Bismarck Tribune

Along U.S. Highway 10 after the March 1966 blizzard. Courtesy of North Dakota State Historical Society

reported that everyone was being well provided for. He was happy that the bar hadn't closed because of the blizzard. Mr. Streeter was westbound, when the storm caught up with him.

The food situation at Sterling Corners wasn't much of a problem. As Mr. Wolt, the Tops Cafe operator reported:

> I've got enough food to hold out for two weeks. As long as the power holds out, we'll be fine. . . There are some places in the state where the power is out, and we'd be in rough shape if it happened here. There was a little resentment among them (travelers) when they first arrived. But as time has gone by, they realize how lucky they are in being here.

Among the vehicles stranded at Sterling Corners were a bus with seventeen passengers (including a lady with a sick child) a dozen automobiles, and about ten trucks. Among the latter were some trucks filled with cattle and hogs. Buried in snowbanks the cars and trucks surrounded the business complex.

All together over 120 people were marooned at Sterling Corners by the blizzard. Singing the praises of the people who helped them and worked there or who lived nearby was Nick Mann of South Beloit, Illinois. This is what he had to say:

> There's probably a lot of unsung heroes all over this state, but these people here are indispensable. These people are a godsend. They're going out of their way to feed us and keep us comfortable and they're even charging us less than normal and giving the food away to those who can't pay.

Not content just to be waited on, Nick Mann and his wife assisted in the cafe. The place was receiving a lot of incoming phone calls to the cafe. The Manns would help out by answering these calls.

They also waited on tables. Nick Mann gave this report:

> There's plenty of room for everyone. There's counter stools, booths, and plenty of chairs to sit on. The people sort of come in shifts for their meals. We're sort of like one big happy family here.

Mann went on to say that the enclave at Sterling Corners were "praying the power stays on."

In reporting the camaraderie of the group, Mann gave the following example:

> A truck driver gave up his motel room for a poorer sleeping spot. That's an indication how we're getting along.

The atrocious weather conditions at Sterling Corners did have a few North Dakota natives worried. Despite this, one of them, James Hugelen (who ran the Tops Motel), was of the opinion that things were "going quite well for all of us." About the storm he had this to say:

> I've lived in North Dakota all my life and I know what these things are like. But this is one of the worst I've ever seen.

Echoing a similar refrain was the operator of the Sterling Corner bar and cafe, Mrs. Lorraine Severson:

> I can't even see across the highway. I haven't been to my bar and cafe since yesterday. It's only 30 feet from my house but drifts have blocked our house doorway and the back door of the bar is completely covered.
>
> It's just myself and two daughters. There's no particular hardship because we're warm and have food, but it certainly is nerve wracking.

Mrs. Harley Albaugh lived in a house on the other side of U. S. 10. She reported that almost all the windows on her house being covered by snowdrifts. Also, enveloped and blocked by snowdrifts was the door to her house. This is what she had to say about her situation:

> My husband's in Fargo and I'm alone, and I don't mind admitting I'm a little scared. I have to get water outside and there's only about two cups left in here.

The majority of stranded travelers were holed up on the other side of U. S. 10 where the bar and cafe were located. The managers of the Tops Cafe and Motel, the James Hugelens and the Albert Wolts, were former Napoleon residents.

Probably summing up the feelings of everyone affected by the blizzard was the heretofore mentioned Nick Mann. As a traveling salesman, Mr. Mann was well aware of the hazards of bad weather. Of others marooned by the storm he remarked, *"We can only hope others who are stranded are as fortunate as we are."*[155]

Driscoll, another NP town, was founded in 1883. It was named for Frederick Driscoll, manger of the *St. Paul Pioneer Press*, the official newspaper of the NP. Era Bell Thompson, a member of one of North Dakota's few pioneer black families, lived here as a child. At one time Thompson was editor of *Ebony* magazine. In 1960, the town had a population of 150.

A sad discovery in the Driscoll vicinity, a town seven miles east of Sterling, was made by a 12-year-old boy on Sunday morning. When he observed a lack of smoke emanating from his neighbor's house, Orien Aucks became concerned about the welfare of 73 year-old Lowell Brown, a Driscoll farmer who lived alone. Auck's son went over to the Brown farm to check on Mr. Brown. The boy found Brown's frozen body with one arm draped over a windmill brace. The time of Brown's death was unknown.

Oliver Knutson farm north of Driscoll on March 9, 1966. Photo by Harley Hettick Courtesy of E.B.R. SC, UND

Oliver Knutson farm north of Driscoll on March 9, 1966. Photos by Harley Hettick Courtesy of E. B. R. SC, UND

Russell Quale farm north of
Driscoll, March 1966.
Both photos by Harley Hettick
Courtesy of E.B. R. SC, UND

Wilton, established in 1899, is different than most North Dakota cities and towns in that it lies in two counties–Burleigh and McLean.(It is considered a McLean County town.) The man responsible for establishing Wilton was General William Drew Washburn, a Minneapolis flour mill industrialist. A one-time U. S. Senator from Minnesota, General Washburn bought 113,000 of NP land in 1898. He was the first president of the Minneapolis, Sault Ste. Marie and Atlantic, better known as the Soo. Washburn named the town after his birthplace, Wilton, Maine.

Wilton was home for 739 residents in 1960.

On Wednesday night, March 2, 1966, Wilton was in the direct path of the storm. Returning from McClusky, basketball fans stopped in Wilton that evening. Wilton residents gave shelter to these stranded travelers.

It took quick action by some men to save the lives of a Wilton couple, Mr. and Mrs. Peter Leif. On Friday, Mrs. Leif became sick. In an effort to get help, Mr. Leif phoned Marvin Johnson, a Wilton druggist, and provided him with a description of her symptoms. After hanging up, Mr. Johnson phoned the Leif's next-door neighbors, Mr. and Mrs. Charles Cowles. Johnson asked them to check on Mr. and Mrs. Leif.

When they reached the Leif's residence, the place was full of gas fumes. After bundling Mrs. Leif up, they picked her up and brought her out onto the porch. To provide the place with fresh air, the Cowles opened the doors and windows.

Needing assistance, Mr. Cowles then phoned William Kilian. Despite the lousy weather it only took approximately fifteen minutes for Mr. Kilian, Bob, Binsfeld, and Mike Hahnzak to reach the Leif home. Trudging through snowbanks they carried Mrs. Leif over to the Cowles residence. As he was in a little better shape than his wife, Mr. Leif, with assistance was able to make the journey to the Cowles home on foot.

Once again, they placed a call to Marvin Johnson. He and Bob Laughlin then brought oxygen to the Cowles residence which was then given to Mrs. Leif. On Saturday, after the gas leak in their water heater had been fixed, the Leifs returned to their home.

A large snowbank in front of Speten's Fairway store in Wilton made entering the store quite a challenge. The situation was alleviated when a tunnel was dug through the drift.

Oliver Borlaug, editor and publisher of the *Washburn Leader* wrote:

Looking Back at the Storm: We Need Our Small Communities!

One of our correspondents for the Wilton News, *Mrs Andrew Luiska, in commenting last week on the Great Blizzard of '66, made a comment worth noting.*

The contribution of the small town merchant to his territory was proved quite well when in spite of storm he made deliveries or at least came down to open the store for the convenience of patrons.

Mrs. Luiska pointed out that if there had been no local merchant, a trip to the city would have been necessary but also difficult, perhaps impossible.

The small town and its merchants are a very necessary party of life in rural America. We need them. We also need to recognize we have a responsibility in supporting them; that the part they play in supporting our community affairs and institutions entitles them to exist and to deserve your trade.

It would have been a sad day if there had been no small town a week or so ago. Besides groceries, we needed fuel oil, service for motor vehicles, drugs, hardware items, service at bank and post office; in fact, as folks dug out after the storm, they found out how valuable was their Main Street.

Your merchants recognized and accepted their responsibility. Our obligation in return is to support them![156]

At the district 27 basketball tournament in Washburn on March 7, the Wilton Miners defeated the Turtle Lake Trojans, 64 to 58. The Miners finished in third place.

Regan was founded in 1911. This NP town was named for a man who resided in Fessenden, J. Austin Regan. He was employed by the Dakota Land and Townsite Co., the firm that founded Regan. That year, the NP finished its rail line from Pingree to Wilton.

Regan supported a population of 104 in 1960.

The Regan area was really buried by the snow from the March 1966 blizzard. As one resident from the Regan vicinity, Mrs. Joe Wold, put it, *"The blizzard itself was a fearsome thing, and living through it was an experience no one will ever forget."*

She was especially appreciative of the service that radio stations provided during the storm. Mrs. Wold said:

The 24-hour radio broadcasts were a wonderful help, and the station staffs deserve a big thank you. Without their news, public service announcements, (and even their music), the long hours would have seemed even more endless.[157]

There were no power outages. Most of the phones worked, as the storm raged.

A bout with pneumonia required that a snowplow be dispatched to Dick Rasmussen's farm to clear the road, so Mr. Rasmussen could be taken to the hospital. Other Regan area residents who were sick were Maretta Engelbretson and Herb Folmer, both hospitalized in Bismarck.

The Regan vicinity came through the blizzard without serious livestock losses. This didn't mean that ranchers didn't have some anxious moments. It took a lot of shoveling, by a lot of people over the course of days, to save the roof of Porter Nelson's barn. A tremendous quantity of snow blew into Glenn Bauer's pole barn that opened to the south. Inspection of it Saturday morning, revealed the cattle and sheep inside of it to be standing up against the rafters. Their backs faced the rafters. As the snow fell, the animals tramped it and rose accordingly.

On the first night of the storm, a few of Willard Backman's cattle skedaddled. On Saturday, Don Ghylin used his snowmobile to round them up. Some of the cattle came through the blizzard in poor shape. Ice and snow driven into the hair on the animal's hides left the hides raw. To allow their stock to breathe, a few ranchers were forced to remove the caked snow and ice from their faces.

At the Lundberg ranch, Everett Dunbar employed a saddle horse for pulling cows from snowbanks. Exit from a straw barn for twenty-three calves at the Lundberg ranch was through the roof. Mrs. Dunbar related this story, *"When we looked out Saturday morning we saw balls of snow everywhere and each ball was a cow that was covered over."*[158]

Mrs. Joe Wold said that her backyard had the appearance of a "real Matterhorn." Windows became an exit for some Regan area families. The Boyd Hedstroms tried a different tack. They kept shoveling snow back into their home until they had carved a small tunnel through the drift which prevented exit via that door.

Wing, 303 residents in 1960, was platted by the Dakota Townsite Company of Carrington, North Dakota. This NP townsite honors a partner of the previously named firm, Charles Kleber Wing. This Vermont native arrived in North Dakota in 1881. Townsites that he laid out include McClusky, Pingree, Regan, Robinson, and Wing.

One motorist was stranded between Regan and Wing for the duration of the storm in his automobile. On Saturday morning, the motorist, Gordon Magnuson, set out for Wing on foot. The result of this trek was frost-bitten feet for Mr. Magnuson.

The blizzard proved to be a trying experience for Ray Moos who had a farming operation north of Wing. His wife was a patient at a hospital in Bismarck. Mr. Moos left his young daughter at the hospital there. On March 2, he was returning to his farm from Bismarck. Due to the blizzard, Mr. Moos was able to get only as far as Regan. The George Schilling home in Regan became Ray Moos's refuge for the remainder of the storm. Fortunately, his other children weren't stuck at the farm by themselves. Staying with them was a Bismarck friend, Ray Hoffman.

Steele, Jamestown, Cleveland, Buchanan, Edmunds, Woolworth, Medina, Streeter, Ypsilanti and Montpelier

The development of the settlement at Steele was started by Colonel Wilbur Fisk Steele (1844-1917) from New York in 1880. He platted the townsite and named it after himself in the fall of 1881.

The NP Railroad went through here in 1872. Steele made a bid for the capital of Dakota Territory in 1883, but Bismarck won that political battle. What would have been the territorial capital became the county court house. Steele paid for the building of it.

In 1960, Steele, the seat of Kidder County, had 847 residents.

The March 1966 snow storm was one for the record books at Steele. The local paper, the *Steele Ozone-Press*, described it thus:

> *Kidder County residents were still digging out here on Wednesday (March 9, 1966) from the worst blizzard the county has seen in years. the storm is said to be worse than the great blizzard of 1888 and may go down in history as the 'granddaddy' of them all.*[159]

Light snow accompanied by some wind began falling in Steele at noon Wednesday, March 2. Intensifying that evening, the storm reached blizzard proportions by the next morning. Before the storm brought cooler temperatures the high that day was 32.

Just as the storm was descending on Kidder County, the District 18 basketball tournament was taking place at Tuttle. On Wednesday afternoon, Steele emerged victorious from its game with Pettibone by a score of 77 to 43. Hurdsfield defeated Woodworth in the other game. The rest of the tournament was postponed until the following Tuesday.

Steele had two lodging facilities, the OK Motel and the Woodlawn Hotel. Mr. and Mrs. Otto Kuss, operators of the OK Motel, had ten cars and one government truck buried in the snow there. While some of the stranded motorists were fed by Mrs. Kuss, others were received their food through grocery deliveries made by the Kusses to their cabins. The last vehicle was dug out on March 7.

After the Woodlawn Hotel was full, Mr. and Mrs. William Smith, proprietors, made telephone calls to private residences in Steele to inquiry if stranded travelers could take shelter there. They were successful. Ironically, one of the marooned travellers at the Woodlawn Hotel was a Grand Forks man who was stuck at the same hotel twenty-five years before, during the March 15, 1941, storm.

A local physician, Dr. Anthony Zukowsky, made a couple of house calls as the blizzard raged. In one case, he provided assistance to a very sick lady. The other situation involved a person with a severe nose bleed. Dr. Zukowsky also imparted quite a bit of medical advise over the phone during the storm.

Steele recorded a whopping 28 inches of snow, 1.10 inches of precipitation, during the blizzard which ended Saturday afternoon.

Members of the Kidder County Sheriff's office were very busy. They directed traffic at Dawson. A snow cut, close to the Allen Thorsness farm, required their assistance in getting stalled cars through it. The Sheriff's office provided assistance at the Peter Glatt and Arlo Nafus farms. In two separate trips, they delivered milk to the George Kraus farm. Val Rohrich was brought to the hospital by Kidder County Sheriff Willard Rawson and Deputy Cliff Nitschke. Curtis Mayphew took Joel Erickson to the hospital, after the Sheriff's office provided help in getting him to the means of transportation.

One Steele family would never forget the March 1966 storm. Mr. and Mrs. Clarence Boschee and their five children resided in a trailer at the west end of Steele. Mr. Boschee was employed by the Wallin Motor Company. On Thursday night, their oil heater exploded. The Boschee family left quickly–there was no time to save anything but the clothes they had on.

Inclement weather prevented the local fire department from saving the trailer. Afterwards, Mr. Boschee and his family stayed at his brother LeRoy's place.

In March 1966, Miles Nelson lived with his family in Steele. On the day the storm hit Steele, Miles was walking home from school. The school was located at the south end of town, and the Nelson home was on the other end of Steele. Miles indicated that visibility was close to zero on his way home, but he made it.

Evacuation of George L. Jackson by helicopter to a hospital in Bismarck from his farm fifteen miles southwest of Dawson. He had sufferd a heart attack, March 1966. Courtesy of Bismarck Tribune

Tuttle area, March 1966. Photo courtesy of E.B.R. SC, UND

The storm had left a drift so high at their house they could climb out on their roof from it. The Nelson's garage was located thirty to forty yards from their house. To reach it, Miles dug a tunnel six feet high through the snow.[160]

On Saturday, the cleanup process was quickly undertaken at Steele. Except from the east all highways coming into Steele were opened on Saturday. It would be Sunday before they were made passable.

Efforts were underway Saturday afternoon in Kidder County to assist farmers and others by opening roads with county plows and equipment. The around-the-clock operation continued through Sunday. Dire situations had top priority. For example, the Herman Mauer farm was out of feed, food, and fuel.

On Sunday, the urgency of the situation led BEK Telephone to ask its patrons to refrain from using their telephones except for emergencies. Compliance with this request would allow telephones to be utilized to direct snow removal operations over the affected area.

Steele received mail again on Sunday afternoon.

For most of the blizzard, Steele did not experience any loss of power. Around 1:30 a.m. Saturday that changed, when a power outage occurred. The source of the outage was between Steele and Driscoll, a town eighteen miles to the west.

To fix the problem, early Saturday, Emil Hockhalter, the local MDU manager was called into action. To restore electricity to Steele, Mr. Hockhalter along with Paul Ritchie and Ed Humann headed north to the vicinity of the Alfred Potts farm. Throwing switches there would bring power from the east through Napoleon.

Just which switch to throw was critical to the whole operation. This was accomplished by having Ed Humann use a Walkie Talkie to stay in touch with his wife. In turn, she communicated with MDU personnel in Bismarck via the phone. This method of communications allowed Mr. Hochhalter to throw the proper switches.

Another hero of this operation was the MDU manager at Napoleon, a town over twenty-five miles southeast of Steele. It was his job to re-direct the power to Steele. Despite the fact of the switch panel being located in Napoleon, he was taking no chances. After tieing ropes to each other, the MDU manager and another man headed out in the storm for the switch panel. By throwing the switch there, power was rerouted north and west to Steele. By 7 a.m. power was back on in Steele.

The line between Driscoll and Steele was repaired by MDU crews from Bismarck Saturday morning.

Later that morning, Ed Humann returned to the switch site by the Potts farm. To get there, he used his 4-wheel drive pickup. Mr. Humann's route took him between the NP track and the elevators to the west edge of Steele. He went by the Skelly gas station and down the highway to the Potts farm. As a footnote to history, Mr. Humann's pickup was the first motor vehicle to depart from Steele since the arrival of the blizzard on Wednesday afternoon.

A barn collapsed at the Andy Engelhardt farm north of Steele. They were able to retrieve only two head of cattle from the barn. The Engelhardt home was so enveloped by snowdrifts above it, the family was fearful the weight of the snow would make the house collapse. To leave the house, the Engelhardts had to use a window as a means of departure. Then, to get back into their home, they had to dig a tunnel. The height of the drifts exceed that of power lines at their place. To top it off, Mr. Engelhardt who had been hospitalized for about a week in Jamestown had just come home on Wednesday, March 2.

Storm related livestock losses in Kidder County were heavy. At the end of March, cattle losses for the county totaled 1,200 head.

After the storm Kidder County Extension Agent Phil Park issued a warning to farmers about removing snow from grain bins. The wind driven snow had made it into nooks and crannies of grain bins, places where it had never been before. Farmers needed to remove the snow, or the grain would be contaminated.

In 1871, engineers and surveyors for the NP directed the laying of tracks west of Fargo across the prairie. They went into winter quarters along the James River.

To protect them, on November 26, 1871, Lieutenant Stafford of the U.S. Army set up a camp at the base of a bluff on the west side of the James River. This place would, in turn, be called Camp Sykes, Camp Thomas, and Fort Cross in the following months. The death of United States Senator, William H. Seward of New York in October 1872 prompted the last change in names. On November 9, 1872, the site became Fort Seward. Although he served as Secretary of State in President Lincoln's cabinet, Seward is better known for having bought Alaska from Russia in 1867. The Fort Seward State Historical Site is located one-half mile northwest of downtown Jamestown.

The year 1872 was a busy one, a tent city sprang up on the west side of the river. However, a population shift was about to occur. That fall, the NP established a depot on the east side of the James River. This forced the majority of the businesses to relocate to the east side of the river.

The man who gave the station the name "Jamestown" was General Thomas Lafayette Rosser, the lead engineer on the project for the railroad. Rosser was a classmate and friend of George Custer at West Point. With the commencement of the Civil War, Rosser joined the Confederate side. Their units met on the battlefield. They renewed their acquaintance in 1873, along the Yellowstone River in Montana. The location of Jamestown reminded Rosser of his hometown, that one was nestled along a river in Virginia.

The Northern Pacific Depot at Jamestown was built in 1917, that landmark building was torn down in December 1981.

In 1960, Jamestown had a population of 15,163 people. Louis L'Amour and Lois Phillips Hudson, acclaimed writers, were from Jamestown. Peggy Lee, a famous blues singer, and H. E. White, drugstore chain founder, also had roots to the city. Darin Erstad, pro baseball player for the California Angels, grew up here. Erstad helped the Angels win the World Series in 2002.

At the time of the March 1966 storm, Interstate 94 was completed through Jamestown.

March 3, 1966
Jamestown Sun
From AP Dispatches:

Winter dealt North Dakota a low card from the bottom of the deck as the worst storm of the season engulfed two-thirds of the state today.

Heavy snow that moved into the southern portions of the state Wednesday afternoon had changed to freezing rain in the southeastern corner early this morning.

The blizzard struck North Dakota from the south about noon Wednesday. Snowdrifts ranged up to 12 inches by 6 a.m. today, and snow was continuing to fall.

Jamestown reported 12 inches of new snow.[161]

Ralph Wood in Bismarck, North Dakota Highway Patrol Superintendent, said the state radio switchboard was jammed at four o'clock Wednesday afternoon with calls of stranded autos. Wood reported that highway patrols had rescued a dozen individuals Wednesday evening between Jamestown and Valley City.

The reading at the FAA Airport showed that Jamestown had a high of 24 degrees on Thursday. Winds in the vicinity of Jamestown were 55 mph.

Traffic and almost all business came to a halt. Main streets were blanketed with several feet of snow. Drifts on sidewalks in front of some business places were 5 feet high. It was said, "Cars stuck in mid-street were a common sight throughout the city."

Local police claimed roads leading into and out of Jamestown were completely clogged, with even the most heavy vehicles having an extremely difficult time negotiating Interstate 94.

Most of Jamestown's street maintenance crews were on standby. Those that worked concentrated their efforts on the vital facilities of the city.

All schools, including Jamestown College, and public buildings were closed.

The *Jamestown Sun* published its paper on Thursday, but it was not delivered to its subscribers. Since 1925, the inability to deliver the paper had occurred only twice.

Medina, a community of 500 people, lost its power early in the storm. On Thursday two Otter Tail employees, Richard Freeberg and Lyle Sjostrom left Jamestown at 6:00 in the morning. It took the men four and one-half hours to travel the thirty miles to Medina. They patrolled the area on foot, looking for the break. The snow blasted their faces and froze their eyes shut. Finally, they located the break and fixed it. Power was restored to Medina at 2:45 p.m. Thursday

On Friday, the storm entered its third day and was more violent than ever. Jamestown had a high of 14, Thursday's night low was 10 above. Another 7 inches of snow fell in Jamestown. Winds gusts reached 63 mph.

The *Jamestown Sun* composed Friday's paper, but left it on the press. Like the day before, weather conditions prevented the delivery of the papers.

Early Friday morning, the NP passenger train, *North Coast Limited* became stuck west of Jamestown. The westbound train left Jamestown about 3:30 a.m. Nine coaches, with about 140 travelers, were pulled back to Jamestown. They were housed in coaches near the NP depot and fed in a dining car and in the Northern Pacific Depot Steakhouse. The cars had steam heat.

Sunday afternoon, the snowbound passengers watched the Jamestown College musical *H.M.S. Pinafore.* They were given complimentary tickets to the performance. Later that day, the passengers were bused to Mandan, so they could make connections on a westbound train.

Jamestown Hospital Administrator, Emil Wieland, faced a serious problem. A newborn baby at the hospital needed a blood transfusion. Time was short. The right kind of blood was not available in Jamestown, so Weiland made arrangements with a blood bank in Fargo. The precious cargo was put aboard a westbound train, but it stalled thirty miles east of Jamestown in heavy snowdrifts.

Hospital personnel reviewed past records of blood donors. They came up with two qualified local donors, their research took them all the way back to 1957. D.O. Nelson agreed to give blood, but he was snowbound.

Hospital officals contacted Otter Tail Power Company and the utility dispatched a four-wheel drive truck to Nelson's home on Thursday. With Nelson aboard, they picked up Dr. James Miles, a pediatrician, on the way back to the hospital.

Weiland reported the transfusion was performed in time, but additional blood transfusions were needed in the following days. On Saturday, Fred Steffen, the other local blood donor match, came to the hospital. On Sunday, blood from the Fargo blood bank arrived in town. On Monday, the patient was "coming along fine."

During the blizzard, the Jamestown Hospital was the lone hospital for the city. On March 1, Trinity Hospital closed its doors. Its patients and some personnel were shifted to the Jamestown Hospital. Four Otter Tail Power Company employees, Jerry Martens, Wes Lee, Bill Trautman, and Wilber Wahl transported many hospital workers in the company's big four-wheel drive truck and pickup. Some medical personnel worked multiple shifts and stayed at the hospital for the duration of the storm. The hospital was so crowded that a cot was set up in one of the men's rest rooms.

On Saturday morning, the skies began to clear. The high was 14 degrees. Another 3 inches of snow fell, .28 inches of precipitation. Overall, Jamestown received a total of 23 inches of snow.

On Saturday, the *Jamestown Sun* was a combination of Thursday's, Friday's and Saturday editions, printed as one. Ron Arness, circulation manager, indicated some carriers would be out Saturday afternoon. Other routes would be attempted on Sunday.

Two Midland Continental Railroad trainmen from Jamestown were stranded in a caboose during the storm. Sam Lowe wrote the following article for the *Jamestown Sun*:

Deck of Homemade Cards, Phone
Were Only Companions For 2 'Rails'

We just sat and looked, watched the snow swirl by, and worried about the people trying to rescue us."

Those were the words of Harry Anderson, a Midland Continental Railroad conductor who sat out last week's storm in a caboose near Nortonville, ND.

Anderson and crewman, Jack Docktor were trapped in the caboose with no food or water for nearly 60 hours before they made a break for it about Saturday.

They became confined at about 11:30 Wednesday night when seven-unit Midland run on which they were riding became stalled. Anderson and Docktor were in the caboose with five cars separating them from the engine.

"We heard the engine whistling for us to come up, and we tried to make it, but just couldn't." Anderson said, "We got out of the caboose and tried one side, but we couldn't breathe. We tried the other side, but saw a snowbank which was up to the top of the boxcars, so we just went back."

The two found out later that fireman Melvin Clemens had tried to get back to the caboose from the engine, but likewise had to turn back. The diesel continued whistling for a while, then cut loose and headed for Jamestown. They stopped at Millarton and called Midland president W. A. Taft for instructions. Taft told them to return to Jamestown so rescue operations could be mapped.

Anderson rigged up a telephone in the meantime, and got contact with the Milwaukee Line depot at Edgeley and made some contact with the Soo Line at Wimbledon. "We heard about the people trying to get to us, and mostly we worried about them. We weren't too worried about ourselves. We weren't about to die out there," Anderson said.

The two had about four tablespoons of sugar in the caboose, but were saving that so they could make some sugar water "in case things really got tough."

Docktor fashioned a deck of cards from some cardboard in the caboose, a project which took about two hours and gave the pair some recreation while they waited.

Finally, on Saturday morning, help arrived–but not much. Arion Rott, Nortonville, started out on a rescue mission with digging out equipment, but that broke down enroute. Rott decided to go the rest of the way on foot, and arrived in the caboose at midmorning.

The three then felt that the storm was getting worse, but decided to make a break for it anyway. They left the caboose and headed for the Aaron Weixel farm, arriving there about noon.

Mrs. Weixel had dinner ready and Anderson and Docktor had their first hot meal since Wednesday.

Looking back, Anderson was full of thanks particularly for "those people in Nortonville who worried so much about us and who tried to get us out.[162]

Jamestown experienced a couple of minor power outages. Otter Tail Power Company personnel had power restored within the hour.

Local manager for Northwestern Bell, R. E. Reibe, reported that following outages in telephone services during the blizzard on March 7. Reibe indicated, "No contact could be made between Janestown and Pettibone via telephone from 5:15 p.m., Thursday until 4 p.m., Sunday; from here and Fessenden from 7 a.m., Thursday and 4 p.m., Friday; from here and Buchanan from 8 a.m. Friday and 4 p.m. Saturday."

There was property damages at the Jamestown Municipal Airport. One of the doors on the hangar was blown open. Snow drifted inside. Snow covered six planes that were being stored there. The heavy snow crushed the aircraft. The planes were owned North Dakota Farmers Union, Vince Buck, Ron Stoltz, Ed Sheetz, and Jamestown Flying Service, all of Jamestown, and Wally Schmidt of Gackle. Another plane not in the hangar, owned by the Flying Service, was destroyed as well. Damages estimates for the planes ran as high as $250,000.

Mr.and Mrs. Clifford J. Kropp and their 11 month-old-daughter lived on a farm, four miles northeast of Jamestown. The place had two houses. They lived in the large house, while Cliff's mother, Mrs. Beulah Kroop resided in the smaller one. Mrs. Beulah Kropp was in Jamestown when the storm hit and was stranded there.

The electricity went off at the farm around 2 a.m. Thursday. The Kropp family moved into the smaller house because it was about 10 degrees warmer. Ten degrees warmer, in this case, was still a chilly 38 degrees. They were there for three days.

Cliff built a tent out of blankets over their daughter's bed. They had eight or nine other blankets on the bed. Vicki Rae was dressed in a snowsuit for the duration of the storm.

The family ate oranges and potato chips during the storm. Vicki Rae drank what milk they had. Mom and dad had no water or milk.

They spent most of their time trying to stay warm. Mrs. Kropp said, *"We played two-handed bridge one day, but we got so cold we couldn't hold the cards."*

Saturday morning, Cliff started his tractor with a bucket attachment, and cleared the snow away the family car. The vehicle started and the heater gave the Kropps their first warmth in three days. The Kropps stayed inside the car four hours.

Later in the day, a snowplow opened the roads to the farm.

Overall, Mrs. Kropp said it *"wasn't too bad. But I think the pioneers were better off in a situation like this. They were prepared for it and used to it."*[163]

Woodworth, originally named Gem, was founded in 1911. It was named for J.G. Woodworth, Traffic Manager and Vice President of the NP. Woodworth's population in 1960 was placed at 221.

Friday morning, 12 year-old Betty Deede, daughter Mr. and Mrs. Raymond Deede, left the farmhouse to close the banging door on a chicken coop 100 feet away. She closed the door, then made her way to the nearby barn where her nephew was waiting out the storm. After a while, Betty tried making it back to the house. To get home, she needed to walk into the wind. From the start, she went in the wrong direction.

Mrs. Deede became frantic when her daughter never made it back to the house. She headed for the barn, located about 200 feet south of the house. With the north wind, gusting up to 70 mph that morning, Mrs. Deede managed to reach the barn. She learned that Betty was gone.

Mrs. Deede headed back into the storm. She fought her way over growing drifts. She hoped it was the direction her daughter had taken. The wind and snow overwhelmed her, but she pushed on anyway. Then, Mrs. Deede fell. She realized she was lost. Her mind was clouded with fear. The menacing whirlwind of snow closed around her, and everything looked the same.

Then, Mrs. Deede remembered the wind was from the north. She knew if she kept the bitter winds in her face, she had a fighting chance of reaching the farmhouse.

The mother crawled face up. She did not know how far she went, possibly 300 feet. Finally, Mrs. Deede caught sight of the farmhouse. She was safe, but her daughter was still missing.

Word of Betty's disappearance spread fast. Woolworth residents organized a search party. They tried to reach the Raymond Deede place late Friday, but the snowplow could not break through the mountainous drifts. The disheartened men returned home. Another attempt was made early Saturday morning, but it ended in failure as well. They did not give up.

The search party from Woolworth finally reached the farm about 10:00 Saturday morning. Visibility was still bad, so the men separated in groups of six and tied themselves together with rope. They fanned out. One of the groups found Betty's body about 45 minutes later. She was lying in an open field near a railroad track, about one-half mile from the farmhouse. Betty Deede was North Dakota's first reported storm victim from the blizzard.

Funeral services were held on March 9 at the Woolworth auditorium. Betty Deede was born on April 7, 1953. Reverend Norman Shawchuck, minister of the Woolworth Methodists and Deede family pastor, said, *"She was a very pretty girl, quiet and well-mannered."*[164]

Mr. and Mrs. James Bennett lived on a farm near Edmunds. On Wednesday, they watched their dog, Rusty, near his doghouse. The Bennetts put out food for him.

The blizzard ran its course in Edmunds. A snowbank, 5 feet high, covered the part of the yard where the doghouse rested. On Monday, the Bennetts continued their search for Rusty. They dug three-foot holes where they thought the doghouse was located. Mrs. Bennett called for Rusty while they worked. Finally, the couple heard some yips and they dug deeper. He was buried for nearly 120 hours. Mrs. Bennett said, *"He was tickled to see us."*[165]

In the mid 1960's NP had only two long-distance passenger trains left in operation. The trains were known as the *North Coast Limited* and the *Mainstreeter*.

On July 13, 1991, members of the Northern Pacific Historical Society attended a convention at Jamestown. They heard railroad stories from one NP conductor and seven NP engineers who ran trains out of Jamestown. All of them had something to say about the blizzard of 1966. Bill Kuebler published an article entitled, *"The Jamestown Veterans,"* in the *"Mainstreeter,"* Winter 1992.

Robert Donegan was promoted to engineer on December 17, 1946. Here's Robert Donegan's story:

> Before Gene Gossett and Jack White left on No. 25 *that night, we left Jamestown on Train No. 603, `a hot shot' freight with about sixty-five cars and three units. The snow wasn't quite as bad when we left, but when we got to the top of the hill at Windsor, you couldn't see three or four cars in front of the engines. You had to keep your eyes glued to the signal blocks, and it was starting to drift pretty bad. Before we got thirty miles out of Jamestown, we were hitting some of those drifts around sixty to sixty-five miles per hour and by the time we got the train through them, we would be down to fifteen to twenty miles per hour. They would pull us down that slow. When we got through a drift, we had to stop, take the scoop shovel out, and shovel the snow off the front of the engine so we could see again. Then we would take off, wind her up, and hit the next snowbank. We went that way for fifty-eight miles to Steele.*
>
> *I knew the passenger train (No.25) was coming out of Jamestown shortly after us. So when we got to Steele, I went in and called the dispatcher and told him he had better not run that passenger train unless he had a snowplow right ahead of it. I said it would never make it because the drifts were getting real bad. He told me that I should run my train and he would run the passenger train. As far as my train was concerned, I said, "I won't move it any further unless you block the train for me from here to Mandan. The storm is getting worse and you can't see anything, not even the signal blocks. I don't want to take a chance of plowing into some other train."*
>
> *We sat at Steele for about a half hour until the dispatcher said the track was clear of trains, we could take off, and we should disregard all block signals. He gave me a train order to that effect, and we took off. The rest of the way to Mandan we were barely able to get through some of the drifts. We made it, but it took us two hours and fifteen minutes going the last forty-five miles. When we got to the Mandan yard, we couldn't get the engines*

Men clearing NP main line west of Jamestown, probably ca 1940's. V.B. Koon Collection. Courtesy of Lori M. Elhard and Family

Snowplow working on main NP line in cut at Oswego between Eldridge and Windsor, probably ca 1940's. V.B. Koon Collection. Courtesy of Lori M. Elhard and Family

to the roundhouse since the switches were all iced up and there was no way they could throw them. So, we just left the power in the yard.

We sat there two days more waiting for the storm to subside. Then, different crews caught snowplows out of Mandan. I happened to catch one that went North on a branch-line up to the coal mines. When we got about twenty miles north of Mandan, found the storm hadn't hit quite as hard up there. So, it was kind of a breeze going up there with a snowplow. But when we came back two days later I caught a rotary and worked on it from Dawson to Medina for about sixteen hours. By that time they had the track open and trains were moving again.

We had snowbanks around the right-of-way that were pretty high. There was so much dirt mixed in with the snow, that when you went in with a rotary, you would just tunnel underneath. Then, you would have to back out and have the section men knock the snow down. Ernie Weise, our brother engineer, was our demolition expert at the time. He dynamited snowbanks so we could plow them out.[166]

Cleveland (169 residents in 1960) lies over twenty miles west of Jamestown. An NP townsite, it was established by settlers from Cleveland, Ohio, in June 1882. Gene Gossett was promoted to engineer on May 21, 1955.

On March 3, 1966, Gossett was the fireman for Engineer Jack White. Here's what Gossett remembered about the blizzard of 1966:

I was firing for Jack White on the North Coast Limited on the night of March 3, 1966. We left Jamestown on No. 25 at approximately 2:00 a.m., against the advice of my brother engineer, Bob Donegon. It was storming to beat the band and it had been for a day and half. We were hitting some pretty heavy snowdrifts. It was some of the hardest snow that I ever seen. The wind was blowing over the bare fields making the snow about fifty to sixty percent dirt which made it like concrete. Later, they brought the diesel-electric drive rotary snowplow (No. 50) out from Washington. The road foreman came with it and said, "We'll plow through that snow like it was butter." Well, he got into it and found out that it was more like concrete. He said, "What the hell kind of snow have you got out here?" When Jack and I got to Cleveland, about 23 miles out, we hit a pretty big bank in a left-hand cut doing forty to fifty miles per hour and got stuck tighter than a drum. They came out from Jamestown with two Geeps and a snowplow. They got to Cleveland and set the plow out, hooked on to the rear of the North Coast Limited, and tried to pull us out. We were in so tight, they couldn't move the engines, the water-baggage car, and the mail-dormitory car which were the first two cars behind the engines. So, they made a cut between the mail-dormitory car and the coaches and pulled the rest of the train back to Jamestown. The three units and two cars were stuck tight. But fortunately, they got the passenger back to where it was warm and they could get something to eat.

Then they came out with new units to rescue us, but they never made it to Cleveland. About eight miles east of us, they hit a drift that took the front window out of the lead unit and knocked the engineer and train-

master out the back door. So, they went back to Jamestown and Jack and I stayed out there for the night, the next day (March 4th) and the second night. We were not that far from Cleveland, and I wanted to walk back and get something to eat. Thank goodness, Jack wouldn't let me go or I wouldn't be here today.

In the excitement and the rush of making the cut and pulling the train back, nobody thought to tell the poor old baggage man what was happening. Here he was sitting in the baggage car and we ran out of water for heating the boilers, so there is no heat going back there. He was back there freezing, but he's got a trunk full of food with a little kerosene stove for cooking it. Jack and I were sitting up in the headend, nice and warm, but we don't have anything to eat. He about froze to death and we about starved to death!

With the snow blowing so bad, after a while you couldn't get through the doors between the units. There wasn't much room there anyhow because of the boilers. I was concerned about the second and third units. I didn't know if they were still operating, or not. In the case they died, I wanted to drain them. So, I crawled down off the lead unit (No. 6702A) and was going to walk back along the engines and check them. When I got to the bottom of the ladder, the first thing I did was slip and fall down into the ditch. I got up and started towards the rear end and all of a sudden I realized that I couldn't see the train. Then, I got scared. So, I stood still for two or three minutes. There was a lull in the storm, and I could hear the engines. Sure enough, I was headed the wrong way. I had been walking right away from them. When I got back to where I could touch the engine, I felt my way back to the head-end, crawled up the ladder, and told Jack what had happened. He said, "Sit down kid. Let them go to hell."

Finally, some farmer came out in a tractor with a front-end loader and got Jack and me off those engines. They hauled us back to Jamestown in a Weasel. I figured that I was all done till the weather cleared up and the snow was gone. I'll be a son-of-a-gun if they didn't send Lewie Boelke and me out to relieve Francis Donegan on the snowplow. I didn't want any part of those rotaries. Anyway, we spent our time plowing snow during the storm, and I spent the next twenty-two years lying like a son-of-a-gun that I wasn't qualified for a rotary.[167]

Ernie Weise, Sr. was promoted to engineer on July 2, 1957. Weise also had a farm west of Jamestown. Here's Weise's 1966 blizzard experience:

I did some blasting when I was in the armed service. I never thought much more about it when the war was over. I had a dental appointment the morning after No. 25 got stuck in the 1966 blizzard. The trainmaster called and got me out of the dentist's chair. He asked if I could blast snow and I laughed and laughed. He said it was no laughing matter. The dirt was so heavy in the snow that it was knocking the Russell plows off the tracks and the rotaries couldn't make any headway at all. A couple of units shoving a rotary three or four inches into a snowbank would stop the wheel dead and then they would have to dig it out.

NP main line west of Jamestown, probably ca 1940's. V.B. Koon Collection. Courtesy of Lori M. Elhard and Family

V plow on NP main line west of Jamestown, probably ca 1940's. V. B. Koon Collection.
Courtesy of Lori M. Elhard and family

I said, "OK, if your serious, I can do that. But what are you going to use for blasting? There isn't much blasting supplies around this part of the country." The trainmaster put a request out over the local radio station for blasting supplies and sent me out to Bloom, east of town. My nephew had worked with me on blasting before, so he was my pick of men for the job. Within a few hours people started bringing in blasting supplies of various kinds that just scared the heck out of me.

You have to keep dynamite turned regularly to keep it safe. To tell you how bad this stuff was, this was 1966 and I was just a little kid when the 'Katzenjammer Kids' comics was in the funny papers. Some of this dynamite came wrapped in 'Katzenjammer Kids' funny papers. All the glycerin was in the funny papers and none in the sticks of dynamite themselves. It was dangerous to handle, because it was really unstable. It was taking your life in your own hands when you handled this kind of stuff. Later that first afternoon, I put all the old stuff in as big a hole as I could make and got rid of it in a hurry. Then, they brought me a whole truck load of new stuff that night and we blasted for a week.

We put the sticks in a hole we made with a ice chipper handle which was about one and one-half inches in diameter with a tool on one end of it. We could push it down into the snow far enough to put six sticks of dynamite in the hole and put the holes about six feet apart. The blast would shake the snow up about ten or twelve feet deep. This allowed the rotaries and Russell plows to come in and clean up the track.

One of our first assignments was out at Cleveland to blast ahead of the rotary working east of there to get to the North Coast Limited. The next day, they sent us over to Medina where a rotary was having a real hard time. The company had rented a snowmobile for us, and during the night we pulled up on the overpass over there. We stopped the snowmobile and took our dynamite out and started setting the charges in the dark. In the morning, we saw that it was about sixteen feet down to the rail about five feet in front of where we had stopped. That would have been a real disaster because we couldn't see ahead of us in the snow. It was easy to see that we had a lot of luck going with us that night.

We got the mainline clear in a few days and went up by Esmond on the Oberon branch where there was an eight hundred foot cut that was pretty deep. It was warming up. We took our snowmobile, three cases of dynamite, our pockets loaded with blasting caps like you shouldn't do. We started off and sure enough, the snowmobile tipped over in a slough of water. I thought that was a disaster. We fished the dynamite out of the water by just reaching down to our shoulders in the water. Our clothes were soaked through to the skin. It was in the evening and just starting to get cold. Our pants froze around our legs, and I thought we would never make it. But as soon as the pants froze, we warmed up and kept right on working on the cut.

We put in about two hundred holes and rigged half of them with wire and the rest with detonating cord which was real fast stuff. We started about six o'clock and finished about midnight. There was a dog at a farm just at the other end of the cut and he had barked for the full six hours that we set the charges. When we fired the charges, we could see about the first three charges lift. From then on, it was just a roar as the two hundred holes went off. The six sticks in two hundred holes going off caused the air to split so it rushed out. That roar was louder any train rushing down the tracks I have worked. The dog heard it too and quit barking about that time. He probably had a heart attack.

Next thing we heard was that air rushing back at us. When it hit us, it whipped our clothes around pretty good. The echo went up the track seven miles to the little town of Hesper and then we could hear it come back again with less velocity. That was quite an experience that I had not had before. We worked day and night for about a week and had terrible powder headaches from handling the dynamite.[168]

NP passenger train west of Cleveland, March 1966. V. B. Koon Collection. Courtesy of Lori M. Elhard and Family

Snow removal at Halfway Lake Interchange on Interstate 94 near Cleveland, March 1966.

Clearing snow off Interstate 94 at Halfway Lake Interchange on Interstate 94 near Cleveland on March 9, 1966. Both photos courtesy of NDDOT

Settlement at Buchanan began when two brothers from Rio, Wisconsin, arrived in the area. John Buchanan came first in 1879, and brother James A. followed in 1880. In 1881, the NP established a station at Buchanan. In 1960, 76 people lived in Buchanan.

John Beardsley, Associated Press journalist, wrote:

Buchanan, N.D., Had A Bellyful of Storm, Snow

The 100 residents of Buchanan, a tiny village marked by a grain elevator on the central North Dakota plateau, fought drifts that buried homes to survive last week's blizzard.

The storm also blacked out power in some homes for 24 hours.

Ralph Cebula, 49, owns Buchanan's only bar, a tiny building barely 20-feet square. He and his wife, Elaine, live in a green frame house, where they rear three children and as many saddle horses.

Ralph and his wife watched the blizzard grow last Wednesday, just as they watched many storms during their lives together in North Dakota. Their son, 8-year-old Scott, watched too, but the 10 month-old twins, Chris and Carrie, weren't aware.

It was 6:40 p.m. Thursday when the lights went off and the furnace stopped.

"How long?" thought Mrs. Cebula, and she looked at the twins.

Through the night the wind screamed. Her husband looked at the living room thermometer. It had dropped several degrees.

He and his wife bundled the twins into snow suits, and wrapped them with blankets. Cebula herded his family into the basement, where it was warmer than upstairs.

Early morning came. The babies were hungry. Cebula took an empty coffee can, stuffed it with rags soaked in rubbing alcohol, and lit it. The makeshift stove heated milk for the babies.

Friday they waited . . . waited.

Near evening, Cebula went up to check the thermometer. It was just above freezing.

(Ed Kulink, a neighbor, swears it was 6:40 p.m. on the dot–24 hours later–when the power sprang to life. "I never even had to set my clock.")

Mrs. Cebula said later, "When I heard the furnace turn on, I felt like I had entered heaven."

Alvin Schumaker, a rural electric repairman, had climbed a 40-foot power pole in 70 mile per hour wind to repair a broken switch. Electricity was restored.

He and Clayton Snitker, a petroleum jobber, had struggled through piling drifts to trace the trouble.

In the blinding snow–unable to open their eyes for more than a moment against the wind–they followed transmission lines from pole to pole, and kept their direction.

Walter Riker, 68, lived alone in a trailer house smaller than an average garage. He watched the storm build, checked his food supply and went to bed.

When he awoke Thursday morning, a crack of daylight showed through one window. His home was smothered under a massive drift, As light fad-

ed, shifting snow drifted down his chimney. It melted and drowned the flame in his oil burner.

Riker turned on an electric heater. Strangely, power on his side of the highway stayed on.

He remained buried in his trailer for three days. The temperature he recalled, dropped to 42 degrees.

Riker stayed in bed with his electric blanket turned on.

"I didn't have much water," he said, "so I sipped it real little. I saved five cans of beer for the last."

The solitude droned on through Friday.

Saturday afternoon, a group of men led by Cebula dug down through the drift and freed the door of his trailer.

"When I heard voices outside," Riker said, "it scared the hell out of me,"

Geraldine Boelter came to Buchanan with her husband to visit his parents. Mr. and Mrs. Gus Boelter.

"I told mum, when we came, I wanted to see snow," said the young woman from Virginia Beach, Va.

"I was scared at first, during the storm, but now I think it pretty," she drawled, gazing out the tunnel dug through a 12-foot drift at the front door.

When the snow started to fall–before the deadly wind came–Geraldine ran out and scooped up handfuls to make what Virginians call "snow cream."

She mixed it with cream, vanilla, sugar, eggs and milk and dished up a treat the elder Boelters had never known.

Ralph Cebula scraped frost from a window of his bar two days after the storm, and gazed outside.

"Storms never have bothered me before," he mused. "But this one did, kind of. I don't think I could take another one.[169]

Gus Boelter service station in Buchanan, March 1966. AP wirephoto Courtesy of Aberdeen American-News

Ypsilanti, another NP town, was founded in 1882. Before that, it was a stopping point for stage coaches on the Jamestown-LaMoure line. William Hartley Colby, the first post master, named it after his hometown, Ypsilanti, Michigan.

In 1960, the community had a population of 130.

Many town and cities had residents missing in the blizzard of March 1966. In the case of Ypsilanti, Miss Candice Gehler, daughter of Mr. and Mrs. Gehler, was unaccounted for a while. Miss Gehler's vehicle stalled in an underpass west of Valley City. After getting out, she returned to Valley City in her car. Miss Gehler came home on Sunday.

Ypsilanti's news correspondent wrote:

> Trent Fisher, son of Mr. and Mrs. Darwin Fischer; Bernice Orr, daughter of Mr. and Mrs. Clifford Orr, and Lindsay Orr, son of Mr. and Mrs. Floyd Orr, spent the duration of the storm at the Carl Erickson farm home as they were unable to get home after school was dismissed.
>
> Most all the streets in town were blocked with snow following the big storm. Part of main street is now open, coming into town around by the school. Our snowdrifts were 15 to 20 feet deep.[170]

J.J. Flint and Bailey W. Fuller platted Montpelier in 1885. Both men had roots from the state of Vermont, so they named the new community after the capital of their home state.

In 1960, the population of the NP town was listed at 97.

Montpelier's news correspondent wrote:

> A light snow began falling about 10 a.m. Wednesday and became heavier as the day wore on with northeasterly winds increasing in velocity. Until mid-afternoon it was called a March squall, but by evening there was no doubt the weather man was having a violent tantrum with no regard for any form of life. Snow continued falling day and night through Thursday and Friday to an accumulation, according to reports to 25 inches, winds becoming northwesterly from 50 to 60 miles per hour. By Friday Mr. weatherman was giving his all. With a window that wasn't covered with snow it was possible at rare intervals to see a faint outline of the nearest neighbor's house (in town).
>
> It is said the record blizzard of 1888 has now been topped by the blizzard of March 2, 3, 4, and 5, 1966. Temperatures were above zero until the winds diminished Saturday afternoon when they dropped somewhat.
>
> About 25 people were stalled at Don and Angies station at the Junction of 281 and 46 south. Mr. Brenman had a narrow escape when making an attempt to reach Millarton for fuel oil. He returned home after being gone about four hours. Mrs. Mary Stott remained at the store and will be unable to get to her house until considerable shoveling is done. Numerous reports are coming in but it would be impossible to list them all. There has been no school for three days.[171]

Litchville, Valley City, Sanborn, Wimbledon, Leal, Rogers, Dazey, Kathryn, Nome and Cuba.

Located in southwestern Barnes County, Litchville is over twenty miles southwest of Valley City. The platting of this NP townsite was done by John C. Olson and Lewis C. Bordwell in 1900.

Hans Jacob Hanson operated a country store and post office six miles south and southeast of here. He moved his enterprises to the railroad town in October 1900. Hanson was from Litchfield, Minnesota. When he named his post office, he liked "ville" better than "field." Hanson talked the railroad officials into the name.

Litchville is where N. D. Governor Fred Aandahl (1945-1950) made his entry into this world in 1897.

In 1960, the town had a population of 345.

Norma Miedema, editor of *Litchville Bulletin* wrote:

> *The storm dumped an estimated 25 inches of snow in this area and was accompanied by winds as high as 60 to 70 miles per hour which resulted in some mighty big snowdrifts here in town, along shelter belts and in farm yards. The blizzard left very little snow on roads with good elevation in rural areas. The winds raged for four days and three nights, starting Wednesday morning and finally diminishing Saturday afternoon. Old timers say this storm even tops those of the thirties, as some of our drifts here in town were from 15 to 18 feet deep. The northern portion of the city was the hardest hit.*
>
> *Most of the cars in town were either snowed into their garages or buried in snowdrifts, thus the traffic was very scarce after the storm was over and roads were opened. ...*
>
> *A break in the city water main during the storm also gave us some trouble as the water had to be turned off and on periodically.*
>
> *School was dismissed early on Wednesday afternoon, and remained closed until Tuesday the following week.*
>
> *Friday was actually the worst day of all with visibility being zero-zero. Saturday morning found the storm somewhat on the decline, but still drifting.*
>
> *The digging out process will be slow and no doubt we will have a goodly amount of water in town, come the spring thaw.*
>
> *People will be talking about the blizzard of "66" for many years to come; it was a king size storm, indeed.*[172]

Valley City had 7,809 residents in 1960. Flowing through the city is the Sheyenne River. Upstream 13 miles is Baldhill Dam and Lake Astabula. That body of water began filling up in the spring of 1950.

At the north end of Valley City is a well known BNSF Railroad trestle bridge (formerly the NP) across the Sheyenne River that is known as the "Highliner."

Notable people coming from Valley City include George Mason and Frank White. The former started American Motors, and the latter would go on to serve not only as governor of North Dakota but also as Treasurer of the United States.

In 1872, the NP established a station here. They called it the "Fifth Siding." In 1878, the townsite was resurveyed and platted. On May 10, 1878, a different name was bestowed on the community. Joel S. Weiser (1834-1925), an early settler, suggested "Valley City," for the town's geographical location.

The Soo Line construction time line for its southeast-northwest mainline in North Dakota: Hankinson to Valley City, 1890; Valley City to Harvey, 1892; and Harvey to Portal, 1893.

On February 25, 1966, the Valley City Hi-Liners defeated West Fargo, 75 to 48. That win gave Valley City a third place finish in the Southeast Region conference race and a 13-5 record.

On February 28, the death toll in Vietnam reached 2,335. The combat deaths for the reported week was 130. The roster, of wounded individuals, increased by 489 to 11,574. Another 151 were reported missing in action and 31 were prisoners of war. The combat deaths passed the totals from three previous wars–in the War of 1812, 2,260, the Mexican War of 1848, 1,733, and 385 in the Spanish-American War of 1898.[173]

Valley City is home to the North Dakota Winter Show, the first one was held in 1937. Its a week-long event with crop and livestock judging events for 4-Hers, high school students in Future Farmers of America, and a open class for adults. The livestock sales have attracted many buyers and the rodeo shows have been very popular.

An attendance record, around 40,000, was set in 1965. That year, the livestock sales brought in $117,095.50. In 1965, two hundred cowboys participated in three rodeo events for $7000.00 in prize money.

In 1966, the 29th North Dakota Winter Show was scheduled to run March 4-11. Four rodeo performances were planned with $10,000 in prize money. Between 50 and 60 thousand people were expected to attend.

It was warm in Valley City on Tuesday, March 1, the high reached 42 degrees. After sunset, the low was 15.

There was an heavy snow warning for southeast and south central North Dakota. Four inches of snow or more and strong northeast winds were predicted for Wednesday afternoon and night. Northeast winds would be strong. The forecast was right on the mark.

On March 2, the mercury rose to 38 degrees. Around noon, snow fell and the weather became treacherous. Wind gusts ranged between 30 and 55 mph.

Wednesday afternoon, Mrs. John Hess attended a birthday party in her neigborhood. Walking home, she fell in the snow and ice. Mrs. Hess broke a bone in her leg. There was no traffic on the street at the time.

Within moments, Curtis Young, a college student, left his apartment house. Mrs. Hess had just left the same building. Young saw someone laying on the sidewalk. He called an ambulance. Then, Young returned with a blanket and covered Mrs. Hess. About that time, William Sowdens who lived in the neighborhood drove by. He stopped and offered assistance.

Driving home, Charles Hill, a member of the Valley City rescue squad, pulled over to lend a hand. To his surprise, the accident victim was his mother-in law.

Four miles west of Valley City is Berea, a community of 10 in 1960. The NP provided service to the Berea elevator in 1966.

Myron Lenning, manager, drove his car over the tracks near the elevator Wednesday afternoon. Heavy snow on the crossing stalled the vehicle. Lenning was busy, working hard to get his car unstuck. A NP switch engine out of Valley City barreled down the tracks toward the crossing at Berea. Lenning looked up, just in time. He jumped out of the way. The switch engine slammed into Lenning's car. The engineer quickly radioed the trailing freight train. The freight train came to a stop, before it came upon the site of the wreck.

Wednesday night, the Barnes County sheriff's office received word that Harry Himmerick, signal maintainer for KXJB, was missing. He was enroute to the television transmitter tower near Pillsbury.

Harold Fowler of Fargo, bus driver for Greyhound since 1937, listened to the storm warnings for southern and central North Dakota, Wednesday afternoon. Later in the day, he would be driving the Chicago-Seattle bus. The weather was a concern, but employees of Greyhound had a "never-give up" policy. He left Fargo on time.

Near Kelly's cafe on the east edge of Valley City, the Greyhound bus carrying 19 passengers hit a big drift. The bus stalled in the snow. It was near midnight. All attempts to free the bus failed. One local passenger was picked up.

Fowler and the passengers waited four hours for a giant four-wheel drive tractor to pull the bus to the Valley City depot. The Char-Mac Hotel was near the depot, but there were no rooms available for the Greyhound passengers. Fowler and his passengers settled in on the bus.

Thursday morning, a post office truck went to the NP station to pick up the mail. Three passengers got off the westbound *North Coast Limited* from St. Paul, around midnight Wednesday. The post office truck brought them into Valley City.

Mayor Lou Bruhn called a special meeting to discuss the out-of-the-ordinary needs of Valley City residents and stranded storm victims. Also, decisions had to be made concerning the opening of 29th North Dakota Winter Show on Friday.

Mayor Bruhn declared a state of emergency after consulting with city commissioners, National Guard officials, Barnes County government representatives, Civil Defense, city department heads, Winter Show officials and businessmen. Theodore Hedstrom was named head of the emergency council. Delbert Tipke, district game warden, and Bill Fagerstrom were appointed to help Hedstrom.

Residents were asked to provide shelter for stranded people. Classes were canceled. Minard McCrea, school superintendent, reported that the schools would be heated in case they were needed for storm shelters. Supermarkets were kept open to provide food supplies.

The emergency coordinators had control of county and city equipment. Fire Chief, Ken Raveling, reported fire and ambulance services had snow removal equipment assigned to the emergency crews.

Valley City oil dealers had 5 gallon cans of fuel oil filled and taken to a central point for distribution. John Carlisle, fuel oil administrator, reported that 15 gallons of oil would pull any homeowner through until the weather cleared up. If a fuel truck was needed a snowplow and a pickup truck manned with extra help would lead the way.

Jack Heimes and Cal Foss, Winter Show officials, worked on a snow removal plan for the grounds of the North Dakota Winter Show.

Throughout the storm, snowmobile owners provided transportation and delivered goods. Valley City implement firms provided their largest tractors for towing and transportation. The Farmers Union Oil Company donated their two tractors.

Colonels Woodrow Gagnon and Bernard Wagner promised the use of the National Guard equipment and men. Equipment operators were notified for standby duty.

On Thursday, the city found private lodging for Greyhound passengers, but they declined the offer. Greyhound indicated that the passengers would be responsible for transportation to the private homes and the bus would leave on a short notice once the storm cleared. Two passengers left the bus. They boarded a westbound NP passenger train which later stalled west of Jamestown. The group ate their meals at the depot cafe and slept in the bus.

Milk was delivered to people who had home service. It was not easy. Tractors pulled the milk vans around town.

The strong winds blew down large signs at the Holiday's, Drugan's and *Times-Record* buildings. Thursday's high reached 25. The first two days of the storm brought 1.63 inches of precipitation.

Late Thursday, Harry Himmerick notified authorities that he was safe. Himmerick's car had stalled on a county road. He spent Wednesday night in the vehicle. On Thursday, he walked to a farmhouse.

On Friday, the thermometer stopped climbing at 16 degrees.

Irvin Koslofsky, secretary-manager for the North Dakota Winter Show scrambled to come up with a new schedule. Rodeo stock was stranded in Fargo. Tons of snow had to be cleared away from Granger Hill.

Northern Pacific's westbound passenger train, *No. 3* stalled at 9 :00 Friday morning, three miles west of the Valley City station.

William R. Kuebler, Jr, drafted a article, titled *"Nature's Fury."* It told the experiences of NP trainmen that were involved in the March 1966 blizzard. Kuebler wrote:

> On Thursday evening, March 3, 1966, the blizzard reached full force. Experienced crews begged officials to halt traffic, but the response from warm and distant headquarters was, "We have powerful diesels. Go!" With trepidation, crews both predicted and experienced the results of this decision. Early Friday morning, in spite of the abundance of first and second-generation diesel-electric power, Fargo Division traffic came to a rather sudden halt in a spectacular manner, and the very lives of passengers and crew were in jeopardy. A brief account follows: ...
>
> **Train No. 3,** Dilworth–Engineer Emil Stumm and Fireman Lyle Rath are ordered on duty early Friday morning. Stumm walks from his Dilworth home to the yard office, but the raging storm is so bad that Rath cannot drive away from his Moorhead home, so he walks the short distance to the Fourteen Street crossing near downtown Moorhead. There, Engineer Stumm stops No. 3, picks up his fireman, and heads west with two units, five cars, and twenty-eight passengers and crew. The power for the trip is 6007D, a freight unit, and 6600, an FP-7, both facing forward. Between Peak and Valley City, No. 3 slams into a deep cut filled with snow and is stuck fast. Passengers and crew survive by donning mail sacks to keep warm. Eventually, they use an ax to chop up the wood floor(laid over steel) of a heavyweight baggage car and burn it in the car's stove. They will not be rescued until two days later.[174]

Heat was maintained in the cars of No. 3 until 6 o'clock Friday night when low water supplies forced its curtailment. All 28 passengers moved to the baggage car. They huddled against a woodburning stove.

At daylight, two members of the traincrew walked over to the nearby Clarence Metcalf farm. They contacted authorities and acquired food for the passengers. Later, a National Guard jeep reached the train. The men transported the passengers and crew members to the Metcalf farm. The Metcalfs prepared a fine dinner for storm victims. After that, school buses took the passengers to the gymnasium of Valley City high school.

After *No. 3* stalled in the snow near Valley City, NP officials ordered another train out of Dilworth on Friday. As events turned out, it needed to be rescued. Three traincrews worked to get *No. 3* back to Dilworth. Here's Kuebler's brief accounts of their service:

Extra 2512 West, *Dilworth–Engineer Doug Anderson is ordered west into the raging storm to rescue No. 3. He has three GE U25Cs and one caboose. Bucking drift after drift of deep snow, he makes it to within two miles of No. 3 where, just beyond Peak, North Dakota, he hits a huge, hardpacked drift. His windshield caves in, filling the cab with snow, and he and his brakeman are nearly buried. Anderson's snow bucking ends, and the new second-generation diesels barely limp back to Peak siding to await their own rescue*

Extra 352 West, *Dilworth–With Anderson and crew immobilized at Peak, Engineer Runyon Peterson, Brakeman Harold "Breezy" Breslin, and Conductor Glenn Lee are ordered to the rescue with two GP-9s pushing a snowplow. They barely make it. After countless hours of digging, they rescued No. 3 by pulling one car at a time back to Peak. The snow is so hard and packed that the brakes on each car of No. 3 must be applied in emergency before the car is pulled back. Sliding wheels cut through the snow, whereas rolling wheels tend to climb the snow and derail. At the scene, officials from St. Paul question Engineer Peterson with great skepticism about this practice, but it works. His twenty-five years' experience railroading against the elements proves superior to the officials' academic prowess.*

Passenger Extra 2509 East, *Peak to Dilworth–By Sunday, No. 3 is reassembled. Pulling on the east end of the train are Anderson's three U25Cs–2509, 2524, and 2512–with Runyon Peterson at the throttle. Pushing on the west end are No.3's two F-units, running in reverse with Emil Stumm in command. Peterson uses radio coordination with Stumm to attack each drift at the highest possible speed, with both sets of units at full throttle. After emerging from each drift, Stumm idles his two F-units. Peterson has covered the front windshields of the 2509 with grain doors to prevent another window cave-in, leaving a tiny hole through which to peek at the*

2509 with grain doors protecting front windshield. Courtesy of Runyon Peterson

approaching drifts. Brakeman Breslin and the St. Paul officials "hit the deck" as each drift is attacked. The 2509 jumps and rocks violently, possibly coming up off the rails at several points–and always returning. Yet, maximum speed is the only means of breaking through the drifts. When the officials complain of the extremely rough ride, the crew tells them not to worry, and that the train will always re-rail itself! The train arrives in Dilworth on Sunday, March 6, 1966, at 2:30 p.m. Stumm and Rath have been on continuous duty for a record 58 hours, 20 minutes.[175]

Peterson and his crew shared candy bars with the passengers. They broke up the walls in the baggage car to burn. Peterson said, *"Getting back to Fargo was the hard part because they left the plow at Valley City,"* Peterson estimated there was one drift, six feet deep and up to three-quarters of a mile long. The train hit the drift going 65 mph. Peterson said, *"The locomotive was jumping up and down like it was running on the ties. The train had slowed to 20 mph by the time it got through the drift, but it still was on the track."[176]*

The storm let up Saturday morning, but before it did another .19 inches of precipitation fell. Overall, Valley City recorded 1.82 inches of precipitation, 25 inches of snow. The *Times-Record* estimated that wind speeds had reached 60 mph.[177]

The digging out process was in full force on Saturday. It was an all-out effort, state, county, city, national guard and private contractors were involved. Unlike many other communities, Valley City merchants closed their doors on Saturday to speed up the process.

Grocery stores in Valley City were open on Sunday.

The Greyhound bus pulled out of Valley City, when Interstate 94 was passable to Jamestown on Sunday.

On Monday March 7, people learned the North Dakota Winter Show had been postponed. The original schedule of events would be followed, only a week later, March 11 through March 18.

The Valley City Hi-Liners knocked off West Fargo, 66 to 44, in the Southeast Regional Tournament.

In a Letter to the Editor of the *Times-Record*, Mrs. G. Kermit Sauer wrote:

My husband and I would like to express our gratitude and appreciation to Ted Curtis, his helpers, the snowplow operators, and the huge "taxi" tractor drivers who fought the blizzard for several hours to get our baby to the hospital.

We would like to write each one an individual thank-you, but as yet we do not know the names of this well-organized team, nor exactly how many men took part in the operation.

We have gone over parts of the route we took to the hospital and I can hardly believe we really got through there.

Little Connie is much improved and should be released soon. it's a wonderful feeling to know that even in an impossible situation, men will attempt the impossible and win.[178]

On Tuesday, Valley City faced Fargo North, the Spartans were ranked 4th in the final Class A poll and they won 14 of their last 15 games. The game was decided in the final seconds.

Overall, the attendance figures for the 29th North Dakota Winter Show were down slightly from the 1965 totals. Although the number of livestock exhibits was less than the 1965 totals, the crops show set a new record in entries. Nine thousand people watched the four rodeo performances.

In 1960, Barnes County had 16,719 residents. Population for the small towns were as follows: Wimbledon, 402; Sanborn, 263; Dazey, 226; Nome, 145; Kathryn, 142; Rogers, 119; and Leal, 70. Except for Sanborn, Dazey and Nome, the Soo Line linked the farming communities together. Sanborn was located on a NP mainline and Dazey and Nome on its branch lines.

According to Cass County Electric Co-op, Cuba, Kathryn, Rogers, Leal, Dazey, and Sanborn reported power outages in their rural areas. The first breakdown occurred at 1:00 p.m. Thursday. Only minor repairs were needed. By Sunday, service was restored to all the communities.

By noon Saturday, Rogers lost all its connections to the outside world. There were forty individual outages in the Nome, Kathryn, and Wimbledon areas. Northwestern Bell Telephone indicated the strong winds wrapped wires together. Repairs were made after the storm on Saturday and Sunday. Most customers had their phones working by Monday.

Tower City, Alice, Kindred, Page, Wheatland, Casselton, Mapleton, Davenport, Fargo, Moorhead, Minnesota, Hunter, Greenfield and Grandin

The NP established a depot in Tower City on August 19, 1879. The community was named after Charlemagne Tower Sr., a NP official and former land owner of the site. Tower City was a boom town, in 1883, the place had a population of 800. In 1960, Tower City had a population of 300.

When the weather turned bad on March 2, 1966, travelers pulled off Interstate 94 and sought shelter at Tower View Cafe in Tower City. Before the storm was over on March 5, forty-eight large trucks and vans were parked at the truck stop. Eighty-one person found refuge at the cafe that was operated by Mr. and Mrs. Don Wilmer.

Shirley Behm of Fingal, a cook, worked Wednesday to Sunday. Waitresses from Tower City made it in during the storm. Young men from NDSU and St. Johns helped the waitresses. Mrs. Thelma Wilner acted as a hostess. She said, *"There were sleepers packed in our dining room so closely you couldn't see the carpeting."*[179]

The restaurant had plenty of food for the visitors. Truckers donated bread, cases of fruit salad and apples to expand the supplies.

Snow drifted around the service station and cafe, the banks blocked all the doors but one. The piles were roof-top high. Saturday afternoon, truckers dug their vehicles out of the snow. Around midnight Saturday, the travelers started moving out as highways opened up.

There was a complete failure of telephone services for Tower City. According to the Northwestern Bell Telephone, the town was completely isolated by noon on Saturday. Repairs were made by March 7.

Alice was established with the arrival of the NP in 1900. The village received its name from R.B. Lewis, a Fargo banker. Lewis once served as North Dakota's Lieutenant Governor. He named the town after his wife's and daughter's name.

Alice had 124 inhabitants in 1960.

For the most part, the residents of Alice came through the March 1966 blizzard in pretty good shape. Snowbanks, around town, were 12 to 14 feet high.

The supply of fuel oil ran out at the Ray Conlon residence. After that, his wife and daughters stayed with the Martin Maruska family. What about Ray Conlon himself? From Wednesday until Sunday, he was marooned in Tower City.

Earl Habiger of Alice lost 30 head of sheep in the storm. It was about half of his herd. Habiger believed the animals died of suffocation, instead of freezing to death. He said, "moisture had frozen over their nostrils which prevented the straying animals from breathing in the high winds."[180]

In March 1966, Debbie Reilly, an eighth grader, lived with her family on a farm near Alice. They raised about twenty Holstein milk cows. The storm left Debbie's family without power for three days. They camped out in their garage, as it was equipped with a fuel burning stove. Since her family did a lot of camping, cooking utensils were not a problem.

Without power, milking the cows proved to be quite a challenge to Debbie's family. They hooked up a generator to the PTO shaft on a tractor to operate the milking machines. They had hay in the barn's loft, so feeding the animals was not a problem.

After the storm had passed, Debbie remembers walking on drifts that reached to the tops of the trees.

Her neighbors had a "breezeway" through their yard. Snow covered their vehicles. Debbie says they used a broom handle to poke down through the drifts to find their cars.[181]

An NP snowplow cleared the tracks through Alice on March 21, 1966. Ralph Corcoran, the local depot agent, expected a freight train for the following day. If so, it would be the first train to make it to Alice in March.[182]

The city of Kindred was home to 580 people in 1960.

Kindred began as a GN townsite in 1880. In September of that year, J. S. Huntington and William S. Kindred, a land examiner for the NP, bought some land and then platted it.

The blizzard interrupted the District 2 basketball tournament. On March 7, the Kindred Vikings, coached by Erling Logan, battled Mapleton. The Vikings lost the double overtime game, 76 to 69. The following day, the Vikings had another tough loss to Oak Grove, 64 to 63. Before the storm, Kindred defeated Davenport, 75 to 63.

The Kindred American Legion Post 117 sponsored an amateur photo contest of the 1966 blizzard for Kindred area photographers. Five dollars, three dollars and two dollars prizes were awarded.

The contestants brought their photos, in sealed envelopes with their name and address, to Jensen's Store, the week of April 23 to 29.

The pictures were displayed between April 30 and May 7. On May 19, the *Kindred Tribune* showed two of the winning photos and published the names of the winners. The results were as follows: Color 1st, Joe Owen, Kindred; 2nd, Mrs. Wallace Graff; 3rd, Mrs. Tallef Lee. Black and white: Carl Knutson, McLeod; 2nd Joe Owen; 3rd, Selmer Johnson.

Buffalo had 234 residents in 1960. The town started out in 1872 as an NP station known as "Third Siding." Around 1875, it took on the name of "New Buffalo", after Buffalo, New York, the birthplace of W. E. Wilkeson, secretary of the NP. Charles A. Wilder, postmaster, shortened the name to "Buffalo" in 1883.

Cass County Electric Cooperative warehouse in Kindred, March 1966. Courtesy of Juli Becker

The village of Buffalo came through the March 1966 blizzard without any fatalities or power outages.

Mr. and Mrs. Harvey Coon sheltered five people during the storm.

Caught by the blizzard in a Holsum Bakery truck near Buffalo were its driver, Clarence Miller, 47, son, Wayne, 21, and Howard Kuvass, 26, his son-in-law. The destination for the Moorhead men was Jamestown. They were transporting a variety of breads, doughnuts and rolls.

Usually, Clarence Miller traveled by himself, as it was against company policy to have passengers. However, his concerns about the weather led him to ignore that policy. As it turned out, Mr. Miller was glad he did.

They departed from Fargo around 6 p.m. Thursday. Their bakery truck stalled near Buffalo. The three men would remain there for the next forty-seven hours.

They took refuge in the van of the truck. For warmth, the men burned bread cartons. They took turns staying awake. For food, they munched on doughnuts.

When the blizzard let up Saturday afternoon, the men headed out on foot. For protection from the wind, the men utilized bread cartons.

The driver of Northern States Power Company snow tractor found them. He took the men to Fargo. Clarence Miller's advice to those motorists caught out in a snowstorm, "stay with your vehicle."

Over five miles west of Casselton lies the village of Wheatland. In 1960, 115 people lived in Wheatland.

The NP set up a station here in 1872 which they called "Second Siding." The settlement was platted in November 1878 through the efforts of townsite owner, Hannah K. Brown, of Cortland, New York. The name of the post office was change to "Wheatland" on July 22, 1879 to reflect the large acreage of wheat being grown on the large bonanza farms in the vicinity.

It began snowing heavily in Wheatland on Wednesday morning March 2. The accompanying winds picked up speed that afternoon. The deteriorating conditions led to the dismissal of school in Wheatland that afternoon.

The worst day of the storm in Wheatland was on Friday, when visibility was nil.

There was a power outage for people residing south and west of Wheatland from Friday afternoon until Saturday.

The blizzard caused a disruption of phone service for Wheatland residents. A week later, it was still a problem.

The let up of the storm on Saturday revealed many black fields in the Wheatland area. Blizzard winds blew so hard, they scoured the ground free of snow. Blown into shelterbelts, the snow was deposited in drifts that were almost as high as the tree tops.

Except for places such as sheltered areas, the same high winds swept township roads bare. In those places, many of the drifts were so huge, the services of rotary plows would be needed to punch a hole through them. Unfortunately, that type of snow removal equipment was needed first on the main roads. Only when they were done there, could rotary plows be employed to open secondary roads.

This was reflected on Monday morning when classes resumed in Wheatland. School buses were not sent out on their routes.

Casselton had 1,394 residents in 1960. Settlers began arriving in this vicinity in 1870. In 1876, the NP set up a station here. It was named for George Cass, president of the railroad, 1872-1875.

Notable residents of the Casselton area included U.S. Senator William Langer, former N. D. Governor George Sinner and M. G. Strauss. He began his chain of clothing stores here in 1897.

Casselton's news correspondent, Dorothy Kapaun, wrote:

> The blizzard that struck the area last week was the worst that anyone could remember. Cars were buried completely by snow and drifts (that) were higher than many homes. Walking over snowbanks and gullies made one think of walking on mountains. The landscape looked almost foreign.[183]

When the storm was at its worst Friday afternoon, Mrs. Martha Paulson heard a loud noise emanating from her stove pipes. Emerging on wing from the stove pipe vent a few minutes later was a blackbird. It was unhurt despite the fact there was a fire going in the stove at the time. Mrs. Paulson used her porch as a shelter for the bird until Saturday afternoon. Then, she moved the bird outside where it took flight.

The storm caught quite a few Casselton area residents on the road. This meant they had to take refuge elsewhere. There were also those individuals who found themselves stranded in the Casselton vicinity. Those local folks who let stranded motorists stay at their homes included Mrs. Amanda Hanson, Mr. and Mrs. James Hobbs, Mr. and Mrs. William Muldoon and Mr. and Mrs. Justus Peterson.

One Casselton home, the Clayton McCartney's on Tenth Ave. N., was buried so completely by drifts that a person couldn't see the doors or windows from the outside.

Saturday morning, Tim Alm, Clarence Krueger, Henry, Lloyd Peck, and George Sinner shoveled snow away from kitchen window so the McCartney family could crawl out. It was still storming at the time. The John Moos home became the McCartney's refuge, until the blizzard abated.

On Monday, in order to alleviate the pressure on the walls of the house, Mr. McCartney employed some boys to tunnel the snow away from the sides of the structure.

The stork was not going to let a mere blizzard slow it up in Casselton. At 8 a.m. Saturday, March 5 William Motter, a resident of Kay Ann Apartments in Casselton, summoned Mrs. William Austin, a registered nurse, to come to the aid of his wife, who was in labor. At the time, Mrs. Austin was residing in the apartments with her sister, Mrs. John Ford.

Although an ambulance and helicopter service were summoned by telephone, inclement weather prevented them from making it to the Kay Ann Apartments.

Later that morning, a snowmobile dropped off Mrs. Wayne West, another registered nurse, at the Kay Ann Apartments to help out.

At 6:05 that evening in the Motter's apartment, their daughter, Rebecca Colleen Motter, weighing 7 lbs. 7 oz., greeted the world.

Finally, at 8:30 that night, West ambulance was able to make it to the Kay Ann Apartments. They took Mrs. Motter and her new born to St. Luke's Hospital in Fargo for checkups.

Casselton had another race with the stork during the blizzard. An automobile was used Thursday morning to transport Mrs. Ed Brandsted of Casselton to St. John's Hospital in Fargo. So that Mrs. Brandsted could reach Interstate 94 south of Casselton, Bernard Baumeister used a snowplow to open that stretch of N.D. Highway 18 from Casselton to the Interstate (about a mile).

Once they had reached that junction, the Bransted car hooked up with the North Dakota Highway Department. That outfit cleared a path to the hospital. A 6 lb. 10 1/2 oz. boy, named Randall Lee, was born to the Brandsteds on Monday March 7.

When the blizzard arrived in Casselton, one of its residents, Mrs. Al Schneider was at the farm residence of her daughter and son-in-law, Mr. and Mrs. Peter Sell. The latter lived near Amenia, a town eight miles north of Casselton.

The problem the storm caused for Mrs. Schneider, a diabetic, was that impassable roads prevented her from reaching her supplies of insulin back in Casselton. In the meantime, the insulin supply she had brought with would run out on Sunday.

On Saturday afternoon, William Kent who had additional insulin with him, drove a car to the Kenneth Anderson farm northwest of Amenia. He then traversed the remaining three miles to the Sell farm on foot. After delivering the insulin he retraced his route (on foot again) to the Anderson place.

Thursday night, the wail of a fire siren was heard in Casselton. A fire had broken out at the Richard Joyce home in Casselton. Answering the call and coming to the Casselton

Fire Hall were thirty volunteer firemen and local townsmen. Blocked roads prevented the fire trucks from leaving the fire hall.

With that option gone, some of the firemen set out on foot for the Joyce home. In this group were Don Barnby, Joe Deutsch, Wayne Geirmann, Chester Hedstrom, Clifford Prischmann, Phil Rieniets, Richard Roth, Dallas Schrock, and Robert Taves.

Once there, the firemen discovered the fire to be almost extinguished. Using a waste paper basket Mrs. Lee Schultz, Curt and Carter Schultz were pouring water on the fire.

The fire, fortunately not a very big one, had been discovered by Curt and Carter Schultz. They had gone to the Joyce residence to check on the furnace. It had overheated and caused the kitchen floor to start burning. There wasn't much damage to the kitchen floor. No one was at home at the time of the discovery of the fire.

In March 1966, Mr. and Mrs. George Loegering resided in a house on the northeast edge of Casselton. Once the blizzard had passed, Mr. Loegering employed a different method to extricate his car from its snowy tomb. First, he shoveled his garage door free. Next, he placed planks and other materials upon the slanting snowdrift in front of his garage. By backing his automobile onto the planks he was able to reach the top of the snowdrift. Surprisingly, the snowbank didn't give way under the vehicle's weight but held it up. Mr. Loegering then proceeded on across the drifts until he made it to the road.

As elsewhere, the snow removal process in Casselton was a laborious slow. Some drifts in the city were as much as 25 feet high.

On March 12, the Central Cass Squirrels defeated Enderlin, 66 to 64, for third place in the Region 1 tournament. Central Cass's leading scorer for the game was Don Bartholomay who had 24 points. Next, came Jerry Pyle with 13 points; followed by Gary Regelstad and Frank Turchin with 7 points each.

Two years later, Jerry Pyle would lead Central Class to the Class B state basketball championship. He would later play college ball at the University of Minnesota.

About ten miles west of Fargo is Mapleton (180 residents in 1960). Mapleton's most famous native son is Mark Andrews. He served in Congress as a U. S. Representative from 1963 to 1981 and as a U.S. Senator from 1981 to 1987. Grand Forks International Airport is named after him.

A post office which was named "Mapleton" was set up here on July 21, 1875. Its name reflected that of the nearby stream, the Maple River.

The appearance of the March 1966 storm led to classes being dismissed in Mapleton at 10 a.m. Wednesday.

After Wednesday night, everything came to a stop. Grocery and milk trucks couldn't make it to Mapleton. By midday Thursday, grocery and milk supplies had run out.

Residents of Mapleton were snowbound in their houses. They required the assistance of their neighbors who had already had made it out.

In order to be able to see over the high drifts one farmer reported that he had to go upstairs.

Places that never held snow before now had snowdrifts.

Mapleton residents were happy to see the snowplow which passed through the village Saturday night.

For the most part by Monday, the job of snow removal around homes in Mapleton was done.

On March 8, the Mapleton Falcons lost the district championship basketball game, 58 to 57, to Central Cass.

Today, Fargo is situated at the intersection of two major interstates, I-29 and I-94. Fargo, the seat of Cass county, is North Dakota's largest city (46,662 residents in 1960).

Settlement at Moorhead began with the arrival of the NP. Its name honors William G. Moorhead, a Pennsylvanian who was an NP director.

Fargo's location was determined by NP surveyors on the evening of July 4, 1871. Officially, its first name was "The Crossing." Unofficially, it was known as the "Tent City."

The name "Fargo" was adopted on February 12, 1872. The person for whom the settlement was named was an NP director and president of the Wells-Fargo Express Company, William George Fargo.

The NP's rail line reached Moorhead in December 1871. After completion of a railroad bridge across the Red River, the NP ran its first engine across the river into Fargo on June 6, 1872.

It was on WDAY-TV in Fargo that physics Professor Daniel Q. Posin of the North Dakota Agricultural College gave the first televised weather forecast in the Red River Valley. On June 1, 1953, that first broadcast emanated from a two-car garage that had been made over into a studio. Professor Posin was the first television weatherman in Fargo. He passed away in New Orleans, Louisiana on May 21, 2003.

Fargo's most colorful television weatherman had to be Dewey Bergquist (1923-1996). He started at WDAY radio in 1947 and then later went on television. He took some remarkable film footage of the 1957 Fargo tornado. Dewey was fondly remembered for his rain gauges (which held over 11 inches of precipitation), "stare downs" and the sunset pictures and weird shaped vegetables he displayed during his weather forecasts. Concerning the forecasts, Dewey would grab his pointer and say, "let's go read 'em".

When WDAZ-TV Devils Lake-Grand Forks, Channel 8 went on the air on January 31, 1967, Dewey did their weather broadcasts too. That tradition continues to this day.

Fargo was hit by a devastating tornado on the evening of June 20, 1957. The area primarily affected by it was the Golden Ridge area of North Fargo. Dr. Ted Fujita of the University of Chicago would later study this tornado extensively. He would use the information from that tornado to help formulate his Fujita scale. That scale rates tornadoes from F1 (the least damage) to F5 (the worst). The 1957 Fargo tornado was classified as an F5.

The March 1, 1966, edition of the *Fargo Forum* gave the following forecasts for Minnesota and North Dakota and Fargo-Moorhead for March 1 and 2, 1966:

> *North Dakota: Partly cloudy to cloudy tonight; Wednesday; scattered light snow beginning west tonight and continuing over state Wednesday; turning colder Wednesday;lows tonight 15-25; highs Wednesday 22-32.*
>
> *Minnesota: Increasing cloudiness tonight, Wednesday; scattered light snow likely to spread across state late tonight and Wednesday; possibly mixed with rain south; not much temperature change tonight and Wednesday; lows tonight 15-25 north, 20-30 south; highs Wednesday 30-40 north; 35-40 south.*[184]

The extended forecast released the same day was for Thursday, March 3 through Monday March 7. Only light snowfall was expected in either Dakotas (and that was to be in the eastern Dakotas) and Minnesota, and that was forecast to fall on Thursday. Precipitation amounts for Minnesota in the form of snow were expected to be between .10 and .30 inches.

Near normal temperatures and light precipitation were expected for the Upper Midwest during March 1966, according to the Weather Bureau's 30-day forecast.

On March 2, heavy wet snow fell in Fargo. The 6.4 inches of snow had .67 inches of moisture. That day, Fargo had a high of 29 degrees. The evening low was 12.

The 1965-66 school year was the inaugural one for Fargo North High School. Strong winds piled the wet snow over three feet high on the lee side of the new gym at Fargo North High School.

Around 7 a.m. Thursday, the gym's roof came down with a deafening roar.

Luckily, the two custodians inside the building were not in the gym that had been open for only nine months.

Schools in the Fargo-Moorhead were closed.

On Thursday, the storm's center was near Fargo. Its situation was like being in the eye of a hurricane. Temperatures remained mild. At 1:30 p.m. Thursday, the reading on the thermometer at Hector Airport was 30 above. Wind gusts at Hector Airport reached 30 mph early Thursday afternoon.

The mild temperatures caused the new fallen snow (8 inches Wednesday night and early Thursday) to melt. A crust then formed on the snow. Unless quite a bit of new snow fell, this was expected to help reduce the drifting of snow. The weatherman at Hector Airport remarked, *"We most likely will have nothing like the winds and snow farther west."*[185]

The low was moving northward. As it did so, it was lessening in intensity. If that trend continued, there would be less chance of lousy weather in Fargo-Moorhead Thursday night. The thermometer climbed to 31 above in Fargo Thursday. At Hector Airport 2.3 inches of snow, .41 inches of precipitation, fell on Thursday. That night, the thermometer bottomed out at 21 degrees.

The storm did not disrupt train service on Thursday through Fargo.

The same could not be said for Hector Airport on Thursday. Clogged runways prevented takeoffs and landings. Crews were busy moving snow throughout the day.

Clogged streets prevented Northern Transit Company from making all its routes in Fargo-Moorhead Thursday morning. They were running in North Fargo. The bus company anticipated having them up and running in south Fargo and Moorhead later that day.

The respite in the weather Thursday allowed street crews in Fargo to open many streets. Included in this was the business district, 4th Street, 13th Street, all of Broadway and some other avenues and streets.

In hopes of having all of Fargo's avenues and streets open to two-lane traffic, Jorgen Miller, Superintendent of Fargo's Street Department intended to keep his snowplow operators clearing snow late into the evening. They were to resume their effort early Friday.

Besides moving wet heavy snow, another problem snowplow operators were encountering was stalled cars on streets. Their drivers had ditched them the previous night.

Thursday morning, only about twenty percent of the people who worked in downtown Fargo arrived at their work places on time,

This number increased to eighty percent by mid-morning. By 9 a.m., around seventy percent of Northwestern Bell Telephone's staff had showed up for work. As of mid-morning, department stores had more employees on hand than customers. The percentage of staffers who had made it to work ranged from thirty to fifty percent. The Internal Revenue Service had a turnout of eighty percent. A similar percentage was being reported at Merchants National Bank.

So, it was around noon Thursday before a semblance of a normal business day returned to downtown Fargo.

Early delivery of the Thursday's morning edition of the *Fargo Forum* was haphazard. In Fargo-Moorhead, impassable streets made early home deliveries impossible. Except for a couple of isolated routes in Moorhead, that edition of the paper was delivered Thursday afternoon. Morning papers for distribution at Devils Lake and Jamestown were placed aboard trains. Other towns serviced by mail trucks did not go out. For paper deliveries to Ada, Barnesville, Detroit Lakes and Halstad, Minnesota, and Wahpeton, North Dakota, the *Forum* dispatched its trucks to those cities.

As for the afternoon edition of Thursday's paper, the Forum's Circulation Department was of the belief that it would be able to make home deliveries in Dilworth, West Fargo and Fargo-Moorhead.

On Thursday, the North Dakota Highway Department office in Fargo advised motorists not to travel outside of Fargo. This was due to the unsettled weather. Road conditions changed every hour. They had no information on stretches of highways away from Fargo.

Many vehicles became stuck on U. S. Highway 10 between Fargo and South West Fargo (West Fargo). Although this thoroughfare was open, it had become heavy.

After a lull, the blizzard resumed with a vengeance in Fargo at 9 p.m. Thursday evening.

There was no motor vehicular traffic out of Fargo or Moorhead Friday morning. Visibility was zero. Within the two cities, except for ambulance and police emergency runs, there wasn't much traffic.

Business establishments open in Fargo included a few restaurants and taverns. Downtown, only an isolated store or two had opened its doors.

Friday morning, Fargo Mayor Herschel Lashkowitz and Claire Simpson, president of the Fargo Chamber of Commerce, directed Fargo residents to remain at home. They asked travelers to stay off city streets and highways.

Northwestern Telephone Bell telephone operators in Fargo encountered difficulties during the storm maintaining circuits between Fargo-Moorhead and Minneapolis. At times the connections were completely broken.

As far as conditions were locally, they were a little better. At times, calls swamped the switchboards.

Northern States Power Company fixed local problems that caused some minor outages on Friday.

The blizzard left all four Fargo-Moorhead hospitals shorthanded on Friday. Doctors, nurses and other personnel worked extra shifts. As one hospital administrator put it, if it wasn't for the effort hospital personnel made in getting to work and then remaining there, he wouldn't have any staff at all. Fargo and Moorhead police received lavish praise from hospital spokesmen for transporting hospital personnel to work.

At 6:25 a.m. March 4, the GN halted its freight trains in the storm-affected area. Yards at Willmar, St.Cloud, New Rockford, Minot, Williston, Grand Forks, and Glasgow held many of the freight trains. GN passenger trains were held at St. Paul, Breckenridge, Fargo, Grand Forks, Minot and Williston. During the blizzard, the GN had no freight or passenger trains stalled between stations.

Catholic college students from St. Procopius, located near Chicago, were enroute to the regional basketball tournament in Grand Forks when the blizzard forced their train to halt in Fargo.

On the train, were two priests, a handful of coeds and 120 students. On the same train were eleven students from Colorado State College of Education and twenty-four students from Valparaiso University of Indiana. Around Fergus Falls, they learned of the postponement of the tournament.

The three basketball teams participating in the tournament and their coaches had come earlier and were staying at the Holiday Inn in Moorhead.

Through the efforts of a couple of *Fargo Forum* reporters, arrangements were made for the students to spend the night at First Lutheran Church in Fargo, only a block from the GN depot in Fargo. The students reclined on padded pews, using their coats for blankets. The four cheerleaders took refuge Friday night at the home of the general manager of the Powers Hotel Company, F. Urban Powers.

After attending mass at St. Mary's Cathedral, located on Broadway across from First Lutheran Church, and eating breakfast, the boys spent the rest of the day at the First Lutheran recreation building. A few of them shoveled the walks encircling the recreation building. As for the rest of them? They played games. Among these was shuffleboard.

Early Saturday, a deal was made. St. Procopius played Valparaiso at Concordia College in Moorhead that afternoon. In that game, Valparaiso swamped St. Procopius 107 to 76.

As of midday Friday, two dozen travelers were stranded at the bus depot in Fargo. They were a hungry, weary bunch. The majority had been there since early Thursday. One lady, Mrs. Joseph Stroppel, had been there since Wednesday night.

Permission was granted to her and the other passengers to spend Thursday night on buses.

Upon learning of their plight, three members of the Minn-Kota chapter of the Red Cross paid them a visit. They were Richard Hall of the disaster committee, Mrs. Irene Thompson, executive secretary of the chapter and John Welton, disaster chairman.

Arrangements were made to feed passengers at the bus depot cafe until they left Fargo.

Better sleeping accommodations for four women and one child were secured Friday night by Mr. Hall. He located three hotel rooms in Fargo for them.

This intervention by the Red Cross improved the bus passengers morale considerably. One of them, Mrs. Joyce Leavenworth who was marooned there with her little girl, lauded the Red Cross's efforts:

> I think the Red Cross has been wonderful to us. They have seeing that
> we got meals, and we had a wonderful hotel room last night. I don't know
> what I can say to them.[186]

Late Saturday afternoon, bus and train passengers became restless. They wanted to leave, but it was too early in the digging out phase. Buses had served as sleeping accommodations for most of the stranded bus passengers since Thursday night. Early Friday morning, roughly 150 passengers aboard GN's *Empire Builder* became victims of the great blizzard when they were marooned at the Great Northern Depot. The passengers spent their time aboard the train doing different things. This included napping, reading or visiting with one another. Since noon Friday, the GN had provided hot meals.

Friday morning, WDAY-TV went on the air one hour and 25 minutes late. A high voltage condenser at that station had to be fixed.

Thursday morning, thirty-two officers and enlisted men of the 119th Fighter Group of the North Dakota Air National Guard (NDANG) reported to their headquarters at Hector Airport. Part of the Air National Guard's mission was to have three aircraft ready to fly twenty-four hours a day. To make sure, lanes were kept open to the unit's fire hall and other buildings, rotary snowblowers were employed.

On Friday, the blizzard forced the NDANG to postpone their regular monthly drills for one week. With roads being impassable, the one shift covered for the others during the storm. At 2 p.m. Saturday, a four-wheel-drive unit was dispatched into Fargo to secure food.

To make emergency runs, Fargo-Moorhead Police traveled in squad cars equipped with chains and two officers in each car.

According to Captain Curtis Langness of the Fargo police Traffic Bureau, policemen transported essential personnel, such as doctors and nurses, to their work places and provided ambulance escort. On an ambulance run, a police vehicle broke trail and another police car followed behind. Heavy snow and poor visibility lengthened the emergency runs. As of 10:30 a.m. Friday, except to the Veterans Administration hospital, poor travel conditions kept Fargo police from traveling north of the fairgrounds.

On Friday, Fargo police put in a shift and a half. Moorhead's night shift continued working Friday morning.

On Friday, both the Fargo and Moorhead Fire Departments were well staffed. For night duty, Moorhead's Fire Department had brought six extra men on board.

Only a few neighborhood grocery stores and supermarkets were open on Friday. The general rule of thumb for neighborhood grocery stores was that if employees could make it there, the stores would be open.

On Fargo's South side, Dahl Super Valu was open. On Friday morning, Dahl said they were enjoying just about "average" business. Another grocery store that was open on Friday was Ted's Northport Super Valu.

Department stores and other retail stores in the two cities did not open their doors on Friday. The majority of Fargo's drug stores were closed Friday. But, a few cafes, banks and taverns were open on Friday.

At one watering hole, there were some patrons, none of whom was dressed for fashion. The bartender related how he had passed the two previous nights:

I slept on the counter over there. This is the second night I have spent here and don't I look it? He had a couple days' growth of beard on his face.[187]

Fargo Street Superintendent, Jorgen Miller, reported that his snow removal crews tried to keep a few of Fargo's main thoroughfares open, but visibility was a real problem and their equipment was too light for the heavy cleaning that was required.

On Friday, William Arndt, Moorhead's Street Superintendent, was only sending snow removal crews only on emergency calls.

Moorhead Mayor Ray Stordahl requested Moorhead residents not drive their automobiles in the business district.

In Fargo-Moorhead, Northwestern Bell was being overwhelmed with phone calls. Except for necessary calls, the company requested that Fargo-Moorhead residents not use their telephones for local calls.

C. H. Hart, building manager of the eight-story Black Building on Broadway reported that only six people came to work there on Friday morning (up to 10:30 a.m.). On a normal business day around 400 people worked there.

One person who made it to work at the Black Building was Gus Magnusson. He was a janitor there. Mr. Magnusson lived in Moorhead. He said, *"I still don't know how I got to work without getting stuck. I guess I was just lucky."* Mr. Magnusson actually was twenty minutes early for work. He served double duty as elevator operator. As he noted, *"the girls couldn't get here."*[188]

On Friday morning, Fargo Mayor Herschel Lashkowitz held a meeting with Fargo Assistant Police Chief Ed Anderson and Leonard Caverly, Cass County Civil Defense Director. They talked about snow removal and using private contractors and their equipment.

Here's what Ronald L. Wood wrote about the March blizzard:

> *I was a student at North Dakota State University in Fargo studying electrical engineering. I was supplementing my income by part time work at the television studio of KXJB-TV, Channel 4, Fargo and Valley City. Their Fargo studio was then located on the south side of Highway 10 between Fargo and West Fargo. My usual shifts were on Thursday and Friday nights and Saturday and Sunday.*
>
> *The "night" shifts were usually 2:30-10:30 PM. The Thursday night that this blizzard started I was on duty at the studio and at 10:30 the blowing and drifting snow was already approaching dangerous conditions. Since we knew what the weather man was forecasting (after all, that was part of our job to broadcast weather reports) four of us from the crew volunteered to stay at the studio for duty the next day should the need arise. The four who stayed were David Dyke, newsman, Lynn Runk, cameraman, Ron Zimbrick, engineer, and myself, Ron Wood, engineer.*
>
> *Little did we know on Thursday night that it would be Sunday afternoon before we would be able to get home. The Fargo police brought us food on snowmobiles and we stayed for a marathon broadcast shift of approximately three days.*
>
> *An interesting sidelight to this is that Channel 4 was in the midst of a major construction project to build their new broadcast tower and transmitter site near Galesburg, North Dakota. Their old site was near Pillsbury, North Dakota and we were still broadcasting from that site. The new site was nearing completion but had not finished all the required testing for approved use.*
>
> *Signals from the studio to the transmitter sites are typically sent via microwave signals. Sometime during this storm, high winds had blown a microwave antenna off a tower on the path between the Fargo studio and the Pillsbury transmitter site causing Channel 4 to go off the air. The microwave path between the Fargo studio and the new transmitter site at Galesburg (which had already been in use for "after hours" testing) was intact and also an engineer who had been working at the new site was marooned there by the storm and was available to put the new transmitter on the air if they could get early approval from the FCC.*
>
> *Station management quickly grasped the situation and (working via phone from their homes) contacted the FCC and outlined the severity of*

the problem that a blizzard was in progress and there was great need for weather information to broadcast to the people of the area. The FCC gave approval and the new transmitter went on the air officially earlier than was planned.[189]

With conditions improving Saturday morning in Fargo-Moorhead, people began emerging from their cocoons. One of them was F. Urban Powers, general manager of the Powers Brother Hotel Company, headquartered in Fargo. He was walking down Broadway Avenue carrying a case of eggs he had purchased from a nearby grocery store, Leeby's Foods. Mr. Powers' destination was the Powers Hotel, not far away.

The *Forum* had this to say about Mr. Powers sojourn:

Powers' lone parade with eggs was only one of many incidents in Fargo-Moorhead Saturday as the two cities struggled from the states of Ghostville into functioning municipalities as the blizzard began to subside.[190]

Mr. Powers was a busy man Saturday morning. Prior to making his journey to get more eggs, he had been looking after the people patronizing the hotel. In the case of its dining room, as soon as some of the students were finished eating, Mr. Powers would escort others to the dining room tables. He also carried dishes to the kitchen to be washed.

As far as its regular staff went, the blizzard had left the Powers Hotel shorthanded. To make sure customers were being served, stenographers doubled as waitresses.

Saturday morning, Don Brantner Sr., a clerk on duty at the Bison Hotel, received a scare around 4:00. While smoking a cigarette, a hotel guest had fallen asleep. The resulting smell of smoke reached the hallway outside the upstairs room. Mr. Brantner called the Fargo Fire Department and the fire was put out.

The scene at West Court on the NDSU campus Saturday was one of deep snow. There were fifty trailers located there. Mrs. James Millman, a resident of the court, didn't know how some of them could exit their trailers. In their own case, Mr. Millman shoveled a path through the huge drift that piled up against their doorway. When a *Fargo Forum* reporter stopped to talk with some trailer residents late Saturday afternoon, he found the occupants within the trailers to be doing OK. Their only hardship was that of blocked views. Snowbanks were window-high.

Because they weren't licensed, snowmobiles were not allowed on Fargo streets at the time of the March 1966 snowstorm. Despite this, one was seen heading south down Broadway Saturday morning.

The March 1966 blizzard was a very busy time for some Fargo-Moorhead agencies. Let *Fargo Forum* staff writer Wayne Lubenow describe their activities:

For three days the wind howled, whipping a blinding curtain of snow across the white landscape.

But babies were born, sick people got to hospitals, the stranded were rescued, and people who were out got food and fuel oil.

That's because at least 1,000 emergency missions were made by agencies such as F-M Ambulance Service, Fargo and Moorhead Police Departments and the Clay and Cass County sheriffs' office.

There were other unsung heroics by Civil Defense departments, the Red Cross and local construction firms who furnished heavy equipment for the mercy errands.

Workers went with little or no sleep, toiled endless hours battling the blizzard to help those who needed help.[191]

Fortune smiled on both Fargo and Moorhead fire departments during the storm. They didn't have to battle any major fires as the blizzard raged. They had their share of ordinary fire calls. Moorhead's fire department took an expectant women to the hospital.

It was a hectic time for Fargo police. Over the three day time span of the storm they made over 500 emergency runs. They picked up a little girl who wandered away in the storm. They found a man lying in the snow with just an elbow sticking up.

Moorhead police had around 250 emergency runs.

Two construction firms, Northern Improvement and Schultz and Lindsay, provided "payloaders" (large tractors equipped with front-end buckets). Their operators ran interference and cleared paths, which then allowed police cars to make it to their destinations.

When such an immense storm like the March 1966 blizzard envelops an area, among the things people become concerned about are road conditions. In an effort to provide answers to questions on that subject or other topics, both Fargo and Moorhead police departments handled more than 500 telephone calls daily during the crisis.

The blizzard had left a couple of young people marooned in an automobile near Baker, Minnesota, north of Barnesville. Clay County Sheriff, Adolph Olsen, dispatched two county plows north from Barnesville to look for them. The rescue mission was a success.

The blizzard left Clay County Civil Defense Director Quentin Keinholtz stuck at his residence in Dilworth. Not being one to sit around, Keinholtz planned snow removal operations for Dilworth from there.

For Leonard Caverly, Cass County Civil Defense Director, the March 1966 snowstorm meant very little sleep. From 7:30 a.m. Thursday until Saturday, he got one hour of sleep.

Caverly was holed up at civil defense headquarters, located in the Cass County Courthouse in Fargo. He coordinated many relief efforts.

By Saturday, Caverly had handled 44 emergency calls. Wayne Lubenow describes Caverly's routine with these calls:

> Caverly got the calls, notified the proper authorities. Typical: Calls to Cass road department crews to clean out areas for emergencies; using a snowmobile with a sled and delivering fuel oil to people who were out.
> About the sleds Caverly had this to say. "The sled holds 2,000 pounds. We pushed fuel oil to county areas and milk to West Fargo.[192]

Friday night, a Northern Improvement snowplow headed a search and rescue mission for a stranded Barnesville motorist who was missing. Their convoy proceeded down U. S. 52 south of Moorhead. But, as time passed, and they didn't find the motorist, they had to give up the effort. The next morning, their "missing" person arrived in Sabin on foot.

The March 1966 blizzard proved to a memorable for Kermit E. Bye and his family of Fargo. He was employed by the U. S. Attorney's office there. Bye and his family had moved to Fargo from Bismarck just the previous Sunday.

With the storm in progress Wednesday evening, Bye's twenty-three month old son became sick. Bye's attempt to transport him to the hospital ran aground when he got his automobile stuck in a snowbank. Borrowing a set of chains from a neighbors, Bye put them on the vehicle's tires. No luck, he got stuck again.

Next, Bye phoned the Fargo Police. They, in turn, contacted F-M Ambulance Service. Enroute to the Bye residence, the ambulance became stuck.

Another neighbor offered the services of his four-wheel-drive vehicle. Placing the boy into that vehicle, they headed for the ambulance.

Let Mr. Bye continue the story:

> *You've never seen anything like it. About twenty people poured out of the apartment buildings in the storm and we got the ambulance pushed out. Around 11 p.m. they arrived at the hospital with the boy.*
>
> *Bye remarked, My wife and I appreciate the help we got more than you'll ever know. This was ironic, because before he left Bismarck, Bye was informed that Fargoans were cold people. After the help, his family had received in the storm, Bye decided to remain there.*[193]

The March 1966 blizzard led six Fargo-Moorhead ham radio operators, in conjunction with forty-four others in the Tri-State area, to furnish emergency communication service to anyone having problems on account of the storm.

Power outages, telephone line breakdowns, and other troubles caused problems which then required emergency calls to deal with them. According to F. S. McCalley, a Fargo resident, the ham operators were taking care of these emergency calls.

South West Fargo began as a settlement south of U. S. Highway 10 in 1936. It took on the name of "West Fargo" on June 7, 1967.

Its population in 1960 was 3,328.

Early Saturday, a fire broke out at the Thore Anderson residence in South West Fargo. Upon awakening around 7 a.m., Mr. Anderson smelled smoke. He and his wife took their three young children across the street from the burning structure.

Even with a snowplow leading the way, the South West Fargo Fire Department had a difficult time reaching the site of the fire. Swirling snow slowed their progress. The firemen could not save the Anderson home. It ended up being a total loss.

Afterwards, Mr. Anderson, a South West Fargo Police officer, and his family took refuge at the Ray Saunders residence in South West Fargo. John Welton, Minn-Kota Red Cross director, picked up the Anderson family and took them to downtown Fargo. The Red Cross supplied the family with new clothes.

Another person putting in marathon hours during the storm was P. C. Davidson, owner of Fargo-Moorhead Ambulance Service. From Wednesday morning until Saturday, Davidson had only three hours of sleep. He had a seven-man crew. They made 28 emergency runs in that span.

For example, at 9:10 a.m. Friday, they received a call concerning a young fellow hemorrhaging in the area of 135h Avenue South and 19th Street. He needed transportation to St. John's Hospital in Fargo. The ambulance service completed the run with the assistance of a Fargo snowplow and two squad cars filled with husky men. Time of the run was roughly 1 hour and thirty minutes.

Fargo had two snowplows on standby for the F-M Ambulance Service. Moorhead allocated one snowplow for ambulance runs. Northern Improvement provided heavy equipment as well. If further assistance was needed, the National Guard placed four-wheel-drive vehicles at their control. An individual offered them a snowmobile and a big toboggan for their usage.

After the storm subsided, one crew member at F-M Ambulance was asked, "Could you handle another blizzard right now?" He said, *"Give me an hour's sleep and we'll try."*[194]

The storm which had moved into the Fargo-Moorhead area around midday Wednesday let up on Saturday. Overall, the March 1966 blizzard dumped 15.4 inches of snow, 1.72 inches of precipitation at the Weather Bureau station at Hector Airport. The blizzard's top wind speed of 55 mph at Fargo was recorded Friday. Temperatures stayed relatively mild throughout most of its duration. It would be Saturday March 5, before temperatures in Fargo dipped to zero. A low of 18 below was recorded Monday morning. After that, there was a big warmup.

Children having fun at Robert Michel's house on U.S. Highway 81. A Fargo Forum photo Courtesy of the Fargo Forum

The snow removal effort in Fargo and Moorhead after the blizzard was a huge undertaking. Their streets crews hauled the snow to dump sites along or in the Red River.

March 6 was a very busy day for Northwestern Bell Telephone Company's Fargo office. That Sunday was the busiest day in history (through March 6, 1966) for that office. The number of long distance telephone calls handled by its operators for residents in the Fargo-Moorhead vicinity came to 18,000. Not included in this total were local calls or direct dial calls. According to Northwestern Bell officials, the number of long distance telephone calls sent out of the Fargo office exceeded the number of calls placed after the June 1957 tornado.

Fargo Forum columnist Wayne Lubenow had the following humorous reflections on the storm:

> *This pal and I were sitting around having a scuttle of suds Monday*
> *(March 7, 1966) and I said, "Well, it was a pretty bad storm, wasn't it."*

He heaved a sigh, wiped the foam off his mouth and answered, "You just don't know how bad."

With that kind of an answer, I figured he had lost a loved one or at least been stranded for three days in a foodless, drinkless area.

"How bad was it?" I prompted.

He wiped his eyes and his hands trembled a bit and he said, "I was snowbound at home for three days."

I thought about that a second and said, "Ran out of food and fuel oil, right?"

"No," he said, "We had plenty of fuel oil and plenty of food and plenty of everything."

I didn't say a thing because I figured he'd continue. He did. His voice actually cracked a bit as he said, "Have you ever been trapped in a house for three solid days with a wife and six kids.?"

No, I hadn't.

He took a long pull of his beer and said, "You wouldn't believe it."

"Oh," he said, "It started out nice enough. Wednesday night was just like usual. I worked and got home around 6. The kids got to bed, and Mary and I watched television.

"And it was still kind of a lark Thursday morning when I couldn't get to work, and the kids couldn't get to school. It was sort of . . . togetherness."

The togetherness deteriorated, he said, rapidly.

"I always thought," he said, "that my children were human. They are fairly respectable on an ordinary day when I come home after work."

"They aren't respectable. They aren't even human. What they do is scream-all six of them. They held screaming contests."

He shuddered again and went on: "And they destroy things. Like on Friday I went down to my workshop in the basement to relax by doing a little upholstering. I had to. I was aa nervous wreck.

He said, "I was working behind a davenport when I heard this pounding noise. I crawled out. It was one of my sons pounding nails into the upholstery I had just finished.

He put his head in his hands and sort of sobbed. "That's how it went for three days-the kids screaming and destroying and beating up on each other and hollering and crying."

He was breaking up now. "And do you know," he choked, "that my wife just ignored it." 'JUST IGNORED IT, DO YOU HEAR.'"

He gulped down a sob and said unbelievingly, "She said . . .she said . . . she said that's how it was at home every day."

He got ahold of himself a bit and said, "Saturday morning I had to get out of there. I just had to get to work. It was madness, but I had to try."

He bundled up, he said, and started mushing the three miles to his job. He never made it.

He said, "I fell exhausted about nine blocks from home. I was lying in the snow-but happy. That's when this nut in a snowplow came along. He picked me up and took me back home."

His voice grew hard, "Oh, I struggled and hollered and told them to leave me alone. Lord knows, I tried."

His eyes got a far-away look as he remembered, "Man, it was peaceful sprawled out there in that snowbank."

But the snowplow crew carried him back home, fighting and kicking. Mary and the kids made him a hot brandy and put him to bed.

Sunday morning dawned bright and sunshiny. The storm was over.

My pal awoke, still in a state of shock. The first thing he heard was the kids screaming.

A rubber-tipped dart from a blowgun nailed him between the eyes. Two small bodies landed on his stomach, "Yahoo, Dad's awake."

He burrowed under the covers.

And that's when Mary came into the bedroom and said calmly, "I think the streets are open. Why don't you go to work, Dear?"

He groaned, "It is Sunday, and the office is closed on Sunday."

Mary smiled sweetly, "Honey, maybe you could get a key and go to work anyway. Maybe you could help shovel around the office or sweep the floor or something."

My pal leaped from bed in one joyous bound. "You're right, I'll go, I'll go, I'll go right now."

Mary smiled again, "That's good. Dear. It HAS been sort of hard on us having you around, you know."[195]

On March 8, in the final seconds of the Southeast regional at Valley City, Fargo North edged Valley City, 51 to 49. At the state Class A tournament in Grand Forks later in the week, the Spartans dispatched Minot Ryan, but then lost to Mandan. In the consolation game Wahpeton topped Fargo North, 60 to 54.

An early victim of the storm was Harlow A. (Jack) Frost, age 64. He was a Clay county deputy sheriff and jailer. Before 1:45 a.m. Thursday, Frost had been in the process of clearing snow with a shovel. While he was on his way to his place of residence in Moorhead, Frost suffered a heart attack. His body was discovered in his stalled automobile early Thursday.

The '66 storm affected the two colleges in Moorhead, Concordia College and Moorhead State College differently. In the case of Concordia College, it touched them hardly at all. The school was on a quarter break, and the students had gone home. It was a different story at Moorhead. There, students were still in class. The blizzard forced the cancellation of classes both Thursday and Friday.

A local newspaper, *The Red River Scene*, wanted an answer to a rhetorical question, *"What do you do with 1,000 college students cooped up in their dormitories for three days while classes are canceled by a blizzard and they have no place to go?"*

They asked Mike Grieve, a part time reporter for the *Scene* to check things out. Besides that job, Grieve was managing editor of the Moorhead State College newspaper. He lived in Ballard Hall, a men's dormitory on the Moorhead State College campus.

Wednesday evening, students heard classes were canceled for Thursday. Instead of hitting the books, students took it easy.

The cancellation of classes on Friday led to more rejoicing and jubilation. An impromptu dance was held at Dahl Hall on Friday. They also played cards. Although the cafeteria in Kise Commons was engulfed by deep snow, students maneuvered their way through deep drifts to get to the cafeteria. All that snow lying around was quite a sight to Joe Kashi, an Iranian who was a sophomore at the college. Others received thrills by leaping from a dormitory balcony down into a soft snowbank.[196]

Moorhead experienced an upsurge in telephone usage. People were asked to limit their calls.

The vast majority of Moorhead businesses closed their doors on Thursday and Friday.

The lull in the weather on Thursday allowed Moorhead's Street Department to have thoroughfares in the business district, plus the majority of through streets open by 2 p.m. Besides this, they opened up many other streets around town. High snowbanks caused problems for snowplow operators.

Business was quite brisk for those grocery stores which did not close during the storm. There were runs on perishable items such as bread, milk, and meat. One store on Seventh Avenue, the Southside Superette, was located next to the Moorhead State College campus. March 4, 1966, was their busiest Friday in history (up to that time). Amazingly, this incredible activity occurred despite the fact only two automobiles were able to get to the store that day.

How did storm bound residents pass the time as the blizzard raged about them? The *Red River Scene* provided a hint. *"Daytime TV programs were probably the most watched in the history of the area as everyone had just no place to go."*[197]

Dave Haakenson remembers being let out of school early on the first day of the blizzard. He was watching TV at a friend's house in the neighborhood. Meanwhile, the storm grew worse. His mom arrived in their car to pick him up. Their vehicle got stuck in the snow. They were close to home, so they started walking in the storm. After walking for a little bit, his mother started going the wrong way. Dave stopped her and led her home. After the storm, the men his neighborhood cleared a path on a field to get to a road that was plowed out.[198]

On Thursday morning, the Moorhead Post Office used snowmobiles to deliver the mail. One such carrier, David Lamb delivered mail on his route on a snowmobile loaned by Froelich Marine of Moorhead. Unfortunately, by Friday conditions were too bad to continue the experiment.

The Moorhead Fire Department beat the stork in a race on Friday. At 3 a.m. that day, Mrs. John Van Sickle decided it was time to head for the hospital.

As the Van Sickles were snowbound, they contacted the Moorhead Fire Department. Firemen arrived in a Civil Defense Jeep. They shoveled and pushed their way through the snowdrifts to the Van Sickle residence.

They took Mr. and Mrs. Van Sickle to St. Ansgar Hospital. Around 8:30 a.m. Mrs. Van Sickle checked in. Her 8 pound son entered this world at 10:33 a.m.

Large drifts also made things difficult for city crews. One stretch of 11 Ave. N. between 17th and 18th Streets in Moorhead had four snowdrifts that encompassed the entire width of the street. Stalled car, hundreds of them, proved to be quite an impediment to Moorhead's snow removal crews. Often the height of snowdrifts exceeded that of car tops. The latter had little choice but to work around such obstacles. In quite a few spots, rotary plows had to be utilized.

As the storm wound down on Saturday, a Moorhead dentist, Dr. Joseph Zbacnik, was skippering his North Dakota curling team to the United States curling championship in Hibbing, Minnesota. Other members of the team were Mike O'Leary, Bruce Roberts, and Gerald Toutant. The Zbacnik rink upended Minnesota 6-3 in the finals.

The symbol of the world curling championship was the Scotch Cup. Zbacnik and his teammates hoped to capture that trophy at the world tournament that was to be held in Vancouver, British Columbia. Tournament play was to start March 21, 1966.

Over 20 miles north of Casselton in northern Cass County is the town of Hunter. Its population in 1960 was 446.

Hunter, an NP townsite, was founded in 1880. John C. Hunter, a big landowner in this area, was honored by having the new settlement named after him.

Several enterprising individuals came from the Hunter area. David H. Houston (1841-1906), local farmer, inventor and poet made an important contribution to film development. "Kodak" is what he called his invention, the roll-type film process. George Eastman bought the rights to this invention from Houston. Bertin C. Gamble, a native of Hunter, who along with Phil Skogmo established a retail chain that, by 1969 had over 4,200 outlets in 39 states.

On March 2, 1966, Mr. and Mrs. Glenn Fletcher of Hunter were in Wahpeton where they attended funeral services for Mr. Fletcher's stepbrother, Elmer Pittner. Enroute home, they made it as far as Mapleton. They stayed with relatives there until Sunday.

In 1960, Grandin's population was 147.

By November 1880, GN rail line being extended south from Grand Forks reached this point. That same month, Grandin was platted. Its name honors John Livingston Grandin, an oil industry pioneer from Tidioute, Pennsylvania, and his brother W. J. Grandin. These men were bankers and owned the Grandin townsite.

Their first acquisition of Red River Valley land, 41,000 acres occurred on June 8, 1876. They secured the land through a credit settlement with the NP. Later, their farm would expand to 72,000 acres. It was one of the most famous of the bonanza farms.

The storm showed up in full force in Grandin, Wednesday evening March 2.

There were a few travelers who took refuge in Grandin for the three day blizzard. Opening their doors for some of them were the homes of Leo Bauer, George Draschner, David Mahars, and Elsie Skinner. One stranded family chose to stay at the fire hall. Sympathetic friends provided them with food.

Conditions were bad enough in Grandin on Thursday morning to prevent Mrs. Molly Hestbeck from walking to the Hi-Way Cafe, an eating establishment she ran. Fellow townsmen came to Mrs. Hestbeck's rescue by utilizing a snowplow and a truck to get her there.

The only business operating in Grandin on Friday was the local garage. That place opened because one of its employees had received a call to rescue a family whose vehicle had stalled on the highway. (probably U. S. 81).

Residents in and around Grandin came through the three day storm in pretty good shape. While supplies of fuel oil for quite a few people ran alarmingly low, timely deliveries by their fuel oil suppliers kept their fires from burning out.

There was only one report of a food shortage in the Grandin vicinity. At the time of the blizzard, Francis Schechenger's wife was a patient at the hospital in Hillsboro. The family wasn't totally without food. But as Mr. Schechenger remarked, *"Pancakes made with water and baking powder are not so hot."*

It was quite a sight that greeted residents in Grandin on Saturday. The depth of snow-drifts across Main Street ranged from 5 to 15 feet.

That afternoon, even though it hadn't quit storming in Grandin, cleanup operations began.

Mrs. Alice Margach described the following scene in Grandin the next morning:

> Sunday morning all the hills were virtually alive with sightseers, cam-era-happy people, oldsters and youngsters, some of them enjoying their very first sled ride.
>
> That afternoon, for the first time since Wednesday, the mail truck came to Grandin.

The Grandin area came through the blizzard with very few livestock losses.

It would be the following Tuesday evening before the cleanup was finished in Grandin. In describing how things looked in Grandin after that monumental task, Mrs. Margach reported, "Now all one can see are the huge blocks of snow that look like boulders."[199]

The Grandin Eagles placed third in the District 6 tournament when play resumed at Mayville by beating Hunter 71 to 61. Craig Hildreth led Grandin in scoring with 20 points. Top scorers for the the Hunter Hornets were John Frost and Larry Ottesen with 25 and 24 points, respectively. John died in Vietnam in 1968.

Washburn, Riverdale, Garrison, Underwood, Turtle Lake, Mercer and Brush Lake

Washburn (population of 993 in 1960) lies on the east bank of the Missouri River in McLean County. It is about forty miles north of Bismarck.

The Lewis and Clark Expedition wintered at Fort Mandan during the winter of 1804-1805. Its location is thought to be over ten miles northwest of Washburn. The Lewis and Clark Interpretive Center on the north edge of Washburn honors the memory of their stay in this area. The Center was dedicated on June 6, 1997.

Washburn was one of the earliest steamboat landing points in the history of North Dakota.

John S. Veeder and John Satterlund founded Washburn on November 1, 1882. They named the town after a man they both personally knew, Cadwallader Colden Washburn. He had served in the Civil War, been governor of Wisconsin from 1872-1874, and been a member of Congress.

In 1904, the Soo purchased an existing rail line from Bismarck to Washburn and Coal Harbor. It was part of the Bismarck, Washburn and Great Falls Railroad.

The March 1966 blizzard showed up at Washburn on the evening of Wednesday, March 2, 1966. It would be late Friday evening, before conditions improved in Washburn.

A Mandan man, Robert Hoff, wouldn't soon forget the March 1966 storm. On Wednesday evening, he took off from Mandan heading for Minot. On his way back, Mr. Hoff's automobile slid off the shoulder of the road. He stayed in the stalled vehicle for the next two days. To stay warm, he burned various items–including floor mats.

Once the blizzard let up late Friday, a rescue team headed north in an attempt to locate Mr. Hoff and any other stranded travelers. It consisted of Highway Patrolman Paul Lowethers and Sheriff Arlin Thompson. Their departure from Washburn was aided by Roy Krebsbach and Roy Yunker. Krebsbach and Yunker had been busy plowing streets in Washburn.

They found Mr. Hoff in his car nine miles north of Washburn. After what he had been through, Robert Hoff was very thankful when the rescuers showed up.

In March 1966, Jeanna Luttrell and her family owned a general store in Washburn. They had just added a laundromat onto the store and were going to have a grand opening the day the blizzard struck. People were going to be able to wash their clothes all day for nothing. The storm, however, delayed the grand opening for a few days.

While it was on, the blizzard slowed business activity in Washburn to a crawl. As of 11 a.m. Thursday, Mr. Areastein, Washburn's postmaster, reported that he had made only one sale that day and that was a one-cent stamp.

Fred Michel delivered groceries and medicine around the city on a snowmobile donated by Nelson Marines of Washburn.

Another way of delivering groceries was used by Leo Schmaltz. He strapped on snow shoes for the task.

The storm dumped 18 inches of snow on Washburn or 2.15 inches of precipitation.

The biggest snowbanks were by the Washburn school. There the snow just about covered the playground equipment. The drifts along the new elementary building were high enough to allow children to be able to stand atop them and touch the eaves of the building. A snowbank blocked old Highway 83 east of the school. The same drift, prevented the John Romanick family from getting a view out of their living room window.

Washburn, March 1966. Photo courtesy of Jeanna Luttrell

After the storm, deep snow in the woods forced deer to leave that sanctuary and head out into the fall plowing and stubble fields in search of food. The Ervin Lahrens who resided east of Washburn reported sighting about 50 deer doing just that.

During the early hours of Saturday, snow removal crews in Washburn began what the *Washburn Leader* termed a "gigantic snow removal project."

Telephone service both in Washburn and outside the city limits was affected by the blizzard. It was still not 100 percent the following Monday.

The *Washburn Leader* thanked those who helped out with the cleanup in the Washburn-Wilton area after the blizzard. The following are some of the *Leader's* musings about the blizzard:

> For the first time in months-perhaps simply, the first time-a lot of people enjoyed the luxury of just staying in bed. Business did not generally go about as usual. Son Larry and the writer, for at least two days saw nobody outside the family except the post office people and a handful of others. Considering that some folks couldn't even go outside, we can well imagine the chafing at the confinement of the youngsters.
>
> Home meant security and comfort. The fireside was never warmer, especially as one deliberated on the plight of those stalled in cars, of the little girls lost in the swirling mass of white.
>
> The power was off for half an hour in Washburn, which obviously was below the average and a tribute to those who bring us our "juice." Some communities experienced obvious discomfort on that score.
>
> Life in our busy communities was almost at a stand- still. There was none of that "gotta" do this or that. And, there was no use complaining about it!
>
> We are a proud race, highly civilized, and also very dependent upon machines and gadgets. We were, during the height of the storm, reminded of the off-stage and likely off-ploy "follow up" to "Nothing can stop the Army Air Corps":
>
> . . . "Except the weather. . ."
>
> the same weather that could ground the mightiest air force the world had ever seen can certainly also disrupt normal living for us all.[200]

North Dakota's 1966 Easter seal child was 7 year old Donna Nelson, daughter of Mr. and Mrs. Morris Nelson of Washburn.

As they had done the year before, the Parshall Braves did it again on March 11, 1966. They beat the Washburn Cardinals, 43 to 41, in the Region 7 championship game and advanced to the state Class B tournament.

Hopes for a bridge across the Missouri River, most probably at Washburn, were raised at a meeting held at Washburn on March 28, 1966. Attending the meeting were business leaders and farmers from McLean, Mercer, and Oliver Counties.

Addressing them was North Dakota State Highway Commissioner, Walter Hjelle. He said there was a 'great possibility' that construction of a bridge at Washburn might begin within five or six years. Such a bridge would cut twenty-five miles off the distance a person traveled from Mandan to Minot.

Highway Commissioner Hjelle's words were prophetic. In March 1970, bids were let for the proposed structure at Washburn. On November 30, 1971, a ribbon cutting ceremony was held, opening the new bridge to traffic.

Washburn was the home of Mary Ann Barnes Williams, author of *Origins of North Dakota Place Names*, one of our sources for this book. The book came out in January 1966.

On top of the bluffs of the Missouri River, just east of Garrison Dam is Riverdale (1,055 residents in 1960).

The Federal Government established Riverdale. This was done by in conjunction with the building of Garrison Dam. The official start of construction of that facility was October 4, 1947. Settlement at Riverdale, the primary boom town during the building of Garrison Dam, began in 1946.

On June 11, 1953, President Dwight Eisenhower came here to dedicate Garrison Dam. Riverdale's population reached a peak of 4,033 in August 1954 before declining. By 1970, only 545 people resided in Riverdale.

The storm showed up at Riverdale on March 2, 1966. Riverdale's high for the day was 33 above.

In the midst of this onslaught were four expectant Riverdale mothers.

That evening, Glen Baldwin, Riverdale's high school boys basketball coach, sent the team to Garrison for the District 27 basketball tournament. Then, he took his wife Sharon to the Hospital in Garrison. He stayed with her as long as he could. Coach Baldwin's Black Knights lost their Wednesday game to Washburn 89 to 57. When the game was over he went back to the hospital. His wait was rewarded, when a 6 pound 6 1/2 ounce son named Scott was born.

Early Friday morning, it was time for Mrs. John Robinson to go to the hospital. Hampton Breeding and Reynold Doerr got a government snowplow ready at 5:30. They led an ambulance transporting Mrs. Robinson to the Garrison Hospital. Driving the ambulance were Lawrence Tice and Ted Walcker of the Riverdale Fire and Police Department. Accompanying them was an attending nurse, Mrs. Cecil McCrorie. They departed from Riverdale at 6:45 and reached the hospital in Garrison at 7:30. At 8:00 p.m., the Robinson became the parents of a 7 pound 11 1/2 ounce son.

On the return journey to Riverdale, the snowplow and ambulance served as an escort for Coach Baldwin and Mrs. Delton Wulf. The blizzard had caught her on duty in Garrison.

Riverdale received 2 inches of snow on Thursday and 3 inches on Friday. It contained .63 inches of precipitation. Temperatures in Riverdale never dipped below zero during the blizzard. A low of 7 below was reached Sunday morning.

Over forty miles southwest of Minot, not far north of Lake Sakakawea, is the city of Garrison.

It had a population of 1,794 residents in 1960.

In 1903, settlers started purchasing the land around the abandoned Fort Stevenson. Two enterprising brothers from Bismarck, Theodore and Cecil H. Taylor, established the original townsite of Garrison. They named it after Garrison Creek. That stream received its name in 1864. It was a reference to the garrisoning or stationing of troops from Fort Berthold along its banks.

In 1905, the Soo Line built their tracks five miles northeast of the settlement. Facing the inevitable, most of Garrison moved to the new townsite.

Garrison Dam has the same name. Completed in 1954, this dam impounds the Missouri River into a body of water known as Lake Sakakawea. As the crow flies, Garrison Dam is about twelve miles south of its namesake.

Garrison was on the edge of the March 1966 blizzard. The storm hit the area in the evening of March 2. The strongest winds came on Thursday. Friday, the blizzard was not as fierce. There was no school on Thursday and Friday.

Some business was conducted. The few places that opened their doors cut back their operating hours.

Among the scheduled Garrison events either canceled or postponed were the Garrison PTA meeting, the regional basketball tournament, the 5th annual Garrison Wagon Train Talent Show, and the NDSU Gold Star Band concert.

Blocked GN and NP rail lines caused a delay in mail service. For example, the *McLean County Independent* March 3 edition was mailed on time at the Garrison Post Office. Quite a few of its subscribers in the Garrison vicinity failed to receive their copy until the morning of March 8.

Determining how much snow Garrison received during the storm was not easy, if not impossible. The strong winds with the blizzard deposited the snow along with dirt from summer fallow (combining to make "snirt") into towns and shelterbelts. The best guess that Mrs. Albert Beierle, Garrison weather observer, could make was that 4 inches of snow fell on the city. That came to 0.45 inch of precipitation.

The *McLean County* Independent noted this about the storm:

> *While Garrison escaped the brunt of last week's severe weather, this community did serve as a gathering ground for most of the snow which fell in the countryside. And as a consequence snow was piled high on many streets and along side many buildings.*[201]

There was a sighting of birds at Garrison after the storm that usually didn't show up there. A flock of hoary redpolls was seen there by Charles Crank.

Garrison had no train service between March 3 and March 7.

On March 7, the Garrison Troopers lost the District 27 championship game to Washburn, 55 to 36.

Underwood lies over eleven miles northwest of Washburn.

The 1960 census gave Underwood a population of 819.

In 1902, General W. D. Washburn extended his rail line (the Bismarck, Washburn, and Great Falls Railroad–later part of the Soo Line) to Underwood. The townsite was set up in 1903 and name after Fred D. Underwood, a business associate of Mr. Washburn.

The first two days of March 1966 brought mild weather to Underwood. Highs of 33 and 29 were recorded there on the first two days of the month. The arrival of the storm brought about a gradual decline in temperatures.

On March 1, Underwood lost to Riverdale, 61 to 65, in the District 27 basketball tournament at Washburn.

The Underwood Fire Department had a standard policy concerning cold weather and high winds. Whenever those conditions prevailed, they maintained a fire watch. A fire watch was kept on both Thursday and Friday night at the fire hall. As the firemen acknowledged, atrocious weather conditions did not allow for the use of fire trucks if and when a call came in. But the firemen could still respond to calls with hand extinguishers and other small equipment.

On Thursday night, the men who maintained the fire watch included Fire Chief Fred Eman, Dan Boyle, Duane Fischer, Max Guenther, LeRoy Hoff, Leonard Lenzen, Gary Miller, Gordon Olson, Carl Radke, Leo Strecker and Neil Walthers.

On duty Friday night were Carl Bader, Hank Goertzen, Burnell Johnson, Harold Lutz, Bob Rasmusson, Robert Schauer, Clarence Simenson, George Werre and Art Wohl.

The firemen were grateful that no calls came into the fire hall during the blizzard. They passed the time with card games and bull sessions.

The local weather observer at Underwood was Ferdinand Koenig. He reported a snow-fall total from the storm of around 10 inches, 1.12 inches of precipitation. The thermometer continued its downward spiral at Underwood. Sunday morning, it bottomed out at 15 below zero.

Underwood had drifts between 5 and 6 feet deep. The snowbanks held many vehicles. On Thursday morning, a man from Minneapolis arrived in Underwood. He left his automobile parked in front of the *Underwood News* office. That building was on the north side of the street. After the storm, Eddie Anderson helped the Minneapolis man dig the car out from its snowy tomb. If he had left the vehicle on the other side of the street opposite of the *News* office, the Minneapolis man would have had to do much less shoveling to get his car free.

A large drift lay in front of Hank's Barber Shop and Lloyd's Bar in Underwood. As was common in places throughout the storm area, the south side of streets with businesses along them were mostly clear of snow.

Emil Wilke climbed out of a basement window after the storm. Then, he shoveled the snow away from the doors of his house.

About fifteen miles east northeast of Underwood is Turtle Lake. The town had a population of 792 residents in 1960.

In July 1905, the NP surveyed a route to the area. That year, the railroad established a station in a place that became Turtle Lake. The NP branch line ended there.

Mrs. John Kraft of Turtle Lake gave this description of the storm that enveloped Turtle Lake in March 1966:

> Yes, North Dakota had a blizzard. This time when we made national
> headlines it was not exaggerated. Old timers cannot remember when there
> was one of such severity, which lasted so long.[202]

The storm reached Turtle Lake on the evening of March 2. Snow began falling around 6 p.m. with blizzard conditions being reached about midnight.

The vast majority of Turtle Lake residents stay in their homes during the blizzard. Only a few headed out in the storm to purchase a quart or two of milk.

Borth's Department Store in Turtle Lake remained open both Thursday and Friday. Holtans, another store, opened for business on Friday. For each day of the storm, at least one Turtle Lake grocery store remained open. They checked with elderly families to inquire about their needs.

A Wednesday delivery of milk and other essentials meant that Turtle Lake's grocery stores went into the blizzard well-stocked. No shortages developed.

With the exception of an army surplus weasel, all motor vehicular traffic in Turtle Lake came to a halt on Thursday and Friday. Willis Britton, that vehicle's owner, along with Clarence Edinger and Emil Neuharth, came to the rescue for several Turtle Lake homes that were short of fuel oil and groceries. The men delivered these much needed supplies in the weasel.

The Turtle Lake Hospital, with thirty patients on Thursday and Friday, needed the services of this trio with their weasel. Besides serving as a taxi for hospital personnel, they brought needed food and medicine to the hospital. As elsewhere, some employees worked extra hours.

Visibility was a problem at times for the trio in the weasel. They just about became lost a couple of times. There were times they "couldn't see any further than their nose."

There was no school at Turtle Thursday and Friday, March 3 and 4. The district basketball tournament had to be postponed.

Turtle Lake became a refuge for nine stranded travelers.

Caught in Turtle Lake on business when the storm arrived were a salesman from Fargo and an auditor from Bismarck. The latter was employed at the state capitol. These two men holed up at the E-V Motel.

Among the guests at the Turtle Lake Hotel were a trio from Cody, Wyoming. This group consisted of a man, his wife, and brother. They had been visiting relatives in Towner and were headed for Bismarck. The blizzard forced them to stop at Turtle Lake.

Two other stranded guests at the Hotel were two men from Bismarck who had been to Velva. Employed by the Vantine Paint and Glass Company of Bismarck, they were enroute home, when the storm forced them to take shelter in Turtle Lake.

The lobby of the Turtle Lake Hospital became the refuge Friday night for a couple heading to Minot.

Around 4 a.m. Friday a Turtle Lake couple, Mr. and Mrs. Leo Cunningham awoke to the sounds of racing motors. Peering out their front window, the Cunninghams noticed six vehicles crawling up Turtle Lake's Main Street. Aboard them were twelve Minot Air Force Base personnel. Their destination was Rugby. The Air Force personnel were looking for three missing persons. The Cunninghams served the men coffee and cookies. With the assistance of Willis Britton's weasel, they were on the road again by 6 a.m.

From around midnight Wednesday until sunset on Friday, visibility in the Turtle Lake neck of the woods varied between zero and a few hundred feet.

Recording temperature and precipitation totals at Turtle Lake while the storm raged proved to be tough going for local weather observer, Walter Renfrow. Blizzard conditions on Thursday prevented him from getting to the weather station located a short distance from his front door.

Renfrow was able to make it to the weather station on Friday. The high and low he recorded for Turtle Lake that day were 22 and 4, respectively.

Renfrow's measurements on Saturday showed that Turtle Lake had received 2.90 inches of precipitation for the two and a half day storm. His estimate of snowfall at Turtle Lake from the blizzard came to about 25 inches. Wind speeds at Turtle Lake during the storm were from 30 to 50 mph. After the blizzard, the thermometer dipped to 11 below at Turtle Lake on Sunday morning.

There was some livestock losses in the Turtle lake area from the blizzard.

With all 99 pens almost completely buried in snow, the livestock ring at Turtle Lake called off its scheduled sale for March 7.

There was an impressive snowbank between Mel's Cities Service station and Miller's grocery store in Turtle Lake.

The snow removal process in Turtle Lake was a rapid one. What made this possible was the Lindteigen Construction Co. Inc., headquartered in Turtle Lake. They employed two of their four-wheel drive payloaders to clear Turtle Lake's streets. One of their payloader operators was Byron Lindteigen.

On March 7, the Turtle Lake Trojans and the Wilton Miners played for third place in the District 27 tournament at Washburn. The Miners came from behind to defeat the Trojans 64 to 58.

Less than ten miles east northeast of Turtle Lake is the village of Mercer.

It enjoyed a population of 154 in 1960.

Mercer began as an NP station in 1905. The village, along with Mercer County were named for a onetime local rancher, a Civil War veteran from Pennsylvania, William Henry Harrison Mercer.

The storm arrived in Mercer around 5 p.m. March 2, 1966. Not everyone from the Mercer vicinity who attended the basketball tournament at McClusky (thirteen miles east of Mercer) Wednesday evening made it back to town.

The blizzard finally abated in Mercer Saturday morning.

Fortunately, the Mercer area came through the storm without any sickness or loss of life.

With the exception of Sidney Nielsens, local ranchers came through the blizzard with a minimum loss of livestock. Mr. Nielsens suffered the loss of eighteen young head of cattle that had strayed.

No church services were held in Mercer on Sunday.

Although school was held in Mercer on Monday, there weren't many children on the school buses. Deep snow, near the school, prevented the buses from letting the children off at their regular spots.

Mrs. Floyd Sprout, Brush Lake's news correspondent wrote:

The storm has passed and we are now in the process of shoveling out. Many drifts of snow are 12 to 15 feet in height. The hay stacks are covered. The shelterbelts are just one huge snowbank. I have never seen such huge and long snowbanks. Many of the trees such as the plum and pine are completely covered. This is a first storm for many of the younger set.

The storm hit about 4:30 p.m. Wednesday and steadily grew worse at 6 p.m. when the basketball boys were preparing to leave for town to join other members of the Bison basketball team to go to McClusky for the sub-district tournament, visibility was very poor. They all made it home safe.

Thursday morning proved to be another story as cattle had to be fed. This task was accomplished by taking bales from the hay loft and pushing them out of a window that had been taken out of the barn. They had to crawl out windows and carry the hay where the cattle were standing. Then the cattle eyes and noses had to be cleaned of ice and snow so they could see and breathe.

Friday night about 10 p.m. it cleared so for the first time in more than 72 hours we could see the garage, barn and the school house across the road.

The clanging of a flag pole chain helped a local youth find his way to safety in the storm. Bennie Schmitt, son of Mrs. Tillie Schmitt, had gone to Drake Wednesday morning.

Bennie stated he left Drake about midnight Wednesday night. It was not storming there, and he could see the vapor light along the road till he got five miles north of Mercer. He kept looking for light at the Jens Glad farm but was unable to locate it. He knew he had gone too far south to make his turn toward home.

He turned around and drove north and seeing an approach he pulled on it. By that time he had lost all sense of direction. He sat on this approach from 1 a.m. till nearly 2:30 a.m. He was running low on gas and decided he must do something. He rolled down his window and drove south again and heard the clanging of the flag pole chain at the Sprout house. He knew he was close to shelter. He tried to back out and turn around as he knew he had parked on the approach which leads to the Sprout farm yard. By this time the car was wet and the motor stopped and he was unable to start it.

Mrs. Sprout had noticed the car lights as they were backing out of the approach so she put the yard light on in case someone could see it. Bennie said he couldn't see it, but knew he was close and struck out for the Sprouts house. Where he stayed till Saturday when he walked home.

Bennie started out Wednesday morning without cap, overshoes or gloves. So he was a cold hungry young man when he reached Sprouts about 3 a.m. Thursday morning. Bennie stated he never was so happy to hear a noise before he heard the clanging of the flag pole chain.[203]

Minot, Velva, Drake, Anamoose and Bottineau

About a hundred miles NNW of Bismarck is Minot. Situated for the most part in the Mouse (Souris) River Valley, the "Magic City" is at the crossroads of three federal highways, U.S. 2, U.S. 52, and U.S. 83. The North Dakota State Fair is held there every July.

Minot is where Dale Brown, longtime men's basketball coach at Louisiana State University (LSU), came from. One of his players at LSU was future NBA star Shaquille O'Neal.

North of the city about thirteen miles is Minot Air Force Base. On July 12, 1955, ground was broken for this base. Its activation came on February 7, 1957. Today, it is the home for B-52 bombers.

In 1960, 30,604 people lived in Minot.

The GN established the townsite of Minot in November 1886. The man for whom Minot was named after was Henry Davis Minot (1859-1890). A GN director, Minot perished in a train accident.

Minot was on the edge of the March 1966 blizzard. It experienced high winds before daylight on March 3. It began snowing around 6:30 a.m. Once it got light outside, the city had squalls of light snow. It became a full blown storm for just a short while, around mid-morning. The city received one inch of snow, .08 inches of precipitation on Thursday. No other precipitation was recorded. It was more of a "snirt storm" in Minot on Thursday, something out of the "Dirty Thirties."

The further west and north a person went from Minot, the better conditions were. A place would get squalls of wind and snow, but then, within an hour, visibility had improved. At these localities, there was a wide variety in intensity of storm conditions, and storm squalls were intermittent. "Blustery" would be the word to describe conditions in these areas on Thursday.

For example, as of 9:15 a.m. Williston was only reporting some wind.

This was reflected in the North Dakota highways being reported open by the state Highway Department to traffic on Friday morning, March 4 when the blizzard was at its height:

U.S. 2 from the Montana line to Rugby, U. S. 83 from the Canadian line to Junction 37 (the Garrison road), U.S. 85 from the Canadian line to Watford City and U.S. 52 from the Canadian line to Drake.[204]

In March 1966, Maureen Puppe of Crystal, ND. was attending school at Minot State College. Although Minot escaped the snowfall points further east had, she remembered the high winds that Minot endured. Maureen recalled being stung by sand as she walked across campus. This, despite being bundled up. The sand came from hills north of town.

Maureen went home on quarter break after the storm. She began encountering deep snow at Cando. While driving down the highway, Maureen found the drifts, in places, to be quite deep. So deep in fact, that it seemed to her, that passing through them was like driving through a tunnel.[205]

Although Minot had escaped the worst of the blizzard, travel through it was still affected by it. GN's eastbound passenger train, the *Western Star*, pulled into Minot at 6:25 a.m. on March 4. The train was held there.

In the meantime, a number of people chose to wait in the depot instead of remaining aboard the train. Quite a few did not leave the train at all. They passed the time either by sleeping in their compartments, reading, or just sitting quietly.

On Friday night, a Minot unit of about forty men of the North Dakota National Guard was informed they were going to assist in helping to restore highways and other places blocked with snow to normal. They were associated with 164th Engineer's Battalion.

Members of National Guard units from Bottineau, Cando, Garrison, and Rugby received orders to get snow removal equipment ready.

Because the 164th Battalion's commander, Col. Robert Dahl was marooned in Grafton by the storm, Maj. Hiram T. Walker took over command until Col. Dahl's arrival.

On Saturday, the *Western Star* was still at Minot. Meanwhile, around twenty more passengers waited at the depot. Their trains were stopped at Williston. These were the *Empire Builder* which was scheduled to arrive in Minot at 9:15 p.m. Friday and the *Western Star* which was due in Minot at 6:05 a.m. Saturday.

The same action was being taken at the other end. Trains that usually went through Minot were being held up in both Fargo and St. Paul.

According to GN officials, no freight trains had run on the Minot Division since Thursday afternoon.

On Saturday, according to the North Dakota Highway Department, all the highways in the northwestern quarter of the state were open and in good driving condition. The highway department hoped to have all highways south and west of the Missouri River passable at a minimum to one-way traffic. Exceptions to this would be sections of Highways 6, 31 and 49, south of 21. U. S. 83 was open from the Canadian border south to Bismarck, and U. S. 10 was open from Bismarck to Sterling. However, no travel was advised east of there. Highways not open at that time included U.S. 2 from Rugby to Grand Forks, U.S. 52 southeast from Anamoose, and the stretch of I-94 and U. S. 10 from Sterling to Fargo.

The letup of the storm meant that mail service to and from Minot from all direction could resume. Mail from Bismarck via that star route came in Saturday. Its driver had been snowbound in Bismarck for two days.

A similar tale of woe was being related by C. G. Allen, who ran the star route to Devils lake. Allen told Lloyd Joyer, Superintendent of mails at the Minot Post Office, that his driver had been stranded in Devils Lake for two days.

A charter plane from Minneapolis carrying 300 pounds first class mail arrived in Minot at 8:20 a.m. Sunday.

However, it would be Sunday night before Minot received mail in any substantial quantities from the east. That is when GN's *Empire Builder, No. 31* reached Minot. Holed up in Fargo by the blizzard since Friday morning, the train came to Minot via Grand Forks. GN's line between Minot and Fargo (known as the Surrey Cutoff) was still blocked at that time. According to Joyer, *No. 31* brought the first big quantity of mail to Minot from the Twin Cities, since the previous Thursday.

The log jam of rail traffic finally broke on Sunday. GN was able to get its line from Minot to Grand Forks open. The *Western Star*, snowbound in Minot since Friday morning, finally headed east at 2:30 p.m. Sunday. GN's *No. 3* which turned around in Grand Forks and returned to St. Paul on Thursday was due in Minot Monday night.

As the *Minot Daily News* noted:

> Making up schedules which had been interrupted by last week's blizzard, trains have been moving through Minot like Grand Central Station since Sunday afternoon.
>
> As of Monday March 7, the Surrey cut-off was still being blocked by five stalled freight trains between Fargo and New Rockford.[206]

As of Monday, March 7, 1966, the North Dakota Highway Department listed the following state highways as being impassable:

N.D. 5, 15 miles east of Langdon.
N.D. 7, (later N. D. 200) from Carrington to Glenfield
N.D. 9, from Melville to west junction 20 and from
Wimbledon to junction 1.
N.D. 11, from west Dickey County line to west junction 1.
N.D. 13, from west LaMoure County line to Edgeley.
N.D. 13, from 10 miles south of Mayville to the North
Cass County line.
N.D. 32, from Nome to east junction 46.
N.D. 34 , from 10 miles east of Napoleon to junction 56.
N.D. 38, from junction 32 to Hope.
All of N.D. 45.
N.D. 46, from junction 1 to east junction 32.
N.D. 56, from east junction 13 to junction 11.

Also blocked at this time, was I-94 and U.S. 52 from West Fargo to the Minnesota line. Traffic was being rerouted through Fargo via U.S. 10.[207]

Minot's two Class A basketball teams did not do very well at the State Class A Tournament being held in Grand Forks. The Minot Magicians lost to Wahpeton 72 to 62, and Minot Ryan was defeated by Fargo North 79 to 58 on March 10, 1966. In consolation action the next day, the Magicians were upended by Cavalier 67 to 61, and Ryan was beaten by Grand Forks Central 75 to 54.

Over twenty miles southeast of Minot, the Mouse River begins its turn back to the north heading for Canada. At this point in the Mouse River Valley, is the city of Velva, North Dakota (1,330 residents in 1960).

CBS radio and television newsman Eric Sevareid (1912-1992) was a native of Velva. Sevareid's 1930 trip with Walter Port from Minneapolis to Hudson Bay via the Minnesota and Red Rivers was related by him in his book, *Canoeing with the Cree*.

In 1893, the Soo Line built its tracks through the Velva area on the way to Minot. They gave the name of the settlement there "Velva." The name reflected the velvet-like appearance of the Mouse River Valley at that locality.

Velva was on the edge of the March 1966 blizzard. It received 2.5 inches of snow, .59 inches of precipitation.

As the storm raged, the Velva Volunteer Fire Department was dealing with a prairie fire. The origin of the fire was thought to be the Velva Dump, a mile and a half east of the city. Pushed along by strong winds the fire moved over the snow. Grass that stuck through the snow was burned off. Before it was contained, the blaze had burned for a about a quarter of a mile. It came close enough to threaten fence posts and other personal property.

Drake (752 residents in 1960) lies about thirty miles southeast of Velva along U.S. Highway 2.

Established in 1899, Drake was located at the intersection of two Soo Line tracks, the Valley City-Minot and the Devils Lake-Max lines. The city's name came from the original homesteader of the townsite, Herman Drake (1860-1947).

No school was held in Drake on March 3 and 4. Drake received 1.41 inches of precipitation from the March 1966 blizzard.

There was no loss of livestock in McHenry County from the storm.

The Drake Trojans won the District 21 tournament at Velva on March 7. Two days later, they beat Minot Model, 45 to 40, in the consolation game of the regional. Jim Isaak scored 18 points and Ron Ziegler added another 13. The Trojans finished the season with a 21-5 record.

Another town along U. S. Highway 52 is Anamoose, located six miles southeast of Drake.

In 1960, Anamoose's population was 503.

Romanians from Saskatchewan established Anamoose about 1893. It was another Soo Line town. The daughter of a Soo official is said to have given Anamoose its name. It comes from a corruption of a Chippewa term for a female dog, "uhnemoosh."

Unlike places northwest of it, Anamoose did not escape the force of the March 1966 blizzard with just high winds. It received quite a bit of snow. Just about everything ground to a halt. This included the closing of schools and any traveling. Despite the lousy weather, roads in the Anamoose vicinity were still passable.

Residents in and around Anamoose came through the storm all right. Apparently, they didn't suffer for lack of food or fuel. Anamoose did not have any power outages during the storm. A few places in Anamoose were buried in the snow.

The further east anyone proceeded from Anamoose, the greater the snowfall became.

On March 7, the Anamoose Royals finished their 1965-66 season with a 68 to 63 loss to Martin in the District 21 tournament held at Velva. Frank Seig had 9 points for Anamoose.

Bottineau (2,613 residents in 1960) is the seat of Bottineau County, located in north central North Dakota. This city is the home to the NDSU School of Forestry.

Established in 1884, Bottineau was named after Pierre Bottineau (1812-1895).

In 1887, GN extended a branch line northwest from the main line at Rugby. That line bypassed Bottineau two miles to its north. So, the town moved to the rail line site that year.

The March '66 blizzard gave Bottineau County a grazing blow. The western part of the county received no snow from the storm. Dust from high winds obscured the sky there (in places like Westhope), but at no time was travel not possible in western Bottineau County.

It was a different story in the eastern part of the county. High winds and several inches of new snow combined to make for blizzard conditions on Friday March 4 in the rest of the county to about six miles west of Bottineau. Traffic was halted as blowing snow reduced visibility and formed humongous drifts. On Friday morning, visibility in Bottineau was down to a block or a block and a half.

But, at the same time, no emergency calls had come into the Bottineau County sheriff's office. As a whole, Bottineau County did not suffer greatly from the storm.

Bottineau received three inches of snow from the storm, .06 inches of precipitation.

Lewis Belisle lived with his family on a farm outside of Bottineau at the time of the March 1966 storm. He was attending high school in Bottineau. Lewis was stranded in Bottineau for three days by the blizzard. He remembers the humongous snowbanks left by the storm.[208]

The disappearance of three students, enroute home on quarter break from the North Dakota School of Forestry, was solved when they were located at a farm home nine miles north of Harvey. The lack of any communications at the farm including telephone service prevented them from telling others of their whereabouts. The three students, Kathy Caine of New Rockford, Lavone K. Fossun of Litchville, and Lynn McCarthy of Drake were reported missing on Friday.

The students, along with other stranded motorists, became stuck near the Arthur Anhorn farm home. The Anhorn place along N.D. Highway 3 was located thirty-three miles south of Rugby. The students along with Berny Waldock, a Swift and Company salesman from Harvey, were located at the Anhorn residence around 1 a.m. Saturday by Highway Patrolman Richard Bercier and Sheriff Walt Miltenberger.

Astonishingly, three other motorists were also stranded close to the Anhorn house. By the time they were rescued, they had been inside their vehicles for over 48 hours. One vehicle sheltered two men from Rugby. Charles Hersey, a druggist, and Charles Liming, a barber had been enroute to Arizona, but did not get very far. They were stranded in their car, only a little more than 100 feet from the Anhorn residence. As Bercier and Miltenberger noted, *"It had stormed so bad, that Hersey and Liming did not even see the Anhorn house."*[209]

The occupant of the other vehicle, Walter Bond, lived in Fargo-Moorhead area. At 10 a.m. Thursday, his car had stalled approximately two blocks from the Anhorn driveway. To keep warm and prevent frostbite, Bond utilized a sweatshirt he had with him. He tore it into several pieces. He wrapped some of the pieces around his feet and then put on his overshoes over the wrapping. Bond wrapped another piece of the sweatshirt around his face. The experience left him with frozen heels.

After locating Bond, Hersey and Liming, the patrolling officers took the three men to the Anhorn residence. Upon entering, the officers discovered the four additional stranded motorists. The unexpected guests had depleted the Anhorns food supply. As Sheriff Miltenberger noted, *"About all they(the Anhorns) had left were a few potatoes."*[210]

On the same night, Bercier and Miltenberger encountered a sad sight on N.D. Highway 19 near Esmond. This highway runs east from N.D. 3. On the highway were thirteen head of cattle with snow drifted around them. Although twelve of them were standing, they were in poor shape. With ice encased muzzles and nostrils, the animals were choking. It appeared to them that one cow that was lying down was going to make it.

McClusky, Hurdsfield, Harvey, Fessenden, Bowdon, Hamberg, Carrington and New Rockford

McClusky, the seat of Sheridan County, is considered to be the geographical center of North Dakota. In 1905, the NP reached McClusky. It was named after William H. Mc-Clusky from Winside, Nebraska, who bought land in this area in 1902. A few miles west of McClusky is the McClusky Canal, a part of the Garrison Diversion project.

In 1960, McClusky enjoyed a population of 751.

One noted resident of McClusky was John E. Davis, Governor of North Dakota, 1957-1960, and later national commander of the American Legion.

The March 1966 storm hammered McClusky. It began snowing there early Wednesday evening. McClusky received .2 inches of snow that day. On Thursday, 10 more inches of the white stuff fell. Winds picked up and residents of McClusky and other Sheridan County towns hunkered down for the duration. Friday, brought an additional 10.3 inches of snow. Wind gusts reached 70 mph.

The *McClusky Gazette* had this to say about the blizzard:

> The storm heaped up 8 to 12-foot snowdrifts in the streets of McClusky and other Sheridan County towns covering windows and doorways of homes and hiding parked cars.[211]

As the blizzard raged, a couple of emergencies came up in the McClusky vicinity. One of them involved expectant parents, Mr. and Mrs. Floyd Murray, who resided on what used to be the Ray Parsons farm southwest of McClusky. To assist with the impending birth, Jerome Lautenschlager employed an REA truck to transport a nurse, Mrs. Froiland, to the Murray home. By the time Mrs. Froiland reached the Murray residence the baby, a 10-pound boy, had been delivered. Assisting with the delivery was Floyd Murray.

In the meantime, on a farm northwest of McClusky, a man had suffered a heart attack. After the storm had let up on Saturday, a snowplow cleared the road to the Wasson farm. He was then taken to Turtle Lake for medical treatment.

According to DeMott Rhoads, Otter Tail Power Company Supervisor at McClusky, the city itself came through the blizzard with only one seventeen-minute power outage. The nearby towns of Denhoff, Goodrich, and Tuttle also suffered the loss of power. They were put back on line Saturday morning.

Including the 1.5 inches that fell on Saturday, McClusky had received a total of 22 inches of snow, 3.11 inches of precipitation. Temperatures dropped from a high of 28 on March 2, to 13 below Sunday morning, March 6. In March 1966, Elmer L. Schielke was the weather observer in McClusky.

The scene in McClusky Saturday morning was of 9 to 14 feet high snowbanks on its Main Street. With that much snow on the ground (24 inches on Saturday) the cleanup process in and around McClusky was a slow one.

Wayne Hankel, Sheridan County Extension Agent, estimated county livestock losses to be around ninety head.

After March 2, McClusky would not see another NP train until March 28. This was due partly to the deep snow. But, another factor was a train derailment. In the previous week, the rail line from Carrington had been opened as far as Goodrich, a town over ten miles east of McClusky.

A diesel engine pulling six boxcars loaded with grain between Carrington and Goodrich came upon a washout six miles west of Carrington on March 20, 1966. Dropping into the washout, the engine took the six cars in with it. Two train crewmen, engineer Christ Fried and brakeman Cy Haffner, received slight bruises in the derailment.

About thirty miles west of Carrington, lies the village of Hurdsfield. It had 183 residents in 1960.

Hurdsfield, an NP station, was platted in 1902. Its name honored Warren W. Hurd, a prominent farmer in this vicinity and land developer for the NP.

Norman Weckerly, a Hurdsfield area rancher, has these remembrances of the March 1966 blizzard:

> I remember the storm of '66, but was too interested in other things to see it as an important "Event."
>
> It was the worst one, I experienced with cattle. Also, the wind was so strong, it was hard to breathe. Here, it was 2 days as I remember.[212]

The blizzard dumped 2 inches of precipitation on Hurdsfield.

In 1960, Harvey, located in the northwestern corner of Wells County, boasted a population of 2,365 residents.

By the spring of 1893, the Soo Line had finished laying its tracks through Minot and onto Portal at the Canadian border. One of the townsite on that line became Harvey.

As to the origin of the name of the townsite-"Harvey" there is some disagreement. The more accepted version has it being named for Colonel James S. Harvey, a Soo Line director and stockholder from Milwaukee, Wisconsin. The other version has the townsite named after Harvey, Illinois.

It hadn't been daylight very long in Harvey Thursday morning, when it was engulfed by the full effects of the storm. Heavy snow, accompanied by a northeasterly wind, was dumped on Harvey. As the local newspaper, the *Harvey Herald*, described it:

> An estimated 20 inches of wet snow came down, twisted and whipped into hard drifts by winds that were recorded at 70 miles an hour at some points in the state.[213]

Normal everyday activity in Harvey shuddered to a stop. Its schools closed, not to reopen until Monday.

Thursday and Friday night, the blizzard brought a dramatic increase in business for the Harvey motels and hotels. The unexpected guests included at least twenty truckers.

The R & R Motel had twenty travelers staying there. They ate at the Coral Lanes Cafe. Employed as their chef was North Dakota state softball commissioner, "Tiny" Schaeffer.

At the height of the storm on Friday morning, nurses at the Sheyenne River Academy, a school two and a half miles from Harvey, placed a call to Dr. Freeman Webber at St. Aloisius Hospital in Harvey. A student at the Academy, Sandra Heinbaugh, 14, from Ridgeview, South Dakota, was suffering an appendicitis attack. At that time, the nurses did not think her condition to be serious.

Around noon, Dr. Webber got ahold of a highway department employee in an effort to secure help in making the trip to the Academy, if the girl's condition warranted it. But the highway department employee wasn't very keen on the idea.

Later in the day, Academy officials phoned Dr. Webber again. In turn, he got ahold of the local Texaco agent, Burnell Dockter. Dockter enrolled the services of Gabe Keller and his "Ski-Doo" snowmobile.

The men left Harvey in a four-wheel drive vehicle, an International "Scout." Coming upon a snowdrift that was too deep, Dr. Webber and Mr. Keller took to the snowmobile. They rode around large drifts until they spied a light. The men set off for it. To their chagrin, upon reaching the light source, they discovered the headlights of the "Scout."

Taking fresh bearings, the men set off once again. They forced their way through the darkness, over large drifts, and near zero visibility to the Academy. Two hours had passed, since they had left Harvey.

They bundled up the girl and placed her on a sled that the snowmobile was towing. On the return trip to Harvey, the sled tipped over once.

Miss Heinbaugh underwent surgery shortly after reaching the hospital at midnight. She recovered nicely.

In thanking Dockter and Keller, Dr. Webber said:

> A real pair of men to make a trip like this under the worst weather conditions you can imagine, to help out a sick girl whom they had never seen before. This was a display of skill and courage.[214]

In another storm related rescue on Friday morning, Mr. Beckory used his tractor that was equipped with a cab, to bring an expectant mother, Mrs. Ray Filler, to St. Aloisius Hospital in Harvey. The Filler Farm was located six miles west of harvey.

With so many people forced to stay indoors for such an extended period of time, what were they to do? According to S. H. Farrington, publisher of the *Harvey Herald*, "it gave people a chance to work on their income tax."

Saturday morning, the photographer for the *Herald* took pictures of Lincoln Avenue after the storm. The paper noted:

> These pictures of just one street in Harvey indicate how heavy was the snowfall, and how powerful the wind that completely covered some homes, and paralyzed traffic for many hours.[215]

It took the services of a caterpillar outfit from Bantry to open the extreme north end of Lincoln Avenue to traffic on Monday.

According to Soo Line employees, the snow from the blizzard did not go beyond Balfour, which is about twenty-five miles northwest of Harvey.

The Harvey Hornets captured third place in the delayed northwest regional tournament by beating Rugby, 51 to 43.

Fessenden, seat of Wells County, boasted a population of 920 in 1960.

The Soo Line reached this place in 1893. The townsite was platted on land homesteaded by Frank Beans, and H. T. Roberts. The town was named for Cortez Fessenden (1825-1910), who was Surveyor General for Dakota Territory from 1861-1885. Under his tenure, the first survey of Wells County was done.

On Wednesday evening, the blizzard arrived here. Everything came to a halt, including the District 16 basketball tournament.

The Fessenden Orioles had finished the regular season ranked as the No. 1 Class B team in North Dakota with a 19-2 record.

Attending the quarterfinal game were some teenagers from Maddock, a town over fifteen miles northeast of Fessenden. They and other travelers ended up staying at the Conner Hotel.

The storm forced the closing of schools throughout Wells County on Thursday and Friday.

Marooned at her business establishment (Tillie's Cafe) from Wednesday until Sunday was Tillie Richardson. Tillie fed many of the stranded travelers in Fessenden. She cooked the meals, washed the dishes and waited on the customers. Her bed for four nights was a combination of booth cushions.

The blizzard deposited 24 inches of snow, 2.45 inches of precipitation, on Fessenden. The town received a trace of precipitation on Wednesday, 6 inches of snow on Thursday, 17 inches on Friday, and 1 inch on Saturday. Fessenden had a high of 20 on Thursday and the thermometer slid to -13 on Monday morning before rebounding.

The front entrances of three Fessenden businesses, Gambles, Clappers Inc., and the Red Owl Agency was completely blocked with snow. Common throughout Wells County were reports of snowbanks up to 20 feet high. Such a drift could be found in the north-west corner of Fessenden.

Amazingly, the cleanup process in Fessenden progressed at a rapid pace. Snow removal began with the opening of single lanes on the majority of Fessenden's streets by Norby Helgesen. To do this he used his bull dozer. Following him, came the city and county snow removal crews. Assisting in this process were a lot of tractors equipped with loaders and a rotary plow. By late Saturday afternoon, the vast majority of Fessenden's streets were open for traffic.

The Corner Hotel in Fessenden enjoyed a lot of business because of the storm. One of its employees, Henry Neibuhr, reported the hotel to be filled to near capacity during the blizzard. Guests stayed longer because N.D. Highway 15, east of Fessenden, remained impassable for several days after the blizzard.

According to J. J. Cummins, Soo Depot Agent at Fessenden, the GN rerouted freight trains through Fessenden. The GN needed time to clear drifts up to 30 feet high in the Pillsbury-Luverne area on the Surrey mainline.

Although schools reopened in Wells County on Monday, many of them let classes out early because of strong winds.

After defeating New Rockford 71 to 46 for the District 16 championship at Fessenden on March 9, the Fessenden Orioles won a berth in the State "B" Tournament at Minot. They did this by upending the Cando Cubs 96 to 79 in Region 4 play at Devils Lake on March 12. Under the guidance of head coach Maurice Railing, it would be Fessenden's first trip to a State Class B Tournament since 1949.

Unfortunately, it proved to be a disappointing trip for the Orioles. The No. 1-ranked Fessenden team started well with an 84 to 61 win over Linton on Thursday, March 17. But, a defeat at the hands of Milnor in the last seconds of the game on Friday by a 73 to 72 score ended Fessenden's title dreams. The Orioles closed out their season with a 69 to 64 third place loss to Langdon.

In March 1966, the Stanley Lund family resided on farm near Bowdon, a town over ten miles southwest of Fessenden. To make it to the barn from their house in the zero visibility of the storm, they attached one end of a rope to a door knob of the house. Whenever the Lunds went to the barn, they held onto the other end of the rope.

A humongous drift across N. D. Highway 30 in Hamberg, a village ten miles northeast of Fessenden, made vehicular traffic through there impossible. To detour around it, Wells County plows cleared other roads.

Carrington, the seat of Foster County, is located about sixty miles south of Devils Lake. Carrington's population in 1960 was 2,438.

In 1883, the NP established a station at Carrington. Coming out of Jamestown, that branch line turned west at Carrington. It ended at Turtle Lake. The Hankinson-Portal mainline of the Soo went through Carrington in 1892. The townsite was platted by the Carrington and Casey Company, townsite developers in central North Dakota. Lyman R. Casey named the settlement after his partner, Miles D. Carrington.

In Class A regional play at Grafton, Grand Forks Central beat Carrington, 78 to 41, on March 1, 1966.

Snow fell in Carrington the evening of March 2. Once the winds picked up, the northeast gusts were between 50 to 60 mph. Along with the rest of Foster County, Carrington was in for an experience that few would forget. The *Foster County Independent* said it was *"one of the worst storms of recorded history."* Furthermore, the newspaper said:

> (The storm) held the area in its grip last Thursday and Friday, causing tragedy, heavy property loss, desolation, deep snowdrifts, and paralysis of traffic. ...The storm had caused virtual standstill to any activity except attending to the home chores, for few people ventured out in the storm which combined heavy snowfall with a high velocity northeast wind.
>
> The numerous acts of heroism and genuine neighborliness are becoming legend in the Carrington area, as the back to normal activity continues. In Carrington the National Guard, the fire department, the Civil Defense organization, the Red Cross, city and county employees, and many other individuals are collaborating in the relief of misery or threats of misery.[216]

Wallace Emerson, Foster County's Civil Defense Director, coordinated relief efforts out of the City Auditor's office in Carrington. Throughout the storm and the following week, his office remained open twenty-four hours a day.

National Guardsmen, firemen and other volunteers offered assistance to those that needed it. Mrs. Ben Will was quite sick in her home. She needed medical attention. They brought Dr. H. A. Fandrich to the Will's residence. They delivered medicines to the hospital and senior citizens homes.

When the blizzard was on, radio station KDAK in Carrington allotted air time for relaying messages of various types. In the days following the storm, emergency personnel depended on KDAK for informing the public of their needs.

No school classes were held in Carrington on Thursday and Friday.

The storm let up in Carrington Saturday morning. It left the city buried under 19 inches of snow, 1.72 inches of precipitation. A high of 37 above was reached in Carrington on March 2. Temperatures fell, but never dipped below the zero mark during the storm. Afterwards, a low of 9 below was recorded on both March 7 and 8.

One Carrington resident, Dennis Ward, relied on the tops of high line poles to guide him on his way home Thursday. He had left the Farmers Union Bulk Station, a mile north of his residence on foot. Ward battled with deep snow and exhaustion, almost became lost, but remained alert and made it home.

It was tough going for a couple of Carrington area men during the blizzard. Friday afternoon, brothers Don and Ron Theis headed for a stack of baled hay a ways from a barn where they had livestock. They headed for the stack with the intention of bringing one or two bales back to the barn with them.

Unfortunately, they lost their bearings. The brothers made every attempt to find out where they were. This included digging through the snow to the ground to find out which crop was planted there. They knew what was planted in all the fields around their farm.

The brothers quickly discerned they had come upon Klindworth land. That property was just a mile from their place. Regaining their bearings, the men headed out on foot in tandem. Upon encountering a fence, the brothers realized they had come to their father's pasture. They used the fence to guide them back to the barn.

The two and a half hour ordeal left them with no more then some frost bite on their faces.

The blizzard meant a lot of anxiety for Ted Clark, Jr., owner of Clark Truck Line of Carrington. He had eight or nine trucks out on the road when the storm descended upon Carrington and he did not know where they were.

On Thursday, two of Clark's truck drivers, Bob Harrington and Jim Schumacher, with a truckload of cattle, became stuck on the highway between Harvey and Fessenden. But, equipped with sleeping bags, the men didn't suffer any frostbite. With the exception of the death of one small animal, the rest of the cattle aboard the truck also survived. A snowplow rescued them on Saturday.

The Vernon Topp family, located about thirteen and a half miles east of Carrington, lost their electricity. A covered shelter provided some protection for sixty of their cattle within it. Hour after hour, the cattle were squeezed into tighter quarters by the wind-driven snow packed in under the roof. The openings to the outside became smaller and smaller. To alleviate the situation, Mr. Topp and his son Richard shoveled snow away day and night.

However, conditions deteriorated to the point to where the cattle had to be evacuated from the shelter. Although it was calving season, the Topps came through the storm without the loss of any cows or calves.

Mrs. Topp had her share of problems in the house. Without power for forty-five hours, the family struggled to get by on their standby electric plant. It lit a small light bulb and prevented the water for the livestock from freezing.

For other lighting purposes, a lantern using fuel oil instead of kerosene was employed. There was no heat for the Topp's house during the electrical outage. They enjoyed but one pot of hot coffee during that time frame.

On Saturday, power was restored on their farm.

In climbing on the roof of their house to shovel off a four feet drift on it, Mrs. Topp found a lot of dead birds in the snow. The following week, assistance was needed to dig out hay and silage from under the snow to feed the Topp's cattle.

Being caught out in the storm in your vehicle was a common refrain in March 1966. Dr. W. C. Voglewede of Carrington could attest to that. His son John, a college student, was returning to Carrington for a short vacation. He was to meet his father in New Rockford. Dr. Voglewede departed for New Rockford on U.S. Highway 281 around 10 a.m. Thursday. But, seven miles north of Carrington the motor on his vehicle stalled in the blizzard. Although stranded, Dr. Voglewede thought that, being stalled on a major highway, he would to be rescued shortly. That didn't happen.

Dr. Voglewede had enough clothes in his car, so he was somewhat warm. He was afraid of falling into a deep sleep, so the doctor remained in the sitting position. In spite of this, he nodded off once in a while.

Finally, after thirty-one hours, help arrived around 6 p.m. Friday evening. It was in the form of two truckers coming from New Rockford. The blizzard had kept them stalled at an intersection close to that city. Afraid of running out of diesel fuel, the truckers made the decision to head for Carrington. The first truck passed Dr. Voglewede's vehicle before he could hail it down. He was ready for the second truck.

That trucker took Dr. Voglewede to the turnoff to his home, a mile north of Carrington. The trek to his house from the highway proved exhausting for the doctor. He weathered the experience okay, the hardest part was being without food all that time.

As for son John? A freight train from New Rockford brought him to Carrington.

Saturday morning, the desolation in Carrington came to an end. Large snowbanks greeted people, as they came out of their houses. The wake of the blizzard left hardships and the need for assistance. The Red Cross helped people by buying gasoline, fuel oil, groceries, medicine, chains and shovels. Members of the National Guard shoveled people out by hand. Their heavy equipment operators and truck drivers made a difference. Equipment of the National Guard was put to good use.

As noted by Foster County Civil Defense Director, Wallace Emerson, the Red Cross had the only available disaster funds in North Dakota.

Foster County experienced significant livestock losses. Continual stamping by cattle in the new snow kept elevating the packed snow until the cattle could step over the top of the feedlot fence. This led to their roaming in the storm and some cattle were lost this way. Robert Montgomery endured a significant loss of cattle this way at his farm. To assist in feeding Montgomery's hungry livestock and check for losses, firemen and National Guardsmen came to his farm on Sunday.

Straight north of Carrington on U.S. 281, is New Rockford (2,177 residents in 1960).

In the spring of 1883, the NP established a townsite that became New Rockford. Charles Gregory, early pioneer, named the townsite after the place he had lived previously, Rockford, Illinois.

In 1912, the GN built the Surrey Cutoff line through New Rockford.

The March 1966 blizzard was one for the record books as far as the *New Rockford Transcript* was concerned. Ed Doherty, editor of the *New Rockford Transcript*, echoed that theme in this manner:

> When the wind and snow started flying about 6 p.m. Wednesday, March 2nd, there was no indication it would continue until the early hours of Saturday morning. Nor was there any indication that it would be the worst storm in the history of North Dakota.[217]

Two sleeping establishments in New Rockford, Klein's Motel and the Rockford Hotel, had lots of guests during the storm. Klein's Motel was located just off U. S. Highway 281. Despite the inclement weather of the blizzard, around thirty of its visitors were able to cross U. S. Highway 281 quite regularly to chow down at Christy's Haven.

Located about a mile south of town is New Rockford's water plant. As the storm raged, Leonard Wells, its superintendent became concerned about the possibility of the development of a water shortage in case of fire. So, when the blizzard was at its worst, he set out on foot for the water plant.

Mrs. Wells was concerned about her husband's safety. In 1965, the Wells had celebrated their golden wedding anniversary.

But she didn't have to worry too long. Mr. Wells made it home Sunday night after a couple days' stay at the water plant.

Imagine Leonard Wells' surprise upon his return. His driveway had been buried under snowdrifts that were 8 to 10 feet high.

When Mr. Wells came back Sunday evening, a 30 foot stretch of it had been shoveled out. Doing the honors were Keith Horning, York Sinkler, and Dr. Willard Varty and his boys.

Quite a few New Rockford homes were unable to pick up a signal on their television sets while the storm was on. What were they going to do? Some people went through their photo albums, refreshing memories and bringing them up to date. In the case of Ed Doherty and his family, they watched home movies. Watching them, brought back memories of forgotten events.

With the tempest raging about them, folks took shelter wherever they could find it. A New Rockford couple, Mr. and Mrs. Bill Lies, found themselves serving as hosts to approximately ten people. Their storm-bound guests were friends and relatives from Fessenden. Mr. Lies, an occasional penny-ante player, remarked that *"this the first time he ever had a full house that didn't make money for him!"*[218]

The storm brought rail and highway traffic in New Rockford to a halt. Being the halfway point on the Fargo to Minot rail line meant that GN trains switched crews at New Rockford. Impassable drifts left five GN trains stalled between Fargo and New Rockford. There were train crews waiting in New Rockford to board trains that never arrived.

Another freight train waited out the storm at New Rockford. Aboard it were a couple of young men "riding the rails." During the blizzard they took shelter in a boxcar and remained there for a couple of days.

On Sunday afternoon, a bit cold and hungry, the men peered outside and made the decision to leave their shelter. Their journey took them from the west end siding into New Rockford. New Rockford's street department employed them through Monday. In that time span, the men shoveled copious amounts of snow. In leaving New Rockford, the men probably took with them indelible memories of the being stranded there in the '66 storm.

GN GP-9 no. 669 moves into the swath cut by a rotary plow on the Surrey line. GN Public Relations photo Courtesy of Stuart R. Holmquist

Wind speeds of the blizzard varied between 30 and 69 mph at New Rockford on Thursday and Friday. They didn't begin to slacken until Saturday. It snowed continuously through this period. What did New Rockford get out all this? Wind packed snowbanks that reached 20 feet in height in sheltered areas. A person could walk on them. Unfortunately, the very hardness of the drifts made it that much more difficult to clear them from roads, streets, and driveways. There was very little foot traffic in New Rockford on Friday, the worst day of the storm.

The residents of New Rockford emerged from their cocoons Saturday morning to a world of white. To do so, many of them were forced to make their exit via windows. Then, if the snow was deep enough, they would have to dig a tunnel to reach their doorways.

Many of New Rockford's business establishments had large drifts in front of them. The snow was piled so deep in front of the Midway City Creamery that its owner, Roy Zweigle, had to dig a tunnel through the drift to gain access to the front door.

As noted elsewhere after the blizzard, because of the prevailing direction of the wind (northeast), snow was piled deep on the south side of business establishment. In many instances, buried underneath all that snow were cars parked along the street. New Rockford had one advantage in the cleanup after the storm. It was the home of Archie Campbell, Inc., a construction outfit with heavy equipment. It took them just a few hours Saturday to have New Rockford's main thoroughfares open to a minimum of one-way traffic.

Eddy County did incur some livestock losses from the storm. The deep snow also made it difficult for farmers to reach feed for the hungry animals.

On March 9, the New Rockford Rockets took second place at the District 16 basketball tournament held at Fessenden. The Rockets lost the championship game 75 to 46 to Fessenden.

The following statement appeared in the *Great Northern Goat*, Volume 36, Number 4, April 1966:

> ...North Dakota was by far the hardest hit. GN's Surrey line in that state experienced the greatest winter buffeting in the 104-year history of the railway. There the tracks were closed until March 11. It was here that hard-packed snow deposited to a depth of up to 35 feet in long drifts that bisected the line at many points. More than 30,000 tons of snow were rotaried out in the initial cut in an 8 1/4 mile stretch. The snow was packed so solidly that a D-8 Caterpillar tractor was able to ride the snow 'wave' and hardly leave a track.

On March 14, all GN main and branch lines were opened, and business was back to normal.

Cooperstown, Luverne, Pillsbury, Colgate, Page, Hope, Finley and Sharon

Almost fifty miles east of Carrington is the seat of Griggs County, the city of Cooperstown.

It had a population of 1,424 in 1960.

Two brothers, Rollin C. Cooper and his brother Thomas, figured very prominently in the early development of Cooperstown. They owned the townsite of Cooperstown which was established in 1882.

In 1882, the Cooper brothers planned on building a rail line north of Sanborn, seven miles west of Valley City. Their enterprise was called Sanborn, Cooperstown, and Turtle Mountains Railroad. It reached Cooperstown in the summer of 1883. That line, was later purchased by the NP.

In 1937, Edward Reiten established a plow manufacturing outfit at Cooperstown.

The arrival of the March 1966 blizzard in Cooperstown was marked by strong northeast winds which sprang up around 3 p.m. Wednesday March 2. It was the beginning of a three-day storm. This was on a day when a high of 35 was reached in Cooperstown.

Cooperstown hosted some marooned travelers. Among them were six Mayville State College students who had driven to Cooperstown to catch first round action of the district basketball tournament taking place Wednesday evening. The storm left them stranded two miles east of Cooperstown at the Ralph Tweed farm (formerly the Charles Young place) on N.D. Highway 7.

The following afternoon, the students who came from Finley, McVille, and Tolna motored to Cooperstown. They stayed there until the blizzard let up.

The storm proved to be a trying experience (including financial) for a family that lived on a farm east of Cooperstown.

The James Luras made it through the first night of the blizzard without any problems.

But, then on Thursday a fuse blew in a transformer located next to the Lura farm. To compensate for their loss of power, Mr. Lura started a tractor to run a standby power plant. After using it that day, he shut it off for the night.

The situation deteriorated for the Luras on Friday. Their tractors iced over because of the blizzard conditions. Now, there wasn't any way for them to restore power. So, Mr. Lura, his wife, and three daughters headed for the shelter of their basement. They remained there until the waning of the storm on Saturday.

After a snowplow cleared the roads, they were transported to Cooperstown. The Luras stayed at the home of Mrs. Lura's father, Herman Solfleld, Saturday afternoon and night.

REA repairman came to the Lura farm and restored power.

In reflecting on their experience, Mrs. Lura said it became cold enough in their home to freeze her house plants. But the same couldn't be said for the water pipes, which did not freeze up.

As if they hadn't suffered enough, the Luras experienced another misfortune. Snow had drifted against a quonset machine shed on their place. The weight of it brought about the collapse of the structure.

The majority of residents in the Cooperstown vicinity didn't stray from the comfort of their homes during the blizzard.

People who worked at the hospital did not have that luxury. Some walked to work and others rode on snowmobiles. Quite a few of them chose to remain at the hospital overnight instead of going home.

The *Griggs County Sentinel-Courier* had this to say about their usefulness:

> The little motor sleds, popular pleasure vehicles in recent winters, served
> as highly practical taxis for anyone lucky enough to catch a ride. Part of
> the fun was in falling off, some passengers reported.

Mrs. Clarence Njaa, a nurse's aid, Mrs. Alma Riste, a laundry worker, and Mrs. Arnold Skofstad, RN, were among those who walked to the hospital.

Mrs. Skofstad wasn't going to let a blizzard, even the worst of the century, keep her from making it to work. Friday morning, Mrs. Skofstad headed off for the hospital. Her four block journey was strenuous for the elderly lady. Half the time, she faced the wind which by now had switched to the northwest. Besides that, her glasses frosted over. But as Mrs. Skofstad commented, *"It didn't hurt me and it was good to know I could still do it."*

The following reflections of the blizzard by "Duna" appeared in the March 10, 1966 edition of the *Griggs County Sentinel-Courier:*

> *When the sun is shining and the snow is thawing and it turns out that only 1.63 inches of precipitation were recorded in the storm, it is hard to believe that just a few days ago we were snowbound. Well, it would be hard to believe, except for the happy fact that we have snow up to our teeth, and will have for a while.*
>
> *A prolonged snowstorm such as we had last week is a legendary event, and as the years go by people will date events by the storm.*
>
> *In our house I was–unwillingly and nervously–the object of a lot of attention. We are expecting a baby soon, and my snowbound family all kept looking at me suspiciously and telling me to sit down and not exert myself.*
>
> *I think they were secretly boiling water, too.*
>
> *We were warm and comfortable and had plenty of food at our house and as I think of the storm, the worst part of it was not being able to see what was going on. Our neighbors' houses across the street were only occasionally visible, and there were only brief glimpses of the drifts building up all over.*
>
> *One thing I'll never forget the sight of, somebody in a red shirt in the house across the street when the storm began to clear Friday night. I felt like Noah when the dove brought back the greenery to the ark.*
>
> *And those snowplows Saturday morning were some of the most beautiful objects I can remember seeing in my life.[219]*

The blizzard began to let up in Cooperstown Friday night. By midday Saturday, it had quit snowing, although there was still a little wind. Cooperstown received 1.63 inches of precipitation from the storm. Temperatures remained moderate in Cooperstown through the course of the storm. A low of 8 above was recorded on Friday. Afterwards, they did plunge to 9 below on Monday morning.

On Saturday, snowbanks as high as 15 feet could be found in Cooperstown and in trees and around buildings on nearby farms. Out in the open, fields and roads were either bare or just about so, due partly to thawing that taken place earlier in the winter.

Although snow removal operations commenced in the Cooperstown area before daybreak Saturday, it was tough going. Before they could open roads, Griggs County crews had to dig their machines out. That afternoon, they embarked on the job of opening roads.

At the Cooperstown Airport, snow drifted into a hangar and onto two planes. The weight snapped the wing off of one plane. The other plane was severely damaged as well.

Cooperstown's team advanced to the state Class B tournament in March 1966. They lost their first game against Milnor in the final seconds. Copperstown defeated Linton, 101 to 81, and New England St. Mary's, 95 to 74. The Lynx came home with the fifth place trophy. Gary Bakken set three tournament records: 49 points in one game; 103 in three games; and 17 free throws in one game. Bakken still holds the record for most points scored in a single game.

Situated in the southwestern corner of Steele County about twenty-five miles north northeast of Valley City is the small hamlet of Luverne (109 residents in 1960).

The Luverne Land Company of Willmar, Minnesota, platted this GN station in 1910 and gave the settlement its name.

The March 1966 blizzard really hammered Luverne. Completely entombed in the snow were a lot of cars and tractors. A few of them had been dug out and had incurred damage. It would take awhile to dig the rest out.

The storm caught an elevator auditor from Moorhead, Minnesota, Chet Kjesbo, in Luverne. He took refuge at the Jacob Gienger residence. The blizzard left the two Gienger automobiles and Mr. Kjesbo's car buried under large drifts.

Huge drifts 31 miles northwest of Fargo, March 1966. GN Public Relations photo Courtesy of Stuart R. Holmquist

Finally, on Sunday, Mr. Kjesbo's partner, Mr. Newman, motored up from Valley City to take him back to Moorhead. The storm had left Mr. Newman, a field representative, stuck in Valley City. They were accompanied on their return by Mrs. Mel Zierke and her daughter.

When the teacherage in Luverne was completely enveloped in snow on Friday, Mr. and Mrs. Esley Ehort and their son had to take shelter at the Richard Rasmussen home. So his family could exit from their house, Mr. Ehort was forced to dig into the house via an upper window.

It was Sunday afternoon before two Valley City residents, Superintendent of School John Conlon and Mr. Ronda were able to depart from Luverne.

The blizzard left twenty-six students, all from St. Mary's vicinity, stranded in Luverne for four days. They boarded at the homes of friends in Luverne for the duration. It would be Sunday before they could leave.

Stuck in Valley City until Sunday were fifteen students from Luverne along with their music teacher, Mr. Hall, and Charley Jensen, their bus driver.

Pillsbury lies a few miles southeast of Luverne.

It enjoyed a population of 76 in 1960.

Pillsbury was established in July 1910 by the Luverne Land Company. C. O. Smith, the original townsite proprietor and others named it after a man associated with the Pillsbury Washburn Milling Company of Minneapolis, Alfred F. Pillsbury.

The March 1966 blizzard caught a GN freight train at Pillsbury. It stalled there on Thursday night. A few of the rail cars were completely buried in the snow. With telephone wires underneath the drifts, there was no outside communications. The train crew was stuck in Pillsbury for the duration. On Sunday, they were treated to supper at the Dale Larson home.

Rotary snowplow X-1507 cutting through a 1 and 5/8 mile-long-drift on March 7, 1966, near Erie Junction on the Surrey line. Fargo Forum photo by Chet Gerbert Courtesy of Loren Charnholm Collection

Rotary snowplow X-1507 chewing inch-by-inch through the heavily packed snow on the Surrey line. Five diesel units supply the "push", March 1966. Courtesy of Loren Charnholm Collection

Dennis Rickard standing next to a large snowbank on the Jim and Millie farm near Hope, March 1966. Courtesy of Jim and Millie Rickard

On Thursday night, Lynn Wilson headed for home from Valley City with the road patrol. Then, no more was heard from him. Finally, on Saturday afternoon, Mr. Wilson reached home. His machine had stalled five miles north of Oriska at the Miller farm. Oriska is fourteen miles east of Valley City and about twenty-five miles southeast of Luverne. Mr. Wilson hadn't been heard from before this because he did not have access to a phone.

Pillsbury had its share of stranded travelers during the storm. The blizzard caught a Cooperstown couple and a child in Pillsbury. The man had just gotten out of the hospital, and they were headed back to Cooperstown when the bad weather forced them to take refuge at the Herman Jess home in Pillsbury Wednesday night.

A South Dakota family was returning from Warwick when they were forced them to pull up at Pillsbury Wednesday night. The Wildlife Hall became their refuge. At midday Sunday, they departed for home.

Long distance phone service in Pillsbury was disrupted by the storm.

Hope lies seven miles northwest of Colgate.

In 1960, 390 people lived in Hope.

The Red River Land Company platted Hope in February 1882. Its named honored Hope A. Hubbard Steele, secretary-treasurer of the Red River Land Company. That outfit purchased 50,000 acres at one dollar an acre from the NP. Steele County is named after Mr. Steele.

The March 1966 blizzard caught many Hope residents elsewhere. These included Mrs. George Thilmony and Jeff who were stranded in Valley City for four days-Wednesday to Sunday.

In Hope itself, guests for a couple of nights at the residence of Mrs. Mabel Chance were Mrs. Ben Nelson and Mrs. Stanley Nelson. Taking shelter at George Thilmony's home were Dave Ihry and the Reed Washburn family. The John Ihrys had their son, Ken, as a house guest Wednesday and Thursday nights. Staying for the night at his parents home (the J. H. McCulloughs) Wednesday was Charles McCullough.

Farms in the Hope vicinity suffered extensive cattle losses. Reed Washburn and Neil Hashbarger had the greatest losses. Many of Hashbarger's cattle died as a result of a barn collapse.

Hope was one of those towns that suffered a loss of long distance telephone service during the blizzard.

In March 1966, Jim and Millie Rickard and their son Dennis resided on a farm near Hope. The following is Millie Rickard's remembrances of the storm:

> We were lambing out our sheep, and my husband Jim had taken the wool to market the first day it started. Barely got home that night and almost didn't make into our yard.
>
> Dennis and I herded the sheep into the barns, and one of our sheep laid down in the doorway and the snow began piling in on top of her. A very busy day for us.[220]

Colgate began as a GN townsite in 1882. It was named after Steele County's biggest landowner, James B. Colgate. In 1880, he had purchased 5,000 acres in Steele County from the NP. His father was William Colgate, founder of what eventually became the Colgate-Palmolive Co.

According to records kept by John P. Burchill, the cooperative weather observer at Colgate, temperatures were mild there leading up to the storm. A high of 39 was achieved on March 1, 1966. The next day, the first day of the storm, a high of 31 was reached. The low for the day was 22. Colgate received .10 inches of precipitation that day. On Thursday, March 3, a high and low of 25 and 18 were recorded in Colgate. The hamlet received .64 inches of precipitation that day.

Unfortunately, that is where the records ended. There were none for the next two days, Friday and Saturday, as the weather equipment was entombed underneath 14 feet of snow.

Page lies over thirty-five miles northwest of Fargo.

It had 432 residents in 1960.

GN set up a station at this location in 1881. Joseph H. Thompson platted a townsite here in June 1882. Colonel M. B. Morton who owned a considerable amount of land in the area named the settlement after his brother-in-law, Egbert S. Page.

A man who spent many years in as a banker and merchant was Louis B. Hannah (1861-1948). He also served as a U.S. Representative and as Governor of North Dakota.

Page came through the March 1966 storm in pretty good shape. Fortunately, there were no emergencies during the blizzard. No power outages occurred. While local phone service remained good during the storm, people were not able to make long distance phone calls.

Helping out in Page, as in other places, were snowmobiles. Their drivers used them to deliver fuel oil in five gallon cans.

With snowbanks in Page as high as 20 feet, the digging out process was a challenge. In order to be able to leave their homes, some Page residents were forced to have others clear the snow away from their doorways.

Not soon forgotten by many Page residents were the efforts of Larry and Ole Erickson, Oscar England and others to see if they needed anything such as fuel, groceries, or other assistance. Among the homes they stopped at were those of retired people.

About fifteen miles northeast of Cooperstown is Finley (808 residents in 1960).

GN arrived in this area on November 3, 1896. They set up a townsite which they called "Walker." Shortly thereafter, the name was changed to "Finley" in honor of W.W. Finley, a GN official from 1889 to 1892.

In what the *Steele County Ozone Press* called "the worst blizzard of the century" showed up at Finley late in the afternoon of Wednesday March 2, 1966, and stayed until Saturday.

Whipped by winds that reached as high as 60 mph, the 15 to 20 inch snowfall was piled into drifts that were as much as 25 feet high. Buildings and trees acted as impediments to the wind driven snow. And that is where the snow piled up both in town and on farms. The drifts were so large, there were a few instances where cars, buildings, and machinery were completely submerged by the white stuff.

The wind driven snow plugged a few chimneys in Finley, forcing the buildings' occupants to take shelter with their neighbors during the blizzard.

A water break occurred in Finley during the storm. Coming to the rescue was an Otter Tail Power Company crew. The men on the crew were Verne Hanson, Palmer Hillestad, Nordeen Sorlien, and Sanford Strand. They kept working on the break until they got it repaired at 3 a.m. Sunday.

As people in the Finley area emerged from their cocoons after the storm, it was an amazing, sometimes disturbing, sight that awaited them.

The weight of the heavy snow collapsed a pole barn that had been built in 1961 on the Archer home farm.

At the George Groseth farm west of Finley an 8 foot high snowbank covered the top of a quonset, damaging the structure somewhat. Also buried under the snow at the Groseth place was his three-stall garage. The impact of that much snow forced the roof of the garage to collapse onto Mr. Groseth's automobile and two tractors.

The weight of snow on the roof of the Finley School cracked a beam in the school's lobby. It took a brace to hold it up.

A bowling alley in Finley, the Hi-Score Lanes, had a ventilator that had snow blown into it. The warmup after the storm melted the snow in the ventilator. The end result was a slight warping of a bowling lane.

There were some livestock losses in the Finley vicinity.

On Saturday, the cleanup by snow removal crews in Finley began.

About six miles northwest of Finley lies the village of Sharon (251 residents in 1960).

Sharon began as a post office in the home of Peter. T. Duncan in 1889. It took its name from Sharon Township. Settlers from Sharon, Wisconsin, gave the township its name.

In 1896, the GN established a townsite, southwest of the post office. At that time, GN was extending its rail line from Hope in Steele County to Aneta, just across the Nelson County line. The rural post office was reestablished in the new settlement.

According to Hugh Lyon, the cooperative weather observer at Sharon, the village received a trace of snow on March 2, 1966. Amazingly, 9 inches of snow fell on Thursday and 9 inches of snow came down on Friday. The moisture content of the precipitation 1.87 inches.

On March 2, Sharon had a high of 32. The thermometer began a gradual drop throughout the course of the storm. Friday morning, the low was 8 above. It would be Sunday before the thermometer dipped below zero. A low of 9 below was reached on Sunday morning.

In March 1966, Steve Bugbee of Sharon raised turkeys. The snow collapsed one of his turkey sheds and the partial collapse of another one. Underneath all that rubble were about 1,200 dead brooder hens. The height of snowbanks in Mr. Bugbee's yard reached up to 20 feet.

The storm kept six ladies from Sharon marooned in Fargo for the duration. On Wednesday morning, the Mesdames Ernie Midstokke, Roy Mikkelson, Mayme Olson, Art Ostenson, P. J. Rund, and Joe Vig drove to Fargo for a day of shopping. The onslaught of the blizzard and the resulting blocked roads prevented their return to Sharon until Sunday night. They watched a showing of *The Sound of Music* in Moorhead on Saturday.

On March 8, Sharon Knights rallied from a 41 to 23 deficit to defeat the Finley Wildcats, 50 to 48, at the district tournament.

Mayville, Portland, Hillsboro, Buxton, Reynolds and Hatton

Mayville, N.D. (1960 population of 2,168) is located in western Traill County along the Goose River.

A native of the Mayville area is Lute Olson. After leading Grand Forks Central to a state basketball title in 1952, Olson went on to college and then coaching. At the latter, he has enjoyed great success coaching the men's basketball team at the University of Arizona.

This city began about a half mile west of its present location as a Hudson Bay Company trading post in the early 1870's. Alvin Arnold arrived in the area in 1871. Shortly thereafter, he set up a post office in the trading post. Arnold gave the new post office the name "May" in honor of his second daughter.

With GN's arrival at the new townsite in 1881, the new settlement needed a name. There are three versions as to how Mayville received its name. One of them has Mrs. Arnold naming the settlement. Her selection was "Mayville", since the name had a pleasing sound, and the word also included the name of her second daughter. Another version has the townsite being named after the Arnold's previous home, Mayville, Ohio. The last version has it being named after Mrs. Anna Marie "May " Weltzin Chantland.

Portland (606 residents in 1960) lies two miles west of Mayville. It is frequently known as "Portland on the Goose."

Surveyors for the St. Paul, Minneapolis and Manitoba Railway (GN) chose to cross the Goose River at this spot. In November 1881, A. Arnold, O. T. Jahr, and S. O. Nordskog donated the land on which present day Portland stands. The platting of the townsite was done in February 1882. Because the new settlement was midway between Portland, Maine and Portland, Oregon, railroad officials selected that name.

On March 1, 1966, the Mayville Lions lost a double overtime game to to Hillsboro in District 6 basketball tournament action at Mayville. The score was 7 to 5. It was one of the lowest scoring game ever recorded in North Dakota in high school boys basketball.

The March 1966 blizzard arrived in Mayville without much fanfare Wednesday evening, March 2. By early the next morning, storm winds were at full strength. All the streets, both in Mayville and nearby Portland, were blocked.

It would be Saturday morning, before the blizzard finally let up in Mayville. Even then, the snow didn't quit drifting until that night.

Especially hard hit by the storm was Mayville State College. That area had the largest snowbanks in Mayville. The height of drifts on both sides of the Fieldhouse reached 20 feet in spots. By standing on top of a snowbank that covered the lower level of the Fieldhouse, a person could make it to the apex of that building.

"OLe Main" on Mayville State College campus, March 1966. Courtesy of Jim Benjaminson

A similar story was being repeated at the students' housing units. Robert Burner faced a hall full of snow at his unit. This, despite the fact that, out in front of the unit was a bare sidewalk. To allow for passage in and out of the unit Burner, teamed with Curt Almlie to remove the snow. Utilizing shovels, Burner attacked the problem from the inside, and Almlie did likewise on the outside.

For others, digging a tunnel was the only way in and out of their units. In this category were Mr. and Mrs. Robert Aasen, Mr. and Mrs. Ray Rosignol and Pat Keenan's trailer home.

The drifts at Mayville State College were so large they completely enveloped student housing units. In other cases, snow filled halls and made doorways impassable.

In quite a few units, ceilings fell as a result of melting snow that had been driven in there by the wind. As of the middle of the following week, no had yet been injured by falling ceilings.

Finding one's vehicle on the Mayville State campus after the blizzard was one thing, but digging it out was something else. In many instances, 2 to 4 feet was the depth a vehicle's owner had to dig through just to reach the top of it.

Trying to start cars in Mayville State College parking lot, March 1966. Courtesy of Jim Benjaminson

In March 1966, Karen Huffman of Walhalla was a freshman attending Mayville State Teachers College. It was the end of the quarter, but Karen had to remain on campus to take an English exam. So, while other students departed for other locales ahead of the storm, Karen stayed in Mayville for the test.

Afterwards, Karen and a girlfriend went uptown. The storm broke as they were on their way back to the college. Conditions grew worse as the ladies approach the school. Finally, exhausted from battling the elements, Karen and her friend got down on their knees. They pulled themselves forward by grabbing onto car door handles of vehicles parked along the street. The ladies finally reached the shelter of the women's dormitory.

Karen remembers that during the storm the vending machines in the dormitories being emptied by students for food. After being stormed in for several days with very poor visibility, students formed a human chain in order to reach the student cafeteria.[221]

Mayville State College Gym and Fieldhouse, March 1966. Courtesy of Jim Benjaminson

Within the first few hours of the blizzard, Mayville's city officials and employees went on round the clock duty.

Praises were being sung in the Mayville vicinity concerning one of the heroes of the March 1966 blizzard, the snowmobile. The following quote from the *Traill County Tribune* sums it up:

> *People of this area have considerable admiration and respect for what many of us thought was merely another toy, the snowmobiles that have been driven through the countryside these past couple of years.*[222]

Among those on snowmobiles coming to the fore to deliver groceries and transport passengers on in both Mayville and Portland during the three day storm were Eric Aasen, Dr. T. L. Christianson, Ted Hagen and his grandson, Ronny Tunseth of Portland, Walter Rindy, two brothers, Harlan and Kenneth Sandvig, plus an employee of theirs, Orville Dakken.

In addition to these trips, the snowmobilers made other excursions. These included giving a guy who worked for KTHI-TV (Channel 11) a ride to the station located west of Blanchard. They deliverd fuel around Mayville. A trip was made to the Chester Viseth farm home. To water his cattle on his farm, located south of Mayville, Bob Elken hitched a ride with Kenneth Sandvig.

On Thursday, a section of Portland didn't have any power. Ted Hagen made a trip on his snowmobile from Portland to Mayville. The highline was his guide along the way. There, he picked up a Northern States Power crewman, took him to Portland, and then gave him a ride back to Mayville when the problem was corrected. In order to procure a tractor for use in hauling snow in Portland, Mr. Hagen gave Allan Kville a ride to the Ardell Strand farm. Mr. Kville drove the tractor back to Portland.

Also stepping to the front to help out was Ted Hagen's grandson, Ronny Tunseth. He transported James Heskin via snowmobile to the Solberg farm in order to feed cattle. It was for the same purpose that Kenneth Christianson hitched a ride with him to the Joe Grinde farm. These were just a few of the many trips on snowmobile this grandfather and grandson duo made in and around the Portland neck of the woods helping people out.

The storm proved to be a harrowing experience for one Mayville area family. Elroy Lindaas and his family resided on their farm two miles east and one and a half miles north of Mayville. Their trouble which came in bunches started Thursday. That day, they lost telephone service at their farm. Their ten month old baby relied on milk from their cow for food and nourishment. About the same time their telephone went out, the cow quit giving milk. Another crisis was brewing at this time also. Mr. Lindaas and his three youngest children came down with the mumps.

Fortunately, Mr. Lindaas was a ham radio operator. On Saturday, he was able to reach Hartwell Burner, a ham radio operator in Mayville. Mr. Lindaas asked Mr. Burner to contact a physician.

Sunday morning, Dr. James Little reached the road that led into the Lindaas farmyard. He covered the remaining distance on foot. Accompanying Dr. Little was Gordon Osland. His purpose in coming with Dr. Little to the Lindaas farm was to do chores and any other work the Lindaas family needed done.

That afternoon, Mrs. James Lyng, Mrs. Lindaas's sister, and her husband deliverd groceries and supplies to the Lindaases.

Restoration of telephone service to the Lindaas farm came Monday morning. The next day, the Lindaases retrieved their car from its snowy imprisonment. The accomplishment of that led Mrs. Lindaas to make this remark, *"Now if I can leave my sick family I can run errands."*[223]

The blizzard proved to be a trying ordeal for personnel on duty at Union Hospital in Mayville. Those who happened to be on duty when the storm arrived Wednesday night were still there on Saturday. Involved in this marathon were registered nurses, nurses aides, a lab technician and the ladies who did the cooking at the hospital. They made it through the storm by working alternate shifts until Saturday night.

Registered nurses on duty when the blizzard hit Mayville were Linda Bergo, Linda Bergstrom, Frances and Norma Lee, and the supervisor of nurses at the hospital, Mrs. Seaver. It was coincidence that Frances Lee was at the hospital when the blizzard made its appearance. Her daughter happened to be a surgery patient at the time.

Nurses aids on duty at the time of the snowy onslaught were Elna Carlson, Mary Eastvold, Barb Gilbertson, Beverly Paulson, Pearl Richtsmeier and Diane Wahl.

Lee Nielsen was the lab technician on duty through the course of the storm.

Also stranded at the hospital was the kitchen help. Their names were Mrs. Orville Dakken, Mrs. Roller and Mrs. Sarah Viseth.

The arrival of the blizzard Wednesday night caught six visitors at the hospital. They remained there for the duration.

Afterwards, Mrs. Seaver praised the hospital personnel for their dedication.

A similar tale was being told at Luther Memorial Home in Mayville. Personnel there also did Herculean duty. All the beds in the place were filled, so the personnel working there had to find other places as beds to sleep on. They slept on davenports and cushions on the floor. Most of them stayed in the solarium. Residents of the home lent them sleeping apparel.

The registered nurses who were at the home included Mrs. Gladys Bjelverud and Mrs. Laura Wegge. Additional help came from Mrs. Gunvor Ellingrud, Mrs. Mildred Finstad, Mrs. Vera Hauge, Edna Haugen, Mrs. Audrey Heskin, Oscar Jemtrud, Mrs. Eunice Klabo, Josie Moen, Mrs. Margaret Otteson, Connie Rogenes, Mark Rye, Mrs. Norma Rye, Dagne Sollid and Thelma Sundeen.

Adrian Knudsvig, another one of the home's personnel had this to say about their performance:

> I feel I received one of the highest compliments ever paid Luther Memorial Home today when a local doctor complimented me on the way the staff at the Home conducted themselves during the storm.[224]

The blizzard dumped 22.5 inches of snow on Mayville. Overall, the precipitation totalled 1.79 inches. Most of the snow came down on Thursday and Friday, 8.5 and 10 inches, respectively. Temperatures fell from a high of 33 on Wednesday March 2, to the teens by Friday March 4. The mercury did not fall below zero until Sunday March 6. The thermometer continued its slide, until 11 below was reached on Monday March 7.

On Saturday, people in Mayville and Portland had to be careful when strolling near power and telephone lines on the high snowbanks. During cleanup, priority was given to main streets, so families could purchase supplies.

Fellow climbing snowbank in Mayville, March 1966. Courtesy of Jim Benjaminson

After the storm, the citizens of Mayville received a thank you from its mayor and city council.

Looking back at the March 1966 blizzard the *Traill County Tribune* had this to say:

> *Mayville with innumerable other localities in the northwest suffered perhaps the most crippling three-day snow storm that this area has known since about 1896, according to George Gunner, one of the oldtimers.*
>
> *Though the actual amount of snow was probably no more than 12 to 15 inches on the level, the 30 to 40 mile an hour winds moved virtually the entire mass into groves, farmyards, and cities, as Mayville and Portland citizens well know.*[225]

Mayville did not receive any mail after Wednesday, March 2 until around 1 p.m. Sunday.

The conclusion of the 1965-66 season for Portland's high school boys basketball team came on March 7. On that date, they were defeated by Hunter 47 to 45 in District 6 tournament action at Mayville. Jim Strand led Portland in scoring with 15 points.

Over ten miles southwest of Mayville, is Clifford.

In 1960, Clifford had 109 inhabitants.

This Great Northern townsite was founded in 1881. It took its name from a promoter of the settlement, Clifford F. Jacobs of Hillsboro. The word "Clifford" has an English origin meaning "dweller at the ford near the cliff."

A resident of the Clifford area, Erwin Ust, had a memorable storm experience. While the blizzard was raging outside, his wife went into labor. Unable to get her to a hospital, Mr. Ust contacted Dr. Carl Oja of Portland, twelve miles north of Clifford. Following the doctor's instruction, Mr. Ust was able to deliver his son around midnight Friday.

Later, a Traill County snowplow cleared a path to Mr. Ust's place. This allowed him to make it to Clifford for supplies.

About half way between Fargo and Grand Forks is the city of Hillsboro (1,278 residents in 1960), seat of Traill county.

In September 1880, modern day Hillsboro was platted by S. G. Comstock and White. There are several explanations as how Hillsboro acquired its name. One of them has the original settlement being on a hill west of present day site. Because of its location, the settlement was known as "Hill City." The other version has the village being named after the president of the GN, James J. Hill (1838-1916).

GN's rail line from Grand Forks made it to Hillsboro on September 14, 1880.

On March 2, 1966, temperatures in Hillsboro reached a high of 37. The blizzard showed up there late that afternoon. Initially, the winds were from the south. They switched to the north, and finally to the northwest at a steady rate of between 30 and 40 mph. Occasionally, wind gust speeds were close to 70 mph. The wind began to abate in Hillsboro on Saturday afternoon.

The city received 1.38 inches of precipitation from the storm. Total snowfall for Hillsboro, an unofficial guess, put it at 25 inches. The northern half of Traill County received more snow than the southern half.

Temperatures remained mild in Hillsboro on both Thursday and Friday. A low of 16 above was recorded in Hillsboro on Friday. Not until after the blizzard, did they drop below zero. On Monday morning, March 7 the thermometer did drop to 18 below in Hillsboro.

As it was located on a major north-south highway between Fargo and Grand Forks (U. S. Highway 81), Hillsboro would become a refuge for hundreds of stranded travelers. Wherever they were on Thursday, would be their home until conditions improved.

One of these places was the Sunset View Motel in Hillsboro. Its proprietors, Mr. and Mrs. Jerry Nysveen, had forty-one guests there during the blizzard. Among them were those who never laid eyes on snow before. They hailed from as far away as Baltimore, Maryland and Oklahoma.

A party was held there for a newlywed couple. For the event, a cake was baked by Linda Nysveen. They received a rolling pin without the handles as a gift. On it were the signatures of all the Motel's guests. Of them, Mrs. Nysveen had this to say,"'they got to know "some wonderful people and made a lot of new friends."[226]

Places of shelter for other stranded travelers during their included the clubrooms at the American Legion and VFW in Hillsboro, the Traill County Court House, Hillsboro's City Hall, in the homes of Hillsboro residents, and the Central Valley School, located on the east side of U. S. 81, north of Hillsboro.

The following are Gary Haisley's remembrances of the March 1966 blizzard:

> I remember the 1966 storm very well. I was 10 years old and living in Hillsboro at the time. We lived about two blocks from the hospital. I was very sick at the time. During the storm, my dad bundled up and made his way to the hospital. It took him a long time to get there and back. He got some penicillin for me.
>
> After the storm, we could not play in the snow behind our neighbor's houses. I heard the radio station say that the electrical wires were covered with snow, and that time was needed to check them out. Mom and Dad warned us, also.[227]

Traill County emerged from the March 1966 blizzard without any major accidents or deaths. Hospitalization was required for one Hillsboro resident. While assisting in righting an overturned snowmobile, the leg of Scotty Way, son of Mr. and Mrs. Bud Way, was cut badly.

Road crews came to the rescue of Mrs. Jerry Muhter, a resident of the trailer court in Hillsboro. They cleared a path to her door and were able to get her to the hospital in Hillsboro not long before her baby son made his appearance to the world.

Once the storm let up Saturday afternoon, the clean up process in and around Hillsboro was under way. In Hillsboro, high snowdrifts and sight-seers caused traffic problems, especially for trucks attempting to haul the snow away. Because of this and safety concerns, Hillsboro city policeman Alvin Nelson and others were placed at the intersection of U.S. 81 and Caledonia Avenue. There, traffic would be directed by those individuals. Unless, there was no other alternative, automobiles were not allowed in the center of Hillsboro.

On Tuesday March 8, Traill County Commissioners and William Meline, the County Civil Defense Director, inspected all of Traill County aboard a helicopter from Minot Air Force Base.

They observed blocked roads and some isolated farms, especially in the northern part of the county. In the case of blocked roads Meline noted that farmers and their neighbors were opening them.

Where there were isolated farms, efforts were being made to get snow removal equipment to those localities. To that end, cooperation was being obtained from the National Guard, Trail County, and private contractors.

The Traill County Civil Defense received quite a few radio calls concerning people whose fuel oil supply was running low.

Snowmobiles were used to deliver fuel oil to farms in Garfield Township.

The Hillsboro Burros lost their chance to go to the state Class B tournament after a 51 to 49 loss to Cooperstown in Region 2 play at Mayville.

Jeff and Brian Johnson, age 3 & 2, in a snowbank in a tree in Blanchard, March 1966. Courtesy of Ruth Johnson

Less than twenty miles north of Hillsboro in northern Traill County is the village of Buxton (321 residents in 1960).

This GN townsite was platted in November 1880 by Budd Reeve.

He honored a business associate of his, Thomas J. Buxton, city treasurer of Minneapolis by naming the settlement after him.

UND benefactor, Chester Fritz (1892-1983), was born here.

A few miles north of Buxton, on the Grand Forks-Traill County line, is the village of Reynolds. Its 1960 population was 269.

Reynolds is one of three North Dakota towns that lie in more than one county. The county line runs down its main street. The townsite was platted by Dr. Henry A. Reynolds, a temperance apostle, in 1880 on land that he had homesteaded. In 1881, GN established a station here.

On the east side of U.S. Highway 81 between Buxton and Reynolds, is Central Valley School. It became the home for almost forty travelers, the majority of them being Canadians, during the blizzard. According to James Flaagan, Central Valley superintendent, they were stuck there for four days from early Wednesday, March 2 until 11 a.m. Sunday, March 6.

As Interstate 29 had yet been completed through this area in March 1966, U.S. 81 was the main north-south travel route between Fargo and Grand Forks.

The travelers weren't at the school by themselves during the storm. They had a host in the form of the school's custodian, Mike Mealy. He lived on the school property.

The travelers were in no danger of running out of food during their stay. Superintendent Flaagan noted that the school's kitchen could have fed the travelers for "five or six weeks."

Concerning the travelers attitude during their confinement Flaagan had this to say:

They were pretty happy to be here. They headquartered in the school library. They also got a lot of use out of the volleyball, basketball and shuffleboard courts in the school gymnasium.

Flaagan also mentioned the fact that the library's floor was entirely carpeted and had comfortable furniture in it.

According to Flaagan, the south end of the school building was buried under snow.[228]

In northwestern Traill County, about midway between Mayville and Northwood, is Hatton (856 residents in 1960).

Hatton began as a GN townsite in 1881, even though the rail line did not reach there until July 1884.

Hatton received its present name when the post office there was given the name of Hatton, after United States Assistant Postmaster General Frank Hatton.

Noted residents born here include polar aviator Carl Ben Eiselson (1897-1929) and writer Agnes Kjorlie Geelan.

The Hatton area was not taken by surprise by the March 1966 storm. Residents there had been listening to storm warnings broadcast over the airwaves all day Wednesday. They knew it was coming from the southwest. People held onto the hope that the blizzard would miss Hatton.

But it was not to be. As the storm progressed northward, it engulfed cities and towns alike with ferocity. Then, late that afternoon, Hatton received word that the blizzard had reached Mayville. But where was it? Hatton wasn't receiving any snow. Finally, around 5:30 to 6:00 p.m. Hatton began receiving light snow. A stiff wind by 8 p.m., made Hatton residents realize they were not going to escape the storm completely unscathed.

Increasing winds and snowfall during the night piled up quite a bit of wet snow in Hatton by Thursday morning. This made it tough to get about. Although the wind was quite strong, temperatures remained mild.

Some business places in Hatton closed their doors early on Thursday. Those individuals who could make it home were happy they had made it. High winds combined with snow enlarged the size of snowbanks in Hatton all day Thursday. Frequently, one couldn't see across the street.

Conditions became worse on Friday as the blizzard became more intense. Snow continued to fall, and snowdrifts increased in height. Visibility was poor all day with the high winds. To see your neighbor's house across the street was just about impossible. By Friday, temperatures had dropped a bit in Hatton, making it feel colder outside.

In spite of the conditions, the majority of stores and gas stations in Hatton remained open most of the time during the blizzard.

Saturday morning, the winds began letting up in Hatton. As the day wore on, conditions improved, and the skies began to clear off. Snowbanks of all sizes blocked city streets. An estimate of the height of one in particular at the north end of Hatton placed its height at between 15 and 20 feet.

At Iverson's Barber Shop, the entrance and stairs there were completely buried in snow. All the business establishments had snow piled up against their windows and doors to a depth of several feet. The height of one drift on the west side of the bank was just about sufficient to touch the awning on the building.

Getting out and about for Hatton residents on Saturday was done mostly on foot. They didn't have other choices. With snow piled up in town as it was, a person would have thought this would prove to be quite difficult. But not necessarily so. Snowbanks were of sufficient hardness to allow people to walk on top of them without sinking in.

Farm yards were chock full of snow. Reports came in from farmers relating to the amazing heights of drifts. Their heights extended to second story levels on houses and to the tops of barns. Northeast of Hatton at the Lewis Huus farm, Kenneth Davidson snapped a picture. His photo in the *Hatton Free Press* showed the view of the Huus home and other buildings being almost blocked by a humongous snowbank.

The familiar story of being forced to make an exit via a window because other home exits were blocked was repeated at several rural Hatton residences. Likewise, people discovered their vehicles to be entirely submerged in the snow. Some farmers needed heavier equipment for snow removal.

The nursing home in Hatton, the Tri-County Home came through the blizzard in good shape. Some employees stayed at the home for the duration of the storm putting in additional hours and helping out where needed. To bring other employees and needed grocery and medical supplies to the home, a tractor was pressed into service.

The *Hatton Free Press* thanked the following nursing home employees for staying at their post for several days while the blizzard was on. They were Mrs. Henning Brandon, Mrs. Leslie Gensrich, Mrs. John Oistad, R.N., Mrs. Leroy Schroeder, Mrs. Stanley Smestad, Mrs. Knute Stensland and Mrs. Carl Teie.

Snow removal in Hatton commenced Saturday morning. Reuben Grande, Hatton's street superintendent headed the operation.

Rugby, Knox, Maddock, Minnewaukan, Graham's Island, Devils Lake, Starkweather, Lawton, Edmore, Lakota and McVille

In addition to being the seat of Pierce County, Rugby (2,972 residents in 1960) is close to the geographical center of North America. A monument to this effect sits just south of U.S. Highway 2 at Rugby. It was erected in 1931.

Rugby was founded and platted in July 1885 as GN was building its main line to the West Coast. Railroad stockholders from England named the town after Rugby, England.

The '66 storm failed to deposit any new snow worth mentioning in Rugby. Instead the city had a four day "snirt" storm.

Areas north and west of Rugby escaped the wrath of the storm.

It was different south and east of Rugby. The effects of the storm began about five miles east of Rugby. One person, Carl Duchscher, resided about nine miles southeast of Rugby. He reported that humongous drifts at his place were hindering his ability to do farm chores.

Another farm family who did not live far from Rugby were the Ned Voellers. There was so much snow at their farm that it took over three hours of shoveling to reach the cattle in their barn.

On March 7, Rugby was defeated by the No. 1 team in the Northwest Region, Minot Ryan, 59 to 52. Rugby finished fourth in the tournament when they lost to Harvey the following day. Rugby's Ray Glesinger scored 30 points in the first game against Williston and 21 points in the loss to Minot Ryan.

Rugby was also the home to a basketball star of the early 1960's. Paul Presthus led Rugby to a state Class A basketball title in 1962. He would later play basketball at the University of Minnesota.

Knox (122 inhabitants in 1960) lies about fourteen miles east of Rugby on the north side of U. S. Highway 2.

This village began as a GN station in 1883.

There are two versions as to how Knox got its name. One of them has H. T. Ober, a GN townsite agent naming it after General Henry Knox of Revolutionary War fame. The other version has Canadian settlers naming the village and township after John Knox, a Scottish religious reformer.

At 2 p.m. March 4, 1966, John I. Johnson, whose place of residence was only seven miles north of Knox went out to his chicken coop to collect some eggs. It was located not far from his house. Johnson's car sat right next to the house. Upon reaching the top of a high snowbank, Johnson came to the realization that he was lost. He remained there, until he regained his sense of direction. Enroute back to his house, Johnson walked into the car. As it was covered with snow, he did not see it.

Maddock is located about thirty-five miles southwest of Devils Lake.

In 1960, 740 people called Maddock home.

Summers Manufacturing company, an agricultural equipment manufacturing operation is located here. Maddock was the birthplace of Merton Blaine Utgaard, a noted bandleader. He was born here in 1914. Utgaard served as the director of the music camp at the International Peace Gardens from 1956-1983.

Maddock was set up as an NP townsite on June 1, 1901 by O. L. Hegge from Minnewaukan. The same year, the NP line extension from Oberon reached Maddock.

There are two versions as to how Maddock received its name. The first one has it being named for a couple early settlers of Viking Township, John R. and David E. Maddock. The second version has it taking its name from another pioneer of the area, Michael Maddock.

Before the March 1966 blizzard enveloped Maddock, it hosted the Maddock Farm Institute. The event was sponsored by the Benson County Extension Service and the Maddock Kiwanis Club. It had a good turnout with 150 people attending.

Serving as Master of Ceremonies was James Kenward, Benson County Agent. The farmers were welcomed by Herb Dahl, president of the Kiwanis Club. Speakers at the event included Julie Gronbeck from the Cass County Electric Cooperative; Bernie Kylo, Assistant State FHA Director; and Vic Sturlagson, Director of the Langdon Experiment Station.

Maddock, in the guise of the Benson County Aggies, was the defending district 16 basketball champions. They had been to state in 1965.

But on March 2, their season came to an end when they lost to Esmond in district 16 quarter-final action at Fessenden. Roger Benson led Maddock scorers with 19 points.

Quite a few people from Maddock and Harlow (a town fifteen miles north of Maddock) were in Fessenden for the tournament when the storm hit. They were stuck there for the duration of the blizzard.

There was some alarm when two Harlow residents, J. V. and Tommy Leppard, were reported missing in the storm. They were returning home from the southern United States. Later on, it was learned they were safe in South Dakota.

Moisturewise, 1.69 inches of precipitation fell at the Maddock Agricultural School from Thursday March 3 to Saturday March 5, 1966. About half of that total came on Friday.

All that snow brought about the collapse of a pole barn at the Fred Rehling farm, located at the edge of Maddock. Three cattle perished and two others were injured.

Minnewaukan, the seat of Benson County, lies on the west edge of Devils Lake. The name of the town comes from an Indian name for Devils Lake. They called the lake "miniwaukon-chante". The literal translation for this word was"the heart of the enchanted water or mysterious water. Whites misinterpreted it as mini (water) waukon (spirit) chante (bad). Their mistranslation came out as Bad Spirit Lake or Devils Lake. This inferred that the water in the lake was salty and of poor drinking quality. The word "spirit" referred to the mirages frequently observed across the lake. The only problem with this, was that Indians did not believe in a devil.

Minnewaukan was originally a steamboat landing, one of the stopping points for the Minnehaha, a boat that operated on the lake. People began moving in around the landing in the early 1880's. Their settlement was about eighty rods beyond the western edge of Devils Lake. This steam boat landing point would later be known as North Minnewaukan. The settlement consisted of some homes and business establishments. People were of the belief the railroad would build a station there. But, they were about to be disappointed. With the platting of a townsite a mile south of them in 1884, the days of their settlement were numbered. Within two years no one lived there.

The new settlement took its name from the lake. It was called Minnewaukon (It was changed to Minnewaukan in 1906). In the spring of 1885, the Jamestown Northern Railway (later purchased by the Northern Pacific) extended its line north from New Rockford through Minnewaukon.

By the 1960's Devils Lake had receded two miles from Minnewaukan. The heavy precipitation since 1993 has brought the lake back to the edge of Minnewaukan.

The March 1966 blizzard moved into Benson County Wednesday evening March 2. It was the beginning of an intense storm that had area residents recalling the March 1941 blizzard. In comparing the two storms, they said the 1966 one was the worse of the two. One person harkened back to an 1893 storm to find one as bad as the March 1966 blizzard.

Just about everything came to a stop in Minnewaukan on Thursday and Friday, March 3 and 4. There was no school in Minnewaukan. Events were canceled, people hunkered down for the duration. Minnewuakan endured a power outage for a little while.

The blizzard left many Benson County residents stranded. One of them, Anton Schaan, had a farming operation between Maddock and Minnewaukan. He was returning from a fishing trip when the blizzard forced him to halt at York. That town on U.S. Highway 2 is about thirty miles north of Maddock.

At home by herself was his wife. Mrs. Schaan was stuck there in their house from Wednesday evening until Saturday morning. With the let up of the storm, she removed the screen door at the front door of their house. Then, she dug an eight foot long tunnel to get through a drift to freedom.

When Mr. Schaan finally made it home, the only portion of the house still visible was a little bit of the chimney and the TV antenna. The rest of the house had been completely submerged in drifts whose heights came close to 20 feet. With so much snow on the roof, it was feared the sheer weight of it would make the roof collapse. To alleviate the situation, on Sunday morning, a crew from Minnewaukan came out to the Schaan farm to shovel the snow from the roof.

So, how did Mrs. Schaan feel after going through such an ordeal? She took it in stride, although she didn't want to go through a repeat of it. What helped Mrs. Schaan keep her cool was the telephone. As she remarked, *"At least I had contact with the outside world, even if I couldn't see it."*[229]

Saturday morning, Minnewaukan woke up to quite a sight. Snow depths around town varied greatly. On Minnewaukan's main street, they were about 4 feet. There were a few snowbanks on the north side of the city whose height's came close to 20 feet.

As far as snow totals around the county from the blizzard, Benson County Sheriff Gordon Burdick said that Maddock had received the most. Next in line came Minnewaukan followed by Esmond. Esmond is more than twenty-five miles west of Minnewaukan. Leeds, on U.S. Highway 2 and over twenty miles northwest of Minnewaukan, received about half as much snow as Minnewaukan.

Livestock losses from the storm were fairly light in Benson County.

Minnewaukan didn't have mail service from Wednesday March 2 until the following Monday.

An outstanding player on the Minnewaukan basketball team was Skipper Johnson. In four years of high school basketball, he scored over 1,000 points. Ted Livetay was his coach.

By late Saturday afternoon, Minnewaukan's main street was open to traffic.

The *Benson County Farmers Press* had this to say concerning how people from that area would compare the March 1966 blizzard to future storms:

> Residents of Benson County will have the opportunity of telling future generations, "Oh heck, this is nothing. I remember the storm of "66."[230]

Graham's Island which is northeast of Minnewaukan was a peninsula on the north side of Devils Lake that in the 1960's extended into the lake.

Graham's Island took its name from a Captain Duncan Graham, a native of Scotland. After fighting for the British in the War of 1812, Graham came to the Devils Lake area around 1814 and set up and ran an independent fur trading post at Graham's Island for awhile.

A resident of Graham's Island from around 1884-1900 was Usher Lloyd Burdick (1879-1960) who served for many years in the U.S. Congress as a representative from North Dakota. His son, Quentin Burdick (1908-1992), was elected to the U.S. Senate from North Dakota in 1960 and held that position until his death.

In taking pictures after the storm, the photographer for the *Benson County Farmers Press* came across a snowdrift on Dick Holz's farm on Graham's Island that he found to be higher than any other ones he had seen. Its height was between 25 and 30 feet.

Copious precipitation in the 1990's led to a rise of Devils Lake and surrounded Graham's Island with water again. A state park is located here.

Located on the north side of Devils Lake, the city of the same name (6,299 inhabitants in 1960) was first known as Creelsburg. Its founder, Lieutenant Heber M. Creel was a topographical engineer who had graduated from West Point. In the spring of 1882, he resigned his army post at Fort Totten and settled on the north side of Devils Lake. There, he platted a new townsite and named it after himself.

In May 1883, the St.Paul, Minneapolis, & Manitoba Railway (later GN) chose to put its station at the head of steamboat navigation on Devils Lake. They named the station after the lake. The name "Devils Lake" is a mistranslation of the Sioux name "MiniWaukon". It was supposed to translate either as "Lake Holy One" or "Lake Great One." The inhabitants of Creel City moved to this new location at this time.

William L. Guy, Governor of North Dakota from 1960-1972, hails from Devils Lake.

One Devils Lake resident, John Howard Disher (1921-1988), led a very distinguished life. A 1939 graduate of Devils Lake High School, Disher went on to earn a bachelor of science degree in mechanical engineering from UND in 1943.

After graduation, Mr. Disher worked for the National Advisory Committee for Aeronautics (NACA), the forerunner of the National Aeronautics and Space Administration (NASA) as a research analyst. As head of their Free Flight Research Section, Disher helped NASA test the first hypersonic flight of a solid rocket.

In 1959, Disher received a NASA appointment to be Project engineer for the task group that was set up to oversee the Mercury Program. It would be this program that would send America's first astronauts into space.

John Disher would later have important jobs in both the Apollo and Skylab programs. He retired from NASA in 1980.

His achievements away from the space program included graduating from the Harvard Business School in 1969 and serving on the Technical Committee of the Indianapolis 500 car race from 1948-1987.

Devils Lake enjoyed a high of 37 degrees on March 2. It began snowing in the Devils Lake vicinity around 10 p.m. that night. At that time, the winds in Devils Lake were in the 23 to 30 mph range. Blizzard conditions began in a few hours.

On Thursday, there was no highway travel or rail service through Devils Lake. Most of the city's businesses were closed. School was called off in Devils Lake. To assist those who needed supplies and could not make it uptown, a few grocery stores stayed open. At radio station KDLR in Devils Lake, 6 inches of snow fell on Thursday. The high and low temperatures for the day were 25 and 9, respectively.

Conditions deteriorated in the city on Friday. School was called off again. A few grocery stores remained open. During the height of the blizzard on Friday, some men from one neighborhood formed a human chain by tying ropes around their waists and to one another. Pulling a toboggan along with them, the men trudged uptown on foot. Once there, they purchased enough groceries to carry them through the remainder of the blizzard.

The thermometer continued its gradual slide in Devils Lake on Friday. It only reached 13 for a high with 5 above for the low. Devils Lake received 17.5 inches of snow on Friday.

The blizzard finally let up in Devils Lake on Saturday. An additional 7 inches of snow fell that day.

For the entire storm 30.5 inches of snow, 3.01 inches of precipitation had been deposited at weather station at radio station KDLR in Devils Lake. Accompanying all that snowfall at Devils Lake were 55 mph winds that gusted to 70 mph.

That snowfall total for Devils Lake differed from the one reported in the *Devils Lake World*. According to the March 9, 1966, edition of that newspaper, 35 inches of snow fell at the weather station at KDLR. The precipitation total, 3.01 inches, was the same as the state climatologist's report. Either way, it was the greatest amount of precipitation recorded at Devils Lake for a winter month in the 61 years (through March 9, 1966) the U. S. Weather Bureau had been keeping records there.

The 3.01 inches of precipitation broke the existing precipitation record for the month of March. That one had occurred in 1956, when 2.29 inches of precipitation were deposited on Devils Lake.

If a person goes by the 35 inch amount, then Devils Lake received more snow than any other reporting station in the storm except Mobridge, South Dakota, which also received 35 inches of snow.

The blizzard caused a power outage to most of the Lakewood community, seven miles south of Devils Lake and part of nearby Camp Grafton. The loss of electric power for several hundred residents of Lakewood came at 5 a.m. Friday March 4.

In March 1966, Ernie Hagen of Devils Lake was Ramsey County Civil Defense Director. Concerning the situation at Lakewood, Hagen had this to report. "People have been gathering in homes that have parlor heat."[231]

Around 4 p.m. Friday, two county snowplows began the task of attempting to open the road south to Lakewood. An Otter Tail Power Company crew trailed behind the plows. But, their efforts to reach Lakewood were in vain.

Not until Saturday morning, were snowplows able to open the road sufficiently to allow Otter Tail Power Company workers through. Power was restored to the affected area at noon Saturday.

In March 1966, Debbie Schenk lived with her family in an apartment in Devils Lake. The storm left a drift that blocked the front entrance to the building. To get out, people had to exit from the rear of the building. They then took shovels around to the front and cleared that entrance of snow.[232]

The March 1966 blizzard was an unforgettable experience for five Soo Line trainmen caught in the storm for twenty-four hours, six miles west of Devils Lake.

The crew consisted of Brakeman Gordon Anderson, Harvey; Roadmaster B. J. Baden, Thief River Falls, Minnesota; Brakeman Bill Dompier, Fordville; Conductor Henry Hirsch, Anamoose; and Engineer Elland Johnson, Fordville.

According to Baden, the five-car freight train had departed from Drake Thursday evening. Despite the fact the storm had been raging for over twenty-four hours, Baden said the weather was "blustery but not severe."

Baden reported the first sign of trouble came when the train pushed through a two-foot drift near Silva in Benson County. Not long after that, the train stalled. Their final destination, Devils Lake, was only fifteen miles to the east of them.

Making their way to the rear of the train, the crewmen spent the remainder of the night in the caboose.

The next morning, they dug the engine out. After uncoupling it from the rest of the train, they headed for Devils Lake.

Unfortunately, with only about six miles between them and safety, they came to a shuddering stop in a 10-foot drift. And howling wind and zero visibility greeted them, if they stepped outside. The men remained in the cab of the engine.

They tried to call for help on the radio but received no replies.

To make sure they had heat, the men kept the diesel running. However, the men became nauseous from the fumes. In order to keep the air fresh, every so often they had to open a window.

The crew had very little food with them to eat, only a few crackers and a can of deviled ham. They ate them sparingly.

The men spent another long night aboard the engine.

Although blowing snow obscured dawn on Saturday, Baden was positive that a farm lay nearby.

As the blizzard began slowly to let up, Dompier and Baden made their way through snowbanks to the Lawton Miller farm. Once there, they called Soo Line personnel in Devils Lake. They wanted a rail snowplow to try and make it to the engine.

While this was going on, Mr. Hirsch once again tried to call out on the shortwave radio set. Eventually, he received a reply–from the caboose the crew had abandoned on Friday.

On Saturday morning, a Minnewaukan farm couple, Mr. and Mrs. Willie Thompson, along with their nephew, Ronnie, noticed the stalled freight train.

Utilizing a snowmobile, the Thompsons made their way to the freight train. They had just made their entry into the caboose when Hirsch's voice came over the radio set.

Upon answering, Mr. Thompson learned where they were stranded. He then went to pick them up. The Thompsons brought the remaining three trainmen to their farm.

It would be around 2:30 a.m. Sunday, before the trainmen finally reached Devils Lake.

Coping with the storm proved to be quite a challenge for the staff at Devils Lake's Mercy Hospital. Counting part time workers, its total work force came to 187 people. But, according to the hospital's administrator, Sister Mary Patrick, there were only between twenty and thirty of them at the hospital during the blizzard.

To handle all the physician's duties there were two doctors at the hospital. For Thursday, Dr. J. H. Mahoney was on duty. Dr. R. D. McBane relieved him that evening, and stayed for the remainder of the storm.

The arrival of the blizzard Wednesday evening found the hospital to be staffed with just four nurses and around eight nurses aides. None of them left the hospital, until the storm was over.

Other workers at Mercy Hospitals rose to the occasion during the blizzard. Among them were eight Sisters of Mercy on the hospital staff who pulled double shifts. Additional help came from St. Mary's high school. From there came eleven other Sisters of Mercy to assist in pediatrics and to run the kitchen and cafeteria.

More help came in the form of fifteen students who were enrolled in the practical nursing program at Lake Region Junior College.

Some of Mercy Hospital's crew reached there on foot during the blizzard. These included laundry man Harold Johnson who washed all the clothing by himself. On Thursday, Charles Wittkop from the purchasing department and pharmacist Sieg Rewald lent a hand wherever it was needed. Others trudging through the elements on foot to reach the hospital included Esther Rader of the housekeeping department, and two of the hospital's maintenance workers, Frank Schiff and Don Soper.

Because of the severity of the situation, wherever possible, hospital patients themselves lent a hand.

Unfortunately, the blizzard piled some of its highest drifts (up to 12 feet) in Devils Lake at the front of Mercy Hospital. That blocked access to the hospital from that direction. So, while the storm was raging, emergency traffic to Mercy Hospital was rerouted to a 10th Avenue entrance via Eighth Street.

Once conditions improved, it was possible to reach the east entrance of the hospital from along 12th Avenue to Seventh Street.

It would be Monday March 7, before rotary plows punched a hole through the huge snowbanks in front of Mercy Hospital.

Seventh Street in Devils Lake, March 1966. Courtesy of Devils Lake World

Temperatures at Devils Lake remained above 0 during the course of the storm. Afterwards, the thermometer fell. The coldest reading was a minus 13 was reached Monday morning.

At the Devils Lake municipal airport, during the week of the March 1966 blizzard, a new VOR (Vertical Omni Range) facility had become operational. Besides weather information, its purpose was to provide other flight information to pilots over a large area.

According to Cliff Hansen, airport manager, installation of the facility by the FAA (Federal Aviation Administration) had begun in the fall of 1965. Its price tag came to about $250,000.

On March 7, Devils Lake St. Mary's high school boys basketball team finished the 1965-66 basketball season with a 67 to 51 loss to Minnewaukan in District 15 tournament action in Devils Lake.

The village of Starkweather (223 residents in 1960) lies over twenty miles north of Devils Lake.

Starkweather began as a farm post office that was set up on February 18, 1886. James H. Boden, its first postmaster named it "Starkweather" after James E. Starkweather, a Michigan native who homesteaded in the area.

In 1902, a new townsite (first known as Davisville) was established three miles northeast of the Starkweather post office on the Farmers Grain and Shipping Railroad line. The rural post office was moved there about 1909.

On Thursday afternoon, March 3, 1966, there was a power failure in Starkweather. It affected the school and around twelve residences. Fortunately, the people who lived in those homes were able to take refuge in dwellings that had not lost power.

The March 1966 storm dumped 34 inches of snow on Starkweather. The new school there had a flat roof. The weight of all that snow made the school's beams creak.

Something had to be done quickly. So, early Saturday groups of men equipped with shovels clambered to the school's roof and removed the snow. Snowbanks on the building's side were removed by them later in the day.

In March 1966, Pat Allard, who hailed from the Williston area, was visiting a college roommate's family who resided in Starkweather. In 2003, he recalled that visit:

We could walk out his bedroom window onto the snow two weeks later.

It was two stories high.

Mr. Allard would go on to serve in the U. S. Navy from 1966 to 1970. In that capacity he worked with the Navy's hurricane hunter squad.

In the early 1980's, Pat Allard became the meteorologist in charge of the National Weather Service's Williston office. He retired from that position on January 2, 2004.[233]

Starkweather's high school boys basketball team ended its season in District 13 action at Cando with a 77 to 71 loss to Leeds. Leading Starkweather with 21 points was Allen Hansen, followed, respectively, by James Rader with 20 points and Tom Erickstad with 15.

Lawton (159 residents in 1960) is located about twenty miles north of Lakota.

GN arrived at this spot with its rail line in 1902. The settlement's name honored a Spanish-American War veteran, General George Lawton. In 1902, he was in charge of a bunch of soldiers in the Philippines known as the "Lawton Scouts." Among those serving in this units were voluntary infantrymen from the North Dakota National Guard. The word "Lawton" comes from Old English and means "from the hillside farm."

The March 1966 blizzard would be one a Lawton area family would never forget. At that time Roger Burt, his wife and children resided in their home eight miles west of Lawton. During the blizzard, the Burt home lost power. At that time a county snowplow came to the rescue of Mrs. Burt and her children.

Later, Mr. Burt, his wife, and four children were traveling in their automobile, when it stalled about four miles from their home. Adding to the Burt's dilemma, was the fact there were no farmsteads close by where they could find shelter.

Once the storm had let up, a search and rescue operation had been undertaken by a helicopter working out of the Minot Air Force Base. Its flight missions covered five counties–Benson, Ramsey, Towner, Cavalier and Pembina.

On one of these flights, they came upon the Burt family and rescued them. It was a good thing, too. The Burts had been stuck there for a "considerable time" and were "plenty cold."

Edmore, a village in northeastern Ramsey County (405 residents in 1960), lies about seventeen miles west of Adams.

As a GN townsite, its origins date to July 1901. The town was named for Edward E. Moore who became the village's first postmaster on August 16, 1901.

The storm arrived there Wednesday afternoon, March 2. As it increased in intensity, activity in the Edmore area ground to a halt. Roads became impassable. The weather forced the closing of the Edmore school and the postponement of the District 11 basketball tournament which was scheduled to be played in Edmore that week.

One Edmore farm family experienced a traumatic experience during the storm. On Wednesday evening, Mr. and Mrs. Andrew Strand, headed out into the storm to do their daily farm chores. Unfortunately, weather conditions became so poor they were forced to take shelter in a chicken coop located roughly halfway between the house and barn. The blizzard forced them to remain there for twenty-four hours, before they could get back to their house. In the meantime, their son Marlyn held down the fort in the house. Despite feeling cold, tired, and hungry, the Strands were okay.

The storm did not leave the Edmore vicinity until Saturday evening. The 33 inches of wet, heavy snow it dumped on Edmore was accompanied by high winds whose gusts reached 70 mph. This was quite a contrast to the half inch of precipitation that William Collins, the local weather observer in Edmore, had recorded for the month of February 1966.

That wet, heavy snow made people nervous. The Arnold Fjalstads could testify to that. Their farm hone located near Edmore was completely buried under the snow; so covered was their house they could not get out any door. Even the chimney on their house was covered with snow. It was like being buried under an avalanche.

To prevent the roof on the Fjalstad home from collapsing and allow them to breathe some clean air, their friends and neighbors removed the wet snow from the roof of the Fjalstad house. In digging down, the shovelers located a door that enabled the Fjalstads to get outside. The Ramsey County dozer labored all night and through the following afternoon in moving snow in their yard. On Monday afternoon, the dozer was followed by some high school boys who shoveled snow away from the Fjalstad home.

It was a laborious process to move the snow. In doing so, the county dozer knocked over the fence, shrubs and trees by the Fjalstad home. There was not a lot of damage to the house itself. Within a few days, the Fjalstads enjoyed a view out their south windows.

As was to be expected, the combination of heavy snowfall and high winds left a deposit of very high drifts in the Edmore area. There were reports of snowdrifts as high as 40 feet in the Adams-Edmore area. They filled in many a farmyard. They buried machinery and buildings. The weight of such large heavy snowbanks threatened to collapse the roofs of buildings, especially barns. To prevent such an occurrence, and to save cattle and machinery, large squads of men used shovels to remove the snow from the roofs of these buildings.

On U.S. Highway 2, twenty-seven miles east of Devils Lake is Lakota.

Lakota, 1,066 residents in 1960, began as a GN townsite. In the fall of 1882 one of their civil engineers, John R. Stevens established its location.

A group of English capitalists, Messrs. Howard and Kane boosted the townsite. After James M. Howard platted Lakota in July 1883, he turned over part of the townsite to Francis J. Kane, a member of the Howard and Kane syndicate.

GN's tracks reached Lakota in 1882, the following year a station was established there.

The name selected for the new settlement was "Lakota." This was done by the governor of Dakota Territory, Nehemiah G. Ordway. for a Teton Sioux tribe. In their language "Lakota" means "allies." According to others "Lakota" translates as "land of plenty." In the Santee Sioux language "Dakotah" is their word for "allies." Common to both "Lakota" and "Dakotah" is the meaning of the suffix "otah" which translates as "many."

The organization of Nelson County in 1883 saw Lakota being chosen to be its county seat at the same time.

The blizzard delayed the plans of six Lakota FFA (Future Farmers of America) boys from taking part in FFA judging events scheduled for March 4 and 5 at the Valley City Winter Show.

The blizzard arrived in Lakota around 9 p. m. Wednesday March 2. At first, the winds accompanying the snowfall were not very strong. Unfortunately, by the following morning a full scale blizzard in Lakota was in progress.

On Wednesday evening, four buses took 150 Lakota high school students to Devils Lake to watch Lakota play Oberon in the District 19 basketball tournament. Another bus carried Brocket high school students. That night, Lakota came away with a 75 to 59 win. Gordon Schroeder popped in 27 points for Lakota, followed by B. Voss's 22 and D. Berg's 12.

The return trip to Lakota was tough for the fan buses. Fortunately, the buses maintained radio contact with the Lakota school office. The five buses reached their final destinations. The students from the two towns made it home, before the blizzard got too bad.

Not so lucky were member's of Lakota's basketball team, their coach Gordon Baumgartner, and Gene Gaffney, the band director. They, along with several carloads of fans couldn't leave Devils Lake. The next day, some of them returned to Lakota by train. The others stayed in Lakota until U.S. Highway 2 was opened.

Lakota was like a ghost town Thursday and Friday. Virtually everyone stayed home. The intensity of the storm was so great that the outlines of houses across the street were not visible to people.

In emergencies, as the storm raged, Lakota city employees helped to deliver fuel.

Berg's Motel and the Lakota Hotel were packed with stranded travelers. Since the inclement weather prevented regular employees from getting to the hotel, guests at the hotel helped in serving meals. Miller's service station on U. S. Highway 2 became a refuge for about ten transport trucks.

The inability of employees to get to work Thursday and Friday kept Lakota business establishments closed those two days.

With the passage of the storm Saturday morning, residents of Lakota and others began coming to grips with what the storm left. Out in the open, most fields were bare. Anywhere the wind encountered an obstruction, it would leave drifts of snow. Humongous drifts blocked the front and rear entrances to some Lakota homes. Snowdrifts higher than 20 feet covered several streets on the edge of Lakota. The rest of Lakota's streets were snow-plugged.

The stupendous cleanup process began in earnest on Saturday. That evening, just about all of Lakota's streets were open to single lane traffic.

The situation along U.S. Highway 2 wasn't any better. Snow removal crews using a rotary snowplow and a v-type snowplow started clearing a 3/4 mile stretch of the highway west of Michigan on Saturday. They were up against snowdrifts that varied between 3 and 15 feet in height. To stay on course, workers on the snow removal equipment would get off the machines. They would then wave their caps as a means of locating the white center line on the highway. As this was happening, highway patrolman helped to control and reroute traffic. Finally, over thirty hours later, around 5 p.m. Sunday, they had that stretch of U. S. 2 open.

In nineteen years on the job, a state highway employee who helped clear that portion of U.S. 2 (Joe Lamb shelter belt area) said that he had never run into problems with blocked roads in that particular stretch of highway. Joe Lamb was a well known Michigan businessman.

After Wednesday, Lakota received no mail until the following Monday. The blizzard interrupted train service through Lakota from just after midnight Friday until Saturday night. Reduced to having just one person operating them, grocery stores in Lakota reopened for a few hours on Sunday.

As with other places in the path of the storm, the digging-out process began in earnest in Lakota on Saturday. Just locating one's vehicle proved to be quite a challenge.

The north and east sides of Lakota were particularly hard hit during the blizzard. This was to be expected since the direction of the wind during the majority of the storm was from the northeast. In those localities, the height of snowdrifts reached as high as the tops of houses.

The situation in the countryside around Lakota was as tough as it was in town.

Storm losses were severe at the Jim Price farm. There, over 7,000 turkey poults expired from dehydration and freezing. In addition to that there was also the loss of eight cattle who froze to death.

Volunteers helped to save chickens on the Ervin Anderson farm. The rafters on a two-story chicken coop began to collapse under the weight of a ten foot high snowbank on the roof. The volunteers helped to shovel off the roof. They also assisted in the removal of the chickens to the barn.

The rafters on the roof of a garage attached to the house at the Kenneth Anderson farm began to crack under the accumulated weight of snow. The day was saved when five men shoveled the snow off the roof.

All in all, livestock losses in Nelson County due to the storm were not as high as expected. According to Morris D. Holm, Nelson County extension agent, about 75 to 100 head of cattle perished in the storm. It was estimated that 175 to 200 sheep died in the storm. Holm advised Nelson County cattlemen be alert for signs of stress in their cattle.

The 1965-66 basketball season for Lakota's squad came to an end on March 9 at Devils Lake. On that date, they defeated Unity of Petersburg 68 to 54 in District 15 tournament action. Gordon Schroeder was top scorer for Lakota with 26 points. Next, came Gary Novak with 14 points. For Unity of Petersburg, Rod Meyer and Jim Arnold had 20 and 16 points, respectively.

Located in southern Nelson County, is the village of McVille. It enjoyed a population of 551 in 1960.

The first part of the last names of two early settlers contributed to McVille's name. There were other "Mc" names in the area as well. Fred W. McDougal operated a rural post office about two miles north of present-day McVille. That post office sooned closed. F. M. McCracken ran a country store and post office in about the same spot four years later. McCracken became McVille's first postmaster. It seems that the prefix from their names was combined with "ville" to give the village its name. The GN arrived in this area in 1906, but its line was about two miles away from McCracken's enterprises, so he relocated to the railroad townsite.

After its arrival in McVille late Wednesday, the storm lasted until Saturday. Copious amounts of snow, accompanied by high winds, reduced visibility to zero. The blizzard conditions brought a cessation of vehicular traffic in McVille. Storm conditions prevented farmers from getting to their barns to take care of their livestock.

In March 1966, Mr. and Mrs. Veron Green and their four children lived on the Bernard Franzen farm near McVille.

Snow completely covered their home on all sides and snow built up on the roof. They were frightened about the possibility of carbon monoxide poisoning, so they let their furnace go out during the height of the blizzard. The snow was good insulation, the temperature in the house never dropped below 50 degrees. A phone call to a neighbor succeeded in bringing the Berg boys to shovel them out. On Sunday, other volunteers arrived and they cleared more snow.

On Saturday afternoon, after the blizzard had let up, snow removal crews began the cleanup process in McVille.

The *McVille Journal* had the follwing to say about the storm:

> *These three days, March 3-4-5, 1966 will go down in history as another Dakota's worst blizzard comparable to the 1888 storm. One would have to actually experience one to realize how bad a storm can get.*[234]

On March 10, Hans Elgin was in McVille's post office. He compared the January 1888 storm (which he rememberd) to the 1966 one. Elgin said "quite a change (had taken place) since then."

The *McVille Journal* agreed with Elgin and went on to say:

> *A farmer(in 1888) would take his wheat to the mill and exchange it for flour and feed. He would get so much flour, shorts and bran for a bushel of wheat and usually took a year's supply of flour home. Butcher a hog and process it into ham, bacon and sowbelly. Bring this up to modern times, each family ran their own Super Valu.*[235]

On March 7, McVille finished the 1965-66 high school boys basketball season with a 70 to 43 loss to Cooperstown in district tournament action at Cooperstown. Dave Reiten led the way for McVille with 14 points.

Northwood, Larimore, Grand Forks Air Force Base, Thompson, Grand Forks and East Grand Forks

Located in southwestern Grand Forks County, Northwood enjoyed a population of 1,195 in 1960.

Northwood began as a farm post office on December 17, 1879. Its first postmaster was Paul C. Johnson. Reflecting on the origin of the majority of the settlers in the area (Northwood, Iowa), Johnson named the post office after that place.

In 1882, a GN townsite was platted two miles northeast of there. As elsewhere, that post office moved to the railroad townsite. It would be 1884, before GN extended its line to Northwood.

On March 2, 1966, in a defensive battle, the Northwood Trojans, finished their season with a 38 to 36 overtime loss to Hillsboro in district tournament play. Daryl Halvorson led Northwood with 16 points.

In an amazing display of longevity, the *Northwood Gleaner* had the same publisher from 1899 until his death, Dan Leroy Clark (1877-1966). Along those same lines, the *Northwood Gleaner* was moving to a new location in Northwood at the time of the March 1966 blizzard.

To best illustrate weather conditions in Northwood, both in leading up to the blizzard and after it got there, let the *Northwood Gleaner* describe them:

> *Balmy shirtsleeve temperatures on Tuesday gave way to slowly dropping mercury. The few scattered flakes of snow drifting in from the South on*

Wednesday rapidly increased to a real snowfall. Then came the wind-and by Wednesday evening "blizzard" was the word.[236]

As the night wore on, the strength of the storm increased.

Not many people were out and about the next morning. Those who did venture out began comparing the March 1966 blizzard with bad storms and winters of the past. Among those mentioned were the winter of 1936 and the March 15, 1941, Alberta Clipper. And the consensus? The March 1966 was up there with the "worst" of them.

Activity in Northwood came to a shuddering halt on Friday.

There had been no reprieve from the blizzard during the night. A person could count on one hand the number of businesses open in Northwood on Friday. The majority of the buildings located along the west side of Main Street had 6 and 8 feet high snowbanks obstructing their entryways.

Just about the only way to get around in Northwood (other than by foot) during the storm was by snowmobile.

The hotel and motel facilities in Northwood were filled with stranded travelers. The depth of the snow on the south side of the motel was too great for the motel's proprietor to shovel out. As a result, the only way people could gain entrance to the rooms on that side of the building was through the rooms located on the north side of the motel.

For the majority of Northwood residents the blizzard did not prove to be much of a hardship as far as food or heat supplies went. For the few that needed assistance, snowmobilers swung into action.

Marooned travelers in Northwood were very thankful for the hot soup and other food items provided by Strande's Bakery.

The storm provided quite a challenge for the staff and patients at Northwood Hospital. Snowmobiles provided a way for doctors to make house calls and take employees to and from work.

It was a situation of "minutes to spare" for an expectant mother from Larimore. She arrived at the Northwood Hospital shortly before the birth of her child.

At one point, it seemed the Hospital's supplies of both fuel and oxygen would run out. A call was made to Grand Forks County officials. A rotary snowplow was dispatched to the rescue.

In the situation of two ambulance calls, 15 foot high snowbanks stood between the patients, their haulers, and the hospital. That didn't stop the haulers though. They carried their patients over the drifts to the hospital without, apparently hurting the patients or themselves.

It would be forty-eight hour stretch on duty without relief for some of the hospital personnel.

After the storm had passed, a query was made to the hospital's administrator, Orren Lee, about how the facility managed during the blizzard. In reply, Lee mentioned the above stories already recounted. Then he said, *"Outside of that, there was nothing unusual."*[237]

Except for very short and minor outages, Northwood came through the blizzard without any disruption to its power and lights.

Conditions in and about Northwood were much improved Saturday morning. The height of drifts around quite a few homes and business places in Northwood was so great it was possible to step onto them from the second story of these buildings. In a few instances, where the height of the snowbank was greater than the upper floor of these places, one stepped "up" to the top of the hard packed drifts.

Snow removal operations in Northwood commenced early Saturday. Involved in the operation were both public and private individuals. There was a big demand for the implement dealers' tractor scoops.

The *Northwood Gleaner* reflected on what a daunting task snow removal crews faced:

> High in moisture as it fell, the snow was driven into solidly packed mounds that defied all but the largest machines.
>
> Biggest problem was to find somewhere to drop the snow being moved. Mostly it was a matter of redesigning the drifts.[238]

For most of those travelers caught in Northwood by the blizzard, Sunday was going to be their day of departure. First things first though, they had to dig their vehicles out. For some of them, this meant probing through the deep snow to find their vehicle. By that afternoon, those who were itching to get moving had left Northwood.

Sitting in western Grand Forks County, three miles south of U.S. Highway 2 on N. D. Highway 18 is Larimore.

In 1960, 1,714 people called Larimore home.

This GN townsite was established in August 1881. Grand Forks County surveyor Alex Oldham platted the townsite on Albert Clark's homestead.

The settlement was named after a Kentuckian, Newell Green Larimore, who along with John G. Larimore, was involved with the Elk Valley Farming Co., of St. Louis, Missouri. They began developing the Elk Valley Bonanza Farm, just south of Larimore. This farm enterprise would eventually encompass 15,000 acres. Although N. G. Larimore was the primary owner and general manager of the operation, his son Clay was in charge of its day to day operations.

Settlers were aware that the GN was extending its line west from Grand Forks, and the NP was pushing its Casselton branch line on to Mayville. Eventually these two lines would intersect and where that happened (according to the settler's supposition) a townsite would be established. So, the townsite of Larimore quickly developed.

The settlers were right. GN completed its tracks to Larimore in 1881. The NP line from Casselton reached there in 1884.

Larimore was enjoying "balmy" weather on March 2, 1966. A high of 40 was reached in the city that day. At noon, the radio was broadcasting reports of a raging blizzard that was hitting southern and western North Dakota. From her place at work in downtown Larimore, a local woman heard this news on the radio. Peering through the window at the gray sky all she could see was a peaceful countryside. Nothing was blowing around. The lady remarked, *"Well, it looks as though the storm has missed us."* She returned to her work. After going home that afternoon, the woman didn't emerge from her residence again until Sunday.[239]

The wind started to pick up in Larimore towards evening.

Worsening storm conditions were a concern to Larimore school officials. Larimore's high school boys basketball team was participating in the regional tournament in Grafton. They played Grand Forks Central that evening. Would they be able to return to Larimore that evening?

No problem. Larimore school officials knew where the storm was and what direction it was taking through their radio contacts with civil defense personnel and the Grand

Forks Police Department. With this information, school officials knew the journey from Grafton to Larimore would be a safe one for the school buses. They gave the school bus drivers the go ahead to return to Larimore. At 9:30 p.m., three busloads of players and other students returned to Larimore without incident.

The full effect of the blizzard arrived in Larimore that night.

The coming of daylight showed Larimore to be one snowed in city. Snowdrifts blocked doorways and motor vehicular traffic was at a crawl. Despite this, the majority of Larimore's stores were open Thursday morning. As the day wore on, deteriorating conditions forced them to close their doors earlier than normal.

The inability of employees to make it to work at the Elk Valley State Bank Thursday morning forced Lee Brandon to man all the tellers' windows by himself. Relief came that afternoon when Mrs. Lloyd Engen was able to make it to the bank to assist him.

One guy really was really having a rough go of it on Thursday. In trying to make it to work, he got his vehicle stuck three times. The fellow decided enough was enough and returned home.

On Thursday. Chuck Hensrud, an employee of Erickson Dairy in Larimore, set out in the maelstrom with his weighted-down pickup. Along the way, he encountered a lady walking down the street and gave her a ride. She was concerned about what appeared to be the flickering headlights of his vehicle. But there was no problem with them. The drifting snow was making them disappear and then reappear. Suffice to say, residents of Larimore didn't receive any milk from Erickson Dairy on Thursday.

In such impossible driving conditions, a local grocer received a phone call from a lady requesting delivery of a pound of coffee and a pack of cigarettes. He was forced to decline her request.

Some clearing in Larimore at noon on Thursday, brought hope to many. Attempts were made to shovel sidewalks. The local newspaper, the *Larimore Pioneer*, expressed their feelings thuswise: *"most people were ready to believe they had seen a quick, not-too-bad storm."*[240]

It was not to be. Conditions grew worse. After a high of 30 was reached in Larimore that day, temperatures began to drop. Late that afternoon, the wind was whistling at a steady 45 mph in Larimore. Gusts reached 63 mph.

With no school being held in Larimore on Thursday, children had time to kill. Downtown Larimore, which had a recently opened Recreation Center overflowed with boys shooting pool.

Larimore's police Chief, Alden Gronlie, wasn't going to let a mere thing such as a blizzard hold him back. The newly purchased Larimore police car was of no use in the deep snow. No problem. Chief Gronlie employed a tractor as a taxi service to haul milk and supplies to restaurants and transport people to and from their jobs in downtown Larimore. The police chief didn't let snowbanks stop him either.

In such weather, there was hardly any traffic in Larimore. Worsening conditions made it harder for fuel trucks to reach fuel tanks. Arrangements were made by some to deliver fuel to homes in 5-gallon cans.

The blizzard provided more than enough excitement for one rural Larimore family. The Gary Cooper family resided north of Larimore along the highway. The time was rapidly approaching for the stork to arrive for Mrs. Cooper. She needed to be taken to the Deaconess Hospital in Northwood.

The Larimore Street Department ran interference for the Cooper automobile through Larimore. Fortunately, the Coopers were able to make it the rest of the way to Northwood.

The next week, the *Larimore Pioneer* had this to say about the incident. *"At press time, it is believed mother and child are doing well; but that stork in this case must have been a penguin."*[241]

On Thursday, Mrs. Glen McDonald, the U.S. Weather Bureau observer in Larimore, recorded snowfall totals to be 8 inches or 1.01 inches of precipitation.

The worst day of the storm in Larimore on Friday. The *Larimore Pioneer* wrote:

> *Winds stayed right around 50 mph, often much higher; snow poured down; visibility was nonexistent. There was no school, no mail, no milk delivery, no travel, nothing but a rip-snorting storm that wasn't of the old fashioned type, because even old timers couldn't remember one like it.*[242]

Inspite of the horrendous conditions on Friday a few Larimore business establishments were able to open their doors. This was due mainly to the fact that some of the businessmen had remained at their posts overnight. These included Harvey Brevik of Harvey's Pharmacy, Chris Eberle at the bank, and Duane Guenthner of Duane's Jack and Jill.

Mr. Eberle worked solo at the bank on Friday. By telephone, he informed customers that yes, the bank was open. Mr. Eberle advised them to use the rear entrance as five feet of snow blocked the front door.

A few people, such as Art Jarman, were able to reach downtown Larimore each day of the storm. It was a struggle for him to make it home Friday against the wind. Twice, Mr. Jarman was forced to seek shelter in homes along his route home.

On one morning of the storm, the cooks at the Melody Room in Larimore hadn't made it to work yet, when Harvey Brevik and Clarence Sobolik arrived there. The men went ahead and made their own breakfast. After they were done eating, the men left some money, and headed for work.

The blizzard didn't prevent Larimore's Red Owl store from being open at least parttime every day of the storm. According to Mrs. Henry Aardahl, there weren't many items that it ran out of.

The intense storm made it quite difficult for Larimore area farmers to feed and water their cattle. One of them, Wilfred Hunt, resided in Larimore. As he was unable to reach his farm, Mr. Hunt's cows didn't get milked for two days.

Even if a person did venture out in the blizzard on Friday, it took the wind driven snow only a short time to fill in his tracks. So, even though it wasn't that cold out on Friday (Larimore had a high and low of 20 and 8, respectively), the strong winds made it feel colder than it was. Larimore receieved 11 more inches of snow, 1.62 inches of precipitation, on Friday.

Despite all this, guys from the trailer court were able get uptown on Friday to purchase some items. The reason these men probably did this was because they were running low on supplies, especially staples such as bread and milk.

Not surprisingly, Larimore's hotels were either filled up with people or were nearly so. It was tough going at the Vel-Mar Motel, managed by Lloyd Hougen, at Larimore during the storm. All rooms were occupied with guests Wednesday night.

Snowbanks blocked the exits for motel guests staying in all the rooms on the south side of the motel. Rescue for its occupants came via tunnels dug through to their doors.

The inhabitants of two motel rooms were served food through the windows. Wind driven snow packed against the rooms' doors made opening them impossible.

After the storm, some motel guests from Fargo-Moorhead went home without their vehicles. The guests caught rides in one of the automobiles and panel trucks they had dug out. These vehicles belonged to other Fargo-Moorhead residents stranded at the Vel-Mar Motel. The hitchhiking guests left their own vehicles buried in the snow. All together, there were seven automobiles completely submerged by snowdrifts.

On Wednesday, three missile workers took refuge at another Larimore inn, the Ace Hotel. It had been a three hours journey to Larimore for them from Finley, which is about thirty miles southwest of Larimore.

By Friday night, the Ace Hotel had no more vacancies and was forced to turn people away. At that time, a few rooms were still available at another Larimore hotel, the Violet.

Watching blizzard images of Grand Forks on national television brought concerns to the mother of one Larimore resident, Bob McLain. He worked at the Larimore Meat and Grocery store. Bob's mother resided in Florida. Worried about his safety, she phoned him one morning. But there was nothing to worry about as Bob lived above the store and didn't have far to go to work.

There were many personal blizzard stories in the Larimore area. Below are some of them.

In March 1966, Doyle Cannon was employed by the H. C. Smith Construction Company. That firm was a Minuteman missile subcontractor. The Wilfred Hunt farm west of Larimore was where the Cannon family lived.

The blizzard caught Mrs. Cannon home alone with her two children. Her fuel oil supply ran out on Saturday. Help arrived the same day and took her into Larimore.

Another emergency arose at a trailer located north of Larimore. The supply of milk ran out for a family with a two-week old baby. A path to the road was cleared by area men. The road itself was opened by a snowplow. This allowed needed items to be deliverd to the family.

The height of a snowdrift in a shelterbelt on Francis Hofer's farm five miles south of Larimore was estimated to be 25 feet. It was located near his granary.

The storm forced the cancellation of a meeting of the board of directors of the Larimore Golf Club. The blizzard had left the greens buried in snow that was 30 inches deep on the level.

There were no shows at the Avalon Theater in Larimore on Friday and Saturday, March 4 and 5. Frank Uika, an employee there, was hoping to have it open on Sunday.

For the first time in 34 years, Johnson Drug Store in Larimore was closed due to the weather. It did not open for business either Thursday or Friday.

The storm caught the Avenue Bake Shop in Larimore shorthanded Friday. Employees were unable to get to the shop. On top of that, two railroad crews stranded in Larimore came there for their meals. Vern Erickson, the shop's proprietor, and Mrs. Andy Burass were there by themselves to take care of the business. They managed to feed not only the railroad crews, but quite a few others too.

In March 1966, Brad Benson was attending high school in Larimore. On the eve of the blizzard, the Bensons attended a snowmobile party at the Legion Club in Larimore. Conditions became so bad the Bensons were unable to return to their home in the country. They were able to travel a block and a half to a friend's place in Larimore. The Bensons remained there for four days. On the fourth day, using their snowmobiles, they were able to get home.

For two weeks after the storm, Brad and his father cleaned out farmyards with a D-8 bulldozer. Many farmers had livestock in barns but could not get to them because of deep snow. To find their vehicles, farmers would push rods into the snow.

Brad Benson operated the dozer during the day, and his father operated it at night. Whenever they changed places, the person taking over would bring out a truck with fuel to fill the dozer.

They cleaned farmyards from Arvilla to Michigan. The snow was melting by the time the Bensons got to the farmer at Michigan. But, it was still deep. The farmer had pigs stranded in a barn. He took a rod to punch through the snow to find his '53 De Soto.

After clearing snow for two weeks, Brad Benson came down with bronchial pneumonia. He was sick for another two weeks. All in all, Brad missed a month of school. However, he was able to pass the nineth grade.[243]

The blizzard made it tough going for the railroads. Ordinarily, GN's passenger train the *Empire Builder*, used the Surrey cutoff to make its run from Fargo to Minot. By early Friday, however, deep snow had made that route impassable. The train was then sent over an alternative route to Minot via Grand Forks and Larimore.

At 12:15 a.m. Friday, Harley "Mick" Mickle, a GN depot agent at Larimore, received notice from GN to return to work.

Clearing the track ahead of the *Empire Builder* was a GN crew with a bulldozer. They reached Larimore at 1:25 a.m. Friday. In the meantime, the engine on the dozer had become wet. The crew could go no further. A relief crew was dispatched from Grand Forks. Unfortunately, storm conditions forced them to remain at Larimore too.

The *Empire Builder* that passed through Larimore at 3 a.m. Friday was the last train to go through Larimore until the blizzard let up.

The snowmobile played an important role during and after the storm at Larimore. The *Larimore Pioneer* gave the following description, both good and bad of them:

> *The popular, and in fact, the only means of transportation during the storm was the snowmobile–little ones and big ones.*
>
> *They scoot over the snow with considerable ease. But they are tricky to operate, tip easily and you can fall off without half trying.*
>
> *One man, with his wife riding behind with nothing to hang onto, lost her twice while coming downtown.*[244]

Having no mail to distribute, didn't keep the Larimore Post Office from being open during the blizzard. Behind the counter by himself most of the time was Joe Meland. He did receive assistance from Jim Sullivan who occasionally came to the post office to help out.

Jack Virden, Larimore's Postmaster, was out of town when the storm showed up at Larimore. It was Sunday before he was able to get back.

The delivery of mail between Grand Forks and Larimore in March 1966 was done by Bob Runyan, a former Larimore and Niagara resident. At the time of the March 1966 storm, he was living in Grand Forks. On his run from Grand Forks to Larimore Thursday morning, Runyon was a few hours late, not arriving there until 10:30 a.m. Because conditions were deteriorating, Runyon departed for Grand Forks at noon. He usually didn't headed out from Larimore until 6 p.m.

Joe Meland was back on duty at the Post office Friday morning. In describing his efforts to reach there, Meland said, "it was a struggle."

The nearby Violet Hotel became his refuge Friday night. Meland stayed there instead of returning home in order that he could make it back to the post office Saturday.

The tie up of trains in Grand Forks meant there was no mail coming in or leaving the Larimore vicinity from Thursday until Monday. With that in mind, why did Joe Meland make such an effort to keep the Larimore Post Office during and after the storm? His answer to that was this:

> The post office is a public service, so I felt we should be open so people
> could check their mailboxes if they wanted to.[245]

Larimore received another 8 inches of snow on Saturday. This amounted to 1.65 inches of precipitation. The March 1966 blizzard deposited 27 inches of snow on Larimore, 4.28 inches of precipitation. The winds let up on Saturday and the skies cleared.

There was deep snow all over the place. There were some huge drifts at the Gordon Brelie farm, five miles southeast of Larimore. They were high enough to allow Mrs. Brelie to screw a light bulb into their yard light. The height of that fixture was 18 to 20 feet above the surface of the ground.

The Brelies had an experience that was common to others after the storm. While perched on top of the huge snowbanks, they could peer down at the tops of their buildings. Snow covered their basketball hoop. It was located 10 feet in the air. In the Brelies barn was a 4-H calf. The huge drifts made it tough for them to haul feed to the animal.

Not surprisingly, as people emerged from their cocoons, they wanted to hear other human voices and exchange blizzard stories. This resulted in a surge in telephone usage. The deluge in calls overloaded the local switchboards of the Northwestern Bell Telephone Company. To be able to place a call, required considerable patience. To deal with this onslaught, additional switches were installed. Unfortunately, even that step proved to be insufficient.

Despite all this, the Larimore vicinity came through the storm in pretty good shape. According to Chuck Conner, Northwestern Bell's local manager, the Larimore area had only one rural line not working.

Larimore came through the blizzard without any major power outages. There were problems with one service line in Larimore, but the other lines fared better. This all came as a relief to Vern Pladson, Northern States Power Company's local representative. He summed up the situation thuswise, "We were very lucky."

After Wednesday, March 2, it would be Monday March 7 before Star Bus Line service returned to Larimore.

An offer by Larimore Boy Scouts to deliver groceries and shovel out doors for elderly people was broadcast on a radio station. According to Scoutmaster Delos Westbrook, hardly anyone took them up on the offer.

The Grand Forks County Home in Larimore came through the blizzard in fine shape. No one remaining there while the storm raged about them got sick. They didn't run out of food or other supplies and didn't experience any power outages. No emergencies arose.

But it was quite tiring for the workers there. The onslaught of the storm prevented the night nurses from reaching the place. and the day shift personnel from getting home. So, the day shift crew toiled from Thursday until Saturday doing both shifts.

Mrs. John Lohse, the home's matron, had this to say:

(the day crew) "*was truly wonderful. They were exhausted, but did all they could.*

Those who couldn't come to work were so concerned, even though they couldn't help it," *she said.*

The home had no emergencies – "*But I was terribly worried, especially about the power going off,*" *she said.*[246]

A housekeeper at the County Home, Mrs. Marius Madsen, wasn't going to let a raging blizzard prevent her from getting to work on Friday. Assisted by her husband, she headed out. Upon seeing them leave, a neighbor, Les Ralston, came out to lend a hand. As Mrs. Madsen was determined to make it work, the men helped her reach the Home.

When evening came, and it was time to go home, the two men were at the County Home to assist Mrs. Madsen with the return journey. Enroute they met Grand Forks County highway employee, Howard Wiegandt. The men put Mrs. Madsen in the scoop of Wiegandt's snow removal equipment. According to the *Larimore Pioneer* "she rode (home) in style."

The blizzard proved to be interesting for a lot of the residents of the McMenamy Trailer Court. They had come to the Larimore area to either work at Grand Forks Air Base or on the missile sites. For those hailing from the southern United States, it wasn't necessarily an enjoyable experience.

Larimore area trailer court, March 1966. Photo courtesy of James Lempe

Looking east from Dick Henry's home in Larimore, March 1966. Photo courtesy of James Lempe

On Sunday, so as to allow the snowplow to pass through the trailer court, its residents were informed they had to shovel out their automobiles. The completion this laborious task took the residents at least three hours. In some instances it took longer. For those who had never shoveled snow before, it had to be quite an experience.

The *Larimore Pioneer* praised the efforts of those who assisted others (including strangers) after the storm in ways such as pushing stalled cars out of the snow. One such individual was Ray Johnson. He made the rounds of all his neighbors making sure everything was going all right. This included their furnaces and adequacy of supplies.

The Larimore Fire Department was quite happy there weren't any fires during blizzard. Its fire chief, Mel Heffelfinger, said:

> *We're mighty fortunate. If there had been a fire, therewas nothing we could have done. To come through a blizzard that had buried the fire station and all approaches to it in deep snowbanks without any calls was indeed fortunate.*[247]

Larimore, March 1966. Both photos courtesy of James Lempe

Swanson Ford dealership in Larimore, March 1966.

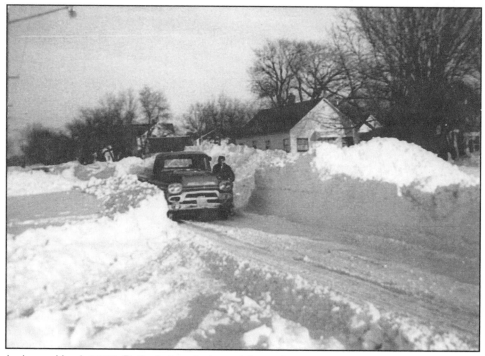

Larimore, March 1966. Both photos courtesy of James Lempe

GN crews faced some humongous drifts to clear after the storm. On the west end of Larimore, a tree-top snowbank a half mile long covered the line. After clearing that drift, the crews ran into a drift west of Niagara, so big a bulldozer couldn't take care it. Reinforcements in the way of larger equipment cleared the tracks.

The Grand Forks to Minot line was open to service at 1:35 p.m. Sunday. Once this was done, rail traffic quickly increased. Between 4:30 p.m. Sunday and 10:30 a.m. Monday, thirteen passenger trains passed through Larimore. These included GN's *Empire Builder* and the NP's *North Coast Limited*. To assist GN's effort to straighten out its snowbound traffic, H. E. Mickle and his associate at Larimore, Virgil Richard, alternated in working almost around the clock.

Windy conditions on Monday filled in the cuts of snow. Freight Train *97* of March 5 stalled in a big drift at Niagara late on Monday night. The Grand Forks-Minot line would be reopened at 7:00 p.m. Tuesday March 8.

Larimore's high school boys basketball team, the Polar Bears, ended their 1965-66 season with a 91 to 42 loss to Grand Forks Central on March 2 in the Northeast Class A Regional tournament being held in Grafton. Dennis Ridgeway and Bill Lee were the leading scorers for Larimore with 12 points each.

West of Grand Forks fourteen miles, not far from Emerado, is the Grand Forks Air Force Base. It is located on the north side of U.S. Highway 2.

The U.S. Congress authorized the establishment of this air base in 1954. Construction of the base started in February 1956 after the purchase of 5,400 acres of land in Meckinock Township. People contributed $65,000 for this transaction.

The activation of the base came in 1957.

The organization of the 321st Missile Wing at Grand Forks, the first Minuteman II intercontinental ballistic missile wing, occurred in 1964. This was followed by the first installation of a Minuteman II missile by Park River the following year. The 321st assumed operational status in 1966 at Grand Forks Air Force Base. It had fifteen launch sites controlling 150 missiles.

In March 1966, Melvin Nybo worked for the Grafton Milk Company. Late on Wednesday, March 2 he made a milk delivery to the Grand Force Air Base. The storm caught him there. It prevented him and several Air Force men from making it to sleeping quarters. They took shelter in an Air Force bus and lived on K-rations throughout the storm. During the storm, if one of them decided to leave the bus and go elsewhere, everyone in the group was tied together by rope to prevent anyone from getting separated.

The housing unit at Grand Forks Air Base suffered a loss of power on the evening of March 3. For the next two days, about 300 housing units had neither heat nor electricity. Affected by this outage were from 1,000 to 1,500 airmen, their wives and children. The base commander ordered the people in the affected housing units to stay where they were.

SMSgt. Phillip Musto Jr. and his family described their experience thuswise:

> We just went down to the basement and huddled together in blankets. We burned candles to give us a little heat.[248]

In some instances, friends and neighbors of those people who were caught in their housing units without either heat or lights took them into their home. Their abodes just across the street hadn't lost power.

According to Major Joe Zainey, the base information officer, there was a paramount consideration at the base while the blizzard was raging. According to him, *"Our first priority out here is to keep the runways open."*[249]

Once in a while, the air base's main traffic loop had snow removal vehicles pass through it. Movement about the base was restricted to those involved with the alert crews and emergency vehicles. Access to the main roads on the base was restricted to alert crews, alert personnel and vehicles.

By Saturday, food supplies at Grand Forks Air Force Base were dwindling. The base commissary was low on supplies, especially bread. At 9 a.m. Saturday, it was reopened for emergency rations. Items in this category included staple items such as bread and milk and baby food. Only those individuals in dire need of food supplies were allowed into the commissary.

There were some enormous drifts around the base to be seen once the storm had passed. One officer on the base gave this description:

> We just can't move by wheels at all. Snow is piled right up to the roof at
> my neighbor's just across the street. The cars are completely buried.[250]

To keep snowplows from hitting their automobiles, all base personnel were requested to attach red flags to them.

One story at Grand Forks Air Force Base had a young lad looking out the window. He then exclaimed to his father, *"Look, that snowplow just gobbled up that Volkswagen."*[251]

Stuck at home during the storm in Meckinock, a village three or four miles northeast of the Air Base, was an wife of an Air Force sergeant and their five-month-old twins. The blizzard kept the sergeant on nonstop duty from Wednesday night to Saturday afternoon. The Air Force gave the sergeant a ride home on a helicopter Saturday afternoon. Along

Grand Forks Air Force Base after the blizzard. Courtesy of U. S. Air Force

Grand Forks Air Force Base, March 1966. Photos courtesy of U. S. Air Force

429

with the backyard landing, came a new supply of food. He came that way because the roads were still blocked in the area.

Grand Forks Air Base personnel received a helping hand from Nodak Rural Electric linemen in getting their power restored. Although Nodak provided Grand Forks Air Force Base with power, the United States government owned the lines on the base and the military personnel managed the power supply. Air Force personnel fixed the electrical problems on the base.

Those personnel on duty when the blizzard hit the base, such as the ready crews, remained there until the storm let up. From Thursday night on, it was nonstop duty for the officer of the day at the base.

After Wednesday, March 3 the storm had prevented delivery of any newspapers to the Grand Forks Air Force Base. On Sunday, a civilian vehicle brought copies of the *Grand Forks Herald* newspaper to the base. The vehicle got no further than the main gate. At that place, the vehicle's driver was told about an emergency ban concerning private vehicles on base.

That afternoon, the base's commanding officer issued a special order allowing the *Herald* vehicle to proceed to deliver the paper.

Thompson lies about eight miles southwest of Grand Forks.

In 1960, Thompson had a population of 211.

GN established a station here in 1879. The settlement was first known as Norton. In 1881, Albert Thompson, postmaster, renamed it for himself and his brother, Robert. Others believed it was named for an early businessman of the area, Alec Thompson.

Around 6 p.m. Thursday, March 3, 1966, two cars were traveling down U.S. Highway 81 when they came upon a transport that blocked the highway. In a couple of the vehicles were Walter W. Gretz from the Grand Forks Air Force Base and John Schatz of Fargo traveling by themselves. Luther Hagen of Stanley and John Hart of Cavalier were in another car with three other NDSU students.

By using the two-way radio in his car, Gretz was able to contact the Reverend Gary Olson in Grand Forks. The latter then notified highway officials, who dispatched a snowplow to the scene.

In the meantime, at least a dozen automobiles were stopped at that location. With snow removal equipment leading the way, the cars followed behind in caravan fashion.

Three of the college students hitched a ride with a highway maintenance truck. Hagen and Hart then hooked up with Gretz and Schatz.

The two vehicles had only gone a few miles, when Schatz went into the ditch. Gretz's car stalled, too. This occurred around 2 a.m. Friday. By using only one vehicle at a time, they were able to keep the automobiles running for another eight hours.

While this was going on, Gretz was able to contact some ham radio operators in Grand Forks. Included in that group were Ken Dobmeier and Dick Spicer.

In conjunction with men from Electronic's Associates, Dobmeier and Spicer helped to set up an effort to reach the men by snowmobile.

Meanwhile, Gretz made contact with another ham radio operator, Ralph Adams, who lived in rural Grand Forks. Gretz informed Adams that his vehicle was located near a certain insurance sign along U.S. 81–immediately north of the Thompson exit.

Being familiar with the area, Adams got in touch with Julian Loiland whose farm house was only 200 yards from the stalled automobile. Loiland and his son trudged through deep snow to the vehicle and brought the men back to his home.

The time was around 1:30 p.m. Friday. It had been three and a half hours, since their cars had run out of gas.

Afterwards, Gretz remarked that he thought he had observed a yard light the previous evening. Unfortunately, even though the farm wasn't far way, Gretz was unable to see it.

An effort to rescue the men by snowmobile was underway at the time. The rescue party consisted of Herb Counterman of the Grand Forks Air Force Base and Kenneth Welter of Grand Forks. They had reached the southern edge of Grand Forks, when they were informed by radio that the stranded men had been rescued.

In March 1966, Jim West was a senior at Thompson High School. He lived with his family on a farm three miles northwest of Thompson. The intensity of the storm prevented them from feeding their livestock. Jim remembers the snowdrifts reaching high enough to cover the power lines. It took considerable effort to dig out after the storm. Their loader was on an International "H". They knew where it was, but it and a truck were still buried in the snow. They got the tractor and loader out by moving the snow one bucket of snow at a time, as the tractor moved forward.[252]

On March 7, Thompson lost to Northwood, 59 to 42, in District 6 tournament play at Mayville. Dan Hanson scored 21 points for Thompson.

Situated at the confluence of the Red Lake River and the Red River of the North is Grand Forks (34,451 inhabitants in 1960).

Almost hundred years before settlers came to Grand Forks, it was visited by French-Canadian explorers and Hudson Bay Company employees. The latter set up an outpost. The former named the intersection of the Red and Red Lake Rivers, "Les Grandes Fourches". In English this means "the Grand Forks."

The arrival of settlers at Grand Forks in 1868 established it, after Pembina, as North Dakota's second oldest permanent white settlement.

Sanford C. Cady served as Grand Forks' first postmaster. He was in charge when a post office was set up in Grand Forks on June 15, 1870. His suggestion to the Post Office Dept. of using an English translation of "Les Grandes Fourches" was accepted by them. In 1871, Capt. Alexander Griggs established squatter's right on land that would eventually become the city of Grand Forks. He filed the original plat for Grand Forks on October 31, 1875.

The organization of Grand Forks County in 1873 saw Grand Forks being chosen to be the county seat.

In January 1880, the GN rail line from Crookston reached Grand Forks.

Grand Forks is home to a few notable North Dakota institutions. These are the University of North Dakota (established February 27, 1883), the State Mill and Elevator (set up in 1922) and the N. D. School for the Blind (relocated from Bathgate in 1961).

Headbolt heaters were invented in Grand Forks by Andrew Freeman, longtime general manager of Minkota Power Company in Grand Forks. In her book, *Echoes*, *Grand Forks Herald* columnist Marilyn Hagerty lets Freeman himself tell the story:

> How did they keep cars running all winter before headbolt heaters?
>
> "Well," says Andrew Freeman, the man who invented the first plug-in. "I remember how the mailman at Upham, N. D. used to keep his car running. He drained the oil out every night. He kept it warm in the house and put it back in the car the next morning."
>
> Born in 1909, Freeman says, "We had a Model A Ford. When we wanted to start it, we would go out and fire up a stove we had in the garage."

There were other ways of starting cars.

"Some people would shovel coals out of the furnace and carry them out to put under the car to heat the engine," Freeman says.

"Others used teakettles of hot water. They would pour the water over the intake manifold."

Canadians, he says, were some of the best customers when he invented the Freeman Headbolt heater in the 1940's. an early customer in Alaska was jubilant when one of the new heaters helped his car take off in 57 below weather.

Although headbolt heaters were replaced by frost plugs and tank heaters, Freeman still feels pride when he sees plugs hanging out of cars. He says the heaters are inexpensive to operate. They take less than a kilowatt an hour.

"That's less than three cents an hour. For ten hours at night, it's between 25 and 30 cents."

"Of course," he says, "the heater doesn't have to be plugged in all night. An hour or so before starting the car generally will do it."[253]

The mayor of Grand Forks at the time of the March 1966 blizzard was Hugo Magnuson (1900-2000). A well known local grocer, Magnuson held that office from 1964 until 1972.

Originally from the Parkers' Prairie, Minnesota area, Magnuson later was a student at Gustavus Adolphus College in St. Peter, Minnesota, for a couple of years.

After that he was employed by Nash-Finch wholesale grocers.

Mr. Magnuson was working in Fargo when he found out about a couple of opportunities, one in Grand Forks (a store for sale), and the other in Greeley, Colorado. Hugo's wife, Dorothy, hailed from Kintyre, North Dakota. The desire to be near family members won out, as Hugo and Dorothy Magnuson picked Grand Forks.

They arrived there in 1939. The grocery store they purchased, Pure Food Grocery, was located on the corner of DeMers Avenue and North Fifth Street.

From that humble beginning, the Magnusons would expand their grocery business into a regional one with additional stores in East Grand Forks, Crookston, Thief River Falls, and Jamestown. They were associated with Piggly Wiggly from 1955 until 1982. Since then their chain of grocery stores have gone by the name of "Hugo's."

One Grand Forks native who went on to achieve fame in country music was Lynn Anderson. She sang on the Lawrence Welk television show at the tender age of 16. The songs Lynn Anderson is best remembered for are "Rocky Top" and "I Never Promised You a Rose Garden."

It started to snow in Grand Forks the evening of March 2, 1966. That night, 2.6 inches of snow fell at the airport.

That same evening, the boys' basketball team from St. James High School in Grand Forks participated in the Northeast Class A tournament being held in Grafton. They finished their season with a 66 to 42 loss to Carrington.

Thursday morning, the residents of Grand Forks woke up to a snowstorm. During the day, another 6.8 inches of snow fell. The thermometer climbed to 26 above.

Starting Thursday afternoon, seven Grand Forks policemen put in a thirty-four hour shift. In addition to their regular duties, they carried out rescue and mercy missions. The operations required the use of snowplows, vehicles from the city and National Guard and snowmobiles.

What did they do?

Besides making a bread delivery to the Deaconess Hospital in downtown Grand Forks, the police picked up and brought a shipment of blood to both there and to St. Michael's Hospital out by the University of North Dakota.

The officers provided assistance in transporting eight expectant mothers to local hospitals. At least, an equal number of other emergency situations, arose that required their help for transportation to a hospital.

For individuals who had too much to drink and were stranded in snowbanks, officers came to the their rescue.

There were people who had never been hemmed in before by such a long lasting snowstorm that blocked their escape from their residences. A feeling of claustrophobia began to set in. They would call the police, and the latter would come over to shovel out their doorways.

Fuel oil was another item the police delivered.

In undertaking one of these missions, a Grand Forks police officer was injured. An employee at the Jiffy Fry potato processing plant on Gateway Drive in Grand Forks was reported missing along that roadway.

Enroute to check out the report on snowmobile was Policeman Larry Bangle, 26. Unfortunately, Bangle's snow machine took an unexpected tumble over an eight-foot drift and landed on the pavement below. Although the accident left Bangle with a bad sprain, he was said to be doing well at Deaconess Hospital.

Officers completing that marathon shift were Sgt. Clarence Gerstner, and Patrolman Wayne Anderson, Orville Gunderson, Arthur Jerome, Marlyn Knuth, Darrell Reese and Robert Sivertson.

As could be expected, Grand Forks hotels and motels were full during the blizzard. Guests and motel management were singing each others praises.

In describing his guests, Neil Smith of the Stardust Manor Motel had this to say:

> We probably have the 85 nicest people in the country right here. We've been marooned out here since Thursday morning and they're still the nicest people in the country.[254]

In downtown Grand Forks, there were no vacancies at the Ryan Hotel. Among the people stranded there were some local residents unable to make it home.

The Ryan Hotel didn't skimp on meals during the snowstorm.

Guests were offered full menus. Employees throughout the hotel put in extra shifts.

The inclement weather prevented some of its bartenders from making it to the Ryan Hotel, so three guests of the hotel filled in. "A wonderful job," was the description of their performance.

So impressed were the Ryan Hotel guests of their hosts efforts on their behalf, they called the *Grand Forks Herald* to let that paper know about it.

Another downtown Grand Forks sleeping establishment, the Dacotah Hotel, was so full that roll away beds were used to sleep on by some folks.

The Dacotah ran out of milk on Friday night, and eggs Saturday morning.

Even though the Dacotah Hotel had an ample supply of labor throughout the course of the storm, employees there still put in additional hours of work.

One evening, the drinkers and nondrinkers got together at the piano bar to sing stirring renditions of "golden oldies."

A skeleton crew took care of the seventy-eight guests stranded at the Westward Ho Motel on Gateway Drive. For the help that couldn't make it home because of the blizzard, six rooms were reserved for them.

Reporting on the morale of the guests Robert McLeod spoke for the hotel's management. He remarked, *"They're in real good spirits and they're a wonderful bunch of guests."*

When doors of the motel units were blocked by snowbanks, some of the guests made their exit via the window.

The lack of eating facilities at the Plainsman Motel didn't affect the thirty-three guests staying there that much. They simply ate at the home of the managers of the motel, William and Gladys Rhodes, In talking about their guests, Mrs. Rhodes had this to say:

> *A real wonderful group. We couldn't ask for anything better. We haven't had any help except my husband and our boy. I've been busy but I'm enjoying every minute of it. We don't have any gripers here.*

To feed all their guests, Mrs. Rhodes had them eat in shifts of six or eight.

Only one guest checked out of the Plainsman Motel after the storm. And that individual returned about fifteen minutes later. On Saturday, none of the guests at the Plainsman Motel was checking out. All twenty-eight units at that motel were occupied.[255]

Gordy Graetz was one of the few paper boys who delivered the *Grand Forks Herald* on Thursday.

On Friday, most of the *Herald* employees stayed home because of the weather. That day, Grand Forks received 17 inches of snow.

A couple of *Herald* employees, photographer Colburn Hvidston III and Peter Wasylow,

Kay Sampson, a storm casualty. Photo by Colburn Hvidston III. Courtesy of Grand Forks Herald

Herald stereotyper, departed from the *Herald* building in downtown Grand Forks on Friday when the blizzard was at its worst. They headed west on a snowmobile. They got to the 2100 block of University Avenue, when they were flagged down by a couple of students.

In a nearby home, was 21 year-old Kay Sampson. The Wahpeton native was UND's 1965 Homecoming Queen. At the home, she was receiving treatment for a foot cut she had suffered in a snowmobile accident.

The *Herald* employees transported Miss Sampson to the Delta Gamma sorority house, located at 2630 University Avenue. She received first aid there.

Next, Hvidston and Wasylow, assisted by a UND student from Grand Forks by the name of Gary Como prepared a toboggan for Miss Sampson. Even though the depth of the snow was up to their hips, the men were able to pull her through it to St. Michael's Hospital. After receiving treatment there, Miss Sampson was released.

One Grand Forks resident, Ron Knotts, using 8 mm film and a home movie camera, shot some scenes from the blizzard.

The blizzard kept one Grand Forks resident hopping. Glen Osbjornson of 702 Lincoln Drive owned a homemade snowplane. He had built the machine three years earlier out at a cost of $125. The materials Osbjornson used to construct the snowplane included scrap iron, an airplane motor and propeller, ski-like runners and a model "T" frame. The snowplane could reach a speed of 70 mph on level ground.

Osbjornson ran a sort of taxi service on Friday, March 4 for people with essential jobs such as at local hospitals. He took people to and from their places of employment.

Glen Osbjorson and Stuart McDonald in Osbjorson's snowplane on March 5, 1966. Courtesy of Grand Forks Herald

Even though the snowplane could reach a speed of 70 mph on level ground, Osbjornson kept the speed down within city limits.

There were a couple of reasons for this. One of them was snowbanks, and the problems associated with them. The other one was pedestrians. While there weren't many of them out in the elements on Friday, he still had to keep an eye out for them. Mother Nature had no answer for Mr. Osbjornson's resourcefulness.

The atrocious weather prevented the *Grand Forks Herald* from being published (for the first time in its history) on Friday, March 4. it wasn't published the next day either. According to Jack Hagerty, a *Herald* employee, copies of Thursday's, March 3 edition were still sitting in the *Herald* mailroom, waiting to be delivered.

Because UND had won the North Central Conference championship, had done well in nonconference play, and had an overall record of 21-3, the school was chosen to be the host for the N. C. A. A. Division II Midwest Regional Tournament. It was to be played on March 4-5, 1966.

The March 1966 snowstorm interrupted those plans. Three of the fours teams in the tournament, Colorado State Teachers College (later the University of Northern Colorado), St. Procopious of Illinois, and Valparaiso University of Indiana were stranded in Moorhead, Minnesota.

Great Northern Depot in Grand Forks on March 5, 1966. Courtesy of E.B.R. SC, UND

Snowmobiler on Conklin Avenue in Grand Forks on March 5, 1966. Drift in background is 20 feet high. Courtesy of Grand Forks Herald

Osco Drug on N. 3rd Street in Grand Forks on March 5, 1966. Courtesy of E.B.R. SC, UND

Carrying groceries in Grand Forks on March 5, 1966. Photo by Colburn Hvidston III. Courtesy of the Grand Forks Herald

The schedule for the tournament had to be rearranged.

In a game played in Moorhead, Valparaiso gained the finals of the tournament with a 107 to 76 win over St. Procopious.

Colorado State's team pulled into Grand Forks Sunday on board a train. Things didn't go their way that evening, as UND beat them 84 to 71. Because Grand Forks streets were still plugged with snow, all 3,550 fans who attended the game, made it there on foot.

The next morning, Phil Jackson poured in a UND one game school record 44 points in a 112 to 82 UND win over Valparaiso of Indiana. UND now had the Midwest Regional Tournament championship under its belt.

Not long afterwards, Jackson received a phone call informing him that he had been chosen for the Little All-America first team. The 6 foot 8 junior from Williston was just the second North Dakotan to win such an award in basketball. NDSU's Marv Bachmeier was a similar winner in 1960.

In response Jackson said, *"I'm really surprised-honored to be chosen."*[256]

In the meantime, Len Marti, UND Athletic Director, had gotten snow removal crews from the city of Grand Forks and the state of North Dakota to open major traffic arteries in Grand Forks. Their efforts gave the UND's men's basketball team enough time to reach the airport to catch a flight and head for the national tournament at Evansville, Indiana.

At that tournament, UND won its first game on March 9, a 63 to 62 hold-your-breath victory over Abilene Christian College.

The next day, UND lost to a strong Southern Illinois University team, 69 to 61. A player on that Southern Illinois squad was a future NBA star and teammate of Phil Jackson with the New York Knicks, Walt Frazier.

UND then played for third place in the national tournament. But they came up short again, as Akron University defeated them 76 to 71.

The 1965-66 team is remembered as one of UND's greatest. Leading the 24-5 squad in both scoring and rebounding, 21.8 points per game and 12.9 rebounds per game, was its Little All-American and Co-Captain Phil Jackson. The 238 field goals Jackson made that season and the field goal percentage of .542 were both school records.

When Phil Jackson finished his basketball career at UND in 1967, he was the all time leading scorer for the mens' teams. It would take 24 years before Dave Vonesh, another outstanding player, broke Jackson's career scoring mark of 1708 points. Presently, that record is held by Scott Gulseth, a great player, who led Edinburg to the 1988 North Dakota State Class B Boys Basketball Championship.

The coach of that great 1965-66 UND mens' basketball team was Bill Fitch. When Phil Jackson was still in high school, Fitch wanted him to play for UND. Coach Fitch showed that he was serious about that when he drove across North Dakota in a snowstorm to speak at a sports banquet in Williston.

Bill Fitch would go on to coach in the NBA. His 1980-81 Boston Celtics won the NBA title that year.

Jim Rodgers, Fitch's assistant coach in 1965-66, succeeded him as UND men's basketball coach. Rodgers would also go on to be a head coach in the NBA. At one time Bill Fitch, Phil Jackson, and Jim Rodgers were all head coaches in the NBA at the same time.

The 1965-66 UND's mens' hockey team had an up and down year. They finished the regular WCHA (Western Collegiate Hockey Association) in second place with a 13-9-0 record.

When tournament time rolled around, the first playoff game for UND was scheduled to be played in Grand Forks on March 3, 1966. Their opponent would be the Minnesota Gophers. In the meantime a snowstorm was brewing.

But the Gophers didn't let that stop them. Traveling by train they made it to Grand Forks early Thursday afternoon.

The game was to be played that night at UND's Winter Sports Arena (known affectionately by locals as the "Barn.") So, as 1,250 hardy fans looked on, and blizzard conditions swirled around them outside, the Sioux upended Minnesota 4 to 2. The Sioux advanced in the playoffs. A member of that Gopher team, Doug Woog, would later coach hockey at the University of Minnesota.

Two days later in Denver, Colorado, the Sioux lost to the Denver Pioneers 5 to 4 in overtime.

The Sioux finished the season with a 17-12-1 overall record.

There were some very talented players on that team. Hailing from Montana was Terry Casey, the team captain. The senior center was UND's top scorer for the 1965-66 season. His 54 points came from 26 goals and 28 assists. In 1967, Casey would play in the World Tournament as a member of the United States national team. Unfortunately, he never got a chance to see how far his talent would carry him. That summer, he died in a car accident in Montana.

Mike (Lefty) Curran was the leading goalie on the 1965-66 squad. Statisticswise, he allowed 3.64 goals per game and stopped 88.4 per cent of the shots he faced. Curan would later play professional hockey with the St. Paul Fighting Saints.

Another UND payer who would go on to a professional hockey career was senior center Dennis Hextall. His 48 points for the 1965-66 season came from 19 goals and 29 assists.

Another member of the 1965-66 team was center John "Gino" Gasparini from Fort Francis, Ontario. He was captain of the hockey in his final season as a player at UND, 1967-68. Gasparini would go on to be an assistant coach under Rube Bjorkman and then take over as head coach in 1978. His men's hockey teams at UND would capture three NCAA Division I championships–1980, 1982 and 1987. The 1987 team was offensively, probably the most explosive in UND history. A few of the outstanding players on that team were Ed Belfour, Tony Hrkac, Bob Joyce and Steve Johnson.

In April 1966, UND hockey coach Bob Peters decided to coach the Bemidji State's hockey team. He was replaced by assistant coach Bill Selman.

In March 1966, Gordon Iseminger was a history professor at the University of North Dakota. He lived east of Columbia Road on Ninth Avenue North. Prior to the start of the blizzard, Professor Isiminger had brought home student term papers in his brief case to grade. As there was no classes being held at UND during the storm, Professor Iseminger corrected the term papers at home instead.

The storm left a large drift in front of Mr. Iseminger's house. It was as high as the eaves on his house. A waste-high drift covered the driveway in front of the Iseminger home. Mr. Iseminger partially shoveled the area in front of the garage. The remainder of the driveway was cleared by Jim Gibbs' son who used a Ford tractor with a scraper to do the job. Jim Gibbs was the owner of A & W Rootbeer Restaurant which was located on Gateway Drive in Grand Forks. He lived kitty-corner across the street from the Iseminger residence. Professor Iseminger walked to and from his job at UND. After the storm, it was particularly hard to make it out to the University.

Mr. Iseminger remembers what happened to William Biggs, a doctoral student in history at UND, during the storm. Biggs and his family lived in married student housing which was located west of the English Coulee on the UND campus. Mr. and Mrs. Biggs' son had undergone an appendectomy at St. Michael's Hospital in Grand Forks. This hospital was located about a block north of the intersection of Columbia Road and University Avenue. William Biggs and his wife went to see their son at the hospital. They were there when the storm arrived. The Biggs could not get home because of the inclement weather. The same conditions prevented the hospital cooks from making it to work. So, the Biggs did the cooking for St. Michael's Hospital during the storm. Nurses who were needed at the hospital during the storm were brought there via snowmobile.[257]

In March 1966, Fred Thoelke was a student at the University of North Dakota in Grand Forks. He stayed at West Hall, a men's dormitory located west of the English Coulee, on the north side of University Avenue. Back then, students living in dormitories west of the English Coulee ate at a cafeteria in Smith Hall. This dormitory was on the south side of University Avenue, just east of the English Coulee. During one of the worst days of the '66 storm, students from West Hall joined hands to form a human chain so they wouldn't get lost in the storm and headed for Smith Hall.

Fred Thoelke remembers looking out of his dorm window at West Hall and seeing one of the married student housing units being completely covered by a snowdrift.

Once the storm had subsided, and snowplows had opened University Avenue, Fred Thoelke drove down that street. The depth of the snow on the sides of University Avenue was much higher than his car. Fred remarked, *"It looked like a tunnel without the roof on it."*[258]

Christus Rex Lutheran Center on UND campus, March 5, 1966. Courtesy of E.B.R. SC, UND

Snowmobiler approaching UND power plant, March 1966 Courtesy of E.B.R. SC, UND

In March 1966, Elwyn B. Robinson, history professor at UND, and his wife, Eva, reviewed proofs for Robinson's book, *History of North Dakota*. The March 1966 blizzard gave the couple some extra time to do this. The book was published by the University of Nebraska Press in October 1966. Elwyn spent twenty years researching and writing *History of North Dakota* which has become highly acclaimed.

In March 1966, Eddy Fladeland worked for the city of Grand Forks. During and after the storm, he operated both a blade and a payloader, although not much during the storm. Eddy remembers the National Guard helping them haul snow.

One of the Guard's officers who rode around with Eddy occasionally on the payloader was Errol Mann. Mann was a kicker on the UND football team. Later on, he would kick in the NFL, mainly with the Detroit Lions. Mann was also on the Oakland Raider team that defeated the Minnesota Vikings in the 1977 Super Bowl.

Eddy Fladeland says that the trucks hauled the snow down 2nd Avenue North and dumped it on the river bank.[259]

At the time of the '66 blizzard, Ted Jarombek and his family lived in Grand Forks. Ted worked as a foreman for GN in their rail yard in Grand Forks. During the first day of the storm, Ted helped clean switches in the Grand Forks yard.

On the second day of the storm, Ted and another worker, rode a switch engine out to the wye located west of town (where today's Amtrak station is located) to clean switches for a passenger train coming from the south. The train had passengers disembarking in Grand Forks. The place where they disembarked was at the train station located along

"You Don't Know The Half Of It I'm Standing On My Roof!"

Stuart J. McDonald's cartoon published in the Grand Forks Herald on March 6. Courtesy of the Grand Forks Herald

DeMers Avenue in downtown Grand Forks.

To reach downtown Grand Forks, the train first had to turn west on the wye and then back up into Grand Forks. Prior to doing this, Ted and the other man cleaned the wye switches. But, their work was undone by the train backing up. It filled the switches with snow. After the train had passed, they had to clean the switches again.

Being a foreman, Ted had to be on duty throughout the storm. The inclement weather created a shortage of workers. Ted caught a ride home aboard a snowmobile once during the storm. Before leaving, he was told by his superiors to make sure that he returned. Stopping at a Valley Dairy Store, Ted picked up milk and other necessities for his family. After he dropped those items off at his house, Ted returned to work via the same snowmobile.[260]

The GN rail yard looked like one big snowbank. Cars had to be pulled out, one or two at a time. Switchmen had a hard time pulling the coupling pins on cars because of all the snow between the tracks. Bulldozers were brought in. The snow was piled on four or five tracks in the center of the yard. It was left there for Mother Nature to melt.

In 1966, UND heated its buildings with coal. Therefore, its power plant had to be kept operating. This meant the university had to have coal delivered to it continuously. Because of this, GN kept its rail spur to UND open throughout the storm.

Mike Lunak, age 13, lost one of his shoes, a boot, in a snowbank during the blizzard. When the storm first started, he said the snowflakes were really big. Barney Lunak, his dad, was really mad at him for doing so. After the storm let up, he went to the local store. There were snowmobiles there and lots of people. There was not much left on the shelves. After all the snow melted, Mike found his shoe.[261]

The blizzard went on and on in Grand Forks. People ran out of cigarettes. Terry Hurst, a strong lad, went to the neighborhood bar to get cigarettes out of the machine for his mother. While there, the bartender asked him, "What will you have?" This turned out to be a moment of opportunity. He answered, "I'll have a beer." Terry had his first beer in a bar. At the time, he was not of age.[262]

One of the more amazing stories that took place during the March 1966 storm involved a registered nurse at St. Michael's Hospital in Grand Forks. At the time of the storm, Mrs. Kirk Blecha was residing at her family's housing unit at the University of North Dakota. She was also awaiting the imminent birth of her first child.

Despite this, Mrs. Blecha volunteered to work at the hospital while the blizzard was in full swing. She trudged through the inclement weather ten block distance from her home to St. Michael's Hospital. Mrs. Blecha put in back to back eight hour shifts as a nurse.

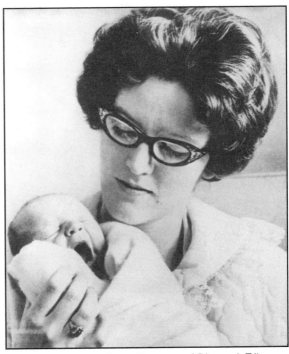

Mrs. Kirk Blecha and son. Courtesy of Bismarck Tribune

On Saturday morning, she switched roles and checked in as a maternity patient. At 2 a.m. the next morning, Mrs. Blecha gave birth to an 8 pound 3 ounce boy. Later, hospital officials reported mother and son to be doing well.

A couple of storm-related trips involved Dr. Curtis Johnson who was a physician at St. Michael's hospital in Grand Forks. He received a phone call from Mr. and Mrs. John Hazlett. Their year- old daughter, Tracy, had a fever for two days and her temperature had reached 105. The snowbound Hazletts were unable to make the fifteen block trip to the hospital.

So, Dr. Johnson and James Puppe, a hospital orderly, set out in the raging storm for the Hazlett residence on a snowmobile. Dr. Johnson drove the machine. After reaching the Hazlett place, they bundled up the ill child. Accompanied by her father, they returned with her to the hospital. On Saturday morning, the little girl was reported to be in satisfactory condition.

On another trip, Dr. Johnson received a police escort for part of his journey. This trip involved an elderly heart patient.

The March 1966 blizzard deposited 27.8 of snow, 2.74 inches of precipitation, at the Grand Forks Airport which was located 4 miles northwest of the city. The greatest snowfall, 17 inches, fell at the airport on Friday March 4.

Temperatures never got that cold at the airport during the snowstorm. A high of 30 above was reached on Wednesday, March 2, the first day of the blizzard. Even on the worst day of the storm, Friday, March 4, the low for the day at the airport was 14 above.

The wind was out of the north at UND on the first day of the blizzard. On the two worst days of the storm, March 3 and 4, it came from the northeast. It switched back to the northwest on March 5.

Jennifer Saul, a UND senior from Crookston, unlocks her snow-covered automobile during the height of the blizzard. Photo by Colburn Hvidston III. Courtesy of Grand Forks Herald

A completely accurate measurement of precipitation totals from the blizzard at the U. S. Weather Station at UND was not possible. High winds accompanying the snowstorm Thursday evening, tilted the instrument with which the weather observer at UND measured the depth of new snow. The observer reported that it wasn't possible for him to even guess at how much snow came down that night. J. R. Schwendeman was the weather observer in charge of the UND

Phyllis Lanes helping Jane Jarman over a drift in University Park area in Grand Forks, March 1966, Courtesy of Grand Forks Herald

Grand Forks, March 1966. Courtesy of Grand Forks Herald

Betty and Ron Knotts exiting from their apartment in Grand Forks on 18th Ave. South, March 1966. Courtesy of Ron and Betty Knotts

Ron Knotts and Lillian Celander on 18th Ave. South in Grand Forks, March 1966

Betty Knotts and Asora Egstad in Grand Forks, March 1966. Both photos courtesy of Ron and Betty Knotts

Roseau snowmobilers in Grand Forks on mission of mercy, March 5, 1966. Left to right: John Miller, Bobby Eastman, Randy Hites, Ray Baumgartner, Edson Brandt. Seated on snowmobile is Roger Dick. Courtesy of Grand Forks Herald

Grand Forks on March 7, 1966. Courtesy of E.B.R. SC, UND

Robert Thorkelson attempting to dig an entrance from the street to his wife's place of business on N. Fourth St., March 5, 1966. Photo by Colburn Hvidston III. Courtesy of Grand Forks Herald

North end worshippers returning from Sunday services in Grand Forks, March 6, 1966. Courtesy of Grand Forks Herald

Snow removal by 231st unit of NDARNG in front of Golden Hour Cafe on N. 5th St. in Grand Forks on March 5, 1966. Courtesy of E.B.R. SC, UND

Snow removal in Grand Forks on March 9, 1966. Courtesy of E.B.R. SC, UND

Snow removal on S. 4th St. in Grand Forks in March 1966. Photo by Colburn Hvidston III. Courtesy of Grand Forks Herald

Curtis Kolbo took time out to give Sister John Elise a ride, March 1966.

Below: N.D. Governor William L. Guy on inspection tour of storm damage in Grand Forks area, March 9, 1966. Both photos courtesy of the Grand Forks Herald

station. According to him, the accident hurt the accuracy of the precipitation figures; they would be off a little.

Snow depth at UND on March 4 and 5 was 27 inches. On March 5, the depth of snow at Grand Forks Airport was 34 inches.

The U. S. Weather Bureau office, located at Hector Airport at Fargo in 1966, was relocated in Grand Forks in 1996.

The snow removal process in Grand Forks was a long slog after the blizzard. National Guard trucks began hauling snow away from the downtown area to dumps around 6 p.m. Friday, March 4, when the storm was still in its fury.

The city of East Grand Forks lies across the Red River from Grand Forks.

In 1960, 6,998 people called East Grand Forks home. The Red Lake River comes from the southeast and flows through East Grand Forks to meet the Red River near the Point Bridge. That structure opened for traffic in 1969. The other two bridges spanning the Red River at East Grand Forks, the Sorlie and Kennedy Bridges, were finished in 1929 and 1963, respectively.

A disaster was averted at the Sunset Acres Motel on Highway 2 in East Grand Forks on Thursday, March 3. The proprietors of the motel, Mr. and Mrs. Page Fassett, noticed a sag in the roof over their living quarters. The motel was completely buried under eight feet of snow. They requested assistance from motel guests.

Coming to the Fassett's aid were four construction workers. From Oksness Construction Company of Fargo came James Beath, Marlton Lindell and Cal Rude. Also helping out was another construction worker, George Duclaunlie of Wales, North Dakota.

The men dug a tunnel, about 3 feet wide, and roughly 60 feet long to reach the Fassett apartment.

Upon reaching their destination, they located several big planks and braced the sagging roof.

Mrs. Fassett said she and her husband were fortunate to have a construction crew staying there. It didn't take long for those men to fix the problem. Otherwise, the roof over the Fassett's apartment would have collapsed.

To relieve pressure on the roof supports, the men dug their way to the roof and shoveled part of the snow off it.

Before they could leave, they had to open a path through a 20 foot high snowbank to the highway. That was an all-day job.

The motel's parking lot was cleared by snow removal equipment Sunday afternoon. A crew of eight finished the job of clearing snow off the motel's roof and away from its front on Monday.

Workers shoveling snow away from Sunset Acres Motel on March 7, 1966. Courtesy of Grand Forks Herald

Left to right: Marilyn, Sandra and Darlene Martell and Mary Gust, all from East Grand Forks, building a snowfort, March 1966. Courtesy of E.B.R. SC, UND

An East Grand Forks newspaper, *The Record*, ran a couple of stories on two individuals impressions of the storm and its aftermath. The first article titled **"Welcome, Sweet Storm"** was by Ann Morton Neale:

> It was a field day for amateur photographers, flood forecasters, school children and proponents of the three-day work week.
>
> Twenty-nine reasons, each more painful then the next, account for the jangled nerves for the city's fathers who spent three days nonstop with their children and who now appreciate more than ever the fate of the housewife.
>
> The snow removal crews worked overtime, and the mail didn't go through. Youngsters learned for the first time
> the wonders of the small box they had never reached, and
> boys booby trapped their yards with tunnels.
>
> Few people had ever walked up to the roofs of their houses, and many shoveled out their cars twice-before and after snowplow.
>
> Snowmobiles slid merrily along snubbing the walker with his toboggan of groceries; snowplows got stuck and the city ran out of places to put the white debris.
>
> With scarfs and gloves and boots and more the photographers made their precarious way up drifts as their delighted children jumped fearlessly from five foot mounds into the winding path which was once a familiar street. We also saw a man with a month's supply of ice cream cones.
>
> A new experience for nearly everyone, no estimates have been made of the loss due to the two-day on-slaught which stymied business, not to mention the snow removal costs and the human toll of lives which fell before it.
>
> And now we look forward to the flood. Last week the weather bureau in Fargo said, "All points north of Halstad probably will have high water. The heavier the precipitation, the higher the water."
>
> So now? we sit and wait and corner the market on mosquito repellent and recall the words of Shelly, worth: "If winter comes, can spring be far behind."
>
> And in Virginia, they tell me that the crocus are blooming.[263]

Joanne Warren, a student at East Grand Forks High School, in March 1966 wrote:

> It didn't take very long to learn Monday morning just what was on everybody's mind. After our 4-day weekend, one filled with snow, snow, snow, it seemed that every person had at least a hundred and one thrilling packed or awesome tales to pass on.
>
> And so on, whenever you happened to find a "listener", (someone who had just finished with his narration) you instinctively knew that your big moment had come, and off you went.
>
> Passing through the halls I heard tales of (how) a weary shoveller fought his way through the mounds of snow adventure to clear his driveway only to find by that time he'd gotten his car started and backed up, the snowplows had cleared the streets and piled the snow (where else) right back in the driveway.

There were even a few "fish stories" floating around, this time in the measure of the tremendous snowdrift around your house. As the day went on it seemed that more and more people had been snowed in or else surrounded by drifts to the tenth power.

Don't get me wrong! The blizzard and all the things that came along with it were (no) joking matters, however it's rather ironic that the events which seemed so serious and hard at the time they're happenings, become treasured anecdotes to be repeated time and again, and with the passage of time the sharpness will vanish, and you might even brag a little of your experiences in the "Cruel winter of '66".[264]

One thing the March 1966 storm did do was make the East Grand Forks City Council look like geniuses. On March 3, 1966, before the city was buried under the terrific snowfall, the city council issued a proclamation declaring that a state of flood emergency existed in East Grand Forks. A part of this declaration was the decision to have a temporary dike constructed.

Grand Forks and East Grand Forks were hit with a major flood after the March 1966 blizzard. The Red River crested at 45.55 feet in Grand Forks on April 4, 1966. At that time, it was the third worst flood for the cities. Only the 1897 and 1950 floods were higher.

After the March 1966 blizzard and subsequent flood, the *Grand Forks Herald* put out a pictorial on them.

RED RIVER RAMPAGE

PICTORIAL STORY OF THE BLIZZARD AND FLOOD OF 1966

U.S. Air Force Photo

Red River Rampage. Courtesy of Grand Forks Herald

Adams, Lankin, Fairdale, Fordville, Park River, Edinburg, Hoople, Minto, Grafton, Nash and Auburn.

Adams is seventeen miles east of Edmore.

It had 360 residents in 1960.

On June 23, 1890, a farm post office was set up in the Adams vicinity. Serving as its first postmaster was Erick T. Grove. At the suggestion of his wife, Christina, the post office was named for the area from which they had come from, Adams County, Wisconsin.

With the building of a rail line through the Adams by the Soo Line in 1905, a townsite was established three miles southeast of the Adams post office. That postal facility transferred its operations to the new townsite.

Adams had a native son who appeared for years with the Lawrence Welk Orchestra on national television. That person was guitarist Neil Levang.

An Adams family found out their newborn was not going to let a storm delay his entry into this world. The blizzard kept Mr. and Mrs. Norvell Richter from making it to a hospital. An R. N. at Deaconess Hospital in Grafton, Mrs. Del Owen, who was helped by her daughter, Connie, delivered the child, a boy, on Friday night, March 4. The delivery was done under the supervision of Dr. M. W. Scheflo, a Grafton physician, whose instructions were relayed to the attendants by Mrs. Sally Ganidagian.

It was probably fortunate the baby arrived when he did. Because for a considerable part of Saturday, all phone connections to Adams were inoperable. On Sunday, Mrs. Norvell and her son (Brettan Lawrence) were admitted to a Grafton hospital. Later, they were reported to be doing well.

The blizzard hammered Adams, but no one from the vicinity was reported being caught stranded out in it. Adams had no water for a few hours during the storm. The pump in the pumphouse froze after drifting snow extinguished the fire in the stove there.

In March 1966, Ole Dahl lived west of Adams. During the storm at his place of residence, he became fearful that his roof would collapse from the weight of the snow. So, while the storm raged, Mt. Dahl climbed up on top of his house to shovel snow off it. The snow was so packed around his door, he had to remove the storm door to get out. When all was said and done, Mr. Dahl ended up shoveling snow four feet deep from his roof.

A snowdrift, about 15 feet high, in front of Mr. Dahl's house covered his two snowmobiles and car. The depth of the snow in Mr. Dahl's yard was great enough to take out the telephone line to his house and power lines to his outbuildings.

In March 1966, Gene Olson had just been discharged from the army. He had been stationed at Fort Knox, Kentucky. On his way home by bus, Gene was delayed for three days in Chicago by the storm. After the bus reached Minneapolis, Mr.Olson was delayed for another five days. These delays were due to blocked roads north and west of Minneapolis.

Eventually, Mr. Olson made it to his parents home on the west side of Adams. To enter and exit their house, one had to climb over a large pile of snow in front of their house. After two days Mr. Olson procured a D-8 dozer and pushed the snow into a vacant lot across the street.[265]

Adams's high school boys basketball met Langdon in the Region 3 championship game being held at Grafton on March 11.

In 1966, Bylin Dam, located a few miles southeast of Adams on the North branch of the Forest River, was completed.

Lankin (303 residents in 1960) lies about ten miles southwest of Park River.

The arrival of the Soo Line in this area in 1905 brought a new settlement here. The new townsite was to be called Lankin in honor of the new postmaster, John Lankin, who took up his position on July 27, 1905.

In March 1966, Frank (Pete) Matejcek and his wife lived on a farm a mile west and a mile south of Lankin.

At the time of the March 1966 blizzard, Mr. Matejcek had four horses on his farm. These along with some chickens, eight or ten milk cows and some beef cattle took refuge in the barn during the '66 blizzard.

Located in a lean-to attached to the barn, the beef cattle were trapped inside by a large snowdrift. Shovels had to be used to dig them out. The Matejceks were able to make it to the barn and feed the animals during the storm. A Walsh County rotary snowplow helped

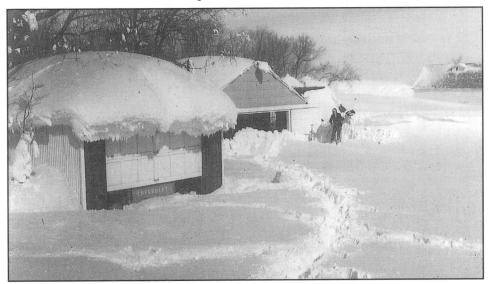

Frank Matejcek farm near Lankin, March 1966. Courtesy of Frank Matejcek

Blowing snow at the Matejcek farm near Lankin, March 1966. Courtesy of Frank Matejcek

to open the road into their yard after the storm. Ben Lala, who worked for Mr. Matejcek, used a rotary snowblower mounted on the front end of an International "M" tractor to clear out the Matejcek yard after the storm.[266]

At Lankin, Dennis Beneda used a tractor equipped with a snowblower mounted on its front end for moving snow. The majority of farm tractors, however, involved with snow removal were ones with front-end loaders.

Fairdale, located in northwestern Walsh County, had a population of 126 in 1960.

In 1905, as the Soo Line was pushing its tracks through this area, they established a station here.

Local residents came up with the name of the new settlement. Its name refers to its nice location in the valley of the Park River.

In March 1966, twelve-year old Allen Skavhaug lived on a farm three and a half miles west of Fairdale. The Skavhaugs had dairy cattle on their farm. The blizzard lasted three days at Fairdale. The milk cows in the barn were restless during the storm and would not milk. So, Allen's father just fed them.

Because of the inclement weather, it was difficult to get from the house to the barn. The Skavhaugs attached a rope to Allen's father, with one end secured at the house. They also put bells on the rope. When Allen's father was done feeding cattle, he would tug on the rope. This made the bells jingle, and let the rest of the family know that Mr. Skavhaug was ready to come in from the barn. The rest of them pulled on the rope until Allen's father made it to the house.

At the Skavhaug farm, the storm covered everything–tractors, cars, trucks, and buildings. Allen said, *"Only the upper part of their two and a half story house wasn't covered."* The Skavhaugs dug tunnels to get around.[267]

Fordville (with 367 residents in 1960) is located in southern Walsh County four miles east of N.D. Highway 32.

Fordville was one of the townsites established in 1905 by the Soo Line as it pushed its line west from Thief River Falls, Minnesota. The name "Fordville", which combined Med-FORD and BelleVILLE, was adopted in 1910.

In 1912, the Soo constructed 132 miles of the so called Fordville-Drake line. Fordville served as the terminal for this line. The resulting grain traffic made for a busy railroad station in Fordville.

On February 24, 1966, the Fordville Flyers basketball season ended with a 70 to 51 loss to Hoople in District 9 tournament play at Grafton. Leading the Flyers in scoring were Lon Enerson and Bob O'Neil with 10 points each.

The March 1966 blizzard arrived at Fordville Wednesday night and lasted until Saturday morning. Wind gusts there climbed to 70 mph.

On Thursday, Fordville's sparse traffic consisted mainly of vehicles moving about town. Very few out-of-town vehicles came to Fordville that day. On Friday, the conditions were so bad, there was no motor vehicle traffic.

Not many Fordville residents ventured outside during the storm. There was no point of going uptown as all of Fordville's businesses were closed for the duration. To compensate for a depletion of their food supplies, some housewives resorted to baking.

The blizzard brought mail and train service to Fordville to a halt.

When it was all over on Saturday March 5, 1966, Fordville had been the recipient of 2 feet of snow. The high winds had whipped the white stuff into huge drifts. Many cars in

Fordville were completely submerged under snowbanks. In some instances, their heights reached above the tops of houses. Where the entrances to homes (including windows) were blocked by snow, people were forced to make their exits via windows. Or, they had to wait inside until their neighbors cleared a path to their doorways.

Entombed in the deep snow was the Walsh County Bank in Fordville. The bank was managed by Harris Trosen. The entrance to it was blocked by a door-high snowdrift. It took quite a bit of shoveling to cut a passageway through the snowbank to gain entry to the front door of the bank. More shoveling was required to remove another large snowdrift, almost 10 feet high, from the roof of the bank.

Two farmers from the Inkster vicinity, George and Henry Amundson, lost seventeen head of cattle and a number of sheep when the roof of their barn collapsed under the staggering weight of all that snow.

The process of clearing roads in the Fordville vicinity began Saturday afternoon.

In March 1966, Rose Potulny lived with her family on the east side of Fordville. In 1993, she published a book of reminisces of her life. The following is an excerpt from that book:

A Three Day Storm

In 1966 we had a three-day snowstorm. Cars standing out on the street were buried under the snow. Men used probes to find their cars. We have a picture of Jerry Gulbranson digging out his car. The school kids got to help, but that was better than going to school. We couldn't get out of the house so we let Jay out through a window and he shoveled the snow from the door. Snowbanks were as high as the roof of the house. Vic and I rode the snowcat right over the top of the fences.[268]

Sixteen miles west of Grafton, along a beach of ancient Lake Agassiz, is the city of Park River (1,813 residents in 1960).

In the spring of 1884, the townsite of Park River was platted. The arrival of GN's branch line later that year led to the abandonment of a settlement known as Garfield, five miles northwest of Park River. The new village took its name from the river that flowed by it.

The residents of Park River banded together to make it through the **"white hurricane."** That's how the *Walsh County Press* described the blizzard of March 1966. The *Walsh County Press* also said:

However, in spite of the havoc and hardships created by the storm, the three-day blast produced some heroic deeds and a host of neighborly acts which forged the surrounding communities into igloos of good will.

Police forces, city employees, county road crews, farmers, businessmen, housewives, children-all pitched in at a hundred different tasks to make the ordeal more bearable.

The Park River police department cooperated 105 percent with the city and county snowplow crews in bringing emergency cases to the hospital.[269]

This cooperation was dramatically illustrated by what happened to Vernon (Shorty) Phelps. He resided at a farm about two and a half miles east of Park River. During the height of the blizzard, Mr. Phelps suffered a heart attack at home early Friday. Although Dr. Piltingsrud was contacted in Park River, terrible road weather conditions prevented the transportation of Mr. Phelps to Park River by car.

To remedy the situation Ray Ellingson of Park River used his snowmobile to deliver the needed pills to Mr. Phelps at his farm home around 3:45 a.m.

Next, Lars Berg and Gilman Seboe, using the Park River city snowplow, plowed their way out to the Phelps residence. At the same time, they towed the Park River city police car with a chain. Police Officer Thomas Bouldin drove the vehicle behind the snowplow. After putting Mr. Phelps in the back seat of the police car, they returned to Park River to St. Ansgar using the same routine, i. e., the snowplow towing the police car.

On March 9, the *Walsh County Press* telephoned St. Ansgar Hospital to ascertain Mr. Phelps' condition. The hospital informed the newspaper that Mr. Phelps was getting along nicely.

In March 1966, Don Flaten, age 9, lived with his family in Park River. Don had to stay indoors because of the inclement weather of the storm. The storm left a drift in Don's backyard at least seven feet high. Don and his friends dug a tunnel into the drift which was long enough to hold twenty people.[270]

In March 1966, Diane Dobmeier lived with her family on a farm west of Park River. At the time of the storm, her mother worked in Park River. The blizzard left her mother and brother stranded in town.

The windows on the second story of their farmhouse were long narrow ones. Diane remembers a huge snowbank by the house. The height of it touched the glass panes on those long narrow windows.[271]

In March 1966, Orville Simon, a North Dakota Game and Fish warden, was stationed at Park River. He remarked, "the high winds that accompanied the blizzard came from the North Pole." For proof, During the storm, Simon said, "he glanced out his window of his home and lo and behold there was Santa Claus in his front yard." Evidently, a plastic Santa Claus had come loose from its mooring at some other place in Park River and with the aid of the wind ended up in Simon's yard.

Edinburg (330 residents in 1960)is located about eight miles northwest of Park River.

Originally located three miles northwest of its present location, Edinburg moved to its present site in 1887. At that time, GN was extending its branch line northwest from Park River. The settlement was named after Edinburgh, Scotland.

In March 1966, Cliff Hilde and his family lived in Edinburg. Cliff worked for Polar Telephone Company which was based in Park River. He rented a garage on his property to the company. This was to be expected, as he drove one of their vehicles. During the storm, Cliff left the garage door open, since he did not want to shovel in front of the build-ing. This policy succeeded, and the front of the building remained free of snowdrifts.

After the storm, Cliff needed to make service calls. So, he went out to the garage to get the company pickup. Even though the vehicle started, Cliff was unable to back it up. Wind driven snow from the storm had lodged tightly underneath the pickup. Cliff had to shovel the hard snow packed snow from under the vehicle. And that was not an easy task within the narrow confines of the garage.

One of the service calls Cliff made after the storm was to the Larson turkey farm west of Union. This small hamlet is located in extreme southeastern Cavalier County. The Lar-son turkey farm had several thousand young polts. Trudging through snow, way over his knees, Cliff Hilde found the problem to be a twisted telephone wire. Soon afterwards, the Larson had the use of their phones again.[272]

In March 1966, Wayne Meyer and his family resided in Edinburg. He was a bulk dealer for Standard Oil. During the storm, Wayne was unable to make any fuel deliveries.

Once the storm had passed, he had to have his delivery truck towed to the International shop in Edinburg. The engine of the truck had become packed with snow from the storm. They used hot water to flush the snow away.

After the storm, Wayne received a phone call from Louie Byers who lived on a farm about a mile southeast of Edinburg. Byers thought he was about to run out of fuel oil. Byers was of the opinion that Wayne Meyer could reach his farm place with his delivery truck.

Wayne Meyer reconnoitered the route to the Byers farmstead. He realized he could not make it because of deep snow blocking the road on a hill west of the Byers residence where the GN tracks crossed the township road.

To clear the road, Carl Peterson brought in his bulldozer. It took Peterson two days to open the road. After the road was made passable, Wayne Meyer was able to reach the Byers home. Once there, he discovered the Byers fuel tank to be still half full.[273]

Hoople lies in northern Walsh County and is seventeen miles south of Cavalier.

In 1960, 334 people lived in Hoople.

A GN townsite, Hoople was established in 1890. Its name honors Allan Hoople (1849-1923), the townsite owner. The GN extended its line from Grafton through Hoople and on to Cavalier that same year.

At the time of the March 1966 blizzard, Nancy Hurtt resided on a farm about a mile southwest of Hoople. She attended school in Hoople. Nancy remembers a huge drift blocking the front entrance to her family's home. Her brothers dug a tunnel through the drift, so people could enter and exit the house. The tunnel was high enough, so that Nancy could walk through it without having to bend over.[274]

In March 1966, Tony Goodoien and his family lived in a house on the Leonard Gryte farm situated along Pembina County Highway 12 northwest of Hoople. At the start of the blizzard Thursday morning, Tony drove his Chevy pickup to his job at the wash plant located on the north side of Hoople. Tony headed east along a road that straddled the Pembina-Walsh County line.

After crossing the North Branch of the Park River, Tony's pickup became stuck trying to climb a hill known locally as Folson Hill. Unable to extract his pickup, Tony walked the remaining distance (about a half mile) to the wash plant.

After getting off work around four o'clock that afternoon, Tony caught a ride with his brother John who also worked at the wash plant. They headed south from Hoople to Walsh County Highway 9 which ran west to Edinburg. From there, the Goodoien brothers headed west. They were able to reach the intersection of Walsh County Highways 9 and 12. Located just north of this intersection was a rural elementary school called Dundee School.

About a quarter mile north of the Dundee school along the east side of the road next to the Middle Branch of the Park River was where the mother of the Goodoien brothers lived. Tony stayed at her place until the storm let up.

Several days later after the storm had passed, Walsh County plows opened Highway 12 to the Pembina County line. John gave Tony a ride in his vehicle as far as the Pembina County line. Tony hiked through the deep snow along Pembina County Highway 12, a mile and a half to his house.

The snow in the Gryte farmyard was so deep that it did not allow Tony any room to maneuver his tractor while moving snow. He was continually backing the tractor up. Later that same day, Tony was able to retrieve his pickup near Hoople.[275]

In March 1966, Jerry Loftsgard resided with his family on a farm west of Hoople. He attended a nearby rural public school known as Dundee School. Jerry distinctly remembers an enormous drift between the yard pole and his family's house. The top of it almost touched the overhead power lines.

Jerry's father, Orvin Loftsgard, owned a snowmobile known as a "Fox" that came equipped with a wide track. During and after the blizzard, Mr. Loftsgard used the snowmobile to deliver food, fuel and medicine to those who needed it.[276]

Minto, (642 inhabitants in 1960) lies along the Forest River, eight miles southeast of Grafton. U.S. Highway 81 runs through the town.

The Canadians who settled the area named the village after a town in Wellington County, Ontario. The year, 1881, was a pivotal one for Minto. Comstock and White, townsite proprietors, purchased the land from James Wilson and platted the settlement. That fall, the St. Paul, Minneapolis, and Manitoba (later the Great Northern) built its line through Minto on its way from Grand Forks to Grafton.

The *Walsh County Record* called the March 1966 storm, the "worst storm in history." After the blizzard, Minto had snowdrifts, 15 feet high. In Jim Gense's neighborhood, the drifts were as high as the houses. Four stakes mark the location of a car buried in the snow next to Gense's home. Also buried in snowbanks in Gense's neighborhood, were electric lead-in lines to homes.

Despite the terrible conditions that stopped virtually all vehicular traffic in Minto, not all was lost. Snowmobiles ("snow-cats") came to the rescue. Among the errands they were used for was to transport people to their farms, so they could take care of their livestock. Snow-bound farms received much needed groceries via snowmobiles. They delivered Minto residents to their business places. Snowmobile drivers in this crisis included Jim Bergeth, Howard Brinkman, Leslie Campbell, J. D. Miller, Ray Silvicki, Louis Slominski and Leonard Wysocki.

During the storm, the Minto Cafe remained open.

Once the storm had let up, the digging out process in Minto began.

Major road construction was taking place close to and in Minto in 1966. At the time of the March 1966 blizzard, U.S. Highway 81 went straight south from Grafton for seven miles, before making a left hand turn to approach Minto from the west. In 1966, the section of U.S. Highway 81 from Grafton to Minto was regraded. The first six miles south from Grafton were as before, but at that point U.S. 81 was rerouted to approach Minto from the northwest.

At the same time, a new bridge was being constructed over the Forest River on the south end of Minto. The old structure had become a traffic hazard.

By late 1966, grading on the Grafton to Minto stretch of U.S. Highway 81 was finished. It was paved in 1967.

Grafton (5,885 residents in 1960) is the county seat of Walsh County.

Thomas E. Cooper was the first white person to settle at Grafton. The land had not yet been surveyed when Cooper arrived here in 1878, so he had only squatter's rights.

Meanwhile, Cooper went ahead and constructed a hotel. In June 1879, the hotel would become the location for Grafton's new post office. Cooper, Grafton's first postmaster, named the post office and surrounding township after his wife's previous home, Grafton County, New Hampshire.

On August 30, 1881, Grafton became the seat of Walsh County. And, in December, the GN rail line reached Grafton.

On March 2, 1966, a new sign was installed at the Grafton National Bank on Hill Avenue. This sign displayed both the time and temperature.

The slow northward movement of the storm allowed many storm warning to be issued Wednesday afternoon, and evening. The blizzard descended upon the Grafton area around midnight that night.

Despite the high winds and falling snow on March 3, vehicular traffic was possible in Grafton until that afternoon when conditions in Grafton had deteriorated considerably. By Friday, Grafton's streets were buried under large drifts which prevented vehicular traffic.

There was no school in Grafton or towns around it either Thursday or Friday. The decision to close schools was made early Thursday. This timely decision meant no school children were left stranded by the storm in the Grafton area.

The lousy weather kept the Walsh County Courthouse in Grafton from opening Thursday and Friday. On Thursday, the deteriorating weather forced many Grafton businesses to close early. On Friday, most businesses in Grafton were closed.

Around 2:00 a.m. Thursday, a fire broke out at two small cabins near the home of Leonard Elshaug. The Grafton Fire Department responded to the call, despite the storm. They made it to the Elshaug residence, but the firemen could not save the two small cabins on the property.

At first, members of the Fire Department feared that Jim Clark, who lived in one of the cabins, had died in the fire. Clark was located afterwards in a Grafton hotel. The blaze forced him to evacuate the cabin. Bob Barr, chief of the Grafton Fire Department, said the fire began in the cabin where Clark lived. An overheated stove was the cause of the fire. Barr estimated the damages at about $2,000. Fortunately, that was the only fire call the Grafton Fire Department received during the storm.

Chuck Johnson, Walsh County civil defense director, went to his office in the beginning of the storm. The latest weather information made it clear that this was not an ordinary blizzard that had swept into the area. Johnson answered many emergency calls. Some farm families ran out of fuel oil. During the storm, he coordinated the rescue of four people who lived in the Grafton vicinity.

To reach them, snowplows were employed to open roads to the homes of the sick people. A lady from Inkster was delivered to St. Ansgar Hospital in Park River as was a lady from Park River. A woman from Ardoch was transported to a hospital in Grand Forks.

Another medical emergency took place on the Abner Stark farm which was located three and a half miles northeast of Grafton. The Norman Hoaby family was living on the Stark farm. On Friday, the Hoaby's young daughter, Christine, had a temperature of 104 degrees. The situation demanded medical assistance. A call was placed to the Civil Defense headquarters in Grafton. Atrocious weather conditions on Friday prevented a snowplow from reaching the Hoabys.

Improving weather conditions on Saturday morning, allowed a snowplow to clear a lane to the Stark's farm. Sheriff Orville Olson and Deputy Sheriff Norbert Hanson followed the snowplow. By the time the police had arrived, the Hoaby girl was very sick. A little blood had crept out of both ears of the girl. In a little while, Christine Hoaby was admitted to the Grafton hospital. The doctors did what to could for the girl. The hospital could not handle this emergency, so the civil defense headquarters was contacted again. Plans for transportation to a Fargo hospital were made.

Late Sunday morning, Mr. Hoaby left the Grafton hospital with his daughter in the car. At the Grand Forks-Walsh county line Duane Bergan, a Grand Forks patrolman, provided an escort to Fargo's city limits. Then, the Fargo police led the way to the hospital. After an examination upon arrival, the Hoaby girl was scheduled for immediate emergency surgery. Christine Hoaby remained in critical condition for two days.

In the western part of Walsh County some farmers had a hard time reaching their their cattle. According to Chuck Johnson, the unavailability of equipment prevented the Civil Defense from helping the farmers. According to Chuck Johnson, while the Civil Defense wanted to help farmers with these difficulties, the unavailability of equipment prevented the Civil Defense from helping the farmers. He said that both the Civil Defense and the National Guard could provide little in the way of assistance in delivering feed to livestock.

Among the farmers with snow problems was Merle Daley, who had a farm six miles west of Adams. On the second night of the storm, Daley was at his barn. On the way to his house, 180 feet from the barn, he became temporarily lost in the blizzard. Daley wound up on top of his garage. The snow was so deep there that only the peak showed above the snow. Daley had two steel bins that were completely submerged in the snow. He had a tractor that was equipped with a snow scoop. Even though the scoop was raised in the air to a height of 14 feet, it was totally covered by a snowdrift.

On Saturday and Sunday, helicopter crews from the Grand Forks Air Base flew over the area. They looked for stranded motorists and farmers in distress. The Air Force planned to continue these flights for several more days.

A former Grafton resident, George DeSautel, had his Grafton relatives worried during the storm and after the storm. He left Minot Friday morning, but then was reported missing. Finally, on Sunday morning, relatives were informed that DeSautel was safe in a small town near Minot.

People inundated the Grafton Police Department with calls during the three-day storm. The majority of the calls were inquiries concerning road and street conditions and when snow removal operations would commence.

Rural homes in the Grafton area received their water from the water plant located in northeast Grafton. Because of the storm, some of these farmers could not get to Grafton to replenish their water supply. There were no rural water systems in 1966. Farmers either had wells on their farms or they hauled water to their farms. To assist them, on Sunday morning, Grafton street crews cleared a lane to the water plant.

On Saturday, noises emanating from the roof of the Lutheran Sunset Home in east Grafton mystified its residents. The mystery was cleared up when they learned the source of the noise. The storm left a snowbank that reached the roof of the building. Children climbed up on the roof of the building and then slid down the high bank.

Class A regional basketball tournament play had begun Wednesday evening at Grafton. In one game, Grand Forks Central defeated Larimore 91 to 42. In the other game, Carrington knocked off Grand Forks St. James 64 to 42.

That night, the basketball teams from Grand Forks and Larimore were able to return home.

Unfortunately, Carrington did not have such luck. As Carrington was a long ways from Grafton, its team, coaches, cheerleaders, and fans, about eighty people in all stayed at Grafton.

After spending the first night at a Grafton hotel, members of the Carrington basketball team took refuge in private homes. Members of Grafton's basketball team opened their homes to quite a few of the Carrington players. The majority of people attending the tournament from Carrington stayed at Grafton motels.

The storm put a major dent in the plans of Stan's Cafe which was located towards the north end of Grafton on the west side of Hill Avenue. The cafe was getting ready to serve 350 people at a banquet Friday night. This was to be followed by their serving another banquet the next evening. On top of all that, the personnel of Stan's Cafe had expected many basketball fans over the course of the tournament.

In March 1966, both Chuck and Mary Wilson attended Grafton public schools. Chuck's family ran an automotive store in Grafton. It remained opened for the duration of the storm. As could be expected, business was terrible. Chuck struggled through deep drifts each day to make it to the store. The blizzard left an eight foot deep drift at the end of the store. After the storm, Chuck leapt from the fifteen foot high peak of the store onto the drift. Chuck's wife Mary remembers the storm blocking N.D. Highway 17.[277]

In March 1966, eighteen-year-old Al Adamsen lived in Grafton. He worked for his father's construction company. Al's father had built the tower for KCND-TV, a Canadian owned television station, located at Pembina. The station which began operations in 1960 went off the air in 1974.

Al remembered the drifts from the '66 storm being so deep, that they were as high as buildings on Main Street (Hill Avenue). There weren't many snowmobiles in Grafton back then. One of their owners, Bill Rogers, used his snow machine to deliver food to various homes. Blocked streets prevented people from reaching grocery stores.[278]

In March 1966, Daryle MacDonald lived and worked in Grafton. She was employed at Polly's Bar. During the blizzard, her employer told her not to come to work. For two days, the storm prevented Daryle from getting to her job.

After the storm let up, Daryle was able to get to work. But she was forced to walk, as deep hard snowdrifts blocked the streets of Grafton.[279]

Mare Thompson lived on a farm outside of Grafton. One morning during the storm, she woke up and looked outside. Her swing set was gone. She could not see it in the yard. Mare's mother told her it was still there. A snowdrift completely covered the swing set. Until her mother reassured her, Mare thought someone took it.

Grafton residents awoke Saturday morning and noticed that it had stopped snowing. In its wake, the storm had left enormous drifts on Grafton's streets.

Despite the inclement weather, Grafton resident Eli Lura (who was in his eighties) was able to make his normal trip uptown. At the peak of the worst blizzard conditions on Friday afternoon, Lura trudged uptown from his residence on Cooper Avenue and Fifth Street. It was slow going though, and about an hour passed before he made downtown. Mr. Lura did not return home the same day but stayed overnight at the Grafton police station.

The next day, Lura did not let huge snowdrifts stop him. using a shovel as means of support, he was seen climbing over some of the larger snowbanks.

In March 1966, weather information about Grafton came from U. S. Weather Bureau instruments that were located on the west side of Grafton at the Grafton State School. Officials from there said "the severity of the storm prevented the weather instruments from being read." This meant that no official information about the storm was available. It was thought that Grafton had received 33 inches of snow or 2.08 inches of precipitation.

Even though Grafton did not have an official record of snow amounts from the storm or what the temperature was during the storm, those Grafton residents with cable television had a good idea as what the temperature and wind speed were. They watched Channel 9, a twenty-four hour weather channel on cable TV. Channel 9 showed that the temperature varied little during the storm. The wind speed and direction were another story, however. At the storm's height on Friday afternoon, on occasion wind gusts would make the needle on the wind velocity panel's jump to close to 70 mph. The needle displaying wind direction moved about constantly.

Four cars became stalled on N.D. Highway 44 over twelve miles southeast of Grafton. At that time (1966), Highway 44 was the main north-south route along the North Dakota side of the Red River. It ran from Pembina to a mile north of Manvel where it joined U. S. Highway 81. Its replacement, Interstate 29, was not completed until the early 1970's. The passengers from the stalled vehicles took refuge Friday at the Peter Kosmatka farm.

Even before the storm let up Saturday morning, snow removal operators in Grafton were being inundated with phone calls from people concerned about their vehicles buried in the snow. The callers wanted their vehicles dug out as quickly as possible. One snow removal operator, Bob Oihus, placed the number of phone calls he received before the storm let up at about seventy-five. He, of course, received quite a few more after the blizzard had departed.

The familiar story of snowmobiles coming to the rescue during the blizzard echoed in Grafton as elsewhere. To help out with emergencies dozens of them were pressed into service Thursday and Friday.

On Saturday morning, with so many vehicles buried in the snow, among the ways Grafton residents got about was the tractor. At that time, people were running low on both food and fuel oil supplies. The tractor was one way of getting fuel oil to where it was needed.

After the storm, some drivers in Grafton attached red cloth to their car's antenna. When they drove through deep cuts in snowdrifts, the red flags gave notice to others that a car was passing through the deep cut.

The '66 blizzard disrupted rail service to Grafton.

Nash (45 residents in 1960) lies six miles northwest of Grafton.

In 1890, GN was pushing a branch line northwest from Grafton. That year, they established a loading station here. The name of the settlement honored the Nash brothers, early residents of the area. Their mercantile career included a fruit store in Grafton. Farther south in Grand Forks the Nash brothers had a wholesale grocery business. This latter enterprise would eventually become the Nash-Finch Company.

In March 1966, Bernice Flanagan and her husband Jim lived in Nash. Jim was the manager of the local grain elevator. After the blizzard had subsided, a medical emergency arose in Nash. A resident there needed some medicine and quickly. There were only two snowmobiles in Nash at the time. Jim owned a Polaris. To obtain the needed medicine, Jim and the other snowmobile owner rode their snowmobiles down the GN tracks six miles southeast to Grafton. After picking up the medicine at a drug store there, they returned to Nash via the same route.[280]

GN Depot at Nash, March 1966. Buried underneath the snowbank was an outhouse.

Kingsbury and Fedje spud house at Nash, March. 1966 Both photos courtesy of M. O. Dahl

GN rail cars at Nash, March 1966.

Cut through snowdrift by the railroad at Nash, March 1966. Both photos courtesy of M. O. Dahl

The town of Auburn, located seven miles north of Grafton, had 35 residents in 1960.

It acquired its name in 1882. The first settlers honored the Walsh County Judge Williams McKenzie who had come from Auburn, Ontario.

The March 1966 blizzard affected the residents of Auburn in the same way as Grafton. Afterwards, one of the favorite stories told by the locals was what had happened to Lorne Larson. During the storm, Larson had stopped his snow sled outside a business. With the motor running, he entered the building. While Larson was inside, the sled took off suddenly. The sled kept going, going and going, until it hit some trees.

Rolla, Bisbee, Cando, Clyde, Langdon, Union, Milton, Osnabrock and Olga

The seat of Rolette County, Rolla (population of 1,398 in 1960) lies twenty-one miles northeast of Dunseith. Rolla is only a few miles east of the Turtle Mountain Indian Reservation.

This city was platted in September 1888 when GN was building a rail line through the area. It became the county seat in 1890.

As to how Rolla got its name, three versions have come down to us. One of them has Arthur Noyes, a GN lawyer, naming the town after his brother. Another one states that Rolla is a contraction of the county's name, Rolette. The third version has early settlers from Rolla, Missouri, naming the town after their former place of residence.

Thursday evening, the storm arrived in Rolla. Late Friday night, the storm was over in Rolla. The city received almost 10 inches of snow, .20 inches of precipitation. This was more than Belcourt, Bottineau or Dunseith received.

Two Rolla boys, out and about, had a nerve wracking experience when they could not locate their homes in town during the storm. They took refuge in a stranger's house.

On Friday, several businessmen in downtown Rolla were either unable to get home or had a difficult time doing so. A driver of a fuel truck tried to make it home during the storm. After getting within a couple of blocks of his house, the driver was forced to take refuge. He spent most of the day "visiting" a neighbor. Quite a few business establishments in Rolla never opened for business on Friday.

Surprisingly, with 10 inches of snow, the main highways in the area were not blocked.

The high winds piled the snow into large drifts in and around Rolla. Some of them reached to heights of seven or eight feet. They covered picture windows and were as high as the eaves on houses. The snow was so deep that some homes were just about completely covered by snowdrifts. The Don Rodland home west of Rolla was buried beneath the snow. The Arne Meyer and Harvey Timmerman farmhouses had very large drifts against them.

It would be Tuesday March 8, before mail service to Rolla was restored to normal.

As the seat of Towner County, Cando (1,566 residents in 1960) is located in the southern part of the county.

Dave Osborn, a star running back for the Minnesota Vikings (1965-1975) came from Cando. He played high school football at Cando and later at the University of North Dakota.

At a Commissioner's meeting on February 14, 1884, Cando was picked to be the seat of Towner County. Some people did not like that choice. To prove a point, at a later meeting, County Commissioner P. T. Parker came up with a name for the new county seat, "Can-do".

On March 3, 1966, the blizzard showed up in Cando. At first, it was just a "snirt" storm. In this case, the "snirt" was primarily dirt.

With zero visibility, everything ground to an almost complete halt. School in Cando was let out at noon Thursday, not to be held again until Monday March 7. By 3 p.m., a full-scale blizzard was underway.

All sorts of events were either canceled or postponed. Business establishments in Cando remained closed Friday or operated with skeleton crews.

By the time the blizzard left the Towner County area on Saturday, it had piled considerable drifts in many localities. It was the worst storm to hit Cando during the 1965-66 winter.

Under the guidance of their coach, Curt Johnson, the Cando Cubs defeated Leeds, 69 to 55, for the District 13 basketball title on March 8. Cando hosted the tournament. Cando received balanced scoring in the game from John Parker, Tim Learned, Dan Lipp, and Vernon Humble. They scored respectively 19, 18, 13, and 10 points.

Cando advanced to Region 4 play in Devils Lake. On March 12 the Cubs played in the championship game. They were beaten 96 to 79 by the No. 1 ranked team in the state, the Fessenden Orioles. Cando finished the season with an 18-5 record.

Bisbee, which lies a little over twenty miles northwest of Cando, received 3.31 inches of precipitation from the storm.

The cleanup in Towner County began in earnest after the storm's departure. The North Dakota National Guard unit stationed in Cando was mobilized Saturday morning. Equipment operators put in long hours opening streets, roads and farmsteads.

Farms in Towner County needed help in snow removal. According to Robert Curl, head of the Towner County Civil Defense, everything possible was being done to assist everyone with what available equipment they had.

About twenty-five miles west of Langdon is the village of Clyde (100 residents in 1960).

Clyde began as a GN townsite in 1905. There were a lot of Scottish settlers residing in the area at the time. To please them, J. Peter Larsen, the settlement's first postmaster, named the place after the River Clyde in Scotland.

The March 1966 blizzard brought events at Clyde to a standstill. The Ken Bittner home served as a three-day refuge for a Fairway truck driver from Fargo.

Another refuge in Clyde was the Great Northern depot. With hardly any water to drink and only a few candy bars to eat, three men waited out the storm there all day Friday.

People in the Clyde vicinity were stranded for quite a few days. Well into the following week, local farmers were unable to leave their farm yards.

The local township board called on the Bill Sparks Construction Company of Calvin to come to Clyde to clear their streets.

Langdon had 2,151 residents in 1960.

The city became the seat of Cavalier County on July 6, 1884. GN's branch line reached Park River in 1884. Not long afterwards, they began surveying a line northwest from Park River. The rail line from Park River to Langdon was completed October 24, 1887. Langdon was named for R. B. Langdon of Minneapolis, the contractor and surveyor who built this GN line.

Cavalier County received the full impact of the '66 blizzard. The storm's arrival on Thursday, brought winds that gusted close to 80 mph. Langdon recorded a snowfall of 20 inches. At the height of the storm on Friday, activity in the county was at a virtual standstill. Having 12 inches of snow on the ground, before the storm did not help matters.

Cavalier County had its share of stranded travelers during the storm. According to Vic Kertz, owner of the Nodak Hotel in Langdon, his establishment was full. Among the guests at the hotel were three people who had originally checked into the Terry Motel. Although this motel was located just three blocks from uptown Langdon, atrocious weather prevented the three customers from returning there. A GN freight crew also stayed at the hotel.

One guest stranded at the Nodak Hotel had a reason to remember his stay. His last name was the same as the place where he was stranded. L. D. (Lou) Langdon worked for Bayer Brokerage of Sioux Falls, South Dakota.

The Paul Ratzlaff farm home near Wales, North Dakota (northwest of Langdon) took in quite a few stranded travelers. Among them was the Bartlett family of six from Tioga who were on their way to a funeral. Another "guest" was W. G. Ackling of Breckenridge, Minnesota. He hauled grain for a living. After riding out the storm in his rig, Ackling joined sixteen other people as the Ratzlaffs' dinner guests Saturday night.

The E. C. Christie home in Langdon became the destination for five Canadians from the Pembina Hutterite colony near Darlingford, Manitoba. The Canadians (Mr. and Mrs. John Meindel, Sr. and their daughter Mary and Mr. and Mrs. John Meindel, Jr.) lost their bearing in the storm. But, they had visited the Christies before and set out to find their home. They were successful and stayed at the Christie home from Thursday until Sunday.

There were four travelers "holed up" at the Ray Chaput farm. Included in this group was Mrs. Hugh Scott who had been to Grafton and was trying to get back to Langdon. Inspite of having the extra company, the Chaputs did not lack for bread. One of their "guests" was Corey Haats of Grafton who was driving a Holsum bread truck at the time. Mrs. Chaput told the Cavalier County Republican they were running out of cigarettes at the Chaput home.

The inclement weather forced the closing of Langdon's two high schools Thursday and Friday. School activities including basketball games had to be rescheduled.

Cavalier County suffered no fatalities from the storm. This was due mainly to the temperatures. It never got below 3 above in Langdon during the storm.

Cavalier County suffered little in the way of livestock losses. Many roads in rural areas were impassable. Concerned individuals called the Cavalier County Civil Defense for assistance. According to its director, Dr. Harold Blanchard, people wanted roads, cleared so feed could be hauled to cattle and fuel tanks be filled. City and county crews handled the snow removal tasks without incident.

A power outage at the Stewart McDonald farm near Langdon was the only one encountered by Cavalier Rural Electric. A forty minute outage of power Friday afternoon was the only loss of power experienced by Otter Tail Power Company.

Residents of Langdon had telephone during the blizzard. There was one exception. Friday afternoon, when the Ottertail Power experienced its outage, around 500 people telephoned the power company at the same time. The calls overwhelmed the United Telephone's system and blew fuses at their Langdon office. This resulted in an hour and a half break of telephone service.

It was a different story out in the country. Telephone service to about forty farms was restored Saturday and Sunday. According to Frank Solberg, manager of United Telephone, *"In order to maintain services at such times, it will be necessary to place the cables underground."* Buried telephone cables from Wales, Langdon, Osnabrock, and Milton to Grafton enabled those towns to maintain telephone service. Microwave from Grafton and beyond provided storm-proof service. Solberg noted that high snowdrifts between telephone poles and homes could break the connecting telephone line.[281]

Solberg noted that during a considerable period of the storm callers could not get dial tones. This was due to overloading of central office equipment. All of United Telephones exchanges suffered this experience. Their exchanges were not set up to handle all the calls. He estimated 12,000 to 14,000 calls were attempted per day during the storm

When the power failure was on, United Telephone's offices in Langdon, Munich, Wales, Osnabrock and Milton operated on emergency power, but the overload of calls prevented many people from getting through to complete their calls.

Although Cavalier County did not suffer much wind damage from the storm, high winds did tear down the awning at the Memorial Courthouse and the big neon sign at Langdon Motors.

The conclusion of the storm brought Langdon's snowfall total for the 1965-66 winter to 50 inches, 8 inches more than normal. Having so much drifted snow around created problems. It buried houses and trailers. At the Harvey Sand trailer court located east of Langdon, the John Flaten family had to move out of their trailer. Snow covering their trailer prevented its heating system from working properly.

On Saturday morning, Dick Berancek, managing editor and photographer for the *Republican* borrowed a snowmobile from John Ramage. Driving around Langdon he took pictures showing the effects of the storm. The pictures he took along with those by Ken Kleven of Kleven Studios showed up in the next week's *Republican* paper.

Vehicular travel in and out of Langdon was at a standstill Saturday morning. Frank Solberg got downtown on skiis. Langdon's postmaster, John Delebo, put on a pair of snowshoes and walked downtown to the post office. Lawrence Thielbar drove downtown on a snowmobile. Dr. N. J. Kalueniak of Langdon to make some house calls on foot.

The digging out process in Cavalier County began in earnest on Saturday.

In March 1966, Dean Stone lived with his family in Langdon. Snow drifted quite high on their house. So high in fact, that for them to exit their home, required the assistance of neighbors who shoveled an exit for them.[282]

On March 19, the Langdon Cardinals closed out their basketball season with a 69 to 64 win over Parshall for third place honors in the state Class B tournament at Minot. The leading scorer in the game for Langdon was Kent Krom who had 17 points. The Cardinals who were coached by Ken Towers finished the season with a 24-4 record.

Ken Towers enjoyed success in basketball both as player and a coach. As a high school basketball player, he led Nekoma to the 1957 North Dakota Class C title. After departing Langdon, Mr. Towers guided Grand Forks Red River to three consecutive appearances at state. His Roughriders teams finished second twice (1968 and 1970) and won the state Class A championship in 1969. Outstanding players from those teams were Craig Skarperud (1968) and Reed Monson (1968-1970).

In March 1966, the Storebo Brothers of Langdon were offering that year's model of Polaris snowmobile for prices as low as $550.00 (a 10 horsepower Polaris Colt).

Langdon Businesses, March 1966. Both photos courtesy of James Zettel

Langdon Businesses, March 1966. Both photos courtesy of James Zettel

Hartz Grocery Store in Langdon. Courtesy of James Zettel

House east of Langdon on Highway 5. Courtesy of James Zettel

Children of James and Laurette Zettel and friends. Both photos courtesy of James Zettel

Buried trailer on Highway 5 east of Langdon, March 1966. Courtesy of James Zettel

Union, a tiny hamlet in southeastern Cavalier County, enjoyed a population of 25 in 1960.

It was founded in 1881.

There are two versions as to how Union got its name. One of them has Henry Felix, a Civil War veteran, coming up with the name. He suggested the name "Union" to honor the fact that the United States or "Union" was still together. The other version has the Union postmaster submitting a list of names to the Postal Department and that organization chose "Union."

GN's rail line from Park River was extended through Union in 1887.

In March 1966, A.J. Johnson and his family resided on a farm southwest of Union. They raised both beef and dairy cattle. The cattle were in the barn at the time of the '66 storm. Snowdrifts piled high enough around the barn to worry the Johnsons. They feared the animals might suffocate. To give the cattle ventilation, A.J. and his father opened an upstairs window, and the hay mow door. This door was used to bring hay into the barn.

The Johnsons sold the cream, but not the milk from their dairy cattle. Storm conditions prevented the Johnsons from getting the milk to market, so they fed it to the animals.

The blizzard left a 17 foot high snowbank at the pole that held their yard light. It was high enough to touch the light and short circuit it. Somebody climbed the snowbank and replaced the yard light.

The road into the Johnson yard was opened by Walsh County dozers.[283]

Located in southeastern Cavalier County, Milton had a population of 264 in 1960.

Milton was settled at its present location in 1887, as GN was pushing its rail line from Park River to Langdon. As for its name, there are a couple of versions. The more acceptable one has Milton taking its name from Milton, Ontario. Early Milton area settler,

Steven Sophar, hailed from there. The other versions has Milton being named for John Milton (1608-1674), a famous British writer.

In March 1966, Norma Hallgrimson and her family resided on a farm southeast of Milton. During the storm, the Hallgrimsons were able to get out to their barn to feed and milk their cattle. The water trough the cattle drank out of was buried in snow. To water the cattle, Norma, Howard, her husband, and their son Larry carried water from a nearby well in five gallon pails. They had to pump the water from the well by hand utilizing the hand pump.

The heavy weight of the snow collapsed the roof of a lean-to attached to the barn. Inside it were twelve young stock. None were injured in the roof collapse. The Hallgrimsons were able to move the cattle into the barn.

Once the storm had passed, the Hallgrimsons had their road opened by Richard Otto of Osnabrock. He used a homemade combination blade and rotary plow mounted on a tractor to open their yard and the road leading into it. The storm deposited large drifts on Highway 66 in the Milton-Osnabrock vicinity. Richard Otto also used his homemade plow to open the streets of Milton. Where other plows couldn't get through, his could.[284]

Raymond Hallgrimson attended school in Milton in March 1966. He remembers shoveling snow off the roof of the community center in Milton after the storm.

To reach their barn northeast of their home, the Hallgrimsons tied a rope from a gate about fifty feet northeast of their house and extended it approximately another 200 feet to their barn. The south facing entryway to that place was blocked by a large drift. To gain entry to the barn the Hallgrimsons were forced to climb the drift to a second floor hay loft. From there a person would descend a ladder to the first floor.

Raymond Hallgrimson remembers that while feeding hay to the cattle the barn creaked from the effects of the high winds of the storm. After feeding the livestock, Raymond fell asleep in the hay. Upon awakening, he discovered that he was surrounded by fourteen cats that had also been sleeping.[285]

At the District 11 tournament being held at Edmore, on March 9, St. Alphonsius of Langdon defeated Milton, 87 to 42. While Duane Gellner poured in 38 points for St. Alphonsius, Handt Hanson led Milton with 12 points.

Osnabrock (289 residents in 1960) lies about six miles northwest of Milton in Alma Township. Osnabrock was established in 1882. It took its name from Osnabrock, Ontario.

It was tough going for two Osnabrock families during the early stages of the March 1966 blizzard. The Charles Lundeby and the William Regner families resided on the northwest edge of Osnabrock. On Thursday night, March 3 they endured a night without heat in their homes.

In addition to that, the Lundebys and the Regners, along with two of their neighbors, the Carl Monsons and Lloyd Wakefords, all were without any lights that night.

The next morning, Joe Giles and Clarence Heck employed shovels to make their way to the Lundeby home. Next, they shoveled a path between the Lundeby and Monson homes. Once that was done, they moved the Lundeby family over to the Monson residence.

By forming a human chain six men, Gordon Heck, Harland Johnson, Dale Keena, John Smith, Gerald Tharaldson and Jim Wakeford made their way through the elements to the Regner home. From Mrs. Katherine Johnson's trailer house they extended an electrical cord over to the Regner home. This was done to allow the Regners to get their furnace working again.

Meanwhile, another drama was playing out by the cemetery south of town. A semi-transport truck had become stalled there. On Saturday morning, after three days' confinement, its driver who hailed from Bemidji trudged into Osnabrock. Other than being weak from being without food, the man was OK.

On March 9, third place honors in the District 11 tournament at Edmore went to the host team. In that game, Edmore beat Osnabrock 64 to 45. Ron Hammer was Edmore's top scorer with 20 points. Barry Lovgren led Osnabrock in scoring with 19 points

Olga is located about fifteen miles northeast of Langdon.

It was founded in 1882. The first school teacher in the Olga vicinity, Ernestine Mager, gave the settlement its name. She was an admirer of Norway's Princess Olga.

In March 1966, Roger Gratton resided with his family in Olga. He attended school at Walhalla. Because of the storm, school was let out early. West of Hank's Corner along N.D. Highway 5, the school bus became stuck. Someone went down to Hank's Corner and called for help. The school children made it home in other vehicles.

After the storm had passed, Roger helped get the town of Olga moving again. First, he crawled out of a second story window and shoveled out the front door of his house. Then, Roger climbed up a snowbank and shoveled snow away from in front of neighbors' second story windows. Next, he removed the storm window, so they could exit from their houses. Roger also helped that family dig out their house. Then, he helped another neighbor dig out a shed where his cattle were kept. The shed was so entombed with snowdrifts, the cattle only had a small opening above them for air. By four o'clock Saturday afternoon, Roger was one tired fellow.[286]

The Tongue River crosses N. D. Highway 5 about fifteen miles east of Langdon. Through erosion, it has created a couple of ravines that Highway 5 must cross. Olga is four miles north of this location. Among the hills here is one known as the Olga Hill.

The March 1966 storm deposited a humongous drift in this locality, which measured up to 25 feet high in places, and was several hundred feet long.

N.D. Highway 5 near Olga, March 1966. Courtesy of Don Dalzell

Snow removal crews working on N.D. Highway 5 near Olga, March 1966 .

Rotary snowplow in action on N. D. Highway 5 near Olga, March 1966. Both photos courtesy of Don Dalzell

Snow removal crews clearing N.D. Highway 5 near Olga, March 1966. Courtesy of Don Dalzell

To punch a hole through this drift was going to take a Herculean effort. State highway crews received some assistance in the form of Don Davidson's large payloader and Walter Schefter's mammoth rotary plow. Even with that assistance, it took snow removal crews four days to punch a hole through the drift. They started early Saturday morning and made it through the drift mid-afternoon Tuesday.

Gardar, Mountain, Walhalla, Crystal, St. Thomas, Drayton, Hensel, Cavalier, Leroy and Pembina

Gardar, in southwestern Pembina County, had a population of 65 in 1960.

The Gardar vicinity was settled in 1879, primarily through the efforts of Eiriker H. Bergman. The name Gardar came from one of the early discoverers of Iceland, a Swedish Viking named Gardar. The poet Stephen G. Stephenson thought this might be an appropriate name for the new settlement.

The Northern Dakota Railway completed a rail line through Gardar in 1908. This line ran from 1908 until 1919. It was torn up in 1922.

In March 1966, John H. Johnson lived on a farm southwest of Gardar. He remembers that he had cattle both inside and outside his barn. The ones outside took refuge in a shed. During the storm, Mr. Johnson was able to feed his cattle small square bales he kept in the hay loft. He remembers that it was never cold during the storm. After the three day storm had let up, Mr. Johnson cleaned out his yard with an International "M" tractor equipped with a loader. He recalls seeing huge drifts in some places, while others spots remained bare.[287]

In March 1966, Orval Holliday and his family lived in Gardar. The fury of the storm there reduced visibility to zero. Mr. Holliday said "You couldn't see your hand in front of your face." The intensity of the blizzard prevented him from getting his wife to a doctor. Mrs. Holliday was suffering from mumps. Orval gave her aspirin which helped to alleviate her condition somewhat.

The ferocity of the storm made it impossible for Orval to feed his cattle on the Holliday farm northeast of Gardar. When he reached the farm after the storm, Orval found drifts there to be as much as fifteen feet deep.[288]

Mountain (218 residents in 1960) lies in western Pembina County on a beach of ancient glacial Lake Agassiz.

A group of Icelanders from Canada under the leadership of Rev. Pall Thorlakson founded Mountain in 1878.

On June 6, 1999, an F4 tornado grazed Mountain. Two months later the city celebrated one hundred years of a locally known event called "August the Deuce." Among the guest was the President of Iceland.

In 1949, Ripley's "Believe It or Not" listed Mountain as being only one of two villages in the United States with a cemetery on its main street.

In March 1966, twelve year old Alvin Bjornson lived with his parents at the south end of Mountain. Alvin's eighty-three year old aunt resided at the north end of town. She was in poor health. During the storm, Alvin and his twelve year collie "Sandy" struggled through deep snow to check up her.

The Bjornson's had a farmstead a mile southeast of Mountain. On the place was a barn without a roof. There were deep snowdrifts in and around the barn. Alvin would climb up the side of the barn to where the roof would have met the barn's walls. From that height he would jump down into the snow inside the barn's walls.[289]

At the time of the March 1966 storm, Duane and Lorraine Byron operated a bar towards the north end of Mountain. In 1970, they would build a new one at the same location. The storm left a huge drift that blocked the south entrance of the building. Duane was able to enter the building from a rear entrance. Even then, he had to cut steps into the drifts, so bar patrons could climb up the drift and then down steps to enter the bar.

At that time, the main street of Mountain had been plowed open. But later, in cleaning up, plows completely blocked the front entrance to Duane's Bar. He exited the bar from the rear and talked to the snow removal operators. Duane told them a fire trap had been created by their actions, as there were still people inside the bar. The operators quickly removed the snow they had piled in front of the bar.

Lorraine Byron remembered her father's car behind the bar being completely covered up with snow. Only a small portion of the top showed.[290]

In March 1966, Lori Cameron resided in Mountain with her parents, Duane and Lorraine Byron. Lori remembers the 1966 blizzard since it occurred on her birthday, and she was unable to have a birthday party. Lori remembers a snowdrift next to their home being as high as the house. Her uncle's De Soto automobile was buried so deep in the snow, that she had to dig down from above to find it. Lori helped him dig it out of the snow.[291]

Walhalla (1,432 residents in 1960) is located about six miles south of the Canadian border where the Pembina River emerges from the Pembina Hills.

The early history of Walhalla is intertwined with the fur trade. First known as St. Joseph, the name of the city was changed to Walhalla on July 21, 1871. That name came from an army officer who had visited the site. Admiring the place, he exclaimed to George Emmerling, a St. Joseph promoter, "This place should be called Walhalla, the home of the gods."[292]

GN's rail line from Cavalier finally arrived in Walhalla on August 26, 1897.

Under the sponsorship of the Walhalla Civic Club and its president, J. C. Soeby, a successful snowmobile event was at Walhalla on Sunday February 27, 1966. Over 2,000 people attended the event. During the day, around 100 machines took part in races and tours. The snowmobilers came from as far away as Winnipeg, Crookston and Greenbush. A temperature of 42 above did not help the snowmobilers.

The growth in popularity of snowmobiling had grown exponentially in just a few years. Only two years earlier, the world's first snowmobile derby was held near Eagle River, Wisconsin. The brainchild of local resident, John Alward, it took place near Dollar Lake on February 9, 1964. Cross country races, oval track races and hill climbs were staged. Between 2,000 and 3,000 people showed up for the event. They overwhelmed the small concessions stand there. In January 2003, the 40th edition of the Eagle River Derby was held.[293]

It began snowing in Walhalla Thursday, March 3. The onslaught of bad weather forced Walhalla to close school at 12:30 p.m. that day. Because of the deteriorating weather, not all the buses were able to complete their runs. In one instance, a bus with thirty-five children aboard returned to Walhalla. The students stayed with friends and relatives in Walhalla.

Once the storm descended on Walhalla, visibility was reduced to zero until Friday night. At its peak, storm winds were estimated to range between 35 and 70 mph. Although there was some let up on Saturday, the countryside around Walhalla experienced heavy ground drifting until Sunday morning.

Walhalla did not suffer from extreme cold during the blizzard. The highs and lows for Walhalla on Thursday, March 3 and Friday, March 4 were respectively, 18 and 14, and 19 and 11.

Walhalla suffered one power failure during the storm. A break in a power line outside of town caused an electrical power outage in Walhalla around 4:30 p.m. Friday. It lasted only a half hour. Ernest Chaput, Otter Tail Power Co. serviceman for the Walhalla vicinity, restored power by utilizing a local standby plant.

Some truckers from the South who were in Walhalla to pick up potatoes were forced to hole up for the storm.

Rail service to Walhalla was also affected. A freight crew stayed in Walhalla not only for the duration of the storm but well into the following week. The GN needed time to clear snow, 5 to 6 feet deep in many places, off the line.

While people could get by without mail during the storm, going without food was another matter. This was where snowmobiles came in. Quite a few people who went uptown to get food returned home on the sleds ("snow machines" as the Walhalla Mountaineer called them). Walhalla's Chief of Police, Floyd Johnson, was in charge of the machines during the storm.

The storm forced the staff at the Pemblier Nursing Center to put in long hours. The ones who came to work Friday morning stayed there until Sunday night. In that stretch of time, they worked in shifts as long as sixteen hours.

In March 1966, Sam Huffman and his family lived on a farm northeast of Walhalla near the Canadian border. Sam had about forty cows. He lost about six head to the storm, as the animals froze to death.

During the blizzard, the Huffmans extended a rope that had knots tied in it from their house to the barn. This allowed them to travel back and forth from the house to the pole barn to feed the cattle during the storm.

To provide water for the cattle, Mr. Huffman burned hay in the snow so as to melt the snow. The three sided pole barn provided shelter for the cattle.

Mr. Huffman had another building where he stored square bales of hay. There were doors on opposite sides of the building. Depending on the wind direction, he would toss bales of hay to the cattle on the on the side opposite from where the wind came from.[294]

In March 1966, Larry Longtin and the rest of his family lived on a farm northwest of Walhalla. Their farm was located east of the North Branch of the Pembina River. The March '66 blizzard left huge drifts at the Longtin farm. They raised cattle and chickens. The livestock came through the storm in relatively good shape. The wooded terrain around the Longtin farm had ravines in it that provided good shelter for the cattle.

During the storm the Longtins were unable to get to their well for water. So, they melted snow instead.

The large drifts left by the storm isolated the Longtins for two weeks. The Longtin children were unable to get to school because of blocked roads. Finally, a Pembina County bulldozer opened a road to the Longtins.[295]

By the time the storm began letting up Saturday in Walhalla, the city had received about 15 inches of new snow. Walhalla was about out of bread and milk. The situation forced many people to make homemade bread. The blizzard had left Walhalla with snowdrifts 10 to 12 feet deep on Main Street. Of course, such large drifts stopped virtually all business for two days in Walhalla when the storm was on. There were reports of even deeper drifts on the edges of town and in nearby rural areas.

Looking east on Central Avenue in Walhalla, March 1966. Courtesy of Don Dalzell

Central Avenue in Walhalla, March 1966.

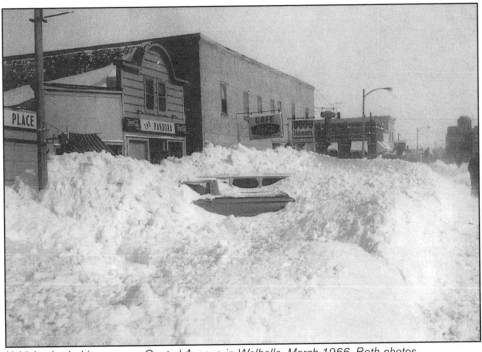

Vehicles buried in snow on Central Avenue in Walhalla, March 1966. Both photos courtesy of Don Dalzell

Looking north at Karel Sales near Walhalla's east side, March 1966. Courtesy of Don Dalzell

By Sunday, the digging out process was going on in earnest in Walhalla.

The Walhalla Eagles, under the tutelage of Coach Dennis Pfeifer, shared the District 10 title with Neche. Each team suffered only two losses in district play.

The blizzard interrupted the District 10 basketball tournament being held at Cavalier during the first week of March 1966. Only one game, was completed that week. On Wednesday, March 2 Neche defeated Hamilton.

Walhalla's season ended on March 11 in Region 3 tournament action at Grafton. On that date, Hannah beat them 63 to 61 in overtime. Duane Schurman paced Walhalla's attack with 16 points.

Crystal in southern Pembina County had a population of 372 in 1960.

In May 1879, members of the Greenway Expedition from Ontario arrived at Crystal. On May 28, 1880, a post office was established. A.F. Appleton, Crystal's first postmaster, named the town after the "crystal clear" water found in Cart Creek which flowed through the hamlet.

GN would build a rail line through Crystal in the fall of 1890.

In March 1966, Camburn Shephard lived on a farm northwest of Crystal. He attended school at Crystal. Camburn remembers the storm leaving a snowdrift at least 15 feet high that was up against a white granary of theirs. If a person wanted to, he could climb the snowdrift and touched the overhead power lines. As their house faced west, that side of the house was free of snow. But, it took a dozer owned and operated by nearby neighbors, the Olafson Brothers, to clear the Shephard yard of snow.[296]

In March 1966, Bill O'Sullivan resided with his family in Crystal. He remembers going to visit his grandparents during the storm. They lived a couple of blocks from Bill's home, around a bend of Cart Creek. Bill set out for their place in the inclement weather. Bill made his way around the bend in the river to his grandparents place by going from bush to bush. Wet snow stuck to his clothes. But he made it. After visiting with them for awhile,

Bill returned home. He also recalls the large drift in front of Johnny Salwei's grocery store on Appleton Avenue.[297]

In March 1966, Harold Johnston of Crystal attended the University of North Dakota in Grand Forks. Harold remembered it being a cold winter. In February 1966, he recalled the thermometer mounted on the wall of the depot in Crystal reading -40 degrees F.

Harold lived in West Hall, a dormitory on the UND campus. The storm kept students confined to their rooms.

Harold's roommate came from New Orleans, Louisiana. He had come to North Dakota to go to school, because he wanted to experience a North Dakota winter. The student would not be disappointed. Harold remembers him keeping a thermometer on the outside of their dorm room window, so as to allow him to check it to see what the outside temperature was.[298]

In March 1966, Danny Salwei lived with his family in a house towards the east side of Crystal. Danny was a student at Crystal High School. The storm deposited such large drifts around the Salwei house, their only means of exit from the house was through a door on the second floor. This led out onto a balcony. From there, the Salweis would climb over a railing and descend to the ground via a snowdrift

Salwei remembers a long drift that extended from Tommy's Bar on the south side of Appleton Avenue north across the street to the Louis Dietrich Garage. He said streets in Crystal were plowed open for only one lane. If a vehicle encountered another vehicle coming from the opposite direction, one of them would be forced to back up to let the other vehicle pass. He noted that the only way to get rid of some of the snow was to let it melt.[299]

In March 1966, Glenn Ralston resided with his family on a farm northwest of Crystal. Glenn remembers that after the storm his older brother Hugh and his sisters shoveling a path across their yard to a shed. His father, Gordon, wanted a 770 Oliver tractor that had been outside during the storm put inside. The road into the Ralston farm yard was opened by their neighbors, the Olafsons.

Snowdrifts in the Ralston yard were so deep they reached from the trees on the north side of the farm to cover corrals more than a hundred feet south of them. The Ralston children were able to slide down these drifts to Cart Creek which ran through their farm.

One time, Glenn's sister fell into a hole in the drifts. They extracted her after considerable difficulty.

After the storm, Gordon Ralston and his neighbor, Ray Becker went to Bergman Implement (an International Harvester dealer) in Hoople where Gordon purchased a snow bucket for his farmhand. It was larger than his other snow bucket.[300]

In March 1966, Lyle Shephard was a junior in high school at Crystal. He lived on a farm northwest of Crystal. As a sideline, Lyle raised fourteen head of sheep. He recalled digging them out of the snow, once the storm had passed.[301]

In the evening just before the March 1966 storm hit, Walter Ortlip (1913-1998) and his wife attended a church meeting. Afterwards, they returned to their home in Crystal. Being thirsty, Walter went out to the kitchen to get a drink of water. He then looked out the window. *"You couldn't see anything."* Walter remarked.

That same evening some Crystal students attended the basketball tournament in Cavalier. They rode in a school bus to get there. On their way back, the bus missed the turn to Crystal from N.D. Highway 18 onto N.D. 66, two miles east of Crystal. The bus proceeded onto Hoople where the students were forced to remain for the night.[302]

In March 1966, Georgia Maize (1920-2003) lived on a farm west of Crystal. Her house was heated their house with a combination of fuel oil and coal. Georgia remembered that she lost neither heat, power, or phone service during the storm. She knew N.D. Highway 66 was open Sunday morning when her neighbors, George and Mary Rathbun, showed up to see how they were getting along. The Rathbuns went to check on two other neighbors, the Mathesons and Russums.[303]

In March 1966, Alice Poehls lived with her family on the west side of Crystal. She attended Crystal Public School. Alice's home had large narrow windows on it. As the storm progressed, she remembers the snow building up towards the top of the windows until it completely covered them. The scene reminded Alice of Noah's ark. The blizzard left large drifts on Crystal's streets. Alice recalls Gerald Almond heading north for uptown on a snowmobile across the top of snowbanks from his home at the south end of town.[304]

The Crystal Bulldogs finished the 1965-66 basketball season on March 8, when they lost to Drayton 60 to 58. Eric Dietrich, with 24 points, was Crystal's top scorer.

St. Thomas lies thirteen miles north of Grafton.

This Pembina County city had a population of 660 residents in 1960.

A couple of hometown boys from St. Thomas are Edward K. Thompson and Thomas E. Whelan. A couple of Thompson's notable achievements were serving as editor of *"LIFE"* magazine and his establishment of the Smithsonian magazine. Under pressure from U. S. Senator William Langer, President Truman appointed Thomas Whelan to be ambassador to Nicaragua in 1951. He held that post until 1961.

It all started for St. Thomas when a couple of GN townsite proprietors from Moorhead, Minnesota, Comstock and White, platted the site in 1881. Pioneer settlers from St. Thomas, Ontario gave the new settlement the name of their home town.

In May 1882, GN's line being constructed north from Grafton made it to St. Thomas.

In March 1966, Roy Bigwood and his family were housebound for three days by the blizzard. His primary memory of that storm was all the snow.[305]

During a lull in the March 1966 blizzard, Duane Larson made his way uptown in St. Thomas to a bar. Upon entering, he found the place to be filled with people.[306]

Nestled in the southeastern corner of Pembina County, Drayton had 940 residents in 1960.

Drayton began as a stopping point for steamboats plying the Red River. The place was known as Hastings Landing, after Captain Hastings, a steamboat operator. When Canadian settlers from Ontario arrived in April 1878, they gave it a different name. They called the place and the surrounding township Drayton, after their home town of Drayton, Ontario.

After the decline of steamboats and the coming of railroads, the next major transportation change to come to Drayton would be roads and bridges. A bridge that would lift in the center served Drayton from 1911 until 1954. It was located in the middle of town.

The new bridge that spanned the Red River opened for traffic on November 22, 1954. It was built to withstand the height of a flood as devastating as the one in 1950. This one was located about a mile northeast of the old one.

In the late 1950's, construction of Interstate 29 north of Drayton had begun. By 1966, the highway was completed a few miles south of the Drayton.

Commencing in 1958 and continuing through 1963, the high school baseball team at Drayton enjoyed amazing success on the baseball field. They won six consecutive state high school baseball championships (still a record). During that span, their baseball team was 68-1. Only Hatton, with seven high school baseball championships, has more titles. They also competed against the likes of Bismarck, Fargo, and Grand Forks in Legion baseball. On that level, Drayton wracked up state championships in 1958 and 1962. That remarkable 1958 team also won a region title. In the Section C tournament they were ahead of four-time defending national champion Cincinnati 7-4 as late as the sixth inning, before succumbing 9-7. Last names that graced those teams included Brosseau, Halcrow, Knoff and Van Camp.

Things were looking up in Drayton as the fall of 1965 approached. Although the harvest had been delayed by almost a month of rain, American Crystal Sugar Company's recently completed sugar beet plant, located about a mile north of town on the east side of N.D. Highway 44, was open and ready for business. Before 1965, local growers had to take their beets to the East Grand Forks plant. This was usually done by rail.

On September 21, 1965, history was being made when the piling of beets at the new plant began.

Beets were being hauled into the plant both by truck and by rail. The train loading started September 20 at Cavalier, Neche, Pembina, Forest River and Voss the following day.

In February 1966, several notable events occurred in Drayton.

On February 17, the first sugar processing campaign at the American Crystal Sugar plant north of town came to a close after 139 days. Two days later, Arthur Fleckten, who was instrumental in establishing the Drayton beet plant passed away.

On Friday night, March 4 snowmobiles which were driven by Paul Stennes and Jerry Botlet were able to bring a pregnant woman, Mrs. Milton Saltviedt of Robbin, Minnesota, to St. Elizabeth's Hospital in Drayton. From there, Erlan Evanson and Tim Sullivan took snowmobiles to the home of Dr. W. A. Pinsonneault. Tim Sullivan remained at the Pinsonneault home to babysit as Mrs. Pinsonneault was stormbound in Grand Forks. Erlan Evanson brought Dr. Pinsonneault to the hospital, where he delivered Mrs. Saltviedt's baby daughter.

After walking to Drayton's water plant Friday morning, Tim Sullivan returned via snowmobile that evening. As the storm conditions prevented fuel trucks from making deliveries, there were several instances where snowmobiles were used to bring needed fuel to customers.

In March 1966, John Ebertowski was working at the Drayton sugar beet factory. To get to work, he car pooled with three other guys from the Warsaw area. I-29 had been only partially built at that time, so John and the others took N.D. Highway 44 to and from work. This highway ran from Pembina to one mile north of Manvel. At that point, it joined up with U.S. Highway 81.

The March 1966 blizzard forced John and the others on his shift to work twenty-four hours instead of eight. This was because workers from the other shifts being unable to make it to work. After working, John and the others drove into Drayton. They stayed at the home of Henry Lizakowski, a foreman at the sugar beet factory, until their next shift. By the time they had completed that shift, eight hour, the storm had let up enough to allow them to go home. The men had been either at the factory or in Drayton for over forty hours.[307]

In March 1966, Don Matter taught school in Drayton. During the early part of the storm, he and another man embarked on a mission of mercy by walking uptown. Don could see that large drifts were already forming. After completely the job, Don returned to his residence and remained there for the duration of the storm.[308]

In March 1966, Jim Pilon lived with his family on a farm southwest of Drayton. Jim attended school in nearby Oakwood. He remembers the huge drifts the blizzard left in their yard.

The Pilons had a couple of milk cows that provided them with some of their dairy needs. The Pilons didn't let the horrendous weather conditions of the storm prevent them from milking their cows. When it was time for milking, one way or another, someone made it to the barn and got the job done.

The Pilons came pretty close to running out of fuel oil for their furnace during the storm. When it was all over, their stock of fuel oil had dwindled to just five gallons.[309]

On March 5, on N.D. Highway 44 about twenty five miles south of Drayton, a state highway department crew stationed in Drayton came to the rescue of a family in a stalled car near the Soo Line tracks. The parents and their three children were almost completely out of gas and milk for their baby. The state department crew took the family to a neighboring farm.

After the letup of the storm, came the cleanup. Drayton had help from nearby American Crystal Sugar plant. Using company equipment, crews from the plant helped with snow removal on Drayton's streets Saturday night and Sunday.

A storm ordeal occurred north of Drayton on Interstate 29. Five Canadians from Winnipeg, Mrs. J.W. McKeague, Mr. and Mrs. John McMillan, and Mr. and Mrs. Jim Searle, headed for a skiing trip in Colorado were stranded for forty-two hours, two miles north of the Bowesmomt interchange. Stuck there since 5 p.m. Thursday, they were not located until Saturday morning. Although trapped by the storm, the five people inside were well prepared. Besides having warm clothing on hand, they ate a rationed menu of cheese-horseradish and crackers. Their coffee came from snow melted on a Fondue Burner. To stay warm, they started their car at four-hour intervals.

Despite the rationing, by 11 a.m. Saturday, they were very low on hopes of rescue and supplies. Mervin Holter, a local farmer, found them. To the stranded motorists, Mervin Holter was "a heaven sent messenger."

The Canadian motorists were taken to the A. D. Dunklee farm located near Bowesmont to stay until they could warm up and wait for the snowplows to clear the highways.

On March 9, the Drayton Bombers won the consolation game of District 10 in Cavalier by beating St. Thomas, 76 to 54.

At Langdon, N.D. in March 1966, the Doris Holler curling team lost at the state ladies curling tournament ending its two year reign as the North Dakota Ladies Curling Champion. But, Mrs. Holler won reelection as president of the North Dakota Women's Curling Association.

North of Crystal six miles is the village of Hensel. The 1960 census shows Hensel with a population of 160.

Hensel began as an Icelandic settlement in 1879. Townsite officials gave it the name of "Canton" in reference to it being a "canton" or small territorial division for some rural Tongue River headwaters settlements.

On November 1, 1887, a rural post office was set up three miles northwest of Canton. Serving as its first postmaster was Joseph Irwin. Since he came from Hensel, Ontario, Irwin applied the name of his hometown to the new post office. Two years later, the post office relocated to Canton. Today, Canton is still the legal name of Hensel. For the most part though, the latter name is used for the village.

In March 1966, Neal Heuchert lived with his parents and brother Donnie in Hensel. Their farm was three quarters of a mile south of town. The arrival of the storm in Hensel found Neal's father near death in a hospital bed. So, it was Neal and his brother Donnie's job to feed their cattle at their farm. As the blizzard raged about them, they would trudge through it to their farm to feed the livestock.

Once the storm had let up, Neal and Donnie began digging out with shovels. They had to free a horse named "Trixie" who was stuck in a snowdrift next to a shed.

At that time, the Pembina County Highway Department had a maintenance shed on the south side of Hensel. Herman Rickbeil used a dozer from that facility to dig out both Leonard Schwartz's (a neighbor of the Heucherts) and the Heuchert's farmyards.[310]

In March 1966, Herman Ratchenski, a resident of the Cavalier area, was out of state, serving in the U. S. military. He recalls Lawrence Anderson, who resided northwest of Hensel, sending him a blizzard photo. It showed Mr. Anderson's son standing atop a snowdrift. The snowbank was high enough to allow the boy to touch the top of a light pole in the Anderson yard.[311]

Cavalier is the seat of Pembina County.

In 1960, 1,423 people lived there.

Cavalier was founded on July 31, 1875, by settlers coming overland from Missouri in covered wagons. They detoured from their original destination of Manitoba upon learning that Mennonites had settled there ahead of them. That same year, a flour mill and store were opened on the present site of Cavalier by their leader, John Bechtel. The city would be named after Cavalier Township which in turn was named after Charles Cavileer. In August 1851, he became the first permanent white settler of Pembina County.

GN's rail line from Grafton reached Cavalier in the fall of 1890.

The March 1966 storm began slowly in Cavalier. Stiff winds Thursday morning blew the light now that fell. At 2 p.m. the snowfall was heavy and the winds became stronger. The blizzard did not let up until late on Friday.

The storm forced many Cavalier business establishments to remain closed on Friday. The ones that did stay open got by with skeleton crews. People who had to be out and about in Cavalier and other hardy souls took shelter in these places.

Cavalier's mayor had this to say about snowmobiles:

> During the storm we were very fortunate to have eight of our local fellows with snowmobiles to transport groceries, fuel, and also people to and from work. I noticed even some of the people that cursed these machines in the past were riding them Thursday and Friday.[312]

Jim Benjaminson was a student at Mayville State Teachers College in March 1966. Quarter break at the school was at hand, so Jim decided to go home. He received a ride from two girls from Crystal, Dorothy and Phyllis Beattie. Jim's parents came to their farm near Crystal and picked him up. He was at home when the storm arrived. Jim said "You could not see across the street."

When it came time to go back to Mayville, Jim's parents drove south from Cavalier and then headed east down Pembina County Highway 3. Upon finding it blocked with snowdrifts, the Benjaminsons turned around and returned to Cavalier. They took N.D. Highway 5 east to U.S. 81 and then headed south to Mayville.

At Mayville State Teachers College, Jim remembers the drifts being deep enough to enable students to write their names on the under side of lamp shades on light poles.[313]

In March 1966, Andy Nupdahl lived with his parents at their home, three and a half miles west of Cavalier. The blizzard left snow piled, so deep that the only way Andy's family could get of their house was by an upstairs window.[314]

In March 1966, Lorraine Martinson lived with her husband and three children one and a fourth miles northwest of Cavalier. The children were respectively, in the first, second and third grades in Cavalier.

The school bus took the children home early on March 2 because of the oncoming storm. The buses got back to Cavalier, just ahead of the storm. The storm piled snow up to the second story on their house. Lorraine and her family had to go up to the second floor of the house to see out because of all the snow.[315]

The storm deposited over 11 inches of snow, 1.43 inches of precipitation, on Cavalier.

The *Chronicle* summed up what the blizzard had done to Cavalier with this description:

> *Although less severe than in other sections of North Dakota, the March 3 and 4 storm here did a thorough job of disrupting business, education, athletics, transportation, and perhaps in isolated instances, the regularity of meals and bedtimes.*[316]

As with many other localities the "big" story of the March '66 storm in Pembina County were the enormous drifts of snow it left behind. People took many pictures both in town and out in the country. The *Chronicle* noted:

> *Eager photographers jostled each other to get angles showing the drifts. Members of parties perched on snow, level with or above rooftops, there to be pictured in surroundings described in any history of North Dakota.*[317]

The storm left huge drifts on Cavalier's Main Street. On Thursday, March 3, Mrs. Edward Werner, bookkeeper for the *Cavalier Chronicle*, parked her car across the street from the Chronicle office. It was buried completely by snowdrifts from the storm. To help snow removal crews find it, a tall stake was driven into the snow to show its location.

There were more automobiles covered entirely by snow further east along Main Street. Despite the conditions, snow removal crews were able to extricate them without damaging the cars. The north end of Cavalier had the highest drifts from the storm.

The height of snowdrifts at a place east of Hamilton reached to the top of the house. If there hadn't been an antenna present, a person wouldn't have known if anyone lived there.

At a farm southeast of Cavalier, a lady there compared the dips and whorls in snowdrifts there to those displayed for tourists in Arizona mountains.

Snow removal began in earnest in and around Cavalier before noon Saturday.

On March 12, Cavalier's high school boys basketball season ended with a 62 to 59 loss to Grand Forks Central in the consolation game at the state Class A tournament being held at the UND Fieldhouse in Grand Forks.

As the crow flies, Leroy is about eight miles east of Walhalla and south of the Pembina River.

A trading post was built here in the 1850's and called Leroy's Trading Post in honor of Julien Leroy, a well known French author and horologist.

In March 1966, Don Dalzell and his family lived on a farm west of Leroy. The storm piled large drifts in their yard. There was an enormous drift in front of their house. The

Dalzells did not lose electrical or telephone service during the storm. Using a John Deere tractor equipped with a loader, it took Mr. Dalzell until Sunday afternoon, March 6 to clean out his yard.[318]

Pembina (625 residents in 1960) is the oldest white settlement in North Dakota. It had the first church and school in the state. Located about a mile south of the Canadian border, Pembina sits at the junction of the Pembina and Red River. Its name is generally recognized as coming from a Chippewa word "anepemian" meaning summer berry. Today, we know it as high bush cranberry.

Permanent white settlement at Pembina dates to 1812. That year, William Douglas, the Earl of Selkirk brought displaced Scotch and Swiss colonist to Pembina. He did this through an arrangement with the Hudson Bay Company.

It wasn't until 1843 when Norman Kittson established a large well stocked fur trading store at Pembina that it began to flourish. After purchasing the furs, Kittson would ship them to St. Paul. In 1844, as postmaster, Kittson gave the town its name.

Don Dalzell farm west of Leroy after the blizzard. Courtesy of Don Dalzell

Don Dalzell farm, March 1966. Courtesy of Don Dalzell

In October 1960, a new television station went on the air in Pembina. Its call letters were KCND-TV Channel 12. It was an ABC affiliate. Channel 12 would stay on the air until 1974, when it moved to Winnipeg. The station's primary market was Winnipeg. Liquor and tobacco advertising was not allowed on Canadian television stations. To get around this, the station's owners built the station on the American side where such advertising was allowed.

There has been a bus plant in Pembina since the fall of 1963.

The snowstorm began Thursday afternoon at Pembina. It lasted until Saturday. It dumped 6 inches of snow on Pembina and left snowbanks, 8 feet high. Temperatures between 10 and 17 above helped to alleviate some of the hardship the blizzard caused in the Pembina area.

Pembina's schools were forced to close because of the storm, as did several Pembina business establishment.

The letup of the storm on Saturday led to what the local newspaper (*Pembina New Era*) called "snow shoveling day" in Pembina.

On March 8, Pembina suffered a 62 to 60 loss to St. Thomas in District 10 tournament action taking place at Cavalier. Lyle Parker led Pembina in scoring with 19 points.

Chapter III
The Minnesota Experience

Pipestone, Redwood Falls, Ortonville, Willmar and Morris

Pipestone, the seat of Pipestone County, is located in the southwestern corner of the state. It enjoyed a population of 5,324 in 1960. Pipestone was platted in October 1876.

Pipestone's name came from a red stone Indians quarried at a site about a mile north of the city. They used the stone to make bowls of their pipes, hence the name pipestone. George Catlin, a famous Indian painter, visited the quarry in 1836. The red stone, known today as catlinite, was named in his honor. Following in Catlin's footsteps were explorers Joseph Nicollet and John C. Fremont. In July 1838, Nicollet, Fremont and four other members of their party inscribed their names in the stone which is known today as Inscription Rock.

Indians have quarried the pipestone from the ground for hundreds of years. The layer of pipestone, about 18 inches thick, is found in a strata of red quartzite. The quarrying has been done north to south for a distance of almost a mile. To ensure that only Indians, in this case the Yankton Sioux, would be able to quarry the stone from the ground, a one mile square reservation was established on April 19, 1858. The quarrying for pipestone continues to this day.

Pipestone missed the brunt of the '66 storm. After reaching a high of 50 degrees on March 1, temperatures dipped slightly during the storm. Even on March 3 and 4, a high of 42 was recorded in Pipestone.

What snowfall Pipestone did receive was light. It fell on Friday and Saturday for a total of 2.6 inches. For the period of March 3-5, a total of .28 inches of precipitation was recorded. Ironically, the .32 inches of precipitation that Pipestone received for the month of March 1966 made it the driest spot in Minnesota for that month.

It wasn't until March 4 that temperatures began to fall in Pipestone. After reaching a low of 16 that day, the thermometer climbed only to 18 on March 5.

The *Pipestone County Star* called the '66 blizzard a **"Great Storm"** that came within a few miles of Pipestone on the evening of March 4. Blowing snow reduced visibility to zero for those who drove to the basketball game in Luverne, twenty-five miles to the south, that evening.

Pipestone's third annual Pork-A-Rama went on as scheduled at the Armory March 3 and 4, despite the weather. The storm did lessen attendance on March 4. Russ Stevens, Chairman of the Subcommittee of the Agriculture Committee for the Chamber of Commerce, considered the promotional event to be a success. Activities included a speaker on land management, a food auction and a demonstration on cooking.

Although Pipestone had missed the full effect of the storm, it suffered a setback soon after the blizzard had passed. A fire broke out during the cold weather after the storm. It was termed "one of the worst fires in Pipestone's history" by an older fireman.

A clock that stopped at 1:44 a.m. on March 7, at the S & L store in Pipestone gave firefighters a clue as to when the fire started. After observing smoke coming from Riteway Cleaners, Pipestone Policeman Chester Reimers turned in the alarm.

For just over five hours, thirty-five fireman fought the blaze. The inferno demolished Riteway Cleaners and damaged two other business establishments.

At 7 a.m. Pipestone Fire Chief, Lee Longstreet said the fire was under control. But, to be on the safe side, firemen remained at the scene until noon.

The cold weather made it difficult to fight the blaze, as everything turned to ice after the water hit it. There was icy slush six inches deep by Gerald's Shoe Store.

Assistant State Fire Marshal, Mel Hardy, was in Pipestone the following day to check the damage. He believed the fire damage ranged between $150,000 and $200,000. Hardy said the cause of the fire was "strictly accidental." Fire Chief Longstreet determined that a short in the boiler feed pump at Riteway Cleaners precipitated the fire.

In March 1966, there was the merger of two prominent independent bakeries, Pan-O-Gold and Regan. Pan-O-Gold, which maintained a plant in Pipestone, was founded there in 1906.

Pipestone's high school boys basketball team ended their season with a 70 to 52 loss to Worthington at Luverne on March 4.[1]

Redwood Falls is the seat of Redwood County.

Among the people who settled Redwood Falls in 1864 were Col. Samuel McPhail and J. S. G. Homer. The platting of Redwood Falls was done in October 1865.

Its name comes from the falls of Redwood River. In its last three miles, before it joins the Minnesota River, the Redwood River, by means of rapids and vertical falls, makes a descent of around 140 feet. Most of this descent occurs in a scenic gorge below the city.

The March 1966 snowstorm only grazed Redwood Falls. Only rain fell there on Wednesday, March 2 (.10 inches) and Thursday, March 3 (.31 inches). The reason for that was the temperatures. Highs and lows of 38 and 34 on Wednesday and 49 and 36 on Thursday were recorded in Redwood Falls that day.

But lousy highway conditions forced a Greyhound bus to stay at Redwood Falls Thursday night.

Cooler temperatures on Friday brought snowfall to Redwood Falls. As a precautionary measure, at 12:30 p.m. Friday, Vesta students who rode the bus to attend school in Redwood Falls, were sent home. At 2:35 p.m., other bus students were let out of school. A high and low of 36 and 26 were reached in Redwood Falls on Friday.

The precipitation total for Friday in Redwood Falls was .12 inches.

Temperatures continued their gradual descent in Redwood Falls on Saturday. The high and low for the day were 28 and 7.

Another .05 inches of precipitation fell in Redwood Falls on Saturday. Snowfall totals at the Redwood Falls Federal Aviation Administration (FAA) Airport from the storm came to 1.7 inches. This fell on Friday and Saturday.

Heading west from Redwood Falls, one encountered slippery roads. On Saturday, because of ice and lousy visibility, conditions were poor enough in the Marshall vicinity on Saturday, to force the postponement of several district basketball tournament games.

In the aftermath of the storm, a low of -1 was reached in Redwood Falls on Monday, March 7.

Redwood Falls high school boys basketball team, the "Cardinals", finished their season in District 10 tournament action on March 7 at New Ulm. Gibbon, which trailed Redwood Falls at halftime, rallied to beat the Cardinals 65 to 43.

Ortonville (population of 2,674 in 1960) lies at the lower end of Big Stone Lake. From this lake, the Minnesota River emerges to flow southeast and then northeast to join the Mississippi River in the Twin Cities.

There is a continental divide between Big Stone Lake and Lake Traverse to the north. Water from Big Stone Lake end up in the Gulf of Mexico. Runoff from Lake Traverse eventually flows into Hudson Bay. At one time the valley in which both lakes are located in was part of a glacial river. Known as River Warren, it flowed south.

The first settlers to come to Ortonville Township arrived in 1871. A Wisconsin man of Norwegian descent gave the township and city their names. Cornelius Knute Orton (1846-1890) moved to Minnesota in 1857. He established a claim on land in Ortonville Township in 1871. Orton platted the village of Ortonville in September 1872.

The storm hit Ortonville late Thursday night and lasted until Sunday.

On Friday morning, poor visibility forced motorists in Ortonville to turn on their headlights. For the greater part of Friday evening, visibility in town was reduced to zero. The brunt of the storm in Ortonville lasted from Friday night into Saturday morning.

These conditions forced the closure of all highways in the Ortonville vicinity. They even forced the official closure of the Ortonville school-something that had not occurred for a long time. Few businesses were open in Ortonville on Friday afternoon. That evening it was virtually impossible to drive in town. The Ortonville area suffered no loss of power or phone service during the storm.

On Friday night, a snowplow helped Mrs. Gene Cloos from Big Stone City, who was in a car, reach the Ortonville Hospital.

There, her sixth child, a girl, was born.

Conditions were bad at Big Stone Lake that evening. On the dike road that ran along its foot, seventeen cars were said to have been "shoveled out."

The blizzard had resulted in a crisis, not only for area dairy farmers, but also for the Big Stone Cheese Factory. Impassable roads prevented its bulk trucks from picking up milk from dairy farms in the Ortonville area.

Once the roads were opened, the factory was "swamped with cheese-making over the entire weekend."

On the northern end of Ortonville, drifts from the wet, heavy snow reached levels as high as the roofs on many houses.

Bill Miles, who kept track of the weather in Ortonville recorded a snowfall of almost 14 inches. The precipitation amounted to 1.52 inches. But, as he stated, "This could have been more, as it was hard to measure in such blizzard conditions."[2]

The city appeared deserted Saturday morning with almost no businesses open.

The Cy McCormick family lived on Minnesota Street in March 1966. Snow locked the family in their house. They left through a window.

The Ortonville hospital was completely blocked by snow. Fortunately, there was a gap by the front door, so people could get into the hospital.

Large drifts buried vehicles in Ortonville. A pile of snow in front of a store enveloped most of a parking meter. Not only did it prevent any parking, but also any parking tickets from being given out.

A common refrain Sunday morning by those digging out from the storm was "we've done more shoveling today than we've done in the past 10 years."

Ortonville's high school boys basketball team season ended at Madison on March 1. There, in subdistrict tournament action, they were defeated by Marietta 64 to 54.

Willmar lies about forty miles south of Sauk Centre and over ninety miles west of the Twin Cities. In 1960, 10,417 people lived in Willmar.

The arrival of the St. Paul and Pacific Railroad in 1869 led to the establishment of Willmar. The townsite was platted the same year.

The locating and naming of Willmar was done by the President of the St. Paul and Pacific Railway, George F. Becker. At that time (1869) European bondholders owned the St. Paul and Pacific Railroad. Their agent, a Belgian native, was Leon Willmar, who lived in London at that time. He was the individual that Becker named the village of Willmar after.

Willmar was on the edge of the March 1966 blizzard.

The forecast for Willmar for Thursday March 3, 1966, was this:

Cloudy, windy and mild today with occasional rain and a few thunderstorms mixed with snow. Cloudy, windy and turning colder tonight with occasional snow accumulating two to four inches north and inch or less extreme south. Colder Friday with snow ending. Highs today 32-48. Lows tonight 15-25. Shifting winds 15-35 m.p. h. today.

Outlook Saturday, fair to partly cloudy. Temperatures below normal.[3]

Temperatures in Willmar remained mild for most of the duration of the storm. Daily high temperatures of 37, 36 and 35 were recorded consecutively on March 2, 3 and 4 at the Willmar State Hospital. The thermometer dipped down to 28 above on both March 2 and March 4. Not until Saturday, March 5, did the temperature slide down to 10 above. Even then, Saturday's high was 29. A low of 3 below was reached on March 7, before temperatures began to rise again.

Precipitation-wise, because of the mild temperatures, most of what Willmar received from the storm came in the form of rain. The city received a half inch of snow on Wednesday. Its precipitation total for that day came to .06 inches. The precipitation on Thursday (0.36") was almost exclusively rain, except for a trace of snow.

Willmar endured blustery weather on Friday, March 4. As of that morning, the city had received only a trace of snow. Temperatures were just below freezing.

Many schools in the Willmar closed early Friday afternoon in anticipation of a blizzard that was supposed to hit the Willmar area that afternoon.

But it never did. Willmar received only two inches of snow that day.

It was still windy in Willmar on Saturday morning. That morning, wind speeds varied between 20 and 25 mph with gusts up to 35 mph.

Precipitation totals at Willmar for the four days of the storm came to .76 inches of precipitation.

On March 5, in Region 13 Junior College basketball playoff action at the Willmar High School, Willmar lost to Fergus Falls 86 to 79 in consolation action to end its season. Willmar was paced by Mike George's 24 points.

Located in west-central Minnesota, Morris is the seat of Stevens County. It had a population of 4,199 in 1960.

The city of Morris would take its name from Charles A. F. Morris (1827-1903), a man who worked with the engineering departments of different railroads. Included in this group was the St. Paul, Minneapolis, and Manitoba and the Northern Pacific.

In 1869, Morris was platted.

Morris was on the edge of the '66 blizzard. First it rained, then the precipitation changed to a wet snow Thursday evening. It kept on snowing through the night. The snowfall was accompanied by winds that rose through the night to reach blizzard velocities. In Morris wind speeds reached about 55 mph, reducing visibility almost to zero.

The storm brought transportation in and out of Morris virtually to a standstill. Despite this, some streets in town remained open for the duration of the blizzard. Plows kept some routes open during the storm. County and state highway department plows were kept on standby during the storm for emergency calls.

Except for the University of Minnesota at Morris, schools in the Morris area were closed on Friday due to the storm. Although some offices closed in Morris on Friday, most businesses stayed open Friday and Saturday.

The Greyhound bus from Minneapolis only made it as far as Benson, twenty-five miles southeast of Morris. There was no Greyhound bus service from Morris either Friday or Saturday.

The Zephyr bus was able to make it to Morris both Friday and Saturday. But, it then remained there and did not go on to its destination of Sisseton, South Dakota.

Rail traffic came to a halt in Morris during the storm.

Many school and social activities were canceled or postponed.

The blizzard did not let up until Saturday night.

The storm dumped 15.3 inches of snow inches of snow, 1.26 inches of precipitation, on Morris.

Temperatures in Morris fell from 35 above on Friday to 11 below zero Monday morning.

Browns Valley, Beardsley and Wheaton

Just east of the south end of Lake Traverse, which separates Minnesota and South Dakota, lies the city of Browns Valley (1033 inhabitants in 1960).

The founder of Browns Valley, Joseph R. Brown (1805-1870), was one of Minnesota's greatest pioneers. At the age of fourteen and a soldier in the U.S. Army, Brown arrived in Minnesota. In the November 12, 1870 issue of the *St. Paul Press* Joseph A. Wheelock listed occupations Brown had during his lifetime. He was "a drummer boy, soldier, Indian trader, lumberman, pioneer, speculator, founder of cities, legislator, politician, editor, inventor..."[4]

Joseph Brown established Browns Valley in 1866-7. It was first known as Lake Traverse, but the name was changed following Mr. Brown's death on November 9, 1870. The first person to serve as Brown's Valley mayor was his son, Samuel J. Brown, who held the job from 1867-1868.

The village of Brown's Valley served as the first county seat of Traverse County. In 1886, Wheaton replaced Brown's Valley as the county seat.

The March 1966 blizzard did not arrive in the Browns Valley area until around 10 p.m. Thursday, March 3. So, unlike people in other areas, the residents of Browns Valley were fortunate in missing the first full day of the storm.

But, it was only a respite. Because, the storm unleashed its wrath on Browns Valley and the surrounding area for the next two days. It would be the city's first blizzard of the 1965-66 winter.

By Friday morning, most activity (including schools) in and around Browns Valley had either stopped or was shutting down. Heavy snow and 60 mph winds reduced visibility to zero. All the roads around Browns Valley (rural, county, and state) were impassable Friday morning. Visibility remained at zero in the Browns Valley neighborhood for the majority of the time Friday and Saturday.

These sort of conditions led to the closing up shop for the large majority of businesses in Browns Valley Friday afternoon, and many of them stayed closed on Saturday.

Vehicular traffic ground to a halt in the Browns Valley neck of the woods on Friday and for most of Saturday. Deep snowdrifts were the order of the day in Browns Valley. They were 8, 10 and 12 feet high. As of Friday night, 8 to 10 feet high snowbanks had blocked Browns Valley's Main Street completely.

During the worst of the storm, high winds blew shingles off the roofs of some homes. One Browns Valley business establishment, Valley Implement, Inc. (previously known as SchiefelBein's Implement Company), suffered the loss of a large northerly facing display window just before 7 a.m. Saturday.

Beardsley, Minnesota, is a few miles southeast of Browns Valley on Minnesota Highway 28. There, winds from the storm tore a big neon sign from what used to be the Klein Cafe.

Some Browns Valley residents were among the 100 motorists who spent two consecutive nights marooned south of Sisseton, South Dakota, at Brooks Corner Service Station.

To have a fire break out in such atrocious weather as residents of the Northern Plains were experiencing in March 1966 was a tragedy. Such a tragedy occurred at Peever, South Dakota, not far from Browns Valley. Around 6:45 a.m. Friday, a call was made to the Browns Valley Fire Department to assist in fighting the blaze at Peever. Responding to the call and riding in their white fire truck was Browns Valley's Fire Chief Bob Hansen and Vern Domarus. Ed Butals, Jim Ecker and "Buzz" Krone used a pickup to make it to the fire. The lousy visibility of the snowstorm hampered the firemen's efforts to get to Peever and it took them a half hour to reach there.

Quite a bit of damage had occurred before the Browns Valley fire crew reached Peever. The blizzard hindered efforts to battle the fire. The firemen returned to Browns Valley around 10 a.m.

Conditions began to improve in Browns Valley Saturday afternoon. By late afternoon, skies had begun to clear. The blizzard had dumped 4.5 inches of snow on the city. In a refrain that was familiar throughout much of the storm area, sheltered areas in and around Browns Valley were buried under huge snowdrifts, while storm winds had blown nearby fields clear of snow. The U.S. Weather Bureau reported that it was the worst blizzard to hit the Upper Midwest since the one of 1888.

Initial snow removal efforts Saturday morning, other than individual Browns Valley residents' efforts at their homes, were concentrated on clearing snow from the sidewalks on the north side of Main Street. The sidewalks there were submerged under eight to ten feet of snow. To accomplish this, any city snow removal equipment ready for use was put to work removing snow.

That afternoon, the snow removal equipment of the Layden Construction Company was used to clear residential streets. On Main Street, their equipment pushed the snow into huge piles along the sides of the street.

At noon Monday, the process of removing the humongous piles along Main Street was begun. To accomplish that task additional trucks were employed. It would be Wednesday afternoon before that job was completed.

The Browns Valley area came through the March 1966 blizzard without any reports of loss of livestock.

Unfortunately, the pheasant population did not come through the storm in as good of shape. Estimate of pheasant losses in the Browns Valley area were as high as eighty percent.

Browns Valley experienced considerable flooding after the March 1966 blizzard. During the spring runoff, ice jams formed on the Little Minnesota River. To break them up, dynamite had to be employed.

Wheaton, the seat of Traverse County, lies about 30 miles south of Breckenridge, Minnesota. Nearby are Mud Lake and Lake Traverse. These two lakes form the boundary between Minnesota and South Dakota.

In 1960, 2,102 people called Wheaton home.

The city of Wheaton was named in honor of Daniel Thompson Wheaton, a surveyor.

At the time of the founding of Wheaton, Thompson was a surveyor for the Fargo Southern Railway Company. The land on which Wheaton was located was owned by two Swedish men, Ole and Swan C. Odenborg. Wheaton said the new settlement should be called Swedenburg in honor of the Odenborgs. However, they disagreed, preferring to name the village after Wheaton. So it was done.

Wheaton and Traverse County were not in the direct path of the worst part of the March '66 blizzard, but were more towards the southern edge of it.

Mild weather leading up to the big storm had melted much of what little snow Wheaton had received so far during the 1965-66 winter. The city enjoyed a high of 42 on March 1, 35 on March 2 and 35 on March 3.

So, they had quite a surprise in store for them when they awoke Friday morning. A blizzard was raging outside. High winds reduced visibility to less than 100 feet and piled the falling snow into humongous drifts.

The atrocious weather conditions disrupted community events such as scheduled meetings. The district basketball tournament had to be rescheduled.

The Traverse County Highway Department made a concerted effort to keep county highways open during the storm. Their snow removal effort meant ten hour days for all Traverse County snow removal equipment. Traverse County Engineer Ken Paulson stated that the cost for using all county snow removal equipment over a ten hour workday was almost $1,500.

Despite the lousy weather Friday morning, the majority of business establishments in Wheaton were open. Store personnel struggled through the drifts to make it to work. They might as well have stayed home. Business was almost nonexistent.

That morning, store employees in Wheaton tried to clear the snow from in front of the business establishments. Myrl Bender tried to clear a large drift in front of the Dr. Weickert building with a shovel. But the falling snow and high winds frustrated hers and others efforts. They were forced to abandon their efforts. By early afternoon, most of the stores had closed, and their personnel had departed for their homes.

The ferocity of the storm continued unabated in Wheaton throughout Friday. Snow fell most of the day, accompanied by high winds. Vehicular traffic in Wheaton ground to a halt.

Saturday brought little snow to Wheaton, but the high winds continued.

They slackened late that afternoon. This allowed residents of Wheaton to trudge through the deep drifts to the grocery stores to stock up on depleted supplies. This increase in business traffic did not pertain to most of the other businesses in Wheaton. Few of them were even open on Saturday.

Despite the huge snowdrifts in the Wheaton vicinity, it came through the storm without suffering any serious damage. Wheaton hadn't seen that much snow in a long time.

The part of Wheaton which probably that got the worst of the storm were homes along 5th Avenue North. There were no windbreaks north of them to slow the wind driven snow, just open fields. So, the high northerly winds of the storm whipped the snow around the homes and deposited it on the south side of them in the form of large drifts.

On Sunday morning, 5th Avenue North had been partially cleared of snow up to an elementary school corner. At that location, traffic was stopped by a humongous snowdrift that had a car buried inside of it.

Snow removal equipment cut a path through a large snowdrift that lay between Johnson's Welding Shop and Wheaton Lanes in Wheaton. The drift was higher than cars passing through the cut.

As elsewhere, the majority of fields around Wheaton were blown clear of snow by the winds accompanying the blizzard. Instead, the snow piled up in farmyards and tree claims. One place enduring such a fate was the Willard Krumweide farmstead north of Wheaton.

On Sunday, the cleanup in Wheaton was going full blast. Early that morning, Wheaton's street crews began tackling the mammoth job of snow removal. There was so much snow to haul away out of town; the cleanup was still going on three days later.

Wheaton's high school boys basketball team, the Warriors, ended their season in District 21 tournament play when they lost to Starbuck 70 to 61 at Benson on March 8. The game had been postponed by the storm of the previous weekend. For Wheaton, John Hennen had 28 points in a losing effort.

Breckenridge, Rothsay, Barnesville, Wolverton and Sabin

As the crow flies, Breckenridge is just across the Red River from Wahpeton, North Dakota. It is the seat of Wilkin County.

In 1960, 4335 people lived in Breckenridge in 1960.

Its platting as a village came in the spring of 1857. The surrounding township of the same name was organized on May 23, 1857.

Breckenridge was named after a prominent American politician before and during the Civil War, John Cabell Breckenridge (1821-1875). This Kentuckian served as a member of the U.S. Congress from 1851-1855 and then as Vice President from 1857-1861. Breckenridge ran for the Presidency in 1860 but lost. He then joined the Confederate side in the Civil War. Breckenridges's service to that cause included duty as a general in the Confederate army from 1861 to 1864. From January to April 1865 he was the Confederate Secretary of State.

The city of Breckenridge was enjoying spring-like weather prior to the March 1966 storm. On Tuesday, March 1, a high of 40 above was recorded. The snow was melting so fast that catch basins (which were probably frozen over) in the streets couldn't handle it. So, the Breckenridge Street Department came to the rescue and got the water to go into the catch basins.

People in Breckenridge responded to the mild weather with smiles and open coats and jackets. Spring had sprung, hadn't it?

Well, not quite, as the blizzard descended on Breckenridge the very next day.

But a person would never have guessed it from the forecast for Breckenridge for March 3, 1966. This is what it said:

> It's back to the old "winterish" grind again. Below average temps will drop from 8 to 15 degrees. Normal highs for our snow-capped are from 30 to 40. Normal lo's usually range between 9 and 16. It'll turn much colder today (Thursday) and remain bone-chilling until a moderating period the first of next week. Precipitation, occurring as snow, will dump from .01 to .13 inches melted. Most of the accumulation should occur today.[5]

Despite the arrival of the storm, temperatures in Breckenridge rose into the 30's Wednesday, Thursday and Friday. In fact, not until the last day of the storm, Saturday, did the mercury level in Breckenridge fail to break the 30 degree mark. On that day, a high of 22 was recorded in Breckenridge.

The blizzard's appearance led to school closings in the Breckenridge area Wednesday afternoon and Thursday morning, and the curtailing of most business activity in the city. Those business establishments that chose to remain open enjoyed very little traffic. About the only business they had was from people who endured the storm elements on foot. Vehicular traffic was almost nonexistent.

For Breckenridge and Wilkin County, the March 1966 blizzard did not produce any major catastrophes. That didn't mean there weren't any emergencies-there were. For the duration of the four day storm , Breckenridge's city snowplow had to respond to just two emergency calls. Both incidents happened on the worst day of the blizzard, Friday.

One of them occurred at the Douglas Coen residence at 220 N. 10th St. The Coen's one-year old son, Phillip, had suffered second degree burns from an accidentally spilled cup of coffee. The boy was forced to remain in the hospital overnight.

In the other case, fuel oil supplies at Wayne Slotten's place in the Park Addition at 701 Main St. were almost completely depleted.

The blizzard left Edward Hicks marooned in LaMoure, North Dakota. Mr. Hicks, his wife and their three youngsters, ages 5, 4 and 2 lived in Trailer City in Breckenridge. Unable to find them, Mr. Hicks placed a call to the Wilkin County Sheriff. That department couldn't locate them either, so an alert was put out reporting them to be missing. Fortunately, they were found to be safe and sound in Morris.

Concerns about the safety of loved ones as the blizzard engulfed Breckenridge led to an exponential increase in the number of telephone calls made to the Breckenridge Police Department. From March 1 through noon March 9, they received 411 telephone calls. As Charles Lambert, Breckenridge Chief of Police, observed:

> This compares to 455 calls received during the entire month of February. This shows how the number of telephone calls greatly increased during the storm.[6]

While the storm raged, two emergency calls came into the Minnesota Highway Department in Breckenridge. In the one instance, the Highway Department had to go to the Charles Bucholz farm in southwestern Wilkin County and get Mrs. Bucholz to St. Francis Hospital in Breckenridge.

The other call came in at 11:45 p.m. Friday. Mr. and Mrs. Walter Thimjon lived on a farm near Foxhome. Foxhome is a village on Minnesota Highway 210 and is a little more than twelve miles (as the crow flies) north-northeast of Breckenridge. It was vital that Mrs. Thimjon be taken to the hospital.

Because of the zero visibility, the decision was made to make the trip with two snowplows. At times, visibility was so poor that it was impossible to see the side of the road. These conditions necessitated that a member of the snowplow crew scout ahead of the plow on foot. To show how tough it was outside, it would be 7 a.m. Saturday before the snowplows returned to base after delivering Mrs. Thimjon to St. Francis Hospital in Breckenridge.

The March 1966 blizzard had a definite impact on Great Northern train crews originating from Breckenridge. No freight train departed from Breckenridge from March 3 until March 7. The last freight train to leave Breckenridge was on March 3, before the full impact of the storm descended on Breckenridge. It got not further than the vicinity of Pillsbury, North Dakota, a hamlet that lies about ninety-eight miles northwest of Breckenridge.

A week later, the snowbound train was still there. Reports had it that snowmobiles were being used to deliver food and other supplies to the train crew. Among them were Howard Morris from Wahpeton, engineer, Bill Junge, conductor and Duane Enkers, Breckenridge, fireman. Rounding out the train crew were Ernest Johnson, Wesley Rittenhouse and Elroy Schwankl.

According to Great Northern's station master in Breckenridge, Paul Ruppels, as of March 9, about twenty-five miles of track from Erie Junction to Luverne, both in North Dakota, still had not been opened to traffic. To clear that stretch of track, two rotary plows, one at each end, were chewing through twenty-five foot high drifts towards each other.

Because of snow-blocked tracks west from Breckenridge, freight trains were being detoured through Devils Lake via Grand Forks.

Another Breckenridge crew escaped injury in the Niagara, North Dakota, area when a snowdrift with a fifteen foot high cut through it collapsed upon their freight train. The crew was made up of James Kuehn, fireman, Oran Lord, conductor, Richard Mikkelson, engineer, and Jim Schmitt and R. W. Lee, brakeman.

Weather related difficulties held up the westbound *Western Star* for thirty-six hours in Breckenridge, before it proceeded on to suffer a head-on collision near Chester, Montana with GN's *Empire Builder* on March 7.

As of March 9, seven Great Northern crews from Breckenridge had been stuck at New Rockford, North Dakota, since March 3. From there, on the same day, two other train crews from Breckenridge were progressing eastward.

The storm vacated the Breckenridge area Saturday leaving 10 inches snow. Precipitation-wise the city received .20 inches on Wednesday, .12 inches Thursday, .35 inches Friday and .05 inches Saturday for a total of .72 inches of precipitation for the four day storm.

In the storm's aftermath, it could be seen that northwestern Wilkin County had been hit the hardest by the blizzard. There, the depth of snowdrifts reached to the roofs of outbuildings (and in some cases on top of them).

In Breckenridge itself, some homes also had snowbanks as high as their roofs.

The cleanup in Wilkin County after the storm was quick and efficient. As of Sunday evening, all county roads were open to vehicular traffic. According to James Burgess,

Wilkin County Highway Engineer, by the following night, the same could be said for those township roads, with a few exceptions, that enjoyed some sort of regular traffic.

The cleanup proceeded rapidly in Breckenridge too. There was much snow to haul away. To give an example, Bud Stollenwerk, Superintendent of Breckenridge's Street Department, related the following statistics to the *Valley Alert*. To clear a one block portion of 5th Street between Minnesota and Nebraska Avenue, entailed the removal of 153 truckloads of snow. That worked out to about 1200 yards of snow.

It wasn't all work for the Street Department workers. Taking advantage of a large pile of snow in front of City Hall, Gordon Millbrandt, Dick Neppl, Bud and Mike Stollenwerk and Gordon Strom dug waist deep holes in the pile of snow. After climbing into the holes, they had their picture taken showing them standing in waist deep snow.

As the northwestern part of Wilkins County had received the greater brunt of the storm, snowdrifts were deeper there. Residents of the Wolverton area wanted the Wilkin County Civil Defense to have the area declared a disaster area so help could be procured to help them dig out from the effects of the blizzard.

In response to this on March 8, A. W. Gruenberg, Wilkin County Civil Defense Director, along with Al Humann of the Wilkin County Soil Conservation Department, toured the county by air.

Afterwards, Gruenberg made his decision by saying, "We're not a disaster area." His conclusion was that Wilkin County had not suffered damage of disaster proportion.

The *Valley Alert* carried Gruenberg's explanation for his decision:

> Before Civil Defense can take action, all local effort must be exhausted according to Gruenberg who added, "by that is meant that all local equipment must be in use and not able to handle the job. We saw many farm yards with lots of snow in them and covering their equipment but a real good job was being done in opening their yards.[7]

There was flooding in Wahpeton-Breckenridge after the March 1966, but it was not record setting.

The Don Yaggie family had an unexpected visitor at their farm just off Minnesota Highway 210, seven miles east of Breckenridge around 5:00 p.m. Friday. Mr. Yaggie, his wife and six children were safely ensconced in their house when there was a knock at their door. Upon opening the door, a man tumbled inside. He was Ben Kaufman, 27, a *Minneapolis Star* reporter. His boss at the newspaper had dispatched him on an assignment to get a story on the blizzard. Kaufman informed the Yaggies that his automobile had stalled down the road a half mile west of the Yaggie house. The walk to the Yaggie place had chilled Kaufman, so they invited him in stay awhile.

It would be 3:30 p.m. the next day before Don Yaggie and Mr. Kaufman were able to return to the latter's car, a little English made convertible.

Don Yaggie towed the convertible back to a shed. There, Mr. Kaufman and him cleared snow away from the engine and the car's interior. Once they had the motor dried out, Don Yaggie was able to get Mr. Kaufman back on the road.

While stranded at the Yaggie farm place, Mr. Kaufman took a lot of pictures. The subjects of his camera included the Yaggie family, buildings, snowbanks, and the snow filled interior of his car on the highway.

Some of these pictures appeared in the Monday (March 7, 1966) evening edition of the *Minneapolis Star*. One photo taken in front of the barn shows three of the Yaggie children, Kayla, 8, Kevin, 7, and Mike, 6, perched on top of a snowdrift. Another picture shows

Don Yaggie moving snow with a tractor and loader. Mr. Kaufmans snow -filled car also appears in the *Star*.

Two Clay County schools, Barnesville and Hawley, closed for the day at 1 p.m.

Close to 30 miles southeast of Moorhead, on U.S. Highway 52, is the village of Rothsay (457 residents in 1960). No other place in the United States has this name. Rothsay was named after a Scottish seaport of the same name near Glasgow, Scotland.

Rothsay became a stopping place for several motorists during the storm. Snowbanks reached heights of eight feet in the northeastern corner of Rothsay.

Situated about fifteen miles southeast of Moorhead, Barnesville, Minnesota enjoyed a population of 1632 in 1960. Founded by George S. Barnes in 1874, Barnesville was one of the stops on the NP line. The surrounding township also had the same name.

The local newspaper, the *Barnesville Record-Review*, had this to say about the March '66 storm:

> One of the worst blizzards in history roared across the Dakotas last week and battered the Barnesville area for four days, piling up huge snowdrifts, stranding travelers and bringing anxiety into the lives of many families. . . driving winds and snow cut visibility to zero and many cars on the highways became stalled in the drifts or went off the road due to the blinding snow.[8]

Weather conditions in Barnesville began to deteriorate on the morning of March 2.

The decision was made to let school out early in Barnesville. At 11 a.m., telephone calls to Barnesville area radio stations were made informing them of the decision to dismiss classes early.

But, the radio stations were slow to put the announcements on the air. The earliest any of them aired the announcement was around 12:10 p.m. By that time, the buses had departed from the schools. The sluggishness in reacting to the schools' announcement by the radio stations upset Barnesville Superintendent of Schools Harold C. Grams. He had this to say about the event:

> In an emergency weather situation, it is important that somebody be at home or at the bus stop to meet the little ones. Some of these children have to be let out as much as a quarter mile from their house.
>
> If the emergency broadcast stations failed to provide better cooperation down the road, Grams said other stations might get the nod.[9]

City snow removal crews in Barnesville kept working for the duration of the storm in an effort to keep streets (including Front Street) open.

When all was said and done, a Barnesville City Hall spokesman thought the cost of plowing, loading, and hauling the snow away would be over $1,000.

There were many storm related stories in the Barnesville vicinity. The *Barnesville Record-Review* thanked its correspondents for collecting them.

Wolverton is on U.S. Highway 75 over 20 miles south of Moorhead.

There was supposed to be a wedding there on Saturday March 5, 1966, at the Wolverton Lutheran Church between Agnathia Kragerud and Orland Stephenson. But, with the groom aboard a train that had stalled near Mandan, North Dakota, the wedding had to be rescheduled.

Another couple and their children, Mr. and Mrs. Jim Kragerud and daughters, Kari and Tami of Brownsberg, Indiana encountered problems enroute to the wedding. Their automobile had gone off U.S. 75 into the ditch between Kent and Wolverton and had become stuck. Kent is eleven miles south of Wolverton. It would a thirty-six hour wait in the car for the Krageruds. But, they and the groom made it to the wedding which was held in Wolverton at 8 p.m. Sunday.

A Barnesville couple, Mr. and Mrs. Alfred Kluck, would never forget the March 1966 blizzard. On Wednesday, March 2 ,they were in Fargo. Because of the arrival of the storm that day in the Fargo-Moorhead area, the Klucks made the decision not to leave town but chose instead to stay in Moorhead at the home of her sister, Mrs. Frank Weaver.

Unfortunately, on Friday, in the middle of the storm the child Mrs. Kluck was carrying decided to make his entrance into this world. She was rushed to a Fargo-Moorhead hospital in an ambulance. All the while a tv camera crew filmed the trip. The final leg of the trip for Mrs. Kluck into the hospital was made on a stretcher.

Just an hour after her arrival, Mrs. Kluck gave birth to a 7 pound 15 ounce son, whom the Klucks named Jay Alfred.

Mrs. Kluck's journey through the storm to the hospital was shown to a nationwide audience on Sunday night on the NBC network news.

A medical emergency on Saturday involving a rural Baker, Minnesota person, Richard Thompson, required the use of two snowplows and a police car to reach him at his farm residence.

After picking Baker up, they made it to Barnesville via the Comstock road.

As U.S. Highway 52 was open, a police car was able to take Mr. Baker to St. Ansgar Hospital in Moorhead.

That evening, an appendectomy was performed on him.

The blizzard disrupted mail service in and out of Barnesville. But resourceful postal employees found other ways to deliver the mail or get to work. Utilizing his snowmobile, Ken Christensen was able to deliver the mail to several rural Barnesville families. Snowshoes helped postal employee Vernon Seefeldt get to work.

Although it came in late to the post office, Barnesville did receive its mail on Thursday. It would be Monday before the mail came to Barnesville again.

Means of transportation in and around Barnesville while the blizzard raged included snowshoes, snowmobiles and tractors.

Although stores in Barnesville were open on Friday, they enjoyed almost no business, and they all shut down for the day about 5 p.m. A business promotion, the "Bonanza", scheduled for that week was rescheduled for the following week.

After four days, the storm finally let up in Barnesville. Barnesville residents were either low or out of items such as bread and milk. To help them resupply their needs, grocery stores in Barnesville were open for business on Sunday.

One of the most dramatic stories of the '66 blizzard involved Kenneth Durensky of rural Barnesville. He worked as a firemen for GN.

Durensky headed out from his home around 10:30 p.m. Thursday to go work in Fargo. He never made it there. After a time, Durensky was reported missing.

Friday night a rescue party was formed by Durensky's brother-in-law, Fargo banker Stewart Turing. To lead the rescue effort, he procured a 23-ton front-end loader (also known as a payloader) that came equipped with an enclosed cab and bucket. The other two vehicles in the rescue party were a truck and a radio-equipped Minnesota Highway Patrol car. One of the two officers in the patrol car was Clint Foslien of Barnesville.

As Durensky had been seen passing through Sabin on his way to Fargo, the search party concentrated its efforts on Highway 52 north of Sabin.

Mr. Foslien stated that the rescue effort was "real slow going." The stretch of Highway 52 from Moorhead to Sabin had many stalled automobiles along it. Checking all of them took quite a bit of time. As soon as anyone left the safety of their vehicle and stepped out into the elements of the storm, the wind driven snow would penetrate their clothes, leavening them soaking wet. But, they found no one in the abandoned cars.

Becoming lost in the blizzard the rescue party ended up turning off Highway 52 and onto a gravel road. They were forced to remain there until daylight. Regaining their bearings they were able to locate Highway 52 again.

It would be noon Saturday before the rescue party reached Sabin. They had left Moorhead at 8 p.m. Friday. The nine mile journey had taken them sixteen hours.

But where was Mr. Durensky? It turned out that he had turned around north of Sabin and headed back for Barnesville. Unfortunately, no one saw him drive back through Sabin.

Mr. Durensky's vehicle ended up in the ditch off Highway 52 southeast of Sabin. By putting on an extra parka and exercising every hour, he managed to get through the night. The following morning Mr. Durensky trudged into Sabin. The only effects he suffered from his ordeal were frostbitten cheeks.

The last vehicle to get through on U.S. 52 from Barnesville to Moorhead, before storm conditions forced its closure Thursday night, was an ambulance driven by Don Dobmeirer. The ambulance was making a return trip to Barnesville after transporting Mrs. Ray Fankhanel to St. Ansgar Hospital in Moorhead. She was suffering from pneumonia. Accompanying Mr. Dobmeirer in the ambulance were Ray Fankhanel and Rev. Dietrich.

Having the ambulance equipped with a radio was of a great benefit to Dobmeier. This allowed him to make contact with snowplow operators. They would then know that the ambulance was coming through. This gave them time to pull over and allow the ambulance to proceed on its way.

The ambulance made it back to Barnesville around 9:30 Thursday evening. By then weather conditions were so poor, that according to Mr. Dobmeier, "anybody in their right mind would not have attempted the trip."[10]

Mr. Dobmeier also shed light on what may have forced Kenneth Durensky to turn around north of Sabin. On its way to Barnesville, about a mile and a half north of Sabin, the ambulance met two semitrucks.

Within a few minutes of passing them, Mr. Dobmeier was of the belief that the two trucks had blocked Highway 52. This prevented Mr. Durensky from continuing on to Fargo when he came upon the scene later that evening.

Star Route mail carrier, Milton Brett of Fargo, didn't let the blizzard stop him. He spent Thursday night at his cottage on Cotton Lake. That body of water lies ten miles northeast of Detroit Lakes. After picking up mail in Detroit Lakes Friday morning, Brett headed out in his three-quarter ton pickup truck. Heading down U.S. 59, his destination was Fergus Falls. He dropped off mail at various towns along the way.

Once he had reached Fergus Falls, Brett filled his truck with mail and set off for Moorhead on U.S. 52.

Although his vehicle went into the ditch one time, Brett was able to extricate it without shoveling.

Since U.S. 52 was impassable north of Barnesville, Brett traveled on county roads. West of Barnesville, he resumed his journey on U.S. 52.

Brett found U.S. 52 to be blocked two miles east of Baker.

With the pickup's engine becoming wet and running low on gasoline, Brett made the decision to walk to Baker before the onset of darkness.

For the most part, Brett had been trudging backwards, when he came upon a car in the ditch. It was around 6:15 p.m., and Brett had gone about a half mile.

Brett found two people inside the car. Their names were Joe Thorsanson and Sandy Erickson, and they were enroute from Minneapolis to Dickinson.

Their car had run out of gas, and the couple lacked heavy clothing. Huddled in a couple of cotton blankets, they were happy to see Brett.

Brett informed them that he would continue his journey into Baker. After reaching there, he would either return or have help dispatched to them.

Brett got ahold of Fran Iverson and told her to contact the sheriff. Barnesville men rescued the couple. They had been stranded in their vehicle for a few hours.

That weekend Mr. Thorsanson and Ms. Erickson stayed at the Donald Boone home.

Immediately north of Barnesville, the storm left great big drifts that halted all traffic through the underpass located there. Motor vehicles could not get through on U.S. 52 because of these drifts. This area was one of the last ones to be opened for traffic.

The huge drifts in and around Barnesville after the blizzard forced people to use tractors to clear them. Shovels could do little against such large drifts.

A large snowdrift along side the home of *Record-Review* editor Barry Prichard allowed his son, Chuckie to stand on top of it and say that he was higher than the roof.

A varsity basketball player on the NDSU men's basketball team hailed from Barnesville. Tom Noyes, a senior, earned his third letter from the school. He was a 6'3" center for the Bison. Noyes averaged 1.9 points per game over 18 games with the Thundering Herd. The 1965-66 Bison finished the season with a 14-10 record. It was their first winning season in nine years. Mr. Noyes parents were Mr. and Mrs. Russell Noyes.

Sabin, a Great Northern (GN) Railway village lies nine miles southeast of Moorhead in Elmwood Township. This township took its name from the numerous elm trees found along the banks of the South Branch of the Buffalo River. U.S. Highway 52 runs through Sabin.

The village of Sabin was named after a Minnesota businessman and politician, Dwight Sabin (1844-1902).

The March 1966 blizzard stranded two Sabin couples in Moorhead on Thursday. Prevented from making their return that night, Mr. and Mrs. Darryl Dickelman and Mr. and Mrs. Harold Schenck took refuge in Moorhead with Mr. and Mrs. Gale Teiken. On Saturday, they rode the train back to Sabin.

A bus filled with passengers became stuck on U.S. 52 northwest of Sabin. After a twelve hour wait, Eugene Fitzgerald came to their rescue and got the bus into Sabin Friday morning. The Sabin Cafe became their place of refuge.

Their food needs were taken care of by Mr. and Mrs. Eddie Buth. The Alfred Krabbenhoft residence supplied needed sleeping rooms. The train provided transportation back to Fargo for some of the passengers.

In another emergency, a Sabin boy, Steven Sellent, become sick with a pain in his right side at home Friday morning. Although concerned there was no way Steve's parents, Mr. and Mrs. Ed Sellent, could get Steve to the hospital with a terrible blizzard roaring just outside their home.

But when the pain failed to let up the next day, Steve's parents knew they could not wait any longer. But, they had a dilemma on their hands. With no doctors in Sabin, the boy needed to be transported to Moorhead quickly for medical treatment. And the storm had left roads (specifically U.S. 52) blocked.

Then Steve's parents came up with a bright idea. Why not transport him to Moorhead via the train? GN's line passed through Sabin.

So they contacted Willard Pectal, the Great Northern depot agent in Sabin. Pectal had GN's *Western Star, No. 3*, headed from Minneapolis to Minot stop in Sabin to pick up the group. Before this happened, however, the Sellents faced another dilemma. The four blocks from the Sellents home to the depot were impassable. They telephoned Harry Buth, Mayor of Sabin, who got ahold of Eugene Fitzgerald. Mr. Fitzgerald came to the rescue again with his payloader and opened Sabin's Streets enough to accomplish this task.

At noon Saturday, the *Western Star* stopped in Sabin and young Mr. Sellent was brought aboard. A waiting ambulance in Moorhead took him to St. Ansgar Hospital where an appendectomy was performed on him. It had been a near thing for young Sellent, as his appendix was close to rupturing.

The Sellents really appreciated all the help, including the unscheduled stop by the train in Sabin, they had gotten from everyone. Mr. Sellent (who was an algebra instructor at Moorhead's South Junior High) made this statement, "We had tremendous cooperation from everybody who helped us out. It is impossible to thank them enough."[11]

Elbow Lake and Fergus Falls

As the crow flies, Elbow Lake, the seat of Grant County, is about twenty miles southeast of Fergus Falls.

There were 1,521 people living in Elbow Lake in 1960.

The city and township of Elbow Lake derived their names from the lake that lies next door to them in Sanford Township. Two members of an 1849 expedition, Major Samuel Woods and Captain John Pope, were the first to name the lake which was "shaped like an arm bent at the elbow."

Grant County was named after the Civil War hero, Ulysses S. Grant (1822-1885). Its setup and organization came in 1868 and 1874, respectively. At the latter date the townsite of Elbow Lake was picked to be the seat of Grant County. The platting of the Elbow Lake townsite occurred on October 28, 1886.

Elbow Lake escaped the brunt of the March 1966 blizzard. It was on the southern edge of the storm.

Temperatures remained on the mild side in Elbow Lake, throughout the duration of the blizzard. The highest temperature recorded during the storm was 35 above on Thursday. A low temperature of 20 above was registered on Friday.

Precipitation-wise, Elbow Lake received .08 inches on Wednesday, .21 inches Thursday, .26 inches Friday and .03 inches Saturday. This amount came to about 6 inches of snow.

On March 8, Elbow Lake's high school boys basketball team ended their season with a loss to Alberta in district tourney quarter-final action at Fergus Falls. The final score was 61 to 36. Elbow Lake shot only nineteen percent from the field during the game were and had twenty-two turnovers. It was the worst performance, the team had put on all season. When it came to rebounds, Alberta had only a 38 to 34 edge. Perry and Johnson led Elbow Lake in scoring with 8 points apiece.

Fergus Falls, the county seat of Otter Tail County, lies at the eastern edge of the Red River Valley, about twenty-five miles east of Breckenridge.

In 1960, 13,733 people called Fergus Falls home.

The city of Fergus Falls owes its origins to a man by the name of James Whitford. He made a journey in the winter of 1856-57 to establish a townsite at Graham's point along the Red River. Informed by an Indian family of a better location twenty miles away, Whitford went there and staked off a new townsite.

Whitford's expedition had been outfitted by a Scotsman by the name of James Fergus (1813-1902). The exploring party named their proposed settlement after him. The word "Falls" allured to the continuous series of rapids over which the Otter Tail River flowed. The river drops almost seventy feet in a three mile stretch within city limits.

After being platted in August 1870, Fergus Falls became the seat of Otter Tail County two years later.

Fergus Falls received heavy wet snow plus freezing rain and winds up to 45 mph during the first part of the storm Wednesday night and early Thursday. Around 7:50 p.m. Wednesday, a flash of lightning and some claps of thunder produced strange sound effects, to mix with a roaring wind during the blizzard. The noise produced, led to speculation by some Fergus Falls residents, that jets were flying overhead. With the thermometer climbing to 35 above that day in Fergus Falls, one could easily see why the city received freezing rain.

At midnight Wednesday, Fergus Falls city crews went to work clearing streets, and continued to do so during the daylight hours on Thursday.

There were the usual reports of stalled vehicles due to the storm and icy roads.

Schools were closed in Perham on Thursday, after it had received six inches of snow. Rothsay schools closed at 12:45 p.m. Wednesday, and it received no mail Thursday.

While other towns near Fergus Falls closed their schools because of the storm, Fergus Falls did not. It had a policy of keeping its schools open even during blizzards. In response to numerous phone calls as to why Fergus Falls schools stayed open while those of other towns closed, Superintendent L. E. Weimager had this to say. Of the 3700 students enrolled in the Fergus Falls school district, 3300 lived within the immediate city area. This meant that only ten percent of the students had to be transported any distance.

As a result, Fergus Falls was able to hold school and maintain a good attendance rate even on very stormy days. On such days, the attendance rate would still be eighty to ninety percent. Attendance at Fergus Falls schools during the height of the storm ran at eighty percent.

The Fergus Falls area suffered power and telephone outages due to ice coated lines that snapped in the high winds.

Trains coming and going from Fergus Falls were operating way behind schedule. In some instances, they had to be rerouted. When a Northern Pacific freight train from Wahpeton arrived in Fergus Falls at 10:30 Friday morning, its crew stated that visibility was zero on the trip. A passenger train that was due in Fergus Falls, Friday morning, was kept in Minot until the weather improved.

By Friday, snowdrifts were covering cars in Fergus Falls and plugging rural roads so hard, they could not be opened.

By Saturday morning, many roads in and out of Fergus Falls were blocked. Snow removal crews worked all night both Thursday and Friday to open streets and haul away snow from the downtown area.

That same morning, U.S. Highway 52 between Fergus Falls and Elbow Lake could be driven by truck, and Interstate 94 was open as far as Evansville. But, as the *Fergus Falls Daily Journal* noted:

It was possible to drive to Minneapolis or Pelican Rapids today if you were careful, lucky, and somewhat foolish.[12]

Mail carriers in and out of Fergus Falls started to deliver backlogged mail Saturday morning. Even then, they had their problems, as one carrier's vehicle became stuck at the rear of the post office.

The March 1966 blizzard dumped 11 inches of snow on Fergus Falls. The breakdown in snowfall was as follows, 3 inches on Wednesday, 3 inches on Thursday, 4 inches on Friday and 1 inch on Saturday. Precipitationwise, this came to 1.16 inches. The 0.74 inches of precipitation received on Wednesday and Thursday in Fergus Falls included freezing rain.

After recording a high of 40 above on March 1, temperatures in Fergus Falls declined only slightly. Highs of 35 and 34 and 33 were recorded successively, on March 2, 3 and 4 in the city. Even during the worst of the blizzard on Friday the thermometer managed to climb above the freezing mark. The thermometer never dipped below 20 above in Fergus Falls either Thursday or Friday.

Glenwood, Alexandria, Long Prairie and Wadena

Glenwood (2,631 residents in 1960), the seat of Pope County, lies seventeen miles south of Alexandria.

Glenwood sits at the northeast end of Lake Minnewaska. It lies in two townships, Glenwood and Minnewaska.

While most of Pope County is prairie-like, this is not the case with that part of the county where Lake Minnewaska lies. It lies in a large glen or valley and is tree-lined. The geography of Lake Minnewaska helped to name both the city and township of Glenwood.

Glenwood was partially platted on September 28, 1866.

The March 1966 blizzard left a slippery mess in Glenwood. Precipitation from the storm began as rain and then turned to a wet heavy snow on Thursday.

The snow did a number on highways in the Glenwood vicinity on Thursday, by freezing to them. By that evening, although the highways remained open to traffic, they had turned into skating rinks. There was just about no way motorists could drive on them. Because of these conditions, motorists were told to limit their driving to emergency situations only.

Although, in some cases, the lousy weather reduced traffic flow on the trunk highways in the Glenwood area to a single lane, it failed to close them. They remained open for the duration of the storm.

The height of the storm in Glenwood came Friday morning and afternoon. Because of the poor weather conditions, the Villard schools did not open on Friday. While the Glenwood and Starbuck schools actual held classes on Friday, they closed before noon.

Many activities had to be postponed.

As with other cities and towns in the Upper Midwest, stores in Glenwood traditionally opened up for a couple of hours on Friday nights (until 9 p.m.). A dearth of people and traffic kept some of them from opening. Other retailers stayed open but shut down early. A die hard few remained open until 9 p.m.

Early Saturday the snowfall let up. The storm had dumped 11 inches of heavy wet snow on Glenwood. A mile west northwest of Glenwood 1.46 inches of precipitation fell from March 3 to the 5. Problems with drifting snow that day came from high winds that climbed to speeds of 25 mph and higher.

The city of Glenwood came through the blizzard without any major crises. Because of the inclement weather, a few automobiles ended up in the ditch on Thursday and Friday. Their drivers were forced to leave their cars there. Weather conditions left some travellers stranded on Friday night.

Meeting up with a ridge of snow on Minnesota Highway 104 ten miles south of Glenwood proved to be the undoing for a partially filled Glenwood Creamery Company milk truck. The driver of the truck, Gary Fiala, lost control of the vehicle. It went into the ditch and tipped over. Thankfully, Fiala came through the ordeal without any injuries. But, the milk truck suffered tremendous damage.

It would not be until Monday morning that travel conditions on highways in the Glenwood vicinity were anywhere close to normal. Due to rising temperatures and outstanding work by the Minnesota Highway Department, by the following afternoon, highways in the Glenwood vicinity were both snow and ice free.

Despite the havoc the blizzard had wreaked on Glenwood, it was fortunate to be only on the edge of the storm.

Over fifteen miles north of Glenwood, not far from Interstate 94 is the city of Alexandria, seat of Douglas County.

In 1960, 6,713 people called Alexandria home.

The first settlers who came to Alexandria were two brothers from Maryland, Alexander and William Kinkaid. They moved here in 1858. The settlement was named after Alexander Kinkaid, but the spelling of the name follows that of Alexandria, Egypt.

On November 5, 1878, the first passenger train arrived in Alexandria.

The FAA Airport at Alexandria was the recipient of 12 inches of snow from the March 1966 storm. In order, 1 inch fell on Wednesday, 4 inches on Thursday, 6 inches on Friday, and 1 inch on Saturday. This came to 1.05 inches of precipitation.

A daytime high of 31 was recorded at the airport on Wednesday March 2. A high of 33 was reached on both Thursday and Friday. The thermometer never dipped below 20 on any of those days.

Long Prairie, the seat of Todd County, lies north of Sauk Centre and west of Little Falls.

In 1960, 2414 people called Long Prairie home.

The city and township of Long Prairie took their name from the Long Prairie River. That stream courses through Todd County before emptying into the Crow Wing River. A long and generally narrow prairie that borders the river on its east side and whose width varies from a half mile to a mile gave the river its name. This prairie, which is about twenty miles in length, extends from the west line of Fawn Lake township southward to Lake Charlotte and the city of Long Prairie.

Permanent white settlement came to the village of Long Prairie with its platting in 1867.

It began snowing in Long Prairie at 7:30 p.m. March 2 and continued until March 5. Temperatures hovering just below the freezing mark made for a heavy wet snowfall in Long Prairie.

When all was said and done, 13.6 inches of snow had been deposited on Long Prairie. The official weather observer in town measured 2.65 inches of precipitation due to the storm.

As one went south from Long Prairie the snowfall amounts decreased quickly. They increased as one traveled north from the city.

The thermometer began to slide in Long Prairie after the storm. It reached a low of -19 on Monday morning before rebounding.

Long Prairie's high school boys basketball team ended their season in March 1966 with a 67 to 52 loss to heavily favored Henning in first round action of District 22 tournament play at Alexandria. Pacing Long Prairie in a losing effort was Mr. Eldred with 21 points and Mr. Hillman with 15 points.

Wadena lies about forty-five miles southeast of Detroit Lakes in Wadena County.

In 1960, 4,381 people called Wadena home.

Both the city, county, and township were named after the Wadena trading post which lay between the Leaf and the Partridge Rivers. They, in turn, disgorged into the Crow Wing River. At the same locality, a ferry crossed the Crow Wing River. A trail ran from Crow Wing past the Wadena trading post on to Otter Tail City and Pembina. This trading post sat atop a bluff on the west side of the Crow Wing River. The origin for the word "Wadena" is supposed to be an Ojibway on, meaning "a little round hill." Most likely, they were referring to the roundness of these bluffs.

The city of Wadena, situated fifteen miles west of its namesake trading post, owes its existence to the Northern Pacific Railroad. The construction of the rail line through the area led to its settlement in the fall of 1871. The following year Wadena would become the county seat.

The March 1966 blizzard really let Wadena have it. It began snowing in Wadena on Wednesday, and did not let up until Saturday.

The *Wadena Pioneer Journal* referred to Thursday's weather as being "winter's severest blast." Conditions were so bad in the city on Thursday, no schools were open in Wadena County. These included all parochial and public schools and the Wadena Area Technical Institute (WATI). Driving conditions for motorists Thursday morning were exacerbated by a light rain.

In New York Mills, the lousy weather forced Lund Metalcraft Company to shut down on Thursday.

Despite the frightful conditions, snow removal crews in the Wadena area worked Thursday night and Friday. They made this effort to keep driveways, streets, and roads open, in order that people could get to work. One of those participating in this job was Thorval V. Johnson, member services director for Todd-Wadena Electric Cooperative.

Local businessmen made a Herculean effort to keep the walks in front of their stores in Wadena snow free.

Conditions weren't any better out in the open countryside. Wooded areas along U.S. Highways 10 and 71 were conducive to large drifts that had been formed by wet snow. Areas of concern on U. S. 10 that forced motorists to slow down, included the viaduct between New York Mills and Perham (northwest of Wadena) and the Wing River Bridge at Verndale, seven miles southeast of Wadena. It was a common sight to observe drifts 8 feet high on county and state highways in the Wadena vicinity.

In spite of the weather, people really made an effort to make it to work or go about their business. It would be in these conditions that snowmobiles really shined. A snowmobile was employed by Roger Hosek of Jacobson Oil Company to travel the fourteen miles from his residence located on Minnesota Highway 210 three miles east of Hewitt to his place of work.

Employees of the *Wadena Pioneer Journal* had problems getting to work. It would be mid-morning Friday before three of them reached the office. Another employee never did show up that day. One member of the *Journal* staff, Sharon Limanen, took extra precautions on Thursday afternoon to ensure that she got to work on Friday. She had George Payne of Menahga bring her part of the way by snowmobile.

On Friday morning, Orlan Lien, Route 3, Wadena used a snowmobile to cover the eleven miles to Wadena, in order get his mail and stock up on groceries. Mrs. Howard Fulz, his aunt, caught a windy ride with Mr. Lien from her farm residence to her job at Modern Cleaners in Wadena.

During the storm employees of Bell Telephone Company used a snowmobile to inspect telephone lines.

Despite the inclement conditions on Friday, both the WATI and the Wadena Public School were open for classes. All the other schools in the county were closed that day.

On Friday, the roof on the turkey sheds at the Taves East Farm suffered considerable damage from the buildup of heavy wet snow.

Snowmobiles came to the rescue for some of the players on the Menahga Braves and Verndale Pirate basketball teams on Saturday. They were trying to get to the Sub-District 24 semi-finals being held at Staples Saturday evening. By riding on snowmobiles, they were able to get to their buses.

On Saturday, Roger Folkestad traveled from his residence on the airport road to work via a tractor.

Once the storm had passed, residents of Wadena could get out and see just how high the snow had been piled about town. Snow depths about the entrance to Wadena's Senior High School came within a few inches of the roof of the place.

To help with the snow removal in the Wadena area after the storm, the following advice was provided to the public. Those individuals who had vehicles parked on streets or along roadsides, were cautioned to attach a red flag to the top of the radio aerial. The sight of the red flags gave snow removal crews advance notice of the location of the vehicles.

By Monday morning, despite the poor road conditions, milk delivery to the Equity Creamery in Wadena was ninety percent of normal, according to its manager Joe Hansen.

It was quite a storm to remember for Ken Hall, the weather observer in Wadena. By 7 a.m. Friday, March 4, Wadena had received 22 inches of snow. Up to that time (March 1966), there had never been that much snow fallen on Wadena in a forty-eight hour time span. If more snow had fallen on Wadena in that time frame, Hall could not find it in the record books.

Mr. Hall arose at 5:45 a.m. Saturday to check his instruments. At that time, his anemometer was recording wind speeds from 56 to 58 mph. Unfortunately, just moments later, the anemometer was toppled by the high winds.

Precipitationwise, Thursday was the worst day of the storm for Wadena. The city had 13.5 inches of snowfall on it that day. Combined with the rain that fell the same day, Wadena's total precipitation for Thursday came to 1.32 inches.

In succession, over the next three days, Friday, Saturday and Sunday Wadena received 8.5, 6.1, and .8 inches of snow. When all was said and done, 28.9 inches of snow, 2.86 inches of precipitation, which also included Thursday's rain, were dumped on Wadena by the storm.

From September 26, 1965, through March 6, 1966, Wadena had received 65 inches of snow. Concerning the snowfall, Mr. Hall stated:

> *If 4.4 inches (of snow) falls during the rest of this month, it will match last year's March production of 33.3 inches, or the most snow within the county to fall in any month on record since 1905.*[13]

The thermometer registered pretty steady temperatures in Wadena during the blizzard. From Wednesday March 2 through Friday March 4, the thermometer varied only 9 degrees at Wadena. A low of 24 above was recorded all three days. A high of 33 above was recorded on March 3.

Dilworth, Hawley, Ulen, Ada, Twin Valley, Detroit Lakes and Mahnomen

Dilworth (1960 population of 2,102) lies three miles straight east of Moorhead.

It was a division point for the Northern Pacific whose officers gave the village its name.

One of the most terrifying stories of the March 1966 storm occurred three miles east of Dilworth. Living at that location were Mr. and Mrs. Dale Hendrickson and Cheryl, their two-and-one-half month old daughter in their trailer. Residents of Clay County since June 1965, the following November, the Hendricksons moved their trailer to its present locality.

In March 1966, Dale Hendrickson was employed by Ytsebo Drywall of Moorhead.

Around 9 a.m. Friday, the drifting snow began to envelop the trailer. About 11 a.m., with the belief that he could push the trailer's door open and lead his family to freedom, Dale tried to do just that and failed. The trailer was entombed in the snow.

Attempts by the Hendricksons to contact the outside world via telephone failed. Snow had shorted that out. Their next problem came when they lost both their heat and lights. The weight of all that snow had unplugged the trailer's electrical outlet.

When it rains, it pours (or snows). Next, the pressure and weight of the wind-driven snow started to buckle the trailer's walls. Time was running out for the Hendricksons.

Then, just when they needed a break, the Hendricksons got one. Around 11:30 a.m., their phone rang. It was a call to another party on the Hendrickson's party line. Interrupting the telephone conversation between the two parties (you could do that on party lines), Dale made a request for assistance. His appeal worked, as Clay County Sheriff Adolph Olsen and two deputies, with the assistance of two county snowplows, answered his call.

The rescuers were directed to the snow pile under which the Hendrickson were buried by their landlord, Lawrence Rehder. They began digging steps in the snow down to the trailer.

Trapped in their trailer the Hendricksons could hear the rescuers digging above them. To help them locate the easiest place to get out, Dale Hendrickson started to pound on the trailer's door.

Deliverance for the Hendricksons came at 2:30 p.m. when the lawmen got them out of their trailer.

Upon reflection of their ordeal, Mrs. Hendrickson remarked:

> *We didn't think that we were in too serious a trouble, but when we got outside, we found it hard to get our breath. The sheriff told us that if we*

had been inside much longer we probably would have used up all the oxy-
gen.[14]

On Sunday, it took the Hendricksons and his friends over half a day to dig out their ten by fifty foot trailer. They were trying to prevent food and water pipes from freezing. Unfortunately, their efforts were hampered by heaters that wouldn't work. Snow blocked vents were the problem.

Hawley (1,270 residents in 1960) lies about twenty miles east of Moorhead.

The city of Hawley owes its beginning to the Northern Pacific Railroad (the NP). That rail line completed a line from the east through Hawley to Fargo, North Dakota, in 1872. That same year, English colonists were the first to settle in Hawley.

The village and the surrounding township were known at first, as Bethel. But, then, as a tribute to General Joseph Roswell Hawley (1826-1905), the name was changed to Hawley. A resident of Connecticut, Hawley was one of the NP's original stockholders.

Around the Hawley area, with the exception of snowmobiles, trains were able to run longer than other modes of transportation. But, eventually the blizzard stopped even them. As the *Hawley Herald* noted:

> *Northern Pacific RR gave it the old college try, but the Blizzard of '66*
> *finally brought it to a halt.[15]*

Richard Palmer was the NP agent at Lake Park, Minnesota, in March 1966. Leaving his home in Hawley for work on Friday morning, March 4, Palmer got no further than the Becker County line. Because of whiteout conditions, he could no longer see U. S. Highway 10. Palmer hitched a ride back to Hawley in a truck. He never did make it to Lake Park that day. It would be the next day before Palmer was able to return his car.

The Northern Pacific agent at Gary, Minnesota, in March 1966 was Wes Cresap. On Thursday morning, March 3 he tried to make it to Gary from Hawley via State Highway 32. Finding it blocked, Cresap returned to Hawley and headed north on a county highway. Unfortunately, near the Lloyd Burnside farm, Cresap's automobile hit a snowdrift in the middle of the road. The encounter damaged the grill of his car.

Cresap headed out on foot for the Burnside farm. On the way he was picked up by a snowplow which brought him back to Hawley. Cresap then borrowed a car to take him to Gary. He did not make it back to Hawley until the following afternoon.

In March 1966, Bob Voss was a NP operator in Detroit Lakes. He departed from Hawley at 10 p.m. Thursday, March 3 aboard an NP passenger train. After completing his shift, Voss returned to Hawley the next morning on a freight train belonging to the Milwaukee Railroad. This was quite amazing, considering that the Milwaukee Railroad did not pass through Hawley. With its own line blocked, the Milwaukee Railroad freight train was attempting to continue on via another route. The NP gave the Milwaukee Railroad permission to run on its tracks.

After depositing Voss in Hawley, the train proceeded onward. It never made it to Fargo. As the *Hawley Herald* noted:

> *It was a valiant trip, but somewhere around Dilworth...the Milwaukee*
> *train disappeared into oblivion and was never heard of again. Trainmen*
> *are wondering if it will become the Flying Dutchman of the railway.[16]*

On Thursday night, a light engine took Timan Bakken, Tully Jacobson, and Lester Nelson, all of Lake Park, to Gary to clean switches. Their efforts allowed Train *No. 13*, destined for Winnipeg, to return to Dilworth.

The storm piled huge drifts onto rail lines, wreaking havoc. A local freight train encountered one on the Winnipeg line between Fertile and Gary. Disconnecting six of its thirty-one cars, the train proceeded on with them to Fertile. When the train returned for more cars, it derailed. After spending the night in the engine's cab, the three crewmen aboard the derailed train returned to Fertile aboard snowmobiles.

By the following Tuesday, conditions had improved considerably. According to Maurice Sperling, NP agent in Hawley, the NP's trains *No.1* and *No. 2* were running between Fargo and St. Paul. the NP's westbound *North Coast Limited* train remained stuck near Cleveland, North Dakota. This blocked westbound traffic between Fargo and Bismarck.

To get around this problem, on Monday the NP sent a train on Great Northern tracks to Grand Forks and then to Sidney, Montana. The train did not return to NP tracks until it reached Billings, Montana.

An equipment shortage prevented the NP from dispatching a train via the same route on Tuesday. Also, by Tuesday evening the Winnipeg Line was up and running again.

When snowdrifts get very large and hard, only rotary plows can cut through them. Unfortunately, a rotary plow the NP sent to work on the drift at Cleveland, North Dakota broke down. It was soon repaired and joined by a second rotary plow. While these plows worked at the drift from the east, another one from Washington state was going to chew on the west end of the drift. Until the train was freed, the NP could not resume its normal train schedule.

Further west, the NP's westbound *Mainstreeter* was moving again. The blizzard had stopped it at New Salem, North Dakota. The one hundred passengers aboard it took shelter in New Salem until the train could move again. The same was true for an NP *North Coast Limited* that was forced to stop at Glen Ullin, North Dakota. It was moving again.

The March 1966 blizzard dumped 1.03 inches of precipitation on Hawley.

Ulen is located about twenty-five miles northeast of Moorhead.

In 1960, 481 people called Ulen home.

The first person to take up residence at Ulen, and from whose name the town received its name, was Ole Ulen (1818-1891). He came to Clay County in 1872 and settled at Ulen.

The March 1966 blizzard descended on Ulen on Wednesday, March 2. Poor weather conditions forced Ulen's schools to let out classes at noon. Community activity in Ulen came to a grinding halt. The *Ulen Union* called it "the worst snow storm in 50 years."

A stalled NP freight train between Fertile and Gary prevented any rail service through Ulen from Thursday until Tuesday.

Having temperatures that remained fairly "mild" for the duration of the storm were a great benefit to emergency crews who had to be out and about during the blizzard.

Wind speeds of the storm reached 50 to 60 mph at Ulen. The wind whipped snow was pounded into drifts whose heights reached up to the eaves of quite a few buildings in Ulen.

For those who lived in trailers, the storm was especially troublesome. In some instances, the trailers were so buried in the snow, the residents within them were forced to call their neighbors for assistance. Their neighbors had to come over and dig them out, so they could make their exit from the trailers.

It would be late Saturday before conditions started to improve in Ulen. Almost two feet of snow had been dumped on this Clay County village.

On Saturday, the cleanup in Ulen began. Rotary plows were used to cut through the huge drifts quickly on the highways that passed through Ulen. The State of Minnesota dispatched a rotary plow to Ulen, and the machine arrived there Saturday afternoon.

There was such a large snowdrift in front of Harry Hilde's place, at the east end of Ulen, that clearing a single lane path through it required working at it from two different directions.

Snow had drifted so deep at the *Ulen Union* newspaper shop, that, on Saturday, the services of a mechanical snow scoop were required to clear a path to gain entrance to the building. On top of that, the newspaper's camera was not working. As a result, they were unable to get pictures of the large snowdrifts around town.

As late as Monday, blocked roads kept some Ulen area schools from reopening.

Conditions were so tough in the Ulen vicinity, it was Tuesday before some area farmers were able to have their driveways cleared of snow.

The storm forced the cancellation of most religious services in Ulen on Sunday, March 6. One exception to this was Bethlehem Church which held a service at 11 a.m. that day.

The blizzard had kept Ulen area farmers from getting to town to shop and take advantage of specials that stores were advertising. To accommodate the farmers, Ulen stores extended a lot of the shopping specials for another week.

A Clay County rotary plow helped with snow removal at Ulen on March 8 and 9.

Ulen's high school boys basketball team ended its season on March 8 with a loss to Battle Lake 89 to 65 in sub-district play at Detroit Lakes. Leading Ulen's scoring were Ardean Swenson with 22 points and Jerry Knutson with 12 points.

Minnesota State Highway 9 angles south from U. S. Highway 2 east of Crookston. About forty miles south of this intersection is Ada, which enjoyed a population of 2,064 in 1960.

Established in 1874, Ada is the seat of Norman County. During Ada's early days, a St. Paul man, William H. Fisher wore two hats for the St. Paul and Pacific Railroad. Not only was he its attorney, but also its superintendent. It was through his efforts in this latter capacity that a rail line to Ada was built.

The name "Ada" honors the memory of a daughter of William Fisher. Ada Nelson Fisher was only six years old at the time of her death in 1880.

The arrival of the storm in Ada was marked by 3 inches of snowfall on Wednesday, March 3. Schools in Ada and around Norman County let out early that day.

It was still possible to drive around Ada on Thursday. Travel conditions weren't impossible yet. The majority of store owners in Ada were able to make it downtown on Thursday to open their stores. The only thing they lacked were shoppers.

Unfortunately, the weather continued to deteriorate. Ada was on the receiving of 12 inches of new snow that day.

With vehicular travel around Ada impossible after Thursday, it would be the snowmobile that stepped up to help out in various capacities. Ada's City Hall served as the base of operations for a number of Ada's snowmobilers. They ran a sort of taxi service, delivering people and goods to where they were needed. For emergency runs, Dr.Kinkade didn't hesitate to utilize the services of a snowmobile. These machines were the means of travel for nurses going to and coming from the Ada Municipal Hospital.

On Friday, downtown Ada had the appearance of a ghost town. Few, if any businesses were open on Friday or Saturday. An additional 6 inches of snow fell on Ada.

Ada experienced a scare for a short while Friday afternoon. At the height of the storm, there was a fire alarm at 1:05 p.m. As things stood at that time chances of fire engines being able to make it to the scene of a fire on time were doubtful. Imagine, everyone's relief when it turned out to be a false alarm.

It was a nervous time for the family and friends of Thomas Habeck of Ada who was employed in Fargo. During the worst of the storm, he was reported missing. But, this story has a happy ending. Habeck found shelter at a farm in the Georgetown vicinity. When conditions improved, Habeck was able to get to a phone and let them know that he was safe.

The atrocious weather forced the cancellation of community events going on in and around Ada. Until conditions improved, people were told not to go outside.

By Saturday, food supplies for many Ada residents, especially bread and milk, were running low. No problem, snowmobilers stepped up to the challenge and stayed busy making grocery runs for them. Ada was the recipient of five more inches of snow that day.

The velocity of the wind during the blizzard at Ada varied from 30 to 60 mph.

The storm dumped 26 inches of snow on Ada, 2.65 inches of precipitation.

Temperatures at Ada during and after the storm ranged from a high of 32 on March 2 to -20 on March 7. But, the fact remains, as the storm raged, it simply did not get that cold in Ada. On Friday, March 4, when the intensity of the blizzard was the greatest, Ada recorded a low of 16 above.

Blocked roads and snowed in homes made travel impossible for many people who lived in the Ada vicinity. This led to the cancellation of Sunday church services in the majority of the area churches.

With 31 inches of snow on the ground at Ada, the digging out process was a slow laborious one. A very popular item in and around Ada after the storm were tractors equipped with scoops.

With the snow removal process complete in downtown Ada by Monday morning, business was returning to normal. As a rule, there was a lot of activity in stores-particularly grocery stores.

Ada schools were able to reopen Monday, March 7. Deep snow in certain places made for tough going for two of their bus drivers.

Two neighboring towns, Gary and Twin Valley, didn't have quite as smooth going. Another storm came through the area Monday night. Roads in their area that had just been opened on Monday became impassable again when drifting snow filled cuts that had been made through snowdrifts from the four day storm. As a result, they were unable to hold classes in Gary and Twin Valley on Tuesday.

The name Detroit Lakes has a French origin. A French missionary camped on the north shore of the lake one night. He saw the sandy bar that divides the lake into two sections and leaves a strait. In French, the word "detroit" means strait.

The city of Detroit Lakes (5,978 residents in 1960) was settled by Civil War veterans in 1871. Since its beginning in 1871, when Becker County was formed, Detroit Lakes has served as the county seat.

The arrival of the storm late Wednesday morning meant three days of "snowbound" activity for residents of the Detroit Lakes area. As with Frazee, the blizzard started with a mixture of rain and snow. By midafternoon, it was all snow. The inclement weather conditions forced the closure of all schools in Becker County for the remainder of the week.

Around noon Friday, as the storm raged, Mrs. O. H. Bursa, a Detroit Lakes resident, saw eight to ten robins in her yard. She told the *Detroit Lakes Tribune* "they (the robins) perched in a tree and a honeysuckle bush before disappearing into a patch of woods west of us."[17]

The lousy weather forced the postponement of the subdistrict basketball tournament, slated to begin Thursday night in Detroit Lakes. But, the continuing bad weather first pushed it back to Friday and Saturday, and then to Monday and Tuesday.

Because of poor road conditions, only seven jurors were able to make it to Detroit Lakes Thursday for the March general term of the Becker County district court. This forced Judge Chester G. Rosengren to postpone the term until 9:30 a.m. March 7.

Weather conditions stopped a dozen semi-trailers near Detroit Lakes. On Saturday morning, they were parked along U.S. Highway 10 east of Detroit Lakes. They had been moved off the highway by highway patrolmen. There was no travel of any kind in any direction from Detroit Lakes Friday night or Saturday morning.

Snow removal crews in the Detroit Lakes vicinity were unable to keep up with the blizzard, as roads and streets became impassable. They were open only between Detroit Lakes, Lake Park, and Mahnomen. But, stalled vehicles at Mahnomen blocked traffic beyond that point.

As could be expected, the storm wreaked havoc with snow removal efforts in Becker County and neighboring counties. On Friday night, conditions became so poor in western Becker County that snow removal crews from the Minnesota Highway Department were taken off the highways. As Vernon Johnson, Minnesota Highway Department District Maintenance Engineer at Detroit Lakes put it, "they just couldn't see"[18]

As of Saturday, U.S. Highway 59 north of the Mahnomen County line had been blocked for two or three days. In another direction U.S. Highway 10 was impassable east of Lake Park.

In order to expedite the snow removal, Johnson was trying to have equipment brought in from other parts of Minnesota. Once the storm let up, the plows intended to work around the clock to open the highways. Until then, as Johnson noted, "people will have to be patient-and stay home.[19]

Activity in Detroit Lakes during the storm was curtailed. Stranded travelers filled up the city's hotels and motels. Detroit Lakes itself did not shut down during the storm. Many businesses remained open. The number of downtown businessmen who chose not to go home at noon helped increase restaurant business there substantially.

Cars were buried under drifts in Detroit Lakes.

Many Detroit Lakes residents, unable to get their vehicles out of their garages, elected to travel via taxi. Operating from 7 a.m. to 9 p.m. each day, the taxis ran only where the streets had been plowed. As Robert Arnold of Courtesy Cab noted, business for taxis was quite brisk.

Weather conditions halted city and rural mail delivery in the Detroit Lakes area. Because of this, G. W. Magle, Detroit Lakes Postmaster, requested that customers pick up their mail at the post office.

Because of the atrocious weather, the majority of Detroit Lakes business establishments closed at 3:30 p.m. Friday. This action was a boost to employees trying to make it to their homes. As always, banks and grocery stores maintained their regular Friday night schedules. The banks were open from 7 to 9 p.m., and grocery stores stayed open until 9 p.m.

On Thursday, Northwestern Bell Telephone Company reported a dramatic increase in the number of long distance calls at its Detroit Lakes exchange. They went from a normal rate of 2,000 calls a day to 3,548 on Thursday. Telephone exchanges at Bemidji, Brainerd, Crookston, Detroit Lakes, Fergus Falls, Thief River Falls and Wadena averaged 1,200 long distance calls above their usual number.

To get employees to work so they could operate switchboards at the various exchanges, snowmobiles and company trucks were employed. The blizzard failed to disrupt Northwestern Bell's telephone service, and the company reported that it had suffered little damage from the storm.

Train service through Detroit Lakes was also affected by the weather. A re-routed Milwaukee Road freight train passed through Detroit Lakes on the NP tracks Friday morning but was stopped in Fargo at 1:28 p.m. the same day. Friday, NP's *Mainstreeter* went through Detroit Lakes, but got no further than Fargo. On the same day trips for NP trains *No. 2* and *No. 4* were canceled. The disruption of rail service amazed R. L. Petit, NP's agent at Detroit Lakes. He remarked, "I've never seen anything like it, and we've never been tied up like this before."[20]

The Soo Line was also having its share of problems with the weather. Although two of its freight trains passed through Detroit Lakes on Friday, they got no further than Glenwood and Thief River Falls, respectively. The Soo Line had two other trains with problems. Trains 9 and 10 (known collectively as the *"Winnipegger"*) did not make it to Detroit Lakes Friday or Saturday. The former stayed in Minneapolis, and the latter remained in Winnipeg.

Weather conditions could not prevent 100 students from attending the National Forensic (debating) League district tournament being held in Detroit Lakes March 4 and 5. Some of them came a considerable distance to make it to the tournament. Attenders came from Brainerd, Cloquet, Duluth Central, Duluth Denfield, Hibbing, Proctor, St. Cloud and Detroit Lakes.

On Friday night, the students were put up in private homes. Accommodations were made if they had to stay longer. Co-chairmen of the event were Mrs. Mary Adams and Martin Eia.

Events in Detroit Lakes had to be rescheduled because of the storm. The Detroit Lakes Jaycees had to postpone a planned orientation dinner and party from March 5 to March 19.

A March 4 meeting of the Detroit Lakes Barracks 2174, World War I veterans, had to be rescheduled. The commander of the group, Art L. Waldon, said the meeting would be held at 1 p.m. on March 11 at the American Legion Clubhouse in Detroit Lakes.

In two and a half days, the blizzard dropped 12 inches of snow on Detroit Lakes.

A total of 16 inches of snow, 0.67 inches of precipitation, fell a mile north-north-east of Detroit Lakes.

The temperature there stayed mostly in the 20's during the storm. A high of 30 degrees F. was recorded at that location both Thursday and Friday. On the days leading up to the blizzard, the thermometer climbed to 36 and 35 on March 1 and 2, respectively.

In high school boys basketball, Detroit Lakes enjoyed a good 1965-66 season. They defeated Moorhead, the No. 3 rated team in Minnesota, for the District 23 title. The team was coached by Orin Schueler.

On March 17, in Region 6 play at Concordia College in Moorhead, Detroit Lakes ended their season with a 73 to 56 loss to the Henning Hornets, the No. 2 team in the state.

Mahnomen County was organized December 27, 1906, from the eastern portion of Norman County.

Both Mahnomens, the county and the city of Mahnomen (population of 1,462 in 1960), take their names from the Chippewa word for wild rice.

The blizzard descended upon Mahnomen about noon Wednesday, March 2. Described as "the worst blizzard in 50 years", its path across the Dakotas and Minnesota, could be followed by listening to announcements of school closings and cancellation of a variety of public functions.

The movement of the storm into Mahnomen County on March 2, forced the closure of schools in the county that afternoon.

The storm brought vehicular traffic in the Mahnomen area to a standstill. Both Trunk Highways 31 and 59 were blocked most of March 3 and 4.

Blocked highways were a problem during the storm. On Friday morning, a state rotary plow dug out eight or ten trucks stalled about three miles south of Mahnomen on Trunk Highway 59. A similar problem occurred along U.S. Highway 59 between Mahnomen and its intersection with Trunk Highway 2 at Erskine. Impassable conditions resulted in the stalling of two or three dozen trucks along that stretch of road.

As elsewhere, one of the significant heroes of the storm in Mahnomen, was the snow-mobile. Utilizing Jack's Texaco as a headquarters, snowmobile owners responded to over 250 calls during the storm. They delivered fuel oil, groceries, medicine and other supplies. During shift changes at MCV Hospital, snowmobilers delivered the hospital staff to and from work. They helped others get to work.

Rudy Tupa, Mahnomen County Sheriff, appreciated the work of snowmobile owners, operators of emergency vehicles and snowplow operators. Because of them, no serious emergencies surfaced. As Tupa explained:

> This (lack of life-threatening situations) was because we were able to get help to take care of the requests we had before any of the situations became critical.[21]

The blizzard had quite an impact on Mahnomen area farmers. Storm conditions forced several dairy farmers to dump milk after they had used up all their storage on their farms.

By Friday, very little milk or cream was being processed at the Mahnomen Cooperative Creamery. Vern Hedman, manager of the creamery, reported that only nine farmers had brought milk or cream to the plant. The farmers used tractors to deliver their produce. One customer utilized a snowmobile for taking extra milk cans back to his farm for usage in storing milk or cream.

In spite of the fury of the storm, Mahnomen escaped without any bad shortages of food or other supplies. The last available milk supplies were delivered on Sunday, March 6. Kenny Johnstad employed a snowmobile to make home and retail deliveries. The arrival of new supplies of milk early Monday helped alleviate the shortage.

The storm forced the postponement of the subdistrict basketball tournament, scheduled to be played March 3 and 4, until March 7. On that date, the Mahnomen Indians were defeated in tournament action by Ada 78 to 46.

The demand for snow removal equipment in Mahnomen after the storm overwhelmed their operators. People wanted their sidewalks, service entrances, driveways and approaches cleared. There was such a demand that snow removal operators reported a backlog of forty to fifty calls.

By Saturday night, most of Mahnomen's streets and quite a few of its alleys were open.

By the afternoon of March 5, snowplow crews had opened both Highways 31 and 59. Round-the-clock work by snowplow crews opened all the trunk highways and over half of the county highways in the Mahnomen vicinity by March 7.

Once roads were opened dairy farmers came to the Mahnomen Cooperative Creamery in a steady stream. On Monday, March 7, despite the isolation of a few farmers, milk trucks were able to make it to most of their customers.

According to Oscar Nelson, U. S. Weather Bureau observer in Mahnomen, 16 inches of snow, equivalent to 3.50 inches of precipitation fell on the city during the storm. He said that ordinarily that much snow would yield about half as much precipitation.

Temperatures in Mahnomen dropped from a high of 38 on March 1 to -19 on March 7. It stayed in the teens there during the height of the storm.

A south wind on the night of March 7-8, helped bring in warmer temperatures. Unfortunately, the strong southerly wind also blocked many of the recently opened roads in the Mahnomen area.

Some schools in Mahnomen County reopened March 7. Blocked roads kept other schools closed. Nevertheless, school bus drivers, except for a very few instances were able to make their stops.

Crookston, Thief River Falls and Oklee

Less than twenty-five miles southeast of East Grand Forks is Crookston (8,546 residents in 1960), the seat of Polk County.

The American Crystal Sugar Company has a plant on the southwest side of Crookston that opened up in 1954.

Crookston's first settlers arrived in 1872. That same year a railroad, known as the St. Paul and Pacific, built a rail line from Glyndon through Crookston and then on to a place on the Snake River that would later be known as Warren, Minnesota. The village was named after Colonel William Crooks (1832-1907) who was the engineer primarily responsible for bringing the railroad to Crookston.

In 1862, in acknowledgement of Crooks railroad service to Minnesota, the first locomotive to operate in the state was named "William Crooks."

Crookston was in the group of Minnesota cities, such as Detroit Lakes and Fergus Falls, that received the 6 to 8 inches of snow that began falling on Wednesday.

Crookston received the full blast of the storm. It would last three days there. Even with the use of snowmobiles, Crookston police could hardly keep up with requests from people needing medical attention, fuel oil and with other emergencies. Stores were closed, and many businesses did not open, as employees were unable to get to work.

Although the wet snow was heavy and sticky, it would not support a person's weight. This made it extremely difficult to try walk through the drifts.

A snowplow was kept in front of the Crookston fire station to open a path in case there would be a need for the fire trucks. It was estimated that about ten cars were stalled on U.S. Highway 2 between Crookston and Erskine, a distance of thirty miles.

Stalled semi-trailer trucks caused the worst types of drifts to form on highways. Their height and length made for snowdrifts 5 feet high and 500 feet long along the trucks.

The blizzard forced an abbreviated edition of the *Crookston Daily Times* to be published on Friday. Making their way through the blizzard to the office via snowmobile driven by Lee Halverson, a *Times* employee, the *Times'* employees were able to put out that day's edition.

By Friday, most of Crookston's streets were blocked. Cars couldn't move around, and the city plows only worked on the main streets, trying to keep them open for emergency purposes. The Minnesota Highway Department refused to send out its plows until the storm let up and visibility improved.

A major problem was stalled cars and trucks on highways. Snowplows couldn't see them in zero visibility and accidents could result from this situation. Because of the storm, drugstores and clinics in Crookston were closed. To take up the slack, the hospital in Crookston handled emergency calls.

The storm also caused problems for Northwestern Bell Telephone Company. So many calls were being made during the blizzard, Bell's automatic circuits couldn't handle all the calls being made. So, Northwestern Bell made a request of its patrons to limit their telephone usage. If they had to make a call, the patrons were asked to keep their conversations short.

The duration of the blizzard led to shortages of items such as bread, milk and cigarettes. To alleviate the shortage, the residents of one Crookston neighborhood came up with a solution. They called around their neighborhood to find out who had either a shortage or surplus of these items, or had run out of them completely. After this was done, a swapping of these items was done around the neighborhood. Men with toboggans went from house to house around the neighborhood to complete these transactions.

At the Northwest School of Agriculture in Crookston, 5 inches of snow fell on Thursday, March 3, 7 inches on Friday, March 4 and 1 inch on Saturday, March 5. Collectively, this came to 13 inches of snow or .64 inches of precipitation.

Temperatures at that location before, during and after the storm, varied from a high of 33 above on Wednesday, March 2 to -23 on Monday, March 7.

Thief River Falls (population of 7,151 in 1960) is the seat of Pennington County. The Thief River coming from the north and the Red Lake River flowing from the southeast meet at Thief River Falls.

The platting of Thief River Falls was done in 1887. At one time above a dam in the city, steamboats operated on the Red Lake River all the way to Red Lake. The name for the city has a Chippewa source, which means "Stolen Land River or Thieving Land River."

Pennington County, the youngest county in Minnesota, came into existence on November 23, 1910. It was a part of Polk County from 1858 to 1896 and was a section of Red Lake County from 1896 to 1910. It was named after Edmund Pennington, president of the Minneapolis, St. Paul, and Sault Ste. Marie Railway (Soo Line).

Riding on easterly winds, the March 1966 storm began to drop snow on Thief River Falls Wednesday evening.

Despite the continuing snowfall on Thursday, highways remained open, though heavy with snow. Schools in Thief River Falls were closed Thursday. The wind picked up with gusts reaching 65 miles per hour.

Temperatures stayed relatively mild during the storm, falling to 16 on Friday and 0 on Saturday.

When it was all over, 25 inches of new snow (2.32 inches of precipitation) lay on the ground at Thief River Falls municipal airport.

The airport remained closed from Wednesday evening until Saturday afternoon. At that time, once the snow had been cleared away, it reopened.

At Thief River Falls, many cars and trucks became stalled because of deep drifts or wet wiring.

Arctic Enterprises, maker of the Arctic Cat snowmobile, provided an emergency snowmobile service the last two days of the storm, Friday and Saturday. Around 200 calls were received by the service, and from three to six snowmobiles operated steadily those two days.

Streets were plugged, and city plows did not venture out, until the worst of the storm had abated.

More than 1,000 telephone calls were made to Thief River Falls police from Wednesday evening on into Saturday.

Unfortunately, because of the road conditions, the police could only relay messages and contact the appropriate authorities who could provide the needed assistance. Conditions around Thief River Falls were so bad during the storm, that even with chains on their tires, the police were unable to drive their cars around town.

Radio station KTRF in Thief River Falls, which normally went off the air at midnight, stayed on the air through the night on Thursday to give weather information and notice of any cancellations and to broadcast emergency messages.

Oklee, a Red Lake County village, lies straight north of McIntosh and northeast of Crookston.

There were 529 people living in Oklee in 1960.

In 1909, the Soo Line Railroad began constructing a line from Moose Lake, Minnesota to Plummer, Minnesota. The line reached Federal Dam in 1910. That same year the line was extended through Bemidji, Clearbrook, Gonvick, Gully, Oklee and on to Plummer.

Oklee took its name from Ole K. Lee, on whose land the village was established.

The March 1966 storm was a three-day affair in Oklee. It arrived there Wednesday evening when it began to snow. The next morning, travel conditions had deteriorated to the point where about the only transportation possible was via snowmobile. This was because wind whipped snow filled in roads and streets as quickly as snowplows cleared them.

No school classes were held in Oklee Thursday and Friday.

The Oklee school reopened on Monday.

Oklee came through the blizzard in relatively good shape. A rural area east of Oklee experienced a short power outage. People in the Oklee area were happy about the fact they had come through the storm without any fires. Because, if any had occurred, blocked roads would have prevented fire trucks from getting to them.

One emergency did come up in the Oklee vicinity during the blizzard. Otto Kvasager, a resident of rural Oklee, was laid low by an appendicitis attack. Kvasager's home was located north of Oklee.

Taking him to the hospital in Thief River Falls was going to be quite a challenge. But, the Oklee ambulance, led by a county snowplow, answered the call. In the snowplow, was Ed Bernier, Ed LaJambe and Luaine Johnson. Mr. Kvasager rode in the ambulance driven by Herb Bakke. After a three hour trip, they delivered him to the hospital.

Mr. Kvasager came through the surgery in good shape. It was a good thing the rescue crew got him to the hospital when they did. Because, according to the doctor who looked after him, "He couldn't have made it through another night." [22]

Otto Bakken, Oklee's weather recorder, reported that the village had received 13 (1.16 inches of precipitation) inches of snow from Wednesday through Saturday. The storm had left snowdrifts as high as 20 feet in the Oklee vicinity. Fortunately, temperatures remained moderate during the blizzard.

As elsewhere, the blizzard left many residents of Oklee short of staples like bread, eggs and milk. These grocery store items quickly disappeared from shelves and were about gone Saturday afternoon. Like everything else, the supply trucks that replenished them were delayed in getting to Oklee.

Storm-blocked roads prevented dairy operators from getting their product to town. As a result their storage capacity was filling up quickly.

In cases where roads had been cleared and vehicular traffic was possible, farmers lost no time in getting their product to market. To catch up on the backlog of deliveries, on Sunday the Brooks Cheese Factory churned out 40,000 pounds of cheese.

By putting in long hours, snow removal crews got streets and highways in and around Oklee open again. Huge piles of snow (up to 12 feet high) on both sides of Oklee's streets made for poor visibility and hazardous driving in the days following the storm. A week later, snow depths in Oklee were still 2 feet on the level.

Oklee did receive a small amount of mail Thursday afternoon. After that they were shut off. On Sunday, a mail truck made it to Oklee. Even on Monday, not all of Oklee's mail and school routes were open.

In rural areas around Oklee, the snow removal process was a slow going one. As of Sunday, a lot of farmers had yet to clear their driveways of snow. To get from his farm about two miles southeast of Oklee to town, Archie LaCoursiere found another way. He employed a horse-drawn sled.

People were of the belief that the blizzard had been the cause of an explosion in an oil heater at the Don Stenberg residence north of Oklee. It was thought that the chimney had become blocked by wind driven snow, resulting in the explosion. The interior of the house suffered considerable smoke and soot damage. Fortunately, the Stenbergs were away from home when the explosion occurred.

The Jensen Mink Ranch at Oklee also encountered problems with wind driven snow from the storm. Snowdrifts formed in sheds where the Jensen mink cages were located, almost completely burying them in snow. Several days were required for a group of men to shovel the snow out of the sheds.

All in all, things could have been worse. An Oklee area resident put the March 1966 blizzard in perspective. That person remarked, *"It's better than a tornado or a cyclone."*[23]

Park Rapids, Walker and Backus

Park Rapids (3,047 residents in 1960), the seat of Hubbard County, is located in Minnesota's lake country, forty miles east-northeast of Detroit Lakes. It is surrounded by woods, especially those of the coniferous type.

Frank C. Rice gave Park Rapids its name. After platting the railway town of Riceville, Iowa he came to Minnesota. A couple of geographic features about the Park Rapids vicinity inspired Rice's choice of a name for the town. One was the parklike woods and prairies in the Park Rapids neighborhood. The other choice concerned rapids that used to be in the Fish Hook River before it was dammed.

Park Rapids received the full brunt of the storm. Accompanied by 25 to 50 mph winds, the blizzard dumped 27 inches of snow, 2.25 inches of precipitation, on the city. School classes were dismissed early on March 2 at Park Rapids, and they did not resume until March 8.

At Park Rapids on March 2, the storm began with a mixture of rain and snow.

But, as the weather began to deteriorate, it made things tougher and tougher for highway crews trying to keep the roads open.

Finally, on March 4, snow removal crews from the Minnesota Highway Department were pulled from roadways in the Park Rapids-Detroit Lakes area. As Vernon Johnson, district maintenance engineer explained it, "They just couldn't see."[21]

Rail and vehicular traffic in the Park Rapids vicinity ground to a halt March 3 and 4. The atrocious weather forced many truck drivers to park their rigs along highways in the Park Rapids area and wait out the storm. All highways in and out of Park Rapids were blocked. There was no rail service on the Northern Pacific and Soo lines.

To help people in need during and after the storm, the Park Rapids sheriff's office rented a snowmobile from Gulbranson Equipment Company in Park Rapids. They took sick people to the hospital and delivered feed to farms.

After the storm let up on Saturday, the digging out process in Hubbard County began. By Monday, highway crews had opened the main highways. Warmer temperatures on Tuesday greeted snow removal crews as they worked to open secondary roads.

Blocked roads in the Park Rapids area did not prevent one mail carrier from delivering the mail. By utilizing a horse from his riding stable, Walter Erickson was able to deliver mail to customers on his route.

The storm created a serious situation at the Schoolcraft Game Refuge near Park Rapids. Snow depths reached 47 inches at the refuge. There were 200 starving deer gathered or "yarded" in and around Jack Pine cuttings. The deep snow made it difficult for the deer to get around.

The problem was exacerbated by logging operations in the management area earlier in the year. Deep snow forced the deer to move into the cutting area. They ate the tips of Jack Pine slashings. Although the tips filled the deer's' stomachs, they were of little nutritional value.

On March 6, Park Rapids area sportsmen opened trails and delivered hay to the deer. Unfortunately, due to a hay shortage in Hubbard County, this was the last of the hay they had on hand. The sportsmen used snowmobiles to haul the hay bales, donated by area farmers, to the deer.

It was thought that an additional fifty to sixty bales would really help the deer make it to spring. So, the sportsmen were looking for more hay, preferably alfalfa.

On March 12, in high school boys basketball play, the Park Rapids Panthers lost to Littlefork-Big Fork Vikings, 60 to 58, in District 29 tournament action at Bemidji State College. They ended the season with a 72 to 47 victory over Walker on March 14.

Walker is located near Leech Lake and is twenty-eight miles northeast of Park Rapids. In 1960, Walker had 1,180 residents.

Walker was named after Thomas Barlow Walker.

Walker came to Minnesota in 1862. As a surveyor, Walker helped to locate parts of the St. Paul and Duluth rail line route.

In 1868, Walker started to buy large acreages of pine forests in northern Minnesota. Among those counties where Walker purchased land, was Cass County. In later years, Crookston, would be one of the many places where Walker constructed and ran a big lumber mill.

Established on September 1, 1851, Cass County took its name from a noted American statesman, Lewis Cass (1782-1866). After service as a brigadier general in the War of 1812, Cass became governor of Michigan Territory in 1813. He held that position until 1831.

Cass led an exploring expedition in 1820 that journeyed through Lakes Huron and Superior. His party continued on to the Upper Mississippi River via Sandy Lake. They followed that river up to Red Cedar Lake. At that time Red Cedar Lake was considered to be the source of the Mississippi River.

Later, the name of the lake was changed to Cass Lake in honor of the general. This was done by a member and narrator of the expedition, Henry Rowe Schoolcraft (1793-1864), who would discover the source of the Mississippi River, Lake Itasca, in 1832.

The *Walker Pilot* called the March 1966 storm, "the worst blizzard in the history of Cass County." The city of Walker did not have the privilege of being on the edge of the blizzard as places further south did. The storm gave it the full treatment.

It began snowing in the Walker area on Wednesday, March 2. Schools were forced to close.

Temperatures at Walker remained fairly close to the freezing point during the storm. This meant the snowfall coming down tended to be of the heavy wet variety.

The accumulation of this type of precipitation was hard on roofs. In Walker the roof of a building being utilized for boat storage gave way under the weight of the snow. Surprisingly, boats underneath it, escaped without any damage to them.

In a similar incident in Walker, the crush of wet snow brought down a big steel portico at the entrance of Gordon's Department Store (previously known as Lundquists). Fortunately, the sidewalk beneath the portico was empty of people when the structure fell down.

Backus, Minnesota, is on U.S. Highway 371 about fifteen miles south of Walker. Heavy wet snow forced the roof of a garage there to collapse on top of a car and tractor being stored in the building.

The storm lasted four days at Walker. Weather records for the Walker vicinity were kept at nearby Ah-Gwah-Ching. There, a total of 23.5 inches of snow, 2.57 inches of precipitation, had fallen during the blizzard. The Ranger Districts of both Outing and Backus tallied up a snowfall total of 22 inches. A snowfall of 17 inches left Pillager State Forestry with 29 inches of snow on the ground.

One Walker family, the Hollis Baileys, came home from the southern United States in time to be caught in part of the storm.

The blizzard really caught the timber operators at a bad time. Prices for pulpwood had risen to a level that had not been seen in years. The operators wanted to get the pulpwood shipped out before spring road restrictions went into effect on highways. One of them had planned on sending out twenty carloads of pulpwood.

However, the storm left the Walker area with blocked roads. Because of this and the road restrictions, it would be May before the operators could ship out the pulpwood. It would not be until then that the road restrictions would be lifted.

With such a heavy snowfall being hammered into hard drifts by ferocious winds, snow removal in Cass County would not be easy. And it wasn't. Even when the storm was raging, small plows worked nonstop.

The same could not be said for the rotary plows. They would shut down around 8 p.m. Their inability in the storm to see to turn around, and the fact they often became stuck led to this decision. Drifting snow filling in cuts just after the plows had passed through did not help matters.

With blocked roads and streets, residents of Cass County employed other means to get to work or go about their daily routine. Snowshoes were one way residents of Cass County getting about. Vernon McAllister used them to make a three and a half mile trek to Backus in order to get to work.

Impassable roads led to the cancellation of many church services on Sunday, March 6.

Mail service for rural areas did no resume until Monday, March 7. Although the trains bringing the mail were getting through, snow plugged tracks were not responsible for the several hour delay in the trains arrival. Rather, it was the difficulty encountered in removing the mail from snow-blocked depots.

The snow removal process in Cass County was a slow one. Jim Worcester, Assistant Cass County Engineer, noted that although in some cases their larders were getting low, residents of Cass County had remained patient and understanding. Large, hard snowdrifts were causing problems for both county and state snow removal equipment. The smaller snowplow equipped trucks were unable to make a dent into these hard drifts. The only recourse involved patience, i. e; wait until larger snowplows could be released from other places that had a more pressing need for them.

For example, the Crookston and Thief River Falls districts had very high snowdrifts. The only way roads in those areas could be opened was by using rotary plows. So, six state rotary plows were dispatched up there. One of those state rotary plows being sent to northwestern Minnesota was from the Walker area. This action meant that snow removal operations in Cass County would take longer than it would have otherwise. It was hoped that by the weekend following the storm that all county roads in Cass County would be open, and they would open private roads as quickly as they could.

A medical emergency led to one snowplow operator, Roy Mills, being dispatched from Walker to the Gull Lake vicinity (down by Brainerd) to clear snow from roads. The snowplow operator down there was in the hospital. Mr. Mills rode the last mile and a half on a Ski Doo snowmobile to the snowplow.

The piled up snow in Walker was sent by truck out onto Leech Lake.

Generally speaking, it was tough going in the Walker district after the storm. For a day, motor vehicles could not get through on Minnesota Highway 87 east of Walker towards Park Rapids. Snowdrifts on Highway 6 at Cohasset brought traffic there to a standstill.

Hard packed drifts south of Longville on Minnesota Highway 87 delayed snow removal there for half a day. As the small snowplow equipped trucks were enjoying little success in snow removal on Minnesota Highway 64 between Akeley and Motley, ten-ton trucks were dispatched to do the job.

Stuck snowplows on Minnesota Highway 64 north of Leader forced a man coming from Minneapolis in his car to turn around and go through Brainerd in order to reach Akeley.

Temperatures at Ah Wah Ching during the storm stayed between 24 and 33 above. Once weather conditions improved the thermometer began to slide to reach a low of ten below on Monday morning.

McIntosh, Gonvick, Fosston, Bagley, Shevlin and Leonard

Mcintosh is close to forty miles southeast of Crookston on U.S. Highway 2.

McIntosh enjoyed a population of 785 in 1960.

The Great Northern Railroad ran its line through McIntosh. The individual for whom the town derived its name was a man by the name of McIntosh. In addition to being part owner of the townsite, he also had a hotel in the village.

Accompanied by easterly winds it began to snow in McIntosh Wednesday afternoon March 2, 1966. By 11 o'clock that night, the winds had veered to the northeast and were increasing in strength.

Despite the snowfall and winds, it was still possible to travel on highways, fairly deep in snow, in the McIntosh area Thursday morning. But, deteriorating conditions brought that traffic to an almost complete stop that afternoon. Hotels and motels in towns along U.S. Highway 2 filled to capacity with stranded motorists.

There was no school in McIntosh on either Thursday or Friday.

As with so many other places in the path of the storm, the fury of the storm in McIntosh was at its greatest on Friday.

The blizzard continued to leave McIntosh with new snow and strong winds on Saturday. It began to letup that afternoon. It quit snowing. But the heavy ground drifting was slower to die down. In spite of the continuation of the ground drifting, conditions had improved sufficiently to allow snowplows to commence with the humongous job of opening roads and highways.

The high winds made it difficult to measure total snowfall in eastern Polk and Northern Clearwater Counties. But, a total of around 19 inches was a figure that most sources agreed upon.

Snow removal crews went quickly to work. East of McIntosh on U.S. Highway 2 on Sunday morning, rotary plows cut through a snowbank. With some exceptions, the plows had the main highways in the McIntosh vicinity opened for traffic by noon Sunday. They were also able to get some county highways open.

As there were still roads blocked with snow on Monday, no school classes were held in McIntosh that day.

As the cleanup continued in McIntosh in the aftermath of the storm, snow removal equipment left huge piles of snow all over the place. Single lane paths were cleared down streets. These two factors reduced visibility for drivers quite a bit. So they were urged to use a cautious approach when coming up to intersections.

One McIntosh resident, Mrs. Willies Role, was storm bound for three days aboard a passenger train in North Dakota. After being gone for a month to California, she was returning to McIntosh. Out in California she visited her three sons and their families. During her and the other passengers ordeal aboard the train, railroad officials kept them warm and well fed.

Gonvick lies in Pine Lake Township in western Clearwater County northeast of McIntosh. A railroad town, Gonvick took its name from a pioneer Norwegian settler of the area.

There was a storm related tragedy at a farm six miles southwest of Gonvick. A fire had broken out at the home of an elderly woman, Mrs. Anna Rud, age 80.

Living not far away from Mrs. Rud was her daughter and husband, Mr. and Mrs. Carl Hoven. Their contact with Mrs. Rud earlier in the evening revealed nothing out of the ordinary. When she woke up about midnight, Mrs. Hoven noticed her mother's house in flames. Intense heat drove Carl Hoven back when he tried to enter the building.

A call was placed to the Gonvick fire department. But, the road to Mrs. Rud's place was so heavily drifted with snow that a snowplow had to lead the way for the fire truck behind it. As they were coming into the farm, the snowplow slid off the road. This was due to the side pressure on the plow caused by very heavy drifting of snow.

There were not enough snow shovels on hand for all the volunteers along (about twenty-five) to shovel. As the road was being opened, some firemen trudged through four foot deep drifts with fire extinguishers. They proceeded on into the farmyard. They did this to keep the fire from spreading. Their efforts were successful as they kept the fire from spreading to other buildings. Unfortunately, Mrs. Rud did not survive the fire.

Fosston (1,704 residents in 1960) lies along U.S. Highway 2 in eastern Polk County, eight miles southeast of McIntosh. Fosston has been described as "where the pines meets the prairie." In this area the woods of Minnesota give way to the prairie.

It took its name from the first merchant to establish a business in the village, Louis Foss.

In the early days, horses and oxen were the means by which supplies were brought to the Fosston area, either from Crookston or Detroit (later Detroit Lakes).

Pioneer settlers made quite an effort to lure railroads through their vicinity. They finally interested the St. Paul, Minneapolis, and Manitoba Railroad (Great Northern).

The idea of a rail line connection between the Great Lakes and Red River Valley grain fields appealed to them. So, in 1886 a route from Crookston to Fosston was surveyed. The construction of the forty-five mile between the Crookston Junction was done two years later. The line reached Fosston on November 24, 1888.

For the next ten years, Fosston which was at the end of the rail line enjoyed a lot of business. But, the completion of the Great Northern line to Bagley in 1898 ended that status for Fosston. Great Northern continued to push the line east across Minnesota through Cass Lake, finally reaching Duluth in 1907.

The storm descended upon Fosston Wednesday evening. Poor weather on Thursday forced the cancellation of school in Fosston and the rescheduling of the sub-district basketball from Thursday and Friday to Monday and Tuesday.

There was no mail delivery in or out of Fosston from Wednesday until Monday. Even then, the inability to get around meant a much reduced mail delivery.

Being on a major highway like U.S. 2 meant there were a lot of stranded motorists in Fosston. The situation was exacerbated by a truck that had jack-knifed on U.S. 2, blocking the road. The accident which occurred in the vicinity of an outdoor theater that was located between Fosston and McIntosh.

Snowdrifts piled up around the truck. A traffic snarl ensued with around 100 automobiles piling up behind each other. These stalled cars proved to be a good snowfence, as the blizzard whipped up drifts on and around them.

By Thursday afternoon, it was evident that Fosston did not have sufficient housing for all the stranded motorists. However, by employing emergency measures, this crisis was solved. This involved locating private homes that would give stormbound motorists shelter for the duration.

The coming of age for snowmobiles, which occurred in other hamlets in the path of the March 1966 blizzard, was repeated in Fosston. They made emergency runs delivering fuel oil and milk on toboggans pulled by the sleds.

Blocked roads prevented cattleman from getting to their farms to feed their livestock. As a result, snowmobiles were pressed into service to do that job.

Milk trucks couldn't get out to dairy farms to pick up milk during and after the storm. Snowmobiles alleviated this situation. Toboggans hitched to the snowmobile had empty milk cans on them. Their drivers delivered the cans to the dairy farms where the milk could then be placed in storage.

As usual, while one place is getting hammered by lousy weather, another one is enjoying fabulous conditions. Such was the case at Fosston. The local newspaper, the *Thirteen Towns*, had this story to relate about such an incident that happened as the March 1966 storm raged:

> Some people just don't have a heart. In the middle of our snowstorm Thursday night, Albert Johnson called from Texas and said that he and Ed Haugstul had just finished a round of golf. He added that the temperature was around 90.[24]

A couple of Fosston residents, Dr. and Mrs. E. L. Sather, spent more time away from home than they intended. They departed for Fargo on Wednesday, expecting to return the same day. But events did not go as they had planned. Storm conditions in Fargo on Wednesday forced the Sathers to remain there for the night. A lull in the storm on Thursday allowed them to leave Fargo at noon.

Unfortunately, deteriorating storm conditions prevented the Sathers from getting any farther than Crookston. Once there, they found the motels to be snowed in. Luckily, for stranded travelers like the Sathers, there were rooms available at the hotels.

The Sathers were not the only Fosston residents stranded in Crookston. Among the others were students who were attending Concordia College in Moorhead. As with the Sathers some of them made it back to Fosston on Saturday. For others it would be Sunday before they made it home.

The storm finally left the Fosston area Saturday. There were 22.5 inches of new wind driven snow on the ground at the Fosston Power Plant (2.36 inches of precipitation). That brought the depth of snow at the power plant on Saturday to 35 inches. In terms of snowfall, the daily breakdown was this: 0.5 inch on Wednesday, 10 inches on Thursday, 9 inches on Friday and 3 inches on Saturday.

From a high of 33 above on Wednesday, March 2 at the Fosston Power Plant, the thermometer gradually fell, until a low of -19 was reached on Monday, March 7.

The snow removal process in Fosston commenced Saturday morning. Initial efforts concentrated on clearing one-way "tunnels" or lanes through drifts on highways and Fooston's streets. That afternoon, n U.S. Highway 2 was opened for traffic between Fosston and McIntosh.

The editor of the *Thirteen Towns*, Franklin Vikan, rode around on a snowmobile driven by Jerry Speckeen Saturday morning to take pictures of the storm's effects. He did this before the snow removal process began on Fosston's streets. The March 10, 1966, edition of the *Thirteen Towns* had photos of what he had seen. The following stories tell what Mr. caught on film.

Piled up snow in front of the *Thirteen Towns* newspaper office forced employees to "tunnel" their way to the building's entrance.

The parking lot of the Red Owl store had a large drift in it.

The depth of a snowdrift in front of the bank in Fosston reached almost to the bank's canopy. In a photo at that location, Fosston police chief, Adolf Retzer, can be seen pointing at a sign that reads "15 minute parking." However, on Saturday morning before Fosston's streets were plowed, the only automobiles parked on Fosston's Main Street were storm-stalled ones.

Utilizing a snowmobile is how Dr. McNeil reached his office in Fosston Saturday. He parked the machine on top of a snowbank that sat in front of his office.

Not much was showing of Mrs. Norman Dokken's automobile Saturday morning in the aftermath of the blizzard. Parked in front of her residence on Second Street the car was pretty well covered with snow.

In northeast Fosston, a humongous drift sat in front of the Bill LaVoi home. From street level only the upper floor windows could be seen.

In the same neighborhood, drifts as high as 12 feet encircled the Kenneth Moody residence.

There was a snowdrift whose height was close to that of the apex of the southeast school addition.

At Fosston's main intersection, the Mobil Oil and Standard Oil stations were across the street from each other. The intersection there was buried in snow. But, through quick action by snow removal crews Fosston's downtown was "snow-free" by Monday.

When the March 1966 storm arrived in Fosston, Clarence Offerdahl still had Christmas decoration up in front of his house. After the blizzard had departed the Fosston vicinity, not much of the decorations, among them a "Joyous Noel", could be seen above the snow.

It would be the next morning before the cleanup really got under way full bore. Among the equipment being pressed into service were large earth moving machines, better known by their moniker as "turnapulls." Other snow removal equipment being utilized were bulldozers and front-end loaders.

Once the cleanup was underway, trucks and turnapulls were employed to haul the snow out to the fairgrounds. It was calculated that 528,000 cubic feet of snow was moved from about ten blocks of Fosston' streets.

The March 1966 blizzard prevented subscribers to the *Thirteen Towns* from getting their March 3 copy of the paper until March 7, 1966. The four day delay in delivering the paper to patrons was possibly the longest in the eighty-two year history of the newspaper.

Fosston's high school boys basketball team ended their season on March 7, when Bagley defeated them 58 to 46 in Sub-District 30 Tournament action at Clearbrook.

School classes did not resume in Fosston until Tuesday morning.

In March 1966, Jim Hanson and his family lived on a 40 acre farm a mile from Fosston. Jim's father worked for Land O Lakes. Jim remembers watching television during the storm. As any school kid, he was happy to get out of school because of the storm.

The blizzard had left a large snowdrift in front of Jim's house. A rotary snowplow clearing the road in front of the house deposited even more snow on the drift, making it higher.

Jim remembers that when the school bus came to pick him up for school, he could only see the running lights located high on the sides of the bus.

In cutting through the drift the rotary snowplow left the side of the drift next to the road with the face of a sheer cliff. The Hansons cut steps in the drift on the side of the drift next to the house to enable them to climb up it.

But the vertical cut on the other side of the drift made it too steep to descend. So, Jim and other members of his family dug a tunnel through the drift. Therefore, when the school bus came, the Hanson children would climb up the steps they had cut in one side of the drift and slide down through the tunnel onto the road to meet the waiting school bus.[25]

Lying 17 miles southeast of Fosston along U.S. Highway 2 is Bagley, the seat of Clearwater County. The lumber business is an important industry at Bagley.

In 1960, 1,395 people called Bagley home.

The city's name honors a pioneer lumberman who worked along the Clearwater River in the Bagley area, Sumner C. Bagley. Later, (1885) he made Fosston his home until his death in 1915.

Before the coming of the railroad to Bagley, only one wagon trail passed through Clearwater County. Beginning in Fosston the trail passed through Bagley and then angled north to the Red Lake Agency. Bagley did enjoy a connection with Bemidji on a narrower less travelled route. West of Bagley was a rail head at Fosston. To the southeast, over sixty miles away, was a rail connection to Leech Lake.

That all changed in 1898. Starting at Shevlin, GN constructed a line east and west from that village. The line was built through Bagley west to Fosston and south to Ebro. People enjoyed watching the progress of the construction. They would put on their finest clothes and check out the construction of the rail line on Sunday afternoons. James J. Hill himself, was aboard the first passenger train that passed through Bagley on September 21, 1898..

Bagley really got hammered by the March 1966 storm. No classes were held in schools in the Bagley vicinity Thursday and Friday. The basketball tournament had to be postponed twice.

Through the raging blizzard, city crews worked to keep Bagley's streets passable for traffic. While they were unable to keep all of them open all the time, the snow removal crews didn't give up.

For the duration of the three-day storm, the ability to travel around Bagley was not impossible. This can be shown by a picture on the front page of the *Farmers Independent* taken of Bagley's Main Street during the height of the storm. The photo shows the street to be pretty well plowed out. The end result of the continuous plowing was that, by the time the blizzard was letting up Saturday morning in Bagley, its primary thoroughfares were open for traffic.

An attempt to do a Good Samaritan deed backfired Thursday on Harvey Courtney, a cashier at First National Bank in Bagley. He thought any customer who made it to the bank through the blizzard should be rewarded for their efforts. So, he journeyed through the storm to a local bakery, purchased rolls, and then returned to the bank. A pot of coffee was brewed up by the ladies working at the bank. Courtney didn't think many "hardy souls" would brave the elements and come to the bank.

But Mr. Courtney was in for a surprise. Over a hundred bank patrons made it to the bank before it closed for the day. This necessitated a second trip to the bakery, at which time, the bakery's entire bismarck supply was purchased.

The storm left a 4 feet deep snowbank in front of the Faith Lutheran Church in Bagley.

The blizzard forced the Bagley High School Music Department to reschedule their annual Mid-Winter Pops Concert from March 3 to March 10, 1966.

As was the case throughout much of the storm area, snowmobiles performed an important service in Bagley as the blizzard raged. A good example was a couple of Bagley grocery stores, Olson's Grocery and Hartz Supermarket.

Olson's Grocery and Curtis Lundell came to the rescue for Bagley residents who needed groceries as the storm raged but couldn't get to the store. Lundell employed both his pickup and snowmobile to make deliveries. Where it became impossible for him to get through with his pickup, Mr. Lundell pressed his snowmobile into action.

A similar emergency service was performed during the blizzard by employees of Hartz Supermarket in Bagley. One of them, Bradley Hanson, delivered groceries on his "Sno Cat."

Telephone line repairs were needed at Ebro. But, impassable roads ruled out getting there via motor vehicles. So Aron Trandem, the individual making those repairs, enlisted a driver on a snowmobile to take him there.

The REA in Bagley reported no power outages during the course of the storm.

Clearwater County had few emergencies during the blizzard. The Clearwater County Sheriff answered one emergency call and transported a lady to the hospital.

On a sad note a Bagley area resident, Mrs. Elsa Iverson, age 61, perished in the March 1966 blizzard near Cook, Minnesota. After her vehicle had become stalled, Mrs. Iverson headed out into the storm to get assistance. She never made it. Snow removal crews recovered her body.

The passing of the storm Saturday morning revealed that one Bagley street, a block south of U.S. Highway 2, to be open to only one-way traffic in the middle of the street. This was because deep snow prevented cars from parking within ten feet of the curb. However, because of hard work done by Bagley snow removal crews, by the next morning, this street was completely open. The street a block north of U.S. Highway 2 also opened for traffic on Sunday.

The scene leading to and around the Clearwater County Memorial Hospital in Bagley Saturday morning was one of huge snowdrifts. A road leading from Minnesota Highway 92 to the hospital had snowbanks on it that just about completely enveloped it. Roof-high snowdrifts completely hid the reception room entrance to the hospital.

The storm left high snowdrifts in front of the Benny Bestul residence on the west side of Bagley. Once snow removal operations commenced, piles of snow around seven feet high almost blocked the Bestul home from view.

At the Bagley public school, snowdrifts just about completely enveloped a driver training car, a station wagon and two school cars. School entrances were blocked with snow. Both motor vehicles and school entrances were dug out on Saturday.

The snow removal process in the countryside around Bagley was not completed as quickly as that in town.

The blizzard had forced the closing of U.S. Highway 2 west from the Mileage Gas Station to Fosston from Thursday March 3 to Saturday March 5. The problem there was exacerbated by cars that had tried to drive that stretch of road and had become stalled. The presence of them on U.S. 2 prevented snowplows from getting through.

Conditions east of Bagley allowed for some traffic on U.S. 2. Thicker woods, especially coniferous trees east of Bagley, also helped. Heading west, the nearer one got to Bagley, the more open the countryside became.

As of Saturday morning March 5, there were fifteen trucks and as many cars stranded at the Mileage Station in Bagley. They were waiting for U.S. 2 to be opened west to Fosston. And it was-that afternoon.

The blizzard had kept snowplows from reaching Clearbrook on Thursday. On that day, they could get no further than the Braget place. On Saturday the plows reopened the stretch of Minnesota Highway 92 from Bagley to Clearbrook.

Because of the high winds and the immensity of the snowfall in Clearwater County, as of March 10, a few of the county roads were still closed. There were people in rural areas who still could had trouble getting out.

Concerning the snow removal process the *Farmers Independent* had this to say:

> County crews are working and doing a good job, but they have a lot of territory to cover, so it will take a little time.[26]

The *Farmers Independent* compared the March 1966 storm with those of the past:

> There are still a few long-lived souls around who can remember the storm that has gone down in history as "The Great Blizzard of 1888." It was something to remember! The toll it took in human suffering makes the other "great blizzards" of the past look like pikers. Books could be filled with tales of experiences in that storm, tragic stories of heroism and pathos, of miracles of survival, and horrible? death.
>
> Those who remember are generally glad to tell such stories-even, if need be, without narrative embroidery. But never again, after the storm that hit northern Minnesota and North Dakota last week can the oldsters smugly play narrations on the theme "you just don't get winters like we did when I was a boy."
>
> The famed blizzard of '88 did have two elements that the blizzard of 1966 fortunately lacked. One of these was temperatures below zero, which some people consider a prime requisite to justify the name "blizzard". The other was the heavy loss of life: 400 died in that storm 78 years ago. In this immediate area, no lives were lost, but two were reported dead in North Dakota.
>
> The Great Blizzard of '66 will give youngsters something awesome to tell their grandchildren some years hence.[27]

In a rescheduled tournament being held at Crookston, Bagley's high school boys basketball team, the Flyers, ended their season on March 11, with a 70 to 51 loss to Ada. Both teams were playing for the District 30 championship. Seniors Greg Olson and Harlan Highberg paced Bagley's scoring with 13 and 8 points respectively.

Shevlin is located seven miles straight east of Bagley on U.S. Highway 2.

Both the town and the township it lies in took their names from a Minneapolis businessman, Thomas Henry Shevlin (1852-1912).

Shevlin's activities in the timber industry included both logging and lumber manufacturing. In fact, he served as president of several such companies. His businesses did a lot of harvesting of pine trees in Clearwater County.

The Shevlin area had its share of people (especially elderly) isolated by the deep snow of the '66 storm. Young men on snowmobiles and toboggans came to their rescue. Included in this group were three guys from Bagley, Don Higginbotham, Austin Larson, and Gene McBain. Their deliveries included fuel oil to the Bill Olsons and groceries to other people. They encountered a blocked door at Anna Reiten's place.

On Thursday, March 3, a snowplow had to answer a call from the Frank Ballek farm near Shevlin. The Ballek's daughter, Annie had suffered a staple induce eye injury. She was taken through the storm to a hospital in Bagley.

A Clearwater County resident, Mrs. Melvin E. Johnson, reported that in Popple Township people were still dealing with snow removal a week after the storm and wouldn't be done for quite some time either. Her children were sure enjoying playing on 7 foot high snowbanks. She said that it took photos of the snowdrifts to make a person comprehend how tough things were.

Located directly north of Shevlin in Dudley township is the village of Leonard which is on the Soo Line. George H. French, was a pioneer merchant in Leonard. Leonard French was his first child, and the village was named after the lad.

Leonard came through the '66 blizzard without any fire or medical emergencies. The Leonard vicinity was buried in deep snow. There was no school in Leonard on Thursday or Friday, and the town was without mail service for a couple of days.

The digging out process was a slow one. Blocked roads prevented dairy farmers from getting their milk to market. They were forced to dump it. One of them had to dump his milk until the road to his place was opened on Sunday.

Glen Langseth, a Leonard area dairy farmer, really had a tough time after the blizzard. As the storm raged, Langseth labored to get milk and cream to take to town. While enroute Monday morning, with six cans of milk and four cans of cream in the back his pickup, the vehicle began sliding and went backwards off the road. Out the back-gone were the milk and cream, spilled out onto the snow.

Monday morning, a snowplow passed through Leonard clearing the Soo Line of snow.

That same day school classes resumed in Leonard. School buses picked up school children where possible.

The Clearwater County township of Bear Creek took it name from Bear Creek from a local stream. That brook's claim to fame is that it flows into the Mississippi River in Section 26 of Bear Creek Township.

One Bear Creek resident, Mrs. M. Trigland, had this to say about the March 1966 blizzard:

> Our Spring was rather short-lived, wasn't it? Now it's snow, snow, yes, mountains of it, wherever you look. The blizzard of '66 will be long remembered by the younger generation.[28]

Bear Creek Township came through the '66 storm without any major emergencies. As elsewhere in Clearwater County, this was fortunate. This was because so many roads were impassable, and it took some time to open them. Throughout the duration of the blizzard, electrical and telephone service was maintained in Bear Creek Township.

Before the storm arrived, some Bear Creek Township area residents left to attend a funeral for Merle Frazee at Pelican Rapids, Minnesota. Herman Evermoen, Mrs. Tom Haug, Almer Hole, and Mr. and Mrs. August Lundeen departed for Pelican Rapids early Wednesday. Unfortunately, before they arrived in Pelican Rapids weather conditions had begun to fall apart. So, instead they dined at the Frazee residence and stopped at the Funeral Home. After that, they immediately departed for home.

Two other couples, the Andersons and Johnsons, also headed for Pelican Rapids to attend the funeral. But inclement weather forced them to head for home before they reached Pelican Rapids.

Warren, Argyle, Stephen, Kennedy, Hallock, Karlstad, Strandquist and Middle River

Warren, the seat of Marshall County, is about thirty miles northwest of Crookston.

In 1960, Warren had 2,007 residents.

Warren took its name from the general passenger agent of the St. Paul, Minneapolis and Manitoba Railway, Charles H. Warren. By the summer of 1878, that railroad and its tracks had reached Warren. By the end of the year, there was train service through Warren all the way to Winnipeg.

The city of Warren was platted in 1879-1880.

A wet snow began falling on Warren about 6 p.m. Wednesday, and it continued to snow all day Thursday. The snowfall on Friday was accompanied by 30 to 40 mph winds, with gusts over 60 mph.

The blizzard prevented some employees at the Good Samaritan and Emmaus Lutheran Homes and Warren Hospital from getting to work, as they lived in the country. So, other employees who either lived in Warren or couldn't get home stayed on to work around the clock Thursday and Friday. Many were able to get to and from work via snowmobile.

Warren ran out of both milk and bread during the storm. The creamery and stores expended their milk supplies on Friday, and did not receive any more milk until Sunday.

By Saturday morning, the Warren Bakery was out of bread. The previous day, Mayor Fournier (also the baker) reported that he had 300 loaves of bread remaining. That was why he did not make any bread Saturday morning. However, with all the bread gone, and people wanting more, Mr. Fournier baked more bread Saturday afternoon.

On Saturday, it quit snowing, with the sun coming out at noon. The winds died down about 5 p.m.

Temperatures during the storm varied between 21 and 26 above on Thursday and 17 to 22 degrees on Friday.

Warren received 12.35 inches of snow from the storm or .98 inches of precipitation.

It was estimated that the blizzard left twenty stalled cars on U.S. Highway 75 between Warren and the Canadian border.

In the largest snow removal operation in Warren's history, City Engineer Wendell Larson's crews had most of the downtown area cleared of snow after five days of work. Some of it was around the clock. Residential streets were to be made passable, but not cleared of snow. As time permitted some back alleys were to be plowed out.

Although, overtaxed at times, Warren's telephone facilities kept operating practically uninterrupted during the storm. But, people did have to wait until someone got off the telephone so, they could make a call.

The blizzard disrupted mail service to Warren. On Monday, March 7 city carrier John Carlson used a snowmobile to deliver the mail. The post office received more mail that day (through March 7, 1966) than on any other day in its history. A lot of it consisted of magazines and newspapers. The next day, the Warren post office handled the most first class mail it had ever received (through March 8, 1966).

Roads in the Warren area were generally blocked from Wednesday evening until Saturday afternoon. On the level in Marshall County, snow depths averaged about 30 inches.

A snowplow, pushed by two diesel units, opened the railroad tracks Saturday night at Warren, Angus, and Stephen.

According to Marshall County Civil Defense Director, John O. Peterson, the county experienced very few emergency calls.

Argyle lies about nine miles north-northwest of Warren.

It boasted a population of 789 in 1960.

The origins for the name of this Minnesota city, a township in Maine, and cities in nine other states comes from a county in western Scotland with the same name. Solomon G. Comstock, a Great Northern Railway Company lawyer, gave Argyle its name. Comstock entered this world on May 9, 1842, in Argyle, Maine. After his arrival in Minnesota in 1869, Comstock took up residence at Moorhead, Minnesota.

The thermometer reached a high of 36 in Argyle on March 2, 1966. But, that night it began to snow in Argyle and continued to do so for the next four days.

The onrushing blizzard kept Argyle's two schools from opening their doors Thursday and Friday.

Except for snowmobiles, vehicular traffic in and out of Argyle during the storm was nonexistent.

Those businessmen who tried to work as the blizzard raged Thursday and Friday faced 12 foot drifts as obstacles.

Once again, snowmobiles and their drivers came to the rescue to a city under a wintery siege. Deliveries by them included fuel oil, groceries and other needed goods. For those individuals who had to be out and about in the blustery weather, snowmobiles provided a needed taxi service.

Because of the storm, Argyle had no mail service.

Supplies of bread and milk were completely used up at local grocery stores.

The *Marshall County Banner* noted Argyle's good luck in relation to any emergencies as the blizzard hammered the town.

As it stated, "Argyle fared much better than the rest of the storm area with no reported emergencies requiring hospitalization, no fires, no lost individuals."[29]

When the snow finally ceased on Saturday, almost twenty-five inches of the white stuff had been dumped on Argyle. Unfortunately, for us, the weather records for those four days in Argyle are missing.

Despite the reemergence of the sun on Saturday, wind gusts up to 65 mph frustrated the snow removal effort on Saturday.

When they emerged from their homes on Saturday, what residents of Argyle saw were huge snowdrifts. Snowbanks at the Valley Oil Company's building in Argyle were so high that one could almost cross from them to the top of the building. The height of the drifts there were as high as the top of the company's signs.

But, the weather improved, and much enlarged snow removal crews were out in force on Sunday. Because of the extraordinary amount of snow, trucks had to haul the excess out of Argyle.

On Monday, Argyle residents facing the huge job of plowing out driveways in Argyle received assistance from farmers who had snowblowers mounted on their tractors.

Sadly, there was one local storm-related accident during the cleanup in the Argyle area. Late Saturday, Aime St. Germain was using a tractor for snow removal in his yard. When making a final pass, he ran over his 11 year old son, Joel St. Germain. The boy had been utilizing a four foot tin ski to slide down piles of snow. One of his downhill slides carried Joel into the path of the tractor.

Joel St. Germain was quickly rushed to the Warren Hospital and then on to one in Crookston. Surgery was performed that evening. Fortunately, the boy survived the ordeal. Besides a three to four week hospital stay, Joel emerged from the accident with a lot of bruises and a cracked pelvis.

Although Argyle's Public School resumed classes on Monday, the St. Rose School did not start up until the following day.

Strong winds and drifting snow Monday evening started to undo the cleanup effort in Argyle by filling plowed out streets and driveways. The results of these winds were the school closings north of Stephen on Tuesday. More inclement weather for Argyle was forecast for Wednesday. But, rising temperatures into the 40's that day in Argyle ended that threat. Spring was on its way.

The city of Stephen (858 residents in 1960) is located in Tamarac township in Marshall County about nine miles northwest of Argyle.

Stephen began as a Great Northern village, as that rail line built its line through this area in 1878.

Stephen took its name from George Stephen, who along with James J. Hill, Norman Kittson, and Donald Smith (later Lord Strathcona) were instrumental in opening this area to settlement. Born June 5, 1829, at Dufftown, Scotland George Stephen emigrated to Canada in 1850 and settled at Montreal, Quebec. His business activities there included the dry goods business and the cloth manufacturing.

From his position as President of the Bank of Montreal (1876-1881), Stephen was able to give Jim Hill financial backing for the construction of the St. Paul, Minneapolis, and Manitoba Railway (later, the Great Northern R. R.).

Later endeavors for Stephen included serving as president of the Canadian Pacific Railway from 1881 to 1887, and with Donald Smith, starting the Royal Victoria Hospital in Montreal. During his tenure as president of the railroad, the Canadian Pacific was pushed to the west coast of Canada. Completion of this railroad occurred in 1885.

Queen Victoria knighted Stephen in 1886, and two years later he moved to England. Another honor bestowed on Stephen came in 1891 when he was given the title of Baron Mount Stephen. This was a reflection of what had occurred during the building of the Canadian Pacific across Canada. As its construction was going on, Stephen's name was chosen for one of the peaks in the Canadian Rockies.

The Stephen area was one of the vicinities hardest hit by the March '66 blizzard. People living in and around Stephen called it the "worst in history" for that area. The 31 inches of snow dumped on Stephen was accompanied by winds that had gusts reaching up to 80 mph. The results were snowdrifts that were up to 20 feet high in towns and on farms. Of course, the combination of heavy precipitation and high winds blocked all the highways in Marshall County.

Impassable roads would have made it impossible to get to fires in the Stephen area during and immediately after the storm. Fortunately, no fires were reported. Nevertheless, as the blizzard raged, the Stephen Volunteer Fire Department provided the necessary manpower to be on call twenty-four hours a day. Emergency service via snowmobile was available to those who needed it. Among those getting about via snowmobile was Edmund Pietruszewski on his Polaris Sno-Traveler.

Community activities at Stephen virtually stopped altogether during the storm and after the storm. The cancellation list included churches, schools, and sports events. Quite a few businesses in Stephen closed down because of the inclement weather. Even if they needed something at the store, customers would not have been able to get there.

It was quite a scene in Stephen on Saturday, once the storm had left. Snowbanks on the main street of Stephen varied between 8 and 12 feet in height. Wind driven snow piled so high against the entrances to homes in Stephen, the occupants inside faced a difficult, if not impossible task of getting out of their residences.

For some Stephen residents, their rescue from their snowbound homes came from Pastor Walter Anderson. He was an old hand at snow removal having one time served as a missionary in Alaska. Since that time, Anderson had never found it necessary to use those skills. But, the '66 storm gave him a chance.

On Saturday morning, bundled up in an Eskimo parka and a pack on his back, Anderson set out on snowshoes to help people trapped in their homes by blocked entrances. He went door to door shoveling snow away from the entrances to homes. This allowed the residents inside to open their doors. As could be expected, people were very grateful for his services.

Another Stephen resident, Frances Swanson, a former editor of the *Stephen Messenger*, was not going to let a "mere" blizzard keep her home snowbound. Snow blocking the front door prevented her from using that exit. After a struggle with the back door Ms. Swanson was able to make her exit that way. But, then she found the snow too deep to walk through. So, Ms. Swanson shoveled her way through snowdrifts to her garage.

There, she located a pair of skis that hadn't been used in years. Strapping them on, Ms. Swanson took off for uptown. As the *Stephen Messenger* put it:

> *Not many ladies would attempt such a feat but to Frances Swanson,*
> *your former editor, nothing seems impossible.*[30]

With such deep snowbanks on its streets, it was going to take more than conventional snow removal equipment to open them. The first step entailed using big caterpillars and machines equipped with rotary blowers to clear a path. Next, came snowplows, followed by front-end loaders and trucks.

Snow removal equipment had opened the majority of roads in the Stephen vicinity by Monday morning. Unfortunately, a 30 to 35 mph south wind that evening blocked most of the county roads. Starting the next day, a fast warm-up helped to alleviate the situation.

The March '66 blizzard had a devastating effect on the ability of deer to get around in an effort to locate food. The Minnesota Conservation Department stated that once snow depths reached eighteen inches, serious deer losses could be expected. And, after the storm, many places had snow depths that exceeded thirty-six inches on the level.

Help was needed quickly. To remedy this the Central Marshall County Sportsmen's Club at Middle River offered to coordinate the feeding operation in their area under the chairmanship of Ing Gullickson. People interested in helping out with the feeding program were to contact Mr. Gullickson or the Middle River Record Office. Donations were also a must, as the Minnesota Conservation Department lacked the money for this crisis.

The *Stephen Messenger* had this take on area residents reaction to the '66 blizzard:

> *As most of the local residents look back at the storm, it now appears*
> *to be quite an experience and something to remember. However, most of*
> *them would rather not be involved in another for some time to come, as*
> *we now have approximately 40 to 50 inches of snow on the level in this*
> *area.".*[31]

There was considerable flooding in the Stephen area that spring after the blizzard.

The last passenger train to come through Stephen was Burlington Northern's (BN) *Winnipeg Flyer* which passed through Stephen on its way to Winnipeg on April 30, 1971. Ironically, the very next day May 1, 1971, Amtrak began its service.

About fourteen miles north of Stephen is the village of Kennedy.

In 1960, 458 people called Kennedy home.

Kennedy took its name from a railway director, John Stewart Kennedy (1830-1909).

On Saturday morning, Mr. Keene, the mayor of Kennedy, reported that drifts on the highways in Kennedy were as deep as 6 feet, and they were quite long. In the Kennedy neighborhood, the highways had been, for the most part, blown clear. But, there were places where only snowplows could proceed.

Hallock (1,527 residents in 1960), the seat of Kittson County, lies ten miles north of Kennedy.

As he was building his rail line to Canada in 1878, the tracks of Jim Hill's St. Paul, Minneapolis and Manitoba Railway were built through Hallock. They reached Canada in December of that year. The village of Hallock was platted in 1879-1880.

The person for whom Hallock was named for led an interesting life. Charles Hallock was one of the founders of the city of Hallock. He made his entry into this world in New York City on March 13, 1834. In 1854 he graduated from Amherst college. He served for a long time as editor of *Forest and Stream* magazine, a publication he began in 1873. A prolific writer, Hallock penned quite a few articles and books on fishing, hunting and travel in Alaska, Florida and other locales. A large hotel he built in Hallock in 1890 acquired a reputation as a resort for sportsmen. Fire consumed it in 1892.

The city of Hallock took the full brunt of the storm. As the *Kittson County Enterprise* noted:

At the height of the storm one could barely see his hand in front of him.[32]

Despite round the clock plowing, streets became blocked. As the storm progressed, more and more homes lost vehicular access to the outside world. To compensate for this, people were forced to go, either on foot or by snowmobile.

By plowing continuously during the storm, crews were able to keep some streets open. These included ones to doctors' homes, the hospital, the fire hall and main business streets. However, if a person's vehicle lacked snow tires or tire chains, he or she had little chance of going anywhere. This was because the blowing and drifting snow began filling fresh cuts quickly.

Hallock was fortunate there were no outbreaks of fire during the storm. But, if there had been, the Hallock volunteer fire department would have been ready. They made sure that equipment was ready, vehicles would start, and the driveway to the fire hall clear of deep snow. The firemen passed their time during the blizzard playing cards.

The blizzard stranded some Kittson County ASC (Agricultural Stabilization Committee) officials at a meeting in Moorhead. They had gone there on Tuesday to attend a Cropland Adjustment Program meeting. In the group were Clarence Beck, office manager of the Kittson County ASC, committeemen Kenneth Berg, Canon township, Mrs. Leonard Nelson and Mrs. Pat Russell of Hallock and W. C. Gundstrom of Kennedy.

Dean Younggren (1922-2004), a Kittson County farmer, made a short film of the first day of the blizzard, March 3, at his farm.

Lloyd Clow, who had a farm in Hill Township, lost his entire herd of six cows during the storm. They were being kept in a 16 by 26 foot shed. Sometime either late Friday night or early Saturday morning the roof of the building collapsed. The cause of the roof cave-in was either high winds or heavy snow. It might have also been a combination of the two.

Storm conditions Friday evening prevented Mr. Clow from reaching the shed to feed the cattle. Upon his arrival there early Saturday morning, he learned the fate of the cattle and his shed. The collapse of the shed's roof dropped the power lines across the milk and water line pipes. When the animals came to drink, they were electrocuted.

As elsewhere, one of the heroes of the March 1966 storm was the snowmobile. As the storm progressed, travel conditions in Hallock grew worse. Drifts from 3 to 8 feet or higher blocked alleys and streets. Unusual drifts reached greater heights. One such drift, a 25-footer called "Mount Mead", was located on the north side of Hallock.

To combat the deteriorating conditions, the Civil Defense, Hallock police, and the Kittson County Sheriff's Department combined forces and formed a taxi service utilizing snowmobiles. They also had the use of a four-wheel drive Jeep owned by Uptown Standard. This vehicle came equipped with a hydraulically operated snowplow.

As the *Kittson County Enterprise* remarked:

> *The snowmobiles worked around the clock and did a magnificent job, making delivery of groceries to homes all over Hallock, milk for children and babies, medicines, took sick persons to the hospital or doctors' offices, drove businessmen from their homes to places of business and return to check their furnaces, and they made deliveries to farms in this immediate vicinity and under blizzard conditions."*[33]

The *Enterprise* praised the work they had done. The storm had kept them, the city council, civil defense, and law enforcement personnel busy. The newspaper gave special recognition to the following: Dean Anderson, Peter Anderson, William Ingebrigtsen, Ruggles Clay, Curtis Johnson, Glen Johnson, Miles Johnson, Al Kile, Bruce Larson and Lee Pemberton. Lloyd Agman and Tommy Baker were recognized for working nonstop through the duration of the storm.

Because of deep snow, the Kittson County Courthouse became isolated during the storm. So, Kittson County Sheriff Trygve Ingebrigtsen and Civil Defense Director Clyde Haines moved their offices as related to storm activities to the police department, located at City Hall. Good connections around Kittson County allowed these men to respond to any emergency twenty-four hours a day during the blizzard. The end result of their work was no storm-related deaths and not many drastic emergencies in Kittson County. It was a job well done.

Because of the severity of the storm. state highway patrolmen, local police and the sheriff's department could not use their vehicles while it lasted. The Hallock police department obtained a four-wheel drive Jeep with a hydraulically operated snowplow to help them get around.

The depth of snowdrifts around the hospital in Hallock varied between six and ten feet. Blocked roads prevented many nurses who lived in other towns from reaching the hospital. Several nurses had to work from Wednesday on until the storm abated. As the *Enterprise* noted;

> "It will be readily understood how the hospital staff has been hard-pressed."[34]

The storm really pounded Hallock. People in town woke up Saturday morning to quite a sight. As the *Enterprise* described it:

> Here in Hallock the snow accumulation has presented a picture never before equalled in the history of Hallock. The streets everywhere were blocked with snow in spite of the fact that plows worked every day and night during the blizzard to try and keep the roads open.[35]

Snow drifted so high on the new elementary school in Hallock that, by climbing up drifts, children could slide down from the roof.

The storm finally began to wind down in Hallock on Saturday. Even though skies had cleared, the wind still blew at 30 to 45 mph with gusts higher than that on Saturday morning. Hallock had received 13 inches of snow or 1.29 inches of precipitation. The end of the snowfall and the slackening of winds meant that the plowing of city streets in towns around Kittson County could begin.

It was a different story out in the countryside. Late Saturday morning Arthur Chard, Kittson County Engineer, dispatched the county plows out to clear the county highways. These consisted of both V plows and rotary plows.

Unfortunately, the plows could not finish their work and had to return. Drifting snow filled in highways as fast as the plows could open them. Many of the drifts on the highways in Kittson County were of enormous size. Only a rotary plow could cut through them. The bad thing about rotary plows was that they worked slowly. So, the clearing of snow from highways in Kittson County was slowed up. Fortunately, the U. S. Weather Bureau said the winds would taper off that (Saturday) evening. Utilizing that information, Mr. Chard intended to send the plows out to open the main county highways.

Plowing efforts in Hallock Saturday morning were hampered by vehicles either parked or stalled along streets or in front of houses. Because of this, only a single track was plowed out. Even then, deep snow in some places rendered the ability of a vehicle to proceed questionable.

Out in the open country many highways had blown clear. But, in other spots the *Enterprise* was informed that in some places the state highways were covered by 5-foot drifts that reached 400 yards in length. On Saturday morning, a farmer residing near Hawkeye's Corner six miles east of Hallock, reported 6-foot drifts on the county highway there and extending as far as he could see. Sheltered areas were really hammered by large drifts.

As could be expected, telephone lines in the Hallock vicinity were buzzing with activity during the storm. In fact they were so busy the local telephone company could not handle all the calls coming in at one time. According to Mr. Leibnitz, manager of the local telephone company, the dial board for the telephone company was capable of handling only a certain number of calls at one time. Any call coming in above that number was not put through. The caller would have to wait a few minutes for clearance. Despite minor delays, telephone service in the Hallock area was not disrupted by the storm.

There was no train service through Hallock during the storm. After GN (Great Northern) train *No. 7* passed through Hallock on Wednesday morning, there was no more train service to the city. As of Saturday morning, because of high winds, GN's snowplowing equipment remained in Grand Forks. As soon as the weather let up, they intended to start out. GN's *Winnipeg Flyer* also remained in Grand Forks for the duration. It would be Sunday morning before train service was restored to Hallock.

As with other areas clobbered by the storm, dairy farmers in the Hallock vicinity were having their problems. Ordinarily, milk trucks made daily trips to dairy farmers to pick up the milk and cream. Farmers put their milk in bulk tanks from which the milk was transferred to the milk truck. The blizzard prevented the milk trucks from reaching the dairy farms for several days. In the meantime, the milk turned sour, forcing the dairy farmers to dump it.

During the week following the storm, a quadruple warning was sounded in the Hallock neighborhood. Hallock police warned motorists to slow down to speeds of one or two miles an hour at intersections. The huge piles of snow, from 4 to 6 feet high, left at such localities by snow removal equipment made for blind intersections. There had already been some close calls.

These and other piles of snow lewd to the second warning. Children were burrowing tunnels into the piles. Men who were removing snow would not be able to see the children if they were in the tunnels.

A tragedy was narrowly averted at Crookston the week before. After a child had climbed inside a tunnel in a snowpile, a snowplow came along. Just as the operator lowered the wing on the plow, the child emerged from the snowpile. At the last second the operator lifted the plow, missing the child. If he hadn't seen the child and lifted the wing, the child could have been buried and suffocated in the snow. The child may not have been found until the snow had melted. So, snow removal operators in Hallock wanted parents to keep their children off the streets while snow removal operations were underway.

The third warning came from Otter Tail Power Company to parents. The blizzard had piled drifts high enough so as to allow children climbing on them to touch the high voltage power lines. If they did so, the children could either be electrocuted or terribly burned.

Shop on Carl Hedlund farm near the Red River west of Hallock, March 9, 1966. Courtesy of Dean Younggren

Carl Hedlund farm, March 9, 1966. Courtesy of Dean Younggren

Dean Younggren farm, March 7, 1966. Courtesy of Dean Younggren

Business District on 2nd St. S. Hallock. March 7, 1966. Courtesy of Dean Younggren

Second St. S. (the business district in Hallock), March 7, 1966. Courtesy of Dean Younggren

Looking north along U.S. Highway 75 in Hallock, March 7, 1966. Courtesy of Dean Younggren

Elementary school in Hallock, March 7, 1966. Courtesy of Dean Younggren

Kittson County Memorial Hospital in Hallock, March 7, 1966. Courtesy of Dean Younggren

The last warning was also to parents. Coming from the local telephone company, it involved telephone lines and poles. Damage to lines and cross arms on telephone poles was resulting from children climbing drifts and playing with telephone wires. They were not supposed to be doing this.

On March 7, in the midst of the cleanup, Hallock Police Chief Gerald Jackson submitted his resignation to the Hallock City Council. His resignation became effective March 21. Jackson had been police chief in Hallock for six years. He was taking a job as a security officer with the Boeing Aircraft Company.

Karlstad, which enjoyed a population of 720 in 1960, lies about twenty-eight miles east of Drayton, North Dakota. This northwestern Minnesota city is located about five miles east of the eastern edge of the Red River Valley.

The Soo Line Railroad, whose services Karlstad, pushed its line through here in 1904. Karlstad took its name from the Swedish city of the same name.

The March 1966 storm really hammered Karlstad.

There was no school in Karlstad from the evening of March 2 until the morning of March 9. Even then, many side roads remained closed. It was feared that it would take the spring thaw to open them again.

There was almost no business in Karlstad from Thursday thru Saturday. Weather conditions forced the cancellation of all meetings.

There was some personal drama during the storm. The storm forced seven large transports to remain in Karlstad from 1 p.m. Thursday until Saturday evening. The opening of U.S. Highway 59 at that time allowed them to proceed. State Highway 11 was not opened until the next day.

People became worried about the fate of seven or eight transports that had departed west from Karlstad on Highway 11 on the afternoon of March 3. However, later it was learned that they were staying at the Leonard Dagen farm, located four miles east of Donaldson. The transports had all become stalled in that vicinity. The Dagens had some twenty unexpected visitors staying with them. These included the drivers and their riders.

The event caught the attention of the *Minneapolis Tribune* which called the Dagens. Mrs. Dagen informed the paper that "the food was still holding out." If conditions deteriorated to that of an extreme emergency, the Dagens and their "guests" had access to one of the stalled trucks that was hauling a load of frozen meat.[36]

There was some excitement during the storm in the Karlstad area. On the evening of March 3, it appeared that Mrs. Dale Grandstand, who lived with her family about six miles west of Karlstad, was going into labor. She needed a ride to the hospital in Thief River Falls. So, Morris Koland and Ardene Sandberg drove the state plow out to the Grandstand home. After Mrs. Grandstand was picked up, the plow led the way to Thief River Falls.

But, it turned out to be a false alarm, and Mrs. Grandstand eventually returned home to await the delivery of her baby. The ferocity of the storm prevented the return of the snowplow to Karlstad until Saturday morning. On the way home, it helped to open U. S. Highway 59. The snowplow made it back to Karlstad around 11 a.m. Saturday.

During the height of the storm Friday night, Ervin Dagen and Connie Stallock took the county plow out to the Ivan Holland farm which was located east of Halma. In their attempt to reach the Holland farm, they slipped into the ditch and became stuck several times. But in the end they made it. With the snowplow leading the way, Mr. and Mrs. Holland drove to the Karlstad hospital.

Impassable street conditions in Karlstad forced Mrs. Holland to travel the last block or two on a snowmobile. (The *Karlstad Advocate* called it a "snowcat.")

At the time of the March 1966 blizzard, the Karlstad Hospital lacked a doctor. So, calls were made to Mrs. Thelma Thompson, Mrs. Damon Renstrom and Harold Ploemphen of the Karlstad Hospital. With their assistance, delivery of Mr. and Mrs. Holland's baby, an eight pound girl named Diane Joy, was made at 9:20 a.m., March 5.

The saga of the coming of age for snowmobiles was very evident in Karlstad as it was elsewhere. With blocked roads and streets, other than walking, snowmobiles became the mode of transportation for getting around. They brought food to the elderly and delivered fuel oil in five and ten gallon cans to wherever it was needed in the Karlstad vicinity.

But, they did have their mishaps. Mrs. N. O. Folland was going to take a ride on a snowmobile. But upon mounting one, she wrenched her back. The resulting muscle spasm forced Mrs. Folland to go to the Karlstad Hospital. There she was one of three patients who were looked after by two nurses. But, without a doctor, the hospital was not "open." On the evening of March 6, Mrs. Folland was taken to a hospital in Thief River Falls where she was put in traction.

The amount of snowfall and the long duration of the storm made for very large snowbanks that covered many homes in Karlstad area. Deep drifts blocked exits from many peoples' homes. Such conditions at the Allan Olson farm on Friday morning, March 4 forced them to break a storm window to secure an exit. The Olsons could not exit by either door on their house.

An unofficial headquarters for snowmobile operators during the storm was the Carlson Oil Company in Karlstad. Among those who used their machines to help throughout the storm were Elmer Anderson, Bob Carlson, Doug Norden, John Oistad, Don Parker, Gordon Sollund, and Dave Berg. Berg and his boys rendered assistance to the drug store in Karlstad by delivering prescriptions via snowmobile. As the *Karlstad Advocate* noted, "*There were others flying about all the time, and the little machines really proved their worth in this greatest of all blizzards.*"[37]

There were other stories of people using snowmobiles during and after the storm. Luverne Dagen owned a large potato warehouse in Karlstad. His farm was located eight miles west of town. Dagen didn't let blocked roads prevent him from checking things out at his warehouse. He simply drove his snowmobile to Karlstad.

In a familiar refrain, storm conditions prevented dairy farmers from bringing their milk to town. One farmer, Harley Clark, used his snowmobile to help him out. He drove his machine from his farm to Karlstad about five miles away to pick up cream cans.

In March 1966, Norman Johnson lived on a farm about six miles west of Karlstad. He remembers the '66 blizzard being a three-day storm.

Large drifts blocked Minnesota Highway 11 which passed near the Johnson farm. This was due in part to stalled semis on the road. The truckers kept the semis running until they ran out of fuel. Because of the huge snowbanks on the highway, the ditches were cleared to allow the passage of vehicles.[38]

Youngsters in Karlstad had a great time with snowmobiles during and after the storm. They had never before encountered so much snow that had been pounded into all sorts of shapes.

Karlstad was the recipient of 2.85 inches of precipitation from the storm.

On Thursday, March 3 a high of 29 and a low of 19 were recorded in Karlstad. For the next day, 21 and 14 were the maximum and minimum temperatures reached in Karlstad. After the blizzard, a low of -20 was reached on Monday, March 7.

By March 10, the job of snow removal in the business district on the main street of Karlstad was almost done. But many streets had cuts only in the middle of them. There were large piles of snow all over the place. The opening of highways in the Karlstad area required a "round the clock" effort by plow crews. High, long drifts required the use of a larger rotary plow that had to be brought into the Karlstad area.

In March 1966, the Soo Line Railroad was cutting back on section crews (they maintained the rail lines) in the Karlstad vicinity. It eliminated section crews at Lake Bronson and Newfolden. Only those at Karlstad and Lancaster remained.

Karlstad's high school boys basketball team, the Rabbits, had a great season in 1966. They defeated the Lancaster Cardinals on March 7 to win their first subdistrict championship in a long time. Lancaster and Karlstad were co-champions of the Northern Lights Conference for the 1965-66 season. This subdistrict game had been originally scheduled for March 4. But the inclement weather at the time forced it to be rescheduled.

Storm conditions on Monday evening, March 7 made it difficult for fans to get back from the game at Kennedy. Some recently opened roads became blocked, forcing people to seek alternate routes home.

Karlstad's high school boy's basketball team finished their season with a 77 to 56 loss to Bemidji on March 19, in Region 8 tournament play at Grand Forks.

It had been quite a season for the Rabbits. After a slow start to the season, the Rabbits went from a 4-3 record to a 20-4 one. The Rabbits finished the season at 20-6. Co-captains of the team were David Henry and Neil Wikstrom.

The village of Halma is located seven miles northwest of Karlstad.

How the storm had affected the condition of potato cars at Halma was a concern of Halma depot agent, Walter Anderson. Orrin Abbey and George Wikstrom helped to get him there via snowmobile.

In March 1966, Paul Kurowski resided with his family on a farm near Halma. After the storm had passed, Paul took a sled and two 5 gallon cans and walked two miles to a neighbor to get fuel oil for the furnace in his family's house. Then, he returned home.[39]

Another resident of the Halma area in March 1966 was Harvey Baker.

At the time of the storm, Harvey had milk cows in a barn. He was able to milk the cows through the duration of the blizzard.

Harvey had a holding tank for the milk. But, it's capacity was only 400 gallons. So, after four milkings (twice a day), the tank was full. After that, Harvey had to dump the milk.

Despite the inclement weather, the temperature in the barn remained at 60 degrees during the storm.

The storm left a drift so high at the south end of Harvey's barn, it completely covered the 9 feet high doors at that end.

After the blizzard had let up, Harvey opened his yard with a snowblower mounted on the three-point hitch of his tractor.

Harvey could have cleared a path to a county highway, three quarters of a mile away, but he felt the distance and depth of snow on his township road was too much work. So, he called the Kittson County engineer. Harvey told him that he needed his road opened, so the milk truck could get to his place. A snowplow dispatched to Harvey's farm cleared the road shortly afterwards.[40]

Strandquist, a Soo Line railway town, lies seven miles southeast of Karlstad, Minnesota in Marshall County Strandquist The 1960 census showed Strandquist to have a population of 160.

Strandquist took its name from J. E. Strandquist, a local merchant. Entering this world in Sweden in 1870, Mr. Strandquist moved to Marshall County in 1892.

John Lofstrom was attending school in Strandquist in March 1966. He remembers school being canceled, and the incredible amount of snow the storm deposited on Strandquist. There was a huge drift that banked up against the school.

John recalled "cats" (bulldozers) being used for snow removal in and around Strandquist. With the help of Henry Pettis and four or five other kids, John dug a tunnel from his house over to the Pettis residence about a block away.[41]

Strandquist celebrated its centennial on June 26, 2004.

Middle River (1960 population of 414) lies in northeastern Marshall County over twenty miles north of Thief River Falls. Both the city and township of Middle River took their names from the river that courses in a westerly direction through the middle of Marshall County. That river flows through both the towns of Middle River and Argyle. It joins up with the Snake River shortly before that river joins the Red River.

Weather conditions in Middle River were blustery on Monday February 28, 1966. The next two days brought sunshine and little or no winds.

The March 1966 storm arrived in Middle River Wednesday evening, March 2. The wind was out of the east, and it began to snow. Conditions did not improve overnight, and on Thursday the wind began to pick up speed. The Middle River vicinity was now engulfed by a full scale blizzard. As a result, schools in the area were forced to close. There was also the cancellation or postponement of scheduled activities.

Despite the lousy conditions, there was still motor vehicular traffic on the major thoroughfares in the Middle River area on Thursday. The same could not be said for side roads. They were impassable.

On Friday morning, the wind picked up in speed from the north and northwest. Wind driven snow was now forming humongous drifts. As a result motor vehicular traffic in and around Middle River ground to a halt.

Finally, on Saturday morning, the snow quit falling in Middle River. A total of 25 inches of the white stuff had been deposited on Middle River. The drifting of snow, accompanied by strong northerly winds, would last all day.

In the storm's aftermath, the depth of snowdrifts on Middle River's Main Street varied between 4 and 15 feet. The front windows on Overvold Motors located near the corner of Main Street and Highway 32 were engulfed by snowdrifts.

The Middle River high school boys' basketball team, the Skippers, ended their season on March 12 in Roseau. They lost the District 32 basketball championship to Karlstad, 66 to 55. Bobby Englestad, Steve Holmes and Eldon Sparby were the co-captains of the Middle River team. In a losing effort, Sparby and Holmes scored 17 and 14 points, respectively.

Considering everything, not a single major crisis occurred in the Middle River area during the storm. It wasn't smooth sailing for everyone. Dairy farmers in the Middle River vicinity suffered some inconvenience. Ordinarily, milk from their farms was picked up every other day by bulk milk trucks. Unfortunately, the blizzard disrupted this schedule. This forced several dairy farmer, whose bulk milk tanks were already full, to dump a portion of their milk.

Something had to be done. Even though it had its own regular customers, the Middle River Creamery came to the rescue for dairy farmers who usually sold to Minnesota Dairy in Grand Forks. Their trucks picked up those farmers milk.

The drivers for the Middle River Creamery, Ray Ness and Al Risberg, worked nonstop in picking up the milk and hauling it to Roseau.

Some farmyards were snowplugged, and Ness and Risberg could not pick up the milk at those places. The day was saved by three young men. They delivered the milk from the farms to the creamery in cans. They did this by utilizing a snowmobile and a pickup. Mylan Erickson employed his Sno-Cat, and Dale Risberg used his pickup. Also helping out was Harold Peterson. As the *Middle River Record* noted:

This was an emergency where everyone pitched in to help.[42]

About the March 1966 blizzard, the *Middle River Record* had this to say:

Old timers here say this is the worst blizzard they can remember. It brings to mind the disastrous blizzard in March 1941 which brought much more tragedy in the short time it lasted. The fact that this was such a lengthy storm, with the heavy snowfall made it the worst since the Blizzard of 1888.[43]

Cleanup operations in Middle River began on Saturday. Any and all heavy equipment went to work clearing the snow. Having a construction company, the Schenkey Construction Co., as a neighbor benefitted Middle River greatly. Their first priority in snow removal operations was the Middle River vicinity. The cleanup proceeded quickly in Middle River. By Sunday motor vehicular traffic was possible on its streets. The Highway Department opened side roads.

A major deer feeding program, (the Deer Survival Project), was underway in the Middle River area after the March 1966 blizzard. They used bulldozers, Sno-Cats and men on skis to cut browse for the starving deer and feed them alfalfa bales.

Greenbush, Roseau, Warroad, Baudette, Borders, Carp, Wayland and Pitt

Greenbush (population of 706 in 1960) lies nineteen miles northeast of Karlstad in Roseau County.

Minnesota State Highway 11 runs through it. The highway curves along a gravel ridge and follows an older trail that ran along the ridge. Lake Agassiz formed this gravel beach ridge. Early travellers used this "ridge road." In turn, a wagon road, a rail line and then Highway 11 followed it.

Greenbush took its name from a stand of spruce trees located about two miles northeast of town. They were the first evergreens seen by travellers coming from the west. This was quite a contrast for people after traveling through the mostly treeless Red River Valley.

The *Greenbush Tribune* compared the March 1966 blizzard to the storms of 1888, 1909 and 1941. In comparing the 1966 storm to the 1941 blizzard, long-time residents of the Greenbush area remembered that one (1941) as being "more sudden, stranding more people, and causing more deaths." But to them, the 1966 blizzard lasted the longest, with the most snowfall and longest sustaining winds.[44]

Around midnight with the wind blowing from the east, snow began to fall in Greenbush. There had been snow drifting across roads in the Greenbush vicinity prior to this, but the arrival of the snowfall exacerbated events. The continuing deterioration of the weather forced the closing of school in Greenbush on Thursday.

Despite the conditions, few business establishments in Greenbush failed to remain open on Thursday. As could be expected, business was poor.

As long as anyone could remember, there had never been a single day when at least one farmer had not come to Greenbush. This tradition continued at least for March 3, when some people reported seeing a local farmer, James Efta, in Greenbush.

Blizzard conditions the following day, March 4, forced the cancellation of school classes in Greenbush. Not all businesses in Greenbush opened on Friday. As elsewhere, snowmobile operators (called "snowcats" by the *Greenbush Tribune)* and snow removal operators were the heroes of the storm. They assisted in getting the staff to the Greenbush hospital and helped with other emergencies in the Greenbush area. Townspeople and those who lived in the country were grateful for their assistance.

The blizzard kept some staff members of the Greenbush Community Hospital from reaching the hospital as they lived in the country. Bad weather forced many staff members to sleep at the hospital. This was especially true Friday night, when poor visibility prevented snowmobile operators from taking them home after the end of their shift at 11 p.m. Others worked on their days off to make sure the hospital had a full staff.

The duration of the storm had members of the Greenbush Fire Department worried. The longer the storm lasted, the less chance they would be able to get out to help in emergencies. To combat against this, they organized on March 4. Members of the Fire Department made preparations to be ready for any emergency. A caterpillar with a man to keep it running at all hours was leased from Reese's. The Greenbush school loaned a four-wheel drive truck to the Fire Department. Personnel from there got it ready for any emergency. Fortunately, the Greenbush area escaped the storm without any reports of fire.

The let-up of the storm on Saturday March 5 signalled the beginning of the arduous task of snow removal in the Greenbush area. The effort was slowed by wind and an inch of new snow Monday evening. Driveways and roads that had been plowed out filled in again.

Classes in Greenbush did not resume until March 9. Road conditions on Monday and Tuesday, March 7 and 8, were still too poor to allow buses to reach enough students to have school, according to Superintendent Louis E. Allen. About eighty of the students were in class in Greenbush on March 9.

As to be expected, mail service to Greenbush was disrupted by the storm. Not until Sunday March 6, did it resume. As of March 9, no freight trains had made it to Greenbush.

Temperatures remained steady at Greenbush during the storm. Highs were in the 20's The thermometer sank to a low of -20 on March 7 before rebounding to a high of 37 above the following day.

Two medical emergencies occurred just as the storm let up. On March 5, a county road plow cleared a route through deep snow to allow Adolph Tomnock, who had suffered a heart attack, to be brought to the Greenbush hospital. The plow repeated the procedure the next day to bring another sick person, Alice Owens, to the hospital. Later, Dr. Kiefstad, who was on the hospital staff, said both patients were doing well.

Despite the cancellation and postponement of many events, the *Greenbush Tribune* was thankful for the lack of deaths, fires and power failures during the storm.

A heavy deer loss resulting from the storm was a concern of the Western Roseau County Sportsman's Club in March 1966. They purchased over 1,000 bales of hay to help feed the deer.

Roseau is the seat of Roseau County of. A river with the same name flows through Roseau.

Roseau has had its share of great hockey players. The list includes the Broten brothers, Neal, Aaron and Paul.

In 1960, 2,146 people called Roseau home.

The word "Roseau" is a French translation of a Chippewa word which means "the-place-of-rushes-river." Many lakes in the prairie regions of Minnesota and Manitoba have numerous stands of this reed or very coarse grass. They border the edges of lakes. It has been known to attain heights of twelve feet.

In the early days, access to the Roseau County region from the Red River Valley was by means of a trail that followed a sand ridge formed by glacial Lake Agassiz. Indians used it first then the white man. The area was known as one that had fertile soil but there was a lot of swampy ground too. In the 1890's, getting to the Red River Valley via this ridge trail with oxen and horses often proved to be difficult.

Efforts to persuade James J. Hill of the Great Northern Railroad to bring a railroad to Roseau were at first, not successful. In 1899, he said:

> I have felt that a milk run is better than a wheat run for your part of the state. Let the Northern Pacific build your railroad."[45]

It would be a long slow process before Roseau received rail service. The Great Northern pushed its line to Greenbush in 1904. Two years later it graded the road bed from Greenbush to Warroad. In 1908, GN extended the line onto Badger, Roseau, and Warroad. On October 23, 1908, the first train came to Roseau.

To celebrate, the farmers and merchants of Roseau threw a party on December 18, 1908. A chartered Great Northern train with 100 people from Crookston hooked up with people from Roseau and Warroad. The train chugged down the line through Roseau and onto Warroad. It was greeted in each town by flag waving and a band. Also included in the festivities were speeches and a banquet.

The *Roseau Times-Region* described the March 1966 storm as Roseau County's "Worst Blizzard." The newspaper went on to describe it as the following, "An 'old fashioned blizzard' of unprecedented proportions struck Roseau county last weekend bringing practically every form of activity to a complete halt by Friday."[46]

It began snowing in Roseau Wednesday evening. The winds picked up the following morning. By mid-morning, gusts were reaching speeds of 50 to 60 mph. The wind whipped the falling snow into drifts that quickly stopped traffic. Motorists abandoned their stalled vehicles and headed for the closest available shelter.

The Roseau Creamery was not going to let a storm keep its milk trucks from making their runs. Even during the worst of the storm, the trucks made a fairly successful effort to up milk from dairy farmers. With more roads open on Sunday, 17,000 pounds of milk was delivered to the Roseau Creamery. Unfortunately, blocked roads and lack of storage space forced some dairy farmers to dump their milk.

About a hundred people took refuge in Roseau's three motels during the storm. These were the Evenson Motel, The Great House, and the Godden Hotel. Pleased with their treatment during the storm, many guests thanked their hosts.

The storm forced the closing of all schools in Roseau County Thursday, Friday, and Monday. The majority of them reopened Tuesday. The basketball tournament scheduled for Monday and Tuesday at Roseau was pushed back to Tuesday and Wednesday.

The Law Enforcement Center in Roseau was a busy place during the blizzard. Its phones hummed with activity. The Center recorded twenty-four incidents where people were stranded, and their relatives did not know their whereabouts. Rescuers found three boys in a house. On their way home from their cabin in the woods, the boys had taken shelter in the house. Another three boys on their way home from college were located. Four people requiring medical treatment were transported to the Roseau hospital.

The Roseau County sheriff's office handled many inquiries about road conditions. As Roseau County Sheriff Paul Knochenmus put it, "All in all the storm was safely weathered by the Roseau County citizens, and though there were some anxious moments for some, there were no serious problems."[47]

By working overtime, Honl's Bakery in Roseau prevented a low supply of bread in the Roseau area from becoming a shortage. Because of the storm, milk supplies in Roseau also ran low.

One of the heroes of the March 1966 blizzard in the Roseau vicinity were snowmobiles made right in Roseau by Polaris Industries. As in other localities, the machines provided invaluable service in and around Roseau. From delivering medicine, fuel and food supplies to isolated residents, to transporting essential personnel to hospital, rest homes, rest homes, restaurants and hotels, snowmobiles proved their worth.

Edgar Hetteen, the man who helped to start Polaris and later founded Arctic Cat, came from Roseau. In the fall of 1944, Hetteen founded Hetteen Hoist and Derrick which he named after an invention of his. Later, Hetteen would be joined by two partners, David Johnson, his brother-in-law, and younger brother, Allen Hetteen.

During its early years of operation, Hetteen Hoist and Derrick specialized in manufacturing agricultural equipment, items such as grain elevators, post setters, and straw choppers. But, the company could and would make about anything upon demand.

Upon returning from a vacation to California during the winter of 1955, Edgar Hetteen discovered a contraption in the company shop that David Johnson had built. He called it a "snow machine." Johnson enjoyed the outdoors and wanted a way to be able to move around in the snow.

Additional impetus had been provided by a neighbor of Hetteen's, Pete Peterson, the owner of a lumber yard across the street from Polaris Industries (a recent name change to the company by Edgar Hetteen). He made a request of David Johnson to build him a "gas-powered sled." Pete Peterson would be the first in a long line of buyers of Polaris snowmobiles.

Although skeptical of the snow machine at first, Edgar Hetteen soon became intrigued by it. The machine would go on to have a major impact on his life and the others associated with.

In 1956, Edgar Hetteen traveled to Alaska to sell the machine first known as "Sno-Cats" and "Pole-Cats", and finally as "Sno-Travelers." He sold one at Point Barrow, Alaska.

Sales of the snow machine were slow at first. To improve sales and obtain more credit from banks, the machines needed publicity. So, in March 1960, Edgar Hetteen, Bessie and Rudy Billberg, and Erling Falk made an historic eighteen day 1100 mile trip partly on the Yukon River from Bethel in southwestern Alaska to Fairbanks on Polaris Sno-Travelers.

Unfortunately, for him, many people back in Roseau were not impressed with the trek across Alaska. They wanted Polaris to give up on making snow machines and concentrate on manufacturing farm-related items. Fed up with the whole mess, Edgar Hetteen cut his ties with Polaris on June 1, 1960.

After knocking about Alaska for awhile at different jobs Hetteen realized that he wanted to get back to making snowmobiles. He wrote a letter to L. B. Hartz, a prominent grocer in Thief River Falls. The previous spring, Hartz had come to Roseau with a group of businessmen from Thief River Falls. They offered to bankroll Hetteen, if he moved Polaris Industries to that city. At that time he turned them down. But, by December 1960, Hetteen was ready to take up their offer. He reached Thief River Falls by Christmas.

On January 2, 1961, Polar Manufacturing Company opened its doors in an unused grocery warehouse that Hartz owned that was situated along the banks of the Red Lake River. Their first snowmobile which had a rear mounted engine was known as the "Polar 500." To emphasize the company's cold weather orientation and make note of the fact that it offered a wide range of product types, its name was changed to "Arctic Enterprises Inc." in 1962.

Arctic Cat's Model 100 was the first American snowmobile to have the engine mounted in front of the driver. Early Arctic Cat snowmobiles had slide rails made of maple. Edgar Hetteen tested the Model 100 snowmobile out on Ruth Glacier on Mount Mckinley, Alaska in the summer of 1963.

Edgar Hetteen left Arctic Cat Enterprises on September 1, 1965, after selling his interest in the company to Lowell Swenson. After other business ventures, Hetteen would return to the company in an advisory capacity in 1967 and become vice president of marketing in 1970.

In 2000, using modern snowmobiles, Edgar Hetteen, along with personnel from Polaris, retraced the route of his famous 1960 Alaskan snowmobile trip.

In 2004, Polaris Industries celebrated its fiftieth birthday.

A Polaris snowmobile was instrumental in rescuing a stranded motorist. When the storm began, Larry Gross's vehicle became stalled in a forested area near Roseau. Gross took shelter in a cabin in the woods. On Sunday, after the storm had let up, Ronald Hedlund and Robert Hetteen set out on a Polaris snowmobile to the cabin which was located over seven miles southeast of the River Fire Tower. By the time they reached Gross, his food supply was almost completely gone. Out of firewood, and trying to keep warm, Gross was forced to burn the furnishings of the cabin.

It was on a mission of mercy that five Polaris employees, Roy Baumgartner, Edson Brandt, Bobby Eastman, Randy Hites, and John Miller, ventured out into the blizzard at noon Friday. *(See photo on page 447)*

In January 1966, Edson Brandt took second place in the Winnipeg to St. Paul snowmobile race which was a part of the Winter Carnival in St. Paul.

Departing from Roseau they were headed for Grand Forks to bring Roger Dick, who was in Seattle, back to Roseau. His father, Kenneth Dick, had suffered a heart attack on Wednesday and was in critical condition at a Roseau Hospital.

Kenneth Dick operated a Polaris snowmobile dealership in Roseau. In conjunction with working with his father, Roger Dick, he also raced the Polaris snowmobiles a lot. This required much traveling.

Late Wednesday, Roger Dick received the news about his father's condition. His flight from Seattle arrived in Minneapolis that night. A train brought Mr. Dick to Grand Forks on Thursday. For the duration of the storm, he stayed at the home of his in-laws in Grand Forks, the Glenn Wrights.

Enroute, the snowmobilers made stops at Greenbush, Newfolden, and Warren. These stops consumed five hours. They spent more time at Newfolden than expected. A farmer from Newfolden needed to reach his farm. His cattle there didn't have any feed. So, Edson Brandt gave him a ride out to his farm.

They reached Grand Forks at eleven o'clock that night. Actual travel time came to about six hours. Roy Baumgartner described the trip as "fun."

Randy Hites said the hardest part of the trip was from Warren to Grand Forks. How come? He replied:

> We had the wind at our backs." Having a high wind at their backs wasn't necessarily a good thing. The snow was blown forward from the snowmobile drive belt and reduced the driver's visibility.[48]

Along the way the men noticed quite a few stranded automobiles on the highways, with the most being on the twenty mile stretch between Alvarado and East Grand Forks.

Snowdrifts encountered by the snowmobilers on their journey varied between six and ten feet. They saw a lot of snowbanks whose heights reached up to thirty feet.

Around two o'clock Saturday afternoon, the snowmobile caravan, accompanied by Roger Dick, set out for Roseau. By 9:30 that evening, they had made it to Greenbush. In the meantime, Minnesota Highway 11 had been reopened between Greenbush and Roseau. So, Mr. Dick traveled that distance by automobile. As for the snowmobilers, they intended to drive their machines all the way to Roseau.

The snowmobiler's machines came through the whole experience with frozen carburetor and a stuck throttle.[45]

The storm piled 15 inches of snow on Roseau. A mile east of Roseau 1.46 inches of precipitation fell. At the same location, temperatures during the worst of the storm varied between 16 and 28 degrees. By Monday morning, March 7, the thermometer had dipped to 25 below.

In front of Manfred Holm's place of business in Roseau was an extremely high drift. By driving his Polaris Sno-Traveler on top of the drift, Holm and his machine sat at the same height as the sign in front of his store.

At a Roseau City Council meeting March 7, snowmobile operators were notified that, since the storm emergency was over, the usual rules governing the use of the machines in Roseau would now be enforced.

The storm forced the postponement of the Tenth Annual Lion's Fishing Derby from March 13 to March 20. The Derby was to be held at Long Point Resort on Lake of the Woods.

Situated on the southwest corner of Lake of the Woods, Warroad enjoyed a population of 1309 in 1960.

Warroad incorporated as a village on November 9, 1901.

The Warroad River flows through Warroad on its way to empty into Lake of the Woods. The Ojibways and Sioux tribes were enemies who warred with each other. The Warroad River was considered to be neutral territory by them. Explorer Jonathan Carver (1732-1780), who explored Minnesota in the 1760's, described the name like this: "All countries not possessed by any one nation, where war parties are often passing, is called by them the road of war."[49]

In 1902, the rail line the Canadian Northern Railroad was building around the south side of Lake of the Woods reached Warroad. It then went on to Baudette and back into Canada. This was the only Canadian rail line that crossed over into the United States.

In 1918, the Canadian Northern was acquired by the Canadian National Railroad. They discontinued passenger service to Warroad in 1977 and turned their depot over to the city of Warroad. They, in turn, converted the depot into their city hall.

In 1908, Great Northern Railway extended its line from the west to Warroad. GN discontinued passenger service to Warroad in 1952.

Warroad is home to Marvin Windows and world-famous Christian Brothers Hockey Sticks. The latter company came into existence in 1964. It's founders were Billy and Roger Christian and their brother-in-law, Hal Bakke. The Christian brothers were on the 1960 United States hockey team that won the gold medal at Squaw Valley, California. Billy Christian's son, Dave, was a member of the U.S. Olympic squad that won the gold medal at Lake Placid, New York in 1980.

At that time (1964), the Christian brothers were employed by their family's construction company. The U. S. government had contracted with their company to construct border stations. Meanwhile, Hal Bakke was in charge of a radio station in Roseau.

The inspiration for starting a company that made hockey sticks came from Hal Bakke. He thought the combination of the Christian brothers being carpenters and hockey players made for a "natural fit." In 1965, they adopted the motto "Hockey Sticks by Hockey Players." The following year, before any other North American company, the Christian Brothers brought forth a 21-ply stick handle.

The Christian brothers and Hal Bakke only worked evenings during the company's formative years. In the meantime, they hung onto their day jobs. It would be 1969 before they devoted their energies to the company full time. In August 2002, they sold the company to Platinum Group, a Twin Cities firm. Although Christian Brothers Inc. had new owners, it would remain in Warroad.

Billy, Roger and Dave Christian were inducted into the U. S. Hockey Hall of Fame in 1984, 1989 and 2001, respectively.

The temperature in Warroad reached 29 above on Wednesday March 2, 1966. The *Warroad Pioneer* described what happened next:

> *a storm... swept viciously into the area late Wednesday night. Unmerciful winds drove the falling snow into mountainous drifts and brought the Northland to its knees in complete submission in what was probably the worst storm seen in this country in 60 or more years.*
>
> *About all residents could do in the three days and nights the storm howled, was to look out the windows and marvel at the unrelenting way Mother Nature chose to show she was not about to give up and say it was time for spring.[50]*

As could be expected, transportation in and around Warroad deteriorated as the storm progressed. After Thursday a person could forget about automobile and truck traffic in Warroad. People abandoned their stalled vehicles stuck in drifts and sought refuge wherever they could find it.

Visibility was so bad on Friday, that it didn't make any sense to send out the snowplows. On Friday, the only real options people had for getting about Warroad was either on foot or by snowmobile. Even as far as the latter was concerned, the lousy visibility made operating them dangerous.

But they got the job done. Practically any snowmobile that was available, was put into service. When all else failed, they were the means of transport for conveying people and supplies to where they were needed.

Even though the Grey Goose bus line ran Thursday, the inclement weather on Friday forced them to discontinue service at Warroad.

One person who took advantage of the Grey Goose bus service on Thursday was Willis Nelson of Angle Inlet. This village is part of the Northwest Angle. This part of Minnesota lies along the west side of Lake of the Woods. The only access to it by land is through Canada.

When Nelson departed from Angle Inlet Thursday, weather conditions appeared okay. But, they deteriorated so badly that Nelson was forced to abandon his pickup at Middlebro, Manitoba. Continuing on foot, Nelson made it to the border station. A Grey Goose bus took Nelson from there to Warroad.

To demonstrate the length of the storm, consider the case of Jim Bishop of the U.S. Border Patrol. He worked at the border station near Warroad. Bishop's shift started at 8 a.m. Thursday. It would be 1 a.m. Saturday, before he returned to Warroad. Even then, the only reason Bishop made it back to Warroad was because of a five truck caravan from the Northwest Angle. They were following a Mando plow.

Even if the truck caravan hadn't come through, the men at the border station were in good shape. With lots of food to eat, they were in no real danger.

From late Thursday onward, border traffic declined considerably. Jim Bishop said that virtually all cars crossing at the border station became stuck there.

Another person, Roy Hill, had been cooling his heels at the Canadian National Railroad (CN) depot in Warroad since 10 a.m. Friday. He was hoping that a train would come through and give him a ride to the border station. Hill's wishes came true that evening, when the CN plow passed through Warroad.

Many stranded travelers in Warroad took shelter in Cal's Motel and the Warroad Hotel, filling up those establishments.

As Cal's Motel was located on the east side of Warroad near Lake of the Woods and not uptown where there would be restaurants and grocery stores, the supply of food for all the people taking refuge there wasn't going to last very long. To assist them Maynard "Swede" Carlson and Danny Carlson, his nephew, did the cooking and washed dishes. Snowmobiles brought needed food supplies from Warroad.

The proprietor of Cal's Motel was Cal Marvin (1924-2004). Although related to the Marvins of Marvin Windows, Cal Marvin struck out on his own. He is best remembered for his association with hockey. As a student at the University of North Dakota in 1946, Cal Marvin and Dan McKinnon helped get the ball rolling when it came to setting up a men's hockey team at that institution.

He held various positions with the Warroad Lakers, an amateur hockey team in Warroad that he established in 1947. These roles included ones as a founder, player, coach and manager. In 1994, 1995 and 1996 the Lakers won the Allen Cup, the trophy for the Canadian Senior Amateur Champions.

In addition to being a member of the U.S. Hockey Hall of Fame, Cal Marvin gave Warroad the status of "Hockeytown U.S.A."

Emerging from Warroad's outstanding hockey tradition were great players. Besides Olympians, these included both amateur and professional players. Along with the Christians, names that come to mind include Henry Boucha and Allen Hangsleben. As a member of the Minnesota North Stars in 1972, Boucha scored the fastest goal in a regular game in NHL history. The game was only six seconds old, when Boucha put the puck in the net. As a freshman at the University of North Dakota (1971-1972), Hangsleben earned All-American honors.

The '66 blizzard hampered operations at Marvin Millwork (Marvin Windows). In 1966, they employed 127 people. To illustrate the severity of the weather, about twenty people came to work Thursday, March 3, ten on Friday March 4 and thirteen on Saturday March 5. The intrepid souls who did make it to the Marvin plant got there either by walking or via snowmobile.

The blizzard left many people stranded in Warroad. Among them was Charles Payor, production manager for the Warroad Pioneer. He spent the night in the back shop of the Pioneer office. Setting up a bed on the floor, Payor used his parka as a blanket. He claimed he was quite comfortable with the setup.

The March 1966 snowstorm deposited 20 inches of snow, 1.70 inches of precipitation, on Warroad. The greatest snowfall, 10 inches, occurred on Thursday, March 3.

Only six reporting stations in Minnesota reported temperatures below zero on Wednesday, March 2, 1966. Warroad was one of them. After a low of -8 that morning, the thermometer rebounded to reach 29 later in the day. Temperatures at Warroad on Thursday, March 3 and Friday, March 4 varied from a high of 28 on Thursday, to a low of 12 on Friday.

No school was held at Warroad from Thursday through the following Tuesday. A storm Monday night brought in more snow and high winds that blocked roads, which had just been opened that evening.

According to Richard Nelson, Warroad postmaster, there was some mail delivery to and from Warroad on the Blackduck route on Thursday and Saturday. Nothing came in or left the Warroad post office on Friday. Warroad did receive mail on a run from Thief River Falls on Sunday. Rural mail delivery on Tuesday, March 7, was not helped by the new snowstorm.

A Warroad physician, Dr. Russ, received a couple of calls during and after the blizzard that could have been life threatening. One call from the Williams depot reported that a woman on the passenger train was very sick. When the train arrived in Warroad, Dr. Russ was there ready to take the ill person to the Warroad hospital on a snowmobile. But the lady had recovered sufficiently to continue on her journey to Winnipeg.

In another instance on Sunday, Dr. Russ rushed the home of Mrs. Leo Ulwelling. After trudging through deep snow from the road to her house, Mrs. Ulwelling had collapsed. Concerned over the possibility that she had suffered a heart attack, Dr. Russ had brought to the hospital. Within three days Mrs. Ulwelling was convalescing at home.

On Saturday night, Carl Larson plowed open a road that enabled Mrs. Lloyd Olson to get to the Warroad Hospital. The next day the Olsons became the parents of a baby boy.

The March 1966 storm was hard on mink ranchers in the Warroad neighborhood. Deep snow covered parts or all of mink shelters. This made it hard for the ranchers to get to the shelters to feed the mink. The animals were also suffering from sickness. As a result, the ranchers suffered the loss of some of their mink.

An additional problem was the fact that, in the week after the storm, most of the mink ranchers had planned to start breeding their animals. The blizzard had set this timetable back, although not by much.

By the middle of March, things were pretty much back to normal for the mink ranchers. They had come through the storm without losing a lot of mink. And the mink breeding was now under way.

There was at least one death suffered in the Warroad area during the storm. On Friday morning, Lawrence Budd was on his way to work. Riding a snowmobile from his home, he reached Marvin's (Millwork) office.

Budd was advised not to try make it to work that day because of the weather conditions. Despite the warning, he continued onto Warroad, where he stopped at the village office.

Budd was again advised not to try continue on to work. Accepting a ride on a snowmobile, Budd went on to Cal's Motel. Upon getting off the snowmobile, Budd walk only a short ways before collapsing and dying of a heart attack.

As the blizzard raged, another story that involved the Warroad Bantams' hockey team was unfolding. They were out to recapture the Minnesota state championship, a title they had last held in 1964. Unfortunately for them, the tournament was being held in South St. Paul, Minnesota.

The hockey players arose at 5 a.m., Friday to get ready to travel to South St. Paul, in case, a decision to that effect was made. At 11 a.m., it was decided that they would try make it to tournament.

So, in what the *Warroad Pioneer* called "the worst storm to ever hit northern Minnesota" an automobile caravan left immediately for the Twin Cities. Leading the way was

John Landby, driving a snowplow. Accompanying the team were Coach Dick Roberts, Manager Jack Marvin and Warroad Mayor Morris Taylor. Bringing up the rear were Jim Bishop of the U.S. Border Patrol and Dick Florhaug of the Minnesota Highway Patrol, in a radio-equipped patrol car.

By 3 p.m., they had made it to Wadena.

Upon reaching South St. Paul fifteen hours later, the players were informed that their hockey game would start in six hours.

Needless to say, it was a tired Warroad hockey team that faced a talented Eveleth the next morning. Lyle Kvarnlov gave Warroad a 1-0 lead in the first period. But, it was downhill after that. Sam Sabeitti scored four goals for Eveleth, as they skated past Warroad 6-2. Eveleth would go on to win the tournament.

It wasn't surprising then, when they lost both of their games in the hockey tournament. But it would be the trip to the tournament that would always be in their memories.

The snow clearing process required a round the clock effort for snow removal crews in the Warroad vicinity. With the possibility of emergencies in mind, they kept at least one entrance to the Warroad Hospital open. The *Warroad Pioneer* praised them for their efforts.

Impassable roads due to the storm, forced some Warroad area farmers to dump milk. This was not the case at the Rudy Hegstad farm, where there were forty-one milk cows. The Hegstad's were able to obtain over 3200 pounds of milk from their cows, without having to dump any of it. They brought the milk into Warroad on Saturday. As was to be expected, the creamery in Warroad was deluged with milk after the storm.

A Warroad couple, Mr. and Mrs. Harry Brewster, escaped unpleasant weather both in the South and in the North in March 1966. After staying in Louisiana for most of the winter, they headed back home just before a terrible tornado outbreak in the South. They made it back to Warroad Saturday night, just missing the '66 blizzard.

Others weren't so lucky. After spending a month in Mesa, Arizona, where she had been visiting, Mrs. Chet Feick returned to Warroad February 26, just in time to experience the terrible storm.

Concerned friends and relatives from other parts of the country called their loved ones in Warroad to ask how they got along during the storm.

After the storm had passed, the *Warroad Pioneer* tried to put a positive spin on the '66 blizzard. It noted that:

> *youngsters are having a real time playing on the huge drifts of snow, parents will eventually recover from sore backs acquired from shoveling snow, and all residents hope it will be another 60 years before a storm like this comes along again.*[51]

By the middle of March, the Warroad area was well on its way to recovery from the devastating storm. The snow had piled up so deep that a lot of people living out in the country or wooded areas were snowbound for a week or longer. While Warroad itself was pretty well dug out, it was taking a longer time to complete the job in rural areas. The snow removal process was being hampered by warm temperatures. Melting snow was harder to move than cold dry snow.

The story telling began in earnest after the storm. It seemed that everyone had a story to relate. A familiar refrain concerned people encountering snow too deep to walk through, as they tried to complete some needed chore. They were forced to crawl on top of the snow.

Tales of cattle and sheep buried in the snow came from Warroad area farmers. Surprisingly, some of the animals survived being submerged in the snow with little or no ill effects.

Over thirty miles southeast of Warroad is Baudette (1,597 residents in 1960). It lies along the Rainy River across from Rainy River, Ontario.

Both it and Baudette township took their names from Baudette River, a tributary of Rainy River. The word "baudette" is thought to have come from a personal French surname.

One person residing in Baudette in March 1966 was Wally Olds, a junior at Baudette High School. Following his graduation in 1967, Olds attended the University of Minnesota. There, he was a three-time letter winner, achieving All-American honors in hockey in 1970. Olds' scholastic career was just as outstanding. His graduation in 1972 in engineering was noted for achieving a perfect 4.0 in that area of study.

Perhaps, Wally Olds' greatest recognition came in being a member of the 1972 U.S. Olympic hockey team that won a silver medal. For his achievements, Olds' jersey (#6) from his days of playing high school hockey, was retired in ceremonies at the Baudette Hockey Arena on October 26, 2002.

The *Baudette Region* gave the following description of the March 1966 storm:

> *A storm center which moved northeastward from the plains states and eventually blew itself out over Canada seized the Rainy River country in a strangling grip Thursday and held grimly on for nearly two days.*

Fortunately, warnings about the oncoming storm had been issued well in advance. This allowed local residents time to take necessary precautions.

No school was held in Baudette on Thursday or Friday. On Thursday, local stores were open. But, conditions were much worse on Friday. Quite a few store owners, either closed their doors that morning and returned home, or remained at their establishments to get caught up on unfinished jobs.

While pedestrian and vehicular traffic came to an almost complete stop out in the countryside, the same could not be said for vehicular traffic with in Baudette. Unless an automobile was buried in or was sitting behind a substantial snowdrift, people could get around with their vehicles.

This mode of transportation may have even been easier than getting around on foot. For many of those on foot, out and about in the storm walking in the streets proved easier than attempting to navigate through deep snow on nearby sidewalks.

The Baudette area had its share of food shortages, medical emergencies and livestock feed emergencies. However, in each case, events concluded successfully. The *Baudette Region*, listed the reasons for this:

> *Each turned out all right, owing to skill and cooperation of such agencies as neighbors, civil defense, power toboggan operators, the medical people, and last but certainly far from least, the men who have kept plows going when and where they were badly needed during the storm, and on a 24-hour basis ever since.*

Concerning snowmobiles, the *Baudette Region* sang their praises:

> *Snowmobiles came into their own, buzzing around town with ease as operators awaited calls for emergency services.*[52]

These machines did encounter problems maneuvering through deep snow. A picture in the *Baudette Region* shows Bud Moorhead riding down the Main Street of on a Polaris snowmobile. What made that stand out was that his machine was an older model with the engine mounted on the rear of the snowmobile.

Two other ways of getting about in and around Baudette were skis and snowshoes.

The storm caught many people who resided in the country but worked in Baudette in the city when it arrived. They were forced to take refuge with friends until conditions improved.

Mail service to and from Baudette was disrupted by the storm.

Wind speeds at Baudette during the blizzard were from 25 to 45 mph. The height of snowbanks was as much as 15 feet.

It definitely wasn't easy for snowplow operators attempting to keep roads in the Baudette region open for traffic. The *Baudette Region* enumerated the problems they faced:

> *The snow was so heavy, drifts so deep, surface so slippery, and visibility so limited that removal equipment has on many occasions been stuck either on or off the road.*[53]

In neighboring Koochiching County, a snowplow became the refuge for Irvin Davidson and Morton Ebeltoft, a couple of state plow operators on one of the storm nights. They had been unable to keep their machine on the highway.

Problems were also being encountered by county plow operators. Rural roads had large drifts on them. It was a struggle to keep equipment up and running.

Baudette was the recipient of 18 inches of snow from the storm. The *Baudette Region* noted that the relatively mild temperatures of the storm prevented it from being called a "blizzard." But few were complaining.

As to how it was decided that Baudette had received 18 inches of snow from the storm, the answer lay with Harland Pickett. He had kept a weekly measurement of snowfall depth in Baudette in a stand of popple. They were dense enough to prevent any apparent drifting of snow. Mr. Pickett's last measurement, prior to the storm, showed that Baudette had a snow depth of 24 inches. A snowshoe trek by him into the popple stand right after the storm revealed a new snow depth of 42 inches.

Weather records indicated that Baudette had received 4.03 inches of precipitation from the storm.

Temperature data for Baudette was during and after the storm was hit and miss. Highs of 32 were reached both Wednesday and Thursday, March 2 and 3. But such information for Baudette was missing for the next three days. A low of -27 was recorded on March 7.

Traffic was reopened across the International Bridge at Baudette Sunday afternoon. The majority of main roads in the eastern part of Lake of the Woods County were open to traffic on Monday.

An attempt was made to reopen school in Baudette on Tuesday. Unfortunately, a high wind had come up during the night that drifted roads shut again. As a result, when the school doors were opened in Baudette Tuesday morning, a couple hundred school children were missing. Those pupils who had made it to school were sent home.

Surprisingly, for the most part, rural schools were open on Monday.

Communications and power lines in the Baudette vicinity remained in working order through the course of the storm.

By Tuesday evening, the snow removal process in the business section of Baudette was, for the most part finished.

In nearby Wabanica Township on Wednesday March 3, Terry Ebeltoft rode on the school bus to Eugene Molberg's place. He was planning on staying there for the night.

But the onslaught of the storm left him stranded there for the next three days. Finally, on Sunday the two boys were able to extract a car from its snowy grave at the Molberg residence and return to Baudette.

The storm forced Mrs. Oscar Maus, a Wabanica Township resident and a nurses aid at the hospital in Baudette, to remain in that city for a couple of nights.

A couple of Wabanica Township residents, Mr. and Mrs. Bjarne Anderson, were able to get their driveway opened by Paul Gugal and his son Jay on Saturday March 5. The Gugals had trudged from Wabanica Hall on foot to retrieve their "Cat." That blade-equipped machine was on John Benits' land south of Bjarne Andersons. It was employed to bring pulp loads out of the woods. Upon their return, the Gugals used their "Cat" to plow out the Anderson driveway.

The John Benits had a ski equipped visitor for coffee on Sunday March 6. That was Mrs. Marvin Anderson, who used skis to make the trek to the Benits place.

Blocked roads from the storm left Wabanica Township without mail service for three consecutive days.

Activity at Baudette's airport was adversely affected by the storm. Snowdrifts covered most of the planes there. But, on Saturday, March 5 four airplanes stopped at the airport. Their pilots and passengers were returning from a wolf hunting trip in Canada. They had been stuck there for the duration of the blizzard. On their way back, the planes' occupants stopped at Baudette to check through Customs & Immigration.

Unfortunately, all roads between the airport and the customs offices at the bridge in Baudette were impassable. No problem. Inspector Ernie Peterson donned a pair of cross country skis and skied over to the airport to do his inspection.

The next day a call was received from Arnie Skrivseth at Williams, a hamlet seventeen miles west of Baudette. His daughter, Trenda Lee, required transportation to Trinity Hospital in Baudette. Mr. Skrivseth wanted her flown to Baudette. So, in response to his plea, Bob Griffen flew to the Skrivseth farm.

But upon his arrival, Mr. Griffen discovered that someone else had taken the girl to the hospital in Baudette. Bringing some medicine with him, Vern James made it to the Skrivseth farm on a snowmobile. He transported the girl to the highway from which place an automobile took her to Baudette.

In the meantime, Bob Griffen's plane had become stuck. However, with some help by Kenneth Baade, it wasn't long before he was winging his aircraft back to the Baudette Airport.

Because snowplows were needed elsewhere, a few days passed before the road to the Baudette Airport was opened. One way to reach the airport was by foot from a nearby county road.

That was part of the reason there was little activity at the Baudette Airport on Sunday, March 6, 1966. Usually, there was a lot going on at the airport on Sundays. A couple of visitors to the airport that day were Ted Rowell and his son Joe. They made it there aboard a snowmobile. With Joe Rowell behind the wheel of the airport Jeep, the two men worked to clear the snow away that was piled up against the large doors of the hangar. It was a slow laborious process.

About ten miles east of Baudette is the village of Borders.

On Thursday, March 3, on the first day of the blizzard, twenty-two students made it to school in Borders. Even then, one of the school buses had not ben able to make it to all its stops. Deteriorating conditions forced school to be let out school at noon. The transportation of the pupils home on the high school bus was done almost on the heels of the snowplows.

No classes were held at the Borders school on Friday. Plowing of roads in the Borders area was in full swing on Sunday. By Wednesday school buses were back on their normal schedules.

For those fellows in the Borders vicinity who worked in the woods, the blizzard proved to be quite an inconvenience. They headed out Thursday morning, ready to embark on another work day. The arrival of the storm led most of them to quit early and head for the safety of home.

Upon returning to the woods Sunday with his dozer, Alvin Hasbargen found the wood roads to be buried in snowdrifts. To reach the wood was going to entail an enormous snow removal effort.

Albert Hasbargen, a local farmer, was forced to use skis for transportation on Saturday, March 5. The fan belt on the tractor he was using for transportation between his two farms three quarters of a mile apart broke. Mr. Hasbargen was using the tractor to check on his livestock. Unable to procure a fan belt at the time, Mr. Habargen opted to use skis.

As it was, Mr. Hasbargen couldn't have driven his tractor much further anyway. To discern where the road was becoming harder.

To keep an eye on his lambs and the twice a day feeding of his sheep at the sheep barn, Willie Hanson, another Border area resident, employed snow shoes to make the trek. At Mr. Hanson's place and a couple of others, snow was piled high enough to cover the clothes lines.

In March 1966, the U. S. Air Force maintained a radar station at Baudette. It was known as the 692nd Radar Squadron Air Force Base. At that time the Air Force was looking for houses to lease for military personnel who were assigned to the station. The base closed in 1979.

Carp is a small village over fifteen miles south of Baudette. A resident of that community, Mrs. Harold Hansen, gave the following description of the recovery effort in Carp after the storm:

> Everyone shoveling snow and you never get done. It was hard for those
> who have cattle. Am glad to say our little community came through fine.
> The snowmobile was just the ticket.[54]

An example of this occurred on Saturday, after the storm had let up. On that day, Chub Hancock used his snowmobile to make it to the county garage at Carp. Along the way he picked up Frank Lystad. From there, they set off on a snowplow to tackle the huge job of opening roads.

The storm caught two other fellows away from home. Marooned at a camp at Wayland, a village over thirty miles southeast of Baudette were Harold Duitscher and Ed Thurerson. As with the case of Mrs. Janicke, they faced the monotony of having little variety of food to eat. However, they came through their stay at the camp in good shape and returned home Sunday night.

On Minnesota Highway 11, six miles west of Baudette, is the village of Pitt. The atrocious weather kept Pitt residents home for the duration of the storm. People who lived in the Pitt vicinity and worked in Baudette were forced to remain there until the storm had passed. The teachers at the local school remained there for the entire weekend.

On Saturday, snowplows were doing double duty. They opened a few roads to one-way traffic. And, in some instances where people had run out of fuel and livestock feed, they cleared a few driveways. While making deliveries of groceries on Ski-Doos to the Pitt vicinity on Saturday, Kenneth Baade and Vernon James came upon Roger Lindstrom. He had left Pitt earlier and was headed for home on skis. Baade and James gave him a lift for the remaining distance to his home.

St. Cloud and Minneapolis-St. Paul

St. Cloud, the seat of Stearns County, lies about fifty miles northwest of the Twin Cities. It is actually located in three different counties–Stearns, Benton and Sherbourne. The "Father of Waters", the Mississippi River flows through St. Cloud.

In 1960, 33,815 people called St. Cloud home.

The first settlement at St. Cloud occurred in October 1851. John L. Wilson, "the "Father of St. Cloud" platted the village in the fall of 1854. He named the town after a grandson of Clovis, St. Cloud. Clovis was a renowned French King. St. Cloud set up a monastery near Paris, France and did many good works before his death around 560 A. D.

St. Cloud escaped the brunt of the storm and received less than 1 inch of snow.

But, it did receive quite a bit of rain Thursday afternoon, March 3. Thunderstorms pummeled St. Cloud between 2:30 p.m. and 3:30 p.m. that day. Thunderheads bellowed to 45,000 feet over St. Cloud which was "very unusual" according to weathermen. A combination of sleet, rain, and snow pellets fell during the thunderstorm. At 2:32 p.m. lightning hit the 500 foot KFAM radio tower in St. Cloud knocking the station off the air for five minutes. KFAM's chief engineer said, *"It was the first time in my life I've seen so many fuses go out at once."* By the time the thunderstorms were through, St. Cloud had received 0.95 inches of precipitation.[56]

Unfortunately, because of frozen ground and frozen storm sewer catch basins, quite a bit of flooding occurred in St. Cloud. Many home basements were flooded. and there was ponded water all over St. Cloud. The flooding forced at least two dozen people to flee their homes in St. Cloud, mainly in the north and west sides of the city. City crews couldn't keep up with all the flooding on Thursday as everything came in at once. The crews worked through the night thawing out the storm sewer catch basins.

According to Edward L. Henry, mayor of St. Cloud, as of late Friday, over 100 reports of flooded basements had been reported. He said inadequate drainage was the main reason for this.

On Friday, March 4 the U. S. Weather Bureau expected St. Cloud to receive the full force of the blizzard. As of 10:30 a.m., heavy snow was reported to be falling along an east-west line only five miles north of St. Cloud.

However, blizzard conditions expected for Friday and Saturday failed to materialize. While St. Cloud recorded high winds, it received less than an inch of snow. As a U. S. Weather Bureau spokesman stated, *"We have gotten by about as easy as we could have expected with something as wicked as this was."* St. Cloud was in the center of the eye of the storm which passed over the city at 8 a.m. Friday. The end result was milder weather for the city.[57]

The Twin Cities escaped the wrath of the '66 blizzard. At the Weather Bureau station at the Minneapolis-St. Paul International Airport in Bloomington most of the precipitation that fell was in the form of rain. On Wednesday, March 2, 0.08 of precipitation was received. The next day, .72 inches of rain fell.

The type of precipitation received in the Twin Cities during the storm is reflected in the temperatures they had. The high and low for Thursday, March 3 were 43 and 36, respectively. On Friday, March 4, the high and low at the airport was 40 and 27, respectively.

The Minneapolis-St. Paul International Airport did not receive any recordable snowfall until Saturday, March 5. At that time, 0.4 inches fell. Only a trace of snow was received at the airport on each of the three previous days. The high and low for Saturday at the airport was 27 and 15. The lowest temperature recorded at the airport after the storm was 6 above on Monday, March 7.

An explanation as to why the southern third of Minnesota received less snow and more rain from the storm than the northern two-thirds of Minnesota was provided by Joe Strub, climatologist with the U.S. Weather Bureau office in Minneapolis. Here is his explanation:

> Snow on the ground tends to beget more snow. When you have snow on the ground, the air temperature can be 10 to 15 degrees colder. Warm air tends to retain moisture and cold air will dump it. So with colder temperatures in the northern two-thirds of the state, they're likely to get more of the snow up there.[58]

Bemidji, Grand Rapids and International Falls,

Bemidji, (9,958 residents in 1960), located near the headwaters of the Mississippi River along the south shore of Lake Bemidji. The Mississippi River flows through Lake Bemidji on its way to the Gulf of Mexico.

The city took its name from an Ojibway Chief named Bemidji. He and his band of fifty Ojibway Indians lived in the proximity of the south end of Lake Bemidji. Translated into English, Bemidji means *"the lake where the current flows directly across the water."* Chief Bemidji passed away in April 1904 at the age of 85.[59]

In March 1966, the State College Board of Minnesota approved the moving of the Minnesota Vikings training camp from Bemidji to Mankato. The Vikings wanted to move to Mankato to be closer to the Twin Cities and southern Minnesota fans. Mankato was eighty miles from the Cities versus Bemidji's 220 miles. The Vikings players were unhappy with the five hour drive from the Twin Cities to Bemidji. The Vikings had been holding their summer training camp at Bemidji since 1961. The people most upset with the move were some the Bemidji area resort owners. Their brochures featured the Vikings training camp at Bemidji State College as a tourist attraction.

On March 3, over 2,200 students were in class in Bemidji, compared to the usual 2,600 to 2,700 students on an average day. According to Ray Witt, Superintendent of Bemidji Public Schools, the most noticeable decline in attendance was at Bemidji High School. This was because forty-eight percent of those attending Bemidji High School were from outside the city.

Despite the inclement weather, the Bemidji schools were going to try to remain open. Since Bemidji belonged to the North Central Association of Accredidation, Superintendent Witt said that it was required to have a minimum of 175 class days a year. As best he could remember, Bemidji schools had been closed only about three times in the last twenty years. If the schools had to close, an announcement would be made over Bemidji radio station KBUN.

Unfortunately, the next day, Friday, March 4, everything was either slowing down or grinding to a halt in Bemidji. For only the fourth time in twenty years, Bemidji schools had to close.

Bad weather forced the curtailment of city bus service in Bemidji for most of the day. Despite being open, most retail stores in Bemidji enjoyed very little business and intended to close early.

Bemidji's streets became virtually impassable. In spite of this, city crews did their best to keep the city's main thoroughfares open. People were advised to drive only in case of an emergency.

Blue skies on Saturday, March 5, in Bemidji meant an end to three days of snowfall. With the better weather, came a decline in winds and improved visibility. The storm deposited 11.8 inches of snow, 1.30 inches of precipitation, on Bemidji. Temperatures in Bemidji during the storm varied between 10 above and the upper 20's.

The digging out process now began. Crews from the Minnesota Highway Department were out in force. They did not intend to stop plowing, until they had opened all roads.

By the afternoon of March 5, the majority of primary roads around Bemidji were open. These included U.S. Highway 2 from Deer River to Bagley. Unfortunately, blockage of U.S. Highway 2 at Bagley kept motorists from proceeding west. State Highway 371 was open to the south from Bemidji. The stretch of State Highway 72 from Baudette to Blackduck was expected to be opened quickly. Reported to be in very poor condition was State Highway 92 south from Bagley and the La Porte cutoff. It was thought that by March 6, secondary roads in the Bemidji vicinity would be open.

West of Bagley, large snowbanks formed along the shoulder of roads. This did not give ordinary snowplows any place to push snow. To alleviate this situation, three rotary plows were dispatched to the scene from St. Paul.

A drift, 8 feet high, 200 feet long, completely blocked U.S. Highway 2, west of Fosston.

In Bemidji itself, plowing continued nonstop for the duration of the storm. With most of the main traffic arteries open Friday night, city crews concentrated on streets in residential areas. Their efforts were hampered by abandoned vehicles stuck in the middle of intersections or streets. The plowing by city crews left windrows eight to ten feet high in downtown Bemidji. To assist in the snow removal, Lake Bemidji was utilized as a repository for snow.

Bemidji's low of -25 on March 7 tied Roseau for the nation's low for the day.

A sign of the changing times was occurring in Bemidji in March 1966. The Northern Pacific Railroad, which ran passenger trains *No. 11* and *No. 12* from St. Paul to International Falls through Bemidji, wanted to discontinue passenger service on that line. It cited increasing competition from airlines, buses and automobiles as reasons for declining traffic on passenger trains. Bemidji's Chamber of Commerce and the Brotherhood of Railroad Trainmen took issue with the NP's figures and opposed the discontinuation of passenger rail service.

In years to come, there would be more changes. Up until the latter part of the 1980's, U. S. Highway 2 ran through Bemidji along the shore of Lake Bemidji. Construction of a U. S. Highway 2 bypass in the late 1980's directed some highway traffic south around Bemidji.

On March 3, Bemidji native Gerry Suman was chosen as an honorary captain for the NDSU's men's basketball team. Suman, a 6'6" junior, majoring in electrical engineering, averaged 15.3 points a game and garnered 210 rebounds for the 1965-66 team which finished with a 14-10 record. What was remarkable about Suman's play was being forced to learn to play center after playing as a forward the year before.

In 1966, Bemidji State College hired Bob Peters away from his job coaching the University of North Dakota men's hockey team. Over a 35 year career at Bemidji (1966-2001), Peters would win over 700 hockey games.

Grand Rapids (1960 population of 7,265) is the seat of Itasca County. U.S. Highway 2 connects it to Bemidji, about seventy miles to the northwest. The Mississippi River turns at Grand Rapids, to head west to its headwaters at Itasca State Park near Bemidji.

Itasca County was formed on October 27, 1849. It was named after Lake Itasca, the source of the Mississippi River. That body of water was discovered by Henry Rowe Schoolcraft in 1832.

Mr. Schoolcraft gave Lake Itasca its name. Before he discovered the source of the Mississippi River, Schoolcraft was canoeing along the south shore of Lake Superior with his friend, the Rev. William T. Boutwell. Schoolcraft asked Boutwell for the Latin or Greek word for the headwaters of a river. Unable to remember one in Greek, Boutwell came up with two Latin words, "Veritas" and "Caput", which means "Truth" and "Head".

Getting rid of the first three letters of "Veritas" and the last three letters on "Caput", Schoolcraft combined the remaining letters to come up with "Itasca."

The city and township of Grand Rapids took their names from rapids in the Mississippi River at that spot. In one third of a mile these rapids drop five feet. At one time, steamers on the Mississippi River from Aitkin made it this far up the river.

Snow began falling in Grand Rapids Wednesday afternoon, March 2. It continued to snow Thursday and Friday, and did not quit until Saturday. The blizzard dumped 14.5 inches of snow (1.78 inches of precipitation) on Grand Rapids.

It was the second major snowstorm to hit Grand Rapids during the 1965-66 winter. The city had received 14.1 inches of snow on November 26 and 27, 1965. This brought a total of 70.1 inches of snow to Grand Rapids for the 1965-66 winter. During the 1955-56 winter, 73.2 inches of snow fell on Grand Rapids. It was the second major storm in a year to hit Grand Rapids in early March. On March 1-3, 1965, Grand Rapids received 14.5 inches of snow (1.51 inches of precipitation) during a snowstorm. For that entire winter, Grand Rapids was the beneficiary of 67.5 inches of snow.

Because of the inclement weather, classes were not held in School District 318 on Thursday and Friday. Also closed on Friday, were Itasca Junior College and the Coleraine schools. But, stores and public buildings in Grand Rapids were able to stay open during the storm. There was also mail service. This, however, was delayed in some rural districts which had not been plowed out.

The local telephone system at Grand Rapids was overloaded with calls during the blizzard.

Grand Rapids experienced few power outages during the storm. The ones they did have, were due to broken branches and snowplows striking pole guy wires.

By Sunday, the weather had cleared, and the thermometer skidded to 15 below at Grand Rapids on Monday morning.

The city of International Falls (6,778 residents in 1960) lies along the south side of Rainy River, across from Fort Francis, Ontario. International Falls is not that many miles upstream from where the Rainy River flows into Rainy Lake.

On December 19, 1906, Koochiching County was formed, and International Falls became its county seat.

As a village, International Falls was also known as Koochiching. Later, it changed its name to International Falls. The name change took into account both the city's location on the Canadian border and its proximity to a waterfalls.

The completion of a dam in 1908 above the falls increased the level of the river to Rainy Lake. This enabled steamboats from Rainy Lake to advance upriver to International Falls. The dam provided waterpower for International Falls large paper mills.

Across the Rainy River from International Falls is the Canadian city of Fort Francis, Ontario. It took its name from the wife of Sir George Simpson (1792-1860), a legendary governor of the Hudson Bay Company. Her name was Frances Ramsey Simpson. It would be under his leadership of the Hudson Bay Company (1821-1860) that much of the Canadian northwest was explored.

On February 26, 1966, in St. Paul, International Falls whipped Roseau 5-0 to win the Minnesota High School Boys Hockey Championship for the fifth time in the twenty-two year history of the tournament.

It began snowing at International Falls around 6 a.m. Thursday. By Friday morning, 13 inches of heavy, wet, wind driven snow had fallen. Activity in and around International Falls quickly slowed to a trickle. There was no school in International Falls on Friday. The scheduled Friday night high school performance of *South Pacific* was canceled.

Highway travel in and out of International Falls was out of the question.

The airport runways at International Falls were blocked. The scheduled North Central Airlines afternoon flight was held up at International Falls Thursday.

Getting to work was hard or virtually impossible. The Minnesota Highway Department pulled its plows off the roads in many parts of northern Minnesota on Friday due to restricted visibility. They advised no travel west of a line running from Breckenridge to Baudette. North of this line visibility was very poor, and many roads were closed.

By the time the storm was over, International Falls had received 21.2 inches of snow or 2.12 inches of precipitation at the Weather Bureau station at the airport. At the same location, the depth of snow on the ground went from 17 inches on March 3 to 38 inches on March 5.

From noon Wednesday March 2 to noon the following day, the temperature in International Falls oscillated between 26 and 31 degrees. The thermometer ranged between 22 degrees and 27 degrees in the 24 hour period from noon Thursday to noon Friday. After the storm had passed, temperatures began to sink in International Falls, reaching a low of -22 degrees Monday morning.

Over the weekend highway crews worked nonstop to open roads in the International Falls area.

Brainerd and Aitkin

Brainerd is about fifty miles north of St. Cloud and is also on the Mississippi River.

In 1960, 12898 people lived in Brainerd.

Brainerd was established in 1870, when the NP decided to locate their place for crossing the Mississippi River here. The first NP train to reach Brainerd, arrived there on March 11, 1871.

It's name honors the wife of the NP's first president, J. Gregory Smith (1818-1891). His wife's maiden name was Ann Eliza Brainerd (1819-1905). Before serving as president of the NP (1866-1872), Mr. Smith was governor of Vermont from 1863 to 1865.

During the first 24 hours of the storm Brainerd received 7 inches of snow. This turned to a drizzle, and the mushy combination made for treacherous driving on roads. It was reported that schools within a fifty mile radius of Brainerd were forced to close.

From Thursday, March 3 through Saturday, March 5, 2.55 inches of precipitation fell at the Brainerd Ranger station.

Temperatures remained mild through the storm. The precipitation that fell in the form of a mist is reflected in Thursday's temperatures. The low for the day at the ranger station was 29. The thermometer did fall to 11 above for a low on Friday.

Nestled along the south side of the Mississippi River fourteen miles north of Mill Lacs Lake is Aitkin.

In 1960, 1,829 people called Aitkin home.

The person for whom the city of Aitkin was William Alexander Aitkin, a prominent fur trader in Minnesota who worked for the American Fur Company.

In 1870, the NP was constructing a rail line through Aitkin County. They established a station on the south (east) bank of the Mississippi River which they called Aitkin. When Aitkin County was organized in 1871, the village of Aitkin became the county seat.

As elsewhere, a familiar story was heard in Aitkin, when the snowstorm blew into the area on March 2. Since the first part of the snowfall was wet, it did not drift. This helped in Aitkin County.

The wetness of the snowfall during the first stages of the snowstorm at Aitkin is re-elected in the temperatures recorded at the Aitkin Ranger Station. On Thursday, March 3 and Friday, March 4 high and low temperatures reached there were 33 and 19 and 33 and 26, respectively. A low of -15 was recorded at the Aitkin Ranger Station on Monday, March 7.

Deteriorating conditions forced the cancellation of quite a few meetings and school Thursday and Friday. Despite the inclement weather of those two days, snowplow operators did manage to keep the primary roads open. Then, the process of digging out began.

The storm deposited 2.56 inches of precipitation at the Aitkin Ranger Station. Most of this, 1.61 inches fell on Friday, March 4.

In high school boys basketball action, Crosby-Ironton eliminated Aitkin from District 24 tournament play 53 to 30 at Brainerd on February 28.

Hibbing, Cloquet and Duluth

Situated in western St. Louis County, Hibbing (17,731 residents in 1960) is about sixty miles northwest of Duluth. It is located in the world famous Mesabi Iron Range.

The man who founded the city, Frank Hibbing (1857-1897), came to America from Germany as a youngster with his parents. In the fall of 1892, Hibbing located the iron ore beds at Hibbing. Mr. Hibbing made a large financial investment in the Mesabi iron ore mines.

The storm began in Hibbing with freezing rain and sleet. It began snowing around 6 p.m. Thursday. Around midnight, snow started to fall steadily and was accompanied by strong winds.

By noon Friday, 10 inches of wet heavy snow had fallen on Hibbing. At that time, the storm let up somewhat, but then resumed its fury. U.S. Weather Bureau personnel at the Hibbing Airport declared, *"We're due for much more and with heavy winds."*[61]

In the meantime, schools all across the Iron Range closed. Businesses closed, meetings were canceled, bus service was canceled, the Hibbing Airport was closed, mail delivery was canceled, the Hibbing Public Library was closed and the District Court Session was postponed. All sorts of social events were either canceled, postponed, or rescheduled. People couldn't get their cars out of their garages. Motor vehicles were stuck all over the place. Snowplows cleared some of the main streets in towns on the Iron Range.

By Saturday, Hibbing had received 14 inches of snow. Wind gusts up to 36 mph, had piled the snow into drifts 7 to 10 feet in many places, and made driving on highways hazardous. Once the storm was over, Hibbing recorded a snow depth of 32 inches on the ground. Since November 1965, 68 inches of snow had fallen on Hibbing.

Bus service resumed Saturday, and crews began clearing the runway at the airport. Street plowing began again in Hibbing the same day.

Temperatures at the Hibbing airport during the storm stayed between 18 and 32 above. Once the weather had cleared, the thermometer skidded downwards, reaching a low of 10 below Monday morning, before climbing back up.

Less than twenty miles west of Duluth is the city of Cloquet (9,013 residents in 1960).

Cloquet took its name from the Cloquet River. Logs were floated down this river to Cloquet for lumber manufacturing. It is thought the word "Cloquet" originated from the name of some fur trader.

Cloquet did not escape the wrath of the March 1966 blizzard. Sallie Kyle, a reporter for a local newspaper, the *Pine Knot*, gave this description:

> March came in like a lamb-but two days later she bared her fangs and roared like the proverbial lion. With the wrath of that furry animal, the March storm swooped down on the unwary citizens of our area, catching most of us completely unprepared. Hail. sleet, snow-we got them all.[62]

Because of mild temperatures, the precipitation that fell in Cloquet was a mixed bag. The storm arrived there Wednesday evening.

A high and low of 31 and 20 were recorded at the Minnesota forestry center at Cloquet Wednesday.

Because of high winds (35 to 40 mph) accompanying the sleet, Cloquet began losing power around 2 p.m. Thursday. Surrounding communities affected by the outage included Carlton, Duluth-Superior, Esko and Wrenshall.

There was no school in Cloquet, either Thursday or Friday.

People in and around Cloquet got around during the blizzard on foot, on horseback, on skis or on snowmobiles. That's how Boyd Ellis of Boyd's Market in Cloquet got to work Friday morning..

The storm created a run on food staples, such as bread and milk, in Cloquet. Because of this, Boyd's Market was doing a box office business on Friday.

Supplies of such items were running pretty low by 3:30 that afternoon. Mr. Ellis intended to close his store as soon as the last of the necessities was gone. Instead of remaining open late on Friday, as they ordinarily did, the majority of grocery stores in Cloquet intended to close their doors at 6 p.m.

The electrical outage was tough for those people in the Cloquet vicinity who relied on it for heating and power.

For example, farmers who required electricity to operate milking machines or water pumps were in a pinch. Their best hope were reports of the quick restoration of power.

Also hampered by the power outage were those homes which relied solely on electricity for heating and cooking.

The local radio station in Cloquet, WKLK, broadcast offers of assistance to those affected. These included providing coal burning stoves or small wood.

Communications to the outside world had improved enough in the Cloquet vicinity Friday night to provide information to those friends, relatives and public officials who were concerned about loved ones. To assist in sending messages to them, a short-wave radio operation was set up at radio station WKLK. It was manned by volunteers.

During the height of the storm, Carlton County snowplows stayed put and didn't try to go out and clear roads. As soon as the plow operators made cuts through drifts on roads, the drifting snow filled them back in. This made it impossible for the operators to keep the roads open.

As of 2:30 p.m. Friday, with the exception of U.S. Highway 61, virtually all roads within a thirty-five mile radius of Cloquet were impassable. Unless absolutely necessary, people who lived in this area, were being advised to stay off roads.

An around the clock effort was being made by crews from the Minnesota Power and Light Company (MPL) to restore power in the affected area. They were being assisted by MPL crews from Little Falls and the Iron Range. Other help came from Midland Construction Company and Northern States Power Company.

The affected region extended as far south as Barnum; east to the Floodwood area; as far north as the Alborn vicinity and east to Duluth-Superior.

The primary cause of the power outages was snow on feeder lines. Insulators on power poles iced up. To fix the problem, crews had to make pole by pole repairs. Obviously, having to go from pole to pole slowed power restoration considerably.

It never did get that cold in Cloquet during the blizzard. Highs and lows for Thursday, March 3 and Friday, March 4 were 31 and 25, and 32 and 25 respectively.

According to Bruce Brown, from the Minnesota forestry division, up to 6 p.m. Friday, Cloquet had received 15.1 inches of snow from the blizzard. Precipitation totals from the storm came to 1.86 inches.

On March 12, at the University of Minnesota-Duluth in Duluth, Cloquet's high school boys basketball team, lost the District 26 championship to Duluth East 69 to 64. Charles Jensen and Ken Young were co-captains of the Cloquet "Lumberjacks", who were coached by Ben Trochlil.

The port city of Duluth, Minnesota, the seat of St. Louis County, enjoyed a population of 106,884 in 1960. At the western end of Lake Superior, Duluth is next door to Superior, Wisconsin. Together Duluth and Superior are known as the "Twin Ports."

The two cities are connected by the Richard Ira Bong Bridge. This bridge is dedicated to the memory of a World War II fighter pilot from Superior, Richard Ira Bong (1920-1945). With forty Japanese planes shot down to his credit, Bong is the United States' all time leading "Ace of Aces."

The first white settlers to come to Duluth arrived in 1850-51. The platting and the choosing of a name for the city came in 1856.

Duluth was named after Daniel Greysolon Du Luth, a French explorer. Born near Paris, France in 1649, Du Luth came to North America. In 1678, Du Luth accompanied by seven other Frenchmen travelled by canoe to Lake Superior. Exploration of the country west of Lake Superior was his aim. This area was inhabited by the Assiniboines and the Sioux tribes. For the purpose of fur trading, Du Luth wanted these tribes on the side of the French. To this end, he assembled quite a few Indian tribes at or near the city of Duluth in the fall of 1679. On February 25, 1710, Du Luth passed away at his residence in Montreal.

Of all the cities and towns in the path of the March 1966 blizzard, none was hit harder than Duluth. The storm arrived in the city about 2:30 p.m. Wednesday. The high for the day in Duluth was 27 above at 2 p.m. The storm began in Duluth with a combination of snow and sleet. The city was on the eastern edge of the storm.

By 10 p.m. that evening, the Duluth Public Works Division had salted and sanded the main streets. By 11 p.m., plows in and around Duluth, were clearing snowdrifts off roads and streets. According to the Minnesota Highway Patrol slippery conditions existed on roads south of Duluth, and motorists were urged to use extreme caution.

Elsewhere, while only light snow was recorded in the Virginia-Hibbing-Eveleth areas Wednesday afternoon, heavier amounts were reported at Grand Rapids and other places.

The storm left many parts of Duluth without electrical power Thursday night. There were power shortages everywhere that left many homes with no heat or cooking power. A spokesman for the Minnesota Power and Light Company called it "the worst storm in memory."

At the Duluth International Airport, the thermometer recorded a high of 30 above in Duluth at 7 p.m. Thursday and a low of 26 at 3 a.m. Friday.

The slippery conditions were much worse than a straight snowfall especially for a city with hills like Duluth. It made highways in the Duluth vicinity almost impassable.

The economic damage to Duluth from the storm was dreadful. There was a high rate of employee absenteeism from their jobs. On Friday in downtown Duluth, most of the stores were not open. Impassable roads reduced commercial transportation in and out of Duluth to almost nothing. The word "silent" was used to describe the downtown Duluth area Friday afternoon. Schools were closed.

Downtown Duluth went without lights for nearly two hours Thursday afternoon. The editorial staff of the *Duluth News-Tribune* resorted to candles to provide light after the power failed. The newspapers operation were interrupted by an hour long outage that began at 3 p.m. Thursday and a 45 minute stoppage early Friday.

A Minnesota Power and Light spokesman said most neighborhood power failures were due to ice on the lines (up to three inches thick) and branches covered with sleet that were blown around by the wind. These broke brittle feeder and distribution lines. All available employees of Minnesota Power and Light worked throughout Thursday and early Friday to maintain electricity.

Three Duluth hospitals and one in Superior, Wisconsin, lost regular power Thursday afternoon. Two hospitals, St. Luke's and St. Mary's, were forced to get by with flashlights and emergency power. They used flashlights to take care of some routine patient care. Unfortunately, another hospital, Miller Memorial Hospital, lacked emergency generators. In order that its patients would receive their evening meals a bucket brigade-type operation was employed to relay dinner trays up the stairs.

Emergency utility crews were brought into Duluth from cities on the Iron Range and Little Falls to reinforce local crews.

All Duluth radio and television stations began experiencing power interruptions about 3 p.m. Thursday and were able to return to the air waves only sporadically after that. They said power failures close to transmitters made it almost impossible to broadcast. Despite the inclement weather, some radio and television stations were able to stay on the air.

At 4:45 p.m., Thursday North Central Airlines discontinued flight from Duluth because the power failure had blacked out the runway lights thus making it impossible to fly at night.

While other places near Duluth suffered power outages, none were as severe as those at Duluth.

The power shortage also affected the Duluth-Superior Transit Company. They could only run some buses on the main routes since their electrically operated fuel pumps became inoperable during the power outage. By Friday afternoon, this had been taken care of, and electrical power had been restored.

This was also true of gas stations around Duluth. When power outages occurred, they could not pump gas.

Because of the conditions, Yellow Cab suspended its taxi service in Duluth for Friday.

Auxiliary power units kept power interruptions at Duluth to a minimum for Northwestern Bell Telephone Company. Their greatest problem was the overload on the system due to all the telephone calls made during and after the storm.

The storm kept most of Duluth's downtown and suburban stores closed, as there was few customers.

The combination snow and sleet storm continued in Duluth on Friday. A howling wind coming off Lake Superior piled the snow into 15 to 20 foot drifts in the Park Point district of Duluth.

Duluth's main streets were kept passable both Friday and Saturday. On Friday, the driveway leading into Fire Department headquarters was blocked with snow. A snowplow was sent there in an attempt to open the driveway.

Outside of Duluth's city limits, it was a different story. The accumulation of snow into drifts was occurring faster than snow removal operators could remove it. Because of this, the Minnesota Highway Department district office in Duluth and the St. Louis County Highway Department pulled their plows off the highways.

Blocked roads in St. Louis County included main trunk highways.

By 7:15 p.m., Duluth had 14.7 inches of new snow on the ground. An expected blizzard for Duluth Friday night and Saturday failed to materialize.

Cars needed to have chains on their tires so they could make it up and down hills on Saturday. On the same day, Duluth's thirty-five snowplows were out in force, but making little progress in cleaning up after the storm.

It quit snowing in Duluth on Saturday. At the U. S. Weather Bureau station at the Duluth airport, a snowfall of 16.9 inches, 2.08 inches of precipitation, from the storm was recorded. The depth of the snow on the ground was 28 inches.

A person can see why Duluth was socked by a combination snow and sleet storm. Both, down by the harbor and at the airport, temperatures hovered at or not far below the freezing mark on Thursday and Friday, March 3 and 4. In order, high and low temperatures at the U. S. Weather Bureau station at the Duluth Airport for Wednesday, March 2, Thursday, March 3, Friday, March 4, and Saturday March 5, were 30 and 22, 32 and 26, 31 and 21, 22 and 8.

Chapter IV

The Canadian Experience

As with the American states just to her south, Manitoba did not escape the March 1966 blizzard. Southeastern Manitoba received the brunt of the storm, while southwestern Manitoba was on the edge of it.

Boissevain, Virden and Brandon

Boissevain (population of 1,473 in 1966.) lies in southwestern Manitoba, directly north of the International Peace Gardens and the Turtle Mountains. Every year an international Turtle Derby is held at Boissevain. The name of the races refers to the nearby Turtle Mountains.

Boissevain was first known as Cherry Creek (1881). The Canadian Pacific Railway built a line through the settlement. With the opening of a post office in 1886, came a change in the name of the community. It was now called Boissevain, after Adolph Boissevain of Adolph Boissevain and Company.

The storm arrived in Boissevain in southwestern Manitoba on Friday, March 4. Although on the perimeter of the blizzard, Boissevain still received gale-like winds that brought everything to a screeching halt. Businesses were closed; roads and streets were blocked.

About fifty miles west of Brandon is the city of Virden (2,933 residents in 1966).

In extending its line west across Canada, the Canadian Pacific Railway (CP) reached Virden in 1882. The same year, a post office was established at this site. It was named Gopher Creek, after a local stream that flowed into the Assiniboine River.

How the village got the name Virden, is a much debated one. One story has it being named after a place in Scotland. Another version has the site taking its name after the country estate in the area that had been homesteaded by Sir George Stephen (later Lord Mount Stephen). At the time (1882), he was president of the CP.

Extreme western Manitoba missed the full blast of the March 1966 storm. Virden reported winds up to 40 mph on Friday, March 4 which blocked many market roads.

Brandon, whose location is about sixty miles north of the International Peace Gardens, had a population of 29,981 in 1966. The CP, Canadian National (CN) and the Trans-Canada Highway all pass through Brandon.

After negotiations for a rail site with the MacVicars of nearby Grande Valley fell through, General Rosser of the CP picked Brandon as a railroad townsite in 1881. A post office had opened at Brandon the year before. When the CP line reached Brandon in 1881, a tent city was already in existence.

There are a couple of versions as to how Brandon got its name. The most probable one has the city being named after Brandon House, a Hudson Bay trading post at the mouth of the Souris River. That post most likely took its name from the head of the house of Douglas, the 8th Duke of Hamilton (1756-1799). Upon entering the House of Lords in 1782, his new title became the Duke of Brandon in Suffolk, England. The family owned a considerable amount of Hudson Bay Company stock. It would be this inheritance that Thomas Douglas, 5th Earl of Selkirk would use to finance his 1812 Red River settlements.

Brandon was on the edge of the March 1966 blizzard. None of the major highways in the Brandon district were blocked or covered with deep snow. What little amount of loose snow the Brandon area did have, blew right across the roads. But market roads, school bus routes, and other secondary routes were experiencing heavy drifting. Snowplows intended to clear them as soon as the weather improved.

Highway officials and the Royal Canadian Mounted Police (RCMP) warned motorists, if possible, to stay off highways. They noted that visibility was zero in many places. Also, as one proceeded east from Brandon, the visibility became markedly worse. People took the highway officials and RCMP's warnings seriously. As of Friday, the Brandon RCMP had received no reports of accidents or of cars stuck or abandoned.

Temperatures in Brandon varied between 7 and 13 above Thursday night and Friday morning. The wind speed was between 20 and 30 mph, until 5 a.m. Friday morning. At that time, the snow began to drift, as it was pushed by wind gusts up to 40 mph.

Manitoba's Minister of Education called off school for Friday for all of southern Manitoba. Students who had come to school that day were quickly sent home. With the schools closed, the manager of the Wheat City Arena in Brandon allowed free skating in the arena Friday morning and afternoon.

The storm dusted Brandon with about a quarter inch of snow on Friday. It did not affect highway travel a lot in the Brandon area. Neither Grey Goose nor Greyhound bus services were delayed by the storm in the Brandon area. Heavy truck traffic also had little trouble on the Trans Canada Highway and provincial Highway 10. Deliveries of milk and mail went on as usual.

By Friday evening, the wind had dropped to 15 mph, and the temperature had fallen to 10 above in Brandon.

Pilot Mound, Morden, Crystal City and Winkler

East of Boissevain lies Pilot Mound (767 residents in 1966). A post office in the Pilot Mound vicinity opened for business in 1880. When the CP built a line through the area in 1884, the post office was moved two miles south to its new location.

The first proposed name for the village was Balmoral, but, as that name was already in use, the name Pilot Mound was chosen instead. That name came about from a large hill of shale in the area that could be seen at a long distance by pioneering settlers. They used the mound as a "pilot" or land mark to guide them.

One story has Indians calling the mound "Dancing Hill". To them, the hill was not only a place of dance, but also an observation point, a shrine and a burial mound.

Unlike Boissevain, Pilot Mound received the full effect of the blizzard. On Friday, heavy snowfall and wind gusts up to 60 mph, dropped visibility to zero. As with other towns and cities in the storm's path, Pilot Mound had its share of blocked streets and no traffic. Stores and businesses remained open to provide people with the necessary goods and services, but most people stayed home.

In the Pilot Mound vicinity, people kept their sense of humor throughout the storm. One person was reported to have told his boss, *"Won't be in for work today-haven't been home yesterday yet."*[1]

After the storm had passed, residents of the Pilot Mound area debated whether or not it was the "blizzard of the century." Everyone agreed that the short duration of the storm was its only shortcoming in that respect.

Morden is located pretty much straight north of Langdon, North Dakota. Situated on the edge of the Red River Valley, with the Pembina Escarpment on the west side of town, Morden enjoyed a population of 3,097 in 1966.

Morden took its name from a homesteader of the area, Alvey Morden. Hailing from Bruce County, Ontario, he came to the Morden vicinity in 1874. Mr. Morden stayed put here and passed away in 1891.

Before the CP established Morden as one of its stopping points (1882-1883), there had been two other settlements in the area. To the southwest of Morden was Mountain City. The name of the settlement northwest of Morden was Nelsonville.

Originally, it was hoped that a rail line would be constructed to link Morden and Nelsonville. When it became apparent that wouldn't happen, the CP pushed for the development of Morden (1883). They built a station there.

Morden experienced the full wrath of "the blizzard of the century" or "the big blow of '66", as it was known locally. The storm dumped 18 inches of snow on Morden. This was accompanied by winds that gusted up to 50 and 60 mph.

After 36 straight hours of zero visibility in Morden, the storm finally let up on Saturday.

Of how the blizzard affected every day life in Morden on Friday, the *Morden Times* had this to say:

> Main street was like a ghost town on Friday as local business places and
> schools locked their doors and battened down the hatches to wait for the
> storm to abate.[2]

The city of Morden swung into emergency mode, once the storm descended on it. At the fire hall, fire trucks were ready to roll, just in case an emergency call came in. To ensure that they could get out, the approaches to the fire hall were kept open twenty-four hours a day by maintenance operator Henry Harder. He was also ready to clear a path in front of the fire trucks, if the alarm at the fire hall did ring.

During the height of the blizzard on Friday, and continuing into Saturday, the Morden city police, snow removal operators and the staff at the Morden District General Hospital endured sleep deprivation.

If the situation became a crisis, the Morden city police and RCMP were prepared to function together as a co-ordinated "Emergency measures" team. The police received approximately forty to forty-five telephone calls, most of which were inquiries for information.

The lousy weather did not prevent any of the staff at the Morden Hospital from making it to work. One way or another, the doctors and nurses found a way to get to the hospital. Few of them left, before the storm let up. Any sleep they got during their long stay at the hospital consisted of catnaps on make-do beds.

All in all, Morden came through the "Blizzard of '66" without having a lot of emergencies. A couple of emergencies at Morden involved two pregnant women.

On Friday, it appeared that Mrs. A. R. Neale of Morden was about to have a baby at any time. A Manitoba Telephone System vehicle, with a crew that had been on emergency standby for situations like this, was dispatched to her home on Third Street. They took her to the Morden Hospital.

The other situation concerned Mrs. Murray Nichol of Darlingford. She had come to Morden before the storm hit the city to see her doctor. As there were storm warnings out, her doctor advised her to stay in Morden. This, Mrs. Nichol did.

Unfortunately, during the height of the storm on Friday, it became evident that she had to get to the hospital, and the sooner the better.

To transport Mrs. Nichol to the hospital, the Morden City Police were called. However, every street in Morden was blocked with humongous snowdrifts. To overcome this emergency, Jack McKennit of Morden, who possessed a cutter and a team of horses, was contacted.

Accompanied by Cliff Minty and Constable Ove Larson of the RCMP, Mr. McKennit went to 11th Street in Morden with his cutter and team. After picking Mrs. Nichol up, they set off for the hospital. A reporter for the *Morden Times* observed them passing along Stephen Street in Morden. Equipped with a jingling harness, the horses trotted over snowbanks and past stalled vehicles to deliver Mrs. Nichol to the hospital in plenty of time.

The blizzard depleted most homes in Morden of their larder, particularly bread and milk. So, on Saturday, in addition to the sight of people digging out, they could also be seen walking to grocery stores that had reopened, to buy food. Ones that couldn't get to the stores put through their orders by phone. Then, they had to wait for the delivery trucks to try make it to their residences through snow clogged streets.

At the Jack Zacharias farm one mile south of Morden, the weight of the snow from the storm caused the collapse of a portion of a chicken barn. Some volunteers, under the leadership of Art Heppner of the Pembina Poultry Packers, cleaned out the barn. The building sustained quite a bit of damage.

The *Morden Times* summed up the '66 storm this way:

> *The conclusion of it all seems to be that despite modern day technology, man-made machines grind to a halt when mother nature "really lets us have it". However, given a new dawn and a brighter day, men and their mechanical monsters emerge as they roar to life in the effort to clear the way toward resumption of normal, everyday living. As you read this you won't be feeling nearly as helpless as you did five days ago. The "blizzard '66" is history."[3]*

On March 12, 1966, Morden's high school boys' basketball team lost in the finals of the Manitoba "B" basketball tournament to Brandon's Vincent Massey High school by a score of 41 to 38 in Brandon. The game ended Morden's eight game winning streak.

The Morden team was led in scoring by Tim O'Rourke and was coached by Henry Neufeld.

Crystal City (600 residents in 1966) is located west of Morden. This town lies along Crystal Creek which ambles to the northwest to join the Pembina River. Surveyors had given the creek its name because of the crystal-clear water in it. An underlying shale bed was responsible for the clear water.

A colonizer of the Crystal City area, Thomas Greenway of Ontario, took the creek's name and gave it to the village. Crystal City was settled by the Rock Lake Colonization Company. A member of that organization was reported to have said:

> *Why, we will give it a big name like they do in the States; it is on the Crystal Creek named by the surveyors, so we will call it "Crystal City."[4]*

In 1879, a post office opened in Crystal City.

The March 1966 storm did not last as long in Crystal City as elsewhere. Light snow, accompanied by high winds, descended upon Crystal City on Thursday, March 3.

The next day conditions deteriorated, as heavy snow and winds gusting up to 60 mph left Crystal City with zero visibility.

Vehicular traffic ground to a halt Friday, due to plugged alleys and streets. Despite this, some business establishments in Crystal City, while not fully staffed, were able to be open up on Friday to provide necessary goods and services. As could be expected, business was not booming, since most people stayed home. While an effort to hold school open in Crystal was made on Thursday, no such effort was made on Friday.

The inclement weather interrupted commerce flowing through Crystal City. This included buses, food trucks, mail and milk.

Milk destined for Crystal City did not get there until Sunday.

Wind gusts accompanying the storm reached 70 mph at Crystal City. These blew around the approximately 12 inches of snow that fell on the ground there. As could be expected, the results were drifts that ranged in height from 6 to 14 feet. Snowbanks reached up to the eaves on houses.

A snowbank that completely submerged several windows was high enough so as to allow children to climb up it and get on the roof of the Thomas Greenway Collegiate.

Lousy visibility and drifted on Thursday helped to contribute to a highway accident at the 3A bridge south of Crystal City. There, two cars side sideswiped each other.

The digging out process began in earnest at Crystal City on Saturday. Early that day, snow removal equipment was out plowing out Crystal City's main streets and the highway entrances into town. Their efforts on Saturday allowed for some vehicular traffic in Crystal City that day. The *Crystal City Courier* described their plowing efforts as this, " The village of Crystal City has become a network of trenches dividing huge piles of snow."5

For residents of Crystal City, the back-breaking work of shoveling out their residences and clearing driveways and sidewalks was just beginning. The digging out would continue well into the next week.

In a couple of instances, two Crystal City families were literally snowbound. They could use neither their front or back doors, as these were blocked by deep snow. Their neighbors saved the day to shovel out the entrances to their homes.

A Crystal City area rancher, Sid Vines, came close to losing thirty-six head of cattle to suffocation. They were entombed when deep snow blocked the entrance to their shelter. Vines's neighbors and residents of Crystal City rescued them in the nick of time Saturday morning.

Luckily for Crystal City, it came through the storm with no reports of fires or fatalities.

The relatively mild temperatures during the March 1966 storm kept Canadian weathermen from calling it a "blizzard."

Turning philosophical, the *Crystal City Courier* had this to say about the storm:

> *The past week, nature has reminded residents of this part of the world that although they may be able to circle the world in a space craft in a matter of minutes there are also times when they cannot move very far.*[6]

Located six miles east of Morden is the city of Winkler.

It had a population of 2,520 in 1966.

The CP set up a rail site here in 1892. The land Winkler was established on, was owned by a lumber merchant, Valentine Winkler, who built the village's first structures. Since he gave the CP every second block of land, they named the new townsite after him.

Valentine Winkler entered this world in 1865 at Neustadt, Ontario. Later, he emigrated west, becoming in 1891, the municipality of Stanley's first Reeve (In certain Canadian provinces, a reeve is the elected head of a town council or village). The following year Winkler won election as a representative for Rhineland to the Manitoba legislature. Other service included being a Member of Parliament, and from 1915-1920 as Minister of Agriculture and Immigration.

In the 1950's, a report came out that said Winkler would stagnate and not develop into a growth center. This made city officials and developers see red. According to Walter Siemens, consultant for the Winkler Community Development Corporation, *"That just made us mad."*

They set out to disprove the report-and they did. They started with a garment facility. City officials and developers increased Winkler's industrial base by installing four industrial parks. The continued growth required the development of other sectors of Winkler's economy-housing, medical, retail and recreational.

Assisted by strong leadership and the Winkler Community Development Corporation, the results have been phenomenal. By 2003, Winkler's population had grown to almost 8,000, with expectations of it doubling over the next 10 to 15 years.[7]

The March 1966 blizzard arrived in Winkler Thursday night.

The next day, the raging storm brought almost everything to a halt. Before noon, some Winkler businessmen trudged through the snow to get downtown. But, the continuing onslaught of the storm forced the closing of all businesses in Winkler.

The schools in Winkler were closed on Friday.

The situation was becoming difficult. The Winkler City Council had just met the night before, but they held another meeting Friday to scope things out.

One thing they did was to contact A. C. Wiens who had a large front-end loader. He remained on stand by notice ready to swing into action if any emergency (such as fire or sickness) came up.

As for Town Superintendent Jake Loewen, the City Council requested that he repair to the water plant and stay there overnight. He would be there just in case any emergency came up.

A request was made of the Winkler City Council to assist in helping two expectant mothers, Mrs. Denis Giesbrecht on Crystal Crescent and Mrs. Dave Reimer on 3rd Street get to the hospital. They needed both equipment to clear a path ahead of them and transportation.

Winkler made it through the blizzard without any major fire problems.

The storm let up Saturday morning, and the residents of Winkler were left with 12 inches of new snow and snowdrifts on their streets that, for the most part, were from 4 to 5 feet high. In places such as Crystal Crescent, the drifts soared to heights of 20 or more feet.

Moving rapidly Saturday, the Winkler City Council swung their public works department into action. A. C. Wiens was directed to plow single lanes on Winkler's streets. By doing it this way, they had most of Winkler's streets open to traffic by early afternoon.

The City Council also purchased twenty shovels for the Bible Scholars from the Winkler Bible School. On Saturday, students from there voluntarily cleared snow off sidewalks for Winkler residents. In one good deed, they went over to the Salem Senior Citizens Home and cleared snow from the sidewalks and exits to the place.

To assist residents of Winkler who had run low on food during the storm, Winkler businessmen met and assented to keep their stores open until 9 p.m. Saturday. They also agreed that if any emergency requests for supplies came in on Sunday they would open their establishments. A third item they agreed to was to be open on Monday. This way the businesses would be open to provide service to Winkler area farmers who couldn't get out over most of the weekend because of blocked roads. After three or four days, their larders would be running low. By Monday, some of the area farmers were actually making it to Winkler.

To assist stranded farmers in his vicinity, Abe Friesen used his home-made snow plane. Comprising of large skis, a big aircraft motor, a propeller and a jet plane wing tank, the snow plane helped keep Friesen busy delivering emergency supplies to the farmers. Although snow planes were still fairly common in 1966, they were rapidly being replaced by snowmobiles.

The snow removal effort would have to continue for the majority of the week to make roads and streets in the Winkler vicinity really passable for driving.

The Winkler Zodiacs ended their basketball season in 1966 by defeating Morris, 46 to 32. Don Klassen led the winners with 17 points, and Ike Dyck added 8 points.

The March 1966 blizzard disrupted the new publishing schedule for the *Pembina Triangle Progress* which was to begin with the March 9th issue.

In conclusion, the *Pembina Triangle Progress* had this to say about the March 1966 storm:

> *The Big Storm of March 4th, 1966 is almost history but it will live in the memories of all those who lived through it (there was no loss of life here) and will be talked about long after as "The Storm of the 20th Century."*[8]

By clearing snow from the early hours onward on Monday, Jake Lowen and his snow removal team were able to have two blocks on Main Street cleared of snow by 9 a.m. For their efforts, they were praised by Winkler Mayor John Epp.

In retrospect, Mayor Epp said the March 1966 storm caught the Winkler City Council and the public unprepared. For starters, he mentioned a shortage of snowblowers. Epp also noted the lack of assistance the Emergency Measures Organization had to offer. The failure of the Manitoba Government to have a rotary snowblower stationed in the Winkler area was another thing he was critical of. Despite all this, they were able to get by to a certain extent.

Altona, Gretna and Rosenfeld

Altona is located about 15 miles north of Neche, North Dakota.

In 1966, 2,129 people called Altona home.

The "Sunflower Capital of Manitoba" took its name from Altona, Germany. It translates into English as "old fertile Plain." Altona first showed up on maps in 1902.

The storm blew into Altona about 1 p.m. Thursday, March 3 and did not leave there until 7 p.m. Saturday, March 5, a total of fifty-seven hours. Wind gusts reached 70 mph in Altona. The city suffered the usual problems so many other towns encountered-blocked roads and streets, stalled vehicles, and stranded motorists.

A serious problem that residents of Altona endured was the loss of hydro (electrical) power during the storm. The hydro powered failed at 1 p.m. Friday, and it was not until 11 a.m. Saturday that power was fully restored. Many homes in Altona were without hydro power for as long as twenty-two hours.

Among those without electricity was the Altona Hospital. A 200-foot extension cord from an adjacent building was connected to the hospital, so it could be reheated. Hospital employees, including nurses, used flashlights to supply needed light. There was no need for any emergency operations during the storm, so the light from flashlights sufficed.

Because she was in labor, a woman had to be brought to the Altona Hospital. To accomplish this she was placed in a toboggan and strapped in place. Then, a snowmobile towed her to the hospital in Altona. Her baby entered this world early Monday.

Entombed by 18-foot drifts and cut off from the outside world for thirty-six hours, residents of an Altona apartment block cleared a path to safety.

A farm house became a place of refuge for a bus driver and twenty-seven passengers, after their bus stalled in a snowbank near Altona Friday evening. It would be another thirty-six hours before they could dig the bus out.

When left without electricity due to the hydro failure, families in Altona resorted to using kerosene lanterns and camp stoves to provide heat and light.

Announcers at the local radio station broadcast messages of public interest and of the progress of the storm. They suffered the hydro failure like other people in Altona. However, they had auxiliary power plants at their studio and transmitter site to keep them on the air.

Snowmobiles provided many services to people . These ranged from delivering food to hungry families to transporting women in labor to the hospital.

The flatness of the Red River Valley contributed to the severity of the blizzard in Altona and other towns and farms.

Gretna (561 residents in 1966) lies about a mile north of Neche, North Dakota.

It was settled about 1883, following a CP-GN linkup at the border. It was named for the place of origin of the man who erected the first grain elevator in Gretna, a Mr. Ogilvie. He came from Gretna Green, a Scottish border community that was known for its runaway marriages. Ironically, Gretna, Manitoba was also a border town.

The March 1966 storm dumped 14 inches of snow on Gretna.

Over 15 miles east northeast of Gretna along the Red River is where Fort Dufferin once stood. It was established in September 1872 as a base of operation for the British-Canadian portion of the North American Boundary Commission. This was a joint British-Canadian and American effort to survey and determine the precise location of the United States-Canadian border from Lake of the Woods to the Continental Divide on the Rocky Mountains.

Trouble with whiskey peddlers among the Indians in the Canadian West was one of the reasons for the formation of the Northwest Mounted Police (NWMP) in 1873 (later the Royal Canadian Mounted Police (RCMP)).

The new police force departed from Toronto the following year. They were under the command of Colonel G. A. French, the NWMP's first commissioner.

The NWMP, along with their horses, rode aboard a train until they reached Fargo, Dakota Territory in June 1874. After disembarking there, it took the NWMP six days to ride up the Red River Valley from Fargo to Fort Dufferin. They arrived there on June 18-19, 1874.

Fort Dufferin would be the NWMP's first headquarters in the Canadian West.

After three weeks' of training, Colonel French and his force headed west on July 8, 1874. They followed the route pioneered by the Boundary Commission.

Upon arrival in Alberta, the NWMP set up Fort McLeod and Fort Saskatchewan near Edmonton, Alberta.

Colonel French, accompanied by two troops, made it back to Fort Dufferin in November of that year.

Once the Boundary Commission and NWMP had no more use for Fort Dufferin, they abandoned it.

The fort was purchased by the Canadian government in May 1875. It was used as an immigration center, especially for Mennonites from the Ukraine. The first 500 Mennonites processed through Fort Dufferin arrived there aboard the steamboat *International* on July 14, 1875.

The Canadian government sold Fort Dufferin in 1907.

The trail along the U. S. Canadian border pioneered by the Boundary Commission would later be used by others, including ox carts and wagon trains.

A modern reenactment of the Boundary Commission trail through Manitoba was done in July 1991. A group of people in wagons and horseback followed two Mounties (also on horseback) along the trail. The Mounties were dressed in NWMP uniforms from the 1870's. People can retrace the Boundary Commission-NWMP Trail in the comfort of their own vehicle along marked routes through southern Manitoba today.

Rosenfeld, a Mennonite settlement, became a CN/CP rail junction. In 1882, the CP gave it the name "Rosenfeld." It translates into English as "rose field."

The blizzard left a bus stalled a mile south of Rosenfeld. Inside was the driver and twelve passengers. Along came a municipal snowplow to get the bus moving. Unfortunately, in the meantime, a car ran into the bus. In the ensuing collision, the driver of the car was injured and had to be taken to the hospital.

Carman and Portage la Prairie

Located sixty miles southwest of Winnipeg, Carman (1,922 residents in 1966) began with the opening of a post office in 1880. Shortly thereafter, the CP and CN located railway points there.

The name for the city came from Manitoba Premier Rodmond P. Roblin. Before coming to Manitoba, Roblin had been a student at Albert College in Belleville, Ontario. The Chancellor of the school was the Reverend Albert Carman (1833-1917). Roblin suggested naming the settlement after him. In the course of his career, Carman served as Bishop of the Episcopal Methodist Church in Canada (1874-1883) and General Superintendent of the Methodist Church in Canada(1883-1917).

At first, the settlement did not have a name. But then, a log church, thought to be the first Protestant church built west of the Red River, was erected. While engaged on a tour of western missions, the Reverend Dr. Carman stopped in the community and dedicated the church. To honor his visit, the village was named after Rev. Carman. Initially, it was known as "Carman City", but that moniker was quickly dropped.

Carman shut down completely during the '66 storm. As the (Carman) *Dufferin Leader* noted:

> *Don't bother telling your grandchildren about it; they won't believe it.*
> *Mind you, fourteen -inch snowfalls aren't all that bad, and winds gusting*
> *to a mile a minute(some gusts up to 70 mph) aren't that unusual, but*
> *when you put both of them together you've got weather conditions guaran-*
> *teed to keep great-uncle Smedley from talking about the blizzard of '08.*

The *Leader* also noted that the U. S. Weather Bureau called the March 1966 storm "the worst in recorded history, including the blizzard of 1888."

In describing the effect of the storm on the Carman area the *Leader* said:

> *Everything stopped. Buses were stranded, hockey games were canceled, shops closed, schools shut, snow shoes were dusted off, and in the minds of thousands the weatherman was sent to the seventh level of the inferno.*[9]

The '66 blizzard lashed Carman with wind gusts up to 70 mph and 14 inches of snow.

There were many stories to tell in and around Carman during and after the storm. Below are a few.

The inclement weather on Friday prevented store keepers, several truck drivers and other employees who had gone to work that morning from getting home that night. The majority of them took refuge in hotels.

The atrocious weather conditions forced the abandonment of about a dozen automobiles on the streets of Carman. Unable to proceed any further, their owners abandoned them.

Traveling by bus to Carman for a playoff hockey game, the Thompson Hawks team got no further than Portage la Prairie early Friday. The players took refuge in three hotels there. Saturday morning they dispatched a scout car ahead to check the condition on the highway between Portage La Prairie and Carman. Following by bus they made it to Carman shortly before noon Saturday.

Unable to extricate himself from his home by any other means, a doctor was forced to remove the storm window from a door on his house. He then crawled out through the opening.

During the height of the storm, an expectant mother was brought into Carman on the heels of a snowplow.

There was no bus service in and out of Carman until Saturday afternoon.

Despite the raging blizzard, the movie theater in Carman was open Friday evening. Three people were on hand to see a movie starring Jack Lemmon and Virna Lisi.

On Friday, no school was open in southern Manitoba.

Mink ranchers in the Carman area suffered a few losses during the storm. But, these were minor compared to those losses in the Bird's Hill and St. Pierre vicinities. Because some mink ranchers were in Winnipeg attending an annual mink rancher's meeting, when the blizzard arrived in Carman, they did not get home. And, their mink went to bed hungry.

One of the heroes in Carman during and after the "Blizzard of '66" was the snowmobile ("power toboggan"). Among the items they conveyed were coal, oil, groceries and a baby calf. A man was unhappy that a snowmobile had run over his buried car. A collision with a windshield on a car (the machine went through it) brought another snowmobile to an abrupt stop.

Groceries were delivered to different places in the Graysville region via bombardier.

Snow was piled so deep around one house at the north end of Carman that access to it had to be made through a tunnel. So high were the drifts around it that if it wasn't for chimney, television aerial and little corner of the roof jutting above the snow, a person wouldn't have known there was a house there.

A power outage at 7:20 a.m. Friday at Stephenfield left homes without power. Soft snow kept a Manitoba Hydro snow machine from reaching the trouble spot. Power was not restored until late Saturday afternoon. North of Graysville a telephone line was not working.

First, with such lousy weather on hand followed by such deep drifts (up to 20 feet) people ran out of food. To get to grocery stores in Carman people resorted to skis and snowshoes.

There was such a demand for bread, the bakery in Carman was forced to limit patrons to purchases of five loaves of bread per customer.

There was a run on snow blowers and snow shovels in Carman. Buyers cleaned the stores out of these items, even though they had a large stock on hand.

The blizzard disrupted mail delivery in Carman until Monday March 7.

The snow removal effort in Carman began in earnest on Saturday. Among the extra equipment brought in to help were two snow blowers. That day they concentrated on Carman's main thoroughfares and had most of them passable the same day. The crews worked around the clock until Tuesday. By Monday a majority of Carman's streets were open to at least one lane of traffic. The snow that had been removed was dumped in the river. Despite all this efforts there were still many piles of snow in Carman. The cost of the snow removal effort in Carman was estimated to be as much as $3,000.

School was back in session in Carman on Monday. The student turnout for classes was good. Unfortunately, the same could not be said for all country schools near Carman. Not all of them held classes on Monday.

Portage la Prairie (13,012 residents in 1966) lies sixty miles west of Winnipeg. The Assiniboine River flows through it on its way to join up with the Red River in Winnipeg. The Trans Canada Highway runs through Portage la Prairie.

The history of this Manitoba city is intertwined with the fur trade. The first white person to appear in the Portage la Prairie area was Pierre la Verendrye in 1738. Below is La Verendrye's own account of his trip:

> I pursued my route and entered the river of the Assiniboine, which is fifteen leagues from the fort (Maurepas). I then ascended the river sixty leagues, and not being able to go farther I stopped and built fort la Reine at that place on the third of October.[10]

Once he had established Fort La Reine, La Verendrye set off southwest across the prairie. He reached the Mandan Indian villages along the Missouri River and then returned. He would be the first white person to have entered the state of North Dakota.

In 1742, Fort la Reine would be the jumping off spot for Verendrye's sons' attempt to find the "western sea." They never found it. They buried a lead plate at a spot overlooking the Missouri River near Pierre, South Dakota. That object would be found by some school children in 1913.

Leaving Fort la Reine, voyagers would then portage north from to Lake Manitoba. The French term for this overland trek would one day be used to name the future city. The following is an account of how Portage la Prairie got its name:

> The name Portage la Prairie is derived from the existence of a carrying place nine miles long, between this part of the Assiniboine and Lake Manitoba. It is stated by {Metis} at the settlement, that at seasons of extraordinary high water, canoes can approach each other from the Assiniboine and Lake Manitoba, so as to leave but a very short distance from the portage; and instances have occurred of water, during periods of high

floods, flowing from the Assiniboine into Lake Manitoba by the valley of the Rat River. (now Rat Creek).[11]

The exact location of Fort la Reine is uncertain.

Other trading posts would be established in the Portage la Prairie vicinity. Once the French had departed, the Hudson Bay Company (HBC) established a post at or near the locale of Fort La Reine. Initially, they called their establishment Assiniboine River Fort. Later on, it was known as Portage la Prairie. The HBC would remain at this location until around 1870.

In 1832, two miles east of the center of Portage la Prairie along the Assiniboine River, the HBC set up another trading post. By 1870, this trading post had been moved west and was located on Saskatchewan Avenue.

The Northwest Company also had a trading post in this area. It went by the name either of Fort des Prairies or Fort la Reine.

Permanent white settlement came in 1851 when Archdeacon Cochran of the English Church Mission Society bought land on which Portage la Prairie lies today from Chief Pequakekan. The community had a post office before 1870. Both the CN and CP ran their lines through the city.

Going into March 1966, the city of Portage la Prairie was emerging from a cold winter. The previous month of February had been cold, but mostly dry in the city. January 1966 had been considerably colder in Portage la Prairie than February 1966. For the record, 4.4 inches of snow fell on the city in February. A record low (for that date) of 44 below zero was observed on February 18 at the RCAF's (Royal Canadian Air Force) Portage station aviation forecast office. The thermometer climbed to 39 above in Portage la Prairie on February 27.

The forecast for Portage la Prairie for March 2, 1966, read as follows:

> *Sunny today clouding over this evening. Mostly cloudy Thursday. Little temperature change. Winds northeast 15 increasing to 25 this afternoon. Low tonight and high Thursday 5 and 20 above.[12]*

Giving a hint as to the deteriorating weather conditions that were coming the forecast for Portage la Prairie for the following day March 3, 1966, stated:

> *Cloudy. Light, blowing snow beginning this evening and continuing on Friday. Little temperature change. Winds north 30 (mph) with gusts to 45. Temperature at Gimli, Carman and Winnipeg steady near 20 overnight and dropping to 15 Friday evening.[13]*

The *Daily Graphic* gave the following vivid description of the storm that descended on them on March 4, 1966:

> *Portage la Prairie was turned into a veritable ghost city today as a vicious March blizzard virtually paralyzed the community along with all of populated Manitoba and north-western Ontario.*
>
> *Snow driven by winds gusting at close to 70 miles an hour turned the whole Portage area into a wild and seemingly deserted white wasteland.*

The forecast for Portage la Prairie for such a dreadful day (March 4, 1966) was not for anyone thinking of spring:

> *Weather warning continued-cloudy with snow and blowing snow and blowing snow today becoming sunny with drifting snow Saturday afternoon. Winds north 30 gusting to 50. Low-high zero and 10 above.[14]*

With such atrocious weather occurring Friday, there was little activity or movement either on foot or by motor vehicle in Portage la Prairie.

Because of the zero visibility outside of the city, the RCMP in Portage la Prairie issued a warning to motorists to refrain from driving on any highway.

The storm caught twenty-five people at the Campbell Soup Company Ltd. plant in Portage la Prairie. A rescue effort early Friday morning involving a road patrol and the city-owned snow blower failed to reach the plant. Very poor visibility kept their operators from driving them to the plant.

That afternoon a second attempt was made. To help the snowplow push on through the storm with its zero visibility, men from the public works department trudged through the snow ahead of the machine driven by Stan Zerkee, guiding it and looking for stalled automobiles. "Casey" Bruinaage, Fred Dell and Jim Ostepowich took turns performing this hazardous duty.

Relief workers for those stranded at the plant rode on a Webb Bus Line vehicle that stayed close behind the snowplow, as it worked its way towards the plant.

It took two hours to complete the rescue mission, i. e., from the time the snowplow left Portage La Prairie, drove to the plant and then returned.

The bus was involved in some other rescue missions. It transported people caught by the storm at the shopping center to places of safety. The bus was also used to deliver and help find accommodations in town for transport truck drivers stranded at the Co-op Garage located at the west end of Portage la Prairie.

The blizzard forced a one week postponement of Portage la Prairie's Winter Fun Festival, which had been slated to begin Friday night. Festival committee members held an emergency meeting at 10 a.m. Friday to make the decision. They were of the opinion that a one week postponement was better than taking a risk that the weather would clear by Friday evening.

As with fire departments elsewhere, the one in Portage la Prairie was on "alert" for the duration of the blizzard. However, it would not have the luck of many other places and come through the storm without any fires.

When a call came into the Portage fire station around 10 p.m. Thursday, the storm hadn't descended on the city yet. The call involved trouble with a furnace motor. But, no damage was reported. It would be another call that came in at 11:30 p.m. Friday, just as the storm was beginning to let up a bit, that gave the Portage la Prairie fire department a real challenge. Kent Yee turned in the call.

A fire had broken out at Walt's Tire garage located at the intersection of Lorne Avenue and Tupper Street in Portage la Prairie.

Responding to the call were ten firemen on two fire trucks and the city's rescue truck. Additional help came from men from the Board of Works.

When they got to the fire, the firemen saw a Mr. Lilley trying to put out the fire by shoveling snow through a window onto it.

The firemen's efforts were hampered by various things. Among them were high winds (up to 50 mph), and a large volume of tires and tubes that had caught fire. They proved hard to put out. The situation wasn't helped by a leaking acetylene tank that kept feeding the blaze. Finally, some men were able to enter the building and extricate the acetylene tank from the premises. Another item conveyed from the building was an oxygen tank.

But, the fire wasn't out just yet. Another call to the fire station came in at 4:27 a.m. Saturday. Evidently, the high winds had reignited the fire in the service station's office.

In the second go around, the ceiling and roof of the service station fell within itself. This didn't help an already dangerous situation. By this time, the thermometer in Portage la Prairie had fallen to just above zero. This time, however, the firemen were successful in extinguishing the blaze.

The service station suffered quite a bit of damage in the fire. As of Saturday morning, Portage la Prairie Fire Chief Harold Braden didn't know the cause of the fire. According to him, it was close to a moulding machine for tire repairs, where the fire began.

The lousy conditions almost led to several collisions involving city snow removal equipment. Because of this, at mid-morning Portage la Prairie's snow removal equipment was called in off the city streets. According to the chairman of Portage la Prairie's public works department, Ald. (Alderman) Webster Burton, *they were more a hazard than anything else. The decision was made after several near-accidents.*

In the hope that storm winds would subside to allow snow removal crews to start clearing city streets and highways, the public works crews were not to resume snow removal operations until after the lunch hour.

Mr. Burton went on to declare, *The crews are prepared to work all through the night if necessary to bring the situation back to order.*[15]

The fact that Portage la Prairie's General Hospital was kept staffed through the storm was due mainly to Bud Kitson who had a towing service.

To get the city through the storm crisis, the Emergency Measures Organization (EMO), headed by Portage la Prairie's mayor, H. L. Henderson, swung into action. Stranded travelers needed accommodations. To help them, the EMO dispatched an appeal for emergency accommodations. Within twenty minutes, people were answering the appeal. Their swift reaction to the appeal prompted Mayor Henderson to say:

> *The co-operation of our people in general was absolutely amazing.*
> *When we asked for anything, we got it-right now.*[16]

It was not a dull time for Portage la Prairie's EMO unit during the worst of the storm. In a 24 hour period, the city's four-wheel rescue truck answered fourteen calls. It was able to go places, where vehicles without four-wheel could not go.

The same two units also took supplies southwest of Portage la Prairie to the Indians Students' Residence. Along with a snowplow, it delivered provisions and extra gasoline to the river pumping station. This was done as a precaution, just in case electrical power at the station went out.

Mike Yablonski, superintendent of the water plant, together with two shift employees, was marooned at the water plant early Saturday. They did not get rescued until snow removal equipment clearing a path towards Hillside Cemetery came along.

Other duties performed by the city's rescue truck included transporting stranded public works employees to work, bringing staff to the Portage General Hospital and delivering nurses for standby duty at the Manitoba School.

Because an emergency might arise during the storm, regular firemen of Portage la Prairie's Fire Department remained on the job all day Friday and through the night. For the following day, four of them would be on duty.

Mayor H. L. Henderson sang the praises of those helping out with the emergency measures. According to him they "did a terrific job." For example, secretary-treasurer D. G. Rodgers arranged for Portage la Prairie's City Hall to be manned for emergency work. In another case, Mrs. Campbell and Alf Tarr babysat the radios and telephones throughout the day on Friday and on into the night.

Mayor Henderson said Portage la Prairie's experience with the March 1966 storm displayed the need for a two-way radio hookup; i.e., for equipment operating within city limits.

An attempt to connect the water plant with emergency headquarters via a radio hookup had failed due to the problem of distance. If the connection had been successful and an emergency had arisen, EMO could have contacted the water plant to provide the needed stores.

According to him, the absolute minimum radio hookup setup would involve include a central control, at least one fire truck, the four-wheel drive rescue vehicle, snowplow and the pumping station. The advantage of this system included the elimination of the need to return to emergency headquarters for information and orders. It would also stop a lot of duplicating runs.

Caught by the blizzard near the Assiniboine River, two department of conservation employees found sustenance at the water plant. They remained there until the roads were plowed out. This allowed them to make it into Portage La Prairie.

The forecast for Portage la Prairie for Saturday March 5, 1966 read as follows:

Clearing today. Little change in temperature. Winds decreasing to 20. High today 10 above. Sunny and a little colder Sunday.[17]

There was a storm related fatality in Portage La Prairie. T. St. Cyr, aged 79, lived south of the city. He had gotten severe frostbite from the blizzard. A snowplow followed by an ambulance were dispatched to the scene by Portage la Prairie's Emergency Measures Organization. After battling the elements for three hours, the rescue vehicles reached the victim's home.

St. Cyr was transported by ambulance to Winnipeg's General Hospital. Sunday night, he passed away there.

Just a few hours later, the snowplow and ambulance answered another call. An accidental gunshot victim, 22 year-old Roy Smoke, at the Sioux Indian village which lay four miles southwest of Portage la Prairie needed assistance. He was taken to a hospital in Winnipeg.

The March 1966 storm disrupted weekday mail service in southern Manitoba for the first time since the general strike of 1919, when there was no mail delivery on Friday March 4, 1966. The resumption of airline and rail service on Saturday allowed mail to be delivered to Winnipeg.

The snow removal crews in Portage la Prairie did a Herculean job in getting the city's streets cleared of snow. From early Friday, they worked nonstop until 6 p.m. Sunday. They resumed their snow removal efforts at 6 a.m. Monday.

Early Sunday morning, the snow removal crews began clearing paths through residential areas. Their hard work paid off, as by late that afternoon, there were almost no homes in Portage la Prairie that could not be reached in case an emergency arose.

By Monday morning, Mayor H. L. Henderson was able to report that vehicles could now travel on up to ninety-five per cent of Portage la Prairie's streets.

Mayor Henderson had praise for both the general public and Portage la Prairie's snow removal crews. Of the former he said, *"Everyone was very patient."* Of the latter, he stated, *"There was not a complaint from any of them, despite the long hours and arduous work."*[18]

Although, most of Portage la Prairie's thoroughfares were open Monday morning, this did not mean the streets were completely clear of snow. An open street might have a single lane open through it.

On Monday, Webster Burton, public works chairman, announced that widening of these passing lanes would begin right away. He said that Portage la Prairie residents could help the snow removal efforts considerably by keeping their vehicles out of the way of equipment. Vehicles left on Portage la Prairie streets after 8 a.m. Tuesday were to be towed. A warning to this effect was issued.

As elsewhere, children in Portage La Prairie were attracted by the huge snowdrifts and the deep cuts in them made by snow removal equipment and played there.

This worried Chairman Burton and the snow removal crews. They wanted parents to inform young children of the dangers of playing near where snow removal equipment was working and keep them away from such areas.

As Mr. Burton put it:

> Public works employees have been working under terrific pressure. Let's not give them more worries about our children. They don't want an accident.[19]

Also on Monday, Portage la Prairie's public works department thanked people who used shovels and private snow removal equipment to assist the department in their snow clearing efforts.

By late Sunday, the Trans-Canada Highway between Portage la Prairie and Winnipeg was open, although there were still snowdrifts on it. At the same time, the highway between the Lakehead and Kenora was also open. That stretch of the highway had not yet been cleared to its full width.

As of early Monday all major highways in Manitoba were open to traffic.

Winnipeg, Beausejour and Steinbach

Winnipeg lies at the intersection of the Assiniboine and Red Rivers. European settlement of Winnipeg dates to the arrival of the Selkirk immigrants in 1812. The city's first name was Red River Settlement, so named by Thomas Douglas, Earl of Selkirk.

Winnipeg was later known as Fort Garry. That name came from a HBC Director, Nicholas Garry, who visited the area in 1821. HBC and the Northwest Company merged that same year, and Garry was on the advisory board for that union. From 1822-1835 he served as Deputy Governor of HBC.

A post office was established in Winnipeg about 1870. In 1876, the name was changed to "Winnipeg." The city was named after Lake Winnipeg. The term "Winnipeg" is an Indian one meaning "nasty water lake" or "sea."

Winnipeg recorded a high of 31 above on February 28, 1966, and Brandon came in with a high of 30 above. Although like Americans Canadians had experienced Alberta Clippers, their meteorologists also knew that the heaviest snowfall to Manitoba would come from the south where developing lows could tap into moisture from the Gulf of Mexico. Particularly worrisome were lows emanating from the Colorado Rockies.

This can be seen in a forecast from their Weather Service that ran in the *Winnipeg Free Press* on March 1, 1966. It said, "A new disturbance emerging out of the southwestern United States threatens to bring some heavier snow to southern Manitoba late Wednesday." Their forecast for Wednesday, March 2, 1966, called for "Sunny and a little colder Wednesday. Winds west at 28 mph and gusty becoming light overnight."[20]

On March 1, Winnipeg recorded a high of 30, Brandon reached 25 and Kenora soared to 35.

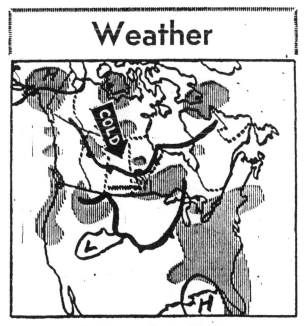

Canadian weather map for March 1, 1966. Courtesy of Winnipeg Free Press

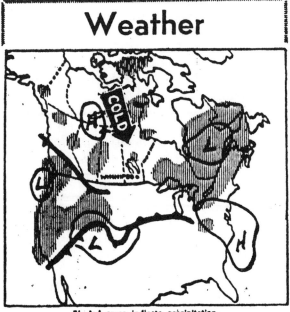

Canadian weather map for March 2, 1966. Courtesy of Winnipeg Free Press

On March 2, the Canadian Weather Service had this to say about the storm:

> A storm brewing in the southwestern United States will move northeast-
> ward into northwestern Ontario by late tomorrow. After a sunny day in
> Manitoba today, skies will cloud over ahead of the system tonight. Light
> snow is expected to develop in the southeastern sections of the province
> by morning. Temperatures in Manitoba will continue near the seasonal
> levels.

The forecast for Manitoba called for:

> Clouding over this evening. Occasional light snowflurries. Thursday,
> little change in temperatures. Winds light becoming northeast at 20 mph
> this evening.[21]

High temperatures in Manitoba on March 2 included 20 above at Winnipeg, 18 at Brandon, and 30 at Kenora.

On Thursday, the Canadian Weather Service still thought that Winnipeg would only get light snow. But, as they noted in the *Winnipeg Free Press*:

> A storm system south of Manitoba moving northeastward will bring
> snow to southern parts of Manitoba today. The storm system affecting
> Manitoba will move far enough eastward by late Friday and begin clear-
> ing in this area. Meanwhile temperatures under cloud cover will remain
> slightly above seasonal normals.

The forecast for March 3 stated:

> Cloudy, light snow and blowing snow beginning this evening and con-
> tinuing Friday. Little change in temperature. Winds north at 30 mph with
> gusts to 45.[22]

Some of the highs reached in Manitoba and Ontario on March 3 included 11 at Brandon, 13 at Winnipeg, and 26 at Kenora.

However, instead of receiving light snow and wind gusts up to 45 mph, Winnipeg was deluged with heavy snow (14 inches) and winds gusting up to 60 mph. Meteorologists admitted their mistake by putting a sign held up by a person buried in snow with the word "HELP" written on the sign.

The Canadian Weather Service's synopsis of the weather (on March 4) stated:

> A fierce blizzard is blowing in southern Manitoba. Blizzard conditions
> are expected to continue until Saturday afternoon as the centre moves
> slowly northeastward through Northwestern Ontario. Temperatures in
> the blizzard area will remain near 10 above. Further north and westward
> conditions gradually improve to clear skies. Saskatchewan will be mostly
> sunny as well Alberta. These provinces are under the influence of a large
> cold high pressure area and temperatures will run 10 to 15 degrees below
> normal today.

The forecast for March 4 for Manitoba read:

> Cloudy with snow and blowing snow today and tomorrow. Little change
> in temperature. Winds north at 35 mph and gusting to 60. Weather warn-
> ings continued. Low tonight for Gimli, Carman, and Winnipeg 5, High
> Saturday 10.[23]

On Friday, wind gusts up to 68 mph were recorded at Winnipeg International Airport.

Weather

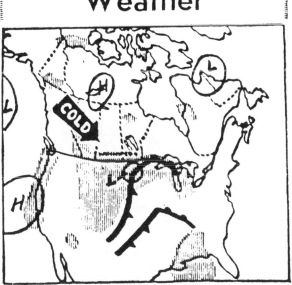

Canadian weather map for March 3, 1966. Courtesy of Winnipeg Free Press

Shaded areas indicate precipitation.

On Thursday, March 3 forecasters thought the storm would miss Winnipeg. On that day, they issued a storm warning for northwestern Ontario. To them, at that time, the northern edge of the storm seemed stationary about fifty miles south of Winnipeg.

Unfortunately, as the storm continued eastward, it suddenly veered north. The forecasters had anxiously watched the storm for twenty-four hours or more and expected it to continue east. They knew it would hit northwestern Ontario. Then, suddenly it turned north and hit Winnipeg. The end result was that Winnipeg was given only a two hour notice, before the storm arrived.

Many people, including the mayor of Winnipeg, Steven Juba, went to bed Thursday night expecting that the storm would miss the city. At 7 a.m., CJOB radio newsman Steve Halinda called the mayor to ask what measures could be used to combat the blizzard. The mayor was unaware of the storm. Thanking the caller, Juba went to City Hall to begin setting up an emergency center from which news bulletins were issued to the news media.

Weather

HELP!

Sign depicting situation in southern Manitoba on March 4, 1966. Courtesy of Winnipeg Free Press

The storm tied things up completely in Winnipeg on Friday. For the first time in the history of Winnipeg, the law courts were closed because of the weather. All Manitoba law courts were closed that day.

During the blizzard, fifty amateur radio operators set up a citizens band network to send needed items including food and medicine all over Winnipeg via skidoos (snowmobiles), tow trucks and private cars.

Shortages of oxygen, bread and milk threatened Winnipeg's Children's Hospital Friday, until the situation was remedied.

City of Winnipeg Mayor Steven Juba conducting a special council meeting to formulate plans on how to deal with the snowstorm that had parlyzed the city. March 4, 1966.
Courtesy of Western Canada Pictorial Index

Pedestrians on a Winnipeg street during the blizzard. March 4, 1966. Courtesy of Western Canada Pictorial Index

Some corner grocery stores, drug stores and cafes were able to stay open during the storm to provide service to those who had to head out into the storm.

The intensity of the storm became clear in its first hours, as orders were quickly given out to close all schools in southern Manitoba. These came via a bulletin from Education Minister George Johnson. They reopened March 7. Classes at the University of Manitoba were canceled.

There was an irregular delivery of bread and milk.

Also shutting down Friday were liquor stores and many businesses. Those that attempted to open, found themselves found themselves lacking both customers and employees.

As of mid-morning, the depth of snowbanks in a few suburban sectors of Winnipeg was waist high. The center of Winnipeg took on the appearance of a "ghost town."

At 10 a.m. Friday, people were told *"to stay at home and keep their cars off the streets."*

An emergency committee was set up that consisted of the mayor, Maitland B. Steinkopf (Manitoba's Public Utilities Minister), metro officials and city department heads. These included Winnipeg Police Chief George Blow, Fire Chief Cecil Leckie and City Engineer. W. D. Hurst. The mayor and the committee were concerned with doing "first things first." This meant fire and police services.

Winnipeg's transit system (Metropolitan Winnipeg Transit) became crippled Friday by huge drifts from the storm. This forced the abandonment of some routes. The schedules on others were worthless.

An 11 a.m. curfew was put in Friday morning, (six hours after the blizzard had descended upon Winnipeg) to stop bus service. This was done because of the inclement weather. The last time that had occurred in Winnipeg was during the general strike of 1919.

Of the 400 city buses in service Friday morning, 135 were still abandoned on the streets as of 9 p.m. Friday. Many of the bus drivers joined their passengers in private homes. Drivers overtime skyrocketed Friday beyond time and a half. It was to be paid to drivers who were stranded with their buses.

The lack of transportation forced a lot of people to return home, when they learned there wouldn't be any to take them to work. The heated shelters of the Metropolitan Winnipeg Transit System became refuges for hours on end for others.

The blizzard snowed in undertakers and cemeteries. This forced the cancellation of scheduled funeral services.

Abandoned automobiles were a major hazard on the streets of Winnipeg during the storm. It was suggested that a ban on automobiles be imposed during weather conditions such as the March 1966 blizzard.

Police Chief George Blow said all abandoned vehicles would be towed away. Constables accompanied each tow truck. Blow wanted the streets cleared for emergency use only. He remarked that if people remained at home and kept their vehicles off city streets, city personnel and other emergency crews would take care of the rest.

On Friday morning, the Manitoba Motor League suspended its emergency services. Hundreds of cars were reported stranded west of Winnipeg. A warning was issued to motorists by the Manitoba Highway Department. They were not to venture out on any provincial highway. People calling taxi firms in Winnipeg for service on Friday didn't receive a reply on the other end.

Originally, it was hoped to have Winnipeg city buses back on the streets between 4 and 6 p.m. Friday. Unfortunately, this proved impossible to do. Mayor Juba asked everyone who hadn't left their homes yet Friday morning to remain there.

The *Winnipeg Free Press* was able to publish on Friday, but it was delivered only to parts of the downtown area, to homes where open streets permitted delivery and by rail. Rural areas did not receive their paper.

More than 1,600 employees of downtown Winnipeg stores, such as Eaton's, Simpson Sears and the Bay, were unable to get home Friday and spent the night in the stores. Other employees jammed downtown hotels.

The weather made things difficult for police, fire and other essential services, and they operated on a haphazard basis. Power toboggans (snowmobiles), bombardiers, and four-wheel drive vehicles were the primary means of transportation in Winnipeg during the blizzard.

The storm forced pregnant women to give birth to their babies at home, as the storm prevented assistance to them from police and fire departments. Suburban fire chiefs were thankful there were no fires in the suburbs during the storm.

The storm put a crimp on crime in Winnipeg. Except for answering emergency calls, Winnipeg police weren't dispatching their cars onto city streets. As long as it continued to storm, the RCMP was suspending all highway patrols. The RCMP asked motorists to also stay off highways. At the time the March 5, 1966 edition of the *Winnipeg Free Press* was going to press, no emergencies, either for the police or ambulance drivers, had been reported to that newspaper during the storm in Winnipeg. The ambulances did become stuck in the growing snowbanks. However, it was reported that in spite of the delays, at no time was anyone's life in danger.

On Friday the Manitoba legislature did not meet. Because of the atrocious weather, the Winnipeg Grain Exchange canceled trading for the first time in its 61 year history.

Only downtown Winnipeg was receiving its mail on Friday.

The snowstorm shut down construction work in Greater Winnipeg on Friday, March 4. Atrocious weather conditions prevented Kam Gajdosik, secretary of Construction Laborers' Local 101 from making it to his office, located in the Labor Temple.

According to a spokesman for the National Employment Service (NES), it was "very, very quiet" at his office in downtown Winnipeg on Friday. To allow workers from the office to make it home before they became snowbound, everyone, but a skeleton staff, was being sent home. Even the skeleton staff would be heading out the door at 4:30 p.m.

The NES spokesman noted that a normal heavy snowfall brought in hundreds of requests for men to remove snow. It wasn't happening this time. People who ordinarily made such requests weren't at their work places. As a result, on Friday, the NES was receiving very few requests for help to clear snow.

On Friday the storm forced the CP discontinue service on its line to Minneapolis. At the same time, there were no airplane arrivals or departures from Winnipeg International Airport.

The Winnipeg Police Department urged residents to leave front porch lights on. This step was being taken in order to guide people who might be lost in the storm. People were also asked to keep snow away from front and back doors because of the chance of fire. They were also asked to use the telephone only in an emergency. The Manitoba Telephone System had a skeleton crew working, and there was a fear that overuse of the lines that were open would disrupt communications.

Simpson Sears employees bedding down in furniture department during the blizzard. March 4, 1966. Courtesy of Western Canada Pictorial Index

Trolley buses on Portage Avenue during the snowstorm. March 4, 1966. Courtesy of Western Canada Pictorial Index

The Canadian armed forces also assisted during the blizzard. Two emergency units were set up in Winnipeg. These consisted of a doctor, nurse, and a dentist who had an autoboggan for their use. They could be reached through the 999 emergency telephone service.

Army trucks helped to transport stranded people home over partially blocked streets..

The Red Cross used trucks to get blood supplies to hospitals.

Motorists who had abandoned their automobiles on Winnipeg streets were asked to put their names, addresses and phone numbers with the writing side facing out on folded pieces of paper under rolled up car windows. This way the drivers could be contacted more easily when conditions improved so that cars could be moved.

By Saturday, the storm had departed from Winnipeg, and the digging out process began. The snow removal process began in Manitoba. It was led by an army of snowplows. Aircraft, trains and intra provincial buses were trying to return to normal schedules by early afternoon. This was after not running at all Friday or being eleven hours late that day.

All available equipment was used to open main routes first for public transportation and food deliveries. This meant that streets in residential neighborhoods of Winnipeg wouldn't be opened until Sunday morning at the earliest.

Winnipeg's city buses returned to work at 10 a.m. Saturday. They passed through narrow lanes cut through snowbanks, of which the height of some reached 19 feet.

For many residents of southern Manitoba, the March 1966 blizzard brought back memories of the November 17-18, 1958 snowstorm. That one dumped 16 inches of snow on Greater Winnipeg.

Machines clearing snow from street following snowstorm in Winnipeg. March 5, 1966. Courtesy of Western Canada Pictorial Index

High snowbanks lining downtown Portage Avenue in aftermath of blizzard in Winnipeg. March 5, 1966. Courtesy of Western Canada Pictorial Index

Snowmobile on downtown Portage Avenue in aftermath of the blizzard in Winnipeg. March 5, 1966. Courtesy of Western Canada Pictorial Index

Children jumping off a building into snowdrifts following the snowstorm in Winnipeg. March 5, 1966. Courtesy of Western Canada Pictorial Index

People gathered outside the Silver Heights Shopping Centre in St. James area of Winnipeg with various means of transportation including snowshoes, skis and toboggans upended in snowdrifts. March 6, 1966. Courtesy of Western Canada Pictorial Index

The city of Beausejour lies northeast of Winnipeg. In 1966, 2,214 people called Beausejour home.

The CP reached this location in 1877.

Accounts vary as to how the city got its name. According to one of them, a French construction engineer named it. Building a rail line for the CPR through brush and swamp, he came upon an elevated grassy area. The Frenchmen called the location "beausejour" which translates into English as "a good stopping or camping place." To the natives this place was known as Stony Prairie.

The Winter Farewell celebration in Beausejour in February 1966 was a big success. Describing the weather before and after the celebration the *Beausejour Beaver* had this to say:

> *The weekend preceding the Farewell broke all records for plain old Manitoba frost, the weekend following broke all records for winter storms in Manitoba.*[24]

The March 1966 storm left Beausejour with a heavy blanket of snow. Beginning on Thursday March 4, the storm lasted in Beasejour until Saturday.

With other modes of transportation grounded by the blizzard, the power toboggan (snowmobile) was the hero of the day in Beausejour. The accolades given to these machines by the *Beausejour Beaver* says it all:

> *Last Thursday's once-in-a-century snowstorm which buried the countryside under millions of tons of fresh snow, proved that the power toboggan is more than just a sport-ing vehicle. Throughout the height of the storm itself on Friday and over Saturday, power toboggans took over the transportation business in Beausejour. They delivered the groceries, taxied people to and from work, got the doctors to their patients and the patients to the doctors, delivered bread and milk to people who were out of provisions, and generally proved themselves an indispensable winter emergency vehicle.*[25]

The inclement weather prevented nurses from getting to work at the hospital in Beausejour. This forced those nurses on duty to work double shifts. Telephone operators at the Manitoba Telephone Office in Beausejour faced a similar situation. At both places, some help came when snowmobiles brought relief workers to the hospital and telephone office. The machines also took workers at these places home.

During the worst of the storm on Friday, a lady from the Green Oak district, Mrs. Nick Ferens, started to experience labor pains. Using a Manitoba Hydro bombardier, Dr. Robbie was able to come to her assistance. He was then able to transport her safely to the hospital. There, at 3 a.m. Saturday Mrs. Ferens gave birth to a 11 lb. 3 oz. boy.

A power toboggan was used by Dr. Giesbrecht to commute between his office and the hospital in Beausejour. As difficult as it may seem to believe, one of the patients brought via snowmobile to Dr. Giesbrecht at his office was his wife. A cut on her hand required some stitches.

Dr. Giesbrecht faced another emergency at Lac du Bonnet, a village on Manitoba Highway 12 north of Beausejour. Not only had a patient of his become suddenly ill, but the town of Lac du Bonnet experienced a power failure. Because of weather and road conditions Dr. Giesbrecht could not get to his patient at Lac du Bonnet.

The day was saved when the good doctor was able to make a diagnosis of the patient's illness from information given to him over the phone. A Lac du Bonnet drugstore then provided the medication that Dr. Giesbrecht had prescribed for the patient. In reflecting about the storm the *Beaver* noted:

> *It's an ill wind that blows no good, according to the old saying, and last week's storm was no exception. . .*
>
> *For once, the rigorous schedule we have subjected ourselves to (in order that our beneficiaries may buy us a better coffin, according to one wit) was broken, and we managed well without. Trucks and buses ground to a standstill. The mail didn't come. Deliveries which always had to be on schedule were not made. Yet we lived and enjoyed it.*
>
> *The man who is beset with a heavy schedule of meetings– the fellow who always complains that he has no time for home life because of his many*

meetings– suddenly found himself at home with his family, strangely ill at ease but suddenly realizing that it didn't change matters one bit.

Certainly the storm helped to prove that our own efforts become pretty puny when the forces of nature are let loose.[26].

Once the storm had passed, snow removal operations started underway in the Beausejour area. But, with so much snow around, the task of snow removal was an immediate done deal. This was shown when a medical emergency took place on Wednesday, March 9 at Tyndall, a village a few miles west of Beausejour on Manitoba Highway 4. Mrs. Mike Zolondek became very sick that day. As their road had not yet been cleared, her husband trudged on foot to the Tyndall Garage to get assistance.

The seriousness of the situation did not allow them to use a bombardier to reach the Zolondek home. Instead, two snowmobiles at the garage were pressed into service. Ted Zygarliski, driving one of the machines, delivered an ambulance driver and stretcher to the Zolondek residence. Dr. Robbie rode on the back of the other snowmobile, which was driven by Rick Riley to the Zolondek's home.

With the stretcher in place on the two snowmobiles, Mrs. Zolondek was delivered to a waiting ambulance. A fast drive by the ambulance delivered her next destination, the Winnipeg General Hospital.

Ironically, just a week before the March 1966 storm, on February 25, 1966, Beausejour firemen made history. For the first time ever, they responded to a fire call via snowmobile. That morning there was a chimney fire at the Fred Wittmeier home, located at the corner of Poplar Avenue and First Street in Beausejour. Firemen placed fire equipment aboard a snowmobile and rushed to the scene of the fire. Their efforts weren't in vain, as they were able to get the fire under control, before it got away on them.

Steinbach (4,648 residents in 1966) is situated southeast of Winnipeg. Surprisingly, for its size, Steinbach is not served by a railroad.

Its settlement by Mennonites dates to about 1874. They named their community after Steinbach, their home in Russia, and their home before that, Steinbach, in Germany. In English, Steinbach means "stone brook". The new arrivals at this locality discovered a small coulee or brook with stones in it.

A Steinbach newspaper, the *Carillon News*, described the entry of the March 1966 blizzard into Manitoba as this:

A roaring blizzard which swept northward out of the Dakotas last Thursday night, carved another notch in the record of the severest winter Manitoba has experienced since away back in the last century.[27]

It was late Thursday afternoon when the storm arrived in Steinbach. Wind speeds increased to blow the newly fallen snow around. A blizzard was on in Steinbach, and many activities, including vehicular traffic, came to a screeching halt.

But, as elsewhere in the storm area, the snowmobile made a vital difference. The *Carillon News* had this to say about the machines:

If it did nothing else, the storm demonstrated that the power toboggan is more than just a sporting vehicle. Throughout the height of the storm on Friday and all day Saturday, power toboggans took over the job of transportation in Steinbach and in most other Southeast communities.

They delivered groceries, taxied people to and from work, got the doctors to their patients and the patients to their doctors, delivered bread and milk to people who were out of provisions, and generally proved to be indispensable emergency vehicles.[28]

Friday, March 4, was a long day for snowmobile operators. The Tom-Boy Store in Steinbach used its own snowmobile to deliver groceries to customers. Unfortunately, after making about fifteen runs, the machine broke down.

In an act of generosity, the J. R. Friesen Garage in Steinbach let its snowmobile, a Sno-Cruiser, be used for public service. With Alvin Reimer at its helm, the machine logged around 100 miles during the day Friday.

One of Reimer's trips involved taking Abe Dirks, a poultryman, to his chicken farm which was located four miles west and a mile south of Steinbach. Returning alone, Mr. Reimer's goggle's were frozen over with snow. Unable to see the road in the storm, he almost became lost.

Mr. Reimer also provided taxi service for the Bethesda Hospital in Steinbach on Friday. Several nurses made it to work at the hospital on his machine. He delivered a load of eggs to the hospital. In addition to that, in the daytime he had three other runs with his snowmobile in which he, either brought doctors to the hospital or took them to patients.

The J. R. Friesen snowmobile concluded its day Friday around midnight by becoming stuck in a snowbank on Creek Road. A wet ignition system was the initial cause for the machine's stalling out. Worn out, Reimer quit for the night and left the snowmobile there.

On Saturday, he had a bombardier pull the machine out of the snowdrift. Mr. Reimer dried off the ignition system and then continued with his taxi service.

In an emergency during the blizzard two Steinbach Creamery employees, Leonard and Peter Friesen, used a snow machine to deliver some milk.

There were others who provided delivery and taxi service on snowmobiles during and after the storm. These included Bob Banman, Doug Barber, William Friesen, Aaron Isaac, Chuck Toews and Gordon Topnik. Runs in Steinbach were done by the snowmobile operators free of charge.

The Manitoba Telephone System maintained a central office in Steinbach. Telephone exchanges that enjoyed its long-distance service included Greenland, Kleefeld, Niverville and Steinbach.

As could be expected with such a ferocious storm, the Steinbach telephone exchange had a tremendous increase in long-distance phone calls. According to a Manitoba Telephone System spokesman it was "the heaviest load ever placed on the equipment since the installation of automatic service in the Steinbach central office."[29]

Friday, March 4, 1966, was a very long day for the six telephone operators who worked in the Steinbach exchange. The outside weather kept them at their posts. In the daytime, Wilf Curtis, service manager for the Steinbach exchange, delivered food to them.

After working all day Friday and well into the evening, three of the operators finally were relieved by Chief Operator Florence Roberts. She had one of the operators napping on an old bed, another slept on a hard chesterfield (davenport) and the third one snoozed on the floor. The six operators spelled each other off all night long. While some of them manned the phones, the others slept. Their outstanding efforts earned them kudos from Miss Roberts.

Both hydro and telephone lines in the Steinbach area remained ice-free during the March 1966 blizzard. Unlike Duluth, Minnesota, temperatures at Steinbach did not reach the freezing point during the storm. A storm in April 1964 in the Steinbach vicinity had left a coating of ice on hydro and telephone lines there.

Among the numerous storm-related incidents that occurred at Steinbach was one involving an expectant mother. As the storm raged on Friday, Steinbach's Police Chief Ben Sobering was informed that a woman from Blumenort, Mrs. Gordon Brown, was having labor problems. Riding in his Diamond Ready-Mix payloader, Bill Giesbrecht cleared a lane through the storm the five mile distance from Steinbach to Blumenort. Trailing behind the payloader, came Chief Sobering in his police car.

Giesbrecht and Sobering made it to the Blumenort Cafe around 8:15 p.m. Mrs. Brown was there already, awaiting their arrival. Leading the way, the Payloader cleared a path for the police car back to Steinbach. Once there, Chief Sobering took Mrs. Brown to the Bethesda Hospital. Around midnight, the Browns' became the parents of a baby girl.

On Saturday, the scene in Steinbach was unbelievable. Cars were buried under snowdrifts, and streets were completely blocked. One of the streets in Steinbach that had the highest drifts was Reimer Avenue East. It was tough going for Steinbach's largest road grader when it came to clearing one large drift on Main Street. The height of a snowdrift in front of Johnny's Grill reached to the awning on the front of the building. A large drift in front of C. T. Loewen's Factory made for a great toboggan slide. A large snowbank in front of Reimer Farm Supplies prevented access to the building by the front entrance. In Woodlawn Park, Rollin Reimer's car was completely submerged in the snow. There was deep snow in front of the Esso Gas Station.

Kenora, Dryden, Sioux Lookout, Red Lake, Reditt, Port Arthur and Fort William

The northwestern Ontario city of Kenora lies about 120 miles east of Winnipeg. Kenora is located on the north side of Lake of the Woods. The women's curling team from Kenora represented Ontario at the Canadian's ladies Curling Championship in Vancouver, British Columbia in March 1966. Skippered by June Shaw, the team finished the tournament with five wins and a fourth place finish. The other members of the team were Joan Lecain, lead, Dorothy Holmgren, second, and Shirley Wiebe, third. A curling team from Alberta won the championship.

The March 2, 1966, weather forecast for Kenora read as follows:

> Sunny today. Clouding over this evening. Snow beginning in the morning.Continuing mild. Winds light becoming east 15 (mph) tonight and east 20 tomorrow. Low tonight and high Thursday at Kenora and Red Lake 15 (degrees Fahrenheit) and 30, at Fort Frances and Lakehead 25 and 35.[30]

The next day, March 3, the *Kenora Daily Miner and News* complained about the failure of the blizzard to show up in Kenora

This is what the newspaper had to say about the storm:

> The blizzard which dumped almost a foot of snow on parts of Minnesota and North Dakota last night, failed to make its scheduled appearance at Kenora. At 2:00 p.m. the temperature at the Airport was 24 degrees, with winds blowing from the northeast at 16 m.p.h., gusting to 28 miles. The forecast low tonight is given as 25 degrees, and the thermometer is stated to remain constant at that figure for most of Friday.
>
> The weatherman predicts snow and blowing snow this evening and tomorrow.[31]

This proved to be true when the storm descended on Kenora early that evening. The new weather conditions forced the *Miner and News* to change its tune the very next day. The paper admitted that "The warning given Thursday that a major snow storm was likely to move from Minnesota into this area, has proven to be all too true." The paper gave the following lament:

> Everyone is talking about the weather… but apart from a from a few valiant men manning the snowplows for the Town and Dept. of Highways, no one is doing much about the unprecedented conditions which exist in the Kenora district today.[32]

The forecast for Kenora for Friday March 4 was:

> Cloudy with snow and heavy blowing snow today and tomorrow. Little change in temperature. Winds northeast 25 gusting to 40. Temperature at Kenora, Fort Frances, and Red Lake 10 above overnight and steady near 10 above tomorrow. Temperature at Armstrong steady near 20.[33]

Friday, March 4, 1966, was definitely not a good day to be out and about in Kenora. There weren't many stores open for business. There weren't many people making the trek downtown to shop on Friday. Delivery of mail and milk were halted. Many people in the Kenora area could not remember the last time weather conditions had forced the closing of schools.

There were no flights in or out of Kenora's airport during the storm. But, the trains kept running. In spite of the lousy weather, snowplow operators were trying to keep roads and streets open. They weren't having much success, as the drifting snow quickly filled the cuts made by the plows.

At 1:00 p.m., the Excel buses began making their runs in Kenora. They intended to keep going as long as possible. Only, if and when road conditions deteriorated to the point where traversing them by bus proved impossible would they stop. Unfortunately, this proved to be the case, and service was discontinued at 4 p.m.

By 2 p.m. Friday, about 14 inches of snow had fallen on Kenora. Atrocious weather conditions prevented any exact measurement. At that time wind speeds in Kenora averaged 30 mph, with gusts to 45 mph.

Except for one instance, the blizzard failed to disrupt telephone and electrical service to the Kenora vicinity. Parts of J-M were left in the dark for about twenty-five minutes by a power failure.

The storm failed to interrupt the printing of the *Kenora Miner and News*. However, delivering the paper took some ingenuity. Quite a few of the newspaper's carriers picked up their papers at the *Miner and News* office. Other carriers normally relied on city buses to drop their bundles off at bus route stops. Because of impassable streets jeeps instead of buses were employed to deliver the papers. Some *Miner and News* readers did not get their copy of the paper until Saturday morning.

Snowplow operators in Kenora fought a losing battle all day Friday in an attempt to keep city streets open. City Fire Chief Len Whiting was not happy with the situation. To have a fire break out under the terrible weather conditions in Kenora on Friday was not one anyone wanted to contemplate. Chief Whiting's concern was easy to see. The storm was predicted not to let up in Kenora until late Sunday. If the blizzard lasted that long, and a fire emergency arose in Kenora, it would have been next to impossible to stop it. To combat the crisis, two power toboggans, one of them loaded down with fire hose, were procured.

After hearing of Chief Whiting's concern, Kenora's Emergency Measures Organization, which was headed by A. M. Delamere, contacted Captain Jack McFarlane of the 40th Field Regiment to have army vehicles stationed at the fire hall. These would help to break a trail for the firemen if the situation called for it and with other emergencies. The stationing of four men and two army trucks from the Kenora Armories at the fire hall pleased Chief Whiting considerably.

The Kenora branch of the Red Cross loaned beds that were placed aboard a four-wheel drive army vehicle to be used if an emergency arose.

Another emergency crew was provided by Superintendent Larry Gartner of the Ontario Provincial Police.

To illustrate just how bad the conditions were, it took a snowplow four hours and thirty minutes to reach Minaki on Friday. As the crow flies, Minaki is about thirty miles northwest of Kenora.

As of 10 a.m. Friday at Dryden, Ontario, the brunt of the storm had not yet arrived. This Ontario city is on the Trans-Canada Highway about fifty miles east of Kenora. At that time 2 inches of snow had fallen on Dryden. But, the situation changed in the afternoons heavy snow was falling at both at Dryden and Sioux Lookout. Located about fifty miles northeast of Dryden, Sioux Lookout sits at the end of Ontario Highway 72.

Although snow free in the morning, there was a possibility of the storm hitting Red Lake that afternoon. That Ontario city was about a hundred miles northeast of Kenora on Ontario Highway 105.

By Friday afternoon, blocked roads prevented any wheeled vehicular traffic in and out of Reditt. This Ontario hamlet lies about twenty miles northeast of Kenora on Ontario Highway 658.

That day wind speeds accompanying the storm reached 60 mph at Port Arthur (Thunder Bay) and Fort William, Ontario. Both cities lie along the north side of Lake Superior.

As the storm was moving in a generally southwest to northeast direction, road conditions east of Kenora were better than those west of the city. On Friday, buses and trucks coming from the east were making it into Kenora. Driving conditions weren't that great, even then. Poor traveling conditions delayed two transports for two hours on Longbow Lake Hill Friday morning.

Because of the slow progress of the blizzard, on Friday weather forecasters thought the storm would hang around the Kenora area until Sunday night.

Yet, in another twist, just as the unpredictable storm had fooled forecasters before, it did it again on Saturday. Residents of Kenora awoke that morning to see that the snowfall had ended and conditions improving. Colder air moving in dropped early morning temperatures below zero. It had been a thirty-five hour endurance contest for Kenorans.

Officially, the March 1966 blizzard dumped 21 inches of snow on Kenora. From 6 p.m. to midnight Thursday, 7.7 inches of the white stuff fell there. Over the next twenty-four hours, another 13.3 inches came down. By 10 a.m. Saturday, the temperature at the Kenora airport had risen to 0. At the same time, the wind was clocked at 15 mph, with gusts to 20 mph.

Kenora had weathered a potential catastrophe successfully. As the *Miner and News* noted, *"Today, with each passing hour, as snowplows are able to open streets, the acuteness of the very critical emergency is lessening."*[34]

There weren't any fire or police emergencies in Kenora during the blizzard. Neither Keewatin, Kenora, nor the Ontario Provincial Police (OPP) reported any incoming emergency calls. If an emergency had arisen, the OPP would have been able to provide a car that had chains for its tires for some use.

Snowplow operators in Kenora worked nonstop through the storm on into Saturday. Kenora Fire Chief Len Whiting was especially effusive in his praise for them and H. W. Cochrane, Kenora's Town Engineer for his direction of them. Of them, the *Miner and News* had this to say:

> A truly magnificent job of keeping equipment on the roads, when roads were difficult to find. The same can be said for the members of the Dept. of Highways.[35]

All through Friday night and on into the day on Saturday, Captain McFarlane stayed at his post.

As could be expected, Kenora's hotels did a great business during the storm. Stranded travelers from automobiles and buses flocked to these businesses on Thursday, with most of them departing on Saturday.

One snowmobile agent reported that many people called during the storm inquiring about the machines. But none of the customers came to pick up their snowmobiles.

No medical emergencies arose in Kenora during the blizzard. Despite this, doctors used snowmobiles for getting around to and from work and patients. On Saturday, in order to make it to her car, a nurse who resided west of Keewatin, resorted to burrowing a tunnel through the snow.

The pulp mill at Kenora didn't let a blizzard stop its operation. The sound of its whistle on Friday signalled the beginning of another day of work. This was possible, as the mill's workers had made it to work on time. Along the Winnipeg River, the storm brought the work of the pulpwood cutters completely to a halt. The inclement weather halted the dumping of logs at Cameron Bay in Normah. But, at Matheson Bay, a fairly well plowed out road allowed for the dumping of logs.

The cleanup was well under way in the days following the blizzard. It was feared that a rise in temperatures would impede the snow removal process. Groups of young men earned money shoveling driveways and walks for Kenora residents.

On Monday March 7, Kenora Mayor, E. L. Carter, thanked the fire department (for being constantly ready through the worst of the storm) and police departments, public works personnel, utilities crews and the 40th Field Regiment.

To illustrate how much snow Kenora had received, Roads Foreman John Zilinski reported that around 290 truck loads of snow had been hauled to the western outlet bridge and dumped into the Winnipeg River. And, this amount came only from an area from Main and Second Streets' to the Fire Hall.

As Mayor Carter noted, such a tremendous storm as the March '66 one, illustrated the value of snow blower equipment.

The *Miner and News* also wanted to thank those who helped out in the blizzard. In reminiscing, the paper had this to say:

> Citizens will long remember the sounds of wind whistling around their houses, but will remember equally, the sound of snowplows and graders, almost carried away in the wild and weird sounds of a blizzard.[36]

In retrospect, it was a huge storm that had blasted southern Manitoba and northwestern Ontario. It had covered 100,000 square miles of this area. Left in its wake were huge snowdrifts carved by winds whose gusts reached as high as 70 mph.

Chapter V
Conclusion

Since the early days of humans, weather has been a major concern for everyone. There was a time when nobody knew what lightning and thunder was. Mother Nature has killed countless numbers of people.

The following account was written by a professional weatherman, Herman G. Stommel, State Climatologist, Environmental Science Services Administration, Bismarck, North Dakota. Stommel's article was published in the October 1966 issue of *Weatherwise*. Stommel wrote:

The Great Blizzard of '66 on the Northern Great Plains

The hardy plainsmen of the northern Great Plains expect unusual and severe weather and are seldom disappointed in their expectation. Summertime brings dreaded, destructive tornadoes and violent thunderstorms accompanied by heavy hail sometimes larger than a baseball, or a kind of hail that, in minutes, wipes out a farmers's nearly realized dream of a wonderful bumper crop.

And winter, which comes early and stays late in the Big Country, brings the fearsome, angry, howling "white death"– the hazardous prairie blizzard with 60-mile-per-hour, bonechilling winds, overladen with snow so fine, so strongly driven, that no crack or crevice is too small to admit what in time becomes an amazing mass. North Dakota averages several blizzards a year, but only three or four severe, widespread blizzards occur during each decade.

Sometimes spring comes early, if only for a few days, with warm balmy chinook winds, rapidly melting snow, with a peek at solid earth again for the first time in months. Such was the promise at the close of February and the first day of March 1966, nature's hint that winter wouldn't last forever.

But the reprieve was short-lived. By midmorning of March 1st clouds began to gather and shut out the welcome sun. A preliminary warning, issued by the Weather Bureau on 28 February, of possible snow and high winds was confirmed when on March 2 a severe weather bulletin was broadcast by radio and television stations warning of an approaching storm. The bulletin was received with an exasperated sigh, prompted by an already too-long winter, and the people resigned themselves to a day, or possibly two, of battened-down hatches. Cattle and other farm animals were brought in close to the farmhouses, into large barns or corrals. Plans for trips of more than a few hours duration were either canceled or rescheduled to avoid the all-too-well-known dangers of exposure in a blizzard.

What prompted the early warning was a small and relatively insignificant low pressure system centered in southwestern Montana at midnight, CST, on 1 March. During the next 24 hours, however, the low steadily deepened and moved rapidly south-southeastward until it was centered over Pueblo, Colorado, at midnight on March 2. At the same time an arctic air mass with temperatures in the teens was slowly advancing southward into northern Montana and North Dakota.

Snowfall early on 2 March had become general over most of Montana, Wyoming, and Nevada and by noon had moved into and spread over much of South Dakota and southern North Dakota.

Twelve hours later the low, now moving on a northeastward course, had advanced into central South Dakota with continued deepening. There it stalled. By 0600, 3 March, it had reached a central pressure of 983mb/29.03 inches. Temperatures in the Dakotas had reached the mid-teens, winds had increased to 20-30 miles per hour, and the snow had already begun to mount into drifts deep enough to stall traffic. Rain or snow were by now falling over most of Minnesota.

The stalling and deepening of the low in South Dakota and its slow eastward movement into western Minnesota prolonged and increased the severity of the storm in the Dakotas. As the center became more intense, increasing winds, now occasionally gushing to 70-80 miles per hour and driving icy snow crystals, reduced visibilities to zero over much of the northern Plains. Typical of widespread conditions was Bismarck: the visibility remained at zero for 11 hours on 3 March from 0200 until 1300. For the next 19 hours, until 1900 on 4 March, the visibility varied from zero to not more than one-eight mile. A continuous period of as long as nineteen hours of one-eight mile, or less, visibility is without know precedent in North Dakota weather history.

By midnight of 4 March, the low center, now in eastern Minnesota, began to fill slowly as it moved eastward and the snowfall had become intermittent in northern North Dakota. High winds, however, continued to stir up and carry considerable snow, keeping visibilities restricted much of March 5, particularly in eastern and southeastern North Dakota.

Bitter cold arctic air, pouring into the Dakotas following the prolonged blizzard, dropped temperatures well below zero by Sunday morning , March 6, a morning which dawned clear and crisp to present a fantastically beautiful fairy world of tremendous grey and white streaked, marble cake snowdrifts that occasionally nearly covered some two-story buildings. Streets and farmyards were completely blocked by solid packed drifts offering stubborn resistance to all but the heaviest types of snowplows to penetrate them.

Although snow depths in North Dakota, were drifts were the deepest, reached a height of 30 to 40 feet, the actual amount of snowfall, impossible to measure accurately, conceivably did not much exceed 30 inches for the storm. The accompanying map shows the total depth of snow which fell between 2-5 March 1966, inclusive, as measured at official observing stations. The northwestern corner of North Dakota received no snow and experienced only some dust storms.

During the storm violent churning wind swept bare some areas, while only a few yards away towering drifts built up downstream from what were sometimes only minor obstructions. Loose wind-borne dirt, mixed with snow, resulted in a greyish mass of snow-dirt, aptly dubbed "snirt."

In some respects, this 1966 blizzard must be considered on of the most severe in the history of North Dakota, where its major violence and impact were felt. The legendary Blizzard of 1888 on January 12 lasted only 14 hours, but at least 112 dead and wiped out cattle herds wholesale. The unusually severe blizzard of 15 March 1941, with 70 mph winds raced across North Dakota from northwest to southeast in only seven hours. Travelers, trapped in their cars, accounted for most of the 39 deaths occurring in eastern North Dakota where the storm was most severe. Estimates of the loss of live chargeable to the 1941 storm ranged from 76 to 90.

The 1966 storm, with up to 80 mph winds occasionally gushing up to 100 mph, continued unabated for as long as four days in some areas. For the first time in the history of many towns, schools were closed, all business was suspended, newspapers failed to publish, and all forms of traffic came to a complete halt. Some roads were not cleared for two weeks.

Minimum temperatures during the blizzard did not, in general fall below the teens. Fortunately, below-zero temperatures were not reported until Saturday or Sunday, after the blizzard had passed. The absence of bitterly cold temperatures of well below zero, which frequently accompany severe North Dakota blizzards, undoubtedly was largely responsible for the fact that relatively few persons lost their lives as a direct result of the storm. Timely and effective dissemination of warnings at least a day in advance of the storm, and modern communications contributed to minimize the impact of the storm and to keep the loss of life at a minimum. No deaths in this storm could be ascribed to any lack of warnings or forecasts, the cause of so many deaths in earlier days, when fastmoving blizzards caught many persons totally unwarned and unprepared.

Before it blew itself out, the Great Blizzard of '66 had claimed the lives of 18 persons. Two women, one in Nebraska and the other in Minnesota, froze to death while walking from stalled automobiles. Three men in South Dakota died from exposure, two from heart attacks, one by asphyxiation. In Minnesota, heart attacks, attributed to exertion while shoveling snow, claimed to lives.

Five persons in North Dakota died as a result of a related effect of the storm. A six-year-old Strasburg girl, fully clothed for the outdoors, became separated from her two brothers when the children went from their home to a barn 60 feet away. She was found two days later only a quarter of a mile from home, frozen to death.

Another girl, age 12, of Woodworth, slipped out of the house to close a chicken-coop door. She was never again seen alive after she started back to the house which was only 100 feet away. Her frozen body was found the next day, half-a-mile from home.

Three elderly men died as a result of heart attacks, probably brought on by overexertion. One was a 60-year old man of Linton who died in his car after vainly trying to extricate it from a ditch after a skid. A janitor was found inside a school where he had collapsed after shoveling snow from the walks. The third man, age 73, a farmer of Driscoll, was found frozen to death in his farmyard, only a few yards from home. Many injuries, directly related to the storm, occurred but none proved fatal.

Deaths during northern Great Plains blizzards are partly due to occasional lapse of several years between severe blizzards. As a result, people forget the hazards of such storms. Through a false sense of security, they do not take proper precautions. Many persons did remain in their stalled cars through several days of the '66 blizzard, but lived to tell harrowing tales of how close they came to death.

The loss of livestock in Nebraska and the Dakotas was appalling, with estimates including 74,500 head of cattle, 54,000 sheep, and 2,400 hogs. On one farm alone in eastern North Dakota, 7,000 turkeys perished. Many cattle suffocated when barns became completely covered and sealed-in by huge snowdrifts. Large barns, into which stock were herded before the storm struck, collapsed, resulting in many dead and injured animals. The total loss of livestock in these three states was estimated at over $12 million. Many thousands of upland birds– grouse, pheasants, and partridge– were killed by the storm.

The continued high winds piled snow in corrals and feed lots. Cattle, as a result of milling around in corrals, tramped down and compacted the snow as it fell until the level of the snow became higher than the fence. Then they wandered off and perished in open fields or against fencelines.

All transportation had come to a standstill by the second day of the storm. Three transcontinental trains, trapped in railway cuts, became nearly covered in a short time with rock-hard packed snow, defeating all efforts to free the trains until well after the storm had ended. Five hundred passengers were trapped for a time without heat or food. Automobile travel, even in the storm, was stopped by huge drifts and near zero visibility.

Power and telephone service were interrupted up to several days in many areas by the high winds and driven snow. Several aircraft hangers collapsed, damaging and destroying a number of airplanes. Many store windows were blown in. Snow, driven into the attics during the storm, melted later with distressing consequences. Chimney vents froze up, causing a number of cases of gas poisoning in homes.

Many all-time records for monthly snowfall, for snowfall during one storm, and for 24-hour snowfall were broken. The duration of the blizzard, particularly in the southern half of North Dakota and in northern South Dakota, set many records as did the severely restricted visibilities.

One serious, delayed result of the Great Blizzard of '66 was the spring flood of the Red River of the North and its tributaries. This near-record flood, which extended through March, April, and May, would have been only minor and local in its effect had there been no March storm. The total cost of the flood was set at $7.9 million, of which $2.2 million was spent for diking and other protection. The damage to roads and bridges exceeded $2 million.

In the Big Country there have been higher winds, colder temperatures, and snowfall has been greater. But it is doubtful if any previous storm, at least in the past nearly 100 years of weather history in North Dakota, hit *so big an area, for so long a time, with such sustained speeds, piling up so many gigantic drifts. The blizzard of '66 will long be remembered on the northern Great Plains, particularly for its sustained severity, low visibilities, and total snowfall over a great expanse.[1]*

Figure 1 depicts the surface maps for March 1-5, 1966. Figure 2 shows the track of the March 1966 blizzard. Figure 3 gives the snowfall totals from it.

Both surface and upper level (850mb (millibars), 700mb, 500mb, 300mb, 250 and 100mb) weather maps and charts that showed the development and track of storms such as the March 1966 one were prepared at the National Meteorological Center in Camp Springs, Maryland.

From Thursday, March 3, 1966, onward, the high pressure system trailing the low of the March 1966 blizzard took on the shape of what meteorologically is known as an "omega block." In the middle or upper troposphere, this is a high pressure ridge that takes on the shape of the Greek letter omega (an up side down "u"). This ridge can become stationary and keep low pressure troughs from moving.

The troposphere is that layer of the earth's atmosphere that extends from the ground to the tropopause (boundary between troposphere and stratosphere). The tropopause is located about 10 kilometers above the earth's surface.

This is what happened during the latter half of the March 1966 blizzard. The 700 (about 3,000 meters or 10,000 feet up in the

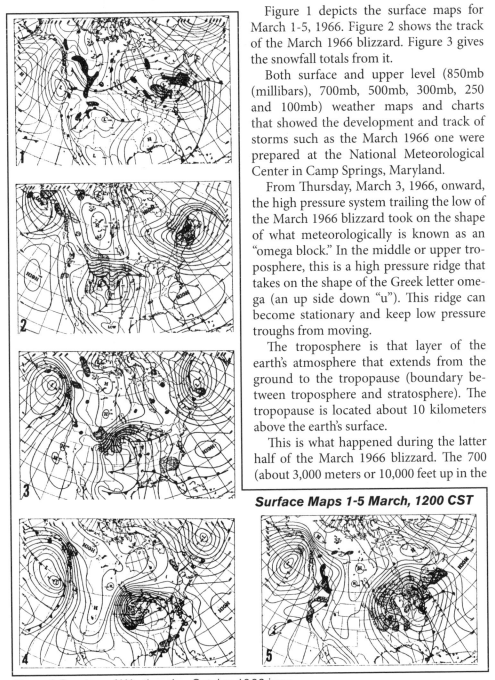

Surface Maps 1-5 March, 1200 CST

Figure 1 Courtesy of Weatherwise, October 1966 issue.

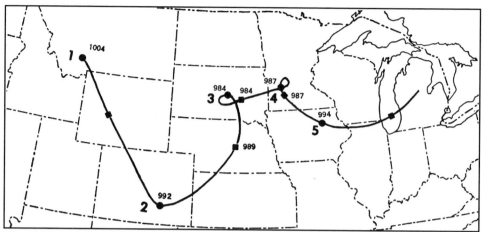

Figure 2 Location and pressure of center, 1-5 March, indicated by circles at 0000 CST and squares at 1200 CST. Lowest pressure: 984mb = 29.06".

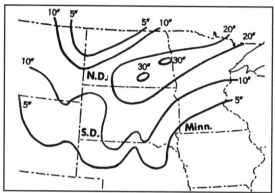

Figure 3 Inches of snowfall in blizzard area. Both Figures 2 and 3 courtesy of Weatherwise, October 1966 issue.

atmosphere) and 500 mb charts (around 5600 meters or 18,000 feet) showed that this ridge assisted in slowing down the blizzard. This stalling action helped to intensify the storm, which increased wind speeds. That is partly, why Friday March 4, 1966, was the worst day of the storm for much of the affected area. Usually, omega blocks persist in the same locale for quite a few days. This did not happen with the one associated with the March 1966 blizzard. See Figure 4.

The following information is a partial meteorological explanation for the development of storms such as the March 1966 blizzard:

> Vorticity helps to explain the development of storms on the leeward side of mountains. We can see why when we examine the flow of air over a mountain barrier. Assume that the wind is westerly and there is no shear, so that the relative vorticity of the air column as it approaches the mountain will be zero. Theoretical studies show that the absolute vorticity of the column divided by its depth is equal to a constant, as long as the air is frictionless and no heating or cooling of the column takes place. (This expression is called the **potential vorticity**.)

> Thus,

$$\frac{\text{Earth's vorticity} + \text{relative vorticity}}{\text{Depth of column}} = constant.$$

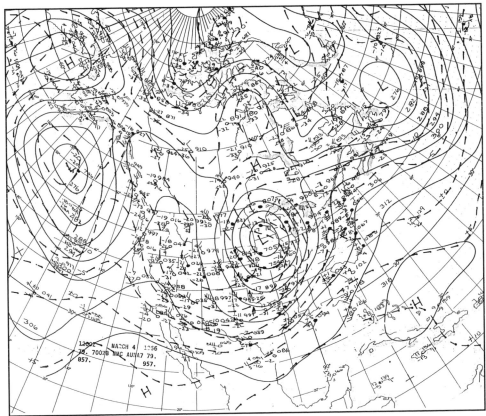

Figure 4 Upper air chart (700 mb) at 6:00 a.m. CST March 4, 1966. Courtesy of National Climatic Data Center

As the column moves up the side of the mountain, the tropopause acts as a lid on the top of the column. This causes the column to shrink vertically and expand horizontally. To compensate for the column's decreasing depth, there must be a similar decrease in absolute vorticity. Since the relative vorticity of the column is zero, the air must curve anticyclonically, or toward the southeast, into a region of decreasing earth vorticity.

Once the column begins to move downslope, it stretches vertically, its depth increases, and so must its absolute vorticity. The relative vorticity of the southeastward moving air is zero, but the air is moving into a region of decreasing earth vorticity. Consequently, there must be a bending of the airflow in the cyclonic sense to increase the column's absolute vorticity. The airflow now swings to the northeast, which creates a trough of low pressure (a **lee-side low**) on the downwind side of the barrier. Now we can see so many wave cyclones form along the flanks of the Rocky Mountains, especially in eastern Colorado, where the crest of the mountains reaches its maximum elevation.[2]

U.S. Weather Bureau surface weather maps, which most people followed, tracked the progress of the storm.

On March 17, 1966, in a report provided by the extension service of South Dakota State University, livestock losses in that state from the blizzard were placed at about 95,000. Broken down, these losses came to 50,000 head of cattle, 1,800 hogs and 44,000 head of sheep.

In North Dakota, the estimate of livestock losses was put at 27,399 animals. This amounted to 18,905 head of cattle, 640 hogs and 7,854 head of sheep.

Many journalists covered this story, most wrote about their friends and neighbors. George Moses, Associated Press reporter, wrote for a wider audience. His story ran in major newspapers on March 13, 1966. Moses's article was published with different headlines. For example, in the *Rapid City Daily Journal*, the headline read: **"Word 'Blizzard' Not Taken Lightly In Dakotas."** In Huron, South Dakota, the *Daily Plainsman* headline stated, **"Great Blizzard Of '66 Dealt Death, Hardship To Plains Area."** The *Aberdeen American-News* headline declared, **"Spring– One Warm Day And Three of Misery."** The *Argus Leader*, Sioux Falls, South Dakota, headline said, **"Blizzard Etches Icy Saga Of Courage and Disaster."**

George Moses wrote:

> Spring is an elusive visitor to the northern Great Plains. It drops in briefly after the cold of January and February to set the snow melting and to remind the hardy plainsmen winter won't last forever.
>
> Then it usually gives way to another blast or two of icy air before it returns to stay.
>
> March of 1966 opened with such a promise. The sun squeezed water out of a sparse snow cover on the Dakota prairies. Children brought out jump ropes and bikes.
>
> But the harbinger was brief. By Wednesday, the second day of the month, gray clouds began to cover the sun. The weather bureau predicted snow ending by Thursday, with possibly heavy snow in western South Dakota. Shortly before noon Wednesday the weathermen took another look, predicting heavy snow and strong wind farther east in the Dakotas. They still said it would end Thursday.
>
> One who heard that snow warning was a hardy rancher named Otto Mettler, who lives 16 miles southeast of McLaughlin, South Dakota, near the North Dakota border.
>
> Mettler, his wife, and their son Lyle, 7, had been visiting a daughter in nearby Lemmon, on her birthday. As a light snow began, the Mettlers started home.
>
> In McLaughlin they stopped for gas, and Mettler bought 50 cents worth of candy bars.
>
> Across the North Dakota line, in Mandan three basketball coaches from the Indian reservation town of Fort Yates were watching a basketball tournament. Their team was to play the next day.
>
> Harlan Wash, Allen Mitzenberger and James Barret eyed the thickening snow and the rising wind, decided to drive the 60 miles home to Fort Yates anyway.

In their car were three sweet rolls.

Southeast of Mandan, across the Missouri River, lies the little town of Strasburg, North Dakota. Fading road signs labeled it the home town of bandleader Lawrence Welk. A cousin, Eugene Welk, farms east of town.

His 6 year-old daughter, Carleen, splashed around the muddy farmyard in her new overshoes. As usual, she was following her two bigger brothers as they did the chores.

Many miles across the prairie to the northeast, at the Raymond Deede farm near another tiny town called Woodworth, a hint of spring had been in the air, too. The Deedes' daughter, 13-year old Betty, was a seventh-grader in the Woodworth School.

Suddenly there was the snow, and the wind.

The weathermen had been watching an odd combination of low pressure cells. One developed in Nevada and a second in northern Colorado. Deepening, they moved slowly northeast on a collision course. They met that day over the northern plains, linking up with a third low already on the scene.

The snow thickened. The wind rose. Quickly, it was hard to see more than a few feet in the white, or breathe in it. Drifts formed on highways and stopped travel dead over all but northwestern North Dakota and southeastern South Dakota.

The weather bureau on Wednesday afternoon added to its prediction a word it doesn't use lightly:

Blizzard.

You can usually get an argument at any corner cafe in the north country on when a snowstorm becomes a blizzard. To the weathermen, the yardstick is simple: Winds of more than 45 miles an hour, great density of snow, and temperatures of 10 or lower.

Though temperatures first were in the teens probably saving lives there was no argument about the storm that swept over the Dakotas from the southwest that day. It packed winds clocked unofficially in some places at more than 100 miles an hour, 69 miles officially. It laid down a blanket of snow ranging up to three feet.

Despite its howling, blinding fury, it lumbered northeastward across the Dakotas and northern Minnesota with punishing leisure.

Before it blew itself out four days later, the great blizzard of 1966 took 18 lives, stopped outside life almost dead in hundreds of towns in its path, and killed unsheltered livestock that still are being totaled.

Homeward bound, the Mettlers and their boy fought mounting drifts and blinding snow until a tire chain broke. Their car went into a ditch. The Mettlers didn't know it, but they were two miles from their ranch.

Wise to the prairie winters, the three put on heavy clothes from the trunk and began a lonely vigil in their car that was to last three dark nights and two snow-white days. "I kept saying, 'we can't leave the car,'" Mettler said later.

To keep his family from suffocating as the drifts closed over them Mettler would roll down a back window and shovel until he could crawl through enough to widen the hole to the top of the drift. Then he'd crawl back into the car.

Often, in the frightening hours, Mrs. Mettler and Lyle sang the Sunday school hymn, "Jesus Loves Me."

Lyle ate the last of the candy bars Friday evening.

Saturday morning the Mettlers stirred under the feather comforter they shared. The snow and wind had stopped, after 60 hours.

They fought their way free of the car and walked the two miles home across crusted drifts.

Some forty miles to the northeast, the three young coaches from Fort Yates were having their own problems. Their car stalled about 30 miles south of Mandan.

Without heavy clothing, they ripped out the back cushion of the car. There, in the back seat, they burned everything burnable– including some wooden fence posts near the road.

"We kept thinking with every sunrise or sunset it would break," said Barret. "Everybody was saying his own prayers. It got pretty quiet in that car."

The men shared the three sweet rolls, grabbed fistfulls of snow for water.

At 2:30 a.m. Saturday a rescue party from Mandan, led by a rotary snowplow, found them. All three were hospitalized for treatment of smoke-irritated eyes from the fire that kept them alive.

Thursday afternoon the blizzard eased momentarily at Strasburg. At the Welk farm, Carleen's two brothers, Alle, 13, and Duane, 11, went to the chicken coop 60 feet away from the house, then to the barn another 20 feet away.

Carleen started out with them. When the boys got to the barn, they stopped, frightened. The little girl was no longer with them.

Welk and the two boys looked for her in the wind and snow until dark. Welk tried it again Friday. Search parties couldn't reach the farm.

The storm dying, Welk went out again Saturday battling foot drifts. A quarter of a mile from home he found Carleen's body. It was in a sitting position, upright in the snow. Her new overshoes were still on her feet, a stocking cap over her brown hair.

At the Deede farm Friday morning, the winds were screaming, the snow still falling. There'd been no school, since the storm broke. Betty slipped out of the farmhouse to close a banging door on a chicken coop 100 feet away. Then Betty went to a barn close by, where a nephew had taken refuge.

The girl started back for the house. She was not seen alive again.

Mrs. Deede, realizing Betty was missing, headed in a frenzy for the chicken coop, then the barn. The boy in the barn pointed in the direction Betty had disappeared– away from the house.

Mrs. Deede followed. She soon realized she to, was lost in the blinding whiteness.

The women remembered the lashing wind was from the north, and home was in that direction. She kept the wind in her face, and dropped on *hands and knees so she could breathe and move. She crawled perhaps 300 feet that way, until her home loomed up in the snow.*

Rescue crews from Woodworth could not break through to the farm until the next morning, when the storm slackened. With visibility still bad, they roped themselves together in teams of six.

One group found Betty's body at 11:15 a.m. half a mile from home. It was lying near a railroad track.

"She was a very pretty girl," said her family's minister, of the brown-haired seventh grader, "quiet and well-mannered."

In the larger Dakota cities in the blizzard's path, traffic signals blinked foolishly for days, directing vehicles that were stuck in drifts, In some, office workers were marooned for days, even though home might be a few blocks away. Some emergency workers caught at home risked their lives to report to duty.

And in at least, one Bismarck residential area, the first shortage that started neighbors bucking drifts to lend or borrow, was in cigarettes.

The blizzard of 1888 is a legendary one on the northern plains. It raced out of Canada on January 12, left at least 112 persons dead, and wiped out cattle herds wholesale.

On November 11, 1940, a sudden blizzard struck Minnesota, which had northern reaches sharing part of the 1966 storm. The Armistice Day blizzard left 49 dead.

And almost 25 years ago to the day, on March 15, 1941, a blizzard pounced on the Red River Valley of North Dakota and Minnesota, trapping unwarned travelers wholesale in their cars. The loss of live in that one is variously put at from 76 to 90.

Better forecasting and the speed and spread of modern radio may have helped keep the 1966 death toll relatively low.

But in terms and ferocity of the storm itself, the blizzard of 1966 may well rank as the worst in recorded Weather Bureau history. The weathermen are still checking their records.

Winds have been higher, and snows have been deeper. But it is doubtful if any other winter storm in history has circled on itself twice, as this one did, or hit so big an area with so much for so long.[3]

Between 1941 and 1966 weather forecasting had improved tremendous. Meteorologists were now aware of the jet stream and some of its effects on weather.

The era of global-satellite coverage began on April 1, 1960, when a 270 pound satellite, *Tiros I*, was released into orbit. This satellite was equipped with two television cameras programmed to take pictures of cloud cover over large sections of the earth, including the oceans and sparsely populated land regions.

Tiros I was followed by eight more satellites. Information was downloaded to United States Weather Bureau stations and weather facilities of other countries.

NASA (National Aeronautics and Space Administration) launched *ESSA I* on February 3, 1966 and *ESSA II* on the 28th of the same month. *ESSA* stood for the Commerce Department's Environmental Science Services Administration. The United States Weather Bureau came underneath that department. The launching of these two satellites inaugurated the first operational space weather reporting network for the planet Earth. Aboard these satellites were cameras which photographed the entire globe at least once a day. They took pictures of clouds and storm patterns and then transmitted them back to earth.

Ironically, the first automatic photo sent back to Earth by *ESSA II* was taken at 9:10 a.m. March 2, 1966 (Central Standard Time). It shows the developing blizzard in north central portion of the United States with the Dakotas beneath a heavy cloud cover. After being transmitted, it would be at ESSA'S National Environmental Satellite Center in Washington, D. C. where the photo was received. See photo below.

At the same time it must be understood that such technology was in its infancy. There was no Doppler radar in 1966.

Among the changes in weather forecasting over the years was the adoption of a new wind chill system by the National Weather Service and Environment Canada in 2001.

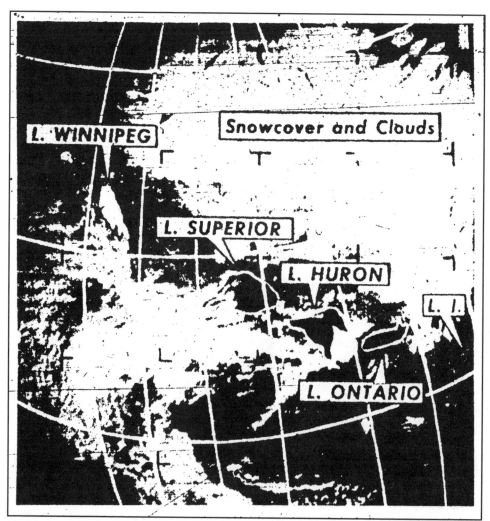

ESSA II satellite photo. 9:10 a.m. CST March 2, 1966. Courtesy of Grand Forks Herald

Temperatures in the new system wouldn't be as low as the old one. According to the National Weather Service the new numbers would be more accurate and realistic.

The old wind chill charts originated from research done in Antarctica in 1945. The accuracy of them was brought into question by Professor Maurice Blumenstein of Purdue University.

A big difference in the two wind chill charts was that wind speed would now be measured at 5 feet above ground, "face height", instead of the previous 33 feet above the surface.

Another difference was that the new wind chill charts were much more precise as to when frostbite occurred. Scientists had discovered that when the wind chill index reached 18 below zero people suffered frostbite in fifteen minutes. The old charts featured graduated zones of danger.

The smaller numbers of the new wind chill index was thought to be of some comfort for operators of ski resorts. Smaller numbers might entice people outdoors who would otherwise stay home.

The single most critical factor that kept the March 1966 blizzard from becoming a real killer was the fact, that while the storm was on, it never got that cold. Temperatures throughout the affected area remained above zero. Also, the 1966 blizzard built up gradually. It didn't hit suddenly, as the '41 storm did.

Forecasting since 1966 has seen the automation of weather forecasting by the National Weather Service. The system is known as AWIPS (Automated Weather Information Processing System). According to Lee Anderson, meteorologist in charge of the Grand Forks office, the adoption of AWIPS meant that warnings and forecasts would be provided to the public in a faster and more accurate manner.

The full automation of the AWIPS system at the Grand Forks weather office occurred on February 10, 2000.

The following editorial by Mike Jacobs, editor of the *Grand Forks Herald* does a nice job of summarizing modern weather forecasting. Although it was written in 1990, his remarks still apply today:

"A sticky surprise," said the Herald's headline Friday morning.

Sticky it was. But a surprise it was not.

The storm struck right on schedule, it dumped about as much snow as had been predicted on the places where it was forecast.

In fact, the forecasts were on the mark all during a week of remarkable weather in a season known for its unsettled weather.

So to the list of marvels of the modern age, let's add weather forecasting.

The accuracy of the weather service's forecast was underscored by a weather coincidence. This storm struck on the anniversary of one of the most tragic blizzards in the history of the Northern Plains.

On March 15, 1941, a storm bore down on the region without warning. It killed 72 people, including several inside the city of Grand Forks.

It's worth remembering, too, that North Dakota's great winter heroine died in a mid-March storm. Hazel Miner was caught in an unexpected spring snowstorm on March 16, 1920. She got lost on her way home from school near Center. Hazel covered her younger brother and sister and protected them, and they survived.

There is a statue of Miner outside the Oliver County Courthouse, and North Dakota Troubador Chuck Suchy has recorded a song about her.

Even the tremendous blizzard of March 1966–which delivered the heaviest daily snowfall ever recorded in Grand Forks–was not as well forecast as this week's storm.

It's popular to chide the weather service for inaccurate forecasts. Of course, forecasters don't always hit the day's temperature exactly right. Nor do they predict exactly how much rain will fall nor where it will fall.

The past week made it clear, however, that modern weather forecasting is amazingly accurate. The storm first appeared in the five-day forecasts, and the weather service issued bulletins about it beginning Tuesday.

Because of the National Weather Service forecasts, the region was spared the tragedy that confronted residents of the Northern Plains in other spring snowstorms.

That knowledge is worth smiling about-just as the sticky snow is worth celebrating for the moisture it contained. Add forecasting to the list of marvels of the modern age.[4]

Sources

Newspapers have provided the bulk of information for this study. We have cited quotes, headlines and stories from them, but information was also used without a footnote.

Many people have shared their memories of the March 1966 blizzard with the authors. We regret not being able to use all of them.

Information on the orgins of place names and other tidbits about about the cities and towns were not cited. Credit belongs to the following individuals and their published works. For South Dakota, the authors consulted *South Dakota Place Names* by South Dakota WPA Writers' Project (Vermillion, SD: South Dakota University of South Dakota, 1941). For North Dakota, we used *North Dakota Place Names* by Douglas A. Wick (Bismarck, ND: Hedemarken Collectibles, 1988); *Orgins of North Dakota Place Names* by Mary Ann Barnes Williams (Washburn, ND: Mary Ann Barnes Williams, 1966). For Minnesota, we relied on *Minnesota Geographic Names: Their Origin and Historic Significance* by Warren Upham (St. Paul, MN: Minnesota Historical Society, 2nd printing, reprint edition, 1979). For Manitoba, we referred to *Geographical Names of Manitoba* by Manitoba Geographic Names Program as of January 2001 (Millenium Bureau of Canada).

The authors have mentioned the names of many local weather observers. They deserve all the recognition. Weather information in this book is the result of their work. The writers gathered the information from the local newspapers of the times. For communites, without a local newspaper, the authors have relied on the weather records compiled by climatologists. In both cases, the local weather observers have provided the data. The special weather summaries for South Dakota, North Dakota and Minnesota for March 1966, were utilized in this study. There were only a few instances where the readings were different. In those cases, we have noted the differences.

The railroads brought growth and stability. The authors have not cited information concerning the dates when they established stations in the communities of our region. For South Dakota, we relied on *History of South Dakota* by Doane Robinson (Chicago and New York: The American Historical Society, Inc. 1930), Volume 1, pages 383-388. For North Dakota and Minnesota, that information came from the place name books already mentioned. Another source was *North Dakota Centennial Blue Book: 1889-1989* (Issued by Secretary of State, North Dakota, Under direction of Ben Meier, 1989), pages 502-513. Data concerning the Soo Line came from *Saga of the Soo: West from Shoreham* by John A Gjevre (Moorhead, MN: Gjevre Books, 1990), pages 152, 153.

Our memories are associated with the popular culture. Although none of the information is cited, the authors have utilized many different sources to assure accuracy. The following is not a complete list of the material we reviewed.

For historical background and other aspects of the 1960s, the authors relied on *This Fabulous Century, 1960-1970,* (New York: Time-Life Books, 1970), Volume 7; *Our American Century, Turbulent Years: The 60's* (Alexandria, VA: Time-Life Books, 1998); *The People's Almanac Presents The 20th Century* by David Wallechinsky (Little, Brown and Company, 1995); and *Our Times: The Illustrated History of the 20th Century* by Lorraine Glennon, Editor in Chief, (Atlanta, GA: Turner-Publishing, Inc. 1995); *Chronicle of America* by John W. Kirshon, Editor in Chief, (Mount Kisco, NY: Chronicle Publications, 1989).

For songs, the best source was *The Billboard Book of Top 40 Hits, 1955-1999*, by Joel Whitburn (New York, NY: Billboard Books, 2000). For movies, the authors referred to the *Twenty-Fifth Anniversary Movie and Video Guide, 1995*, by Leonard Maltin (New York, NY: Penguin Books USA Inc., 1994); *AFI's 100 Years 100 Movies* (Target). For TV programs, *TV Book: The Ultimate Television Book* by Judy Fireman. editor, (New York, NY: Workman Publishing Company, 1977). The sources mentioned in the previous paragraph had much information on the popular culture as well.

Footnotes

A Look Back at the Times
[1] Grand Forks Herald, 7 January 2004, p. 2a.

Chapter I
The South Dakota Experience

[1] Willadene Price, Gutzon Borglum: The Man Who Carved a Mountain, (Mclean, VA: Emp Publications, Inc., 1974), pp. 150, 151.

[2] Edward Patrick Hogan, The Geography of South Dakota, (Sioux Falls, SD: The Center of Western Studies, 1995), p. 40.

[3] Rapid City Daily Journal, 1 March 1966, p. 2.

[4] Ibid., 2 March 1966, p. 2.

[5] Ibid.

[6] Joe Whitburn, The Billboard Book of Top 40 Hits, (New York: Billboard Books, 2000), p. 829.

[7] Rapid City Daily Journal, 4 March 1966, p. 1.

[8] Ibid.

[9] Ibid., 6 March 1966, p. 4.

[10] Ibid., 4 March 1966, p. 1.

[11] Ibid.

[12] Ibid., 6 March 1966, p. 4.

[13] Ibid., p. 3.

[14] Ibid., p. 1.

[15] The Daily Plainsman (Huron, SD), 6 March 1966, p. 3.

[16] Joyce l. Vander Lugt, Behind The Scenes In South Dakota, (Sioux Falls, SD: Think Print Publishing Company, 1994), p. 194

[17] Pennington County Courant (Wall, SD), 3 March 1966, p. 1.

[18] Ibid., 10 March 1966, p. 1.

[19] Ibid.

[20] O. W. Coursey, Beautiful Black Hills, (Mitchell, SD: Educator Supply Company, 1926) p. 217.

[21] Herbert Samuel Schell, South Dakota: Its Beginning and Growth, (New York: American Book Company, 1955), pp. 86, 87.

[22] Hogan, The Geography of South Dakota, p. 34.

[23] Hot Spring Star, 10 March 1966, p. 1.

[24] Hogan, The Geography of South Dakota, p. 41.

[25] U.S. Department of Commerce, Environmental Science Service Administration, Climatological Data: South Dakota, March 1966, Volume 71, No. 3. p. 33.

[26] Hogan, The Geography of South Dakota, p. 34.

[27] Queen City Mail (Spearfish, SD), 10 March 1966, p. 1.

[28] Sturgis Tribune, 10 March 1966, p. 2.

[29] Belle Fourche Bee, 18 March 1966, p. 8.

[30] Ibid., 11 March 1966, p. 2.

[31] Lugt, Behind the Scenes In South Dakota, p. 103.

[32] Kadoka Press, 10 March 1966, p. 1.

[33] Ibid.

[34] Daily Capital Journal (Pierre, SD), 7 March 1966, p. 1.

[35] Bennett County Booster II (Martin, SD), 10 March 1966, p. 1.

[36] Ibid., 17 March 1966, p. 1.

[37] Ibid.

[38] Ibid., 10 March 1966, p. 1.

[39] Pioneer Review (Philip, SD), 10 March 1966, p. 1.

[40] Daily Plainsman, 17 March 1966, p. 1.

[41] Lugt, Behind The Scenes In South Dakota, p. 66.

[42] Rapid City Daily Journal, 6 March 1966, p. 3.

[43] Eagle Butte News, 10 March 1966, p. 1.

[44] Rapid City Daily Journal, 6 March 1966, p. 1.

[45] Eagle Butte News, 10 March 1966, 1.

[46] Lugt, Behind The Scenes In South Dakota, p. 161.

[47] U.S. Department of Commerce, Climatological Data: South Dakota, March 1966, Volume 71, No. 3. pp. 33, 38.

[48] Bison Courier, 10 March 1966, p. 1.

[49] Ibid.

[50] Ibid.

[51] Aberdeen American-News, 15 March 1966, p. 4.

[52] Isabel Dakotan, 17 March 1966, p. 1.

[53] Ibid., 3 March 1966, p. 1.

[54] Ibid., 10 March 1966, p. 1.

[55] Ibid.

[56] Ibid.

[57] Aberdeen American-News, 15 March 1966, p. 4.

[58] U.S. Department of Commerce, Climatological Data: South Dakota, March 1966, Volume 71, No. 3. pp. 32, 33.

[59] Isabel Dakotan, 10 March 1966, p. 1.

[60] Watertown Public Opinion, 5 March 1966, p. 3.

[61] Lemmon Leader, 10 March 1966, p. 4.

[62] Ibid., p. 1.

[63] Morristown World, 10 March 1966, p. 2.

[64] Ibid., p. 4.

[65] Daily Plainsman, 17 March 1966, p. 1.

[66] McLaughlin Messenger, 10 March 1966, p. 5.

[67] Aberdeen American-News, 6 March 1966, p. 1.

[68] McLaughlin Messenger, 10 March 1966, p. 2.

[69] Ibid.

[70] Ibid.

[71] Daily Plainsman, 10 March 1966, p. 2.

[72] Morristown World, 10 March 1966, p. 2.

[73] Winner Advocate, 10 March 1966, p. 1.

[74] Burke Gazette, 10 March 1966, p. 1,

[75] Bonesteel Enterprise, 10 March 1966, p. 1.

[76] Lyman County Herald (Presho, SD), 10 March 1966, p. 1.

[77] Advocate-Leader (Kennebec, SD), 10 March 1966, p.1.

[78] Ibid., 17 March 1966, p. 1.

[79] Hogan, The Geography of South Dakota, pp. 74, 75.

[80] Chamberlain Register, 10 March 1966, p. 1.

[81] Dale Lewis, Roy Houck: Buffalo Man, (Fort Pierre, SD: Buffalo Press, 1992), p. 7.

[82] Ibid., p. 12.

[83] Chamberlain Register, 10 March 1966, p. 1.

[84] Ibid., p. 2.

[85] Ibid.

[86] Ibid., p. 1.

[87] Ibid., 17 March 1966, p. 1.

[88] Ibid., 10 March 1966, p. 1.

[89] Hogan, The Geography of South Dakota, p. 40.

[90] Daily Republic (Mitchell, SD) 3 March 1966, p. 1.

[91] Ibid., 4 March 1966, p. 1.

[92] Ibid., 7 March 1966, p. 3.

[93] Ibid., 5 March 1966, p. 1.

[94] Ibid., 7 March 1966, p. 3.

[95] Ibid,

[96] Salem Special, 10 March 1966, p. 1.

[97] Ibid.

[98] Watertown Public Opinion, 8 March 1966, p. 9.

[99] Lennox Independent, 10 March 1966, p. 1.

[100] Lake Andes Wave, 16 March 1966, p. 5.

[101] Ibid., 9 March 1966, p. 1.

[102] Ibid., p. 2.

[103] Armour Chronicle, 3 March 1966, p. 1.

[104] Ibid., 10 March 1966, p. 1.

[105] Ibid.

[106] Daily Plainsman, 28 February 1966, p. 8.

[107] Parkston Advance, 10 March 1966, p. 1.

[108] Daily Plainsman, 13 March 1966, p. 11.

[109] Bob Karolevitz and Bernie Hunhoff, Uniquely South Dakota, (Norfolk, VA: The Donning Company, 1988), p. 32.

[110] Karolevitz and Hunhoff, Uniquely South Dakota, p. 258.

[111] Freeman Courier, 10 March 1966, p. 1.

[112] Scheel, South Dakota: Its Beginnings and Growth, pp. 258-261.

[113] Argus Leader (Sioux Falls, SD), 6 March 1966, p. 1.

[114] Vermillion Plain Talk, 10 March 1966, p. 1.

[115] Daily Republic, 7 March 1966, pp. 1, 2.

[116] Daily Plainsman, 6 March 1966, p. 1, 2.

[117] Ibid., 7 March, 1966, p. 1.

[118] Woonsocket News, 3 March 1966, p. 1.

[119] Ibid., 10 March 1966, p. 1.

[120] Ibid., 17 March 1966, p. 2.

[121] Daily Republic, 5 March 1966, p. 1.

[122] Daily Plainsman, 27 February 1966, p. 19.

[123] Madison Daily Leader, 2 March 1966, p. 1.

[124] Ibid., 7 March 1966, p. 1.

[125] Ibid., p. 2.

[126] Ibid., pp. 1, 2.

[127] Daily Capital Journal, 3 March 1966, p. 1.

[128] Ibid.

[129] Ibid.

[130] Ibid.

[131] Ibid., 4 March 1966, p. 1.

[132] Ibid.

[133] Ibid., 7 March 1966, p. 1.

[134] Daily Plainsman, 6 March 1966, p. 3.

[135] Daily Capital Journal, 7 March 1966, p. 6.

[136] Ibid., 9 March 1966, p. 1.

[137] Ibid., 8 March 1966, p. 1.

[138] Highmore Herald, 10 March 1966, p. 4.

[139] Onida Watchman, 10 March 1966, p. 1.

[140] Ibid.

[141] Highmore Herald, 10 March 1966, p. 1.

[142] Ibid.

[143] Daily Plainsman, 6 March 1966, p. 3.

[144] Highmore Herald, 10 march 1966, p. 1.

[145] Ibid., p. 6.

[146] Aberdeen American-News, 6 March 1966, p. 5.

[147] Daily Plainsman, 13 March 1966, pp. 13, 17.

[148] Clement A. Lounsberry, Early History of North Dakota: Essential Outlines of American History, Volume I, (Washington: Liberty Press, 1919), pp. 628-630.

[149] Daily Plainsman, 2 March 1966, p. 1.

[150] Ibid., 3 March 1966, p. 3.

[151] Ibid., 4 March 1966, p. 2.

[152] Ibid., p. 1.

[153] Ibid., 6 March 1966, p. 3.

[154] Ibid., 4 March 1966, p. 2.

[155] William T. Anderson, The Story of the Wilders, (Davison, MI: Anderson Publications, 1973), p. 8.

[156] De Smet News, 10 March 1966, p. 1.

[157] Daily Capital Journal, 10 March 1966, p. 1.

[158] De Smet News, 17 March 1966, p. 4.

[159] Brookings Register, 5 March 1966, p. 1.

[160] Potter County News (Gettysburg, SD), 10 March 1966, p. 3.

[161] Ibid.

[162] Ibid., p. 2.

[163] Ibid.

[164] Ibid., p. 5.

[165] Ibid.

[166] Ibid.

[167] Aberdeen American-News, 5 March 1966, p. 5.

[168] Ibid., 15 March 1966, p. 4.

[169] Redfield Press, 10 March 1966, p. 1.

[170] Daily Plainsman, 4 March 1966, p. 1.

[171] Ibid., 6 March 1966, p. 3.

[172] Clark County Courier (Clark, SD), 10 March 1966, p. 1.

[173] Watertown Public Opinion, 3 March 1966, p. 1.

[174] Ibid., 5 March 1966, p. 9.

[175] Ibid., 4 March 1966, p. 1.

[176] Clear Lake Courier, 10 March 1966, pp. 1, 10.

[177] Ibid., 17 March 1966, p. 2.

[178] Karolevitz and Hunhoff, Uniquely South Dakota, p. 200.

[179] Mobridge Tribune, 10 March 1966, p. 6.

[180] Aberdeen American-News, 4 March 1966, p. 8.

[181] Mobridge Tribune, 10 March 1966, p.6.

[182] Selby Record, 10 March 1966, p.6.

[183] Ibid., p. 1.

184 Ibid., p. 2.

185 Ibid., p. 10.

186 Ibid., 17 March 1966, p. 1.

187 Ibid., 10 March 1966, p. 9.

188 Ibid.

189 Ipswich Tribune, 10 March 1966, p.1.

190 Dickey County Leader (Ellendale, ND), 10 March 1966, p. 1.

191 Ipswich Tribune, 10 March 1966, pp. 1, 5.

192 Ibid., 17 March 1966, p. 1.

193 Aberdeen American-News, 15 March 1966, p. 4.

194 Ipswich Tribune, 10 March 1966, p. 6.

195 Ibid., p. 3.

196 Selby Record, 17 March 1966, p. 1.

197 Karolevitz and Hunhoff, Uniquely South Dakota, p. 86.

198 Aberdeen American News, 15 March 1966, P. 4.

199 Ibid., 2 March 1966, p. 7

200 Ibid., p. 7.

201 Ibid., 3 March 1966, p. 1.

202 Ibid., p. 7.

203 Ibid., 4 March 1966, p. 1.

204 Ibid., 8 March 1966, p. 7.

205 Ibid., p. 3.

206 Ibid., 4 March 1966, p. 3.

207 Britton Journal, 10 March 1966, p. 1.

208 Ibid., 17 March 1966, p. 1.

209 Webster Reporter and Farmer, 9 March 1966, p. 1.

210 Ibid., p. 2.

211 Ibid., p. 3.

212 Ibid., 23 March 1966, p. 1.

213 Aberdeen American-News, 15 March 1966, p.4.

214 Wilmont Enterprise, 10 March 1966, p. 1.

215 Watertown Public Opinion, 4 March 1966, p. 9.

216 Milbank Herald Advance, 10 March 1966, p.4.

217 Ibid., p. 7.

218 Ibid., p. 1.

219 Ibid., p. 2.

220 Ibid.

221 Ibid.

222 Ibid., p. 3.

223 Ibid.

224 Ibid.

Chapter II
The North Dakota Experience

1 Bowman County Pioneer, 10 March 1966, p. 1.

2 Morning Pioneer (Mandan, ND) 9 March 1966, p. 7.

3 Mott Pioneer Press, 9 March 1966, p. 1.

4 Billings County Pioneer (Medora, ND), 10 March 1966, p. 3.

5 James A. Vivian, The Romance of My Life, (Fargo, ND: Prairie House, 1989) At Medora, North Dakota while campaigning for the Republican presidential ticket in 1900. (back cover page).

6 Billings County Pioneer, 10 March 1966, p. 8.

[7] Ibid., p. 4.

[8] Harold Flom to Douglas Ramsey, 28 August 2003.

[9] Bismarck Tribune 5 March 1966, p. 2.

[10] New Leipzig Sentinel, 10 March 1966, p. 1.

[11] Letter by Marcella Schock, North Dakota REC/RTC Magazine Volume 44, No 9., March 1998, p. 31.

[12] Hebron Herald, 9 March 1966, p. 3.

[13] Morning Pioneer, 7 March 1966, pp. 1, 2.

[14] Ibid., p. 2.

[15] Ibid., p. 16.

[16] Gary Hellman to Douglas Ramsey, 10 March 2004.

[17] Morning Pioneer, 7 March 1966, p. 1.

[18] Bismarck Tribune, 7 March 1966, p. 5.

[19] Morning Pioneer,

[20] Ibid., 8 March 1966, p. 1.

[21] Bismarck Tribune, 5 March 1966, pp. 1, 2.

[22] Ibid., 9 March 1966, p. 22.

[23] Ibid., 8 March 1966, p. 6.

[24] Morning Pioneer, 4 March 1966, p. 1.

[25] Ibid., pp. 1, 2.

[26] Beulah Independent, 10 March 1966. p. 1.

[27] Emmons County Record (Linton, ND), 9 March 1966, p. 1.

[28] Ibid.

[29] Ibid.

[30] Ibid.

[31] Bismarck Tribune, 8 March 1966, p. 2.

[32] Ibid.

[33] Fargo Forum, 8 March 1966, p.2.

[34] Bismarck Tribune, 8 March 1966, p.2.

[35] Emmons County Record, 22 March 1966, p. 1.

[36] Foster County Independent (Carrington, ND), 31 March 1966, p.9.

[37] Emmons County Record, 9 March 1966, p. 2.

[38] Ibid.

[39] Ibid.

[40] Ibid.

[41] Ibid.

[42] Ibid., 16 March 1966, p. 11.

[43] Ibid., p. 4.

[44] Ibid., 9 March 1966, p. 7.

[45] Ibid., p. 6.

[46] Ashley Tribune, 10 March 1966, p. 1.

[47] Ibid.

[48] Ibid., p. 4.

[49] Ibid., pp. 1, 4.

[50] Ibid., p. 4.

[51] Tim Nies to Larry Skroch, 9 February 2004.

[52] Ashley Tribune, 17 March 1966, p. 1.

[53] Ibid.

[54] Ransom County Gazette (Lisbon, ND), 24 March 1966, p. 2.

[55] Foster County Independent, 31 March 1966, p. 9.

[56] Wiskek Star, 10 March 1966, p. 1.

57 Ibid., 17 March 1966, p. 1.
58 Ibid.
59 Napoleon Homestead, 9 March 1966, p. 1.
60 Grand Forks Herald, 10 March 1966, p. 9.
61 Foster County Independent, 31 March 1966, p. 9.
62 Kulm Messenger, 10 March 1966, p. 3.
63 Tri-County News (Gackle, ND), 10 March 1966, p. 1.
64 Ibid.
65 Ibid.
66 Ibid., pp. 1, 3.
67 Ibid.
68 Ibid., p. 1.
69 Kulm Messenger, 17 March 1966, p. 4.
70 Dickey County Leader, 10 March 1966, p. 4.
71 Ibid., p. 3.
72 Ibid., p. 1.
73 Oakes Times, 10 March 1966, p. 1.
74 Minot Daily News, 5 March 1966, p. 2.
75 LaMoure Chronicle, 9 March 1966, p. 1.
76 Letter, Juli Becker to Larry Skroch, 12 May 2000.
77 Kulm Messenger, 10 March 1966, p. 1.
78 Ibid., p. 3.
79 Ibid., 24 March 1966, p. 2.
80 Ibid., 31 March 1966, p. 2.
81 Enderlin Independent, 3 March 1966, p. 1.
82 Fargo Forum, 5 March 1966, p. 2.
83 Edgeley Mail, 7 April 1966, p. 11.
84 LaMoure Chronicle, 2 March 1966, p. 1.
85 Ibid., p. 5.
86 Ransom County Gazette, 17 March 1966, p. 6.
87 Ibid.
88 Ibid., 24 March 1966, p. 3.
89 Litchville Bulletin, 9 March 1966, p. 8.
90 LaMoure Chronicle, 9 March 1966, p. 1.
91 Kulm Messenger, 10 March 1966, p. 4.
92 Sargent County News (Forman, ND), 10 March 1966, p. 1.
93 Ibid.
94 Mrs. James Kunkle to Larry Skroch, 6 October 2004.
95 Mrs. John Hayen to Larry Skroch, n.d.
96 Sargent County News, 10 March 1966, p. 1.
97 Ibid.. p. 3.
98 Ibid., p. 6.
99 Letter by Doris Gulsvig, North Dakota Rec/RTC Magazine, Volume 39, No. 9., March 1993, p. 43.
100 Sargent County News, 10 March 1966, p. 4.
101 Greg Groettum to authors, 1 September 2003.
102 Prairie Press, (Gwinner, ND), 10 March 1966, p. 2.
103 Ransom County Gazette, 17 March 1966, p. 1.
104 Ibid.
105 Sargent County Teller (Milnor, ND), 8 March 1966, p. 1.
106 Ibid., 24 March 1966, p. 1.

[107] Snorri M. Thorfinnson, Ransom County History, (Ransom County Historical Society, 1975), p. 101.

[108] Ransom County Gazette, 10 March 1966, p. 2.

[109] Ibid.

[110] Ibid., p. 5.

[111] Ibid., 17 March 1966, p. 6.

[112] Ibid., 24 March 1966, p. 1.

[113] Ibid., 10 March 1966, p. 8.

[114] Ibid., p. 3.

[115] Ibid., p. 7.

[116] Ibid., p. 1.

[117] Enderlin Independent, 10 March 1966, p. 3.

[118] Ibid., p. 1.

[119] Ibid.

[120] Ibid., p. 2.

[121] Ibid., p. 5.

[122] Snorri M. Thorfinnson, History of Sargent County, (Sargent County Commissioners, publishers), p. 55.

[123] Lidgerwood Monitor, 10 March 1966, p. 1.

[124] Farmer Globe (Wahpeton, ND), 7 March 1966, pp. A-1, A-3.

[125] Douglas Wick, North Dakota Place Names, (Bismarck, ND: Hedenmarken Collectibles, 1988), p. 121.

[126] Hankinson News, 10 March 1966, p. 1.

[127] Ibid., p. 8.

[128] Ibid., p. 1.

[129] Fairmount News, 10 March 1966, p. 1.

[130] Farmer Globe, 7 March 1966, pp. A-1, A-3.

[131] Ibid.

[132] Ibid., 10 March 1966, pp. 1, 8.

[133] Wyndmere Missile, 10 March 1966, p. 1.

[134] Ibid., p. 2.

[135] Ibid., p. 1.

[136] Farmer Globe, 10 March 1966, p. C-4.

[137] Ibid., 7 March 1966, pp. A-1, A-4.

[138] Grand Forks Herald, 7 April 2004, p. 4B.

[139] Farmer Globe, 3 March 1966, p. A-1.

[140] Gloria Ebertowski to Douglas Ramsey, 8 August 1999.

[141] Bill Mitchell to Larry Skroch, 27 July 2001.

[142] Farmer Globe, 7 March 1966, pp. A-1, A-3.

[143] Bismarck Tribune, 3 March 1966, p. 2.

[144] Ibid.

[145] Ibid.

[146] Ibid.

[147] Ibid., 4 March 1966, p. 1.

[148] Morning Pioneer, 4 March 1966, p. 1.

[149] Bismarck Tribune, 4 March 1966, p. 1.

[150] Ibid.

[151] Ibid., 7 March 1966, p. 4.

[152] Ibid., p. 5.

[153] Ibid., 9 March 1966, p. 7.

[154] Foster County Independent, 31 March 1966, p. 9.

[155] Bismarck Tribune, 5 March 1966, p. 12.

[156] Washburn Leader, 17 March 1966, p. 4.

157 Wilton News, 11 March 1966, p. 4.

158 Ibid.

159 Steele Ozone-Press, 9 March 1966, p. 1.

160 Miles Nelson to Douglas Ramsey, May 2000.

161 Jamestown Sun, 3 March 1966, p. 1.

162 Ibid., 7 March 1966, p. 3.

163 Ibid., p. 8.

164 Ibid., pp. 1, 8.

165 Ibid., 9 March 1966, p. 1.

166 Bill Kuebler, "The Jamestown Vetrans," Mainstreeter, Volume 11, No. 1, Winter 1992, p. 18.

167 Ibid., pp, 13-15.

168 Ibid., pp. 18-21.

169 Jamestown Sun, 8 March 1966, p. 1.

170 Litchville Bulletin, 9 March 1966, p. 7.

171 Ibid., p. 2.

172 Ibid., p. 1.

173 Valley City Times-Record, 7 March 1966, p. 2.

174 William R. Kuebler, Jr., "Nature's Fury," NP Color Pictorial, (LaMirada, CA: Tours Ways West Publication) pp. 31, 34.

175 Ibid., p. 34.

176 Fargo Forum, 3 March 1966. p. 2E.

177 Valley City Times-Record, 7 March 1966, p. 2.

178 Ibid., p. 4.

179 Ibid., p. 1.

180 Enderlin Independent, 10 March 1966, p. 5.

181 Debbie Reilly to Douglas Ramsey, 4 November 1998.

182 Hunter Times, 24 March 1966, p. 2.

183 Ibid., 10 March 1966, p. 1.

184 Fargo Forum, 1 March 1966, p. 2.

185 Ibid., 3 March 1966, p. 1.

186 Ibid., 6 March 1966, B-7.

187 Ibid.

188 Ibid., 4 March 1966, pp. 1. 2.

189 Letter, Ronald Wood to Larry Skroch, 16 April 2002.

190 Fargo Forum, 6 March 1966, p. B-6.

191 Ibid.

192 Ibid.

193 Ibid., p. B-4.

194 Ibid., p. B-6.

195 Fargo Forum, 8 March 1966, p. 9.

196 Red River Scene (Moorhead, MN), 7 March 1966, p. 1.

197 Ibid., p. 2.

198 Dave Haakenson to Larry Skroch, n.d.

199 Hunter Times, 17 March 1966, p. 8.

200 Washburn Leader, 10 March 1966, p. 2.

201 McLean County Independent (Garrison, ND), 10 March 1966, p. 2. 202Washburn Leader, 10 March 1966, p. 1.

203 McLean County Independent, 10 March 1966, p. 9.

204 Minot Daily News, 4 March 1966, p. 2.

205 Maureen Puppe to Douglas Ramsey, 9 August 2000.

[206] Minot Daily News, 7 March 1966, p. 13.

[207] Ibid., p. 2.

[208] Lewis Bellsle to Douglas Ramsey, 4 May 2000.

[209] Minot Daily News, 5 March 1966, p. 1.

[210] Ibid.

[211] McClusky Gazette, 9 March 1966, p. 1.

[212] Letter, Norman Weckerly to Douglas Ramsey, 29 June 2004.

[213] Harvey Herald, 10 March 1966, p. 1.

[214] Ibid.

[215] Ibid.

[216] Foster County Independent, 10 March 1966, p. 1.

[217] New Rockford Transcript, 10 March 1966, p. 1.

[218] Ibid., p. 2.

[219] Griggs County Sentinel Courier (Cooperstown, ND), 10 March 1966, p. 1.

[220] Note, Millie Rickford to Larry Skroch, n.d.

[221] Karen Huffman to Douglas Ramsey, 11 April 1999.

[222] Traill County Tribune (Mayville, ND), 10 March 1966, p. 1.

[223] Ibid.

[224] Ibid., 17 March 1966, p. 1.

[225] Ibid., 10 March 1966, p. 1.

[226] Hillsboro Banner, 9 March 1966, p. 1.

[227] Gary Haisley to Larry Skroch, 24 August 1999.

[228] Grand Forks Herald, 7 March 1966, p. 3.

[229] Benson County Farmers Press (Minnewaukan, ND), 10 March 1966, p. 1.

[230] Ibid.

[231] Bismarck Tribune, 5 March 1966, p. 12.

[232] Debbie Schenk to Douglas Ramsey, 31 December 1999.

[233] Grand Forks Herald, 17 December 2003, p. 2B.

[234] McVille Journal, 10 March 1966, p. 1.

[235] Ibid.

[236] The Gleaner (Northwood, ND), 11 March 1966, p. 1.

[237] Ibid., p. 6.

[238] Ibid.

[239] Larimore Pioneer, 9 March 1996, p. 1.

[240] Ibid.

[241] Ibid.

[242] Ibid.

[243] Brad Benson to Douglas Ramsey, 5 May 1996.

[244] Larimore Pioneer, 9 March 1966, p. 8.

[245] Ibid.

[246] Ibid.

[247] Ibid.

[248] Grand Forks Herald, 6 March 1966, p. 15.

[249] Ibid.

[250] Ibid.

[251] Ibid.

[252] Jim West to Douglas Ramsey, 23 May 1999.

[253] Marilyn Hagerty, "B.P.:Before Plugs," Echoes: A selection of stories and columns., (Grand Forks, ND: Grand Forks Herald. 1994), pp. 134, 135.

[254] Grand Forks Herald, 6 March 1966, p. 15.

255 Ibid.

256 Ibid.

257 Gordon Iseminger to Douglas Ramsey, 11 February 2000.

258 Fred Thoelke to Douglas Ramsey, 30 July 1996.

259 Edward Fladeland to the authors, 8 December 2001.

260 Ted Jarombek to Douglas Ramsey, 14 January 2000.

261 Mike Lunak to Larry Skroch, 1 November 2004.

262 Terry Hurst to Larry Skroch 15 November 2004.

263 The Record (East Grand Forks, MN), 10 March 1966, p. 7.

264 Ibid., p. 3.

265 Gene Olson to Douglas Ramsey, 16 February 1998.

266 R. F. "Pete" Matejcek to Douglas Ramsey, 13 December 1998.

267 Allen Skavhaug to Douglas Ramsey, 30 April 1997.

268 Rose Potulny, The Way It Was, 1993. p. 43.

269 Walsh County Press (Park River, ND), 10 March 1966, p. 1.

270 Don Flaten to Douglas Ramsey, 15 December 1999.

271 Diane Goodoien to Douglas Ramsey, 7 June 2004.

272 Cliff Hilde to Douglas Ramsey, 2 December 1999.

273 Wayne Meyer to Douglas Ramsey, 6 June 1998.

274 Nancy Salwei to Douglas Ramsey, 25 May 2002.

275 Tony Goodoien to Douglas Ramsey, 6 June 1998.

276 Jerry Loftsgard to Douglas, Ramsey 7 July 2003.

277 Chuck and Mary Wilson to Douglas Ramsey, 1 February 1998.

278 Al Adamsen to Douglas Ramsey, December 1996.

279 Daryle MacDonald to Douglas Ramsey, 31 March 1996.

280 Bernice Flanagen to Douglas Ramsey, 9 September 2003.

281 Cavalier County Republican, 10 March 1966, p. 4.

282 Dean Stone to Douglas Ramsey, 17 July 2004.

283 A. J. Johnson to Douglas Ramsey 5 April 2002.

284 Norma Hallgrimson to Douglas Ramsey, 9 March 2000.

285 Raymond Hallgrimson, to Douglas Ramsey, 18 August 2003.

286 Roger Gratton to Douglas Ramsey, 4 February 1997; 5 October 1998.

287 John H. Johnson to Douglas Ramsey, 25 February 1999.

288 Orval Holliday to Douglas Ramsey, 5 May 1996; 4 February 1999.

289 Alvin Bjornson to Douglas Ramsey, 2 July 1999.

290 Duane and Lorraine Byron, 8 June 1999.

291 Lori Cameron to Douglas Ramsey, 14 October 1997.

292 Douglas Wick, North Dakota Place Names,

293 Jenny Hipka, American Snowmobile, February 2003, p. 78.

294 Denis A. Martin to Douglas Ramsey, 1 March 2000.

295 Larry Longtin to Douglas Ramsey, 16 February 2003.

296 Camburn Shephard to Douglas Ramsey, 2 May 2001.

297 Bill O'Sullivan, to Douglas Ramsey, 4 July 1997.

298 Harold Johnston to Douglas Ramsey, 7 March 2000.

299 Danny Salwei to Douglas Ramsey, 5 February 2001.

300 Glenn Ralston to Douglas Ramsey, 11 April 1998.

301 Lyle Shephard to Douglas Ramsey, Fall, 1995.

302 Walter Ortlip to Douglas Ramsey, 4 May 1996.

303 Georgia Maize to Douglas Ramsey, 12 January 1998.

304 Alice Poehls to Douglas Ramsey, 17 July 2004.

[305] Roy Bigwood to Douglas Ramsey, 29 December 1999.

[306] Duane Larson to Larry Skroch, 9 June 2004.

[307] John Ebertowski to Douglas Ramsey, 14 March 1996.

[308] Don Matter to Douglas Ramsey, 23 May 1999.

[309] Jim Pilon to Douglas Ramsey, 23 May 1999.

[310] Neal Heuchert to Douglas Ramsey, 18 March 2003.

[311] Herman Ratchenski to Douglas Ramsey, 18 May 2003.

[312] Cavalier Chronicle, 10 March 1966, p. 1.

[313] Jim Benjaminson to Douglas Ramsey, 5 May 1996.

[314] Andy Nupdal to Douglas Ramsey, 9 June 1998.

[315] Lorraine Martinson to Douglas Ramsey, 9 April 1997.

[316] Cavalier Chronicle, 10 March 1966, p. 1.

[317] Ibid.

[318] Don Dalzell to Douglas Ramsey, 17 February 1998.

Chapter III
The Minnesota Experience

[1] Pipestone County Star, 7 March 1966, p. 1.

[2] Ortonville Independent, 10 March 1966, p. 1.

[3] West Central Daily Tribune (Willmar, MN), 3 March 1966, p. 1.

[4] Warren Upham, Minnesota Geographic Names: Their Origin and Historic Significance, (St. Paul, MN: Minnesota Historical Society, 1969), p. 68.

[5] Valley Alert (Breckenridge, MN), 3 March 1966, p.1.

[6] Ibid., 10 March 1966, p. A5.

[7] Ibid., p. A1.

[8] Barnesville Record Review, 10 March 1966, p. 1.

[9] Ibid.

[10] Ibid.

[11] Red River Scene, 10 March 1966, p. 6.

[12] Fergus Falls Daily Journal, 5 March 1966, p. 1.

[13] Wadena Pioneer Journal, 10 March 1966, p. 6.

[14] Red River Scene, 10 March 1966, p. 6.

[15] Hawley Herald, 10 March 1966, p. 1.

[16] Ibid.

[17] Detroit Lakes Tribune, 7 March 1966, p. 1.

[18] Ibid.

[19] Ibid., p. 4.

[20] Ibid., p. 1.

[21] Mahnomen Pioneer, 10 March 1966, p. 1.

[22] Ibid., p. 8.

[23] Park Rapids Enterrprise, 10 March 1966, p. 1.

[24] The Thirteen Towns (Fosston, MN), 10 March 1966, p. 1.

[25] Jim Hanson to Douglas Ramsey, January 1, 2001.

[26] Farmers Independent (Bagley, MN), 10 March 1966, p. 8.

[27] Ibid., p. 1.

[28] Ibid., p. 8.

[29] Marshall County Banner (Warren, MN), 10 March 1966, p. 1.

[30] Stephen Messenger, 10 March 1966, p. 1.

[31] Ibid.

[32] Kittson County Enterprise (Hallock, MN), 9 March 1966, p. 4.

[33] Ibid, p. 1.

34 Ibid.

35 Ibid.

36 Karlstad Advocate, 10 March 1966, p. 1.

37 Ibid., p. 6.

38 Norman Johnson to Douglas Ramsey, 27 September 1997.

39 Paul Kurowski to Douglas Ramsey, 26 January 1999.

40 Harvey Baker to Douglas Ramsey, 11 June 1999.

41 John Lofstrom to Douglas Ramsey, 22 November 2002.

42 Middle River Record, 9 March 1966, p. 1.

43 Ibid.

44 The Greenbush Tribune, 10 March 1966, p. 1.

45 Hazel Wahlberg, The North Land, A History of Roseau County, (Roseau, MN: Roseau County Historical Society, 1975), pp. 71, 72.

46 Roseau Times-Region, 10 March 1966, p. 1.

47 Ibid.

48 Grand Forks Herald, 6 March 1966, p. 17.

49 Warren Upham, Minnesota Geographic Names, pp. 80, 474, 475.

50 Pioneer (Warroad, MN),9 March 1966, p. 1.

51 Ibid., p. 8.

52 Baudette Region, 9 march 1966, p. 1.

53 Ibid.

54 Ibid., p. 2.

55 Ibid.

56 St. Cloud Times, 4 March 1966, p. 1.

57 Ibid., 5 March 1966, p. 1.

58 Mankato Free Press, 3 March 1966, p. 1.

59 Warren Upham, Minnesota Geographic Names, p. 36.

60 Ibid., p. 281.

61 Hibbing Tribune, 4 March 1966, p. 1.

62 The Pine Knot, 8 March 1966, p. 1.

Chapter IV
The Canadian Experience

1 Pilot Mound Sentinel, 10 March 1966, p. 1.

2 Morden Times, 9 March 1966, p. 1.

3 Ibid.

4 Geographic Names of Manitoba, (National Library of Canada), p. 58.

5 Crystal City Courier, 10 March 1966, p. 5.

6 Ibid.

7 Grand Forks Herald, 26 January 2003, p. 1A.

8 Pembina Triangle Progress (Winkler, MB), 9 March 1966, p. 1.

9 Dufferin Leader (Carman, MB), 10 March 1966, p. 1.

10 Geographical Names of Manitoba, p. 84.

11 Ibid., p. 217.

12 Daily Graphic (Portage la Prairie, MB), 2 March 1966, p. 1.

13 Ibid., 3 March 1966, p. 1.

14 Ibid., 4 March 1966, p. 1.

15 Ibid.

16 ibid., 5 March 1966, p. 6.

17 Ibid., p. 1.

18 Ibid., 7 March 1966, p. 1.

[19] Ibid.

[20] Winnipeg Free Press, 1 March 1966, p. 1.

[21] Ibid., 2 March 1966, p. 1.

[22] Ibid., 3 March 1966, p. 3.

[23] Ibid.

[24] Beausejour Beaver, 8 March 1966, p. 1.

[25] Ibid.

[26] Ibid.

[27] Carillon News (Steinbach, MB), 10 March 1966, Section 2, p. 2.

[28] Ibid.

[29] Ibid., p. 1.

[30] Kenora Daily Miner and News, 2 March 1966, p. 1.

[31] Ibid., 3 March 1966, p. 1.

[32] Ibid., 4 March 1966, p. 1.

[33] Ibid.

[34] Ibid., 5 March 1966, p. 1.

[35] Ibid.

[36] Ibid., 7 March 1966, p. 1.

Chapter V
Conclusions

[1] Herman G. Stommel, "The Great Blizzard of '66 on the Northern Plains," Weatherwise (October 1966), pp. 189-198, 207.

[2] C. Donald Ahrens, "The Development of Lee-Side Lows," in Meteorology Today (St. Paul. Mn.: West Publishing Company, 1991), p. 370.

[3] Aberdeen American-News, 13 March 1966, p. 28.

[4] Grand Forks Herald, 17 March 1990, p. 4A.

Index